Novell NetWare 6.5

ADMINISTRATOR'S HANDBOOK

Jeffrey L. Harris

Novell
PRESS™

Novell®

800 East 96th Street, Indianapolis, Indiana 46240 USA

Novell NetWare 6.5 Administrator's Handbook

Jeffrey L. Harris

International Standard Book Number: 0-789-72984-9

Library of Congress Catalog Card Number: 2003104576

Printed in the United States of America

First Printing: December 2003

09 08 07 06   9 8 7 6 5

Trademarks

Warning and Disclaimer

Bulk Sales

Que Publishing offers excellent discounts on this book when ordered in quantity for bulk purchases or special sales. For more information, please contact

U.S. Corporate and Government Sales
1-800-382-3419
corpsales@pearsontechgroup.com

For sales outside of the U.S., please contact

International Sales
international@pearsoned.com

Acquisitions Editor
Jenny Watson

Development Editor
Emmett Delaney

Managing Editor
Charlotte Clapp

Senior Project Editor
Matthew Purcell

Copy Editor
Kezia Endsley

Indexer
Julie Bess

Proofreader
Mike Henry

Technical Editor
Warren Wyrostek

Team Coordinator
Vanessa Evans

Interior Designer
Gary Adair

Page Layout
Eric S. Miller
Julie Parks

Contents At a Glance

Table of Contents

Part II Enabling One Net

Chapter 6 Users and Network Security   237

Part III Providing Transparent Access

Part IV Delivering Business Continuity

Chapter 11 Multiprocessor and Clustering Support   465

Part V Appendices

Preface

NetWare 6.5 continues the journey begun with the release of NetWare 6 nearly two years ago. Novell is busy embracing the Web, adopting Internet standards, and promoting the vision of One Net; in which the concept of Location is replaced with Identity and users can get what they need, when they need it—regardless of location.

But delivering a transparent Net for your users can make things more complex on the back end. As a NetWare 6.5 administrator, you will be faced with a host of new features and technologies that are extending the applicability and value of NetWare like never before. For you, the question is not only how to make these technologies work, but how to keep your network running smoothly as these capabilities are introduced. To do this you can arm yourself with information from many different resources: architecture manuals, online documentation, magazines, books, technical Web sites, and even the phone numbers of your most knowledgeable acquaintances. With the powerful new capabilities, and Web-friendly focus of NetWare 6.5, you will likely tap all these resources at one time or another to make sure you have a handle on everything you need to properly manage your network.

But you don't always need all of this information. When you are administering a network, there are three principal tasks that will occupy most of your time: installation, configuration, and maintenance. You don't want to wade through periodicals, Web sites, or product docs searching for that one detail that you can't quite remember. You just need quick access to the information about a technology, concept, or utility so you can get the job done. The *Novell NetWare 6.5 Administrator's Handbook* has been written with those needs in mind.

Filled with concept overviews, installation procedures, configuration options, and maintenance schedules, this handbook can be your quick reference to the daily tasks associated with NetWare 6.5. The Instant Access pages at the beginning of each chapter help you immediately identify the information, utilities, and commands necessary to perform common tasks. So, keep this book handy, and spend less time looking for information and more time managing your network.

What's New in NetWare 6.5?

NetWare 6 was a significant step down a new path for Novell NetWare. NetWare 6.5 will take you several steps further down that road. If you have been working with NetWare 6, you will likely be comfortable with where NetWare 6.5 is going. If you are coming from a world of NetWare 5.1, or prior, you are going to be exposed to a whole new paradigm of network management. NetWare 6.5 continues to redefine NetWare as a powerful Web-oriented platform for delivering a consistent, location-independent view of a user's data and systems—One Net. The new features in NetWare 6.5 were designed around three main value propositions:

- ▶ The virtual office
- ▶ Maintaining business continuity
- ▶ Delivering powerful new Web services

Your virtual office lets you have consistent access and views of the data and systems your users need to do their jobs, regardless of location, time, or access method. Virtual office capabilities of NetWare 6.5 include

- ▶ iFolder
- ▶ iPrint
- ▶ Instant messaging
- ▶ Virtual teams
- ▶ Search

Business continuity is the ability to keep your business flowing in the face of constant change and an uncertain world. NetWare 6.5 helps you prepare for most any eventuality, physical or electronic. Business continuity features in NetWare 6.5 include

- ▶ Server consolidation
- ▶ Branch office management
- ▶ iSCSI storage networks
- ▶ Snapshot backup
- ▶ Patterned deployment
- ▶ Secure remote administration and upgrade
- ▶ Environment integration

Web services is probably one of the most overused phrases in the high-tech industry, but the fact remains that there is tremendous value in being able to harness the Web to your business strategies. NetWare 6.5 has several capabilities that will help you do just that:

- ▶ Apache Web server 2.0
- ▶ MySQL database
- ▶ Perl language
- ▶ PHP
- ▶ Remote, Web-based support and management tools

What Is Covered in This Book

The major components and features of NetWare 6.5 are explained in the chapters and appendices of this book. To help organize the chapters for a logical flow, easier for you to navigate, they have been organized into four parts.

Part I: Getting Started

Chapter 1 explains the various installation options available with NetWare 6.5, including new server installation, server upgrade, and the new patterned deployment.

Chapter 2 explains the install and upgrade procedures for the various NetWare clients that ship with NetWare 6.5. As you will see, there is ever-less focus on the traditional Novell client in favor of new Web-friendly ways to access the network.

Chapter 3 introduces the suite of management tools used in Novell Networks. This includes the legacy ConsoleOne management tool along with a greatly improved set of Web-based management tools, including iManager, iMonitor, Novell Remote Manager (NoRM), and Web Manager.

Part II: Enabling One Net

Chapter 4 introduces console-based utilities and commands available with NetWare 6.5. It also presents valuable information for optimizing and maintaining your NetWare servers.

Chapter 5 introduces basic eDirectory administrative tasks and the regular maintenance operations that will keep the directory running smoothly. It also discusses LDAP and DNS/DHCP.

Chapter 6 explains how eDirectory is used to effectively manage network users and groups. It also presents the fundamentals of network security and presents the options available to you for making your network safe from attack—both intentional and accidental.

Chapter 7 introduces Novell Distributed Print Services (NDPS) and iPrint services that leverage the Internet Printing Protocol (IPP) to deliver true print from anywhere to anywhere capability.

Part III: Providing Transparent Access

Chapter 8 introduces Novell Storage Services, NetWare's Distributed File System (DFS), and the new iSCSI-based storage area network capabilities of NetWare 6.5. It also describes NetWare 6.5 Backup/Restore capabilities with Storage Management Services (SMS).

Chapter 9 introduces a powerful new set of Web Services for NetWare 6.5, including a new version of the Apache Web Server, the Tomcat Servlet engineer, Web Search Server, and mySQL database.

Chapter 10 introduces the many ways to access files and data on your NetWare 6.5 servers as well as making Web data much more accessible. Features include: iFolder, NetStorage, NetDrive, Virtual Office, and FTP server.

Part IV: Delivering Business Continuity

Chapter 11 explains the ins and outs of multiprocessor support in NetWare 6.5, including installation, configuration, and available multiprocessor services. It also introduces the newly expanded NetWare clustering services with support for up to 32-way clustering.

Chapter 12 introduces two powerful new additions to NetWare 6.5: Nterprise Branch Office and DirXML Starter Pack. Nterprise Branch Office enables you to create an appliance that delivers branch office users everything they need, but you can avoid those trips into the field to support your far-flung operations. DirXML Starter Pack enables you to synchronize data between the different directories, including Novell eDirectory, Microsoft Active Directory, and NT domains.

Appendixes

In addition to all the material covered in the chapters, there are several appendixes that provide a valuable reference for NetWare administrators:

- ▶ Appendix A provides a comprehensive review of Novell client property pages.
- ▶ Appendix B comprises a comprehensive discussion of login script syntax and construction rules.
- ▶ Appendix C references the NetWare console commands and SET parameters used to configure and optimize server operation.

▶ Appendix D lists the **DSTrace** options available from NoRM. It also describes the most common eDirectory error codes and provides information on how to troubleshoot these errors.

▶ Appendix E provides information on a variety of additional resources you can turn to for more help or information.

What This Book Is Not

The *Novell NetWare 6.5 Administrator's Handbook* is not designed to introduce you to the world of data networking. In order to cover the broad feature set in NetWare 6.5, we have to assume that you, as an IT professional, are familiar with the underlying concepts, technologies, and protocols upon which today's networks are built. You will see some brief introductions to concepts as necessary to introduce features, but this is not a reference work for network theory, protocols, or architectures.

You most likely have an existing network of some sort into which you are, or will soon be, introducing NetWare 6.5. You know the network architectures, topologies, protocols, and clients with which you will be working. The *Novell NetWare 6.5 Administrator's Handbook* helps you understand how to integrate the benefits of NetWare 6.5 into your existing environment.

About the Author

Jeffrey L. Harris, a nine-year veteran of Novell, has worked throughout the Novell organization, including stints in Novell Technical Services, Major Market Sales Operations, Technical/Product Marketing, and Contract Management. Mr. Harris has written books, articles, marketing collateral, and technical white papers on several products and technologies, including directories, network and Internet security, network protocols, and proxy caching. Mr. Harris has a B.S. in Computer Science and a Masters of Business Administration (MBA).

Dedication

For my family—Susan, Tyler, Rylee, Austin, and Joshua—
without whom none of this would matter.

Acknowledgments

As is usually the case, this book wouldn't have been possible without the willing collaboration of many who provided information, support, and encouragement. My support group includes the following Novell folks who lent their talent and resources along the way:

Nancy Cadjan, Ryan Taylor, Ron Warren, Amy Ahlander, Leo Teemant, David Chenworth, Jack Hodge, Jim Short, Todd Davis, Corby Morris, and Jeff Fischer.

We Want to Hear from You!

As the reader of this book, *you* are our most important critic and commentator. We value your opinion and want to know what we're doing right, what we could do better, what areas you'd like to see us publish in, and any other words of wisdom you're willing to pass our way.

You can email or write me directly to let me know what you did or didn't like about this book—as well as what we can do to make our books stronger.

Please note that I cannot help you with technical problems related to the topic of this book, and that due to the high volume of mail I receive, I might not be able to reply to every message.

When you write, please be sure to include this book's title and author as well as your name and phone or email address. I will carefully review your comments and share them with the author and editors who worked on the book.

E-mail: feedback@quepublishing.com

Mail: Que Publishing/Novell Press
800 East 96th Street
Indianapolis, IN 46240 USA

Reader Services

For more information about this book or others from Novell Press or Que Publishing, visit our Web site at www.quepublishing.com. Type the ISBN (excluding hyphens) or the title of the book in the Search box to find the book you're looking for.

Getting Started

1 NetWare 6.5 Server Installation

2 Novell Clients

3 Novell Management Tools

In This Part

NetWare recently celebrated its 20th anniversary, and yet for some of you, NetWare 6.5 might be the beginning of your experience with the network operating system. Others have almost certainly been working with NetWare for many years, and this is another upgrade of the industry's premier net operating system. Yet others lie somewhere in between these two extremes.

One of its most unique characteristics of NetWare is the fact that it was designed specifically for the server tasks of network storage, file sharing, print sharing, and network services. Today, the network is the Internet, and files are shared via Web servers, Web services, and Web browsers, but make no mistake that it's still file sharing, and NetWare 6.5 is eminently qualified to play in this exciting new arena. NetWare operates as part of the network "plumbing," and is performing at its best when users don't even realize it's there. Basic design decisions were made to make NetWare the best at performing these tasks, and more than 20 years later, NetWare continues to be the world's best network operating system. The capabilities of a specialized Net operating system such as NetWare continue to prove their worth in the face of ever-mounting evidence that a general-purpose operating system is incapable of delivering the necessary levels of performance and security required by today's mission-critical Net environments.

Global business networks and the Internet now require distributed Net storage, transparent access to Net data, and a consistent Net experience, regardless of location or access method. These are all requirements well within the original design vision for NetWare, and Novell effectively delivers these capabilities, and many more, in the form of NetWare 6.5.

The three chapters comprising Part I of this book begin by taking you through the NetWare 6.5 installation process. They introduce the major components of a NetWare environment—namely the NetWare server, the latest Novell clients—and the latest generation of management tools designed to keep everything on an even keel.

CHAPTER 1

NetWare 6.5 Installation

Instant Access

Preparing to Install

There are four recommended tasks to prepare your network for NetWare 6.5:

- ▶ Back up your data
- ▶ Update eDirectory (if necessary)
- ▶ Update eDirectory schema (if necessary)
- ▶ Update the Certificate Authority object in eDirectory

Installing

- ▶ To install a new server, insert the NetWare 6.5 Operating System CD-ROM into your server's CD-ROM drive and reboot the server.

Upgrading

- ▶ NetWare 6.0—To upgrade to NetWare 6.5, choose one of these options:
  - **a.** Perform an in-place upgrade by running **INSTALL** from the root of the NetWare 6.5 Operating System CD-ROM.
  - **b.** Use the NetWare Server Consolidation Utility to transfer volumes, directories, users, printers, and printer agents from a

source server to a previously installed NetWare 6.5 destination server.

▶ NetWare 5.1—To upgrade to NetWare 6.5, choose one of these options:

   a. Perform an in-place upgrade by running **INSTALL** from the root of the NetWare 6.5 Operating System CD-ROM.

   b. Use the NetWare Server Consolidation Utility to transfer volumes, directories, users, printers, and printer agents from a source server to a previously installed NetWare 6.5 destination server.

   c. Use the NetWare Migration Wizard from a workstation to move server data only from an existing source server to a new NetWare 6.5 destination server.

▶ Any NetWare 5 or NetWare 4—To upgrade to NetWare 6.5, choose one of these options:

   a. Use the NetWare Server Consolidation Utility to transfer volumes, directories, users, printers, and printer agents from a source server to a previously installed NetWare 6.5 destination server.

   b. Use the NetWare Migration Wizard from a workstation to move server data only from an existing source server to a new NetWare 6.5 destination server.

▶ NetWare 3—To upgrade to NetWare 6.5, use the NetWare Migration Wizard from a workstation to move server data only from an existing source server to a new NetWare 6.5 destination server.

▶ Windows NT v4—To upgrade to NetWare 6.5, use the NetWare Server Consolidation Utility to transfer volumes, directories, users, printers, and printer agents from a source server to a previously installed NetWare 6.5 destination server.

Getting Ready for NetWare 6.5

Whether you are building a new network with NetWare 6.5 or installing it into an existing network, there are certain preparations you should make so that the installation goes as smoothly as possible.

For those rare few of you creating a new network from the ground up, you have the opportunity to do all the little things that will make that network easier to manage down the road. Carefully consider your choices of cabling, protocols, addressing, naming schemes, and access methods, and so forth. As the technical foundation of your network, these are very difficult to change midstream. Consider business factors such as potential company growth, mergers or acquisitions, reorganizations, and all the other business considerations of the 21st century. If you don't, your network might lack the flexibility necessary to adapt to changes at the organizational level.

Unfortunately, the results of all this planning will then have to be weighed against the realities of your budget. There will be inevitable compromises, but this type of advanced planning will make sure those compromises don't come back to haunt you once the network is running.

Server Hardware Planning

Consider the following as you prepare your server hardware for the NetWare 6.5 installation:

▶ *Processor speed:* The server must have an Intel Pentium II or AMD K7 processor or higher. Novell recommends Pentium III 700MHz or higher processors for multi-processor servers.

▶ *CD-ROM drive:* The server must have an ISO9660-compatible CD-ROM drive. Novell also recommends using a bootable CD-ROM drive compatible with the El Torito specification for booting directly from the CD.

▶ *Server memory:* A NetWare 6.5 server must have a minimum of 512MB of system memory (RAM).

▶ The NetWare 6.5 installation routine will properly detect most storage adapters and devices, but you should be familiar with brand and type of your server's storage controllers (SCSI board, IDE controller, and so on), as well as the brand, type, capacity, and so on, of the storage devices (hard disks, CD-ROM/DVD drives, tape drive, and so on) attached to those controllers.

▶ *Size of hard disks:* There are two considerations when determining the appropriate size of your server hard disk(s): the DOS partition and the NetWare partition. The DOS partition is a portion of the hard disk reserved for DOS system files, server startup files, and any other DOS utilities you want to store on the server. NetWare 6.5 recommends a DOS partition of at least 1GB, but a good rule of thumb is to start with the minimum and then add 1MB for every MB of server RAM installed. That way you will be able to do a core dump to the DOS partition if necessary. Similarly, NetWare 6.5 recommends at least 4GB for the NetWare partition. This same amount is recommended for the SYS: volume, so the space needs of additional volumes should be added to this minimum amount.

▶ *Network adapters:* Know the type of network adapters installed in the server and have a copy of the latest LAN drivers available. Note the adapter's settings and the frame type(s) associated with each board. The default frame type for TCP/IP is Ethernet II and the default frame type for IPX is Ethernet 802.2.

NOTE Even though NetWare 6.5 is new in many respects, older drivers from NetWare 5.1 or NetWare 6 may still work just fine with NetWare 6.5. If you have an older adapter for which NetWare 6.5 doesn't include drivers, try the older drivers first before spending the money on a new adapter.

▶ *Display and input devices:* NetWare 6.5 requires an SVGA or better video adapter and monitor along with a standard keyboard and mouse for direct console operation. However, with the powerful Web-based administrative tools available with NetWare 6.5, it is now possible to operate a "headless" NetWare server without any direct input or output devices. This also removes one of the primary sources of mischief in the NetWare environment.

▶ *Server name:* If you haven't already done so, you should define a naming convention for your network resources, and determine an appropriate name for this server within those conventions. The server name can be between 2 and 47 characters in length and can include alphanumeric characters, hyphens, and underscores.

▶ *Special hardware configuration:* If your server supports any special hardware configurations, such as HotPlug PCI or multiple processors, make sure to have current drivers available in case they are needed during the installation.

Remember that installing a new network operating system is a significant undertaking. All hardware configurations should be tested in a lab environment before introducing them to a new version of NetWare in your production network.

Volume Planning

Consider the following as you plan the volumes to be created within your server's NetWare partition:

▶ *SYS volume:* The **SYS** volume is the storage location for all NetWare system files and products. As such, it is absolutely critical that your **SYS** volume not run out of space. You should plan a minimum of 4GB for the **SYS** volume in order to have room for the many additional products and services available with NetWare 6.5.

▶ *Additional volumes:* It is usually a good idea to reserve the **SYS** volume for NetWare files and create additional volumes for network applications and data. NSS provides disk pools that can span physical drives. Multiple volumes can reside inside each disk pool. Once created, these additional volumes can be used in any way you see fit. You can organize data in volumes based on who needs access, on the type of namespace required for the files, or on how you want the data distributed across the network. Remember to keep volume names consistent with your global naming strategy.

▶ *File compression:* You can choose to implement file compression at any time, but once installed it cannot be removed without re-creating the volume.

Remember that the **SYS** volume should be reserved exclusively for system files and nonvolatile files that won't be changing a lot or growing significantly over time. Create as many other pools and volumes as you need to support your non-NetWare applications and data, but try not to mix them into the **SYS** volume.

Protocol Planning

Your biggest considerations as you decide which protocols to run on the NetWare 6.5 server are

▶ What is already out there?

▶ How will network usage evolve in the future?

IP has already been selected as the world's network standard, due to its exclusive use on the Web. However, NetWare's original IPX is still in limited use, supporting legacy applications and queue-based printing for the most part. You will almost certainly be implementing IP in your network, but it's still a good idea to understand the advantages and disadvantages of both protocols, along with some other common protocols and protocol configurations prior to implementing your network.

▶ *Internet Protocol (IP):* Novell made the move to IP as its default protocol with the release of NetWare 5, and if your network is connected with any external network or the Internet, you will be using IP to make that connection. An IP network requires some advanced planning in order to be sure that all devices can communicate, particularly if you are connecting your network to the outside world (see Table 1.1).

TABLE 1.1   IP Considerations

CONSIDERATION	DESCRIPTION
Server IP address	Each device on an IP network must have a unique address. If you are connecting to the Internet, you can reserve a unique address, or block of addresses, through the Internet Network Information Center (InterNIC).
Server subnet mask	The subnet mask identifies a portion of the network. Subnet masks allow you to divide your network into more manageable segments.
Default router address	Also called the gateway, this entry determines where packets with an unknown network address are sent. The default router is often that which connects your network to the Internet. If you want to specify a specific default router, make sure you have that information prior to the NetWare 6.5 installation.
DNS information	If you want to use domain name services on your network, you need to know your network's domain name as well as the addresses of any name servers you want to use. Configuring DNS on NetWare 6.5 is covered in Chapter 4, "NetWare 6.5 Server Management."

▶ *Internet Packet Exchange (IPX):* IPX is a Novell proprietary protocol that became a de facto standard due to NetWare's market acceptance. It's very easy to install and configure, but the Internet has relegated it to a legacy role.

NOTE Each server on an IPX network must have a unique internal net number. This number can be randomly generated during installation or you can specify it manually.

NOTE You can choose to install both IP and IPX protocol stacks on your NetWare 6.5 server in order to support both legacy applications and external connectivity. However, this solution adds significant administrative overhead because both environments have to be managed separately. Furthermore, because IP and IPX services cannot interact, you can run into trouble accessing IPX services from an IP segment and vice versa.

▶ *Compatibility Mode:* If you are still making the move from IPX to IP, Compatibility Mode (CM) can help you make the transition more seamlessly by letting IPX-dependent applications receive the information they need in IPX format, even though the network is running IP. Table 1.2 lists some considerations for Compatibility Mode.

TABLE 1.2 Compatibility Mode Considerations

CONSIDERATION	DESCRIPTION
Compatibility Mode (CM) driver	The CM driver acts as a virtual network adapter to which IPX can be bound. The CM driver can then internally route IPX packets and deliver IPX-based information to IPX applications running on the server. IPX services reach IPX clients by being encapsulated within IP packets.
SLP	In order to properly handle IPX-based routing and service advertisement, CM relies on the IP-equivalent Service Location Protocol (SLP). Make sure SLP is configured on your network if you want to use CM.
Migration agent	The migration agent makes it possible for external systems to interact with the internal IPX network created by the CM driver. The migration agent tunnels IPX packets through the IP network so that IP and IPX systems can interact, or so that IPX segments can communicate across an IP backbone.

NOTE NetWare 6.5 doesn't install Compatibility Mode by default. If you need to configure Compatibility Mode on your network, see the NetWare 6.5 online documentation
for more information.

eDirectory Planning

There are some basic pieces of eDirectory information you have to supply
in order to complete the NetWare 6.5 installation. eDirectory design concepts are presented in Chapter 5, "Novell eDirectory Management."
Additional eDirectory reference material is available in Appendix D.

▶ *Tree name:* You need to know the name of the eDirectory tree into
which the NetWare 6.5 server will be installed.

▶ *Server location within the eDirectory tree:* Prior to installing the
server, make sure you are familiar with the organization of your
eDirectory tree. You need to specify the context within which the
server will reside. This consists of the name of the organization or
organizational unit to which this server will belong.

▶ *Administrator name and password:* If you are installing the first
server in a new tree, an Admin account will be created and you will
specify the Admin password. If you are installing the server into an
existing eDirectory tree, you will need to provide the name, including context, and password of the existing Admin user.

▶ *Server's time zone:* You need to specify the server's time zone and
whether that time zone supports daylight savings time.

▶ *Time synchronization:* NetWare provides its own proprietary time
synchronization service that is largely self-configuring. The first
NetWare server in a network is created as a Single Reference timeserver. Subsequent servers, even if they are installed in a new
eDirectory tree, will default to secondary timeservers. If your
eDirectory tree will span geographic locations or manages a heterogeneous server environment—including Unix, Linux, or Windows
servers—you will probably want to implement a time synchronization scheme based on the standard Network Time Protocol (NTP).
For more information on time synchronization, see in Chapter 4.

NetWare 6.5 includes Novell eDirectory v8.7.1. In order to support this
version of eDirectory in your existing network, you should have the latest
eDirectory service packs installed on your existing servers. You can get
the latest eDirectory service packs from Novell at `support.novell.com`.

Print Planning

NetWare 6.5 continues the evolution of NetWare printing, which has relied on Novell Distributed Print Services (NDPS) since the release of NetWare 5. iPrint, first released with NetWare 6, leverages NDPS to deliver print from anywhere, extremely simple printer configuration, and robust Internet printing options based on the Internet Printing Protocol (IPP). For more information on iPrint and NDPS, see Chapter 7, "NetWare Printing Servicer."

To plan for an NDPS printing environment, consider the following:

▶ *Will NDPS be installed:* If this server will function as part of the NDPS environment, remember to install NDPS as part of the NetWare 6.5 installation.

▶ *Will an NDPS broker be installed:* The NDPS broker provides the management framework within which all NetWare print activities occur. The NDPS installation routine will install an NDPS broker on a server only if there is no other broker within three network hops of the server. If necessary, you can override this setting and specify whether to install a broker on this server.

▶ *Disable any broker services:* The NDPS broker provides three principal services: Service Registry, Event Notification, and Resource Management. Depending on how you choose to configure your NDPS environment, one or more of these services might not be needed on the server.

Network Preparation

Before you install NetWare 6.5 into an existing network, there are a few things you should do to make sure the network is ready for the introduction of NetWare 6.5. Novell includes Deployment Manager (see Figure 1.1) to help identify and automate these tasks. You can run Deployment Manager from any Windows workstation by executing NWDEPLOY.EXE from the root of the NetWare 6.5 Operating System CD.

Deployment Manager is organized into three main categories: Network Preparation, Install/Upgrade Options, and Post-Install Tasks. To prepare your network for NetWare 6.5, you will focus on the tasks listed under Network Preparation.

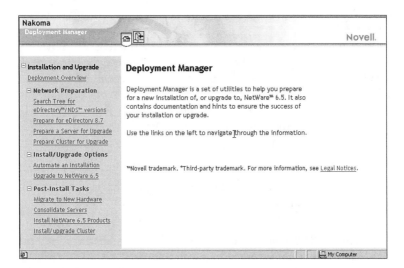

FIGURE 1.1
Deployment Manager installation/upgrade options screen.

You can run Deployment Manager and review its overviews and check-lists from any workstation. However, to actually perform the network checks and updates necessary to prepare your network for the NetWare 6.5 installation, you need to have the latest NetWare client installed. See Chapter 2 for information on installing the NetWare client.

WARNING Before performing any significant work on your network, it is always a good idea to back up your network data. Use your preferred data archive utility, such as NetWare's own Storage Management Services (SMS), to back up eDirectory and server data that might be affected by installation and upgrade processes. For more information on backing up your network data, see Chapter 8, "File Storage and Management."

NOTE Because preparations for NetWare 6.5 will make changes to your servers, install the latest NetWare support packs on the servers that will be associated with the NetWare 6.5 server that you are preparing to install. Failure to do so could result in instability in your network environment. Support packs can be found at http://support.novell.com/filefinder/6385.

Search Tree for eDirectory/NDS Version

Selecting this option lets you search your network for existing versions of eDirectory to determine whether any existing versions need to be updated prior to installing or upgrading to NetWare 6.5. To do this, complete the following steps:

1. From Deployment Manager, select Search Tree for eDirectory/NDS Versions.

2. Select View and Update NDS.

3. Browse to the eDirectory tree or container you want to search for NetWare servers and click Next. Select Include Subordinate Containers to search the entire tree or tree branch you have specified.

4. Deployment Manager will show you the version of eDirectory installed on each server it finds and will indicate whether or not it needs to be updated. If no server needs to be updated, click Exit to return to the Deployment Manager main menu.

5. Click Next to perform the eDirectory update on those servers that require it.

6. Click Next to restart eDirectory on that server.

7. Click Exit to return to the Deployment Manager main menu.

This is an important step because failure to upgrade eDirectory can result in schema corruption and other nastiness.

Prepare for NDS eDirectory 8.7

If you are installing NetWare 6.5 into an existing eDirectory environment, Deployment Manager will review the existing eDirectory schema and prepare it for the installation of eDirectory 8.7. For more information on the eDirectory schema, see Chapter 5.

To review the current schema configuration on your network with Deployment Manager, complete the following steps:

1. From the left pane of Deployment Manager, select Prepare for New eDirectory.

2. Select Extend Core Schema in the right pane.

3. Browse to the eDirectory tree you want to review and click Next.

4. Select one of the servers from the list of servers with Read/Write partitions of the Root partition and click Next. The schema will be extended, as necessary, to support eDirectory 8.7 features and functionality.

5. Click Exit to return to the Deployment Manager main menu.

With the schema updates in place, you can be certain that NetWare 6.5 servers will be able to communicate effectively with the existing eDirectory servers on your network.

Installing a New Server

After you have gathered all the information you need and made the necessary decisions with regards to installation and configuration, you are ready to perform the NetWare 6.5 installation.

This section explains how to install a new server. If you are upgrading from a previous version of NetWare or from a different network operating system, skip to "Upgrading an Existing Server to NetWare 6.5" later in this chapter.

There are three main steps to the NetWare 6.5 installation:

- ▶ (*Conditional*) Configure a DOS partition
- ▶ Install startup files and create the **SYS** volume
- ▶ NetWare 6.5 Installation Wizard

The first step is occasionally necessary to prepare the server for the installation process.

The second step takes you through the hardware setup and creates the **SYS** volume on which the NetWare 6.5 system files will be stored. This portion of the installation is text-based and runs under DOS on the server. This is the "blue screen" installation for which NetWare has become famous over the years. Throughout this portion of the installation, you will be prompted to review the default configuration and to choose Modify or Continue at each screen. Choose Modify to make changes to the default values that the installation routine offers. Choose Continue to accept values and proceed with the installation. In some cases, you will need to press F10 to save your changes before continuing.

The final step sets up the server's environment and switches to a graphical format called the NetWare 6.5 Installation Wizard. The Installation Wizard is a Java-based application that allows you to use a mouse during the rest of the installation.

Configure a DOS Partition

If your server hardware is capable of booting from a CD-ROM, the NetWare 6.5 bootable CD will kick you right into the server installation process. If, for some reason, this option does not work, complete the following steps to create a bootable partition:

1. If there is an existing operating system, make sure that any data you want to save has been backed up, along with CONFIG.SYS, AUTOEXEC.BAT, and any device drivers.

2. Boot the server with the NetWare 6.5 License/Cryptography disk. It is a bootable DR-DOS disk, and has all the utilities you need to set up the DOS partition.

3. Load **FDISK** **/X**. From there you can delete any existing partitions on your server's hard disk(s). Then create a primary DOS partition of at least 1GB plus 1MB for each MB of RAM in your server.

4. Reboot the server from floppy, and use **FORMAT** **C:** **/S/X** to format the partition you have created and transfer DR-DOS system files.

5. Transfer the CONFIG.SYS, AUTOEXEC.BAT, and any required device drivers to your newly formatted **C:** drive. This should enable you to boot directly from the **C:** drive and access the CD-ROM as drive **D:**.

With the bootable partition in place, you are ready to start the actual NetWare installation.

Install Startup Files and Create SYS Volume

Complete the following steps to install NetWare 6.5 startup files and create the **SYS** volume. If you boot directly from the NetWare 6.5 OS CD-ROM, you will see a few questions before the actual installation starts. There are default answers for each question, which will work for most situations:

1. *Default option:* Install a new server. Alternatively, you can create a boot floppy for your server.

2. *Default option:* Search for CD-ROM drivers. This will choose an appropriate CD-ROM driver automatically. Alternatively, you can select the type of CD-ROM driver (IDE or SCSI) and then select a specific driver.

3. *Default option:* Switch **A:** and **B:** drives. This option seeks to ensure that drive letters are properly assigned once the initial boot sequence is finished.

4. *Default option:* Execute INSTALL.BAT automatically. Alternatively, you can launch it manually if you want to specify some optional ·

parameters. Typing **INSTALL** **/?** will show you a list of the available load parameters for the installation.

Now you are ready to get into the installation proper. If you booted from a **C:** drive, simply execute INSTALL.BAT from the root of the NetWare 6.5 OS CD-ROM and continue with the installation routine.

5. At the Languages screen, select the language in which you want the server installed and press Enter.

6. At the Regional Settings screen, make your desired selections and click Continue. The Country, Code Page, and Keyboard settings ensure that NetWare correctly processes keyboard input and extended characters.

7. Review the NetWare license agreement and the GNU General Public License (GPL), and press F10 to accept it.

8. Review the JInfonet license agreement and press F10 to accept it.

9. At the Installation Type screen, choose Default or Manual install and click Continue. If you choose the default install, you can skip ahead to the "NetWare 6.5 Installation Wizard" section, which follows. The default install detects drivers and installs the NetWare server with default settings and default software programs. The manual installation walks you through each step of the server installation and allows you to customize and explore your selections more closely. Default settings include the following:

   ▶ 4GB **SYS** volume (with remaining disk space left as free space)

   ▶ LAN and disk drivers auto-discovered and loaded

   ▶ Country Code is 1 and Codepage is 437

   ▶ Video mode: SVGA Plug N Play

   ▶ Keyboard: United States

   ▶ Mouse: Auto-discovered and loaded

TIP If you want to automate the installation with a response file, press F3 and specify the path to the appropriate file. The NetWare 6.5 installation automatically creates a response file during any NetWare 6.5 installation and saves it to SYS:NI\DATA\ RESPONSE.NI. By making minor modifications to this file, such as changing the server name or IP address, you can use the response file from one server to automatically create another with the same characteristics. For more information on using response files, see the NetWare 6.5 online documentation.

10. At the Prepare Boot Partition screen, make your desired selections and click Continue. Here you can delete any pre-existing partitions in order to make more room for the NetWare partition. You can even delete the DOS partition and re-create one of another size.

11. At the Server Settings screen, make your desired selections as follows, and click Continue.

▶ *Server ID number:* This is a random number for identifying the server on the network. It needs to be changed only if you are filtering addresses or if you have a pre-defined addressing scheme for your servers.

▶ *Load server at reboot:* Specify whether you want NetWare to restart automatically when the server is rebooted. This adds two lines to your AUTOEXEC.BAT to load SERVER.EXE from the NWSERVER folder.

▶ *Server SET parameters:* If your server devices, such as network or storage adapters, require any special load parameters, they can be entered here and stored in the STARTUP.NCF file, which is located in the NWSERVER directory on your DOS partition.

▶ *Video:* Specify the graphics mode for your monitor. The default plug-and-play option will typically work.

At this point, the installation program copies startup files and drivers to the C:\NWSERVER folder on the DOS partition.

12. At the Adapters screen, make your desired selections and click Continue.

▶ *Platform Support Module and HotPlug Support Module:* NetWare 6.5 will auto-detect whether you need Platform Support Modules (for improved multiprocessor support) or HotPlug Support Modules (for HotPlug PCI support). If nothing is listed here, you shouldn't need them.

▶ *Storage adapters:* NetWare 6.5 will auto-detect the appropriate Host Adapter Module (HAM) for your storage adapters. If it is not detected, you can choose the appropriate HAM from the drop-down menu or install one that has been supplied by the hardware vendor.

13. In the Device screen, make your desired selections and click Continue.

▶ *Storage Devices:* NetWare 6.5 will auto-detect the appropriate Custom Device Module (CDM) for your attached storage devices (HDD, CD-ROM, and so on). If the CDM is not detected, you can choose the appropriate CDM from the drop-down menu or install one that has been supplied by the hardware vendor.

▶ *Network Boards:* NetWare 6.5 will auto-detect the appropriate driver for your network board. If it is not detected, you can choose the appropriate network board driver from the drop-down menu or install one that has been supplied by the hardware vendor.

▶ *NetWare Loadable Modules:* Some server and network configurations require you to load special NetWare Loadable Modules (NLM) before completing the server installation. One example is **ROUTE.NLM**, which is necessary for installing a server into a token ring network.

14. At the NSS Management Utility (NSSMU.NLM), specify the size of your **SYS:** volume and select Create.

15. At the NSS Management Utility main menu, click Continue Installation. From this menu, you can see the NSS statistics for your current storage configuration.

At this point, the operating system CD is mounted, and the installation program mounts the **SYS** volume and copies all the necessary system files to it. Then the installation program launches the NetWare 6.5 Installation Wizard—a graphical program that will take you through the rest of the installation.

NetWare 6.5 Installation Wizard

Continue with the following steps to set up the NetWare 6.5 server environment. The Choose a Pattern screen is new with NetWare 6.5. Patterned Deployment is the ability to automatically configure a NetWare server for a specific purpose and avoid additional setup and configuration that might be required for extraneous services that will never be used. Novell has included several patterns with NetWare 6.5. Clicking each pattern in the list opens a description of the purpose of each pattern.

1. At the Choose a Pattern screen, select Customized NetWare Server and click Next.

2. At the Components screen, select the optional NetWare components you want to install on your server, and click Next. Because of the number of optional products with NetWare 6.5, the specific installation steps for each will not be presented here, but will be provided as each product is introduced later in this book.

NOTE The following required components are installed on every NetWare server, and so are not included in the optional components list: Novell eDirectory, Java Virtual Machine (JVM), Novell International Cryptographic Infrastructure (NICI), Storage Management Services (SMS), NetWare Remote Manager (NoRM), and Novell Certificate Server.

3. At the Summary screen, review your component selections and click Copy Files.

   At this point, you will be required to insert the NetWare 6.5 Products CD-ROM in order to install NetWare 6.5 components and any additional products you have selected.

4. Enter a name for this server and then click Next.

5. At the Encryption screen make your desired selections and click Next. Insert the NetWare 6.5 License/Cryptography disk, or browse to the path where your NetWare Crypto License file (.NFK) is located.

6. At the Protocols screen, make your desired selections and click Next. Highlight a listed network board and choose the protocols that will be bound to that board. You can choose IP, IPX, or both. If you choose IP, specify the server's IP address and subnet mask. You can also specify a default router/gateway. (Leave this field blank to have the server locate it automatically.) If you have multiple network boards installed, repeat this process for each board. Similarly, you can select the IPX frame type and specify appropriate network numbers if you are using the IPX protocol on your network.

NOTE The Advanced button opens a page with four tabs:

a. **Protocols** lets you configure your IPX frame types.

b. **IPX Compatibility** lets you configure Compatibility Mode (CM) to permit legacy IPX applications to run on your IP network.

c. **SNMP** lets you set some basic information that will accompany SNMP traps.

d. **SLP** lets you define an SLP Directory Agent (DA) for your network, if one is defined.

7. At the Domain Name Service screen, make your desired selections and click Next. If you are using DNS on your network, specify a hostname for the server, your organization's domain, and then enter the address(es) of the nearest DNS name servers. You can find more information on DNS/DHCP in Chapter 5.

8. At the Time Zone screen, make your desired selections and click Next. Select the time zone in which the server will reside. If this time zone uses daylight saving time, make sure the daylight saving time box is checked.

NOTE The Advanced button opens a page that lets you configure the server as a specific type of NetWare timeserver. Alternatively, you can choose to use NetWare Time Protocol (NTP) for managing time synchronization between servers. For more information on time synchronization and NTP, see Chapter 4.

9. At the eDirectory Installation screen, make your desired selections and click Next. Choose whether this server is being installed into a new eDirectory tree or an existing eDirectory tree.

    For a new tree, you will specify a tree name, server context, Admin object name, context, and password.

    For an existing tree, click the Browse button and select the container into which you want the server installed. You can click Add to create a new container, if desired. You will be required to log in as a user with administrative rights in order to complete this process.

10. At the eDirectory Summary screen, click Next.

11. At the Licenses screen, make your desired selections and click Next. Insert the NetWare 6.5 License/Cryptography disk, or specify the path to your NetWare license files (.NLF). You can also select the Install Without Licenses check box. This option allows you only two user connections to the server. Licenses can be installed after the server installation, if desired. More information on NetWare licensing is provided later in this chapter.

12. At the License Certificate Context screen, make your selection and click Next. NetWare 6.5 uses a User licensing scheme that links a license unit directly to a user object so that users can log in from any workstation at any location without fear of not having a

licensed connection available. License certificates should be installed at or above the users' context in the eDirectory so they are readily available.

13. At the LDAP Configuration screen, make your desired selections and click Next. Default LDAP ports are port 389 for unencrypted communications and port 637 for encrypted communications. Uncheck the Require TLS for Simple Bind with Password check box if you want LDAP clients to be able to log in with unencrypted passwords. This option is not recommended if you believe there is any chance of on-the-wire packet snooping.

14. At the Novell Modular Authentication Service (NMAS) screen, make your desired selections and click Next. You can choose among a variety of password and certificate-based authentication techniques available through NMAS. You can find more information on each of these authentication methods in Chapter 6.

15. At the Installation Complete window, click Yes to restart your new NetWare 6.5 server. When the computer reboots, the server will automatically restart if you made this selection during the installation. Otherwise, change to the NWSERVER directory in DOS and run SERVER.EXE to start NetWare 6.5.

Once the server is running, you will see a graphical screen within which NetWare utilities can be displayed. To bring up ConsoleOne, the primary NetWare management utility, select the Novell button at the bottom of the screen and select ConsoleOne. There are also icons at the bottom of the screen for the Server Console, Editor, File Browser, Console Log, and NetWare Remote Manager (NoRM). To toggle out of the graphical environment and access the various text-based server screens, press Alt+Esc.

Upgrading an Existing Server

There are multiple upgrade options with NetWare 6.5 depending on your current Network Operating System (NOS) and your goals for the upgrade. There are three types of upgrades available with NetWare 6.5: in-place upgrade, server consolidation, and server migration. Not every upgrade option is available for every NOS. Table 1.3 outlines the upgrade options and NOS versions with which they are compatible.

TABLE 1.3   NetWare 6.5 Upgrade Options for Different NOS Versions

UPGRADE TYPE	SUPPORTED NOS	DESCRIPTION
In-Place	NetWare 6.0 NetWare 5.1	Traditional upgrade method in which the server is upgraded directly from the server console.
Server Consolidation	NetWare 6, 5, and 4 Windows NT 4	Uses the NetWare Server Consolidation Utility to transfer volumes, directories, users, printers, and printer agents from a source server to a previously installed NetWare 6.5 destination server.
Server Migration	NetWare 5, 4, and 3	Uses the NetWare Migration Wizard from a workstation to move server data from an existing source server to a new destination server. NetWare 6.5 must be previously installed on the destination server.

Windows NT

The NetWare Server Consolidation Utility migrates NT domain users and local and global groups from a Windows NT v3.51 or v4 server to a destination eDirectory tree. During the migration, the NT users and groups are converted to eDirectory objects and placed in the destination eDirectory tree. Server consolidation also migrates NT shared folders to a NetWare file system while migrating and converting Windows NT permissions to NetWare trustee rights.

NOTE There isn't a direct upgrade or migration path for Windows 2000 at this time.

NetWare 3.x

The Migration Wizard copies the NetWare 3 file system and bindery objects to a destination Novell eDirectory tree. When the bindery objects are copied to the destination eDirectory tree, they are automatically converted to eDirectory objects.

In-Place Upgrade

This is the simplest and most straightforward way to upgrade to NetWare 6.5. The in-place upgrade is available only for the following versions of NetWare. NetWare support packs are available online at `http://support.novell.com/filefinder/6385`.

- ▶ NetWare 6.0 Support Pack 3 or later
- ▶ NetWare 5.1 Support Pack 6 or later with eDirectory 8.85 or later

The in-place upgrade will update the operating system, eDirectory, and additional NetWare components that have been installed on the server, such as Apache Web Server, Certificate Server, and so on.

You should also review and complete the minimum requirements described in this section prior to performing the upgrade.

The server hardware must meet the minimum requirements for NetWare 6.5 as described in the "Server Hardware Planning" section earlier in this chapter. The server to be upgraded should also be in good general health. To check the health of a server, you can use Deployment Manager:

1. Launch Deployment Manager and select Prepare a Server for Upgrade in the left pane.

2. Select Server Health Utility from the right pane.

3. Browse to the server on which you want to run the health check and click Next.

4. Log in as a user with Administrator rights and click OK. A series of tests will be run on the target server.

5. At the Health Check Summary dialog, click Next to continue. This screen shows the results of the tests and will indicate any areas where your server might be lacking, or is in need of attention (see Figure 1.2).

A few other odds and ends you should think about before the upgrade:

- ▶ NetWare maintains deleted files in a salvageable state. Make sure there are no deleted files you want to salvage prior to the upgrade. All deleted files will be purged as part of the upgrade.

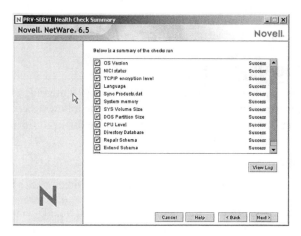

FIGURE 1.2
Deployment Manager server health check results.

▶ Make disk copies of LAN drivers, storage drivers, and the
   AUTOEXEC.NCF from the server's **SYS** volume.

▶ If you are running a NetWare cluster, you can also use Deployment
   Manager to prepare a cluster server for the upgrade to NetWare
   6.5. For more information on NetWare clustering, see Chapter 11,
   "Multiprocessor Support and Clustering."

NetWare 6.5 offers a remote upgrade option for the first time in
NetWare. You can run a remote upgrade from either Deployment
Manager or iManager 2.0. However, once the upgrade is started the
process is the same, whether it is run remotely or not.

No matter how you plan on performing the upgrade, remember that your
existing NetWare server must have a DOS partition large enough to support NetWare 6.5. If your DOS partition is smaller than 1GB, you should
create a new DOS partition and perform a new server installation as
described previously, or consider a server migration, which will be discussed later in this chapter.

In-Place Upgrade from the Server Console

If you are doing the upgrade from the server console, complete the following steps:

1. Insert the NetWare 6.5 Operating System CD-ROM into the server
   CD-ROM drive.

2. From the system console (the server command line), mount the NetWare 6.5 CD-ROM as a NetWare volume by typing CDROM at the server console. You can then type VOLUMES to confirm that the CD-ROM has been mounted.

3. Switch to the GUI console and choose Novell >> Install. This is a change from previous versions of NetWare where the upgrade was performed from the system console.

4. At the Installed Products page, click Add.

5. At the Source Path screen, browse to the root of the NetWare 6.5 CD-ROM. The volume name should be NW650S:. You should see the PRODUCT.NI file in the right pane. Highlight PRODUCT.NI.

6. Click OK to return to the Source Path screen and click OK to continue.

From here, you will continue with the standard upgrade process. See the "Finishing the Upgrade" section that follows.

In-Place Upgrade from Deployment Manager

Deployment Manager now offers the ability to upgrade a server to NetWare 6.5 without ever visiting the console. To upgrade a server through Deployment Manager, complete the following steps:

1. (Conditional) You can use a Windows 95/98 or Windows NT/2000/XP workstation to run Deployment Manager. Make sure the workstation has the latest Novell client installed, and that you are logged in as the Admin user to the eDirectory tree where the server to be upgraded is located. For more information on installing the Novell client, see Chapter 2.

2. On your selected workstation, insert the NetWare 6.5 Operating System CD-ROM. Launch NWDEPLOY.EXE from the root of the CD to start Deployment Manager.

3. Select Upgrade to NetWare 6.5 in the left pane.

4. Select Upgrade a Server Remotely in the right pane.

From here, you continue with the standard upgrade process. See the "Finishing the Upgrade" section that follows.

In-Place Upgrade from iManager 2.0

Novell iManager was introduced with NetWare 6 as a Web-based administration tool. Novell has steadily expanded its feature set since the release of NetWare 6 to make it ever more complete. For information on installing and configuring iManager, see Chapter 3.

To upgrade a server through iManager, complete the following steps:

1. Launch iManager and select Install and Upgrade in the left pane.

2. Select Upgrade to NetWare 6.5.

3. Select Upgrade a Server Remotely in the right pane.

4. Browse to the root of the NetWare 6.5 Operating System CD-ROM and click OK.

From here you continue with the standard upgrade process. See "Finishing the Upgrade."

Finishing the Upgrade

By moving the upgrade routine to the Java-based GUI, Novell has made both remote and console-based upgrades largely identical. There is ever less reason to visit your server directly because the Java tools now let you do most anything remotely from any workstation with a network connection.

To complete the in-place upgrade, complete the following steps:

1. Review the NetWare license agreement and the GNU General Public License (GPL), and click I Accept.

2. Review the JInfonet license agreement and click I Accept.

3. (*Conditional—Remote Upgrade*) At the Target Server screen, specify or browse to the name of the server you want to upgrade. You will be asked to confirm authentication to the target server before proceeding.

4. At the Backup Server Files screen, make your selections and click Next. You can choose to back up your existing server files, and restart the server automatically when the upgrade is finished.

5. At the Components screen, make your selections and click Next. Check all those components you want to install and/or upgrade during the server upgrade. By default, iManager 2.0 is selected, which requires Apache Web Server, so it is best to select Apache Web Server and iManager at the minimum.

6. At the Summary screen, review your selections and click Copy Files. The NetWare 6.5 upgrade process will now copy the new

server files. During remote upgrades, the server will reboot and go through an automated upgrade process. Once completed, Deployment Manager will reconnect to the server.

NOTE If you are performing a remote upgrade, remember that all the installation files will be moving across the network. The data transfer will slow things down significantly.

7. When prompted, log in as the Admin user to complete the eDirectory installation.

8. At the eDirectory Summary screen, review the eDirectory information and click Next.

9. At the Licenses screen, make your desired selections and click Next. Insert the NetWare 6.5 License/Cryptography disk, or specify the path to your NetWare license files (.NLF). You can also select the Install Without Licenses check box. This option allows you only two user connections to the server. Licenses can be installed after the server installation, if desired. More information on NetWare licensing is provided later in this chapter.

10. At the License Certificate Context screen, make your selection and click Next. NetWare 6.5 uses a user licensing scheme that links a license unit directly to a User object so users can log in from any workstation at any location without fear of not having a licensed connection available. License certificates should be installed at or above the users' context in the eDirectory so they are readily available.

11. At the Novell Modular Authentication Service (NMAS) screen, make your desired selections and click Next. You can choose among a variety of password and certificate-based authentication techniques available through NMAS. You can find more information on each of these authentication methods in Chapter 6.

12. At the Installation Complete window, click Yes to restart your new NetWare 6.5 server. When the computer reboots, the server will automatically restart if you made this selection during the installation. Otherwise, change to the NWSERVER directory in DOS and run SERVER.EXE to start NetWare 6.5.

The NetWare 6.5 installation is now complete. The new server will start participating in eDirectory activities immediately. You can start configuring the server for the specific purposes that you might have in mind.

Server Consolidation Utility

With the changes in server hardware over the last years, lots of RAM, and huge drive arrays and network-attached storage (NAS) options, the Server Consolidation Utility 2.5 (SCU) lets you consolidate data from redundant servers into a smaller number of more easily managed NetWare 6.5 servers.

Originally released following NetWare 6.0, the latest SCU lets you copy entire volumes and/or specific directories from NetWare 4, 5, 6, or Windows NT source servers to NetWare 5.1 or later destination servers. The accompanying rights, trustees, ownership, namespace information, and even printers and printer agents can be copied along with the files to the destination server. For many consolidation operations, the servers can even be in different eDirectory trees.

Installing the Server Consolidation Utility

SCU requires a Windows workstation with the following characteristics:

▶ The SCU workstation should be a Windows NT 4, Windows 2000 (support pack 2 or later), or Windows XP Professional workstation with at least 50MB available disk space.

▶ Install the Novell client that ships with NetWare 6.5 or run a minimum of Novell client for Windows NT/2000 version 4.83 or later. You will need supervisor rights to both the source and destination servers.

▶ Microsoft Data Access Components (MDAC) 2.7 or later installed on the workstation. For information on MDAC, and to install the latest version of MDAC, see **http://msdn.microsoft.com/ library/default.asp?url=/downloads/list/dataaccess.asp**.

▶ If the source server is running NetWare 4.x, configure the Novell client for IPX or IPX and the IP protocols.

▶ For best performance, the source server, destination server, and client workstation should be located on a common network segment.

Once the workstation prerequisites have been met, you can complete the SCU installation. SCU files are located on the NetWare 6.5 Operating System CD-ROM, in the **\PRODUCTS\SERVCONS** directory. To complete the installation, follow these steps:

1. Launch the SCU installation by executing NWSC.EXE.

2. At the Choose Setup Language screen, specify the language for the utility installation and click OK.

3. At the Welcome screen, click Next.

4. At the License Agreement screen, click Yes.

5. At the Choose Destination Location screen, specify the path into which you want to install SCU. The default location is `C:\Program Files\Novell Server Consolidation Utility\`.

6. At the Setup Complete screen, click Finish. Check the box next to Yes, I Would Like to Run Server Consolidation Utility Now to use SCU immediately.

With the SCU installed, you can now perform server consolidations in your network. This is described in the following section.

Using Server Consolidation Utility

Before starting the actual consolidation process, make sure your servers are prepared for the consolidation by reviewing the following checklist:

▶ The destination server must be running NetWare 5.1 or later.

▶ The source server must be running NetWare 4.1 or later, or Windows NT.

▶ Make sure that the latest support packs are installed on both the source and destination servers.

▶ (*Conditional*) If you are migrating data from NetWare 4, make sure the source server's volumes are running long namespace support on all volumes to be copied. To add long namespace support to a NetWare 4.11 or NetWare 4.2 volume, enter the following at the server console: `LOAD LONG` and then `ADD NAME SPACE LONG TO volumename`.

▶ Have a current backup of eDirectory files from both source and destination eDirectory trees, if applicable.

▶ Both the source and destination servers must be using the same code page in order to avoid data corruption. If the code pages do not match, Novell only recommends converting an English code page server to a non-English code page. Converting from non-English to English, or from non-English to another non-English, can cause file corruption. For information on converting an English server to a non-English code page, see the NetWare 6.5 online documentation.

▶ *(Conditional)* If there are compressed files on the source server, set Convert Compressed to Uncompressed=0. This will prevent the files from decompressing because of the consolidation process.

▶ Make sure that the latest `SMDR.NLM` and `TSA.NLM` files are loaded on the source and destination server.

▶ *(Conditional)* If you are consolidating from a NetWare 4 source server, make sure the source and destination servers can communicate via IPX. To do this, use the IPXPING utility from the console of both source and destination server to ping the internal IPX number of the other server.

There are also some general consolidation issues that you should consider as you plan your server consolidation:

▶ Open files cannot be copied. However, if you are copying from an NSS volume, you can enable File Copy on Write, which permits an open file to be accessed in the same state as it was in when it was last closed by all processes. You can set this volume attribute from ConsoleOne or from the server console by typing NSS `/filecopyonwritesnapshot=<volume name>`.

▶ If a failover occurs on a NetWare cluster involved in a server consolidation, SCU will stop. The server consolidation will have to be repeated.

▶ NDPS printer agents can be moved as part of a server consolidation, but only within the same eDirectory tree. Print queues cannot be moved. Printer agents that are moved still use the same print broker.

▶ Print Services Managers must be operational during the server consolidation. After moving the printer agents, unload the Print Services Manager on the source server so that the migrated printer agents can establish a connection to the destination Print Services Manager.

Once these pre-conditions are met, use the SCU to perform a server consolidation. You can consolidate from NDS/eDirectory or from a Windows NT domain. The following describes the process for consolidating a NetWare server to NetWare 6.5. For other consolidation options, see the NetWare 6.5 online documentation.

Consolidation from NDS/eDirectory

An SCU project file records your consolidation plan. The details of the consolidation are recorded, letting you run them immediately or save them to run at a later time.

To create an SCU project, complete the following steps:

1. Launch SCU. Once installed, it is available in Windows by selecting Start >> Program Files >> Novell Server Consolidation Utility. The executable file is FC.EXE. You can also launch SCU from Deployment Manager by selecting Consolidate Servers in the left pane, and then selecting Run the Server Consolidation Utility from the right pane.

2. Click OK at the opening splash screen. At the Startup screen, choose Create a New Project and click OK.

3. At the Project Type screen, make your selection and click OK. For a consolidation from a NetWare server, choose NetWare NDS/eDir Tree; for a Windows NT consolidation, choose Microsoft Windows Domain.

4. At the Setup Tasks screen, click Next.

5. Choose a name and location for the project file, and click Next.

6. Choose the source and destination tree for the consolidation and click Next. You must be logged in to a tree to see it in the drop-down list. If necessary you can authenticate to the desired trees by selecting the Login button.

7. Click Create to finish creating the project file.

Once the new project file has been created, you will be taken to the project window (see Figure 1.3). From this window, you model the consolidation as you want it to take place. You select the volumes, directories, and printer objects to move, and drag them to the desired location in the new tree. The source tree is shown in the left pane, and the destination tree is shown in the right pane. Drag objects from the left pane to the right pane.

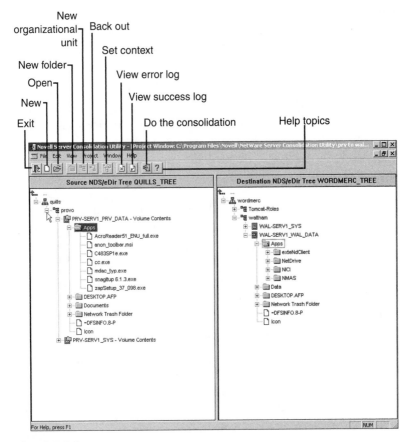

FIGURE 1.3
The Server Consolidation Utility project window.

8. Click Do the Consolidation once you have modeled the consolidation in the project window. There are several conventions you should be aware of as you model the server consolidation in the project window. At any time you can save your project, in progress, by selecting File >> Save As.

   ▶ When moving Volume objects, a Volume Drop Options dialog box will ask you to either migrate the volume contents into the directory or volume that you selected or create a new directory with the name of the volume that is being moved. Select the option you want and click OK.

▶ Once you have dropped a volume or directory to a location in the destination tree, you cannot drag it to a new location. Rather, highlight the volume or directory and click Back Out on the button bar. This will remove the volume or directory from the destination tree and allow you to re-insert it into the correct location.

▶ To create a new container or folder in the destination tree as part of your consolidation process, highlight the parent container or folder in the right pane, and click New Folder on the button bar.

▶ To rename a newly created container or folder, highlight the parent container or folder in the right pane and select Edit >> Rename.

▶ To determine the new location of an object from the source tree, highlight the object in the left pane and choose Edit >> Where Did It Go. The location of the object in the destination tree will be highlighted in the right pane.

▶ To determine the original location of an object in the destination tree, highlight the object in the right pane, and choose Edit >> Where Did It Come From. The location of the object in the source tree will be highlighted in the left pane.

▶ To see all objects currently dropped into the destination tree, choose a container in the left pane, and choose Edit >> Show Dropped Folders. Choose Show Dropped Printers to see printer objects that have been dropped into the destination tree.

This completes the creation of the SCU project. Following project creation you will go through a project verification process, which is discussed in the next section.

Project Verification

Once the SCU project has been created, SCU will launch the Verification Wizard:

1. Click Next to begin the verification process.

2. At the Dropped Folders screen, review the source and destination paths and click Next. If any of the listed information is incorrect, cancel the verification and return to the project window to make the necessary changes.

3. (*Conditional*) At the Create Folders screen, review the new folders you have created as part of your consolidation project and click Next. If any of the listed information is incorrect, cancel the verification and return to the project window to make the necessary changes.

4. At the Duplicate File Resolution screen, make your selections and click Next. If the name of a source file is identical to an existing file in the destination volume or directory, you have three options to resolve the conflict:

   a. *Don't copy over existing files:* The source file will not be copied, thereby keeping the existing destination file.

   b. *Copy the source file if it is newer:* The source file will be copied over the destination file only if it is newer than the existing destination file.

   c. *Always copy the source file:* The source file will always be copied over the destination file.

5. At the Synchronize Files and Folders screen, make your selections and click Next. Select Yes if you want to delete all files and folders on the destination server that do not exist on the source server. The default option is No.

6. At the File Date Filters screen, make your selections and click Next (see Figure 1.4). Choose No to disable any file filter based on file date. If you want to filter the file copy based on file date, choose Yes and provide the following information:

   a. *Attribute*: You can filter files based on the Accessed, Modified, and Created file attributes.

   b. *Attribute Dates:* For each attribute, specify the appropriate dates to define how filtering will be done. The On or After date specifies that only files with an attribute date equal to or later than the date specified will be copied. The On or Before date specified that only files with an attribute date equal or prior to the date specified will be copied. Setting both dates will define a date range, and only files with attribute dates between the two dates will be copied.

NOTE To make the date range work, the On or After date must be set to a date prior to the On or Before date.

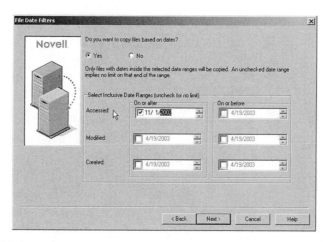

FIGURE 1.4
File date filters in the Server Consolidation Utility.

7. At the Check for Trustees and Ownerships screen, make your selections and click Next. If the source and destination servers are in different trees, browse to the container you want to search. Check Search All Subordinate Containers to include all containers below the container selected. This process will review trustee rights and file ownership information for the objects that have been dropped into the destination tree, and update them as necessary based on their new location in the destination tree.

8. At the Password Verification screen, enter the passwords for the source and destination trees and click Next.

9. Click Next to begin the verification process. Before beginning to consolidate your data, you have the option of verifying that the destination server has enough disk space to accommodate the data from the source server. To do this, click Check for Sufficient Disk Space. This process can take some time if there is a lot of data being transferred from the source server.

NOTE Click Yes to any messages notifying you that an updated TSA.NLM must be copied for the consolidation to work (see Figure 1.5). Selecting No will stop the consolidation.

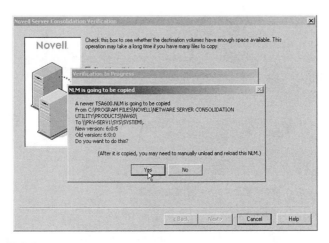

FIGURE 1.5
Sample TSA update message during the SCU verification.

10. *(Conditional)* At the Tree-to-Tree Object Match Up screen, reconcile how SCU should insert the source tree objects into the destination tree and click Next. To complete this process, do the following:

    a. Select the type of objects to display from the drop-down list provided.

    b. Highlight the object(s) you want to match from source tree to destination tree. Use the Ctrl and Shift keys to select multiple objects from the list. If you selected more than one user, right-click the users and then choose Create All Selected Users.

    c. Select the Yes radio button to create new User objects for all selected users. You can browse to the container in the destination tree in which you want to create the selected users.

    d. Click OK to continue.

11. *(Conditional)* At the Destination Object drop-down, select one of the four following options for placing the new objects from the source tree into the destination tree:

    a. *Same Name:* Select this option if the matching object in source tree with an object in the destination tree that has the same name.

    b. *Don't Match:* Select this option if no matching object exists in the destination tree.

    c. *Browse:* Select this option to locate and select a matching object from the destination tree.

    d. *Create:* Select this option to specify a container in the destination tree in which a matching user, with a different name from that of the source tree user, will be created. You will be asked to specify the new name.

12. *(Conditional)* At the Unmatched Objects screen, click Yes to proceed without matching objects or click No to go back and finish the object-matching process.

13. At the Error Resolution screen, click Next to continue the consolidation. If there are any errors during the verification process, they will be listed in the Error Resolution window, along with a possible resolution to the problem. Errors might include name conflicts, insufficient rights, files that need to be updated, required namespaces not loaded, or insufficient disk space. Verification errors fall into two categories:

  ▶ Errors must be resolved before files can be copied. You need to take some action to resolve the problem before continuing with the consolidation.

  ▶ Errors should be resolved but might not affect the copy process.

The project is now completely defined and you are ready to perform the actual server consolidation, which is described in the next section.

Performing the Consolidation

Once the consolidation project has been configured, you can either execute it immediately or schedule it for a delayed start some time down the road.

At the Start Novell Server Consolidation Utility screen, click Proceed to perform the consolidation immediately. During the consolidation, folders and objects are created, files are copied, and printer agents are moved to their destination as specified by the project plan you have just created. When the copy process is complete, the Process Finished screen lets you view the error log, view the success log, and close the consolidation process.

NOTE If you interrupt the copy process before it completes, all changes made to the destination tree will remain. Removing the new objects will require you to delete them manually.

Alternatively, you can use the Windows Scheduled Tasks feature to delay the consolidation to a time that is appropriate. This lets you plan and test a consolidation project during the day, and then schedule it to run during off hours to limit the effect on your production network.

To schedule a project to run at a later time, take note of the project name and location, and then complete the following steps:

1. Launch the Task Scheduler in Windows by selecting Start >> Settings >> Control Panel.

2. Select Scheduled Tasks and then select Add Scheduled Task to launch the scheduler.

3. At the Scheduled Task Wizard screen, click Next.

4. From the list of programs provided, select Novell Server Consolidation Utility and click Next.

5. Specify a name for the scheduled task and select One Time Only as the task frequency, and then click Next.

6. Specify the start time and date for the scheduled task, and click Next.

7. Specify the Windows username and password of the Admin user who will perform the task, and click Next.

8. Verify the scheduled task settings, and check Open Advanced Properties for This Task When I Click Finish, and then click Finish.

9. From the Advanced Properties screen, select the Task tab.

10. Add the following four parameters to the end of the pathname in the Run field, and click OK. Separate each parameter from another by a single space:

    a. *Location and name of project file:* Specify the complete path to the SCU project file you have just created.

    b. *Y:* Indicates that the specified SCU project should be run automatically.

    c. *Password for source server:* Enter the Admin password for the source server.

　　d. *Password for destination server:* Enter the Admin password
　　for the destination server.

The completed Run field should resemble this:

```
c:\program files\novellserver consolidation
utility\fc.exe
"c:\my documents\Prv_to_Wal.mdb" y novell novell
```

11. Enter the Windows username and password of the Admin running
the project once again and click OK.

The scheduled task is now ready to run at the time and date you have
specified.

Server Migration

Introduced originally with NetWare 6.0, the Migration Wizard lets you
migrate a server's file system and all network data, such as NDS or
eDirectory databases, and NetWare 3.x Bindery databases from a source
server to a new NetWare 6.5 destination server.

With the introduction of the Server Consolidation Utility, which replaces
the Migration Wizard in most cases, the primary value of the Migration
Wizard is in migrating those few remaining NetWare 3 servers you might
have. However, it remains possible to migrate NetWare 3, 4, or 5 servers
to a new NetWare 6.5 server with the Migration Wizard.

NOTE The Migration Wizard does not support moving NetWare 6.0 servers to NetWare
6.5. Use the Server Consolidation Utility or an in-place upgrade for NetWare 6.0 servers.

There are several steps to the server migration process:

▶ Prepare the Migration Wizard workstation

▶ Prepare the destination server

▶ Prepare the source server

▶ Copy files and data from the source server to the destination server

▶ Transfer all network data from the source server to the destination
server and convert to eDirectory format

▶ Bring down the source server and allow the destination server to
insert itself into the network and take over the operations of the
source server

Complete the tasks described in the following sections to prepare for the server migration.

Install NetWare Migration Wizard

Migration Wizard requires a Windows workstation with the following characteristics:

- ▶ Windows 98, Windows NT 4, or Windows 2000/XP with at least 50MB available disk space.

- ▶ Install the Novell client that ships with NetWare 6.5 or run a minimum of Novell client v3.3 for Windows 98, or Novell client for Windows NT/2000/XP version 4.8 or later.

- ▶ If the source server is running NetWare 4.x, configure the Novell client for IPX or IPX and IP protocols.

- ▶ For best performance, the source server, destination server, and client workstation should be located on a common network segment.

To install the Migration Wizard software, insert the NetWare 6.5 Operating System CD-ROM into your workstation CD-ROM and complete the following steps:

1. Browse to `PRODUCTS\MIGRTWZD` and run MIGRTWZD.EXE. You can also launch the Migration Wizard software from Deployment Manager by selecting Migrate to New Hardware in the left pane, and then selecting Run the Migration Wizard in the right pane.

2. Choose the setup language and click OK.

3. At the Welcome screen, click Next.

4. At the Software License Agreement screen, click Yes.

5. At the Choose Destination Location screen, click Next. Browse to an alternative installation location if desired. The default is `C:\ PROGRAM FILES\NOVELL\NETWARE MIGRATION WIZARD`.

6. At the Setup Complete screen, click Finish to close the Migration Wizard installation.

Once Migration Wizard has been installed on your workstation, you are ready to set up a server migration. This is described in the following sections.

Prepare the Destination Server

The destination server is the new server hardware that will receive the data from the source server. This server must be installed into a temporary tree. After data is migrated from the source server to the destination server, Migration Wizard automatically modifies the destination server's AUTOEXEC.NCF file to include the source server's name and internal IPX number/server ID. Then, when the destination server reboots, it takes the place of the source server in the network.

To do this, you first prepare the server hardware and install NetWare 6.5 on the new server. To do this, follow the steps given previously in "Getting Ready for NetWare 6.5" and "Installing a New Server." To make sure the destination server is ready for the migration process, complete the following tasks:

▶ Select the Pre-migration Server pattern in the NetWare Installation Wizard.

NOTE When you install a NetWare 6.5 server as a pre-migration server, it does not configure the core management services as it does during a regular NetWare 6.5 installation. Make sure you install the following services after the installation is complete: iManager, iMonitor, NetWare Remote Manager, and Novell Modular Authentication Services (NMAS).

▶ Make sure the destination server is installed into a temporary eDirectory tree with a different server name from that of the source server. If this is not done, the destination server will not assume the identity of the source server after the migration.

▶ Create volumes on the destination server that are the same size as, or larger than, volumes on the source server. Volume names on the destination server must be the same as the volume names on the source server.

▶ Migration Wizard migrates compressed volumes. If you are migrating compressed volumes to uncompressed volumes, Migration Wizard decompresses the volumes during the migration. Make sure you have enough room on the uncompressed volume(s) of the destination server to accommodate the source volumes once they are decompressed.

▶ (*Conditional*) If migrating from NetWare 3 or NetWare 4, install and configure the IPX protocol on the destination server. If desired, you can remove IPX after completing the migration.

▶ *(Conditional)* If you are migrating from NetWare 3, determine whether you want to use a Template object to migrate your users to the destination eDirectory tree. A Template object is used to define additional eDirectory user attributes for bindery or domain users during the migration. Template objects are especially useful for defining additional attributes that are not found in the binderies or domains.

NOTE In order to migrate home directories, you must use a Template object. If there is a conflict between the properties of a Template object and legacy user properties or policy settings, the properties of the Template object will, in most cases, take priority. The last name, full name, and description of every Legacy object is always migrated and these corresponding properties from the Template object are overwritten. If you decide to use a Template object, you can create one in ConsoleOne by choosing File >> New >> Object >> Template. IP addresses for the source server will not be migrated.

Once the destination server is installed and configured in a temporary eDirectory tree, it is prepared to receive the data from the source server.

Prepare the NetWare 3.x Source Server

The source server contains the files, volumes, and network data and objects that will be migrated to the new NetWare 6.5 server. To make sure the source server is ready for the migration process, complete the tasks described in the following sections. Because much of this can be done from the Server Consolidation Utility, discussed previously, only the NetWare 3 migration steps are covered here. For information on using Migration Wizard with other versions of NetWare, see the NetWare 6.5 online documentation.

Complete the following tasks to prepare your NetWare 3.x servers for migration to NetWare 6.5:

▶ Ensure that the source server is running NetWare 3.11 or later.

▶ Update the source server with its latest appropriate support pack or system file updates. NetWare support packs are available online at `support.novell.com/filefinder/6385`.

▶ Load one of the following NLM programs at the server console of each NetWare 3 source server that you are planning to migrate:

    a. NetWare 3.11: load TSA311.nlm

    b. NetWare 3.12 and 3.2: load TSA312.nlm

▶ Use your preferred data archive utility to back up all bindery and server data on the source server so that you can recover should a problem occur during the migration.

▶ Verify that you are authenticated as a user with Console Operator rights to the NetWare 3.x server.

Migrating a NetWare 3.x Server with Migration Wizard

Once the migration workstation, destination server, and source server are prepared, you are ready to start the actual migration process. This process varies, as described in the following sections, with the type of source server with which you are working.

NOTE Migration Wizard should be used only during network off hours due to the bandwidth it consumes during the actual data migration.

Run Migration Wizard from the location where you installed it—by default: Start >> Programs >> Novell >> NetWare Migration Wizard >> NetWare Migration Wizard—and then complete the following steps:

1. Select Create a New Project and then OK.

2. Select NetWare 3 and click OK.

3. Enter a name for the project and specify a place to save it, and then click Next. By default, Migration Wizard saves all projects to `C:\Program Files\Novell\NetWare Migration Wizard`.

4. Select the source server, or servers, from the list of available NetWare 3 servers and click Next.

5. Select the eDirectory tree into which the NetWare 3 bindery objects will be installed and click Next.

6. Have Migration Wizard find any NetWare 3 and eDirectory User objects that have the same name by selecting Yes, and then Next. During the migration, Migration Wizard will look for duplicate usernames in the destination eDirectory tree and on the NetWare 3 source server. Migration Wizard will then display its findings and you can determine whether to merge the matching usernames.

7. To save your project and access the project window, click Create. Migration Wizard will create success and error logs to document the migration process. You can view these logs at the end of the migration process.

8. To initiate the object comparison, browse the tree, select an eDirectory container, and then click OK. Migration Wizard will search this container and all subordinate containers for matching eDirectory usernames.

9. To continue the object comparison, click Next to begin searching for duplicate usernames.

10. Determine how you want to handle each of the matching user-names and click Finish. You have the following three merge options for each duplicate NetWare 3 user. If no selection is made, Migration Wizard will automatically merge the NetWare 3 user with the displayed eDirectory user.

   a. *Merge the NetWare 3 user with the displayed eDirectory user:* To select this option, do nothing.

   b. *Merge with an eDirectory user other than that currently displayed:* Select the arrow by the eDirectory username to view a drop-down list containing all the eDirectory users who have the same username (including context) as the adjacent NetWare 3 user. Select one of the eDirectory names and continue with the next NetWare 3 user.

   c. *Do not merge the NetWare 3 user with any eDirectory user:* If you know that none of the listed eDirectory users represents the same person as the adjacent NetWare 3 user, click the arrow by the eDirectory username and then click Don't Merge.

11. The Project window now appears. Review the three steps in the Using the Project Window screen and click Close.

NOTE The NetWare 3 users who you chose to merge with eDirectory User objects appear automatically in the destination eDirectory tree. Here you can plan the migration process prior to actually performing it. All object modeling is done offline, meaning that none of the changes actually take place until the migration project is actually run.

---

12. Use the project window to plan the migration, as follows. The source server's objects and data are shown in the left side of the project window, and the destination eDirectory tree is displayed in the right side.

a. Determine which NetWare 3 bindery objects and volume data will be copied to which containers in the destination server's eDirectory tree.

b. Create new containers and folders, as needed, for the NetWare 3 bindery objects in the eDirectory tree.

c. Drag and drop NetWare 3 bindery objects, folders, and volumes into eDirectory containers.

13. From the Migration Wizard toolbar, choose Project >> Verify and Migrate Project. The verification will review the proposed locations for the new NetWare 3 objects to make sure they do not conflict with existing names in the destination eDirectory tree.

NOTE You might be notified during the verification that certain NLM files are outdated on your NetWare 3 source server. Those files *must* be updated. The proper versions of these NLMs are supplied with Migration Wizard. They are available in the Products\ NW3X directory that the Migration Wizard installation routine creates. By default, this is C:\PROGRAM FILES\NOVELL\NETWARE MIGRATION WIZARD\Products\ NW3X. Copy only the NLM files that Migration Wizard prompts you to. After copying the NLM files, reboot the NetWare 3 source server and re-launch Migration Wizard.

14. Read the Welcome screen and click Next.

15. *(Conditional)* If you are migrating more than one server, choose the order that you want your servers migrated in and click Next. This matters only if you have duplicate User objects among your source servers.

16. If prompted, specify the volume to which you want to migrate your NetWare 3 print queue and click Next.

17. *(Conditional)* If you want to apply a Template object to newly created users, browse the tree, select the Template object from the tree view, and then click Next. Home directories are not automatically migrated. To migrate them, you must drag and drop the NetWare 3 directory that lists the home directories into the destination eDirectory tree. Then use a Template object when migrating your NetWare 3 users to the destination eDirectory tree and make sure that the specified home directory path in the Template object points to the location where you dropped the NetWare 3 directory in the destination eDirectory tree.

NOTE If you have not created a Template object but you want to use one now, save the project and exit Migration Wizard. Use ConsoleOne to create the Template object, and then restart Migration Wizard and select Open Last Project. Pick up the migration project starting with Step 12.

18. Choose an option for handling duplicate files between the NetWare 3 source server(s) and the destination eDirectory tree and click Next. You have three options:

    a. Don't copy over existing files

    b. Copy the source file if it is newer

    c. Always copy the source file

19. If you are migrating this NetWare 3 server for the first time, click Yes and then Next. If you are continuing with a previous migration, click No and then Next.

NOTE When you migrate users and groups from NetWare 3, Migration Wizard stores a table in the bindery of each source server of the eDirectory names that it associates with the migrated NetWare 3 users as they are migrated to the destination eDirectory tree. This way, you can migrate NetWare 3 objects in phases and Migration Wizard will remember where they were migrated. This also lets Migration Wizard assign the correct file permissions to the appropriate users.

20. Enter the password for the destination eDirectory tree and click Next.

21. Enter the password for the source server that you are migrating and click Next. If you are migrating multiple servers at one time, you will see this screen for every source server that you migrate.

22. Verify that you have enough disk space on the destination volume to accommodate the NetWare 3 file system and click Next. Migration Wizard will also scan the contents of all dropped folders and verify that you have sufficient rights to migrate them.

23. *(Conditional)* Resolve any naming conflicts between objects of different types and click Next. You can choose to rename them or not migrate them. If you are migrating multiple servers at one time, you will see this screen for every source server that you are migrating.

24. *(Conditional)* Resolve any naming conflicts between objects of the same type and click Next. You can choose to merge them or not migrate them. If you are migrating multiple servers at one time, you will see this screen for every source server that you are migrating.

25. Verify that you do not want to migrate the NetWare 3 users listed, and click Next. You will see this screen for every source server that you are not migrating. If you see users who should be migrated, click Cancel to return to the project window and drag and drop those users who should be migrated.

26. Verify that you do not want to migrate the NetWare 3 groups listed, and click Next. You will see this screen for every source server that you are not migrating. If you see groups that should be migrated, click Cancel to return to the project window and drag and drop those groups who should be migrated.

27. Resolve any critical errors and click Next. Warnings, or non-critical errors, can be resolved after the migration. To resolve a critical error or warning, read the description in the text field located beneath it. This description should give you a good idea of what could be the possible cause of the error and a suggestion for fixing it.

28. Read the verification summary and click Proceed to start the actual migration.

29. View the error log and the success log.

This completes the NetWare 3 migration process. Complete the following post-migration tasks to make sure the new server is ready to function in your NetWare 6.5 environment:

▶ Modify the print configuration if you want to convert your queue-based printing to NDPS. For more information on converting from queue-based printing to NDPS, see Chapter 7.

▶ Confirm that all migrated applications are functioning properly.

▶ Install any additional NetWare 6.5 products and services. This can be done from the server console by choosing Novell >> Install from the graphical management interface, or remotely from a workstation using Deployment Manager.

▶ Confirm that each migrated user has the correct Novell client properties so that they can successfully log in to the destination
eDirectory tree.

▶ Modify user login scripts as needed to accommodate the new data
location in the eDirectory tree. For more information on login
scripts, see Appendix B.

▶ Reassign home directories if they were not migrated.

As you can see, this is not a simple process. However, the Migration
Wizard is a powerful tool for bringing legacy servers into the 21st century. Given the powerful tools and features in NetWare 6.5, it really doesn't
make sense to hang on to legacy servers and forego the many advantages
now available through NetWare 6.5 products and services.

Novell Licensing Services

NetWare 6.5 continues to use the User Access License (UAL) model
introduced with NetWare 6.0. In this model, users gain access to network
services by connecting to the network instead of a specific server. The
eDirectory User object for each user on the network receives a license
unit, reserved for their User object, which provides them access to network services at any time and from any network workstation, regardless
of location.

The UAL model replaces the Server Connection License model used with
NetWare 5 and previous versions of NetWare. The UAL model is much
easier to manage because you no longer have to track connections on
individual servers, just connections to the network as a whole.

There are three main components to NLS:

▶ *License Service Provider (LSP):* This is the licensing software that
runs on NetWare 6.5 servers. When you install NetWare 6.5 and its
license certificates, the LSP software is copied to the server and an
LSP object is created in the eDirectory tree. An LSP provides the
actual licensing service. It handles requests from NLS clients and
maintains the license certificates, which are stored in eDirectory.

TIP Any eDirectory partition that will contain License Certificate objects should have at
least one of its replicas stored on a server operating as an LSP.

▶ *NLS client:* This is software that requests licensing services from an LSP. The NLS client will locate and communicate with LSPs as needed to request license information on behalf of NLS-enabled applications. NLS clients are used on both client workstations and NetWare servers. Nothing needs to be done to load an NLS client. The necessary components are installed with the Novell client for workstations and as part of the NetWare installation for servers.

▶ *NLS eDirectory objects:* There are two main licensing objects used by NLS, in addition to the LSP object:

   ▶ *License Certificate object:* When an NLS license is installed, a License Certificate object is created that corresponds to the printed license statement that is typically included in the packaging for software products. The name of the License Certificate object typically corresponds to a serial number or name specified by the software vendor.

   ▶ *License Container object:* The License Container object is a special container object in eDirectory that is used to store License Certificate objects. When you install a license certificate, NLS creates a new License Container object unless a license container already exists. Each license container holds one or more license certificates. License Container objects are named using publisher, product, and version.

NLS requests are handled through the following process:

   1. An application, either from a server or a workstation, issues a request to the NLS client.

   2. The NLS client library packages the request from the application and submits it to an LSP.

   3. The LSP examines the request and determines whether it can fill the request. It does this by checking the eDirectory context of the requesting client for the specific information or license unit being requested.

   4. If the requested resource is available, the LSP fills the request. If the LSP cannot fill the request, it searches for a resource. The LSP will start searching in its current container and then work its way upward in the tree.

5. Once the search is complete, the LSP returns a license status (such as available/not available) to the client library. The library subsequently returns the status to the application.

6. The application determines action based upon the status of license units.

When you install or upgrade to NetWare 6.5, NLS is automatically installed. Actual license certificates can be installed either during the installation or post-installation. NetWare 6.5 uses iManager to install and manage license certificates. You can't do it from ConsoleOne. License certificates enable users to access network resources, including NetWare servers and NLS-enabled applications and services. For more information on iManager, see Chapter 3.

Installing NLS

NLS is installed automatically with NetWare 6.5. To verify that NLS was installed and is running properly, check the following:

▶ At the server console GUI, choose Novell >> Install, and then look for an Novell Licensing Services entry.

▶ Check that NLSLSP.NLM is running on the server. To do this you can type **MODULES NLS*** at the server console or through RConsoleJ.

▶ Check to see whether there is an LSP object installed in the container where the server is installed. It will have the name NLS_LSP_*servername*.

Managing NLS Licenses

Novell typically distributes licenses in an envelope, which is a file with the extension .NLF (Novell License File). The envelope contains one or more license certificates. Envelopes allow you to install more than one license certificate at a time into License Container objects. For example, if you have purchased three products in a suite, you can use an envelope to simultaneously install license certificates for all three products. In some cases you, will also see individual license certificates. They are files with an extension of .NLS.

Installing License Certificates

When adding a license certificate to the eDirectory tree, you should know where in the tree you want to install the license certificate. This location or context determines who can use the license units associated with that license certificate. For more information on installing and configuring iManager, see Chapter 3.

To install license certificates through iManager, complete the following steps:

1. Open iManager and select Roles and Tasks.

2. In the Task frame, select Licenses and then Install a License.

3. Browse to and select the license file and click Next. NetWare 6.5 licenses are normally found on a disk in the folder **A:\LICENSE**. Some NLS-enabled applications also link their license certificates to a separate activation key. This key is stored in a file with a .KEY extension or can be entered manually to unlock the license certificate.

4. Choose the license(s) you want to install and click Next. NetWare 6.5, for example, includes both a server license unit and a group of user license units in each .NLF file.

5. Specify the context where you want the license certificates installed and click Install. If no License Container object exists in the context that you specify, one will be created. If a server license is being installed, you will also need to specify the server to which this license should be applied.

6. Click Done to exit the license installation routine.

You can also use this process to allow only designated servers to grant requests for license units. This is known as a *server assignment*. Some products require that a license certificate have a server assignment before the certificate can be used. The following guidelines apply to server assignments:

▶ Only one server assignment can be made for each license certificate.

▶ No other server can allow use of units from that license certificate.

▶ A server with a server assignment can have multiple license certificates assigned to it.

NOTE If you participate in one of Novell's Master software licensing programs such as the Master License Agreement (MLA) or the Corporate License Agreement (CLA), you will receive special licenses that support an unlimited number of users. Such licenses should be installed in the top of the tree in the Organization container and no further license installations should be necessary.

PART I   Getting Started

Deleting an NLS License

To delete license certificates through iManager, complete the following steps:

1. Open iManager and select Roles and Tasks.

2. In the Task frame, select Licenses and then Delete a License.

3. Browse to the appropriate license and click OK. Remember to browse into the license container to choose a specific License object. You can also select an entire License container, if desired.

TIP You cannot move a license certificate from one location to another. To move a license certificate, delete it from its current location and then install it to the new location.

CHAPTER 2

Novell Clients

Installing/Upgrading the Novell Client

Two Novell clients are available: one for Windows 9x and one for Windows 2000/XP. Novell client files can be accessed directly from the Novell client's CD-ROM, or copied to any convenient location, such as a network server, for installation by any client with existing network access.

Use the Novell Client Upgrade Agent to periodically check for updated client files. When updates are found, the Upgrade Agent will automatically start the client upgrade routine.

If you are upgrading multiple existing Novell or Microsoft clients for NetWare 6.5, you can use the Automatic Client Upgrade (ACU) feature to automate this process. Place ACU commands in a profile or container login script to detect whether the client software needs to be installed, and then the ACU updates the workstation automatically, if necessary, when the user logs in.

To install the Novell client from a Web server, copy the client files to the Web server and use the WRITEIP utility to create a SETUPIP executable that will download the Novell client install files from the Web server and will launch the client install routine.

Configuring the Novell Client

Once installed, you can configure the Novell client by using the Novell client property pages. Right-click the red N icon in the system tray and select Novell Client Properties.

To configure the login for a Novell client user, create a login script. Login scripts can be associated with Container, Profile, and User objects. A login script can control what happens when a user logs in to your Novell network. For information and syntax on login scripts, see Appendix B, "NetWare Login Scripts."

The NICI Client

NICI Client v2.6 ships with NetWare 6.5. The NICI client (Novell International Cryptographic Infrastructure) provides cryptographic services to all client-side applications and services, including Deployment Manager, Native File Access, Novell Modular Authentication Service (NMAS), Certificate Server, and ConsoleOne, when installed on a local workstation.

Integrating NMAS Client

Novell Modular Authentication Services (NMAS) allow you to supplement or replace the traditional Novell password-authentication mechanism with alternative mechanisms such as SmartCards, tokens, and biometrics.

▶ The NMAS client provides a framework within which authentication methods can be configured and integrated with Novell eDirectory to provide a flexible and seamless authentication process.

▶ The NMAS client can be installed from the Novell client's CD-ROM.

Novell NetDrive lets you map a drive to any server without using the traditional Novell client.

▶ With NetDrive, you can access your files on any server and modify them through standard Windows utilities such as Windows Explorer.

▶ The NetDrive client can be installed from the Novell client's CD-ROM.

NetWare 6.5 offers a way to access the NetWare file system using a workstation's native file access protocols.

▶ NFAP supports Windows CIFS, Apple AFP, and Unix/Linux NFS.

▶ NFAP is a core service of NetWare 6.5, and is installed automatically during the NetWare 6.5 installation.

Novell frequently updates its client software. Check on the Novell Support Web site's software download page at `http://download.novell.com/` for the latest versions of the NetWare clients.

Introduction to Novell Clients

On a NetWare network, workstations traditionally use special Novell client software to access NetWare servers. (Workstations are often called *clients* because they request services from the network.) This client software enables the workstation to communicate with the network. However, Netware 6.5 continues its move away from a monolithic client, and toward clientless services and small service-specific clients. Web-based management, iFolder, iPrint, and Native File Access are just a few ways that NetWare 6.5 lets you move your network in this direction.

Does that mean the Novell client is no longer necessary? Absolutely not. The Novell client is still required for advanced authentication and many administrative tasks associated with NetWare and Novell eDirectory. So, although you might not automatically install the Novell client on every workstation, you will still need it for several aspects of your network's operation.

This chapter explains how to install and configure the traditional Novell client software on the both Windows 9x and Windows 2000/XP workstations. This chapter describes how to use the Automatic Client Upgrade (ACU) feature to simplify the process of upgrading numerous workstations to the latest NetWare 6.5 client software. It also explains how to remove the client software, should that become necessary.

NOTE Novell no longer offers a client for DOS or Windows 3.1x. Similarly, the NetWare client for Macintosh, available alternatively through Novell and third-party partners, is no longer available. However, NetWare 6.5 supports Mac users through the Native File Access Pack, described later in this chapter.

In addition to the traditional Novell client software, Novell has collected other modular client pieces on the NetWare 6.5 client's CD-ROM. These include the NICI client, the NMAS client, and the NetDrive client. This chapter will present overviews and installation procedures for these client pieces. This chapter also discusses Novell Native File Access Pack (NFAP), a clientless file access option for NetWare 6.5 that can eliminate the need for the traditional NetWare client for some network users.

The Traditional Novell Client

The Novell client installation program automatically copies all necessary NetWare files to the workstation, and edits any configuration files that require modification. In order to have full administrative capabilities on the NetWare network, you must use Novell's client software instead of the software provided by Microsoft.

You can choose one of three methods for installing the Novell client on your workstation:

▶ Install the client software directly from the NetWare 6.5 client's CD-ROM.

▶ Install the Novell client from a Web server.

▶ Upgrade existing workstations with the Novell Client Update Agent.

▶ You can download the latest Novell client from Novell's software download page at `http://download.novell.com/`. Periodically, Novell releases updated clients with new features, so the client files on the Internet may be newer than those on the NetWare 6.5 client's CD-ROM. It's a good idea to check this location occasionally for updates.

The installation procedure for Windows 9x and Windows 2000/XP work-stations is identical, so you can use the installation, configuration, and removal instructions regardless of the version of Windows you are running. However, before you can install the client, your workstation must meet the following requirements.

For either platform, if you are installing a new client, you will also need either a CD-ROM drive or an Internet connection to access the Novell client install files. If you're upgrading an existing workstation that already has a connection to the network, you can run the installation program from a network directory instead.

Once these hardware and software requirements have been met, you are ready to install the client software.

Installing the Client Software

To install the Novell client software on a Windows 9x or Windows 2000/XP workstation, complete the following steps:

> **NOTE** You can use the following procedure whether you're installing a new network workstation or upgrading an existing one. If you are upgrading an existing workstation, the installation program will detect existing settings (such as the protocol used, the network board, and optional features) and use those same settings as the default settings for the upgraded workstation.

1. Install a network board in the workstation according to the manufacturer's documentation and connect the workstation to the network. It's a good idea to record the board's configuration settings, such as its interrupt and port address.

2. (*Optional*) If you are planning to upgrade a workstation and want to run the installation program from the network, create a directory called `CLIENT` under `SYS:PUBLIC`, and copy the contents of the NetWare 6.5 client's CD-ROM to the newly created network directory. Also, copy WINSETUP.EXE from the root of the CD-ROM to the new installation directory.

> **NOTE** You can create the `CLIENT` directory on any NetWare volume, but make sure users have Read and File Scan rights to the folder so that they can locate the installation files. For more information on file system rights, see Chapter 6, "User and Network Security."

3. Run WINSETUP.EXE.

   ▶ If you're installing from the CD-ROM, insert the client's CD-ROM and WINSETUP.EXE will start automatically. If it does not, run WINSETUP.EXE from the root of the NetWare 6.5 client's CD-ROM.

   ▶ If you're upgrading an existing workstation and are running the installation program from the network, run WINSETUP.EXE from the directory you created in step 2.

4. Select the client you want to install (see Figure 2.1). The installation program will automatically detect your workstation OS and will prevent you from installing the wrong client.

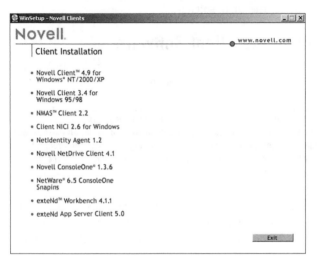

FIGURE 2.1
Novell client install options for NetWare 6.5.

5. Specify the language for the client install.

6. Accept the license agreement by selecting Yes.

7. Specify either Typical or Custom installation and click Install. If you select Custom, continue with step 8. If you choose Typical installation, skip to step 13. The Typical installation configures the Novell client as follows:

   ▶ The Typical installs only the Novell client files, the NICI client, and the NMAS client. If you want to install optional components such as NDPS, Novell Workstation Manager, and ZENworks Application Launcher, use the Custom installation.

   ▶ Both IP and IPX protocols.

   ▶ Directory-based authentication (eDirectory).

8. Select the client components you want to install and click Next. If the installation program detects that any of these options are

already installed on this workstation, those options will be checked.

9. Choose the network protocol(s) to support and click Next.

   ▶ *IP Only*: Installs only the IP protocol. The workstation will be able to communicate only with IP servers, and will not be able to communicate with IPX servers.

   ▶ *IP with IPX Compatibility Mode*: Installs the IP protocol, but allows the workstation to communicate with IPX networks if the servers have IPX compatibility mode and a migration agent installed.

   ▶ *IP + IPX*: Installs both protocols, allowing the workstation to communicate with either type of server.

   ▶ *IPX Only*: Installs only the IPX protocol, allowing the work-station to communicate with IPX servers, but not directly with IP servers.

10. Choose NDS login connection and click Next. Choose a bindery connection only if NetWare 3 is the primary server environment.

11. *(Conditional)* If you selected Workstation Manager as a component to install, enter the eDirectory tree to be used by Workstation Manager, and click Next.

12. Click Finish to complete the installation. The installation program will automatically detect and load most LAN drivers for common network adapters. If it cannot detect your network board, it will prompt you to select one. You will need to specify the location of the driver your network adapter requires.

13. At the Installation Complete screen, click Reboot to restart the workstation and load the Novell client.

When the workstation reboots, it will automatically connect to the net-work and present you with a login screen.

Removing the Client Software

To remove the Novell client software from a Windows 9x or Windows 2000/XP workstation, use the Network control panel. The Novell client uninstall will remove all client components from the workstation, but will leave behind a minimal footprint in the Windows Registry. That way, if you reinstall the client at a later time, the installation program can automatically load the same settings that were used previously.

To remove the Novell client from Windows 9x, complete the following steps:

1. Open the Network Control Panel applet by selecting Start >> Settings >> Control Panel and then selecting Network. Alternatively, you can access this utility by right-clicking Network Neighborhood.

2. Select Novell NetWare Client from the list of installed network services and click Remove.

3. Click Yes to confirm your decision.

4. Reboot the workstation to complete the client removal.

To remove the Novell client from Windows 2000/XP, complete the following steps:

1. Open the Network control panel by right-clicking My Network Places and selecting Properties.

2. Right-click Local Area Connection and then select Properties.

3. Select the Novell Client for Windows entry from the list of installed network services and click Uninstall.

4. Click Yes to confirm your decision.

5. Reboot the workstation to complete the client removal.

NOTE You can also remove the client from the Control Panel by selecting the Add/Remove Programs option, selecting Novell Client for Windows, and then clicking Remove. You will still have to reboot to complete the removal of the client software.

Once the workstation has rebooted, the removal of the Novell client is complete.

Installing from a Web Server

A new option with this version of the Novell client is that you can now set up a Novell client installation from any Web server by completing the following steps:

1. Copy the complete \WINNT or \WIN95 directories from Novell client software CD-ROM to the Web server. You can place the files on up to five Web servers in order to provide faster access.

2. Run WRITEIP.EXE. Using the WRITEIP utility, you can create a small executable called SETUPIP that downloads the Novell client install files from a Web server IP address and launches the Novell client install routine. There are versions for both Windows 9x and Windows 2000/XP, and for all supported Novell client languages.

  ▶ Windows 2000/XP: WRITEIP.EXE is located in \WINNT\i386\admin.

  ▶ Windows 9x: WRITEIP.EXE is located in \WIN95\IBM_<lan>\ADMIN\ where <lan> is one of the languages supported by the Novell client.

3. In the WRITEIP utility (see Figure 2.2), provide the necessary information and click OK.

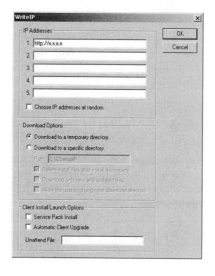

FIGURE 2.2
The WRITEIP utility is used for creating a setup application for installing the Novell client from a Web server.

- ▶ Specify the IP address(es) or DNS name(s) of the Web server(s) that host the Novell client files, and the full path to the client files. For example: `http://www.quills.com/nwclient`. Web servers will be checked in the order listed until a connection is made.

- ▶ Select Choose IP Address at Random to help balance the load of the Novell client downloads across all participating Web servers.

- ▶ Specify download options for the client installation. Files can be downloaded to a temporary or a specific directory.

  Unchecking Delete Install Files After Install Is Complete will leave the Novell Client installation files on the workstation after the installation is complete.

  Allow User to Change the Download Directory lets the user specify the copy location of the Novell client files, and change the default location.

- ▶ Specify the client install options. The Service Pack Install option lets you add service pack files to the Web installation as they are released by Novell. Both the new client software and any service pack software are downloaded and will be installed if needed.

  Automatic Client Upgrade permits the client install to run only if the Novell Client software being installed is a later version than the one currently installed on the workstation.

- ▶ Specify an unattend configuration file in order to fully automate the installation routine. For more information on creating this file, see the section on Novell Client Install Manager (NCIMan) later in this chapter.

SETUPIP.EXE will be created based on the options you have selected. You can then distribute SETUPIP.EXE from a corporate Web site, through email, or by whatever method is most convenient.

When a user launches SETUPIP.EXE, the Novell Client software will be downloaded from the specified Web server, and the client installation routine will run.

Upgrading the Novell Client

There are a couple of options for upgrading workstations with existing Novell Client installations, one has been around for a while, and one is new with NetWare 6.5. You have the option of automatically checking for updates, and running fully or partially automated upgrade routines for your users, depending on their needs.

Novell Client Install Manager

The Novell Client platform-specific installation utilities each read a configuration file in order to properly install and configure the various properties of the client. This file is stored in the same folder as the installation utility, and provides information such as where to copy drivers during installation and the most recent version number. This configuration file is configurable through the Novell Client Install Manager (NCIMan).

NOTE For Windows 9x workstations, options that were previously stored in NWSETUP.INI or were made available from the command line in previous versions of Novell Client are now configured through NCIMan.

To create or modify a configuration file with NCIMan, complete the following steps:

1. Copy the complete \WINNT and/or \WIN95 directories from Novell client software CD-ROM to the server from which users will access the client files.

2. Launch NCIMan (see Figure 2.3) from one of the directories you just copied from the Novell client's CD-ROM:

   ▶ Windows 2000/XP: NCIMAN.EXE is located in \WINNT\i386\admin.

   ▶ Windows 9x: NCIMAN.EXE is located in \WIN95\IBM_*<lan>*\ADMIN\ where *<lan>* is one of the languages supported by the Novell client.

3. Click the New button.

4. Specify the platform for which you are creating a configuration file and click OK.

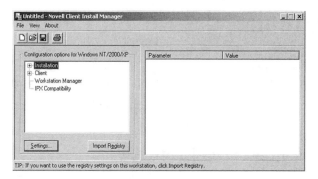

FIGURE 2.3
NCIMan utility from the Novell Client for NetWare 6.5.

5. Double-click Installation in the left pane. Make your installation option choices and click OK. Each of the installation pages contains a list of the configurable parameters for the various Novell Client components (see Figure 2.4).

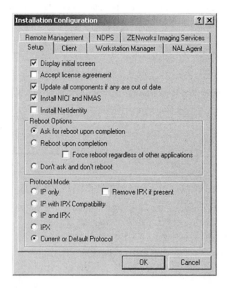

FIGURE 2.4
NCIMan installation pages are used to configure a Novell Client installation.

Any installation options different than the default selections will be listed in the right pane of NCIMan.

6. Double-click Client in the left pane to open the Client tab in the Installation Configuration (see Figure 2.5). From this page you can configure how, or if, each client component will be installed.

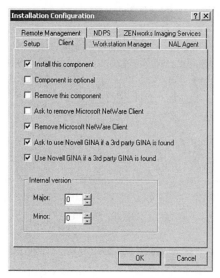

FIGURE 2.5
NCIMan client pages are used to configure default Novell client properties.

NOTE If you have previously installed the Novell client with all the installation and client property options you want, NCIMan can read that information from the Windows Registry if you select Import Registry from the main NCIMan screen.

7. Once you have selected all the installation and configuration options you want, click the Save button. You can save the configuration file with any name you want. Make sure you save the file in the same directory as the SETUP.EXE (Windows 9x) or SETUP-NW.EXE (Windows 2000/XP) file that will run to install the client:

  ▶ Windows 9x: `win95\ibm_language`

  ▶ Windows NT/2000/XP: `winnt\i386`

Once the configuration file has been saved, it can be used as the Unattend file for performing an unattended client installation or upgrade. This option can be used with Web server installations, the Novell Client Upgrade Agent, and Automatic Client Upgrades, all discussed previously in this chapter.

Novell Client Upgrade Agent

New to NetWare 6.5, the Novell Client Upgrade Agent simplifies client upgrades by allowing you to schedule periodic checks for updated client software. The Upgrade Agent will query a specified location for a newer Novell client. If one is found, the install routine will start automatically.

To configure the Novell Client Upgrade Agent, complete the following steps:

1. Create an unattended configuration file with the Novell Client Install Manager (NCIMan), as discussed previously in this chapter.

2. To configure the Upgrade Agent, right-click the Novell N icon in the system tray and select Novell Client Properties.

3. Select the Update Agent tab (see Figure 2.6).

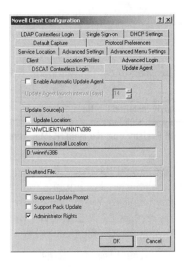

FIGURE 2.6
Novell Client Upgrade Agent configuration options—available from Novell Client Properties.

4. Configure the Update Agent and click OK when you're finished.

► Select Enable Automatic Update Agent, and specify the launch interval, which defines how often, in days, the Update Agent will check for updated client files.

► Specify the source location for the Novell client upgrade files. You can use the previously defined location, specify a new file location, or specify a Web page for the client download if you have created one (see the section "Installing from a Web Server," previously in this chapter).

► Specify the location and name of the Unattend file if one has been created. For more information on unattended configuration files, see the section "Novell Client Install Manager," later in this chapter.

► (*Conditional*) Select Suppress Update Prompt to perform the update without prompting the users.

► (*Conditional*) Select Support Pack Update to have the Update Agent check for client support packs in addition to full software updates.

► (*Conditional*) Select Administrator Rights to grant the client install administrator rights, which are required to install the client, even if the user who is logged in is not an administrator on the workstation. This option is checked by default.

Once these steps are completed, you can use the Novell Client Update Agent to automatically query for and update Novell Client software on your workstations. Once enabled, Update Agent can also be run manually by right-clicking the Novell N in the Windows system tray and selecting Update Novell Client.

Automatic Client Upgrade

Although this functionality has been largely replaced by the Client Upgrade Agent, Novell still offers the Automatic Client Upgrade (ACU) feature to automate the upgrade of multiple existing workstations to the latest Novell client. With the ACU, you place ACU commands in a container login script to detect if the client software needs to be installed, and then the ACU updates the workstation automatically, if necessary, when the user logs in. For more information on login scripts, see Appendix B.

The ACU feature works best in situations when your workstations have similar configurations, because you define a common set of instructions for updating all the workstations in the same way.

To use the ACU process to upgrade a workstation to the Novell client, complete the following steps:

1. Copy the complete \WINNT or \WIN95 directories from Novell client software CD-ROM to the server from which users will access the client files.

NOTE You can create the CLIENT directory on any NetWare volume, but make sure users have Read and File Scan rights to the folder so that they can locate the installation files. For more information on file system rights, see Chapter 6.

2. (*Conditional*) If you want to create an install routine that doesn't require any user input, use NCIMan to create an UNATTEND.TXT file, as discussed previously in this chapter. Save the UNATTEND.TXT file in the same directory from which users will run SETUP.EXE or SETUPNW.EXE to install the new Novell client. If you use a platform-specific configuration file to configure Novell client and you are using ACU.EXE, you must change the [UNATTENDFILE] option to Yes in the ACU.INI file.

3. Use iManager to add the following to the container login script for those users whom you want to receive the updated client. These commands support both Windows 9x and Windows 2000/XP clients.

```
IF OS = "WINNT" THEN
    @\\SERVERNAME\VOLNAME\...\SETUPNW.EXE /ACU
    /u:UNATTEND.TXT
END


IF OS = "WIN95" THEN
    @\\SERVERNAME\VOLNAME\...\SETUP.EXE /ACU
    /u:UNATTEND.TXT
END
```

TIP For Windows 95/98 workstations only, you can back up the old client configuration instead of just replacing it with the new client software. To do this, add the option /RB (for *rollback*) to the end of this command. This option will copy the current software configuration to NOVELL\CLIENT32\NWBACKUP.

4. When the login script executes during a user login, the appropriate
setup program will check the Windows Registry on the destination
workstation to see exactly which version of the client is currently
running. The setup routine will run only if the workstation's
Registry indicates a Novell client version older than the version to
be installed.

TIP If you need to re-install the same client version on a workstation, you can use
NCIMan to modify the Major or Minor INTERNAL version of the client so that it looks to
the setup routine as if the client is newer than that previously installed. The version setting is stored in the UNATTEND.TXT file.

The next time the users in the group log in, their workstations will be
upgraded automatically to the new Novell client. For more information
on ACU options, see the Novell online documentation.

The Client Login

Once the Novell client has been installed, you can view and set login
options from the Novell Login by clicking the Advanced button, as
shown in Figure 2.7.

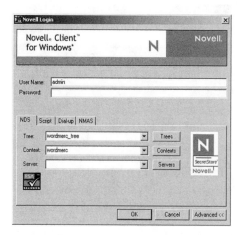

FIGURE 2.7
Novell client login screen with Advanced options.

NOTE The Windows tab, not shown in Figure 2.7, is only available prior to logging in to Windows. From this tab, you can specify the Windows username and workstation name that will be used by the Novell client to transparently log you in to the workstation as part of the NetWare login process.

NDS Tab

The NDS tab, as shown in Figure 2.7, allows you to specify the eDirectory tree, name context, and server to use during login. All users should specify their eDirectory tree and name context. A server needs to be specified only when connection to a NetWare 3 server is needed, or when you are trying to log in to a specific server.

Script Tab

The Script tab (see Figure 2.8) is used to manage the execution of login scripts. It allows you to specify whether or not to run scripts; whether or not to display the login results window (and close it automatically); and which profile and user login scripts to execute. The Variables button allows you to specify values for any script variables that might be included in the login scripts.

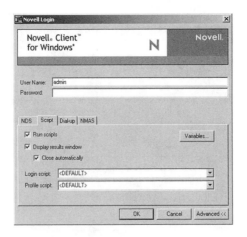

FIGURE 2.8
Novell client Script tab.

Dial-up Tab

The Dial-up tab (see Figure 2.9) is used only when a user is connecting to the network via a modem connection. It allows you to configure a client to automatically dial in to the network whenever a user attempts to login. The Dial-up tab taps into the Windows Dial-Up Networking information. You can select a dialing entry from the Windows phone book and a Windows dialing location profile. This option is used only rarely.

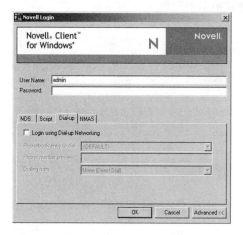

FIGURE 2.9
Novell client Dial-up tab.

NMAS Tab

The NMAS tab (see Figure 2.10) is used to configure a couple of the authentication-related features of Novell Modular Authentication Services (NMAS). For more information on NMAS see Chapter 6.

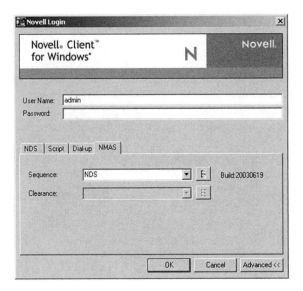

FIGURE 2.10
Novell client NMAS tab.

Configuring the Client

After you have installed the Novell client software, you can configure the
client software by modifying its properties. The client properties enable
you to specify information such as login preferences, protocol settings,
default capture settings, and so on. To open the client property pages,
right-click the red N icon in the system tray and click Novell Client
Properties (see Figure 2.11).

There are several configuration pages available in Novell client properties.
For detailed information on Novell client property pages, see
Appendix A.

▶ *Client*: The Client page lets you define basic login preferences, similar to the NDS tab in the Novell Login screen.

▶ *Location Profiles*: Location profiles allow you to save a specific
login configuration so that users don't have to enter login information manually. Location profiles are especially powerful for users
who log in from multiple locations (such as the office, home, laptop, and so on).

FIGURE 2.11
Configuration options for the Novell client.

▶ *Advanced Login*: Advanced Login options let you hide certain aspects of the Novell Login screen to prevent users from making changes.

▶ *Service Location*: The Service Location page is used to configure the client for the use of Service Location Protocol (SLP). You can specify where and how the client will request network services. For more information on SLP, see the NetWare 6.5 documentation.

▶ *Advanced Settings*: Advanced Settings allow you to configure a host of network communications details. For more information on the Advanced settings options see Appendix A.

▶ *Advanced Menu Settings*: Advanced Menu Settings gives you full control over the client network environment, including which network resources are available, and how they are offered to the network user.

▶ *Default Capture*: This page lets you configure a user's NetWare print jobs.

▶ *Protocol Preferences*: Protocol Preferences let you define the usage order for network protocols and name resolution protocols. The listed protocols are used in the order specified.

▶ LDAP *Contextless Login*: Allows contextless login without requiring the support of a catalog on the backend. When a user authenticates, LDAP is used to search the entire eDirectory tree, or trees, for the specified username. If a username is found, the login process will continue based on the tree and context information associated with that user. If the same username exists in multiple contexts, the user is prompted to select the correct user.

▶ *(Conditional) Single Sign-on*: Novell client for Windows 2000/XP adds the Single Sign-on tab. This allows you to store the workstation-specific password in eDirectory so that it can be automatically presented as part of an NMAS or single sign-on authentication, if available.

▶ *(Conditional) DHCP Settings*: Novell client for Windows 2000/XP adds the DHCP settings to configure the client DHCP environment.

▶ DSCAT *Contextless Login*: Specify the use of an eDirectory catalog for login. This allows users to authenticate using their common name only, rather than having to remember their entire name context. LDAP contextless login is recommended over this option.

▶ *Update Agent*: Configure Novell Client Upgrade Agent options, as discussed earlier in this chapter.

With these client pages you have very granular control over the operation of the Novell client.

NetIdentity

The NetIdentity agent is new to NetWare 6.5. It leverages what is known as the XTier framework used with NetStorage, Apache, and Tomcat services to provide single sign-on across all Novell services that use eDirectory authentication. The only caveat to this is that the first service with which a user authenticates must be NetIdentity-enabled. The list of NetIdentity-enabled services includes the following, with others being added regularly:

▶ Novell Client (v3.4 for Windows 9x, and v4.9 for Windows 2000/XP)

▶ iFolder 2.0

▶ iPrint

▶ NetStorage

▶ Novell Portal Services

Once you have authenticated with one of these services, accessing any other service, such as iManager, that uses eDirectory authentication will prompt a transparent, background authentication so that you aren't required to re-enter your authentication information.

To enable NetIdentity-based single sign-on to Novell services, complete the following tasks:

▶ Make sure that the XTier framework is installed on all NetWare 6.5 servers to which users will authenticate.

▶ Install the NetIdentity Agent on the workstation where you want NetIdentity services enabled.

The XTier framework is installed automatically when you install NetStorage, Apache, and Tomcat services. It cannot be selected and installed separately, so if you want to use NetIdentity, install these services on your NetWare 6.5 server prior to continuing. If you are unsure if XTier is installed on a given server, point your browser to the following URL:

`http://<server IP or DNS name>/oneNet/xtier-login`

If XTier is installed you will see an authentication dialog box, indicating that the server can recognize credentials passed by NetIdentity.

To install the NetIdentity Agent, complete the following steps:

1. From the Novell Clients CD-ROM, or from a shared network drive to which Novell Client files have been copied, run WINSETUP.EXE.

2. From the Client Installation screen, select NetIdentity Agent 1.2.

3. Select the Installation language and click OK.

4. At the InstallShield welcome screen click Next, and then click Install to start the installation routine.

5. When the installation completes, click Finish.

Once installed, NetIdentity will provide single sign-on to all Novell services that authenticate through eDirectory.

Other Novell Clients

In addition to the traditional Novell client, there are three other clients included on the NetWare 6.5 client's CD-ROM. They are as follows:

- ▶ NICI client
- ▶ NMAS client
- ▶ NetDrive client

In addition to these three feature-specific clients, there are a few others that are installed automatically with their respective product software. Each of these clients will be discussed as part of its product overview in other chapters throughout this book.

NICI Client

The Novell International Cryptographic Infrastructure (NICI) is the modular foundation for all crypto-services offered in Novell products and services. NICI client provides cryptographic services to client-side applications and services. NICI client has received FIPS 140-1 (Level 1) certification, which is as good as it gets for client-based cryptographic services. For more information on NICI and other NetWare 6.5 security services, see Chapter 6.

NICI client v2.6 is included on the NetWare 6.5 client CD-ROM. The following NetWare 6.5 services rely upon NICI client:

- ▶ Deployment Manager
- ▶ Novell Advanced Audit
- ▶ Native File Access
- ▶ Novell Modular Authentication Service
- ▶ Novell Certificate Server
- ▶ ConsoleOne (when installed on a local workstation)

To install NICI client, complete the following steps:

1. Insert the NetWare 6.5 client's CD-ROM. The CD-ROM will auto-play and present you with the Novell client installation menu. If the CD-ROM does not auto-play, run WINSETUP.EXE from the root of the client's CD-ROM.

2. Select Client NICI 2.6 for Windows.

3. At the NICI client Welcome screen, click Next.

4. At the License Agreement screen, click Yes.

5. At the Setup Complete screen, click Finish.

This completes the installation of the NICI client.

NMAS Client

Novell Modular Authentication Services (NMAS) allow you to supplement or replace the traditional Novell password authentication mechanism with alternative mechanisms such as SmartCards, tokens, and biometrics. NetWare 6.5 includes the NMAS Starter Pack, which offers two alternative authentication methods. NMAS Enterprise Edition, which is sold as an add-on product, adds support for many third-party authentication methods, multi-factor authentication, and graded authentication.

The NMAS client provides a framework within which authentication methods can be configured and integrated with Novell eDirectory to provide a flexible and seamless authentication process. For more information on NMAS, see Chapter 6.

To install the NMAS client, complete the following steps:

1. Insert the NetWare 6.5 Client CD-ROM. The CD-ROM will auto-play and present you with the Novell client installation menu. If the CD-ROM does not auto-play, run WINSETUP.EXE from the root of the Client CD-ROM.

2. The latest version of the Novell client and the NICI client are required for installation of the NMAS client. Make sure they are installed prior to installing the NMAS client.

3. Select NMAS client 2.2.

4. At the NMAS Installation screen, make sure that the NMAS Client check box is checked and click OK. The installation routine will review the versions of the Novell client and NICI client to make sure that all prerequisites have been met.

5. At the Novell License screen, click Accept.

6. Select the login methods you want to use and click Next. For more information on the NMAS login methods, see the NetWare 6.5 online documentation.

- ▶ *Advanced X509 Login*: This method requires the user to have a PKCS#12 password encrypted file. The private key in this file will be used to authenticate the user by verifying the user's certificate chain to a trusted root that is installed on the server.

- ▶ *Entrust Certificate Login*: This authentication method is used when using certificates provided by the Entrust Certificate Authority.

- ▶ *Simple Password*: This authentication method is used with Native File Access protocols and other services incapable of using the native NetWare password. Simple Password provides support for Windows, Macintosh, and NFS. Simple passwords can now be managed transparently through the use of universal password. For more information on the universal password, see Chapter 6.

- ▶ *Universal SmartCard*: The Universal SmartCard method provides user identification and authentication using a SmartCard and reader connected to a network.

- ▶ *Enhanced Password*: This is the NMAS-enhanced password method.

- ▶ *X509 Certificate*: This authentication method provides digital certificate-based login to the Novell environment.

7. At the Post-Login Methods screen, click Next. You can select NDS Change Password if you want to install that Post-Login Method. For more information on NMAS post-login methods, see the NetWare 6.5 online documentation.

8. At the Install Complete screen, click OK. Select the Restart Later radio button if you don't want the client workstation to restart immediately.

When the workstation reboots, you will see the new NMAS login screen. For more information on configuring and using NMAS login methods, see Chapter 6.

NetDrive Client

Novell NetDrive lets you to map a drive to any server without using the traditional Novell client. This means that with NetDrive, you can access your files on any server and modify them through standard Windows utilities such as Windows Explorer. For more information on using NetDrive, see Chapter 10, "NetWare File Access."

To install the NetDrive client, complete the following steps:

1. Insert the NetWare 6.5 client CD-ROM. The CD-ROM will auto-play and present you with the Novell client installation menu. If the CD-ROM does not auto-play, run WINSETUP.EXE from the root of the client CD-ROM.

2. Select Novell NetDrive client 4.1.

3. Select the language for the client installation and click OK.

4. At the Welcome screen, click Next.

5. At the License Agreement screen, click Yes.

6. At the Destination Location screen, browse to the location where the NetDrive client should be installed and click Next.

Once all files have copied, the installation of the NetDrive client is complete.

Native File Access Pack

Novell Native File Access Pack (NFAP) lets Macintosh, Windows, and Unix workstations access and store files on NetWare servers without installing the Novell client. NFAP is installed by default as part of the basic NetWare 6.5 server installation process, and provides instant network access. Just plug in the network cable, start the computer, and you've got access to servers on your network.

NFAP lets client workstations access the NetWare 6.5 file system using the same protocols that they use internally to perform local file operations such as copy, delete, move, save, and open. Windows workstations perform these tasks using the Common Internet File System (CIFS) protocol; Macintosh workstations use the AppleTalk Filing Protocol (AFP); and Unix/Linux computers use the Network File System (NFS) protocol. This not only eliminates the overhead of a special network client, but also allows users to perform network tasks using the same familiar tools that they use to work on their local drives.

Admin Workstation Requirements

In order to manage Native File Access, there must be at least one administrative workstation with the following characteristics:

- ▶ Windows 9x running Novell client for Windows 9x version 3.21.0 or later *or* Windows 2000/XP Novell client for Windows 2000/XP version 4.80 or later

- ▶ NICI client version 1.5.7 or later—the NICI client is required to perform password administration using ConsoleOne

---

TIP A suitable Novell client and NICI client are available on the NetWare 6.5 client CD-ROM. Alternatively, the latest versions of the clients can be downloaded from http://support.novell.com/filefinder/.

NFAP Client Requirements

To access NetWare servers running NFAP, computers must be connected to the network and running one of the following operating systems:

- ▶ Mac OS version 8.1 or later—Mac OS X.

- ▶ Windows 9x, Windows NT v4, Windows 2000/XP—Windows computers must be running Client for Microsoft Networks, which is a standard Windows networking component. It can be installed by choosing Add >> Client from the Local Area Connection Properties page.

- ▶ Any version of Unix or Linux that supports NFS v2 or NFS v3.

Simple Password

Simple passwords are used to support the local Windows, Macintosh, and NFS password models, which in some cases don't support password encryption. Thus, to prevent the eDirectory password from becoming compromised, Novell created a secondary password suitable for use in these nontraditional situations. To create a simple password for a user, complete the following steps:

NOTE If the simple password is different than the eDirectory password, the user would enter the simple password when accessing the network with native protocols and enter the eDirectory password when logging in with the Novell client software.

NetWare 6.5 introduces a universal password option that manages simple passwords and synchronizes them with the traditional NetWare password. Once enabled, the universal password eliminates the need to manage simple passwords separately. For more information on universal passwords, see Chapter 6.

1. Launch iManager, open the eDirectory Administration link and select Modify Object.

2. Browse to and select the object for which you want to change the Simple Password and click OK.

3. Select the NMAS Login Methods tab and click the Simple Password link.

4. Make the desired Simple Password modifications and click OK. You can create, change, or remove the simple password.

Once created, the simple password will be used by services such as Native File Access and LDAP authentication that cannot be integrated with the native eDirectory-based authentication option provided by NetWare 6.5. Simple passwords are required for these services to function, and removing the simple password may prevent them from using services that rely on the simple password.

Configuring CIFS Access

With NFAP installed and passwords configured, nothing else is necessary to allow Windows users to access the NetWare file system. They can use Windows Explorer to browse and search for files through Network Neighborhood or My Network Places. They can map network drives to their defined share point and assign it a drive letter. Because access to NetWare files is handled by CIFS, Windows users can copy, delete, move, save, and open network files just like they can with any Windows-based drive resource.

You can stop and start the CIFS service on the NetWare 6.5 server by typing **CIFSSTOP** at the server console, or from a remote server connection. Similarly, typing **CIFSSTRT** will start the CIFS service on a given NetWare 6.5 server.

Specifying Contexts in the Context Search File

A context search file lets Windows users log in to the network without specifying their full context. The contexts listed in the context search file will be searched when no context is provided or the object cannot be found in the provided context. If User objects with the same name exist in different contexts, authentication to each user object will be attempted until one succeeds with the user-provided password.

The context search file is stored in the SYS:ETC directory of the NetWare server on which NFAP is running. To modify a context search file, complete the following steps:

1. Open the CTXS.CFG file with any text editor.

2. Enter each context to be searched during authentication, with each context on its own line.

3. Resave the file in the SYS:ETC directory.

4. At the server console, enter **CIFSSTOP**, and then **CIFSSTRT** to reload the CIFS service with the new context search file.

Once restarted, NFAP will be able to use the context search file entries you have provided.

Customizing the Network Environment for CIFS

You can use ConsoleOne to configure file access for CIFS users. For more information on ConsoleOne, see Chapter 3, "Novell Management Tools." Three CIFS configuration pages are available by completing the following steps:

1. Launch ConsoleOne and browse to the appropriate NetWare 6.5 server in the left pane.

2. Right-click the Server object and select Properties.

3. Click the CIFS tab and select one of the three CIFS available pages: Config, Attach, or Shares.

4. Enter the desired parameters in the fields provided.

5. Click OK to save your settings and exit.

The following parameter fields appear on the CIFS Config Page:

▶ *Server Name:* Lets you specify a name, as it will appear in Network Neighborhood, for the CIFS server. It can be a maximum of 15 characters long and must be different from the actual NetWare server name.

▶ *Comment:* Lets you provide a description of the server resource for CIFS users that will be available when viewing resource details in Network Neighborhood.

▶ *WINS Address:* Specifies the address of the WINS server that should be used to locate the Primary Domain Controller (PDC). This is necessary if the PDC is on a different IP subnet than the NetWare server running NFAP.

▶ *Unicode:* Enables international character support.

▶ *OpLocks (Opportunistic Locking):* Improves file access performance using the CIFS protocol.

▶ *Authentication Mode:* Specifies the authentication method used to authenticate CIFS users.

  ▶ *Domain*: If the users are members of a Windows domain, you can have the Windows domain controller perform the authentication. In this instance, the domain and workstation username and password must match.

  ▶ Local: If the users are members of a Windows workgroup, you can have the NFAP server perform the authentication. In this instance, the NetWare and workstation username and password must match.

▶ *Authentication Workgroup Name:* Specifies the name of the Windows domain, or workgroup, to which the NFAP server will belong.

▶ *Primary Domain Controller Name:* Specifies the name of the PDC server, and is necessary only if the PDC is on a different subnet. This option will override WINS or DNS.

▶ *Primary Domain Controller Address:* Specifies the static IP address of the PDC server, and is necessary only if the PDC is on a different subnet. This option will override WINS or DNS.

The Attach page lets you specify the IP addresses to which you want to bind the CIFS protocol. By default, CIFS will be bound to all IP addresses on the NetWare server on which NFAP is running.

The Shares page lets you specify volumes or directories as Windows share points that will be directly accessible from Network Neighborhood. If no share points are defined, all mounted volumes will be listed by default.

▶ *Name:* Specifies a name for the share point, as it will be seen in Network Neighborhood.

▶ *Path:* Specifies the full path to the share point. This will appear as the root, or starting point, for the share. The path must end with a backslash (\).

▶ *Comment:* Lets you provide a description of the share point for CIFS users that will be available when viewing resource details in Network Neighborhood.

▶ *Maximum Number of Connections:* Specifies the maximum number of simultaneous connections allowed to the share point.

Configuring AFP Access

With NFAP installed and passwords configured, nothing else is necessary to allow Mac users to access the NetWare file system. They can use Chooser or the Go menu to access network files and even create aliases. Because access to NetWare files is handled by AFP, Mac users can copy, delete, move, save, and open network files just like they can with any local drive resource.

You can stop and start the AFP service on the NetWare 6.5 server by typing **AFPSTOP** at the server console, or from a remote server connection. Similarly, typing **AFPSTRT** will start the AFP service on a given NetWare 6.5 server.

Context Search Files

If the User object for a Mac user is not in the same container as the server they are trying to access, a context search file lets them log in to the network without specifying their full context. The contexts listed in the context search file will be searched when no context is provided or the object cannot be found in the provided context. This is important because the Mac allows 31 characters for the username. If the full eDirectory context and username is longer than this, you must use a search list so users can access the NetWare server.

If User objects with the same name exist in different contexts, the first one in the context search list will be used. For this reason, it is advisable to have globally unique usernames when using this type of service.

The context search file is stored in the **SYS:ETC** directory of the NetWare server on which NFAP is running. To modify a context search file, complete the following steps:

1. Open the CTXS.CFG file with any text editor.

2. Enter each context to be searched during authentication, with each context on its own line.

3. Resave the file in the **SYS:ETC** directory.

Once restarted, NFAP will be able to use the context search file entries you have provided.

Renaming Volumes

You can also rename NetWare volumes so that they appear with a different name in the Mac Chooser. To rename a volume for Mac users, complete the following steps:

1. Create a file named AFPVOL.CFG in the **SYS:ETC** directory of the NetWare server on which NFAP is running.

2. For each volume you want to rename, enter the current name of the volume and, in quotes, the new Mac name of the volume. For example:

   ```
   prv-serv1.sys "SYS volume"
   ```

3. Save the file.

Mac users will now access the NetWare volume through the name you have specified, rather than the formal name syntax typically used to denote NetWare volumes.

Accessing Files from a Mac

Mac users use the Chooser to access files and directories as needed. They can also create an alias on the desktop that will be maintained after rebooting.

1. In Mac OS 8 or 9, click the Apple menu >> Chooser >> AppleTalk >> Server IP Address. In Mac OS X, click Go >> Connect to Server.

2. Specify the IP address or DNS name of the NetWare server, and click Connect.

3. When prompted, specify a valid eDirectory username and password, and then click Connect.

4. Select a volume to be mounted on the desktop. You now have access to the files on the specified volume. However, these settings are not saved after rebooting the Mac. If you want to create a perpetual link to the volume, you can create an alias.

Once these steps are completed, Mac users will have access to files and directories on a NetWare volume.

Configuring NFS Access

Native NFS file access requires a few more steps before a Unix/Linux client can use it. There are several terms that you should be familiar with if you have not worked with NFS previously and are implementing NFAP for NFS.

▶ *NFS server*: NFS server software is installed as part of the NFAP installation. It enables NFS clients to access a NetWare file system as if it were a local directory on the Unix/Linux workstation. Any client that supports the NFS protocol can also access NetWare files using the NFS server.

▶ *File system export*: Before Unix/Linux users can access the NetWare file system it must be made available to the NFS client. This process is called *exporting* the file system. During the export, you can define who should access the information and how it is accessed.

▶ *File system mount*: Once the NetWare file system has been exported, an NFS client can import it into its local file system. Once imported, the specified portion of the NetWare file system will be available as though it were part of the local Unix/Linux file system.

▶ *Network Information Service (NIS)*: NFAP also permits a NetWare server to function as an NIS server. This is not required for native file access, but is a useful additional service for Unix/Linux clients. NIS is a widely used "Yellow Pages" for the Unix/Linux environment. Similar to eDirectory, NIS servers act as central repositories for common information about users, groups, and hosts that reside on the network. With NIS server software loaded, eDirectory can function as a NIS repository and can respond to NIS requests from any NIS client.

NFAP's NFS support is installed and started as part of the NetWare 6.5 installation. You can stop and start the NFS service from the server console by typing **NFSSTOP**. Similarly, typing **NFSSTART** will start the NFS service on a given NetWare 6.5 server. You can also stop and start the NFS server from iManager by clicking the NFS link under File Protocols. This will open the management page for the NFS server. For more information on iManager, see Chapter 3.

When NFAP is installed, it extends the eDirectory schema to support new NFS objects (see Figure 2.12). There are four new objects that you will see after installing NFAP for NFS.

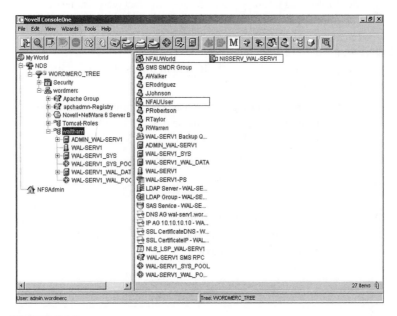

FIGURE 2.12
NFS objects created during the NFAP installation.

▶ *NFSAdmin*: The **NFSAdmin** object is a group object installed at the eDirectory tree root, and gives you access to the exported file structures that will be made available to NFS users.

▶ *NFAUUser*: The **NFAUUser** object is installed in the server context and is used to provide a link between NetWare and the root user on a Unix/Linux client. This link is used internally for managing data flow between the two systems.

▶ *NFAUWorld:* The **NFAUWorld** group object is installed in the server context and provides Unix rights to Other Unix users when they access an exported NFS path. To do this, the effective rights of the **NFAUWorld** object are converted into Unix **rwx** rights. Restrict the effective rights of the **NFAUWorld** object to prevent these NFS users from getting too much access to the NetWare file system.

▶ *NISSERV_<servername>*: The NIS server object is installed in the
server context for those who might want to use Novell eDirectory
as an NIS data repository. It is not used for NFS file access. For
more information on NIS services, see the NetWare online
documentation.

Exporting a NetWare Directory

To export part of the NetWare 6.5 file system for use by NFS clients,
complete the following steps:

1. Launch iManager and log in as a user with administrative rights.
   iManager provides a gadget for managing NFS connections. For
   more information on iManager, see Chapter 3.

2. In the left pane, expand the File Protocols link and select NFS.

3. Click the Export button to open the Export Options screen (see
   Figure 2.13).

4. In the Path field, enter the path to be exported. Use forward slashes
   (/) to separate directories. For example, to export the DATA:
   volume, you would enter **/data**.

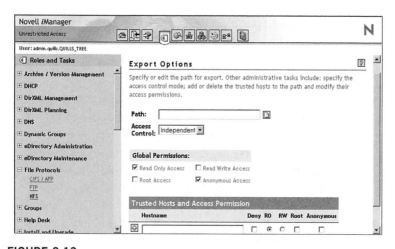

FIGURE 2.13
Creating an NFS export from iManager.

5. In the Access Control field, specify either Independent or NetWare
   mode. Independent mode means that NetWare and NFS rights will
   be managed separately. NetWare mode means that rights will be

managed from NetWare and mapped to NFS accordingly. For more information on access control modes, see the NetWare 6.5 online documentation.

6. The Global Permissions let you specify those permissions that will be granted to all trusted hostnames.

7. In the Trusted Host and Access Permission table, specify the NFS host that you want to make a trusted host for the exported path. Then specify the rights granted to the export host.

   ▶ *Deny* prevents access to the host

   ▶ (Default) *RO* grants read-only access to the host

   ▶ *RW* grants read-write access to the host

   ▶ *Root* grants root, or supervisory, access to the host

   ▶ *Anonymous* grants generic access to the exported directory through the Unix user `NOBODY` and group `NOGROUP`

8. Click the plus symbol (+) next to the hostname to add the host to the trusted host list. This updates the `etc/exports` file on the server and refreshes the NFS server. When you specify access permissions, the default permissions given in the All row are unchecked.

Once created, the newly exported directory will show up in the Exported Paths list on the NFS Server Administration screen. By selecting an exported path from the Exported Paths list, you can see the current path configuration, and modify that configuration by clicking Edit.

Mounting an Exported Directory

Once a NetWare 6.5 directory has been exported for NFS clients, it is imported into a remote file system for access. Unix systems use the `mount` command to accomplish this. To mount an exported directory on a Unix/Linux system, complete the following steps:

1. Use the `mkdir` command to create a directory that will hold the NetWare 6.5 NFS export. For example: `mkdir NW6Files`.

2. Use the `mount` command to link the new directory to the NetWare 6.5 export. For example: `mount <server identifier>:/data/linux /NW6Files`.

PART I   Getting Started

WARNING The server identifier is the IP address or DNS name of the NetWare 6.5 server on which you created the NFS Export. Make sure to use both the colon and forward slash between the server identifier and the volume name. The target import directory must be an absolute path from NFS root and is separated from the source path by a space.

For more information on the Unix/Linux mount command, refer to your system's MAN pages.

CHAPTER 3

Novell Management Tools

Using ConsoleOne

ConsoleOne is a Java-based tool for managing your network and its resources. It can be launched by running CONSOLEONE.EXE from where it was installed (default: SYS:PUBLIC\MGMT\CONSOLEONE\1.2\BIN). By default, it lets you manage Novell eDirectory objects, schema, partitions, and replicas and NetWare server resources.

If you install other Novell products, the appropriate management capabilities are automatically snapped into the version of ConsoleOne installed on that server.

ConsoleOne is installed during the NetWare 6.5 installation, but can also be re-installed or installed locally from the Novell client's CD.

ConsoleOne also supports remote server console access through a Java applet called RConsoleJ.

To access the NetWare 6.5 server console remotely, launch ConsoleOne and browse to the desired server. Select Tools, and then Remote Console.

Accessing Web Manager

Web Manager is a Web-based "home page" for accessing most of the NetWare 6.5 Web-based tools and services.

To access Web Manager, open your Web browser and enter your Web server's domain name or IP address, followed by a colon and the Web Manager port, which by default is 2200. For example:

```
https://www.quills.com:2200
```

or

```
https://137.65.192.1:2200
```

Accessing iManager

iManager provides role-based management of your NetWare network, together with a nearly comprehensive set of administrative tools.

- ▶ You can use either a secure (HTTPS) or unsecure (HTTP) connection to access iManager. However, a secure connection is recommended.

- ▶ Once configured, you can access the iManager Web page by appending the iManager path (`/nps/iManager.html`) to the IP address or DNS name of the server running iManager. For example:

   ```
   https://www.quills.com/nps/iManager.html
   ```

   or

   ```
   https://137.65.192.1/nps/iManager.html
   ```

- ▶ To force iManager into Simple mode to support Federal accessibility guidelines, use the Simple mode path (`/nps/Simple.html`). For example:

   ```
   https://www.quills.com/nps/Simple.html
   ```

   or

   ```
   https://137.65.192.1/nps/Simple.html
   ```

- ▶ You will be prompted to authenticate using a valid eDirectory username. Users can access iManager features only for which they have been assigned rights.

Once loaded, you will use iManager to perform most of the day-to-day administrative tasks in your NetWare environment, including management of most additional services that are available with NetWare 6.5.

Using NetWare Remote Manager

NetWare Remote Manager (NoRM) is used for remote management of NetWare 6.5 servers.

▶ You can launch NoRM from Web Manager, or you can launch NoRM directly by the NetWare 6.5 server's domain name or IP address, followed by a colon and the port number, which by default is **8009**. For example:

`https://www.quills.com:8009`

or

`https://137.65.192.1:8009`

▶ You can also launch NoRM directly from the graphical server console by clicking the red N icon on the icon bar at the bottom of the GUI.

▶ You will be prompted to authenticate. If your user object is in the same context as the server object, you can authenticate by common name only. Otherwise, you need to specify a full eDirectory username, including the leading dot. For access to all NoRM features, the user should have supervisory rights to the NetWare server.

Working with iMonitor

iMonitor is used for Web-based management of Novell eDirectory in your NetWare 6.5 network.

▶ Launch iMonitor from NoRM by selecting NDS iMonitor from the Managing eDirectory section in the left side navigation frame. Alternatively, you go straight to iMonitor by appending the iMonitor path (**/nds**) to the NoRM URL. For example:

`https://www.quills.com:8009/nds`

or

`https://137.65.192.1:8009/nds`

NOTE You can also launch iMonitor directly by appending `:8008/nds` to the end of your server's IP address or URL.

Introduction to Novell Management

Since the release of NetWare 4 in the early 1990s, Novell has been working toward a consolidated management interface from which all administrative tasks can be performed. In that time, the primary issue hampering this effort has been how to deliver that management interface.

From NWAdmin and ConsoleOne

The first version of a centralized management interface was NWAdmin. NWAdmin was a Windows-based utility that delivered a graphical interface that allowed administrators to see the whole network from a directory-centric perspective rather than a server-centric perspective. It relied on the Novell client to provide network communications and access. NWAdmin also defined the standard look and feel for graphical management utilities that is still largely adhered to today.

NWAdmin supported an extendable plug-in architecture so new functionality could be added as necessary to manage new features and new products. This was accomplished through Windows-based programming techniques common at the time.

However, NWAdmin ran only on Windows and used a proprietary architecture. Rather than try to support multiple versions of NWAdmin, Novell moved toward a more open and standards-based management architecture based on Java programming techniques. Java promised the capability to "write once, run anywhere," which was critical to Novell's management plans.

In 1998, with the release of NetWare 5, Novell introduces its second-generation administrative utility known as ConsoleOne. Similar to NWAdmin, ConsoleOne is an extendable management architecture that supports snap-ins to extend its capabilities. Its Java-based design allows it to run on both workstations and the NetWare server itself, providing the first-ever graphical server console. However, it still required some type of Novell client support for network communications and access. In the years since its release, ConsoleOne has achieved respectable performance, a major deficiency in its early versions, and still serves as the preferred tool for managing Novell and third-party products and services.

To iManager

With the release of NetWare 6, Novell started making the final management interface transition necessary to support its One Net initiative by introducing a set of Web-based management tools. Just as ConsoleOne untied the management console from Windows, iManager is untying the management console from the Novell client. iManager promises a true platform-independent management interface that can be used from any workstation at any location to perform network management and maintenance of any kind.

NetWare 6.5 introduces a greatly enhanced set of tools in iManager, nearly equaling that available from ConsoleOne. However, because every feature is not yet available in iManager, you will need to be familiar with the capabilities of each management interface. This chapter provides an introduction to the primary Novell management utilities, from ConsoleOne to iManager. It provides requirements and installation information for each utility, as well as an overview of its features and capabilities.

First, the chapter presents ConsoleOne, which is still the most comprehensive management interface for NetWare 6.5. We show how ConsoleOne can be used for both local and remote server administration as well as full eDirectory management.

Next, a new generation of Web-based management tools is presented, starting with iManager and its closely related sister utilities—NetWare Remote Manager (NoRM) and iMonitor. These browser-based utilities are close to eclipsing ConsoleOne for feature completeness and promise much more flexibility for network administrators looking to get their jobs done from any place at any time.

ConsoleOne

NetWare 6.5 includes ConsoleOne v1.3.6. ConsoleOne is a Java-based tool for managing your network and its resources. By default, it lets you manage

▶ Novell eDirectory objects, schema, partitions, and replicas

▶ NetWare server resources

If you install other Novell products, additional capabilities are snapped in to ConsoleOne automatically. For example, if you install Novell eDirectory, the capability to configure the LDAP interface to eDirectory is snapped in to ConsoleOne automatically.

Because ConsoleOne is a Java-based application, it has a similar look and feel across all platforms, as shown in Figure 3.1.

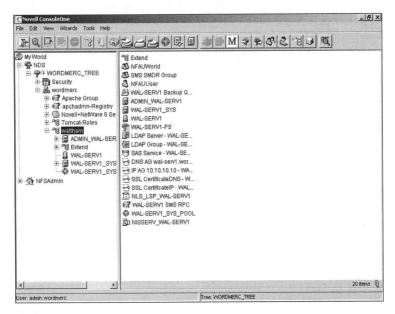

FIGURE 3.1
Novell ConsoleOne v1.3.6.

ConsoleOne Basics

Before looking at specific administrative tasks that are described throughout this book, it's a good idea to get a feel for the basics of ConsoleOne administration. If you need a more detailed introduction to ConsoleOne, see the NetWare 6.5 online documentation.

Organizing Objects into Containers

The whole purpose of using eDirectory to manage your network is that it allows you to organize network resources so they can be managed more easily. A principal way of doing this is to organize objects into logical groupings known as *containers*. Because of inheritance rules, objects in a container are security-equivalent to the container itself; so, general object rights can be managed at the container level rather than the individual object level. For more information on eDirectory tree design, see Chapter 5. For information on network security with eDirectory, see Chapter 6.

Creating and Manipulating Objects

Once you have located the objects you want to manage, you can change their behavior by modifying their properties. You can also create, delete, move, and rename objects as needed. To do any of these, right-click the object(s) you want to manage and select the desired operation from the drop-down menu. For example, to create a new object, complete the following steps:

1. Right-click the container in which you want the object stored, select New, and then the type of object you want to create. ConsoleOne will automatically limit the list of object types to those that are valid for the selected container.

2. Enter a name for the object.

3. Specify any other required or optional information, and then select OK.

WARNING If you are attempting to modify a service-specific object for which you don't have a snap-in, ConsoleOne will only show you a generic list of properties. Make sure you have a snap-in installed for all the objects with which you will be working.

ConsoleOne 1.3.6 lets you modify the properties of multiple objects of the same type simultaneously. To do this, complete the following steps:

1. Select the objects using one of the following methods:

    ▶ In the right pane, Shift-click or Ctrl-click multiple objects of the same type

    ▶ Click a group or template object to modify its members

    ▶ Click a container to modify the objects it contains

2. With the appropriate objects highlighted, select File from the menu bar, and then select Properties of Multiple Objects.

3. (*Conditional*) If you selected a container in step 1, in the Properties of Multiple Objects dialog box, double-click the object type from the Available Classes list that you want to modify.

4. On the Objects to Modify page, make sure only the objects that you want to modify are listed.

5. On the other property pages, make any changes you want to apply to all selected objects, and then select OK.

This greatly reduces the effort necessary to manage objects with similar attributes.

Browsing and Finding Objects

In the left pane, see the eDirectory container, which holds the eDirectory trees you are currently logged in to. If you log in to multiple trees, you will see them all listed here. To log in to a new eDirectory tree, select the NDS Authenticate button on the ConsoleOne toolbar and specify the tree name, context, username, and password.

If you are using DNS tree federation, you can access containers in other trees without logging in. To do this, complete the following steps:

1. In the ConsoleOne menu bar, select View, and then Set Context.

2. Enter the full DNS name for the eDirectory context you are trying to access, including an ending **dns** and period (.). For example:

testing.provo.quills.com.dns.

3. Click OK.

Once you are in an eDirectory tree or context and its objects are listed in the right pane, you typically browse to an object by opening container objects in the left pane until you arrive at the object.

Customizing Views

ConsoleOne gives you the flexibility to customize views in both the left and right panes. However, except for window size, position, and view title, other custom viewing settings are lost when you exit ConsoleOne.

You can define the topmost object in the left pane by doing one of the following:

▶ If the object is a container that's below the current top object, right-click the container object and select Set as Root.

▶ If the object is a container that's above the current top object, double-click in the left pane until the desired container appears.

▶ If you want to reset My World as the Top object, right-click the up arrow in the left pane and select Show My World.

The right pane in ConsoleOne defaults to what is known as the Console view. This is the most-used view for managing directory and server resources. However, you can switch back and forth between the Console view and other views, such as the Partition and Replica view, by right-clicking an object in the right pane, selecting Views, and then the desired view. For more information on the Partition and Replica view see Chapter 5.

Regardless of which view the right pane contains, you can show or hide the view title at the top of the right pane by selecting View from the menu bar and then Show View Title. A check mark is added to or removed from the menu item, depending on whether the view title is being shown or hidden.

Installing ConsoleOne

ConsoleOne will be installed automatically to SYS:PUBLIC\MGMT\ CONSOLEONE\1.2 during the NetWare 6.5 server installation. Furthermore, any products installed on the server will automatically place their ConsoleOne snap-ins in the correct location (SYS:PUBLIC\MGMT\ CONSOLEONE\1.2\SNAPINS) to function with this version. However, this means that different servers with different product sets may not have all the necessary snap-ins to manage services network-wide. So, if you are doing service-specific management, you should run ConsoleOne from a server where the service is actually installed.

If you want to install ConsoleOne on a workstation or an existing server, it is available on the NetWare 6.5 Client CD-ROM.

TIP If you want to synchronize ConsoleOne snap-ins across servers, you can simply copy them from the \SNAPINS directory on one server or workstation to that on another. Some snap-ins may have to register with ConsoleOne, in which case this method may not work.

To install and run ConsoleOne on one of its supported operating systems, complete the instructions in the following sections.

Windows

You can install and run ConsoleOne on a Windows workstation or server, or you can run it remotely from a NetWare or Windows server to which you have a mapped or shared drive.

WARNING If you install and run ConsoleOne from a Windows workstation or server, you should also install the NetWare 6.5 snap-ins so that you will be able to manage all installed services. You will have to manually copy any third-party snap-ins not included on the NetWare 6.5 Operating System CD-ROM from the server on which the third-party service is installed.

The following system requirements apply to ConsoleOne in the Windows environment:

OS version	Windows 95/98 with Novell client 3.2 or later Windows NT/2000 with Novell client 4.9 or later
RAM	64MB minimum 128MB recommended (required for generating ConsoleOne reports)
Processor	200MHz or faster
Disk space	50MB (required for a local installation only)
Video resolution	800×600×256 colors (minimum)

Complete the following steps to install ConsoleOne on a Windows machine:

1. Close any ConsoleOne sessions currently running.

2. Insert the Novell client's CD-ROM. If the CD does not auto-play, run WINSETUP.EXE from the root of the CD-ROM.

3. At the Novell Client Installation screen, select Novell ConsoleOne 1.3.6, and follow the onscreen prompts to complete the installation. If you do not need ConsoleOne reporting, you can choose not to install that snap-in.

4. Once ConsoleOne is installed, you will be returned to the Novell Client Installation screen.

5. Select NetWare 6.5 ConsoleOne Snapins.

6. Make sure you match your install path to that used to install ConsoleOne, and click Unzip to install the snap-in files.

7. Click Close once the file copy is complete to close the installation program. Click Exit to close the Client Installation screen.

TIP If you are installing on a Windows server and you will run ConsoleOne remotely through drive sharing, don't forget to share the folder where you install ConsoleOne.

Once installed, executing CONSOLEONE.EXE from the location where you installed it starts ConsoleOne. If you installed ConsoleOne locally, you will have a shortcut on your desktop.

ConsoleOne Accessibility

To enable the new ConsoleOne Accessibility features for a Windows environment, you must first install the Java Access Bridge. The Java Access Bridge exposes the Java Accessibility API in a Windows DLL so that Windows Assistive Technologies can interact with Java applications that use the Java Accessibility API.

To set up the Java Access Bridge for use with ConsoleOne, complete the following steps:

1. Download the Java Access Bridge from the Java Access Bridge Web site at `http://java.sun.com/products/accessbridge`.

2. Unpack the Java Access Bridge into the `C:\ACCESSBRIDGE-1_0` directory and run the following command:

   `C:\ACCESSBRIDGE-1_0\INSTALLER\INSTALL`

TIP For more information on installing and configuring the Java Access Bridge, see the Java Access Bridge readme (`http://java.sun.com/products/accessbridge/README.txt`).

3. Place a copy of the following files in your `\CONSOLEONEEXT` folder. By default, this folder is at `C:\NOVELL\CONSOLEONE\1.2\`.

   `JACCESS-1_3.JAR`
   `ACCESS-BRIDGE.JAR`

4. Place a copy of following file in your `\JRE\LIB` folder. By default, this folder is at `C:\NOVELL\CONSOLEONE\1.2\`.

   `ACCESSIBILITY.PROPERTIES`

5. Copy the following files to your Windows DLL directory (for example, `C:\WINNT\SYSTEM32` or `C:\WINDOWS\SYSTEM`):

   `JAVAACCESSBRIDGE.DLL`
   `WINDOWSACCESSBRIDGE.DLL`

With this installation process complete, ConsoleOne will now be able to interact properly with Windows Accessibility features.

NetWare

In addition to being installed during the NetWare 6.5 installation, you can install ConsoleOne v1.3 on existing NetWare servers. The following system requirements apply to ConsoleOne in the NetWare environment:

OS version	NetWare 5 Support Pack 6a or later
RAM	Use NetWare recommended minimums At least 128MB recommended
Processor	200MHz or faster
Disk space	38MB available
Video resolution	800×600×256 colors (minimum)

WARNING ConsoleOne v1.3.6 is compatible with existing ConsoleOne v1.2 snap-ins, but *not* with v1.1 snap-ins. If you have any older applications that use these snap-ins, ConsoleOne v1.3 should not be installed on that server.

Complete the following steps to install ConsoleOne on an existing NetWare server:

1. At the Server console, type **JAVA -EXIT** to unload Java and any Java applications running on the server.

2. Make sure network users exit any ConsoleOne sessions currently in use.

3. From a Windows client, map a drive letter to the root of the server's **SYS** volume.

4. From the same workstation, insert the NetWare 6.5 client CD-ROM. If the CD does not auto-play, run WINSETUP.EXE from the root of the CD-ROM.

5. At the Novell Client Installation screen, select Novell ConsoleOne and follow the onscreen prompts to complete the installation. If you do not need ConsoleOne reporting, you can choose not to install that snap-in.

Once ConsoleOne has been installed on the server, you can start the NetWare GUI and ConsoleOne simultaneously by typing the following command:

C1START

If the GUI is already started, select the Novell button in the lower-left corner, and select ConsoleOne from the menu. You will be required to authenticate to eDirectory before ConsoleOne will load.

You can also run ConsoleOne remotely from a Windows computer. First make sure you have a drive mapped to the **SYS:** volume of the NetWare server, and then you can create a shortcut to CONSOLEONE.EXE at the location where you installed it.

Linux

You can access ConsoleOne on Linux locally or remotely from another system through an X terminal session, provided the remote computer has an X Window subsystem.

NOTE This release of ConsoleOne for Linux has been tested only on the IBM 1.3 Java Runtime Environment (JRE). This JRE is included in the ConsoleOne installation package in case you don't have it. If you do have it, you can choose not to install it.

The following system requirements apply to ConsoleOne in the Linux environment:

OS version	Red Hat OpenLinux 6 or later, or Caldera eDesktop 2.4 or later, or Caldera eServer 2.3
RAM	128MB recommended
Processor	200MHz or faster
Disk space	With JRE installation: 32MB; without JRE installation: 5MB
Video resolution	800×600×256 colors (minimum)

WARNING This release of ConsoleOne is not compatible with eDirectory versions prior to v8.5. If the installation routine detects an unsupported version of eDirectory, it will abort the installation.

Complete the following steps to install ConsoleOne on an existing Linux server:

1. At the Linux system, mount the Novell client's CD-ROM and browse to the /`consoleone` folder.

2. Start the installation by typing the following at the system prompt: `c1-install`.

3. Follow the onscreen prompts to complete the installation. Remember, if you already have the IBM JRE v1.3 installed, you can skip that portion of the installation.

NOTE You can uninstall ConsoleOne by entering c1-uninstall at the system prompt. c1-install and c1-uninstall both include some optional parameters for running in unattended mode or installing/uninstalling individual components. For details on the command syntax, type c1-install -h or c1-uninstall -h at the system prompt.

Both the install and uninstall routines maintain a log file in the /var directory that you can review at any time.

Use the following command to start ConsoleOne from either a local session or an X terminal (remote) session:

/usr/ConsoleOne/bin/ConsoleOne

Solaris

You can access ConsoleOne on Solaris locally or remotely from another system through an X terminal session, provided the remote computer has an X Window subsystem.

NOTE This release of ConsoleOne for Solaris has been tested only on the Sun 1.2.2-5a Java Runtime Environment (JRE). This JRE is included in the ConsoleOne installation package in case you don't have it. If you do have it, you can choose not to install it.

The following system requirements apply to ConsoleOne in the Solaris environment:

OS version	Solaris 2.6 or 7 with the latest patch applied (download Solaris patches at http://sunsolve.sun.com/); Solaris 8
Disk space	With JRE installation: 64MB; Without JRE installation: 10MB
Video resolution	800×600×256 colors (minimum)

WARNING This release of ConsoleOne is not compatible with eDirectory versions prior to v8.5. If the installation routine detects an unsupported version of eDirectory, it will abort the installation.

Complete the following steps to install ConsoleOne on an existing Solaris server:

1. At the Solaris system, mount the NetWare 6 client CD-ROM and browse to the `/consoleone` folder.

2. Start the installation by typing the following at the system prompt: `c1-install`.

3. Follow the onscreen prompts to complete the installation. Remember, if you already have the Sun 1.2.2-5a JRE installed, you can skip that portion of the installation.

NOTE You can uninstall ConsoleOne by entering c1-uninstall at the system prompt. c1-install and c1-uninstall include some optional parameters for running in unattended mode or installing/uninstalling individual components. For details on the command syntax, type c1-install -h or c1-uninstall -h at the system prompt.

Both the install and uninstall routines maintain a log file in the `/var` directory that you can review at any time.

Use the following command to start ConsoleOne from either a local session or an X terminal (remote) session:

`/usr/ConsoleOne/bin/ConsoleOne`

Tru64 Unix

This is the first version of ConsoleOne that will run on a Tru64 system. You can run it locally or remotely from another system through an X terminal session, provided the remote computer has an X Window subsystem.

NOTE This release of ConsoleOne for Tru64 has been tested only on the Compaq 1.2.2 Java Runtime Environment (JRE). This JRE is included in the ConsoleOne installation package in case you don't have it. If you do have it, you can choose not to install it.

The following system requirements apply to ConsoleOne in the Tru64 environment:

OS version	Compaq Tru64 Unix 5.0a or later
RAM	64MB minimum; 128MB recommended
Processor	200MHz or faster
Disk space	With JRE installation: 20MB; without JRE installation: 5MB
Video resolution	800×600×256 colors (minimum)

WARNING This release of ConsoleOne is not compatible with eDirectory versions prior to v8.5. If the installation routine detects an unsupported version of eDirectory, it will abort the installation.

Complete the following steps to install ConsoleOne on an existing Tru64 server:

1. At the Tru64 system, mount the NetWare 6 client CD-ROM and browse to the /consoleone folder.

2. Start the installation by typing the following at the system prompt: **c1-install**.

3. Follow the onscreen prompts to complete the installation. Remember, if you already have the Compaq 1.2.2 JRE installed you can skip that portion of the installation.

NOTE You can uninstall ConsoleOne by entering c1-uninstall at the system prompt. c1-install and c1-uninstall both include some optional parameters for running in unattended mode or installing/uninstalling individual components. For details on the command syntax, type c1-install -h or c1-uninstall -h at the system prompt.

Both the install and uninstall routines maintain a log file in the /var directory that you can review at any time.

Use the following command to start ConsoleOne from either a local session or an X terminal (remote) session:

/usr/ConsoleOne/bin/ConsoleOne

ConsoleOne Limitations

Because the newer Web-based management tools are much easier to develop to, some of the newer management features are bypassing ConsoleOne and going straight to iManager. Several of the newer NetWare features, including Licensing and iPrint, are managed through iManager and are not available from ConsoleOne.

Remote Management with ConsoleOne

Much of the server management that previously required access to the NetWare server console can now be done with NoRM, discussed later in this chapter. NoRM lets you perform most management tasks that normally require access to the server console from a remote workstation or even from across the Internet. However, to manage any version of NetWare 5 or NetWare 6 remotely, you can also use RConsoleJ, which is part of ConsoleOne. Although RConsoleJ does not offer the flexibility of NoRM, it can save significant time by letting you manage servers to which you have a LAN/WAN connection.

NOTE If you have NetWare 4.x or earlier servers on your network, you will have to use the DOS-based RConsole utility that shipped with these versions of NetWare. Consult your server documentation for more information.

RConsoleJ is a Java applet that provides a server "window" on your workstation from which you can use console utilities, load/unload NLMs, and change server configuration just as if you were using the server's actual keyboard and monitor. Using RConsoleJ enables you to access the server from any workstation on the network, which gives you greater freedom when administering your network.

RConsoleJ requires the IP protocol to connect to NetWare servers remotely. However, if you want to use it to connect to a server that is running IPX only, you can do so by routing RConsoleJ communications through a secondary proxy server, which has both IP and IPX protocol stacks loaded. The proxy server acts as a gateway between RConsoleJ and the IPX server.

Because RConsoleJ is part of ConsoleOne, you can run it from any platform that supports ConsoleOne, including Windows, NetWare, Linux, Solaris, and Tru64.

To set up your network for RConsoleJ, you have to do the following:

▶ Set up the target server, which is the server you want to access remotely.

▶ *(Conditional)* Install proxy software on an IP server if the target server is only running IPX.

▶ Install RConsoleJ software on the workstation or server from which you want to run the remote console session.

Setting Up the Target Server

The target server is the server whose console you want to access during the remote console session. The target server can be running IP or IPX.

To prepare a target server, complete the following steps:

1. At the server console prompt load the following NLM:

   RCONAG6

2. Enter the password you want administrators to use when accessing the target server from RConsoleJ. You do not need an eDirectory password because RConsoleJ does not use eDirectory.

3. Enter the TCP port number for the unencrypted session. The default value is 2034. If the server communicates using IPX only, enter -1 to disable TCP listening. To enable listening over a dynamically assigned port, enter 0.

4. Enter the TCP port number for the secure session. The default port number is 2036. Ensure the Key Material object named SSL CertificateDNS has been created.

NOTE The secure connection is available only on IP and not on IPX.

5. Enter the SPX port number on which RCONAG6 will listen for a proxy server. The default port number is 16800. If the server communicates using IP only, enter -1 to disable SPX listening. To enable listening over a dynamically assigned port, enter 0.

(Conditional) Configuring an RConsoleJ Proxy Server

This server will act as a middleman between the RConsoleJ client, which only communicates via IP and a NetWare server running on IPX. To do this, the RConsoleJ proxy server must have both IP and IPX protocol stacks loaded.

1. At the server console prompt, enter the following command:
   RCONPRXY

2. Enter the TCP port number on which **RCONPRXY** will listen for
   RConsoleJ. The default value is **2035**. To enable listening over a
   dynamically assigned port, enter **0**.

Once the NetWare server is running the RConsoleJ proxy agent, the
RConsoleJ client can communicate through it with the IPX target server.

(Conditional) Automating RConsoleJ Agents

The default AUTOEXEC.NCF file in NetWare 6.5 will include an optional command that you can uncomment to autoload RConsoleJ modules at
startup. However, because loading these modules requires you to specify
a remote password, it is more secure to use LDRCONAG.NCF, which lets
you encrypt the password so that it cannot be viewed by anyone with
access to the AUTOEXEC.NCF. LDRCONAG.NCF includes all the necessary RConsoleJ commands necessary to support RConsoleJ.

To create an encrypted remote password, complete the following steps:

1. Type the following command:
   RCONAG6 ENCRYPT

2. Enter the password you want to use for remote console sessions.

3. Enter the other required port information as outlined in the previous section. The system will display the encrypted password value
   and a message prompting whether the **RCONAG6** command should
   be written to the **SYS:SYSTEM\LDRCONAG.NCF** file. To include the
   RCONAG6 command with your encrypted password in the
   LDRCONAG.NCF file, enter **Y**.

4. The system places a **LOAD RCONAG** command into the
   LDRCONAG.NCF file with the encrypted password as a parameter.
   To auto-load RCONAG6.NLM with an encrypted password on
   startup, use either **NWCONFIG** or **EDIT** to open the AUTOEXEC.NCF
   file. At the end of the file, enter the following:
   LDRCONAG

5. Save and exit the AUTOEXEC.NCF file.

The server will now automatically load the necessary remote modules
and your encrypted password whenever it is started.

Running the RConsoleJ Client

To run RConsoleJ from a supported workstation or NetWare 6.5 server, do the following:

> **NOTE** If you are running RConsoleJ from a NetWare server, you can start it directly from the server GUI by selecting the Novell button and then selecting Programs and RConsoleJ. You can then continue with step 3.

1. Open ConsoleOne and browse to the server object you want to control.

2. Right-click the server object and select Remote Console.

3. In the RConsoleJ screen, shown in Figure 3.2, specify the required information and select Connect.

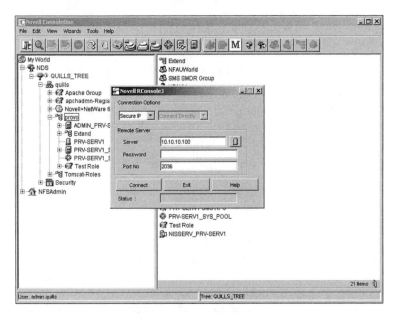

FIGURE 3.2
The Remote Console interface from ConsoleOne.

▶ *Connection Options*: Specify whether you are connecting via Secure or Unsecure IP. If you are using Unsecure IP, you can choose whether to connect directly or through a proxy.

▶ *Remote Server*: Specify the target server's name for a direct connection or the proxy server's name for a proxy connection. Enter the remote password. The port number will be automatically inserted unless you have changed it from the default.

NOTE If you are running ConsoleOne from a different server, or if you have installed ConsoleOne locally, you may be prompted to accept an unknown certificate. If so, click OK to accept the certificate and launch the RConsoleJ window.

For more information on using RConsoleJ, see the NetWare 6.5 online documentation.

NetWare Web Manager

NetWare Web Manager functions as a default Welcome page for a NetWare 6.5 server, and serves as a home page for the various Web services available in NetWare 6.5. As with other NetWare 6.5 Web services and tools, Web Manager leverages the latest version of the industry-leading Apache Web server for NetWare. Two instances of Apache can be installed on your NetWare 6.5 server. The Apache admin server is used by NetWare Web tools, leaving the other instance available for your eCommerce needs without further burdening it with network management overhead. For more information on Apache and other NetWare 6.5 Web services, see Chapter 9.

One of the primary advantages of using NetWare Web Manager is that you can easily access other browser-based management interfaces— including NetWare Remote Manager and iManager—and configure various services from any remote workstation that has Internet access. With Web Manager, you can accomplish the following tasks either locally (from within your WAN or LAN) or remotely:

▶ *Install and configure many of the NetWare 6.5 Web services*: In the left pane, you will see links to install several Web services, including Apache 2.0, UDDI Server, OpenSSH, and eGuide. Once installed, you can also manage the Web services from Web Manager by selecting your server name located under the appropriate service heading.

▶ *Manage user authentication to your enterprise Web server*: Web Manager supports authentication via either eDirectory or a local database. Novell recommends using eDirectory because it will manage both authentication and access rights. However, if your Web server contains mostly public information, authentication will not be a major issue, and the local database mode will work fine.

▶ *Modify Web Manager settings*: To manage NetWare Web Manager settings, select the Admin Server Preferences icon in the gold box of the Web Manager home page. This is available only when using a secure and authenticated session for Web Manager.

Installing Web Manager

NetWare Web Manager is installed automatically during the installation of NetWare 6.5. After the installation, use a Web browser from a client computer in your network to access Web Manager. As you make configuration changes to the Web services available in NetWare 6, configuration files on the NetWare 6.5 server will be modified to support your changes.

In order to access Web Manager from an Internet connection outside your firewall, you will need to make sure that TCP port **2200** is opened through the firewall to the IP address of your Web server. Port **2200** is the default port through which you will access the Web Manager interface. If desired, this port can be changed as long as it doesn't conflict with any other service on the NetWare 6.5 server.

To use Web Manager, you must be using a 4.x or newer Web browser such as Internet Explorer or Netscape Communicator. The browser must have Java or JavaScript enabled on your Web browser to use Web Manager because the configuration forms and other management tools require one or both of these forms of Java to function. To enable Java on your browser, complete the instructions in the following sections that correspond to the browser you are using.

Internet Explorer 4 or Higher

To enable Java on Internet Explorer 4 or higher, use the following steps:

1. From the Internet Explorer browser window, click Tools >> Internet Options.

2. Select the Advanced tab.

3. Under Microsoft VM, check the JIT Compiler for Virtual Machine Enabled box.

4. Click OK. You will have to restart your workstation to complete the installation.

Netscape Navigator

To enable Java on Netscape Navigator, use the following steps:

1. From the browser window, click Options >> Network Preferences.

2. Select the Language tab and make sure Java and JavaScript are checked.

3. Click OK.

Netscape Communicator

To enable Java on Netscape Communicator, use the following steps:

1. From the Communicator browser window, click Edit >> Preferences.

2. Select the Advanced category in the left column.

3. Check the Enable Java and Enable JavaScript check boxes.

4. Click OK.

To access Web Manager, open your Web browser and enter your Web server's domain name or IP address, followed by a colon and the port number, which by default is **2200**. For example:

```
https://www.quills.com:2200
```

or

```
https://137.65.192.1:2200
```

Configuring Web Manager

There isn't a lot you need to do to get Web Manager set up once it is installed. Figure 3.3 shows the Web Manager home page. As Web services are installed, such as Apache Web server, FTP, and Web Search server, links to their specific management interfaces will become active in Web Manager. There are also a few configuration tasks of which you should be aware.

NOTE When you select a Web Manager link, you may be prompted to accept an unknown certificate. If so, select Yes to continue or View Certificate to install the server certificate in your browser. Installing the certificate should prevent this message from appearing in the future.

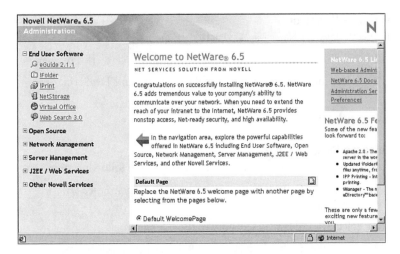

FIGURE 3.3
The NetWare 6.5 Web Manager home page.

By default, Web Manager uses port **2200**, and secures its communications with SSL, using the server certificate that was created during the NetWare 6.5 installation. However, you have control over all three of these settings. To modify any of them complete the following steps:

1. From the NetWare Web Manager home page, click the Administration Server Preferences link. You may need to authenticate as a user with Supervisor rights to the tree.

2. In the Web Manager Port field, type the port number you want NetWare Web Manager to use. If you decide to do this, using a port number of **49152** or higher is the best bet. Ports below **49152** may be assigned for use by other services and should not be used. Pick an unassigned port between **49152** and **65000**.

NOTE For a complete list of registered port numbers, visit the Internet Assigned Numbers Authority (IANA) Web site at http://www.iana.org/assignments/port-numbers.

3. Under Encryption, click On to enable, or Off to disable SSL. By default, SSL is used to secure Web Manager communications by encrypting all information going out of or coming in to Web Manager. When enabled, you must use HTTPS to access Web Manager.

4. From the Server Certificates drop-down list, select the Server Certificate object you want to use for SSL encryption. NICI and Novell Certificate Server provide all the cryptographic underpinnings of Web Manager. They are installed by default as part of the NetWare 6.5 installation. Certificate Server provides the cryptographic key pairs and server certificate used by Web Manager. For more information on NICI and Certificate Server, see Chapter 6.

5. Click OK once all the desired changes have been made.

6. Restart Web Manager for the settings to take effect.

The Apache Web server logs the activities of all services running on it, including Web Manager. These log files track who has visited, what has been accessed, and what errors, if any, have occurred.

The Apache log files are stored in the default Common Log Format (CLF) that provides a fixed amount of information about Apache Web server activity.

The Access log file records information about requests to the server and the responses from the server. The Error log file lists all the errors the server has encountered, including unsuccessful login attempts and any other informational messages.

To view the available Web Manager log files, complete the following steps:

1. From the NetWare Web Manager home page, select the Administration Server Preferences link and choose either View Access Log or View Error Log.

2. In the Number of Entries field, type the number of lines you want the access log to display.

3. If you want to filter the log entries for a specific type of work, enter it in the Only Show Entries With field. The filter is case sensitive, so be specific!

4. Click OK to have your viewing options take effect. Use the Reset button to re-run the search and update the log file view.

Using these steps, you can locate specific errors or types of messages in order to keep track of network events.

iManager

NetWare 6.5 includes iManager 2.0, a Web-based tool for administering, managing, and configuring NetWare products, services, and eDirectory objects. iManager allows Role-Based Services (RBS) to give you a way to focus the user on a specified set of tasks and objects as determined by the user's role(s). What users see when they access iManager is based on their role assignments in eDirectory.

iManager has been re-architected to use Novell's exteNd Web services platform, and is in effect a management portal for Novell's products and services. It runs on the Apache Web server for NetWare. For more information on Apache Web server for NetWare, see Chapter 9.

As you will see, many of the default management tasks formerly requiring ConsoleOne can now be done through a common Web interface with iManager. Among other things, you can define management roles to administer Novell Licensing Services (NLS), iPrint, DNS/DHCP services, and perform eDirectory object management. Over time, iManager will grow to replace ConsoleOne completely as Novell's preferred management platform.

Installing iManager

In some NetWare 6.5 installations and patterns, iManager will not be installed automatically. If you did not select to install iManager during the server installation, it can be manually re-installed through Deployment Manager or the graphical server console. To install iManager via Deployment Manager, complete the following steps:

1. Make sure you are logged in as a user with administrative rights to eDirectory and the NetWare server.

2. At the workstation, insert the NetWare 6.5 Operating System CD-ROM. Run Deployment Manager (NWDEPLOY.EXE) from the root of the CD-ROM.

3. In Deployment Manager, select Install NetWare 6.5 Products in the left pane, and click Remote Product Install in the right pane.

4. Select the target server from the list of available servers, and then click Next. Provide admin user information when requested.

5. At the Components screen, select iManager 2.0 and Apache 2 Web Server and Tomcat 4 Servlet Container and click Next. Make sure

all other products are deselected. All the necessary application files will be copied to the target server. This might take a few minutes. You might need to restart these services manually from the server console. To do this, stop Tomcat by typing **TC4STOP** and stop Apache by typing **AP2WEBDN**. Restart the services by typing **AP2WEBUP** to restart Apache and **TOMCAT4** to restart Tomcat.

6. At the Installation Complete screen, click Reset Apache to restart Tomcat and the Apache Web server. Close Deployment Manager once the installation is finished.

Once the files have been installed on the server, the exteNd environment in which iManager runs must be configured. To perform this initial configuration, complete the following steps:

1. Open a browser and go to the following URL:
   `http://<server IP address>/nps/servlet/configure`.

2. Click the Start button.

3. Provide the LDAP name of an Admin user for the eDirectory tree in which the server resides. Use commas (,) instead of periods (.) in providing the distinguished name of the admin user object.

4. Select the PLATFORM.XAR file and click Next.

5. Accept the Novell exteNd Director 4.1 license agreement by selecting I Accept the Terms of the License Agreement, and click Next.

6. Select Custom Installation and click Next.

7. Specify the portal object to work with and click Next. You can choose an existing object or choose to create a new one. You will be asked to specify a distinguished name and password for the object.

8. At the Configuration screen, click Configure to set up the portal object in eDirectory. All of the portal modules to be configured will be listed.

Once the configuration has been written to eDirectory, and the portal object created, restart Tomcat and Apache 2 at the server console. To do this, stop Tomcat by typing **TC4STOP** and stop Apache by typing **AP2WEBDN**. Restart the services by typing **AP2WEBUP** to restart Apache and **TOMCAT4** to restart Tomcat.

You can now open iManager from its URL, using either HTTP or HTTPS, at `<server IP address>.iManager.html`. You will be required to authenticate in order to access iManager, and will have access to only those features to which you have rights. For full access to all iManager features, authenticate as a user with Supervisory rights to the eDirectory tree (see Figure 3.4).

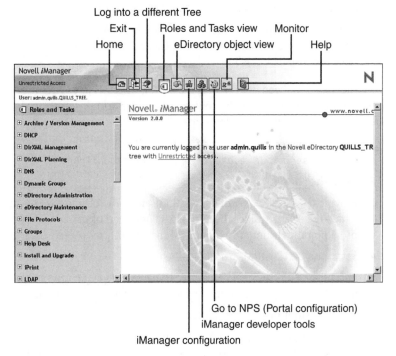

FIGURE 3.4
The iManager 2.0 home page.

You can also open iManager in Simple mode (see Figure 3.5), suitable for compliance with Federal accessibility guidelines. It provides the same functionality as Regular mode, but with an interface optimized for accessibility by those with disabilities (for example, expanded menus for blind users who rely upon spoken commands). To use Simple mode, simply replace iManager.html with Simple.html in the iManager URL. For example:

```
https://www.quills.com/nps/Simple.html
```

or

```
https://137.65.192.1/nps/Simple.html
```

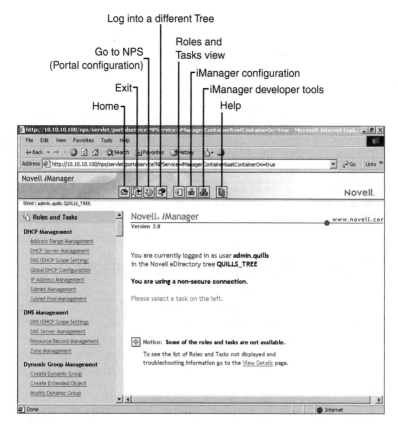

FIGURE 3.5
The iManager 2.0 home page in Simple mode.

Using either interface, you will have access to only those features to which you have rights. For full access to all iManager features, authenticate as a user with Supervisory rights to the eDirectory tree.

iManager Basics

As shown in Figure 3.3, iManager is organized into three main sections, or frames:

> ▶ *Header frame*: The Header frame is located at the top of the screen. It contains links to the Home, Roles and Tasks, Configuration, and Help pages, as well as an Exit link to close the browser window.

▶ *Navigation frame*: The Navigation frame is located on the left side of the screen. It allows you to navigate among the various management tasks or directory objects, depending on the view that is selected. What you see is also constrained by the rights of your authenticated identity.

▶ *Main Content frame*: The Main Content frame occupies the middle-right of the screen. When you select a link in the Header or Navigation frames, the appropriate page will be displayed in the Main Content frame.

TIP If you ever see the Looking Glass icon next to a field in iManager, you can use it to browse or search the tree for specific objects to use in creating, defining, and assigning roles.

Role-Based Management with iManager

Role-based services allow administrators to assign users a group of specific set of functions, or tasks, into Role objects. When users are assigned a given role, what they see when they access Novell iManager is based on their role assignments. Only the tasks assigned to the authenticated user are displayed. The role-based services available through iManager are represented by objects in eDirectory. The object types include

▶ *RBS Collection*: A container object that holds all RBS role and task objects for an eDirectory tree. You specify the location for this object during NetWare 6.5 installation.

▶ *RBS Role*: Specifies the tasks that users (members) are authorized to perform. Defining a role includes creating an RBS Role object and linking it to the tasks that the role can perform. RBS roles can be created only in an RBS Collection container.

▶ *RBS Module*: A container inside of the RBS collection that organizes available RBS Task objects into functional groups. RBS modules let you assign users responsibility for specific functionality within a product or service.

▶ *RBS Task*: Represents a specific function, such as resetting login passwords. RBS Task objects are located only in RBS Module containers.

▶ *RBS Scope*: Represents the context in the tree where a role will be performed, and is associated with RBS Role objects. This object is dynamically created when needed, and automatically deleted when no longer needed.

WARNING Never change the configuration of an RBS Scope object. Doing so can have very serious consequences and could potentially break the system.

Configuring Role-Based Services

During the iManager installation, the schema of your eDirectory tree was extended to support the RBS object types specified previously. It also created an RBS Collection container for your role-based services and installed the iManager plug-ins to support all currently available product packages. However, you can complete these tasks manually from iManager, if necessary.

To install RBS schema extensions, complete the following steps in iManager:

1. Select the Configure button.

2. Under RBS Configuration, select Extend Schema.

3. Select OK to add the new Role-Based Services schema extensions to the tree. If you get a message that the schema extensions have been previously installed, you are good to go.

To create the RBS Collection container, complete the following steps:

1. Select the Configure button.

2. Under Collection Configuration, select Create Collection.

3. In the Create Collection screen, enter the requested information and select OK.

   ▶ *Name*: Enter a name for the Collection object.

   ▶ *Container*: Specify a context for the Collection object.

To install product packages, complete the following steps in iManager:

1. Select the Configure button.

2. Under RBS Configuration, select Configure iManager. This launches the iManager configuration wizard.

3. At the Available Options screen, select Upgrade Collections and click Next.

4. Select the Collection object with which you want to work and click Next.

5. Provide the necessary information and click Start.

   ▶ *Modules to Be Installed*: Specify all RBS modules you want associated with the Collection.

   ▶ *Scope*: Specify the container for which the new role assignments, which will be created for the modules you are installing, will be active.

   ▶ *Inheritable*: Specifies whether the role rights will flow down to all containers under the specified scope.

6. Click Close once the update process has completed. This will return you to the iManager Configure screen.

In most cases you won't have to do this manually, but its nice to know how it's done...just in case.

Defining RBS Roles

RBS roles specify the tasks that users are authorized to perform. The tasks that RBS roles can perform are exposed as RBS Task objects in eDirectory. RBS tasks are created automatically during the installation of product packages. They are organized into one or more RBS Module containers, each of which corresponds to a different type of functionality within the product.

Create and assign a Role object by completing the following steps in iManager:

1. Select the Configure button.

2. Under Role Configuration, select Create iManager Role. Choose Create eGuide Role if you want to define a role specific to eGuide management.

3. In the Name screen, enter the requested information and click Next.

   ▶ *Role Name*: Specify a name for the Role object.

   ▶ *Collection*: Specify a collection to hold the object.

   ▶ *(Optional) Description*: Enter a role description, if desired.

4. From the All Tasks box, select those tasks that should be assigned to the role you are creating and click the right arrow to move them to the Assigned Tasks box. Click Next.

5. Specify the eDirectory objects and scopes for the role you are creating and click Add. You can select multiple objects to occupy the role, and multiple scopes for each object. The scope specifies the container at which the role will be active in the directory tree. Once all objects and scopes have been defined, click Next.

6. Review the role summary, and click Finish to create the new Role object.

Once created, you can modify RBS roles by completing the following steps in iManager:

1. Select the Configure button.

2. Under Role Configuration, select Modify iManager Role. Choose Modify eGuide Role if you want to modify an eGuide-specific role.

3. Make the desired task or role occupant changes. Click Modify Tasks to add or remove tasks from the Role. Click Modify Members to add or remove occupants from the role, or change the scope of an existing role occupant.

To delete any RBS object from your tree, complete the following steps in iManager:

1. Select the Configure button.

2. Under the appropriate RBS object heading, select Delete <object type>.

3. Specify the full name and context of the RBS object you want to delete and click OK.

NetWare Remote Manager

If a good acronym is a sign of a successful product, NetWare Remote Manager (NoRM) is well on its way to greatness! NoRM provides most of the functionality of the console Monitor utility, together with functionality from several other console utilities, but also NoRM makes it available from a Web browser.

You can use NoRM to monitor your server's health, change the configuration of your server, and perform diagnostic and debugging tasks. The following list outlines some of the major tasks you can perform with NoRM:

▶ *Manage server health*: Monitoring the health status of one or more servers, building groups of servers to monitor together, and accessing eDirectory health and troubleshooting tools (iMonitor)

▶ *Configure server environment*: Managing disk partitions; viewing information about hardware adapters, hardware resources, and processor(s); loading or unloading NLM programs, LAN drivers, or disk drivers (also uploading new NLMs from NoRM); monitoring server disk space and memory resources; accessing files on volumes and DOS partitions; managing server connections; configuring SET parameters; scheduling console commands to run; and shutting down, restarting, or resetting a server

▶ *Troubleshoot server problems by*: Finding CPU hogs, finding high memory users, tracing ABEND sources, locating server process hogs, finding disk space hogs, seeing who is using a file

Some of the principal tasks you can accomplish with NoRM include the following:

▶ *Console Screens link*: From this link on the Console Screens page, a Java applet allows you to view and run all the console screens just as though you were using the keyboard at the server console.

▶ *Console Commands link*: From this link you can access a list of all the console commands. Viewing and printing them is now much easier.

▶ *Logging in*: When you point your browser at NoRM, you will be prompted to authenticate before seeing any pages.

▶ *Admin and Non-Admin views*: If you log in to NetWare Remote Manager as a user with Supervisor rights to the server object, you can access and perform all management options. If you log in as a user without these rights, you can see only the volumes, directories, and files to which you have rights. You can view files where you have read access rights and upload files into directories where you have write access. No management functions are available.

▶ *Disk partition operations*: As an alternative to using ConsoleOne to create, change, or remove partitions, volumes, and pools, you can now use the Partition Disks Operation features in NoRM.

▶ *Profile CPU execution per NLM program*: On multiprocessor servers, you can view how each NLM program is distributing its activity across the available processors.

As you can see, NoRM is a very robust management utility that promises extremely flexible operation for today's NetWare administrators.

Installing NoRM

With most installations and patterns for NetWare 6.5, NoRM is installed automatically. After the installation, use a Web browser from a client computer in your network to access NoRM. In order to access NoRM from an Internet connection outside your firewall, you will need to make sure that TCP port **8009** is opened through the firewall to the IP address of your Web server. Port **8009** is the default port through which you will access the Web Manager interface. If desired, this port can be changed as long as it doesn't conflict with any other service on the NetWare 6.5 server.

To use NoRM, you must have a 4.x or newer Web browser such as Internet Explorer or Netscape Communicator. Make sure that Java or JavaScript is enabled on your Web browser. See the section on Web Manager for instructions on how to do this.

NoRM is accessible directly, or from the server console. To open NoRM directly, Open your Web browser and enter your Web server's domain name or IP address, followed by a colon and the port number, which by default is **8009**. For example:

```
https://www.quills.com:8009
```

or

```
https://137.65.192.1:8009
```

You might be prompted to accept an unknown certificate. At the Authentication dialog, enter the full username, with a leading dot, and password of a user with administrative rights to this server, and then select OK (see Figure 3.6).

To open NoRM from the graphical server console, simply click the red N button from the GUI.

NOTE If you don't log in as a user with administrative rights to the server, you will not have access to all pages necessary to manage your server remotely. You will see only pages that display the volumes, directories, and files for which you have trustee rights. In this case, you can view files (where you have read access), and upload files into directories where you have write access. You will not have access to any other management functions.

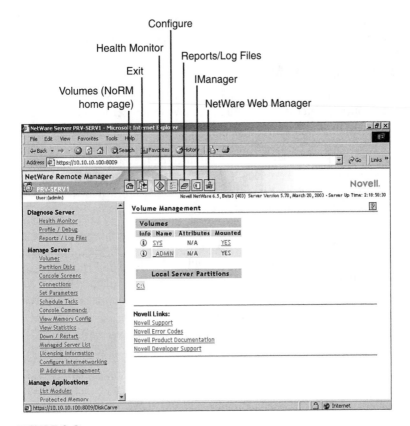

FIGURE 3.6
The NetWare Remote Manager home page.

After logging in, your session for NetWare Remote Manager remains open
until you close all your browser windows at that workstation. To log out
of NetWare Remote Manager, close all the browser windows at the
workstation from which you logged in.

NoRM Basics

Similar to iManager, NoRM is organized into three main sections, or
frames:

> ▶ *Header frame*: The Header frame is located at the top of the screen.
> It provides a semaphore (Green, Yellow, Red) assessment of the
> server's health, in addition to other tools and the Volumes and

Health Monitor pages in NoRM. Clicking the NetWare Remote Manager title in the header will take you to an About NoRM description of the software components of NoRM. Selecting the semaphore icon next to your server name will also take you to the Health Monitor page. By default, the Volumes page is always displayed when NoRM first starts.

▶ *Navigation frame*: The Navigation frame is located on the left side of the screen. It lists different management tasks, organized into groups that you can perform with NoRM. Each link takes you to the specific page(s) for performing that task. The list of available tasks in the Navigation frame can change based on the services and NLMs that you have loaded on the server.

▶ *Main Content frame*: The Main Content frame occupies the middle-right of the screen. When you select a link in the Header or Navigation frames, the appropriate page will be displayed in the Main content frame. If an Information icon appears in the upper-right corner of the page, you can view help for the page that is displayed in the main content frame.

From these frames you will be able to view and modify all features accessible through NoRM.

Configuring NoRM

You can access NoRM configuration options by selecting the Configure button in the header. To access the configuration options you must be logged in as a user with supervisor rights to the server from which NoRM is being run. The NoRM Configuration settings are organized into four groups:

▶ **NetWare Remote Manager configuration options:** The following settings are used to configure NoRM views (see Figure 3.7):

  ▶ *View Hidden SET Parameters*: Toggles whether or not hidden NetWare console SET parameters are visible in the list of available SET parameters in NoRM and on the server console.

  ▶ *View Hidden Console Commands*: Toggles whether or not hidden server console commands are visible in the list of available console commands. This can be helpful for discovering undocumented commands.

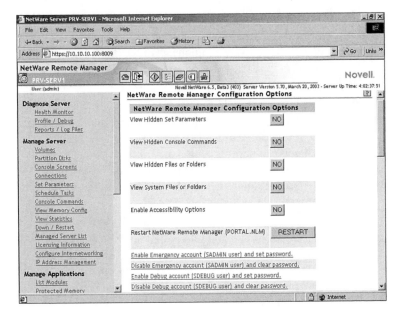

FIGURE 3.7
NoRM Configuration options.

TIP Even if hidden, any SET parameter or console command can still be activated from either NoRM or the server console as long as you know the proper syntax.

▶ *View Hidden Files or Folders*: Toggles whether or not files and folders with the Hidden attribute set will appear in the page lists on NoRM or on the server console.

▶ *View System Files or Folders*: Toggles whether or not files and folders with the System attribute set will appear in the page lists on NoRM or on the server console.

▶ *Enable Accessibility Options*: Disables dynamic refresh of NoRM pages in order to conform to new federal accessibility guidelines. With this option enabled, Health Monitor pages will not refresh until a manual page refresh is performed. For more information on accessibility options, see the NetWare 6.5 online documentation.

▶ *Restart NetWare Remote Manager (PORTAL.NLM)*: If you make any changes to settings in this group, you must reset NoRM for the changes to take effect.

▶ *Enable Emergency Account (SADMIN user) and Set Password*: SADMIN is a backup supervisor account that can be used when the Admin account or eDirectory is not working properly. It lets you perform maintenance tasks that do not require eDirectory. SADMIN is created when NoRM is installed.

▶ *Disable Emergency Account (SADMIN user) and Clear Password*: Disable the emergency user account created by NoRM when it is installed, and clear the password that has been set.

▶ *Enable Debug Account (SDEBUG user) and Set Password*: SDE-BUG is a limited access account suitable for debugging common server problems without granting access to data stored on the server.

▶ *Disable Debug Account (SDEBUG user) and Clear Password*: Disable the emergency user account created by NoRM when it is installed, and clear the password that has been set.

▶ **NetWare Remote Manager Health Logging Controls**: The following settings let you view and control the server health log (see Figure 3.8). From these settings you can view, clear, enable/disable, and restrict the maximum size of the server health log.

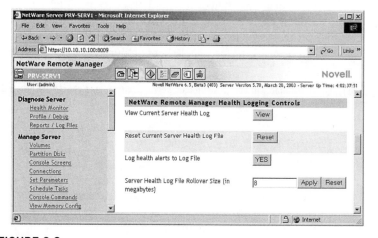

FIGURE 3.8
The NoRM Health logging controls.

▶ **HTTP logging controls:** The following settings control log files in the NoRM environment (see Figure 3.9):

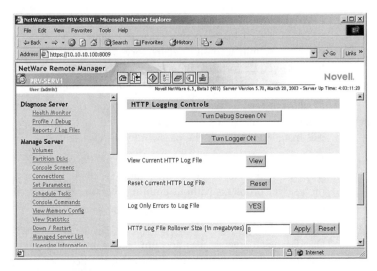

FIGURE 3.9
The NoRM HTTP logging controls.

> ▶ *Turn Debug Screen On*: When instructed by Novell Technical
> Services, turn this setting on to help debug a problem with
> the HTTPSTK module. You must also click the Turn Logger
> On button. The debug console screen journals debug infor-
> mation for the HTTP stack running on the server so that it
> can be reviewed for troubleshooting purposes.

WARNING This option will create significant server overhead and should not be used
under normal operation.

> ▶ *Turn Logger On*: If logging has been turned off, clicking this
> button will turn it on.
>
> ▶ *View Current HTTP Log File*: The log file contains the follow-
> ing information: an entry number; the date and timestamp in
> Greenwich mean time (GMT); hostname; the program mak-
> ing the call; the level of the call (whether it's done by the
> server or by users); and a description of the entry itself with
> information including the IP address of the source machine
> making the request, messages, status, and so on.

▶ *Reset Current HTTP Log File*: This option clears the current log and begins a new one. Restarting the log is useful if you have made a configuration change to your server and want to begin a new logging session.

▶ *Log Only Errors to Log File*: This option controls whether or not all requests are logged to the file. When logging only errors to the file, it will take much longer to fill the file to its maximum size, but casual access to the server is not tracked.

▶ *HTTP Log File Rollover Size (in Megabytes)*: This option sets a maximum size for the HTTP log file. If the available space on your volume SYS: is limited, you might want to limit the log file to a smaller size. If you want to gather more information over a longer period of time in the log file, you might want to increase the rollover size. When the file is full, the file is deleted and restarted. Automatic rollover guarantees that if logging is on, the log file always reflects the most recent activity on the server.

▶ **HTTP Interface Management:** The following settings control the basic configuration of NoRM (see Figure 3.10):

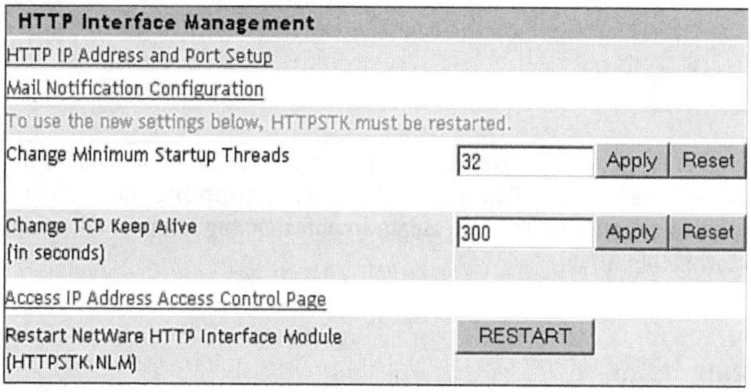

FIGURE 3.10
The NoRM HTTP Interface Management controls.

▶ *HTTP IP Address and Port Setup*: From this link, you can configure the default TCP port for unencrypted access to NoRM (default 81), the alternate TCP port (default 8008), and the default SSL port (default 8009).

▶ *Mail Notification Configuration*: From this page you can specify a primary mail server, an alternate mail server, up to eight users in the notification list, and a Mail From identification. You can control which items to be notified about on the Health Monitor page.

▶ *Change Minimum Startup Threads*: This setting lets you define the number of worker threads that are created for NoRM at startup. At least one thread is required and other threads will be created as needed. These initial work threads will be built between the server and browser-based clients. The default is **32**. However, if memory is low, you might want to set this to **4** and let more threads be created as needed.

▶ *Change TCP Keep Alive (in Seconds)*: This option lets you change the timeout for TCP sessions in NoRM. Default is 300 seconds (five minutes).

▶ *Access IP Address Access Control Page*: From this page you can limit access to NoRM. You can specify IP addresses for workstations or specify a subnet and subnet mask for ranges of workstations from which to give access. Restricting access in this way can help secure remote access to your server.

▶ *Restart NetWare HTTP Interface Module (HTTPSTK.NLM)*: Changes to settings in this group require that HTTPSTK.NLM be reloaded. Select this button to perform the reload remotely.

NOTE By clicking the word Novell in the upper-right portion of the header frame, you can access the Novell Support Connection at http://support.novell.com/. From this site, you can get current updates, locate troubleshooting information, or open an online support incident.

Customizing NoRM

You can add text, graphics, and custom links to the home (Volumes) page of NoRM by creating an HTML file named PRTLANNC.HTM, which contains the HTML code you want to add, and placing it in the server's SYS:\LOGIN directory. Any information in this file will appear at the bottom of the home page. See the NetWare 6.5 online documentation for more information.

NOTE Because this file will be used as part of the HTML code that generates the front page, do *not* include the <body> and </body> tags.

iMonitor

NetWare 6.5 ships with iMonitor v2.1. It is accessible as a component of NoRM, and provides eDirectory management and repair capabilities similar to the server management capabilities offered by NoRM. The goal of iMonitor is to provide a Web-based alternative, and eventual replacement, for many of the traditional eDirectory management and troubleshooting tools such as DSBrowse, DSTrace, DSDiag, and much of DSRepair.

iMonitor is capable of gathering information not only from NetWare 6.5 servers, but from most any version of eDirectory, including NDS version 4.11 or higher, and NDS or eDirectory running on any supported platform (NetWare, Windows NT/2000, Solaris, Linux, and Tru64).

Although iMonitor does provide tree-wide management, it is designed to get "down in the weeds" just like the console-based tools that you may have used in the past. It keeps track of the activities of the DSAgent running on each eDirectory server, so you can get an accurate picture of what is happening at any given time.

The following list identifies some of the major features offered by iMonitor in NetWare 6.5:

▶ *General eDirectory tasks*: This category of features includes search for eDirectory object(s), status of DirXML in your environment (if applicable), both pre-configured and customizable eDirectory reports, and detailed eDirectory error code and troubleshooting references.

▶ *Monitor eDirectory agent health*: This includes synchronization status, detailed synchronization information, known eDirectory servers, and partition and replica status for this server.

▶ *Browse eDirectory agent*: This lets you view eDirectory objects and attributes from the perspective of the server as well as viewing eDirectory schema on the server.

▶ *Configuring eDirectory agent*: Configure partition lists, replication filters, background processes, agent triggers, login settings, schema and partition synchronization, and database cache settings.

▶ *Server-centric tasks*: This includes Web-based versions of DSTrace, simplified DSRepair, and a background process scheduler. These services are available only for the server from which iMonitor is running.

As you can see, much of what was previously accomplished by console-based tools is now available via the Web-based interface of iMonitor.

Installing iMonitor

iMonitor is installed automatically during the installation of NetWare 6.5. Because it shares resources with NoRM, the PORTAL and HTTPSTK.NLM programs must be loaded on the server. Entries are placed in the AUTOEXEC.NCF to accomplish this.

After the installation, use a Web browser from a client computer in your network to access iMonitor. To access iMonitor from an Internet connection outside your firewall, you will need to make sure that TCP port **8009** is opened through the firewall to the IP address of your Web server. Port **8009** is the default port through which you will access the Web Manager interface. If desired, this port can be changed as long as it doesn't conflict with any other service on the NetWare 6.5 server.

To use iMonitor, use a current version of a Web browser, and make sure that Java or JavaScript is enabled on your Web browser. For steps on doing this, see the Web Manager section of this chapter.

To access iMonitor, open NoRM and browse down to the Manage eDirectory heading in the left column, and then select NDS iMonitor.

Alternatively, you can open iMonitor directly by opening your Web browser and entering your Web server's domain name or IP address, the NoRM port number (**8009**), and the iMonitor path (/**nds**). For example:

`https://www.quills.com:8009/nds`

or

`https://137.65.192.1:8009/nds`

You might be prompted to accept a certificate. At the Authentication dialog box, enter the full username, with a leading dot, and password of a user with administrative rights to this server, and then select OK to display the screen shown in Figure 3.11.

As with NoRM, your iMonitor session remains open until all browser windows at your workstation are closed.

Agent Configuration

Agent Summary (iMonitor home page)　Trace Configuration

Logout　Repair

Help　DirXML Summary

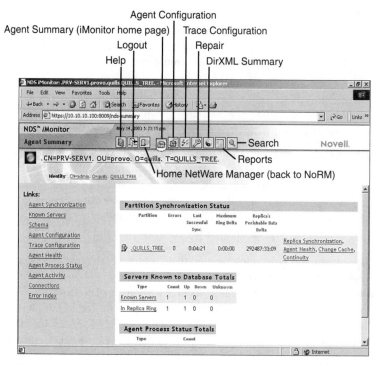

FIGURE 3.11
The iMonitor home page showing a summary of DSAgent information.

iMonitor Basics

Because it is a component of NoRM, iMonitor adheres largely to the same page layout as NoRM and iManager.

iMonitor Interface Layout

There are four possible frames to an iMonitor page:

▶ *Header frame:* The Header frame is located at the top of the screen. It provides a semaphore (Green, Yellow, Red) assessment of the eDirectory tree's health, in addition to access to other iMonitor tools and the iMonitor configuration. Clicking the NDS iMonitor title in the header will take you to an About iMonitor description of iMonitor software components. By default, the Agent Summary page is always displayed when iMonitor first starts.

▶ *Navigation frame*: The Navigation frame is located on the left side of the screen. It lists different management tasks, organized into groups, which you can perform with iMonitor. Each link takes you to the specific page(s) for performing that task.

▶ *Main Content frame*: The Main Content frame occupies the middle-right of the screen. When you select a link in the Header or Navigation frames, the appropriate page will be displayed in the Main Content frame.

▶ *(Conditional) Replica frame*: When needed, the Replica frame will appear in the lower-left corner of the iMonitor frame. This will happen when another replica of the requested data exists, or when another replica has a different view of the information being presented in the Main Content frame. From the Replica frame you can change the replica that you are using to view the requested data.

The amount and type of information that you see in iMonitor is dependent on your current eDirectory identity and the version of the DSAgent with which you are currently working. As new versions of eDirectory are released, they will be updated to provide more information to iMonitor. Therefore, older versions of eDirectory or NDS, while still accessible via iMonitor, will not provide the same level of detail offered by eDirectory 8.7.

Modes of Operation

iMonitor can function in one of two possible modes. You don't need to do anything to select between the two modes; iMonitor handles it automatically. However, it is important to understand them in order to properly interpret iMonitor data and navigate the eDirectory tree.

▶ *Direct mode*: Direct mode is used when iMonitor is gathering information or executing an operation on the same server from which iMonitor is running. The server-centric iMonitor features mentioned previously, which include DSTrace, DSRepair, and Background Scheduler, are available only from Direct mode. Direct mode gives you full access to all iMonitor features and is faster than Proxy mode, which is described next.

▶ *Proxy mode*: Proxy mode is used when iMonitor is gathering information or executing an operation on a server other than that from which iMonitor is running. Proxy mode makes it possible to gather information and statistics from older versions of eDirectory or NDS. Proxy mode is the default method of operation for iMonitor, meaning that once iMonitor is opened, it will continue to run from the specified server until explicitly told to switch to an instance of iMonitor on a different server.

iMonitor chooses the mode based on the URL request submitted from your browser. If the URL contains a server query, iMonitor will use Proxy mode. If no server query is present, iMonitor will run the query against the local DSAgent using Direct mode.

Configuring iMonitor

The default configuration of iMonitor is suitable for most environments. However, iMonitor offers a configuration file, **SYS:SYSTEM\NDSIMON.INI**, that allows you to customize iMonitor if desired. It lets you change both the general execution of iMonitor, as well as customize specific iMonitor features. For more information on iMonitor, see the NetWare 6.5 online documentation.

Enabling One Net

In This Part

Novell's vision of One Net is a world in which all types of networks work together to simplify the complexities of modern business and provide the power and flexibility needed to succeed in the economy of the 21st century.

The one thing you don't have the luxury of doing in today's Net world is dictate the software, hardware, and architecture across the entire reach of your network. By definition, One Net integrates myriad technologies, platforms, and architectures in such a way that the underlying complexity is masked from the user. Users see what they need (and nothing more), when they need it, from any Net connection anywhere in the world!

The three chapters in Part I of this book introduced NetWare 6.5, the various Novell clients, and the suite of management tools that let you keep everything running smoothly. From an administrator's perspective, it is easy to see how NetWare 6.5 helps achieve the goal of One Net. There are several installation and upgrade options; clients no longer demand prerequisites or make assumptions about platform; and management tools are fully Net-enabled, so you can administer from home in PJs and bunny slippers if you want.

But all the One Net love in the world isn't going to change the fact that for you, as a network administrator, the complexity of the Net isn't hidden. You will see it every day, and you will need to know how to perform those tasks that keep the Net functioning smoothly.

Chapter 3 introduced the NetWare 6 administrative tools. Part II of this book introduces the administrative techniques and tasks that keep the foundation of One Net strong and steady. Chapters 4 and 5 demonstrate how to use those tools for day-to-day administration of NetWare 6.5 servers and Novell eDirectory. Chapter 6 provides an overview of managing users and network security, and shows how eDirectory solves many of the traditional problems associated with managing authentication and access control. Chapter 7 introduces the other aspect of network computing that touches just about everybody: printing. With NetWare 6.5, it's easier than ever to configure a robust printing architecture that gives users the freedom to print from anywhere to anywhere with the click of a button.

CHAPTER 4

NetWare 6.5 Server Management

Instant Access

Optimizing Performance

▶ To monitor performance, use NetWare Remote Manager (NoRM). You can also use the legacy server console utility MONITOR.NLM.

▶ To optimize server performance, use NoRM to change server parameters. You can also use the legacy server console MONITOR.NLM, or set parameters individually using **SET** commands from the server console.

▶ You can manage a virtual memory swap file using NoRM.

▶ To see a history of errors that have occurred with the server, volume, or TTS, use a text editor or EDIT.NLM to read the error log files: SYS$LOG.ERR, VOL$LOG.ERR, TTS$LOG.ERR, BOOT$LOG.ERR, and ABEND.LOG.

▶ The Logger utility captures server messages to a separate screen on the NetWare server console so that you can read them for diagnostic purposes. You can also dump the buffered Logger data to a file for offline diagnosis.

Running Java Applications

NetWare 6.5 includes the NetWare Java Virtual Machine v1.4.1 to run Java applications or applets on a server, including the graphical server interface.

Protecting the Server

▶ To use an Uninterruptible Power Supply (UPS) to protect the server from power outages, use UPS_AIO.NLM or third-party UPS-management software.

▶ To protect the server and network from virus infections, use virus-scanning software, assign executable files the Execute Only or Read-Only attributes, and warn users against loading files from external sources.

▶ To keep faulty NLMs from corrupting server memory, you can load them in a protected address space using either NoRM or the **PROTECT** load command from the server console.

Maintaining the Server

▶ If you are unsure of a server's name, you can display it with the NAME console utility.

▶ To display the server's hardware information, use the links in the Manage Hardware section of NoRM. Legacy server console utilities are also available, including **CONFIG**, **CPUCHECK**, and **LIST DEVICES** from the server console.

▶ To determine which version of NetWare is running on a server, look in the header of NoRM. Legacy options for this information include the General >> Server Information tab of the Server object in ConsoleOne, and the **VERSION** console command.

▶ To view a list of the server's volumes and the name spaces they support, open the Volumes page in NoRM or use the **VOLUMES** console command.

▶ To bring down the server, use the **DOWN** console command.

▶ To reboot the server, use the **RESTART SERVER** console command.

▶ Keep abreast of current patches and updated modules by checking http://support.novell.com regularly.

▶ To control the server from a workstation, use Console Screens in NoRM or the RConsoleJ utility in ConsoleOne. More information on RConsoleJ is provided in Chapter 3, "Novell Management Tools."

▶ To control server startup activities, use the server startup files: AUTOEXEC.NCF and STARTUP.NCF. (Edit these files by using EDIT.NLM or NWCONFIG.)

▶ To manage workstation connections, open the Connections page in NoRM. You can also use the legacy console utility MONITOR.NLM.

▶ To monitor or modify a server's time, use the TIME, SET TIME, and SET TIME ZONE console commands.

▶ TIMESYNC.NLM manages time synchronization between servers in an eDirectory tree.

▶ To unload or display currently loaded NLMs, open the Modules page in NoRM. You can also use the UNLOAD and MODULES console commands.

Managing Storage Devices

▶ To add a new hard disk or replace an existing one, use the Partition Disks screen in NoRM. Alternatively, you can use the NSS Management Utility (NSSMU.NLM) from the server console.

▶ CD-ROMs will mount as network volumes automatically when they are inserted into the NetWare 6.5 server's CD-ROM drive.

Managing Routing Between Servers

▶ To list networks, use the DISPLAY NETWORKS console command.

▶ To list servers in a given tree, open the Known Servers page in iMonitor. To see all servers that are contactable via SLP, use DISPLAY SERVERS.

▶ To configure protocols, choose Configure Internetworking in NoRM, or use INETCFG.NLM.

▶ To configure IPX, AppleTalk, and TCP/IP protocols, choose Configure Internetworking in NoRM, or use INETCFG.NLM.

▶ To execute protocol configuration commands made using INETCFG.NLM, use the INITIALIZE SYSTEM and REINITIALIZE SYSTEM console utilities.

NetWare Server Basics

There are many tasks associated with managing a NetWare 6.5 server; from monitoring performance to adding or changing server hardware, to accounting for customer usage. NetWare 6.5 brings a new management paradigm to many of these standard operations. This chapter presents you with the options for performing server maintenance and management. As you will see, many of these options are now Web-based, using the latest one NET-management tool such as NoRM. The move is definitely toward remote, clientless management tools that give you all the power of NetWare's traditional console-based utilities. However, when appropriate, the tried-and-true NetWare methods are provided as well. Specific administrative tasks covered in this chapter include

- ▶ Protecting the server

- ▶ Monitoring and optimizing server performance

- ▶ Performing regular server maintenance

- ▶ Installing or replacing server hardware, such as hard disks and network boards

- ▶ Working with CD-ROMs as network volumes

- ▶ Managing startup files

- ▶ Synchronizing time between all the network servers

The behavior of a NetWare 6.5 server is configured and managed through the use of console utilities and NetWare Loadable Modules (NLMs). NoRM exposes these tools for use from a remote workstation. Similarly, ConsoleOne provides RConsoleJ to make the server console accessible from any workstation on your LAN/WAN.

Console Utilities

Console utilities are used to change or view some aspect of the NetWare 6.5 server. They ship as part of the core operating system. Console commands are accessible either directly from the console or remotely through NoRM or RConsoleJ.

To see a list of all supported console commands, select the Console Commands option in NoRM or type **HELP** at the server console. Figure 4.1 shows the NoRM Console Commands page. To see a brief description and example of any console command, select the Information link next to the command in NoRM or type **HELP** at the server console. Appendix C contains a comprehensive list of NetWare 6.5 console commands.

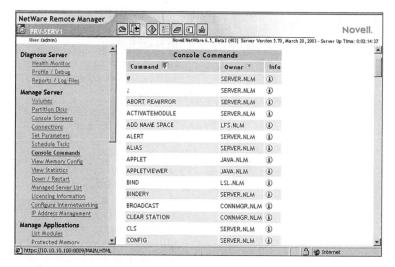

FIGURE 4.1
Console commands list in NoRM.

NetWare Loadable Modules

A NetWare Loadable Module is at its most basic a program that runs on NetWare. Once loaded, an NLM becomes part of the NetWare OS. NLMs can be dynamically loaded and unloaded. Many NLMs are automatically installed and loaded with NetWare 6.5. Others are optional and can be loaded as needed. Four of the most common types of NLMs are listed in Table 4.1.

TABLE 4.1   Common Types of Loadable Modules

TYPE OF MODULE	EXTENSION	DESCRIPTION
NLM	.NLM	Changes or adds functionality to the server. This includes most applications and services that run on the NetWare OS kernel.
Name Space module	.NAM	Allows the operating system to store Macintosh, Windows 2000/XP, Windows 9x, or NFS files, along with their unique file formats, long filenames, and other characteristics.

TABLE 4.1   Continued

TYPE OF MODULE	EXTENSION	DESCRIPTION
LAN driver	.LAN	Permits NetWare to communicate with a network board installed in the server.
Storage drivers	.CDM and .HAM	These drivers are associated with the NetWare Peripheral Architecture (NPA) used to drive specific storage devices and host adapters. The Host Adapter Module (HAM) is used to drive specific host adapter hardware. The Custom Device Module (CDM) is used to communicate with a specific storage device such as a hard disk, which are connected to the host adapter.

NLMs can open their own status screens on the server console when they are loaded. You can view the status screens that are active on your server by selecting Console Screens from NoRM (see Figure 4.2).

If you are at the server console directly, or using an RConsoleJ session, you can toggle through the status screens by using Alt+Esc from the server console. Use Ctrl+Esc to pull up a list of available screens similar to what you can see from NoRM. For more information on RConsoleJ, refer to Chapter 3.

To load an NLM, you can type the name of the NLM on the server console. However, it is often more convenient to use the List Modules link in NoRM. Enter the full name, including path, to the NLM you want to load in the dialog box and click Load Module. Check Display System Console for Module to view the system console while the NLM loads to make sure it loads properly.

Similarly, you can unload NLMs that are not required for the operation of the NetWare operating system by typing **UNLOAD** *<module>* at the server console. Using NoRM, you can select an NLM from the list of loaded modules in List Modules, and click Unload. This option is not available for kernel-level NLMs such as SERVER.EXE or NSS.NLM.

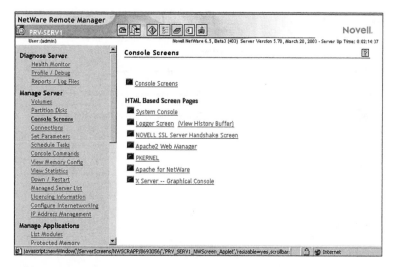

FIGURE 4.2
Viewing active console screens from NoRM.

TIP NoRM has the capability to define groups of servers and create a custom home page from which those servers can be managed. Select the Configure New Group option in NoRM and you can select the server(s) that you want include as part of a management group. Once these groups are created, it makes it easy for you to move from server to server as necessary to perform your administrative tasks.

Stopping and Starting the Server

If you need to shut down or restart your NetWare 6.5 server, first notify users so that they have time to save their work and close any files they are using on that server. Once this is done, select Down/Restart in the navigation pane in NoRM (see Figure 4.3).

TIP You can send a broadcast message to all users attached to a server by selecting the Connections link in NoRM. Simply type your message into the Broadcast Message field and click Send.

▶ *Down*: This option shuts down the server and returns the server console to a DOS prompt. From the DOS prompt, you can turn off the computer, reboot it, or restart the server. This is equivalent to typing **DOWN** from the server console.

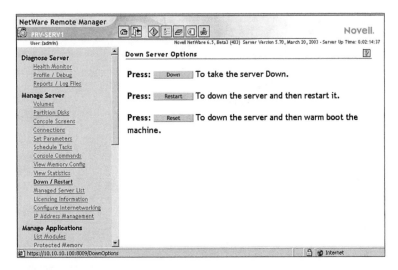

FIGURE 4.3
The Down, Restart, and Reset options in NoRM.

▶ *Restart*: This option unloads and then automatically reloads the NetWare operating system without returning to DOS first. This command is equivalent to typing **RESTART SERVER** from the server console.

▶ *Reset*: This option not only shuts down the server and returns it to DOS, but also performs a reset of the computer hardware (warm reboot). If your server is configured to load automatically on boot up, NetWare 6.5 will automatically reload after the hardware has rebooted. This is equivalent to typing **DOWN** from the server console and then performing a "three-finger salute" (Ctrl+Alt+Del) to reset the hardware.

Running Java Applications on the Server

NetWare 6.5 includes an updated Java Virtual Machine (JVM) for NetWare, version 1.4.1, which makes it possible for Java-based applications and applets to run better than ever. The JVM is installed automatically during the NetWare 6.5 installation and it is used to support graphical server interface, the Apache Web server, and Tomcat Servlet server. To load an external Java application on your NetWare 6.5 server, complete the following steps:

1. Copy the application or applet files, typically a .JAR file, to the default Java directory on the server. The default directory is SYS:JAVA\LIB. This directory is included in the CLASSPATH environment variable, so the server will be able to find the application or applet without users having to specify the path.

2. Specify a Just In Time (JIT) compiler for the server to use. This will improve the performance of Java-based applications. NetWare 6.5 ships with the Symantec JIT compiler v1.3, or you can install another manufacturer's JIT compiler.

3. Java is loaded by default when NetWare 6.5 loads. If it has been unloaded for any reason, you can restart Java by loading JAVA.NLM on the server. Once JAVA.NLM is loaded, you can view Java information from NoRM by selecting Java Application Information under the Manage Applications heading (see Figure 4.4).

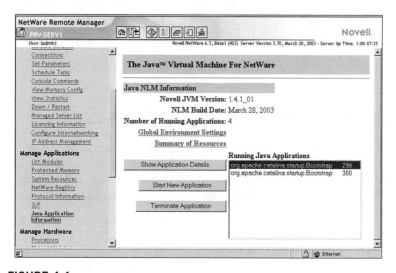

FIGURE 4.4
Java application information and management options in NoRM.

4. You can start a new Java applet by selecting Start New Application and typing the **APPLET <html_file>** command, substituting the applet's filename for <html_file>.

5. To execute a Java-based application, the command you type depends on how you want the application to run. Use one of the

following commands, substituting the application's name for
<*class*>:

- ▶ *JAVA* <*class*>: Use this load format if the application doesn't
  require user input, or if it runs in a graphical user interface.

- ▶ *JAVA* *-NS* <*class*>: Use this load format if the application is
  text-based and requires user input. This will launch a separate console screen for the Java application you are loading.

TIP You can view detailed statistics on any Java application running on NetWare 6.5
by clicking Show Application Details in NoRM.

You can also terminate a Java process from NoRM for any reason from
the Java Application Information screen—select the application from the
list of running Java applications, and click Terminate Application. Click
OK to confirm that this application should be unloaded. This is equivalent to typing **JAVA -KILL** <*id*> at the server console, substituting the ID
of the Java process you want to terminate for <*id*>. The ID of the Java
process is listed next to the process on the Java Application Information
screen.

Managing a NetWare Server

In the preceding sections, you saw how NoRM permits you to manage
most any aspect of a NetWare 6.5 server from any workstation with
browser access to the network, even over the Internet! The following sections review several of the other types of day-to-day server-management
tasks you need to perform on a NetWare 6.5 network.

Protecting the Server

Protecting the server is a very important safeguard that cannot be over-
looked. Damage to the server can affect the entire network. The activities
covered in the following sections can help you protect your server.

Physical Damage

If the server is in an exposed public area where anyone can have access
to it, accidents can, and will, happen. For example, someone might
unplug the power cord or turn off the server, thinking it had been left on

accidentally. For this reason, all file servers should be stored in a locked room. NetWare 6.5 makes this much easier with its comprehensive remote-management tools. Because of this, you should strongly consider removing keyboards and monitors from the servers. This eliminates a major access point for mischief and mistakes.

Today, it is fairly common to purchase customized rack-mountable hardware for your server. This way, many servers can be located in a fairly limited area, with isolated and protected power sources and climate control to keep everything cool. When possible, this type of configuration further limits physical problems that might affect your network.

Electrical Power Problems

If you have been around computers for any period of time, you know the chaos that can be caused by a sudden loss of electrical power. A Uninterruptible Power Supply (UPS) helps mitigate this risk by providing a battery-based power backup for your server. When power is lost, the UPS seamlessly takes over and provides power for a time sufficient to allow you to close things down gracefully.

Several UPS manufacturers provide NetWare-compatible software for their products. However, if your UPS does not come with NetWare software, you can try UPS_AIO.NLM, which allows NetWare to communicate with a UPS attached to a serial port on the server. Complete the following steps to use UPS_AIO.NLM to link your UPS to your NetWare 6.5 server using a serial port:

1. Attach the UPS to the server using the manufacturer's instructions.

2. Load the UPS hardware driver on the server.

3. Load an AIO device driver on the server. AIOCOMX.NLM is the default driver that comes with NetWare.

4. Load UPS_AIO.NLM on the server, specifying the correct options in the UPS_AIO options format (see Table 4.2).

TIP If you want the UPS to be configured the same way every time the server is rebooted, put the LOAD UPS_AIO.NLM in the server's AUTOEXEC.NCF file. Be sure to include the appropriate options (see Table 4.2).

TABLE 4.2   UPS_AIO Options

OPTION	DESCRIPTION
`Downtime = value`	The time, in seconds, that the server will run on battery power before shutting down. Default: 300. Value: Minimum 30 seconds (no maximum).
`MSGDelay = value`	The time, in seconds, before the system sends a message to users about the approaching shutdown. Default: 5. Value: Minimum 0 (no maximum).
`MSGInterval = value`	The time, in seconds, between broadcasts. Default: 30. Value: Minimum 20 (no maximum).
`DriverType = value`	The AIO device driver type. See the manufacturer's documentation for the type. Default: 1 (AIOCOMX). Value: 1, 2, or 3.
`Board = value`	The AIO board number. If you use AIOCOMX, the board number is displayed when you load AIOCOMX. If you use another driver, see the manufacturer's documentation for the number. Default: 0.
`Port = value`	AIO port number. If you use AIOCOMX, the port number is displayed when you load AIOCOMX. If you use another driver, see the manufacturer's documentation for the number. Default: 0.
`Signal_High`	Sets normal RS232 signaling state to High. Use the High setting only if your system uses high values instead of low values to determine whether the power is low. See the manufacturer's documentation for more information. Default: none.

Once configured as noted here, your UPS can communicate with your NetWare 6.5 server through the server's serial port.

Disk Failures

To help isolate your users from the effects of hard disk problems, the NetWare 6.5 offers several powerful storage options, including disk mirroring and duplexing, software RAID support, Storage Area Network (SAN) support with NetWare Cluster Services, and iSCSI. NetWare storage options are discussed in more detail in Chapter 8, "File Storage and Management."

Viruses

Unfortunately, software viruses are a fact of life. Fortunately, the specialized nature of the NetWare architecture has made it resistant to virus infection at the operating system level. However, that doesn't mean that a NetWare server can't host a virus and play a part in its propagation around your network.

The best way to fight the continually shifting assault of viruses is to use a third-party virus-scanning solution to detect and clean network files if they become infected. This solution should also support automatic scanning of Web-based files and email to create a more robust protective barrier.

Because of the rate at which new viruses are being created, keep your virus solution current with both software updates and virus pattern files. Virus scanning won't do much good if it is incapable of detecting the virus that hits your system.

NetWare does offer some protection against viruses infecting executable files through the use of the Execute Only file attribute. You can also remove the Modify right from the directory that contains the executable files and make executable files Read-Only. This will prevent viruses from modifying a file in order to attach themselves to it. For more information on NetWare file system rights, see Chapter 8.

CD-ROMs

With NetWare, a server-mounted CD-ROM can appear as any other NetWare NSS volume. Users on the network can access the CD-ROM just like any other volume, except that it is read-only. For more information on NSS, see Chapter 8.

NetWare uses CDROM.NLM to mount CD-ROMs as NetWare volumes. It supports High Sierra, ISO 9660, and HFS (Apple) extensions for Macintosh clients that might be out there, and the appropriate support module will be auto-loaded with CDROM.NLM (for example, CD9660.NSS). CDROM.NLM is loaded automatically when the server starts. When you insert a CD-ROM into the CD-ROM drive, NetWare will automatically detect and load the drive as a new NetWare volume.

Once loaded, you can use the Volumes page in NoRM to view the CD-ROM volume; it's listed as an active volume on the server. You can dismount and mount the CD-ROM just like any other volume on the server.

NOTE All the manual CDROM load commands that you might remember from previous versions of NetWare, particularly NetWare 5.1 and prior, are no longer available, or necessary, in NetWare 6.5.

Controlling NLMs

Because NLMs load as part of the operating system, it is possible for a misbehaving NLM to cause problems in a server's memory. It could corrupt its own memory space or overwrite memory being used by another process, causing a server *ABEND*, or Abnormal END. An ABEND is a serious error from which the server cannot always recover without your help.

NLMs from Novell should not require that you load them in protected address spaces, but NLMs that execute external applications, including the NetWare JVM, load in protected memory automatically to protect the server from those external applications. If you have an NLM that you don't trust, it is possible to test it in NetWare's *protected address space*.

You can load an NLM into a protected address space from NoRM by doing the following:

1. Select the Protected Memory link under Manage Applications in NoRM. This screen also gives you a view of applications operating in protected memory and settings for memory protection SET parameters.

2. Select one of the following options:

   ▶ *Load NCF file protected*: Many third-party applications will create an NCF script to load the necessary modules. Use this option to make sure all modules loaded from the specified NCF file are loaded into protected memory.

   ▶ *Load module protected*: Use this option to load a single NLM into protected memory.

3. Enter the full name, including path, of the module or NCF file that you want to load in the appropriate field, and then select the corresponding button.

Once loaded in this fashion, the NetWare kernel will be protected from any misbehavior of the module loaded into protected memory space.

Monitoring and Optimizing Server Performance

When you monitor the server's performance, you look for key indicators that the server is functioning at an optimal level. Some of the things you should monitor include the utilization percentage of the server's processor, the number of cache buffers and packet receive buffers being regularly used, and the server's memory allocation.

Every network has different needs and usage patterns. By default, server parameters are set so that the server will perform well on most networks. In addition, the server is self-tuning, meaning that it will gradually adjust itself over time to accommodate changing usage patterns. However, you should be aware of what constitutes "normal" for your server(s). That way, you can effectively plan for future network and server needs as well as notice any unusual changes that might indicate a potential problem.

The best way to do this is to regularly review NoRM's Health Monitor (see Figure 4.5). Health Monitor is broken down into major groupings of server health. Selecting a link in Health Monitor takes you to more specific information about the current state of the server with regard to that category.

Health Monitor also allows you to set thresholds for server performance that can generate automated alerts to the administrative staff when these thresholds are passed.

Server parameters, also called **SET** parameters, control the NetWare 6.5 server environment. They allow you to set Maximum, Minimum, and Threshold levels for many aspects of the server's internal operations. Appendix C contains a comprehensive list of NetWare 6.5 **SET** parameters, and more information on configuring thresholds and alerts.

You can use NoRM to adjust **SET** parameters by selecting the Set Parameters link, as shown in Figure 4.6. This can also be done from the server console with MONITOR.NLM. **SET** parameters come in two types: persistent and non-persistent. Persistent **SET** parameters maintain their state even if the server is shut down. Non-persistent **SET** parameters reset to their default value when the server restarts. You place non-persistent **SET** parameters in your AUTOEXEC.NCF and/or STARTUP.NCF, so they are set automatically to the desired value whenever the server starts.

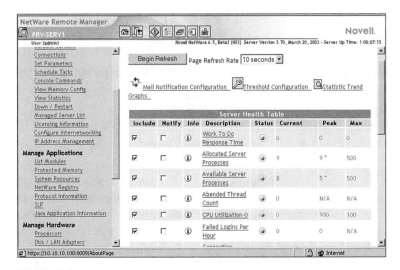

FIGURE 4.5
Health Monitor in NoRM.

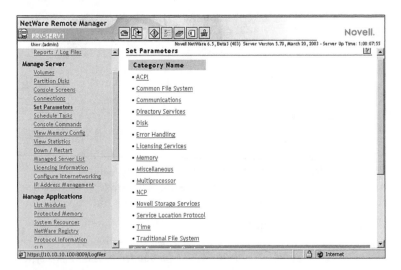

FIGURE 4.6
NetWare 6.5 SET parameters in NoRM.

After NetWare 6.5 is first installed, it will optimize itself over a period of time by leveling adjustments for low-usage times with peak-usage bursts.

Over a week or two, the server will settle on an optimal setting for each SET parameter. However, if you already know where the server should be set, or if you are not satisfied with the server's self-tuned settings, you can configure any SET parameter manually.

The following sections describe some of the ways to monitor and optimize your server's performance.

Cache Memory

Running out of cache memory is one of the biggest causes of poor server performance in a NetWare environment. Prior to NetWare 6.5 there were a number of cache parameters related to directory, open files applications, and the like. One of the major changes between NetWare 5 and NetWare 6.5 is the use of the NSS file system as the default file system for NetWare 6.5 and the SYS volume. With NSS, you get a completely redesigned caching system that eliminates most of the cache monitoring with which you may be familiar.

NSS introduces a much simplified caching system with only two cache pools to worry about: the OS pool and the NSS pool. The OS pool, as its name implies, is used to supply the memory needs of all OS-related processes, including packet receive buffers. The NSS pool is used for everything else, including directory, files, server applications, and so on.

When NetWare 6.5 is installed, the total available cache memory is balanced between the OS and NSS cache pools. The default balance is 60% NSS pool and 40% OS pool. You can change this setting from NoRM by selecting Set Parameters >> Novell Storage Services >> NSS Cache Balance Percent. The NSS system will automatically re-allocate memory between the two pools to keep them functioning at an optimal level.

You can review the current server statistics related to cache memory through the following links in NoRM's Health Monitor. If you are familiar with it, you can also set these values using MONITOR.NLM from the server console:

- ▶ *Cache performance*: Provides both a textual and graphic overview of memory allocation on the server to which you are attached through NoRM. Also provides links to specific memory allocations within the general pools. The Available Memory link brings you to this same page.

▶ *Available ECBs*: Event Control Blocks (ECBs) are another name for packet receive buffers. You can get an overview of ECB allocation from this page. It also lists all modules currently assigned ECBs. The Packet Receive Buffers link brings you to this same page.

If the server seems to be slowing down or losing workstation connections, see how many ECBs are allocated and how many are being used. You might need to increase the minimum and/or maximum numbers of packet receive buffers. To do this from NoRM, select Set Parameters >> Communications and scroll down to the Minimum and Maximum Packet Receive Buffers settings. You can also decrease the New Packet Receive Buffer wait time.

After a couple of days of average network usage, check to see how many packet receive buffers are being allocated, and compare that with the maximum number. If the two numbers are the same, increase the maximum value by 50 buffers. Continue to monitor the buffers periodically and increase the maximum value until the allocated number no longer reaches the maximum.

Virtual Memory

NetWare 6.5 includes support for virtual memory to help utilize memory more efficiently. Any modules that are loaded in protected memory will utilize virtual memory. With virtual memory, data that hasn't been accessed recently can be moved back to disk, where it is temporarily stored in a swap file. When the data is requested again, it is restored back into memory. Data in the swap file can still be accessed more quickly than from its permanent location on the disk, while at the same time allowing existing RAM to be used more efficiently. This helps reduce the possibility of encountering low memory conditions on the server.

A swap file is created automatically for the SYS volume. You can create additional swap files for each volume if you want. The swap files don't necessarily need to reside on the volume for which they're designated, but it's a good idea to have one swap file per volume.

View, create, and delete swap files from NoRM's Health Monitor by clicking Virtual Memory Performance >> To Swap File Information. This will open the Swap File Configuration utility (see Figure 4.7).

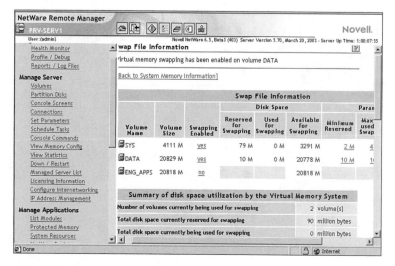

FIGURE 4.7
Swap file configuration as it appears in NoRM.

To create a new swap file, select the No link in the Swapping Enabled column next to the volume for which you want to create a swap file. If you don't specify any parameters, this will create a swap file with a minimum size of 2MB, a maximum size of the entire volume size, and will leave a minimum of 5MB of free space on the volume. However, you can set any of these parameters as you see fit by typing the desired value into the appropriate field.

To delete a swap file from a volume, select the Yes link in the Swapping Enabled column next to the volume for which you want to delete the swap file and select Disable.

Error Logs

You can monitor several error log files to determine whether your network has generated any error messages. They are a valuable source of information and clues when troubleshooting a network or server problem.

You can view the principal log files with NoRM by selecting Reports/Log Files (see Figure 4.8).

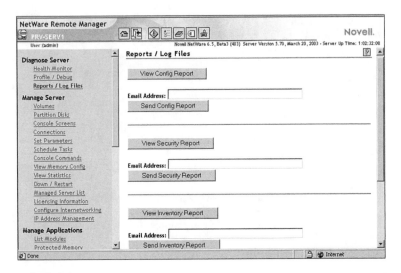

FIGURE 4.8
Report and log file options in NoRM.

You have access to the following information from this screen:

▶ *View Config Report*: Lets you generate and view a NetWare Server Configuration report. This report can help you diagnose problems with your server that might be caused by improper NLM versions. You can print this report from your browser, if desired. Clicking Send Config Report will generate a Config report and email it to the specified email address. The Config report contains the following:

   ▶ Basic server configuration information

   ▶ A listing of all modules currently loaded on the server

   ▶ LAN driver configurations

   ▶ Storage device configuration

   ▶ Statistics for all mounted volumes

   ▶ A listing of all primary server configuration files

   ▶ A listing of current SET parameter settings

   ▶ A listing of the contents of SYS:SYSTEM

   ▶ A listing of the boot directory (C:\)

▶ *View Security Report*: Lets you generate and view a Server Security report. This report can help you monitor potential security risks to a server. To see all the available information, you must be logged as an Admin user. Clicking Send Security Report will generate a Security report and email it to the specified email address. The Security report contains the following:

- ▶ General security-related information

- ▶ Trustee assignments for all mounted volumes

- ▶ Trustee assignments to the common folders on volume Sys

- ▶ Information for all protocols loaded on the server

▶ *View Inventory Report*: Lets you generate and view a NetWare Server Inventory report. Clicking Send Inventory Report will generate an Inventory report and email it to the specified email address. This report can take a while to create, so it is automatically saved on the server where you can view it at a later time. This report contains the following information:

- ▶ Links to volume-specific reports

- ▶ Storage resource management information about the files on the server volumes

- ▶ A list of key statistics

- ▶ Various profiles of the files

- ▶ A list of all the trustee assignments for each volume

▶ *Log File Management*: The links in this table let you view and clear several of the log files available on the server. Simply click the log's filename to view the log. Restart the logging by clicking Clear next to the log you want to clear. The following logs are available:

- ▶ *Server Personal Log Book*: Stored at `SYS:SYSTEM\NRMUSERS.LOG`, this log functions as a journal to let you keep track of changes made to the server, or any other information you might want to keep around.

- ▶ *System Error Log*: Stored at `SYS:SYSTEM\SYS$LOG.ERR`, this log file stores all messages sent to the System Console and Logger screens.

- ▶ *Abend Log*: Stored at `SYS:SYSTEM\ABEND.LOG`, this log file tracks any ABENDs that occurred on the server. Because of the robust recovery features in NetWare 6.5, you might not

be aware that the server has had a problem unless you view
this file.

▶ *Server Health Log:* Stored at `SYS:SYSTEM\HEALTH.LOG`, this
log file tracks the change in health status as they are reported
by the semaphore (traffic light) in NoRM (Green, Yellow,
Red).

There are a few other log files of which you should be aware. You can
view these logs in NoRM by selecting the Volumes link, selecting the volume on which the log is stored—typically SYS: or `C:\`—and then browsing to the file you want to view. The error log files you should keep in
mind include the following:

▶ BOOT$LOG.ERR: Logs all the errors that occur during server start-
up. This file is stored in the `SYS:SYSTEM` directory.

▶ LOGGER.TXT: Many of the console messages that were formerly
sent to the server console are now sent to a new Logger screen
available in NetWare 6.5. All Logger screen messages are maintained in a buffer, so you can scroll up and down the logger
screen as needed. You can dump the Logger buffer file to
`C:\NWSERVER\LOGGER.TXT` by pressing <F2> while in the Logger
screen. Other Logger options can be seen by pressing <F1> in the
Logger screen.

▶ VOL$LOG.ERR: Logs error messages for a volume. This log file is
used only with traditional NetWare volumes. Each volume has its
own log file, which is stored at the root of the volume. Any errors
or messages that pertain to the volume are stored in this file.

▶ TTS$LOG.ERR: Logs all data that is backed out by the NetWare
Transaction Tracking System (TTS). This log file is used only with
traditional NetWare volumes. This file is stored in the SYS volume.
To allow this file to be created, use MONITOR.NLM to turn the
TTS Abort Dump Flag parameter to On.

NOTE Remember, you can also run NoRM from the server GUI by clicking the red N
icon.

To limit the size of SYS$LOG.ERR and BOOT$LOG.ERR, select Set
Parameters >> Error Handling from NoRM and change the appropriate
log file parameters. You can also set these parameters from the server
console with MONITOR.NLM:

- *Server log file state*: This parameter defines what should happen if the server log reaches its size limit. Valid options are 0–2. Default is 2.

    - 0: Takes no action (logging will effectively stop)

    - 1: Clears the log file (all previously saved data is lost)

    - 2: Renames the log file and starts a new one

- *Server log file overflow size*: Sets the maximum size for SYS$LOG.ERR in bytes.

- *Boot error log file state*: This parameter defines what should happen if the boot error log reaches its size limit. Valid options are 0–3. Default is 3.

    - 0: Takes no action (logging will effectively stop)

    - 1: Clears the log file (all previously saved data is lost)

    - 2: Renames the log file and starts a new one

    - 3: Causes a new log file to be created every time the server is rebooted

- *Boot error log file overflow size*: Sets the maximum size for BOOT$LOG.ERR in bytes.

To limit the size of VOL$LOG.ERR and TTS$LOG.ERR on traditional NetWare volumes, select Set Parameters >> Traditional File System from NoRM and change the appropriate log file parameters. You can also set these parameters from the server console with MONITOR.NLM:

- *Volume log file state*: This parameter defines what should happen if the server log reaches its size limit. Valid options are 0–2. Default is 2.

    - 0: Takes no action (logging will effectively stop)

    - 1: Clears the log file (all previously saved data is lost)

    - 2: Renames the log file and starts a new one

- *Volume TTS log file state*: This parameter defines what should happen if the TTS log reaches its size limit. Valid options are 0–2. Default is 2.

    - 0: Takes no action (logging will effectively stop)

    - 1: Clears the log file (all previously saved data is lost)

    - 2: Renames the log file and starts a new one

▶ *Volume log file overflow size*: Sets the maximum size for VOL$LOG.ERR in bytes.

▶ *Volume TTS log file overflow size*: Sets the maximum size for TTS$LOG.ERR in bytes.

Using these log files, you can keep a pretty close eye on events related to your NetWare storage environment.

Performing Regular Server Maintenance

From time to time, you might find you need to perform some type of maintenance on your server. For example, you might need to add a new hard disk, load the latest patches (bug fixes or enhancements) on the server, or clear a workstation connection. The following sections explain how to do some of these common maintenance tasks.

Displaying Information About the Server

Just about all the server information you will ever need is available in NoRM. Utilities with identical functionality are also available from the server console. Table 4.3 lists the types of information about the server you can see and the console utilities you can use to display that information.

TABLE 4.3 How to Display Server Information

TYPE OF INFORMATION	NORM PAGE	CONSOLE UTILITIES
Server name	Header Frame	NAME, CONFIG
Tree name	Access Tree Walker	CONFIG
Network board info	Disk/LAN Adapters	CONFIG
Storage devices	Disk/LAN Adapters	LIST STORAGE ADAPTERS
Loaded NLMs	List Modules	MODULES
Processor speed	Processors	SPEED, CPUCHECK
Processor status	Processors	DISPLAY PROCESSORS
Version number	Reports/Log Files >> View Config Report	VERSION
Current SET parameters	Set Parameters	DISPLAY ENVIRONMENT

TABLE 4.3   Continued

TYPE OF INFORMATION	NORM PAGE	CONSOLE UTILITIES
SET parameters not at default	Set Parameters	DISPLAY MODIFIED ENVIRONMENT
Mounted volumes	Volumes	VOLUMES

Installing Patches and Updates

No software product is going to be perfect, no matter how thoroughly it has been tested. And because of today's tight development schedules and competitive marketplace, the reality is that there is already a list of known defects before the product even ships. NetWare 6.5 is the most thoroughly tested and most stable product ever to be released by Novell, but that doesn't mean that unforeseen flaws or unexpected behaviors won't crop up.

To fix these problems, Novell releases software patches and updated modules that can be installed on your NetWare server. Once tested, NetWare 6.5 patches will be rolled into a support pack. Not all individual patches or updates are needed for every customer, but support packs usually contain enough fixes that they are a good idea for the majority of NetWare 6.5 users.

All NetWare patches come with installation instructions and an automated installation routine to make sure all the files get to the right places.

Novell releases support packs, patches, and updates in a variety of ways. The best way to keep track of the recommended updates is through Novell's minimum patch List. Individual patches are available from Novell's Support Web site, and all patches and updates are also included on the Support Connection Library—a collection of CDs regularly produced by Novell Technical Services and sent to subscribers.

> **NOTE** Novell's minimum patch list is located at http://support.novell.com/produpdate/patchlist.html. Individual patches are available from Novell's Support Web site at http://support.novell.com.

Monitoring Workstation Connections

Some types of server maintenance require that you break a workstation's connection to the server or that you prevent users from logging in while you're completing the maintenance task. Use the utilities listed in Table 4.4 to perform these tasks.

TABLE 4.4 Ways to Monitor Workstation Connections

TASK	NORM PAGE	CONSOLE UTILITY
See connected workstations	Connections	MONITOR
See open files	Connections (select a connection)	MONITOR (select a connection)
Clear connections	Connections	MONITOR (press Del)
Prevent user login	None (use iManager— User Management)	DISABLE LOGIN
Re-enable login	None (use iManager— User Management)	ENABLE LOGIN

Modifying Server Startup Activities

When you start up or reboot the NetWare server, its boot files execute in the following order:

1. The DOS system files load, including CONFIG.SYS and AUTOEXEC.BAT, which sets up a basic environment and can be set to automatically execute SERVER.EXE.

2. SERVER.EXE runs the NetWare operating system on the computer, which turns the computer into the NetWare server. NWSERVER.EXE is located in the \NWSERVER directory.

3. STARTUP.NCF, which is stored in the Boot partition with SERVER.EXE, automates the initialization of the NetWare operating system. It loads disk drivers, name space modules to support different file formats, and may execute some SET parameters that modify default initialization values.

4. AUTOEXEC.NCF, which is stored in SYS:SYSTEM, loads the server's LAN drivers, sets time parameters, specifies the server name and ID (formerly the IPX internal net number), mounts volumes, and then performs optional activities—such as loading application or utility NLMs you specified to load automatically, and executing additional SET parameters.

5. Additional .NCF files, if they've been created, can be called from the AUTOEXEC.NCF file or executed from the server's console. They are normally stored in SYS:SYSTEM.

The STARTUP.NCF and AUTOEXEC.NCF files are created automatically during the installation process. They contain commands that reflect the selections you made during installation. Several other .NCF files are created during the NetWare 6.5 installation or when other services are installed.

You can edit these .NCF files after installation to add new commands or modify existing ones. Table 4.5 describes the utilities you can use to edit the STARTUP.NCF and AUTOEXEC.NCF files.

WARNING When using a text editor, make sure you save the NCF file as a plain text document to prevent any formatting characters from being inserted, and be sure the .NCF extension is preserved.

There are several ways to modify .NCF files, both from the server console and from a client workstation. Furthermore, any server-based method can be accessed remotely through RConsoleJ in ConsoleOne.

TABLE 4.5   Tools for Editing .NCF files

TOOL	DESCRIPTION
Text editor	Any text editor can be used to modify an .NCF file from a Windows workstation. Simply browse to the desired file and open it with your editor. You might have to use the Open With option to specify the editor for the .NCF file extension.
EDIT.NLM	A text editor on the server that lets you manually edit the files. Type EDIT at the server console, and then enter the full name, including path, of the desired file.
NWCONFIG.NLM	Lets you modify the same options you set during installation. Automatically updates the appropriate file with the new information you've specified. Also lets you manually edit the files by choosing NCF files options.
MONITOR.NLM	Lets you add, delete, or modify SET parameters by selecting them from menus. Automatically updates the appropriate file with the new information you've specified.

TIP You can also open EDIT.NLM from console screens in NoRM and edit an NCF file from there.

NetWare Time Synchronization

Although time synchronization is vital to the proper function of Novell eDirectory, it does not implement time synchronization. Rather, eDirectory requires the underlying Network Operating System (NOS) platform to provide a fully time-synchronized environment in which eDirectory can operate.

Novell implemented a proprietary time sync model for NetWare with the release of NetWare 4. However, because eDirectory is now used across multiple NOS platforms, it must be able to synchronize time with non-NetWare servers and/or networks. To do this, Novell has extended the NetWare time sync modules to support an industry standard time synchronization protocol known as Network Time Protocol (NTP).

There are four types of timeservers supported in a NetWare 6.5 environment:

▶ *Single Reference*: Uses its own internal clock, or an external time source, to determine network time. This eDirectory time is then communicated to secondary timeservers and network clients. The Single Reference timeserver is the master source for network time.

▶ *Reference*: Uses its own hardware clock, or an external time source, to determine network time. Reference servers replace the Single Reference timeserver in more complex network environments. The Reference server participates with other timeservers in a voting process to determine a consensus time. When a reference server is used, NetWare uses a hybrid time sync strategy. However, as you'll see, other participants in the time synchronization process will converge toward the Reference server time.

▶ *Primary*: Name notwithstanding, a Primary timeserver does not generate network time. Primary timeservers participate in a polling process with other primary servers and the Reference server. During the polling process, each Primary timeserver votes on the correct network time. From this process, a consensus network time emerges. Each primary timeserver synchronizes its internal clock to the consensus network time and helps distribute that time to all interested parties.

▶ *Secondary*: Secondary timeservers receive network time from Single Reference, Reference, Primary, or other secondary timeservers.

Secondary timeservers are slaves that do not participate in the time polling process, but simply receive and pass on the consensus network time.

The choice of a time synchronization strategy is largely dependent on the size and complexity of your network. You have your choice of a default strategy, appropriate for smaller networks, or a more complex Time Provider Group strategy, which is more efficient in a large network environment. Configuring either of these environments is done with the TIMESYNC.CFG file, as shown in Figure 4.9. TIMESYNC.CFG is stored in **SYS:SYSTEM**.

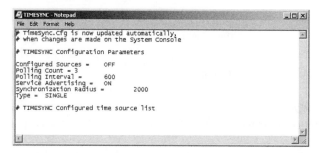

FIGURE 4.9
Sample TIMESYNC.CFG file.

Default Time Synchronization

The default time synchronization strategy is suitable for smaller networks with fewer than 30 servers in the network and no WAN connections. The default time synchronization strategy utilizes SAP in an IPX environment and SLP in an IP environment to locate and query the Single Reference server. Figure 4.10 shows a default time sync configuration.

Under the default strategy, the first server installed into an eDirectory tree is designated as a Single Reference timeserver. All subsequent servers installed into the tree are designated as Secondary timeservers. In this scenario, the Single Reference server defines the network time and responds to all queries regarding network time. Obviously, as the network grows and/or WAN links are added, this single source for network time will become a bottleneck. If this Single Reference server has to be contacted across a WAN link, this time synchronization method will also add unnecessary traffic to expensive WAN links.

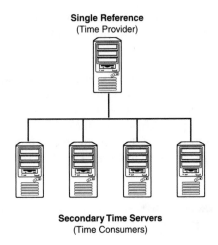

Single Reference
(Time Provider)

Secondary Time Servers
(Time Consumers)

FIGURE 4.10
Logical time sync architecture (sample).

Time Provider Group

More complex environments should implement a Time Provider Group
(TPG) or groups. A TPG consists of a centrally located reference server,
and between two and seven primary servers that will distribute the network time to all servers in the network, as shown in Figure 4.11. This
strategy spreads the task of distributing network time out across multiple
servers. It also makes it possible to limit the amount of time synchronization traffic that needs to traverse costly WAN links.

In a well-designed network environment, it is easy to determine the optimal locations for the various timeservers. The Reference server should
exist at the hub of the network, perhaps at a corporate headquarters to
which all satellite or branch offices are connected. The Reference server
will normally receive its time from a highly accurate external time source
such as an atomic clock, radio clock, or Internet time source. These time
sources can be contacted through dial-up connections or across the
Internet.

Primary servers should be strategically placed at the largest branches and
distribute time information to Secondary servers at their own site as well
as any small satellite sites in their area.

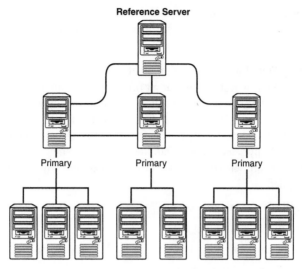

FIGURE 4.11
Sample TPG configuration.

Time Sync Advertisement

In addition to these synchronization strategies, you will have to decide on automatic or manual advertisement of time synchronization. The following describes the advantages and disadvantages of each method:

▶ *Automatic advertisement*: By default, NetWare 6.5 advertises its configuration automatically using SLP in TCP/IP networks or SAP in IPX networks. The advantage of automatic advertisement is ease of implementation. Timeservers will communicate without any intervention from the administrator. However, this background communication consumes network bandwidth, which can be a big issue on WAN links and other slow network connections.

▶ *Manual advertisement*: Also known as *configured lists*, the administrator manually defines the source of network time for each server in its TIMESYNC.CFG file. Reference and single timeservers can get their time from either their internal clocks or from an authoritative time source such as an atomic clock, radio clock, or Internet time source.

Your choice of advertisement method depends on how much you want the network to do automatically, at the expense of some network bandwidth.

Configuring Your Time Sync Environment

TIMESYNC.NLM is responsible for all time sync operations that take place in the NetWare environment. It loads automatically when the server starts. At that time, TIMESYNC.NLM reads the TIMESYNC.CFG file to determine how it should act. You can modify TIMESYNC.CFG settings through NoRM by selecting SET Parameters and clicking Time. Eight of the parameters are set when the server is installed and will seldom have to be modified:

► TIMESYNC configuration file

► Start of daylight saving time

► End of daylight saving time

► Daylight saving time offset

► Daylight saving time status

► New time with daylight saving time status

► Time zone

► Default timeserver type

The remaining parameters are used to configure and reset the time sync environment. They are outlined in Table 4.6.

TABLE 4.6   TIMESYNC.CFG Parameters

PARAMETER	DEFAULT	VALUES DESCRIPTION
Configured sources	OFF	Set ON if a list of time sources is used.
Polling count	3	Defines how many time packets to exchange during time polling cycle. Increasing this number will add network traffic needlessly.
Polling interval	600 sec	Defines the time to wait between time polling cycles. This value should be the same for every server in the tree.

PARAMETER	DEFAULT	VALUES DESCRIPTION
RESET	OFF	Resets internal time sync variables and clears the configured server list.
Restart flag	OFF	Restarts the time sync service. Similar to unloading and reloading TIMESYNC.NLM.
Service advertising	ON	Determines whether SAP/SLP advertisement will be used. Turn this off when using configured lists.
Synchronization radius	2000 msec	Defines how close a server's time has to be to network time in order to be considered in sync.
Time adjustment	[+ | -]hh:mm:ss [AT date and time]	Schedules a time adjustment on a single, reference or primary timeserver.
Time sources	Timeserver to query	Configured list of timeservers that this server will query for network time. Multiple time sources can be configured so that if one does not respond, the server will query the next on the list.
Type	Single, Reference, Primary, Secondary	Defines the type of timeserver.

Using NTP with NetWare 6.5

The first decision you need to make when integrating TIMESYNC and NTP environments is the direction of the time flow. Do you want NTP to receive time from TIMESYNC or vice versa? Both options are equally valid, but some environments lend themselves more to one method over another. The random mixing of NetWare and NTP servers is not recommended.

Novell time sync experts recommend using NTP over WAN links and then letting the NetWare TIMESYNC environments at each site receive their time by NTP. To configure TIMESYNC to receive time from NTP, edit the TIMESYNC.CFG file on the reference or single server and change the time source to point to an NTP server.

CHAPTER 5

Novell eDirectory Management

Instant Access

Managing eDirectory Objects

▶ To create and manage eDirectory objects, you can use iManager for most tasks. However, ConsoleOne is still available and more efficient in some cases. Use what you like.

Managing Replicas and Partitions

▶ To manage replicas and partitions, use iManager.

▶ To manage the eDirectory schema, use iManager.

Managing WAN Traffic

▶ To prevent WAN links from being kept open excessively, use iManager to configure WAN Traffic Manager to restrict routine WAN traffic to specific times or days (or to other limits you specify).

Using Indexes

▶ eDirectory manages most popular indexes automatically, with no intervention on your part.

▶ You can view the list of default indexes with ConsoleOne by selecting the Indexes tab in Server object >> Properties. You can also create custom indexes from this page.

Merging eDirectory Trees

▶ Use iManager to merge eDirectory trees by selecting the Merge Tree option under eDirectory Maintenance. You can also use the console-based DSMERGE.NLM.

Using Additional Services with eDirectory

▶ LDAP services for eDirectory provide robust eDirectory access to LDAP clients. Using ConsoleOne or iManager, configure LDAP through the LDAP Server and LDAP Group objects in eDirectory.

▶ Use iManager to configure DNS and DHCP services for eDirectory.

Troubleshooting

▶ To monitor eDirectory messages, use Trace from iMonitor or one of the DSTrace utilities from the server console.

▶ Use iMonitor to repair an eDirectory tree (click the Repair icon in the header frame). You can also use the eDirectory option in iManager. Some repair operations will also require the use of console-based DSREPAIR.NLM.

What Is eDirectory?

In order to understand Novell eDirectory, you must first invert the standard view of network architecture. Many people assume that because the directory requires a Network Operating System (NOS) on which to run that it is part of the NOS. In reality, it is just the opposite. The directory defines the "world" of your network. As such, network servers are part of the directory, not vice versa. This is a critical shift in thinking if you are going to work effectively with directories in today's complex computing environments.

In the simplest of terms, eDirectory is a distributed and replicated database of network information that provides your network with four key services:

▶ *Discovery*: eDirectory makes it possible to browse, search, and retrieve information about the network. You can search for objects such as users, printers, and applications, or for specific properties of objects such as names, phone numbers, and configurations.

▶ *Security*: eDirectory provides a central point for authentication and access control across your entire network. You can grant specific rights to users or groups of users, control the flow of data across the network, and protect sensitive or personal information through the use of cryptographic technologies. Most importantly, eDirectory provides the foundation for managing security across networks, so you can safely and efficiently communicate with partners, suppliers, and customers without having to create a separate infrastructure to do so.

▶ *Storage*: eDirectory is at its heart a database. As such, it includes the capabilities to safely and securely store network data and protect it from corruption. It also provides a way to classify different data types, so you can manage the type of data in eDirectory and determine how it can be used. Finally, eDirectory allows you to split the database into discrete pieces and distribute those pieces across multiple servers to provide fault tolerance and improved performance for network users.

▶ *Relationship*: eDirectory allows you to model relationships between objects on the network. This allows you to move configuration information away from specific devices and make it global. Practically, this means that users can receive the same profiles, privileges, and services regardless of location, type of connection, or device. Furthermore, users no longer have to connect to each server with a separate user account. eDirectory moves authentication to the network level from the individual server level.

Novell released its first version of eDirectory, then known as NetWare Directory Services, in 1993 with NetWare 4. It has been in constant improvement since that time, making it the most advanced and used directory in the world. The name was changed to Novell Directory Services with the release of NetWare 5 in 1998. In 2000, Novell's directory was rechristened Novell eDirectory, and was modularized so that it can be installed on platforms other than NetWare—including Windows 2000/XP, Sun Solaris, Linux, Compaq Tru64, and IBM AIX. The following sections provide you with an overview of eDirectory architecture, design considerations, and common administrative tasks and the tools for doing them.

eDirectory Architecture

There are three main aspects to the eDirectory architecture:

▶ Physical eDirectory database

▶ Rules governing eDirectory data

▶ Organization of data in eDirectory

Each of these is addressed individually in the sections that follow.

Physical eDirectory Database

At its lowest physical level, eDirectory is a database. A typical database comprises a dataset together with methods of searching and retrieving specific data from the dataset. eDirectory is an object-oriented, hierarchical database. A hierarchical database maintains data (objects) in a logical tree structure. Specific objects are located by traversing (walking) the tree. Each object in the eDirectory database is uniquely identifiable by a combination of the object name, or Common Name (CN), together with information describing the location of that object within the tree, or Context. Figure 5.1 shows a possible tree structure and the relationship between object name and logical position within the directory. The combination of Common Name and Context is known as the *Distinguished Name*.

The underlying eDirectory database is organized as a *b-tree*, which those of you with a programming background will recognize as a well-known type of data structure. B-trees are ordered, or sorted, trees in which the root node always stores values at the midpoint of the sorted value set. As new elements are added, the tree automatically re-orders itself. The eDirectory b-tree nodes contain multiple elements, each of which is a directory object.

The result of these two characteristics is a data structure in which a huge number of elements can be stored, and elements that are stored can be located very quickly.

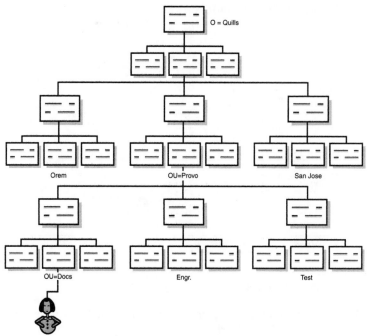

FIGURE 5.1
A sample eDirectory tree structure showing how location determines name.

The eDirectory database also makes extensive use of indexing. Data is sorted in a variety of ways in order to decrease the time required to locate a given piece of data even more. Each index is a smaller b-tree structure that is automatically updated whenever any relevant piece of the database is added, changed, or deleted. When a query is received by eDirectory, internal logic determines what index, if any, should be used to most efficiently respond to the query. Figure 5.2 shows you the default indexes created by eDirectory. You can also add custom indexes by completing the following steps:

1. Launch ConsoleOne and browse to a NetWare 6.5 server.

2. Right-click the Server object and select Properties.

3. Select the Indexes tab. This will show you all current indexes and their state.

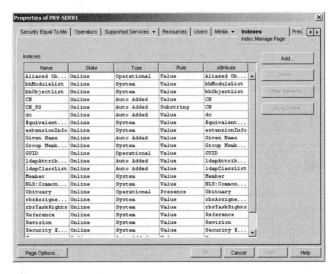

FIGURE 5.2
Default eDirectory indexes.

4. Click Add. Enter a name for the new index, and select the attribute on which it should be sorted.

5. In the Rule field, select Value to create an index based on values of the specified attribute. Select Presence to create an index based on whether the specified attribute has a value.

6. Click OK to save your index configuration. Click OK again to save the changes.

eDirectory will automatically create the index based on your configuration choices.

Rules Governing eDirectory Data

Rules defining valid object types, where they can be stored, and what can be done with each of the object types are maintained within the eDirectory schema. The schema provides the structure to the eDirectory tree. The schema is comprised of a set of object classes. Object classes describe the types of objects that can be created in eDirectory. Each object class contains a set of attributes that specifies the type(s) of data that can be stored within each object. In this way, the schema creates the logical view of the eDirectory data that network administrators and users make use of every day.

Novell provides a base set of object classes in eDirectory but has recognized that it cannot account for every possible use of the directory. To address this, the eDirectory schema is extensible, meaning that third parties are free to define new object classes and attributes in order to extend eDirectory capabilities.

Organization of Data in eDirectory

eDirectory organization has two aspects: the physical organization and the logical organization. Physical organization of data in eDirectory revolves around its distributed nature and the need to provide fault tolerance for the eDirectory database. Each piece of the total eDirectory database is known as a *partition*.

In order to make the data contained in a given partition more secure and accessible, multiple copies of that partition can be stored across the network. This process of creating and maintaining multiple partition copies is known as *replication*, as shown in Figure 5.3. Replication is an extremely powerful capability, and Novell has designed eDirectory with a complex set of checks and balances in order to maintain the integrity of directory data across the distributed environment.

The logical organization of data in eDirectory determines how data will be presented to users and administrators. The logical organization is what you see when you look at eDirectory. The schema controls this logical eDirectory organization. The schema essentially defines the types of data that can be stored in eDirectory and the acceptable set of operations that can be performed on that data.

The eDirectory schema defines a class of objects that can store other objects. These are known as *Container objects*, or simply as *Containers*. Containers are the building blocks used to create the structure of the eDirectory tree. Objects that cannot hold other objects are known as *Leaf* objects. Leaf objects define the actual network resources available in the eDirectory tree.

Each class of Leaf object contains a unique set of attributes that describe the data and functionality associated with that object. Leaf objects can include users, printers, network routers, applications, or even other databases. Because the eDirectory schema is fully extensible, new object classes can be defined and created within eDirectory by anyone who might need them.

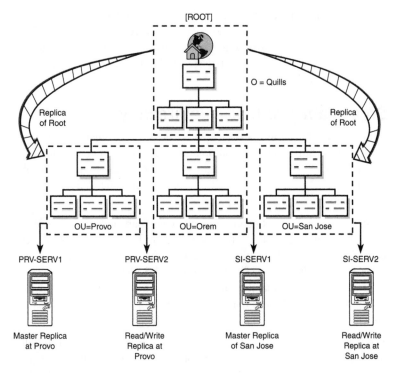

FIGURE 5.3
eDirectory partitions and replicas.

eDirectory Tree Design

A key purpose of implementing a network directory is to make the operation of the network more efficient and easy to use. Unfortunately, this means that the directory cannot be rolled out without any consideration for the environment into which it is being inserted. There are a few basic rules that should be followed when designing an eDirectory tree:

- ▶ The top of the tree reflects the physical layout.
- ▶ The bottom of the tree reflects the organizational structure.
- ▶ Organize objects to facilitate access and administration.
- ▶ Partition and replicate for scalability and fault tolerance.

Each of these issues is addressed in the sections that follow.

Top of the Tree Should Reflect Physical Layout

The top one or two levels of an eDirectory tree form the foundation for everything that comes later. If these levels are not configured properly, the whole tree suffers. Similar to the construction of a house, the eDirectory tree foundation needs to be stable and not prone to changes in structure.

The stable part of an organization tends to be its capital assets (buildings and equipment). Organizational structure might change and merge, but it still generally uses the same physical facilities. Make use of this stability by designing the foundation of the eDirectory tree around physical locations.

There are four main points to address when designing the top levels of the eDirectory tree:

- ▶ Name the tree [Root]
- ▶ Determine use of Country and Locality objects
- ▶ Define the Organization object
- ▶ Define location-based Organizational Unit objects

When you name your eDirectory tree, you are naming the [Root] object. Make the name descriptive and unique. It should also be different from other Container objects. Many use the following tree name convention: Organization Name_TREE.

Next you have to decide how to create the first level in your eDirectory tree. This involves determining whether you are going to incorporate the use of a Country (C) or Locality (L) object into your eDirectory tree design, as shown in Figure 5.4.

Country and Locality object use is optional, and may not make sense depending upon your directory structure. However, if it is important to comply with X.500 naming syntax in order to interact with external X.500 directories, these objects can be used. Other than that, it is probably easier to start with the Organization (O) object and define geographical regions under the organization as Organizational Unit (OU) objects, as shown in Figure 5.5.

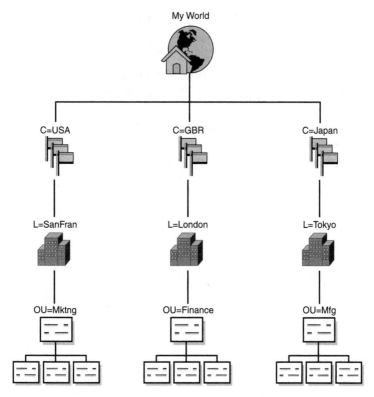

FIGURE 5.4
eDirectory Country and Locality objects.

Next you must determine the name of your Organization object. Every eDirectory tree must have at least one Organization container. Normally, this is the first level of the tree, so using the organization name is a good way to go.

Finally, define subsequent levels of the tree around the physical network infrastructure currently employed (or planned) by the organization. Regional sites are usually defined as level-two organizational units. A third level may also be appropriate for larger organizations to designate branch offices. Usually, three levels dedicated to the geographical structure of the organization will accommodate even the largest organizations.

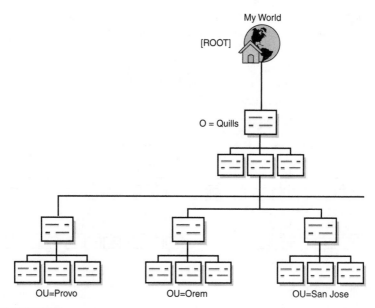

FIGURE 5.5
Sample eDirectory tree.

The opposite is true for smaller companies. In some cases where the company is located at a single site, the physical levels can be eliminated altogether, if desired. However, this strategy is not recommended if there is any chance the company will grow into multiple sites in the future because the lack of containers based upon physical sites will make it more difficult to expand the eDirectory structure as the organization grows.

The Bottom of the Tree Reflects Organizational Structure

The bottom portion of the tree is where all the action is. Unlike the top of the tree, we fully expect adaptation and evolution to occur over time at the lower levels of the tree. This means we need to design flexibility into the system.

For this reason, the lower levels of the eDirectory tree will grow based not on physical locations, but on organizational structure, as shown in Figure 5.6. The best way to visualize the eDirectory tree at this point is to look at a current copy of your company's org chart. You will need to understand the divisions and/or departments that operate at each physical site in order to create the lower levels of the eDirectory tree.

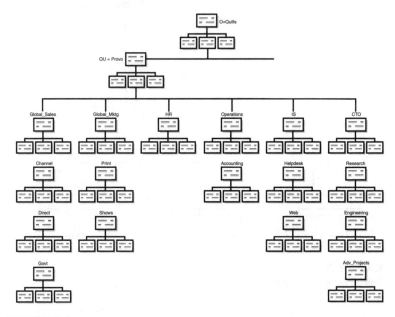

FIGURE 5.6
The lower levels of an eDirectory tree mirror the organizational structure.

The reason that organizational unit containers are so useful at this level is that they allow you to group resources together. You can put the users in the Marketing department together with their printers, servers, and applications. Then those users and resources can be managed together. As you will see in the next section, this grouping also allows you to minimize the overhead associated with maintaining replica integrity and currency.

Locate Objects to Facilitate Access and Administration

Now that you have the general tree design and containers created, the consideration becomes how to organize the Leaf objects that will populate the eDirectory tree. The two primary considerations for this are

▶ Make it as easy as possible for users to access the resources they need

▶ Make it as easy as possible to centrally control and administer network resources

In most cases, you will be able to place resources such as servers, printers, and departmental applications in the same container with the users who will need access to those resources. However, if users in multiple containers will share resources, place those resources one level above the user containers. This makes the resource much easier to locate.

Furthermore, if you group users based upon common needs, you can manage things like access controls, login scripts, and policies from the container level, rather than managing each user individually. Only the exceptions to the general container rules need to be specifically managed. Management by exception is tremendously powerful as a tool for reducing complexity and increasing efficiency.

Partition and Replicate for Scalability and Fault Tolerance

As a distributed database, eDirectory requires a mechanism for dividing the entire database into discrete chunks that can be installed on different servers across the organization. This is done through a process of partitioning and replicating the database.

Partitions

eDirectory allows the creation of partitions in order to distribute the directory database across the network. A copy of a given eDirectory partition is known as a *replica*. By creating multiple replicas of a given partition, you build fault tolerance into the directory architecture. If a server holding a partition replica fails, the partition is still available from other replica servers.

Locating those portions of the eDirectory database close to those users who make use of them dramatically increases eDirectory performance. It also greatly reduces network traffic associated with directory queries. This is particularly important when multiple sites are connected by costly WAN links. The last thing you want to do is use WAN link bandwidth for background operations like searching for a server or printer.

When the first eDirectory server is installed, a [Root] partition is automatically created and a replica of that partition is stored on the eDirectory server. Once [Root] exists, the rest of the directory can be built by adding the necessary Container and Leaf objects.

As other eDirectory servers are installed, replicas of [Root] should be created to provide fault tolerance. If you maintain a small network at a single site, the [Root] partition might be all you need. Replicate it to two or three servers for fault tolerance and you are done. However, if your network environment is more complex, more work should be done to create an efficient eDirectory environment.

Planning your eDirectory partition strategy is similar to planning the top levels of the eDirectory tree. Partition creation should follow the physical network infrastructure. WAN links should always be considered boundaries between partitions. This eliminates the need for eDirectory to pass background traffic across these links. Refer to Figure 5.3 for a view of partitioning along geographical lines.

Each Child partition should then be replicated to multiple servers at the site that partition is serving. Once partitions have been created based upon the physical boundaries, it is not usually necessary to partition the bottom layers of a tree. However, there are two possible exceptions to this:

▶ A Child partition might also be further partitioned in order to limit the number of partition replicas that exist across the network. A large number of replicas for any given partition will increase the background traffic required for synchronization. It also complicates partition repair operations that may be necessary. A good rule of thumb is to try to limit the total number of replicas of a given partition to 10 or fewer.

▶ If you are using Filtered replicas to create specific views of eDirectory information, it is entirely acceptable to further divide a Child partition.

The goal of your partitioning strategy should be a small [Root] partition and a Child partition for every physical site in the network. The [Root] partition should end up containing only [Root] and the Organization object. The reason for this is explained in the next section.

Replicas

A *replica* is a physical copy of an eDirectory partition. By default, the first replica created is designated as the Master replica. Each partition will have one, and only one, Master replica. Other replicas will be designated as Read/Write, Read-Only, and Subordinate references. There are five types of eDirectory replicas:

▶ *Master replica*: The Master replica contains all object information for the partition. Objects and attributes maintained in the partition can be modified from the Master replica. These changes are then propagated to other servers holding replicas of this partition. Furthermore, all changes to the partition itself, such as creating other replicas or creating a Child partition, must be performed from the perspective of the server that holds the Master replica.

▶ *Read/Write replica*: A Read/Write replica contains the same information as the Master replica. Objects and attributes maintained in the partition can be modified from the Read/Write replica. These changes are then propagated to other servers holding replicas of this partition. Any number of Read/Write replicas can be created. However, for the sake of overall directory performance, it is recommended that the total number of partition replicas not exceed 10. This type of replica cannot initiate partition operations.

▶ *Read-Only replica*: A Read-Only replica contains all the same information as the Master and Read/Write replicas. Users can read, but not modify, the information contained in these replicas. The replica is updated with changes made to the Master and Read/Write replicas. In practice, Read-Only replicas are seldom used because they are unable to support login operations. The login process requires updating some directory information. Because a Read-Only replica does not support directory updates, it cannot provide login services. One potential use is maintaining a backup copy of a partition. The Read-Only replica will receive all partition updates but will not participate in the update process in any way.

▶ *Filtered replica*: A Filtered replica can be either a Read-Only or a Read/Write replica. They are designed to provide specific services or applications, including other directories, with only the eDirectory information they need. Creating replicas that contain only certain types of objects and/or specific subsets of object attributes accomplishes this goal. For example, a Filtered replica might hold only User objects with their associated names, phone numbers, and email addresses for a corporate directory application.

NOTE These replica types exist primarily to eliminate the single point of failure in an eDirectory environment. A recommended design goal is three replicas—one Master and a combination of Read/Write and/or Read-Only replicas. As stated previously, the Read-Only replica is seldom used, so most eDirectory implementations will focus on Master and Read/Write replicas in their production environments.

▶ *Subordinate references*: Subordinate references are special replica types that provide connectivity between the various partitions that exist in an eDirectory environment. Subordinate references are internal replicas and are not visible to users or configurable by administrators. A Subordinate reference contains a list of all servers that hold replicas of a Child partition. eDirectory uses this list to locate the nearest replica of a Child partition so that it can walk down the tree when searching for an object. Figure 5.7 shows how Subordinate references are distributed across servers.

A partition's Subordinate reference is stored on all servers that hold a replica of that partition's parent. Subordinate references effectively point to Child partition(s) that are not stored on that particular server. The distributed nature of eDirectory allows servers to hold replicas of the Parent partition but not all of the corresponding Child partitions.

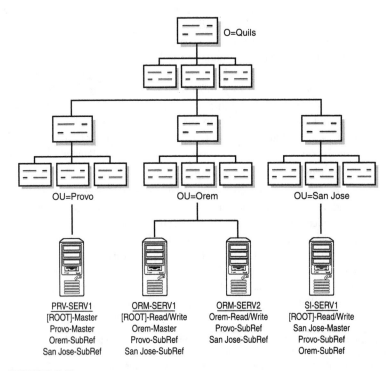

FIGURE 5.7
eDirectory Subordinate references.

The eDirectory replication strategy is a balancing act between the need to provide consistency across the directory and the limitations of network hardware and bandwidth. You should follow three rules when creating your replication strategy:

- ► *Don't replicate across WAN links*: WAN links represent one of the most costly network resources. To clutter up these links with unnecessary eDirectory traffic would be a terrible mistake. To avoid this, all copies of a given partition should be maintained locally. The one situation where this rule might not apply (there's always at least one exception, isn't there?) is the case of a small satellite office with only one server. In that case, it is more important to protect the eDirectory database by placing a replica across a WAN link than it is to preserve the WAN link bandwidth itself. Fortunately, a partition that contains only one server will not usually generate a lot of eDirectory traffic.

- ► *Replicate to limit subordinate references*: Even though Subordinate references don't participate in the normal eDirectory replica update process, it's still a good idea to limit the number of Subordinate references to reduce complexity. There are two ways to do this:

  - ► Limit the number of Child partitions that are created. This is only partially controllable because you always want to define WAN links as partition boundaries. However, this does argue for limiting the number of additional partitions that are created within a single site.

  - ► Store both Parent and Child partition replicas on the same server wherever possible. If multiple partitions are going to exist at a single site, try to distribute replicas such that Parent and Child partition replicas are stored together.

- ► *Replicate to improve eDirectory performance*: The final reason to replicate is to provide the best possible performance for network users. If the partition and replication guidelines in this chapter are followed, a user will find most of his or her resources within the local partition. Occasionally it may be necessary to access a resource on the other side of the world. These situations require eDirectory to traverse, or walk, the tree to locate the requested resource. As previously noted, these searches start at [Root] and proceed down the tree until the requested object is located. Placing replicas of [Root] at strategic locations, such as communications hubs, can facilitate these searches. In order to do this without significantly increasing the overall replication burden, the [Root] partition must be small (only the [Root] object and the Organization object) and the number of [Root] replicas should not exceed three or four.

TIP To avoid many issues associated with the cost and complexity of eDirectory replication at satellite offices, you can use Nterprise Branch Office. For more information on Nterprise Branch Office, see Chapter 12.

Managing eDirectory

Once you have an understanding of the basics of eDirectory architecture and design, it is important to understand the activities and tools necessary to maintain eDirectory on a day-to-day basis.

As with the rest of NetWare 6.5, eDirectory management is now available through ever-more-powerful Web-based utilities. NetWare 6.5 includes much more comprehensive eDirectory management options in iManager and iMonitor. For information on installing and configuring both iMonitor and iManager, see Chapter 3, "Novell Management Tools."

iManager provides comprehensive role-based management capabilities for the entire NetWare 6.5 environment. iMonitor consolidates the monitoring and data gathering aspects of several console-based tools, including DSTrace, DSRepair, and DSBrowse. It also includes the reporting functionality of DSDiag. The iMonitor interface is shown in Figure 5.8.

iManager now provides a complete set of eDirectory management tools and functions for object, partition, and replica operations (see Figure 5.9). Much of this functionality is also available from the Partition and Replica view in ConsoleOne. You can also use RConsoleJ for remote access to the server console from ConsoleOne, from which you can run any of the legacy command-line-based utilities.

This section gives you an overview of common eDirectory tasks and the tools used to perform them. eDirectory management tasks can be organized into six main categories:

- ▶ Partition operations
- ▶ Replica operations
- ▶ Tree operations
- ▶ eDirectory repair
- ▶ Monitoring eDirectory
- ▶ Managing synchronization

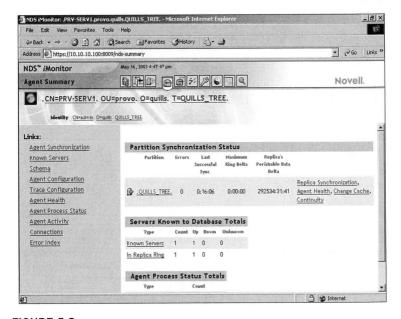

FIGURE 5.8
The iMonitor user interface.

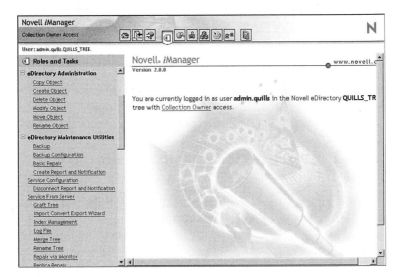

FIGURE 5.9
eDirectory management options in iManager.

NOTE Managing specific eDirectory objects is covered in the appropriate chapter on that topic. For example, User and Group object management is covered in Chapter 6, "Users and Network Security," whereas Printer object management is covered in Chapter 7, "NetWare Printing Services."

Partition Operations

There are three primary partition operations that you will be required to make:

▶ Create a partition

▶ Merge a partition

▶ Move a partition

WARNING eDirectory does a great deal of work when performing partition operations. In larger eDirectory environments, each of the operations described in the following sections can take a significant amount of time to process completely. Furthermore, each operation has to complete before the next can begin. Make sure you take this into account when planning these tasks.

Create a Partition

The first operation we want to look at is creating a partition. As mentioned earlier, partitioning the tree serves to break up the eDirectory database into chunks that can be distributed across multiple servers for fault tolerance and increased performance.

If you want to create a new partition, complete the following steps:

1. Under Partition and Replicas in the navigation frame of iManager, select Create Partition.

2. Browse to and select the container that will be the root of the Child partition, and then click OK.

3. Select Close at the message that eDirectory is processing your request.

By default, the Master replica of the new partition is created on the server that maintains the Master replica of the Parent partition. Read/Write replicas are stored on servers that maintain Read/Write replicas of the Parent partition. You can move or change replica placement after the partition has been created, if desired.

Merge a Partition

Sometimes you want to consolidate partitions, such as when moving from an older NDS environment to a much more scalable eDirectory tree. To merge a partition with its parent, complete the following steps:

1. Under Partition and Replicas in the navigation frame of iManager, select Merge Partition.

2. Browse to and select the container that is the root of the Child partition, and then click OK.

3. Select Close at the message that eDirectory is processing your request.

Once merged, all replicas of the Child partition are removed and the Child partition data will be replicated to the existing Parent partition replicas.

Move a Partition

The partition move operation is commonly known as a *prune and graft*. It involves moving a partition and all its associated containers and objects from one location in the tree to another (pruning a branch from one part of the tree and grafting it in somewhere else). This is the most complex of the partition operations, so note the following qualifications before attempting a partition move:

▶ You cannot move a container unless it is a partition root. If you want to move a container that is not a partition, you first need to define it as a partition. Then you can move the container to its new location and merge it with its new Parent partition.

▶ This operation is available only to partitions that do not have any subordinate (Child) partitions. If you want to move a partition with subordinates, you will have to merge the subordinates into the Parent partition first.

▶ When you move a partition, you must follow eDirectory containment rules that define what type of objects can be placed in each type of eDirectory container object. For example, you cannot move an organizational unit directly under the root of the tree because the containment rules for [Root] allow only Locality, Country, Organization, and Security objects, and not Organizational Unit objects.

If you want to prune and graft a partition, complete the following steps:

1. Under Partition and Replicas in the navigation frame of iManager, select Move Partition.

2. Provide the required information and click OK.

   ▶ In the Object Name dialog box, browse to and select the container you want to move.

   ▶ In the Move To dialog box, browse to and select the new location for the partition. This will be the container within which the new partition will be placed.

   ▶ Check Create an Alias in Place of Move Object if you want users to be able to continue accessing those objects from their original directory context. This is usually a good idea at least until all users have been notified of the location change.

3. At the Move summary, click Move to perform the prune and graft.

The summary screen lists all servers involved in the Move operation so that you can make sure everything is in good shape before attempting the move.

Replica Operations

Now that you have eDirectory partitions created and situated within the tree, you might notice that the default placement for the replicas is less than perfect. After all, you probably don't want all Master replicas on one server, and you want to avoid replicating across expensive WAN links, as discussed previously. Similar to partition operations, replica operations are accomplished from iManager in Partition and Replica Management. There are four primary replica operations:

▶ Add a replica

▶ Change the replica type

▶ Delete a replica

▶ Create a Filtered replica

Selecting Replica View in iManager shows you all servers that hold replicas of the selected partition. These servers form the *replica ring*.

NOTE You will likely see Subordinate reference replicas listed in the iManager Replica View. However, Subordinate references are not manageable in iManager, so their placement is purely informational.

Add a Replica

If you want to place a partition replica on a server that does not currently have a copy of that partition, complete the following steps:

1. Under Partition and Replicas in the navigation frame of iManager, select Replica View.

2. Browse to and select the partition for which you want a new replica and click Add Replica.

3. Specify the server on which you want to create the replica, select the type of replica you are going to create, and then click OK.

4. Click Done to exit the Replica View.

Once created, the new partition will participate in all replication processes for that partition. Too many replicas can slow down partition operations significantly, so try to limit the number of replicas to three.

Change the Replica Type

Sometimes it is useful to be able change the type of an existing replica. For example, if a Master replica is stored on a server and it is going down for a hardware upgrade, you can change an existing Read/Write replica to be the Master so that eDirectory partition operations can continue normally.

NOTE You cannot change the type of a Master replica because a Master replica must exist for every partition. If you want to change a Master replica, change an existing Read/Write replica to be the new Master, and the existing Master will automatically be converted to a Read/Write.

If you want to change the type of a replica, complete the following steps:

1. Under Partition and Replicas in the navigation frame of iManager, select Replica View.

2. Browse to and select the partition for which you want to change a replica type, and then click OK.

3. In the Type column, select the replica that you want to change.

4. Specify the type of replica to which you want to change the replica and click OK.

5. Click Done to exit the Replica View.

The replica will immediately start behaving as the new replica type you have selected.

NOTE You cannot create a Master replica from a Filtered replica.

Delete a Replica

Sometimes, when partitions have been merged or moved, a given replica is no longer necessary. To delete an existing replica from a server, complete the following steps:

1. Under Partition and Replicas in the navigation frame of iManager, select Replica View.

2. Browse to and select the partition for which you want to delete a replica, and click OK.

3. Click the red X next to the replica name that you want to delete, and click OK in the delete replica window.

4. Click Done to exit the Replica View.

The replica is removed from the server on which it was stored, and all future partition operations will include only the remaining replicas.

Create a Filtered Replica

If you are using Filtered replicas in your network, you can configure them with the Replica Wizard option in iManager. To create a Filtered replica, complete the following steps:

1. Under Partition and Replicas in the navigation frame of iManager, select Filtered Replica Wizard.

2. Browse to and select the server on which the Filtered replica will reside, and then click Next.

3. Click Define the Filter Set to specify the object classes and attributes to include in this Filtered replica. Only one filter can be configured per server, meaning that you can only have Filtered replicas of one type on any given server.

4. Click The Filter Is Empty, select the eDirectory objects and classes that you want included in the Filtered replica, and then click OK.

Alternatively, you can select Copy Filter From to specify an existing server with the type of Filtered replica you need, and it will be copied to the new server.

5. *(Optional)* Click Next to continue. You can click Define Partition Scope to add partitions for which you want to create Filtered replicas on this server. This opens the Replica View so that you can add replicas to the server.

6. Click Finish to create the Filtered replicas as defined.

Filtered replicas are often used when eDirectory is sharing data with an external system, such as another directory or database, but only a subset of eDirectory information is shared.

Tree Operations

There are a few operations that you can perform on an entire eDirectory tree, and these are available from iManager as well. Each of these operations is available under eDirectory Maintenance:

▶ Rename a tree

▶ Merge two trees

▶ Graft one tree into another

NOTE Tree operations are complex operations that are *not* recommended for those who are not experienced eDirectory administrators. You can easily damage trees with these operations, so be very careful and perform these types of tree operations only when it is absolutely necessary.

Rename a Tree

Once in a while it might become necessary to rename an eDirectory tree. Perhaps an organizational name change has occurred, or you are moving to match your directory naming scheme to that being used on the Web. Whatever the reason, you can rename your tree by completing the following steps:

1. Under eDirectory Maintenance in the navigation frame of iManager, select Rename Tree.

2. Specify the name of the server that will perform the rename operation and click Next. You can specify the server by NetWare server name, DNS name, or IP address.

3. Specify suitable authentication information for the tree and click Next. Make sure you authenticate as a user with Supervisor rights to the tree.

4. Provide the necessary information and click Start. Specify the new tree name, the Admin username (with context), and the Admin password. Remember that the tree name can be up to 32 alphanumeric characters (dashes and underscores are also allowed).

5. Click Yes to rename the tree.

The utility will first perform a check on the tree to be sure that it can be renamed successfully. Once the rename is complete, you will be prompted to log out and log back in to the "new" tree.

Merge Two Trees

iManager moves the capability to perform a tree merge away from the command-line utility DSMERGE.NLM for the first time. During a tree merge, a source tree is inserted into a target tree such that the tree branches at the Organization level, with each branch corresponding to the contents of one of the formerly distinct trees. To perform a tree merge from iManager, complete the following steps:

1. Under eDirectory Maintenance in the navigation frame of iManager, select Merge Tree.

2. Specify the name of the server that will perform the merge operation for the trees and click Next. You can specify the server by NetWare server name, DNS name, or IP address.

3. Provide suitable authentication information for the both the source and target eDirectory trees and click Next. Make sure you authenticate as a user with Supervisor rights to the tree.

4. Provide the necessary information and click Start.

   ▶ *Source Tree:* The source tree is the tree to which you are currently authenticated. It will be merged into the target tree. Specify the name and password of the Admin user for this tree.

   ▶ *Target Tree:* The target tree is the tree that will remain after the merge. The source tree information will become part of this tree. Specify the name and password of the Admin user for this tree.

5. Click Yes to rename the tree.

The utility will first perform a check on both trees to be sure that they can be successfully merged. If you encounter an error during this check process, follow the instructions to resolve the conflict and try the merge again.

Graft One Tree into Another

A graft is a subset of a merge, in which you can choose the insertion point for the source tree objects. During a tree graft, a source tree is inserted into the specified location of a target tree. The source tree is then converted into a Domain object and it and all of its contents become part of the target tree. To graft one tree into another, complete the following steps:

1. Under eDirectory Maintenance in the navigation frame of iManager, select Graft Tree.

2. Specify the name of the server that will perform the graft operation and click Next. You can specify the server by NetWare server name, DNS name, or IP address.

3. Specify suitable authentication information for the tree and click Next. Make sure you authenticate as a user with Supervisor rights to the tree.

4. Provide the necessary information and click Start.

   ▶ *Source Tree:* The source tree is the tree to which you are currently authenticated. It will be grafted into the target tree. Specify the name and password of the Admin user for this tree.

   ▶ *Target Tree:* The target tree will receive the source tree information as a Domain object after the graft. The source tree information will become part of this tree. Specify the name and password of the Admin user for the target tree. Specify the point at which you want the source tree inserted in the Container field.

5. Click Yes to perform the graft operation.

The utility will first perform a check on both trees to be sure that they can be successfully merged. If you encounter an error during this check process, follow the instructions to resolve the conflict and try the merge again.

Monitoring and Maintaining eDirectory

This section identifies some common administrative tasks that will help you effectively monitor the operation of eDirectory in your network and make little repairs as they are found. After all, the one thing more impressive than resolving a serious network problem is preventing it from occurring in the first place. Although this is not always possible, a program of active monitoring and proactive maintenance will go a long way toward getting you home on time at night. For more information on Novell management tools, see Chapter 3.

The following tasks are a starting point for maintaining your eDirectory environment. By monitoring eDirectory process execution, you can see every type of communication activity and determine whether any errors are being reported. The best way to keep track of the activities of eDirectory processes is through iMonitor (see Figure 5.10). iMonitor provides comprehensive trace capabilities for eDirectory. More detailed information on DS Trace capabilities in iMonitor is available in Appendix D, "Novell eDirectory Reference."

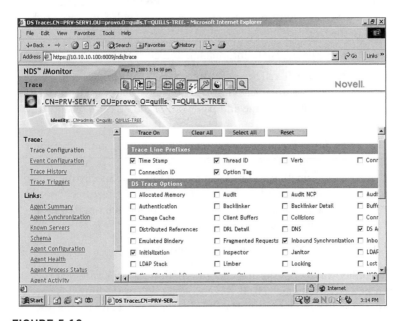

FIGURE 5.10
The eDirectory process monitoring configuration in iMonitor.

To access the iMonitor Trace page, select DS Trace from the NoRM navigation frame, or click the Trace Configuration icon in the iMonitor header frame.

Trace in iMonitor gives you access to all the process monitoring capabilities formerly available solely through DSTRACE.NLM. Tracing eDirectory activity involves the following tasks:

▸ From the Trace Configuration page, check the eDirectory process(es) that you want to monitor and click Trace On. Note that Trace pre-selects some of the more common processes. For more information on the individual options listed here, see Appendix D.

▸ To see a live view of the trace, select Trace History in the left side of the navigation frame, and click the View icon next to the current trace session.

▸ To stop a trace, click Trace Off in the Trace Configuration screen. Because of the added overhead and the size to which log files can grow, you usually want to run DSTrace for only enough time to gather the information for which you are looking.

eDirectory traces provide a powerful tool to track eDirectory processes and monitor operations when troubleshooting directory issues.

Verify the Version of eDirectory

Even if you don't apply updates immediately, it's a good idea to be aware of what updates exist and, more importantly, those issues they are intended to resolve. Keep track of the versions that you have installed on your servers, so as you review Novell support documents, you can keep an eye out for any problems that might relate to your environment.

NOTE With the release of NetWare 6, Novell implemented a new versioning scheme in an attempt to eliminate inconsistencies in the previous model. Although still known as eDirectory v8.6 or 8.7 to provide eDirectory customers with a version context they are familiar with, the build version takes a considerably different format. For example, the build version of eDirectory that ships with NetWare 6.5 is 10510.64.

You can check the version of eDirectory that you are currently running on any server in the following ways:

▸ *iMonitor*: Select Known Servers. The DS revision for all known eDirectory servers is listed.

▶ *DSREPAIR.NLM*: Look in the header for the DS version.

▶ *Server console*: Type **MODULES ds*** and look for the entry for DS.NLM.

NOTE Review Novell's support Web site, http://support.novell.com, on at least a quarterly basis for updates to eDirectory files and utilities.

Verify That Time Is Synchronized

Check the time sync status for each partition in the tree every couple of weeks. Keep an eye out for synthetic time messages that might keep background processes from completing properly.

You can check the status of time synchronization in the following ways:

▶ *NoRM*: Select Health Monitor. Browse to and select TimeSync Status. This will show you the time sync status for the server to which you are currently connected. To check another server, switch to it by selecting Managed Server List, under the Access Other Servers heading, and select the server to which you want to connect.

▶ *DSREPAIR.NLM*: Select Time Synchronization from the main menu. This method will show you the synchronization status of all servers known by the server from which you run DSRepair.

▶ *Server console*: Type **TIME SYNC** and review the server's time sync information. This method lets you know only if this single server is synchronized.

If time is not synchronizing properly, you can run into problems with the timestamps that are maintained on eDirectory objects. Timestamps indicate when the object was last synchronized.

Probably the best-known eDirectory timestamp issue is *synthetic time*. Synthetic time is when an eDirectory object has a modification timestamp ahead of current network time. If the period between current time and synthetic time is small, this problem will correct itself. However, if the period is large, it is possible to resolve the problem manually by reviewing the eDirectory communications processes to be sure that all replicas are communicating properly. From iMonitor, review the status of the Master replica from Agent Summary. You can drill down on the Master to review current state and a detailed set of statistics. Make sure the Master does not contain any errors, and that it is receiving current updates properly.

Timestamps can be repaired in two ways:

▶ Use DSREPAIR.NLM to repair timestamps and declare a new epoch. To use this option, load DSREPAIR with the -a parameter. Select Advanced Options >> Replica and Partition Operations. Select the partition with which you want to work, and choose Repair Timestamps and Declare a New Epoch.

▶ Identify the replica(s) with the synthetic timestamps and rebuild those replicas using the Receive All Objects operation:

▶ *iManager*: From the eDirectory Maintenance Utilities group in the left pane of iManager, select Replica Ring Repair. Specify the server that you want to receive correct replica information from the Master replica. Select the Receive All Objects option.

▶ *ConsoleOne*: Open the Partition and Replica view in ConsoleOne. Browse to and select the container on which you are going to work and select the Partition Continuity button from the toolbar. In the Partition Continuity table, highlight the replica you need to repair and select Receive Updates.

▶ *DSREPAIR.NLM*: Select Advanced Options >> Replica and Partition Operations. Select the partition to work with and select View Replica Ring. Select the replica to be repaired and choose Receive All Objects for This Replica.

WARNING This operation generates a large amount of eDirectory-related traffic as timestamps for all replicas are reset.

Verify Replica Synchronization

You can view synchronization status from several perspectives. However, making sure that all replicas of a given partition are synchronizing properly is probably one of the best ways to keep track of things. Check this every couple of weeks.

You can check the sync status of a replica ring in the following ways:

▶ *iMonitor*: From the Agent Summary, select a replica in the ring you want to check for synchronization. Under Partition Synchronization Status, select the Continuity link on the right, as shown in Figure 5.11. This will show you the status of the replica ring in general as well as the status of each replica in the ring.

▶ *DSREPAIR.NLM*: Select Advanced Options >> Replica and Partition Operations. Select the partition you want to check, and choose Report Synchronization Status of All Servers.

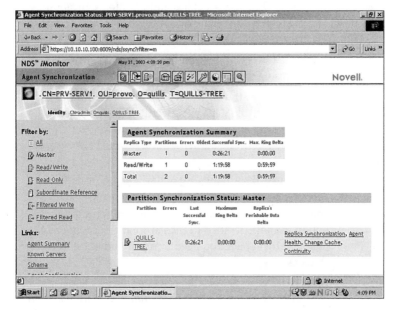

FIGURE 5.11
The Agent Synchronization summary page in iMonitor.

If you begin to notice inconsistencies in replica rings, you can use the following general steps to diagnose and resolve the problems:

1. Identify all servers that host replicas of this partition and the type of replica on each server.

   ▶ *iMonitor*: Select Agent Synchronization, and then select the Replica Synchronization link beside the partition with which you need to work.

   ▶ *DSREPAIR.NLM*: Select Advanced Options >> Replica and Partition Operations. Select the partition to work with and select View Replica Ring.

2. Examine the server hosting the Master replica because it functions as the authoritative source for partition information. If the Master replica is the source of the problem, designate one of the Read/Write replicas as a new Master:

- ▶ *iManager*: Follow instructions outlined in the previous section on replica operations.

- ▶ *DSREPAIR.NLM*: From the server that you want to host the new Master replica, load DSRepair with the -a parameter. Select Advanced Options >> Replica and Partition Operations. Select the partition with which to work, and choose Designate This Server as the New Master Replica.

3. Once a healthy Master replica exists, you can receive updates on the server that is having synchronization problems to eliminate any inconsistent objects:

  - ▶ *iManager*: From the eDirectory Maintenance Utilities group in the left pane of iManager, select Replica Ring Repair. Specify the server holding the Master replica for the partition and select the Send All Objects option.

  - ▶ *ConsoleOne*: Open the Partition and Replica view in ConsoleOne. Browse to and select the container on which you are going to work and select the Partition Continuity button from the toolbar. In the Partition Continuity table, highlight the replica you need to repair and select Receive Updates.

  - ▶ *DSREPAIR.NLM*: Select Advanced Options >> Replica and Partition Operations. Select the partition to work with and select View Replica Ring. Select the replica to be repaired, and then Receive All Objects for This Replica.

4. Monitor the replica ring after making repairs to make sure that it is successfully sending updates between all replica-hosting servers. You can perform a send updates operation from the Master replica by doing the following:

  - ▶ *iManager*: From the eDirectory Maintenance Utilities group in the left pane of iManager, select Replica Ring Repair. Specify the server holding the Master replica for the partition and select the Send All Objects option.

  - ▶ *ConsoleOne*: Open the Partition and Replica view in ConsoleOne. Browse to and select the container on which you are working and select the Partition Continuity button from the toolbar. In the Partition Continuity table, highlight the server with the Master replica and select Send Updates.

> ▶ *DSREPAIR.NLM*: Select Advanced Options >> Replica and
> Partition Operations. Select the partition to work with, and
> then select View Replica Ring. Select the Master replica, and
> then Send All Objects to Every Replica in the Ring.

You should regularly use the preceding techniques to monitor synchronization activities and make sure that eDirectory is performing properly.

Check External References

External references are pointers to eDirectory objects not stored in replicas on the current server. The check examines each external reference
and makes sure that it links to a valid eDirectory object. Performing this
check on a weekly basis makes sure that queries can traverse the tree
properly.

You can do one of the following to check external references:

> ▶ *iMonitor*: Select Agent Process Status and review the data under the
> External Reference Status heading.

> ▶ *DSREPAIR.NLM*: Select Advanced Options >> Check External
> References.

One nice thing about the external reference check is that it will list any
obituaries in your tree. *Obituaries* are references to deleted objects that
are maintained until word of the deletion has been propagated to all
servers hosting replicas of the affected partition. It is possible for obituaries and other types of external references to become corrupt or get stuck
in the tree.

One thing that can cause this is problems with network addresses. To
resolve network referral problems, do the following:

1. Identify the actual assigned IP or IPX addresses for each server
involved.

> ▶ *iMonitor*: Select Known Servers. Select the link for the server
> you want to look at, and then browse down and select
> Network Address in the left side of the navigation frame.

> ▶ *CONFIG.NLM*: Run this console-based utility on each server
> you want to check.

2. Check network addresses to make sure that the addresses stored by
eDirectory match those being reported by the servers in their SLP
or SAP broadcasts. In iMonitor, click the Repair icon and select

Advanced. Select Repair Network Addresses and click Start Repair. Use the Known Servers option in iMonitor to repeat this process for each server hosting eDirectory replicas in the network.

3. More severe problems might require a rebuild of replicas that have received invalid network address information, as described in the previous section on verifying schema synchronization.

Checking External References in this way will help ensure the health and smooth operation of you eDirectory environment.

Check the eDirectory Schema

Anytime you make changes to the eDirectory schema, confirm that all servers hosting eDirectory replicas are properly receiving schema updates. You can check the schema synchronization status in iMonitor by selecting Agent Process Status, and then reviewing the data under the Schema Sync Status heading.

It is possible that an eDirectory server, due to communications problems or corruption of synchronization timestamps, will fail to receive schema updates as they are applied to the eDirectory environment. The resulting schema inconsistencies can be resolved by doing the following:

▶ Identify the server that is reporting schema errors. This will be the server that has not received the schema updates properly. In iMonitor, force schema synchronization by selecting Agent Configuration and Agent Triggers. Check the Schema Synchronization box and select Submit. Before doing this, make sure that DSTrace is configured to report Schema Sync messages and that it is currently logging in to iMonitor.

TIP You can also view the schema sync in iMonitor as it occurs with Trace. Using Trace is described previously in this chapter. For information on specific Trace options, see Appendix D.

▶ Once the server has been identified, one potential solution is to declare a new epoch on the server. Load DSREPAIR with the -a parameter. Select Advanced Options >> Replica and Partition Operations. Select the partition with which you want to work, and then choose Repair Timestamps and Declare a New Epoch.

Unless you are making frequent changes to the schema, these types of activities shouldn't be necessary, but you should be aware of how such schema issues can be resolved.

Review Tree for Unknown Objects

On a monthly basis, search eDirectory for unknown objects. You can do this from iManager by completing the following steps (you can also search for unknown objects from ConsoleOne):

1. From iManager, click the View Objects icon.

2. In the left pane, select the Search tab.

3. Select Unknown in the Type field. Make sure that you are searching from [Root] and that the Search Sub-containers option is checked.

Unknown objects can indicate resources that have not been properly installed or removed from the tree. However, they can also indicate that iManager or ConsoleOne does not have a snap-in capable of recognizing that object type, so don't immediately assume that unknown objects need to be deleted.

It is also possible to get eDirectory object and attribute inconsistencies when replicas of the same partition, for whatever reason, have different information stored about the same eDirectory object or object attribute. In order to isolate the server(s) that have the faulty information, it is necessary to unload eDirectory on other servers. This type of troubleshooting can only be done during off hours.

In order to troubleshoot this type of problem, do the following:

1. Identify all servers that host replicas of the partition, and note the type of replica on each server.

   ▶ *iMonitor*: Select Agent Synchronization, and select the Replica Synchronization link beside the partition with which you need to work.

   ▶ *DSREPAIR.NLM*: Select Advanced Options >> Replica and Partition Operations. Select the partition to work with and select View Replica Ring.

2. Select one of the servers and unload eDirectory by entering **UNLOAD DS.NLM** at the server console. This can be done remotely through iManager or RConsoleJ.

3. Use ConsoleOne to query the tree for the faulty objects and/or attributes. If they are still faulty, you know this server's replica is not the source of the error.

4. Repeat step 3 until the faulty server(s) is (are) found.

5. To attempt to repair the problem, first attempt to receive updates at the faulty server:

   ▶ *iManager*: From the eDirectory Maintenance Utilities group in the left pane of iManager, select Replica Ring Repair. Specify the server that you want to receive correct replica information from the Master replica. Select the Receive All Objects option.

   ▶ *ConsoleOne*: Open the Partition and Replica view in ConsoleOne. Browse to and select the container on which you are going to work and select the Partition Continuity button from the toolbar. In the Partition Continuity table, highlight the replica you need to repair and select Receive Updates.

   ▶ *DSREPAIR.NLM*: Select Advanced Options >> Replica and Partition Operations. Select the partition to work with and select View Replica Ring. Select the replica to be repaired and Receive All Objects for This Replica.

6. If that fails, attempt to send all objects from one of the known good servers. If possible, use the Master replica for this operation.

   ▶ *iManager*: From the eDirectory Maintenance Utilities group in the left pane of iManager, select Replica Ring Repair. Specify the server holding the Master replica for the partition and select the Send All Objects option.

   ▶ *ConsoleOne*: Open the Partition and Replica view in ConsoleOne. Browse to and select the container on which you are working and select the Partition Continuity button from the toolbar. In the Partition Continuity table, highlight the server with the Master replica and select Send Updates.

   ▶ *DSREPAIR.NLM*: Select Advanced Options >> Replica and Partition Operations. Select the partition to work with and select View Replica Ring. Select the Master replica, and then Send All Objects to Every Replica in the Ring.

7. If that fails, the replica has to be destroyed. At this point you might want to involve Novell Technical Support, unless you are comfortable with the use of advanced DSRepair switches. Load DSREPAIR with the -a parameter. Select Advanced Options >> Replica and Partition Operations. Select the partition with which you want to work, and then select the Destroy the Selected Replica on This Server option.

These tasks will help you ensure the object health within your eDirectory tree, and stay on top of the health of your eDirectory environment.

Managing eDirectory Traffic

Replication is an event-driven process, meaning that it is initiated by the occurrence of some external trigger. A few of these trigger events include adding, deleting, and moving directory objects, as well as modifying object attributes. Each trigger event is flagged as being high convergence or not. *High convergence* means that eDirectory considers this event to be more significant than others, and it should be replicated as quickly as possible.

High convergence events are scheduled for fast synchronization (Fast Sync). Fast Sync occurs every 10 seconds by default. Other events are replicated using slow synchronization (Slow Sync). Slow Sync occurs every 30 minutes by default. Both of these sync processes serve to send the changed information out to each server that maintains a replica of the affected partition. Because only the actual database changes are replicated, as opposed to sending the entire partition, replication operations are generally small.

Because each directory operation is timestamped, the synchronization process relies heavily on the time synchronization processes described earlier in this chapter. During the eDirectory synchronization process, each operation will be ordered based upon its timestamp and will be applied to the eDirectory database in that order.

Using WAN Traffic Manager

If your network spans geographical areas, you might want to use the WAN Traffic Manager to control how often eDirectory information is synchronized across the network. WAN Traffic Manager enables you to control when routine eDirectory synchronization takes place, so that the traffic is minimized and/or confined to less active times of day.

WAN Traffic Manager is an optional feature of NetWare 6.5. You can
select it for installation during the NetWare 6.5 installation process or
you can install it after the fact using iManager.

You need to install WAN Traffic Manager on each server whose traffic you
want to control. If servers that share replicas of the same partition are on
opposite sides of a WAN link, all those servers should have WAN Traffic
Manager installed if you want to control their traffic.

Creating a WAN Traffic Policy

To control the eDirectory traffic, you need to create a WAN traffic policy,
which defines the rules that control how the traffic goes out on the network. This policy is stored as a property of each server object. If you
have several servers that all require the same policy, you can create a LAN
Area object, which contains a list of all the affected servers. Then you can
assign the policy to that single LAN Area object, instead of to multiple
individual servers.

NetWare 6.5 includes several predefined policies that may suit your situation. For example, one commonly used policy specifies that all routine
updates should be performed between 1:00 and 3:00 a.m. You can also
edit those policies to create customized policies for your network. For
more detailed information about these predefined policies, see the Novell
online documentation.

WARNING Creating and using WAN traffic policies can have adverse effects on your
eDirectory communications if done incorrectly. Make sure you understand the consequences of the policy before you enact it. For more information on using WAN Traffic
Manager, see the NetWare 6.5 online documentation.

The following predefined policies are available in NetWare 6.5:

► *1-3AM Group*: These policies limit eDirectory traffic to be sent
  between the hours of 1:00 a.m. and 3:00 a.m.

► *7AM-6PM Group*: These policies limit eDirectory traffic to be sent
  between the hours of 7:00 a.m. and 6:00 p.m.

► *COSTLT20 Group*: These policies allow traffic to be sent only if the
  cost factor is less than 20. You can assign cost factors to destinations in units, such as dollars per hour or cents per minute.

► *IPX Group*: These policies allow only IPX traffic.

▶ *NDSTTYPS Group*: These policies are sample policies for limiting traffic to specific types of eDirectory traffic and events.

▶ *ONOSPOOF Group*: These policies allow eDirectory traffic to be generated only across existing WAN links that are already open.

▶ *OPNSPOOF Group*: These policies allow eDirectory traffic to be generated only across existing WAN connections that are already opened, unless the connection hasn't been used for at least 15 minutes. (It assumes the connection is being used for another purpose and is not available.)

▶ *SAMEAREA Group*: These policies allow traffic only between servers in the same network section (servers sharing a common network address).

▶ *TCPIP Group*: These policies allow only TCP/IP traffic.

▶ *TIMECOST Group*: These are additional policies that cover different types of time and cost restrictions.

The following sections explain how to set up a LAN Area object and how to assign a WAN policy to a server or LAN Area object.

Creating a LAN Area object

If you want to assign a single WAN policy to multiple servers, you can save time by creating a LAN Area object that contains a list of all the servers, and then assigning the policy to the LAN Area object. Complete the following steps to create a LAN Area object.

1. Launch iManager and select WAN Traffic in the left side of the navigation frame. Click Create LAN Area.

2. Specify the name of the LAN Area object and the context in which you want it stored.

3. Click Create.

4. Select WAN Traffic Manager Overview in the left side of the navigation frame, and click the LAN Area object you have just created.

5. Configure the LAN Area object as needed and click OK.

   ▶ *Policies Tab*: From this page, you can define the policy that will govern your eDirectory background process communication. Click Add Policy to select a pre-defined policy, or browse to your own custom policy. Once you have chosen a policy, you can modify the policy specifics in the Policy window.

▶ *Costs Link*: From this page you can associate costs with specific network destinations that WAN Manager can use in its policy calculations. The cost value is simply a number that might represent cents or dollars per minute, or packets per second. Click the Add (+) icon to set a cost value and assign it to a TCP/IP or IPX address or address range. You can also define a default cost that will be applied to all addresses that are not specifically assigned a cost in the cost table.

▶ *Server List Link*: From this page you can add or remove servers as members of this LAN Area object.

When you are finished, the new LAN Area object, along with its associated eDirectory traffic policies, will be active.

Using LDAP with eDirectory

Lightweight Directory Access Protocol (LDAP) services for eDirectory lets LDAP clients access information stored in eDirectory. LDAP is currently the preferred directory access protocol on the Internet. Because eDirectory lets you give different clients different levels of directory access, you can manage external, internal, and confidential information from the same directory. eDirectory also supports secure LDAP connections so that privileged users can access internal or private information securely without any special client software. All they need is a browser with LDAP support and connectivity to the LDAP server.

Installing LDAP Services

Novell LDAP Services for eDirectory are installed automatically during the NetWare 6.5 installation routine. For more information on NetWare 6.5 installation options, see Chapter 1.

Two types of objects are defined in the eDirectory schema to support LDAP Services:

▶ *LDAP Server object*: Use this object to configure the LDAP environment for a single LDAP server.

▶ *LDAP Group object*: Use this object to configure LDAP client access to eDirectory.

LDAP Services for eDirectory can be loaded and unloaded manually by loading or unloading NLDAP.NLM on the NetWare 6.5 server.

LDAP Server Object

The LDAP Server object stores configuration information in eDirectory about an LDAP server. Figure 5.12 shows the LDAP Server object configuration page. The LDAP Server object is created in the same container as your server object. Each LDAP Server object configures one LDAP server.

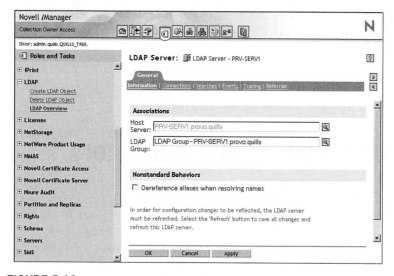

FIGURE 5.12
The LDAP Server object configuration page in iManager.

To configure an LDAP server, complete the following steps:

1. Launch iManager and select LDAP in the left side of the navigation frame. Click LDAP Overview.

2. Select the View LDAP Servers tab, and click the LDAP Server object with which you want to work.

3. Enter the configurable parameters in the property pages, and click the Refresh button to reset the LDAP server. Click OK when you're finished.

There are six pages of configuration parameters for the LDAP Server object:

▶ *Information*: Set the general configuration of your LDAP server on this page. The following entries are available:

- ▶ *LDAP Group*: Specify the name of the LDAP group to which this server should belong.

- ▶ *Dereference Aliases When Resolving Names*: Check this option to force the LDAP server to resolve to the actual object whenever it encounters an alias object.

▶ *Connections*: Sets the secure connection settings for this LDAP server with the following options:

- ▶ *Server Certificate*: Specifies the digital certificate that is used for secure connections on this server. Certificate server creates this certificate during the server installation routine. You should not have to change this value.

- ▶ *Client Certificate*: Specifies how the LDAP server will work with client certificates. Options include Not Requesting Certificates; Requesting, but Not Requiring Client Certificates; and Requiring Client Certificates.

- ▶ *Trusted Root Containers*: Specifies the container(s) in which trusted root certificates are stored for those clients capable of using Transport Layer Security (TLS).

- ▶ *Require TLS for All Operations*: Check this box to require TLS protected connections for all LDAP server communications.

- ▶ *Enable and Require Mutual Authentication:* Check this box to force the LDAP server to mutually authenticate when using SSL.

- ▶ *Enable Encrypted Port*: Sets the TCP port used for SSL connections on this server. Default is port **636**. This should not be changed unless another service is already using port **636** on this server. Uncheck this box to prevent LDAP clients from using secure connections on this server.

- ▶ *Enable Non-encrypted Port*: Sets the TCP port used for LDAP on this server. Default is port **389**. This should not be changed unless another service is already using port **389** on this server. Uncheck this box to force LDAP clients to use SSL connections on this server.

- ▶ *Concurrent Bind Limit*: Sets the maximum number of simultaneous LDAP connections. This should be set based on the amount of available memory in the LDAP server. Each LDAP request takes about 160KB of memory. Default is no limit.

▶ *Idle Timeout*: Defines the maximum time in seconds that an open LDAP connection can remain inactive before being closed. Default is no limit.

▶ *Bind Restrictions*: Specifies whether users must supply a username and password in order to connect. This is useful if you want to prevent anonymous or public access to eDirectory.

▶ *Searches*: Defines the search settings on this LDAP server with the following settings:

▶ *Filtered Replicas*: If you have configured a Filtered replica with specific search data, such as a corporate directory, you can specify that LDAP use this replica to perform its searches. If your Filtered replicas are configured for this purpose, they can improve search time significantly.

▶ *Persistent Search*: Persistent search is an extension to the LDAP search operation that allows an LDAP client to receive active updates to a given query from the LDAP server. As data on the LDAP server changes, the client will be automatically notified of changes that affect its search. These settings let you enable/disable persistent searches, and limit the number of concurrent persistent searches.

▶ *Restrictions*: Sets the maximum values for searches in both time and number of entries returned.

▶ *Nonstandard Behaviors*: Two check boxes let you support ADSI and legacy Netscape schema requests, and provide operational as well as user attributes when a request for user attributes is made.

▶ *Events*: This page lets you enable event monitoring for external applications that may want to monitor certain eDirectory events. This monitoring can place a significant load on the LDAP server, so you can also specify a maximum server load for event monitoring.

▶ *Tracing*: This page lets you enable tracing of certain types of LDAP events. LDAP tracing can place a significant load on the LDAP server, so it should be used only when necessary to gather troubleshooting information.

▶ *Referrals*: This page lets you configure referral options that define how this LDAP server will react if it is unable to process an LDAP request directly:

▶ *Default Referral URL*: Specify the LDAP URL that will point the LDAP client to another LDAP server when no specific referral information is available.

▶ *Conditions Which Return Default Referral*: These three check boxes let you enable/disable situations under which this LDAP server will return a default referral to the client.

▶ *Referral Options: Always Chain/Prefer Chaining*: Chaining causes the LDAP server to contact other LDAP servers to locate the requested data for the client, and then return the data to the client. Query work is server-intensive. *Always refer/Prefer referrals*: A *referral* is a message returned to the client that tells it where it can go to get the requested information. Both LDAP clients and servers must support referrals, but this eliminates the first LDAP server as a middle man for the LDAP request. The chaining and referral preferences can be set separately for eDirectory searches as opposed to other eDirectory operations.

Using the pages just described, you can configure the LDAP Server object as needed to fit your specific environment.

LDAP Group Object

The LDAP Group object allows you to configure user access to the LDAP server. By default, an LDAP Group object will be created for each LDAP Server object, but if you want to use the same user configuration for multiple LDAP servers, you can combine them into a single LDAP group. The LDAP Group configuration page is shown in Figure 5.13.

To configure the LDAP Group object, complete the following steps:

1. Launch iManager and select LDAP in the left side of the navigation frame. Click LDAP Overview.

2. Select the View LDAP Groups tab, and click the LDAP group object with which you want to work.

3. Enter the configurable parameters in the property pages, and click OK when finished.

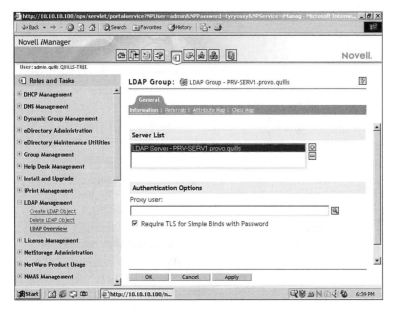

FIGURE 5.13
LDAP Group object configuration page in iManager.

There are four pages of configuration parameters for the LDAP Group object:

▶ *Information*: This page lets you set a couple of general settings for the LDAP Group:

   ▶ *Server List*: Use this option to add/remove LDAP servers from this LDAP group.

   ▶ *Proxy User*: Specifies the eDirectory user object to use as a proxy for anonymous LDAP bind requests. For more information, see "Connecting via LDAP," later in this chapter.

   ▶ *Require TLS for Simple Binds with Password*: Check this option if you want to prevent unencrypted bind requests that contain a password. This is recommended to prevent passwords from being sent across the network in clear text.

▶ *Referrals*: This page lets you configure referral options that define how this LDAP server will react if it is unable to process an LDAP request directly:

▶ *Default Referral URL*: Specify the LDAP URL that will point the LDAP client to another LDAP server when no specific referral information is available.

▶ *Conditions Which Return Default Referral*: These three check boxes let you enable/disable situations under which this LDAP server will return a default referral to the client.

▶ *Referral Options: Always Chain/Prefer Chaining*: Chaining causes the LDAP server to contact other LDAP servers to locate the requested data for the client, and then return the data to the client. Query work is server-intensive. *Always Refer/Prefer Referrals*: A *referral* is a message returned to the client that tells it where it can go to get the requested information. Both LDAP clients and servers must support referrals, but this eliminates the first LDAP server as a middle man for the LDAP request. The chaining and referral preferences can be set separately for eDirectory searches versus other eDirectory operations.

▶ *Attribute Map and Class Map*: These pages let an administrator associate LDAP schema classes and attributes to corresponding eDirectory schema classes and attributes. A default set of mappings is defined when the LDAP group is created, but it leaves many LDAP classes and attributes unmapped. If you have specific needs, you can map LDAP classes and attributes as needed.

NOTE Because there are certain LDAP attributes (such as CN and Common Name) that map to the same NDS value, LDAP services support multi-value associations. However, the LDAP server will return the value of the first matching attribute it locates in the list. If you map multiple LDAP attributes to a single NDS attribute, make sure you order the list with the most important attributes at the top; they will take precedence.

Connecting via LDAP

All LDAP clients bind or connect to eDirectory as one of the following types of users:

▶ [Public] user (anonymous bind)

▶ Proxy user (proxy user anonymous bind)

▶ Directory user (eDirectory user bind)

The type of bind the user authenticates with affects the content the LDAP client can access. LDAP clients access a directory by building a request and sending it to the directory. When an LDAP client sends a request through LDAP Services for eDirectory, eDirectory completes the request for only those attributes to which the LDAP client has the appropriate access rights. For example, if the LDAP client requests an attribute value (which requires the Read right) and the user is granted only the Compare right to that attribute, the request is rejected.

Standard login restrictions and password restrictions still apply; however, any restrictions are relative to where LDAP is running. Time and address restrictions are honored, but address restrictions are relative to where the eDirectory login occurred—in this case, the LDAP server. Also, because LDAP does not support grace logins, users can log in to the server yet not be able to bind to LDAP.

Connecting as [Public]

An *anonymous bind* is an LDAP connection that does not contain a user-name or password. If an anonymous client requests an LDAP connection and the service is not configured to use a Proxy user, eDirectory authenti-cates the client as a [Public] user.

[Public] is an unauthenticated eDirectory user. By default, [Public] is assigned only the Browse right to the objects in the eDirectory tree. [Public] can see only objects; it cannot browse object attributes. This is typically too limited for most LDAP clients. Although you can change the [Public] rights, this will give those rights to all users. To avoid this, use Proxy user (anonymous bind).

Connecting as a Proxy

Proxy user (anonymous bind) allows LDAP to connect as a pre-defined eDirectory user. This gives you the flexibility to offer an anonymous con-nection that may actually be useful for something—such as accessing public information—without potentially causing security problems by changing [Public].

The key concepts of Proxy user (anonymous bind) are as follows:

▶ All anonymous LDAP access is managed through the Proxy User object. Assign the Proxy user appropriate rights to all objects and attributes in eDirectory.

▶ The Proxy user cannot have a password or any password restric-tions, such as password change intervals, because LDAP clients do not supply passwords during anonymous binds. Do not allow the Proxy user to change passwords.

▶ If desired, you can limit the locations from which a Proxy user can log in by setting address restrictions on the Proxy User object. For more information on creating and configuring eDirectory User objects, see Chapter 6.

The Proxy User object is enabled from the Information tab of the LDAP Group object, as described previously in this chapter. There is only one Proxy User object for all servers in an LDAP group.

Connecting as a Directory User

LDAP clients can also connect using regular eDirectory User objects. Once authenticated, the LDAP client is allowed access to any information to which the eDirectory user has rights.

The key concepts of eDirectory user binds are as follows:

▶ eDirectory user connections are authenticated to eDirectory with a username and password entered at the LDAP client.

▶ If secure connections are not required for password-based connections, the eDirectory password can be transmitted in clear text on the path between the LDAP client and LDAP server.

▶ If an eDirectory user password has expired, eDirectory bind requests for that user are rejected.

You have the flexibility to leverage any of these types of LDAP bind operations to give LDAP users access to eDirectory information they might need.

DNS and DHCP Services

Novell DNS/DHCP services in NetWare 6.5 integrate the Domain Name Service (DNS) and Dynamic Host Configuration Protocol (DHCP) into the eDirectory database. Integrating these services into eDirectory provides centralized administration and enterprise-wide management of network (IP) addresses, configuration, and hostnames.

DNS and DHCP manage the assignment and discovery of IP addresses on a network. By integrating this information into eDirectory, network administrators can manage both DNS and DHCP information together with regular eDirectory information from a single, centralized location. The DNS/DHCP information is stored in the eDirectory database, so it is distributed and replicated just like other eDirectory data, making it easier to access and manage. The DNS/DHCP Management utility is available through iManager.

Installing DNS/DHCP Services

DNS/DHCP services can be installed as an optional service during the NetWare 6.5 installation routine. It can also be installed as a post-installation task through iManager. When you install DNS/DHCP services as an optional product during the server installation, the eDirectory schema is extended to support a variety of DNS- and DHCP-related objects. These objects help keep track of IP addresses, DNS and DHCP servers, configurations, host addresses, zones, and the like.

To install DNS/DHCP services from iManager, complete the following steps:

1. Launch iManager and open the Install NetWare 6.5 Products link, and then select Install and Upgrade

2. Click Remote Product Install in the right frame.

3. Browse to the location of the NetWare 6.5 Operating System CD-ROM and click OK.

4. Browse to and select the server to which you want to install DNS/DHCP services. Click Next. Authenticate as an Admin user to the server you selected.

5. At the Components screen, select only Novell DNS/DHCP Services and click Next.

6. At the Summary screen, select Copy Files to install DNS/DHCP services. You will need to insert or specify the location of the NetWare 6.5 Products CD-ROM.

7. Specify the context for the three main DNS/DHCP objects and click Next. More information on each of these objects is provided later in this section.

TIP These objects should be located close to the top of the tree where they can be quickly located.

8. At the Installation Complete screen, click Close to complete the installation.

With DNS/DHCP services installed on the network, an IP client can establish a connection with the network by leasing an IP address from a pool of available addresses, rather than requiring that the workstation be assigned a fixed address individually. This makes IP address management much easier.

Once connected to the network, the IP client can automatically detect available DNS name servers, through which it can translate domain names—for example, `www.novell.com`—into its corresponding IP address(for example, `137.65.168.1`). This enables the client to communicate with the server properly. Domain names are a benefit to the human users of computers, not the computers themselves.

All DNS/DHCP configuration and management is handled through iManager. For more information on the basics of iManager, see Chapter 3.

There are several aspects to the configuration of DNS/DHCP services for your NetWare 6.5 network, but the four primary tasks are

▶ Planning for DNS/DHCP

▶ Setting DNS/DHCP scope

▶ Configuring DHCP

▶ Configuring DNS

Planning for DNS/DHCP

There are three objects to which all DNS/DHCP servers need to have access:

▶ DNS/DHCP Group

▶ DNS/DHCP Locator

▶ RootServerInfo Zone

Locate the DNS/DHCP objects near the top of your eDirectory tree. You might also want to create an administrative role for DNS/DHCP. Once created, you can assign any User objects you want to be able to use iManager to configure DNS/DHCP, as members of this group. For more information on creating iManager roles, see Chapter 3.

Consider the following eDirectory issues to maintain optimal performance when providing DNS/DHCP services on your NetWare network:

▶ *Where to locate DNS and DHCP servers*: Plan to locate your DNS
and DHCP servers so that they are physically close to the hosts
that require their services. Plan to have one DHCP server in
each partition of your network to minimize impact on WAN
communications.

▶ *Which replication strategy to employ*: Replicate the partition containing the DNS/DHCP Group and Locator objects to all parts of
the network that use DNS/DHCP services to ensure access in the
event of system unavailability or hardware problems.

▶ *How to provide fault tolerance*: When planning your DNS replication strategy, consider that replication is employed for load balancing when you provide multiple name servers within the DNS zone.
Well-planned replication is the best way to provide fault tolerance
for DNS/DHCP services.

Keeping these issues in mind will help ensure the integrity and performance of your DNS/DHCP environment.

Setting DNS/DHCP Scope

Setting the scope of the DNS/DHCP services specifies the context of the
Locator object and the administrative scope for the iManager session.
Defining these two values first will improve performance in larger
eDirectory environments because it eliminates the need to search for the
Locator object and it restricts the retrieval of DNS/DHCP objects to the
scope you specify, instead of searching the entire tree.

DNS/DHCP Scope settings will normally last only for the duration of the
DNS/DHCP session. However, if you configure DNS/DHCP Scope settings for either DNS or DHCP Management, the settings apply across the
session to both roles.

To configure DNS/DHCP Scope settings, complete the following steps:

   1. In iManager, open either the DNS or DHCP link and select
   DNS/DHCP Scope Settings.

   2. Specify the eDirectory context of the DNS/DHCP Locator object.

   3. Specify the eDirectory container object that will provide the administrative scope of the current session.

4. Click OK.

Setting the DNS/DHCP scope effectively constrains the DNS/DHCP environment within which you will be working during this iManager session.

Configuring DHCP Services

Configuring the DHCP environment involves the following steps:

- ▶ Planning DHCP
- ▶ Creating DHCP objects
- ▶ Starting DHCP services

Planning DHCP

Before using DHCP for the first time, you need to gather a lot of network information:

- ▶ Make a list of all IP hosts to be served by the DHCP server. Include all devices that use network addresses on every segment of your network.

- ▶ Compile a list of current IP address assignments. Organize your lists of hosts and IP addresses by geographic location. For example, if your network is spread over a WAN, make a list for each location to help you organize the distribution of DHCP resources.

- ▶ You must have a list of all permanently assigned network addresses. You might also want to make a list of devices that are to be denied IP addresses and those hosts that are to receive strict address limitations.

Another major issue is deciding how long to set your client leases. You must strike a balance between the amount of network traffic and the amount of flexibility in the system. The longest lease provided by a DHCP server determines the length of time you might have to wait before configuration changes can be propagated within a network. Consider the following issues when setting lease times:

- ▶ Keep leases short if you have more users than IP addresses. Shorter leases support more clients, but increase the load on the network and DHCP server. A lease of two hours is long enough to serve most users, and the network load will probably not be significant. Leases shorter than this start to increase network and server load dramatically.

► Leases should be set twice as long as typical interruptions, such as server and communications outages. Decide how long your users should be able to go without contacting the DHCP server, and double it to get a recommended lease duration.

► Hosts that are advertising services on the network, such as Web servers, should not have an IP address that is constantly changing. Consider permanent assignments for these hosts. The deciding factor should be how long you want the host to be able to keep an assigned address.

The default of 3 days is usually a pretty good balance between the need for a shorter and a longer lease.

Creating DHCP Objects

After you gather the necessary information, you need to create eDirectory objects to represent this information in eDirectory. Create a DHCP Server object from which to configure the DHCP environment. Create Subnet objects to represent each LAN segment. Create one or more Subnet Address Range objects to represent all your contiguous strings of IP addresses for each LAN subnet.

When a DHCP server makes or modifies address assignments, it updates the database. The partition where this database is stored should have at least two writeable replicas. Having only one replica might be unsafe due to a lack of fault tolerance, but three can be too costly in terms of replication overhead.

To create the necessary DHCP objects, complete the steps in the following sections.

Creating a DHCP Server Object

Use iManager to install a DHCP Server object in any of the following container objects, based upon the needs of your network: Organization, Organizational Unit, Country, or Locality.

1. From iManager, open the DHCP link and select DHCP Server Management.

2. Select Create Server from the drop-down menu and click OK.

3. Browse to and select the server that will act as a DHCP server, and select Create.

4. At the Request Succeeded message screen, click OK.

The DHCP Server object will be used as part of the management infra-structure for DHCP.

Creating a Subnet Object

Use iManager to create and set up a DHCP Subnet object for each of the subnets to which you will assign addresses, by completing the following steps:

1. From iManager, open the DHCP link and select Subnet Management.

2. Select Create Subnet from the drop-down menu, and select OK.

3. At the Create Subnet screen, enter the required information and select Create.

   ▶ *Subnet Name*: Specify a unique name for this Subnet object.

   ▶ *eDirectory Context*: Specify the eDirectory context where the subnet record will be stored.

   ▶ *Subnet Address*: Specify the IP subnet address.

   ▶ *Subnet Mask*: Specify the IP subnet mask.

   ▶ *Default DHCP Server*: Specify the DHCP server that will manage this subnet. By default, this server is assigned all address ranges created under the subnet.

4. At the Request Succeeded message screen, click OK.

IP Address objects are simultaneously created to exclude routing and broadcast addresses.

Creating Subnet Address Range Objects

Use iManager to create and set up Subnet Address Range objects for each pool of addresses you want to be dynamically assigned by DHCP. To cre-ate and set up a Subnet Address Range object, complete the following steps:

1. From iManager, open the DHCP link and select Address Range Management.

2. Select Create Address Range from the drop-down menu, and select OK.

3. At the Create Address Range window, enter the required informa-tion and select Create.

> ▶ *Select the Subnet*: Specify the subnet for which the address range is required from the drop-down menu.
>
> ▶ *Address Range Name*: Specify a unique name for the subnet address range.
>
> ▶ *Start Address*: Specify the beginning of the address range.
>
> ▶ *End Address*: Specify the end of the address range.

4. At the Request Succeeded message screen, click OK.

Optionally, you can also use iManager to create specific IP Address objects if you have certain addresses that need to be assigned to specific devices, or excluded from dynamic assignment. This requires you to specify the client's Media Access Control (MAC) address or client ID.

Starting DHCP Services

Once you have created the necessary DHCP objects in eDirectory, you can start DHCP services on your server by entering the following command at the server console prompt:

```
LOAD DHCPSRVR
```

You typically won't need to anything beyond this, but DHCPSRVR.NLM does support some command-line parameters for specific functions, as noted in Table 5.1.

TABLE 5.1   DHCPSRVR.NLM Command-Line Parameters

PARAMETER	DESCRIPTION
-d1	Turns on a screen log of DHCP packets on the NetWare server.
-d2	Turns on a screen log of debug statements and DHCP packets on the NetWare server.
-d3	In addition to -d2, this parameter sends the DHCP log to a file called SYS:ETC\DHCPSRVR.LOG.
-h	Displays the command-line syntax.
-py	Sets the global polling interval to every *y* minutes.
-s	Forces the DHCP server to read and write from the Master replica.

To enable DHCP services on a client workstation, simply configure the TCP/IP properties to obtain an IP address automatically. The next time

the client starts, it will send a request to the DHCP server for an IP
address.

WARNING Client configuration settings will override the configuration received from
a DHCP server. The only exception is the hostname parameter set on the DNS
Configuration tab of the TCP/IP Properties window.

For detailed information on DHCP configuration parameters, see the
NetWare 6.5 online documentation.

Configuring DNS Services

Similar to DHCP, configuring the DNS environment involves the following steps:

- ▶ Planning DNS
- ▶ Creating DNS objects
- ▶ Starting DNS services

Planning DNS

Consider the following issues and recommendations as you plan your
DNS environment:

- ▶ You will configure a primary DNS name server, which is considered
  the authoritative source for DNS information. For load balancing
  and fault tolerance, plan to install one primary and at least one secondary name server.

- ▶ Secondary name servers receive their zone data from the primary
  name server. When it starts, and at periodic intervals, the secondary checks with the primary to see whether any information has
  changed. If the information on the secondary is older than that on
  the primary, a zone transfer occurs to update the secondary name
  server's information.

- ▶ If you are running a primary name server and providing DNS service for a zone, the size or geography of your network might require
  creating subzones within the zone.

- ▶ Novell recommends installing your NetWare 6.5 DNS name server
  as a primary to most efficiently take advantage of Dynamic DNS
  (DDNS). By doing this, if you make changes to the DHCP environment with iManager, those changes can be dynamically recognized

by the primary DNS server. Secondary name servers, even non-NetWare secondary name servers, can transfer that revised data in from the primary server.

▶ If your NetWare servers will operate as secondary DNS servers to a non-Novell master name server, one Novell secondary name server must be specified as the Dynamic DNS or *Zone In* server (a server that receives zone transfer information from the master name server and updates eDirectory accordingly). Other NetWare secondary name servers can then transfer the information from eDirectory.

▶ If a name server cannot answer a query, it must query a remote server. This is particularly relevant for Internet domain queries. Novell's DNS/DHCP services allow you to configure primary and/or secondary name servers to act as forwarders. Forwarders that handle the off-site queries develop a robust cache of information. When using forwarders, configure the other name servers in your zone to direct their queries to the forwarder. The forwarder can typically respond to any given query with information from its cache, eliminating the need to pass an outside query to a remote server.

Considering the issues discussed here will help make sure your DNS environment is planned properly.

Creating DNS Objects

There are three main types of DNS objects that you will create for your DNS environment. The following sections provide the steps for creating each type.

DNS Server Object

The DNS Server object allows you to configure the operation of your DNS servers through eDirectory. To create a DNS Server object, complete the following steps:

1. From iManager, open the DNS link and select DNS Server Management.

2. Select Create Server from the drop-down menu and click OK.

3. At the Create DNS Server screen, enter the required information and select Create.

   ▶ *NCP Server Name*: Browse to and select the NetWare server that will act as a DNS server.

▶ *Hostname*: Specify a unique hostname for the DNS Server object.

▶ *Domain Name*: Specify a domain name for the DNS server object.

4. At the Request Succeeded message screen, select OK.

Once created, the DNS Server object will allow you to manage your DNS environment through eDirectory.

DNS Zone Object

Zones define the group of domains and/or sub-domains for which you have authority. All host information for a zone is maintained in a single, authoritative database. To create a DNS Zone object, complete the following steps:

1. From iManager, open the DNS link and select Zone Management.

2. Select Create Zone from the drop-down menu, and select OK.

3. At the Create DNS Zone screen, enter the required information and select Create.

▶ *Zone Type*: Select Create New Zone. The IN-ADDR ARPA zone is used for reverse look-ups, translating an IP address into a domain name. For more information on IN-ADDR ARPA zones, see the NetWare 6.5 online documentation.

▶ *eDirectory Context*: Specify a location for the Zone object.

▶ *Zone Domain Name*: Specify a domain name for the Zone object.

▶ *Zone Type*: Select Primary if this zone will be associated with the primary name server and will function as the authoritative source for domain information. Otherwise, select Secondary.

▶ *(Conditional) Name Server IP Address*: If this is a secondary zone, enter the IP address of the primary DNS name server from which this zone will receive its updates.

▶ *(Conditional) Assigned Authoritative Zone Server*: If the primary DNS server is a NetWare server, select it from the drop-down list.

▶ (*Conditional*) *Name Server Information*: If the primary DNS server is not a NetWare server, specify its complete hostname and, optionally, its domain.

4. At the Request Succeeded message screen, select OK.

You can create multiple DNS Zones to better manage more complex DNS environments, and each can be managed separately.

(Optional) Resource Records

A *resource record* is a piece of information about a domain name. Each resource record contains information about a particular piece of data within the domain. To create a new resource record, complete the following steps:

1. From iManager, open the DNS link and select Resource Record Management.

2. Select Create Resource Record from the drop-down menu, and select OK.

3. At the Create Resource Record screen, enter the required information and select Create.

   ▶ *Domain Name*: Select the domain in which the resource record is to be created.

   ▶ (*Optional*) *Hostname*: Select the name of the host server. This binds a domain name with a hostname for a specific name server.

4. Specify the Resource Record (RR) type and select Create. Depending on the type of RR you are creating, you will be required to specify different types of record data. For more information on RR types, see the NetWare 6.5 online documentation.

5. At the Request Succeeded screen, select OK.

You can create as many resource records as needed to properly describe and configure your DNS environment.

Starting DNS Services

After you have created and set up a DNS Server object and a DNS Zone object, enter the following command at the DNS server console:

```
LOAD NAMED
```

After NAMED.NLM is loaded, the DNS server can respond to queries for the zone.

You typically won't need to do anything beyond this, but NAMED.NLM does support some command-line parameters for specific functions, as noted in Table 5.2. You can issue the **LOAD NAMED** command repeatedly to invoke different command-line options. Although the different features will toggle on/off, NAMED.NLM is loaded only the first time.

TABLE 5.2   NAMED.NLM Command-Line Parameters

PARAMETER	DESCRIPTION
-rp	This option can be used to add characters to the list of characters prohibited from use in DNS names. All characters in the list will be replaced by dashes (-) before storing them in eDirectory.
-r [ON¦OFF]	Dynamic reconfiguration option tells the DNS server to periodically (every 15 minutes by default) reload the configuration data for the server and zones, and automatically check for added, deleted, and modified zones.
-ft [ON¦OFF]	When enabled, the DNS server will start using the backup files if eDirectory is inaccessible. When off, the DNS server will not service the zones for which eDirectory is inaccessible.
-?	Displays usage information.
-dl	Sets the level of detail to be logged. Values are –1 to –5 for information, notice, warning, error, and critical respectively. You can also indicate the specific categories of messages that you want logged. For a complete list of log categories, see the NetWare 6.5 online documentation.
-n <number of CPUs>	Specifies the number of CPUs available for use by DNS. Can specify from 1 to 32.
-p	Specifies the port number used by DNS. Default port is 53.
-mstats	Saves the DNS server's memory usage information to SYS:ETC\NAMED.MEM. This is useful for determining DNS server load.

TABLE 5.2   Continued

PARAMETER	DESCRIPTION
-qstats	Saves the DNS server's query statistics information to SYS:ETC\DNS\NAMED.STA. Can be used with -mstats information determine DNS server load.
-pa	Purge all cache on the DNS server.
-info	Provides information about all zones currently loaded in the DNS server.
-v *<volume name>*	Enables clustering support for DNS by allowing DNS information to be stored on a volume other than SYS.
-zi *<zone name>*	Forces named zone for zone-in transfer.

To enable DNS services on a client workstation, simply configure the TCP/IP properties to obtain DNS server addresses automatically. The next time the client starts, it will dynamically query for DNS information on the network.

CHAPTER 6

Users and Network Security

Instant Access

Creating Users and Groups

▶ To create User and Group objects, use iManager or ConsoleOne.

▶ To set up a template so that all users you create receive a set of common characteristics, use iManager or ConsoleOne to create a Template object.

Ensuring Login Security

▶ To create account restrictions, access the user or group properties through iManager or ConsoleOne.

▶ To set or change passwords, access User object properties with iManager or ConsoleOne.

Working with eDirectory Security

▶ To view or change eDirectory object or property rights, use iManager or ConsoleOne.

Dealing with Directory and File Security

▶ To view or change file system rights, use ConsoleOne.

▶ To view or change directory and file attributes, use ConsoleOne.

Securing the Network from Intruders

▶ To use NCP packet signatures, use NoRM to set the Packet Signing parameter on the server to the appropriate signing level. Use the

Advanced Settings page of the Novell client property pages to configure the appropriate packet signing level on your Windows workstations.

▶ To set intruder detection, use iManager or ConsoleOne.

▶ To lock the server console, use SCRSAVER.NLM.

▶ To remove DOS and prevent NLMs from being loaded from insecure areas, use the **SECURE CONSOLE** command.

An Overview of Network Security

Like no other time in the history of computing, regular users and small network administrators are being confronted with the issues of securing their networks. The Internet has uncovered the deficiencies in standards, protocols, and operating systems by allowing hackers and other n'er-do-wells the opportunity to test networks from distant locations. Malicious viruses, worms, and Trojan Horses seek to infiltrate your network to harm and destroy.

And yet the most likely source of network attack is from your own users, whether out of malice or ignorance. Viruses can be introduced, security procedures circumvented, and sensitive systems and data left unprotected. Clearly, any effective security program has to protect from both internal and external threats.

NetWare 6.5 offers a broad set of security features. Many of these features are implemented and managed through Novell eDirectory, which helps you develop a robust network security infrastructure without creating a management nightmare. NetWare 6.5 security concepts and features can be organized into five main categories:

▶ User-related objects

▶ Authentication

▶ Authorization

▶ Data security

▶ Other security features

Novell has always been adept at providing effective network security, primarily because NetWare is not an operating system that lends itself to simple security attacks. However, today's network security involves a lot more than assigning passwords to network users. Today's complex computing environments require advanced techniques for assuring that only those persons required to access network resources are able to do so. It is important to understand these basic topics in order to lay the groundwork for discussions of specific security products and features.

NOTE ConsoleOne has traditionally been the method for performing most object administration in eDirectory. However, because Novell's direction is to move all of this functionality to the browser-based iManager environment, all object manipulation that is currently available in iManager will be discussed from the perspective of that utility, rather than from ConsoleOne.

User-Related Objects

This might seem like an odd place to talk about User objects and related features, but critical security problems can arise from a misunderstanding of the ways in which eDirectory users can be assigned trustee rights. There are three main objects that are used to organize your network users. You can use iManager or ConsoleOne to create and manage each of these types of objects (for more information on both iManager and ConsoleOne basics, see Chapter 3, "Novell Management Tools"):

- ▶ User object
- ▶ Group object
- ▶ Organizational role

These objects form the foundation from which network services and privileges are ultimately delivered. After all, user-related objects define the human elements of your network. Immediately after a new NetWare 6.5 and eDirectory installation, the only User object that exists is Admin. Although it might be comforting to think of a network of one, you are going to have to create user accounts for every one of your users. Once users have been created, they can begin working on the network. In most cases, users on a network will notice very little difference from working on a stand-alone computer. They still use the applications they were using before. They still open, save, and delete files the same way. They can still play the same games—but only if you let them!

And that's the goal of network security: to prevent users from taking some action, either unintentionally or intentionally, that might compromise the integrity of the network or expose network resources in such a way that can cause harm to the network or the organization. There are several levels of network security in today's networks, and NetWare 6.5 gives you a great deal of control over each.

The User Object

To create an eDirectory User object, complete the following steps:

1. *(Optional)* Create a directory for all users' home directories. For example, you might want to create a network directory called Users on volume **VOL1**. For more information on NetWare volumes, see Chapter 8, "File Storage and Management."

2. From iManager, select the Users link and click Create User (see Figure 6.1).

3. Specify the desired information and click OK. You should pay particular attention to the following fields:

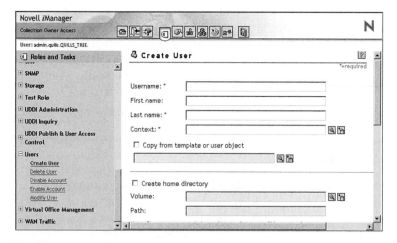

FIGURE 6.1
Creating a new user in iManager.

> ▶ *Username*: (Required) Enter the desired login name for this user. This is the name the user will enter when he or she authenticates to eDirectory.

▶ *Last Name*: (Required) Specify the last name of this user. This field is required so that you can perform name-based searches on eDirectory.

▶ *Context*: Specify the container in which the User object should be created.

▶ *Password*: Select this option and you can either specify the user password or force eDirectory to prompt the users for a password upon their first login.

WARNING It is possible to create an eDirectory User object without a password, but it is highly discouraged due to the network security breach that results.

If you plan to assign many of your users certain identical properties, you can use a User Template object. The Template object will automatically apply default properties to any new user you create using the template. However, it does not apply those properties to any users who existed before you created the user template. Network administrators often use a template to automatically grant default eDirectory and file system rights to users.

To create a User Template object, complete these steps:

1. *(Optional)* Create a directory for all users' home directories. For example, you might want to create a network directory called Users on volume VOL1. For more information on NetWare volumes, see Chapter 8.

2. From iManager, select the View Objects icon in the Header frame.

3. In the left navigation frame, click any container object and choose Create Object from the task list.

4. Select Template from the list of available objects and click OK.

5. Specify the name of the Template object, and the context in which it should be created, and click OK.

Once created, you configure any of the common characteristics you want assigned to all users you create. To do this in iManager, browse to and select the object in the left frame. Modify the template by selecting the appropriate task and providing the desired information. Most of the template information will be specified in the Modify Object and the Rights to Other Objects tasks.

The Group Object

Group objects are used to apply a common set of trustee rights to different User objects. User objects assigned to a group are made *security equivalent* to that group, meaning that any rights given to the Group object will also be applied to each of its member users. Creating a group is very similar to creating a user. Complete the following steps to create a group and assign group membership to a user.

1. From iManager, select the View Objects icon in the Header frame.

2. In the left navigation frame, click any container object and choose Create Group from the task list.

3. Specify the name of the Group object, and the context in which it should be created, and click OK.

4. Click Modify to access the Group object properties pages. From there you can provide any object-specific information, and add members to the group by selecting the Members link. Click OK when finished to save the Group properties.

The Organizational Role

Organizational roles function like groups of one. (They can have multiple occupants for process redundancy.) They use explicit security equivalence to provide specific rights to a user who needs to be able to perform a specific task. Organizational roles are generally used to grant some degree of administrative capability for a tree or branch of the tree. Although similar in some respects, an organizational role should not be confused with the role-based services of iManager. The iManager roles are much more flexible in their application than Organizational roles. For more information on iManager roles, see Chapter 3.

Complete the following steps to create an organizational role and assign occupancy to a user:

1. From iManager, select the View Objects icon in the Header frame.

2. In the left navigation frame, click any container object and choose Create Object from the task list.

3. Select Organizational Role from the list of available objects and click OK.

4. Specify the name of the Organizational Role object, and the context in which it should be created, and click OK.

5. Click Modify to access the Organizational Role object properties pages. From there you can provide any object-specific information, and specify the occupant of the Organizational Role. Click OK when finished to save the Organizational Role properties.

Once created, you can assign any User object to an organizational role to grant specific rights related to specific responsibilities within your organization.

Authentication

Authentication provides the doorway for access to network resources. Without a strong authentication mechanism, sensitive network resources are essentially laid bare for anyone to access. The primary authentication method currently used with eDirectory is the username/password combination. Novell Modular Authentication Service (NMAS) makes it possible to integrate more advanced authentication and authorization techniques into your NetWare environment. Furthermore, NMAS offers a feature new with NetWare 6.5 that improves the traditional password-based authentication method, which is known as *universal password*.

Novell Modular Authentication Service

NMAS is designed to help you protect information on your network. NMAS offers a more robust framework for protecting your NetWare 6.5 environment. If you're not familiar with the different pieces of NMAS, you should get to know the following concepts. More information about each of these is provided in the NetWare 6.5 online documentation.

Phases of Operation

There are specific times when NMAS can be useful in helping to secure your network environment:

▶ *User identification* occurs prior to the actual authentication process. It provides a way to automatically gather a user's authentication information and use it to populate the Novell Login dialog in the Novell Client.

▶ *Authentication* is the opportunity for users to prove they are who they claim to be. NMAS supports multiple authentication methods.

▶ *Device removal detection* is the capability to lock down a workstation after authentication when it becomes clear that the user is no longer present.

Each these phases of operation is completely independent. You can choose to use the same, or completely different, identification techniques for each phase. To provide this functionality, NMAS introduces a few additional concepts to NetWare authentication:

▶ Login factors

▶ Login methods and sequences

▶ Graded authentication

Login Factors

NMAS uses three approaches to logging in to the network, known as *login factors*. These login factors describe different items or qualities a user can use to authenticate to the network:

▶ *Password authentication*: Also referred to as "something you know," password authentication is the traditional network authentication method. It is still responsible for the lion's share of network authentication that goes on, including LDAP authentication, browser-based authentication, and most other directories.

▶ *Device authentication*: Also referred to as "something you have," device authentication uses third-party tokens or smart cards to deliver the secret with which you authenticate to the network.

▶ *Biometric authentication*: Also referred to as "something you are," biometric authentication uses some sort of scanning device that converts some physical characteristic into a digital pattern that can be stored in eDirectory. When users attempt to authenticate, their biometric patterns are compared against the stored version to see if they match. Common biometric authentication methods include fingerprint readers, facial recognition, and retinal scans.

NOTE NMAS provides support for password authentication only. Device and biometric login factors are supported with NMAS Enterprise Edition.

Login Methods and Sequences

A *login method* is a specific implementation of a login factor. Novell has partnered with several third parties to create a variety of options for each of the login factors described earlier in this chapter. A *post-login method* is a security process that is executed after a user has authenticated to eDirectory. One such post-login method is the workstation access method, which requires the user to provide credentials in order to unlock the workstation after a period of inactivity.

Once you have decided upon and installed a method, you need to assign it to a login sequence in order for it to be used. A *login sequence* is an ordered set of one or more methods. Users log in to the network using these defined login sequences. If the sequence contains more than one method, the methods are presented to the user in the order specified. Login methods are presented first, followed by post-login methods.

Graded Authentication

Another important feature in NMAS is *graded authentication*, which allows you to grade, or control, access to the network based on the login methods used to authenticate to the network. Graded authentication operates in conjunction with standard eDirectory and file system rights to provide very robust control over data access in a NetWare 6.5 environment.

There are three main elements to graded authentication:

▶ *Categories*: NMAS categories represent different levels of sensitivity and trust. You use categories to define security labels. There are three secrecy categories and three integrity categories by default: biometric, token, and password.

▶ *Security labels*: Security labels are combinations of categories that assign access requirements to NetWare volumes and eDirectory objects and properties. NMAS Enterprise Edition comes with eight security labels:

  ▶ Biometric and password and token

  ▶ Biometric and password

  ▶ Biometric and token

  ▶ Password and token

  ▶ Biometric

  ▶ Password

- ▸ Token

- ▸ Logged in

- ▸ *Clearances*: Clearances are assigned to users to represent the amount of trust you have in them. In the clearance, a read label specifies what a user can read and a write label specifies locations to which a user can write. Clearances are compared to security labels to determine whether a user has access. If a user's read clearance is equal to or greater than the security label assigned to the requested data, the user will be able to view the data.

By configuring these elements of graded authentication, you can greatly increase the security of your network data, and apply different types of security to data of different levels of sensitivity.

Installing NMAS

NMAS requires both server- and client-side software in order to perform its authentication services. Installation of the NMAS client happens during the installation of the Novell Client, and is described in Chapter 2. On the server, NMAS is one of the default services, and will be installed automatically with any service that requires its services, such as Native File Access Protocols (NFAPs). However, if necessary, you can install NMAS manually from iManager or from the graphical server console.

To install NMAS from iManager, complete the following steps:

1. Launch iManager and open the Install and Upgrade link, and then select Install and Upgrade.

2. Click Remote Product Install in the right frame.

3. Browse to the location of the NetWare 6.5 Operating System CD-ROM and click OK.

4. Browse to and select the server to which you want to install NMAS and click Next. Authenticate as an Admin user to the server you selected.

5. At the Components screen, select only Novell Modular Authentication Service and click Next.

6. Select the NMAS Login Methods you want to install and click Next. Mouse over each method name to see a brief description of how the method is used.

7. At the Summary screen, select Copy Files to install NMAS. You will need to insert or specify the location of the NetWare 6.5 product's CD-ROM.

8. At the Installation Complete screen, click Close to complete the installation.

Once NMAS is installed, there are several configuration options, depending on your specific environment and needs. Server-side configuration is available through either iManager or ConsoleOne. Once the NMAS server options are configured, you can configure the NMAS client to leverage NMAS capabilities. Generally, the process involves the following:

▶ *Create a login sequence*: This process identifies the specific login methods that will be used for login and post-login operations, and the order in which they will be applied if multiple login methods are specified.

▶ *Assign a login sequence to a user*: Once created, a login sequence is available for use by a user. A default login sequence can be defined, and users can be forced to use a specific login sequence, if desired.

▶ *Graded authentication*: With the login environment configured, you can now define those network resources that are available with each login method. Graded authentication lets you label network resources and require certain levels of authentication in order to access those resources.

▶ *Customize the user login*: The Novell Client supports several customization options based on the type of authentication that is being used. For more information on the Novell Client, see Chapter 2. You can also review Appendix A for detailed information on the Novell Client property pages.

For more detailed information on each of these NMAS configuration steps, see the Novell online documentation.

Universal Password

In addition to its other authentication and authorization options, NMAS also provides a new way of dealing with the different password requirements of some of Novell's cross-platform services. The traditional Novell password, although quite effective for NetWare-based authentication, is limited by its weak capability to integrate with non-NetWare systems.

Universal password proposes to resolve this problem by simplifying the management of different password and authentication systems with your NetWare 6.5 environment.

Universal password resolves several deficiencies in the current password authentication model across the various NetWare 6.5 services, including:

▶ *Native file access*: Native file access protocols such as CIFS, AFP, and NFS cannot interoperate with the traditional NetWare password. Rather, they use a separately administered Simple Password, which is less secure than the NetWare password and must be managed separately. For more information on NFAP, see Chapter 2.

▶ *LDAP*: Similar to NFAP, LDAP binds are largely incompatible with the traditional NetWare password, and also run the risk of sending unencrypted passwords.

▶ *LDAP user import*: It is possible to import users from foreign directories via LDAP, but imported passwords conform to the rules of the native system and are encrypted in the native format. This makes them largely incompatible with the traditional NetWare password and forces them to be managed through the Simple Password mechanism.

▶ *Password synchronization*: With the availability of meta-directory tools such as DirXML and Account Management, you often end up with multiple passwords stored as different object attributes. These passwords can be synchronized as long as changes are performed using the proper interface, such as the Novell Client. Changes made in other ways can cause synchronization problems.

If these issues mentioned, and the use of international characters in passwords, are not problems for you, you might not need to enable universal password. However, as your network becomes increasing Web-integrated and managed, universal password will likely become more attractive.

Universal password leverages NICI for cryptographic services, and NICI now includes special cryptographic key that can be shared across multiple servers. Known as the *SDI domain key,* it removes the problems associated with encrypting data using server-specific keys. The SDI domain key can be shared across multiple servers so that any server in the domain can decrypt data.

Preparing for Universal Password

The universal password environment requires NetWare 6.5 on at least one of the servers in any replica ring that holds User objects that will leverage the universal password. To do this, identify the container(s) that holds the objects of those users who will be using universal password, and then locate the eDirectory partition in which that container resides and identify the server(s) that hold replicas of that partition. At least one of those servers will have to be a NetWare 6.5 server.

Because of this requirement, universal password is not enabled by default in NetWare 6.5. However, as you plan your NetWare 6.5 migration, plan to upgrade at least one server in each partition first, and then move to other replica servers. This strategy will help smooth the way for using universal password throughout your network.

NOTE If you want to use NFAP with universal password, NFAP servers should be upgraded as described previously for SDI domain servers.

Configuring the SDI Domain

NetWare 6.5 includes SDIDIAG.NLM for configuring the SDI domain in preparation for enabling universal password. Prior to creating the SDI domain, you should check any non-NetWare 6.5 servers that you want in the SDI domain to see if they meet the minimum requirements:

1. From the server console, load SDIDIAG.NLM.

2. Authenticate as an Admin user in the tree and click OK.

3. Enter the following command. If any problems are noted, use the information in `SYS:SYSTEM\SDINOTES.TXT` to help you resolve them, and then continue with the configuration.

   `CHECK -v >> sys:system\sdinotes.txt`

4. *(Conditional)* Verify that each SDI domain key server that is not running NetWare 6.5 is running NICI v2.4.2 or later. To do this, enter the following command at the server console of each server in the SDI domain:

   `M NICISDI.NLM`

   The version must be 24212.98 or later. If not, you must either upgrade the server to NetWare 6.5 or update the NICI on this server to v2.4.2.

NOTE NICI v2.4.2 requires eDirectory 8.5.1 or later, so if you are not running a fairly current environment, the preparation for universal password can be significant. You can download NICI v2.4.2 from Novell's support Web site at http://support.novell.com/filefinder/.

Based upon the results of the configuration tests, you can add or remove servers SDI domain key servers with SDIDIAG.NLM as well.

To add a server to the SDI domain, complete the following steps:

1. Load SDIDIAG at the server console.

2. Authenticate as an Admin user in the tree and click OK.

3. Enter the following command to add a server:

   ```
   AS -s <Full Server Name>
   ```

   For example: `AS -s .prv-serv1.provo.quills.quills-tree`

   To remove a server from the SDI domain, use the same process, but use the following command:

   ```
   RS -s <Server Name>
   ```

   For example: `RS -s .prv-serv1.provo.quills.quills-tree`

Once you have placed all the necessary servers in the SDI domain, use SDDIAG to check that each server has the cryptographic keys necessary to securely communicate with the other servers in the tree. To do this, complete the following steps:

1. Load SDIDIAG at the server console.

2. Authenticate as an Admin user in the tree and click OK.

3. Enter the following command to add a server:

   ```
   CHECK -v >> sys:system\sdinotes.txt -n <Container DN>
   ```

For example, to check the container **provo.quills** in **quills-tree**, you would type the following:

```
CHECK -v >> sys:system\sdinotes.txt -n provo.quills.
➥quills-tree
```

This operation will report any inconsistencies between the cryptographic keys on the various SDI domain servers. If any problems are noted, use the information in **SYS:SYSTEM\SDINOTES.TXT** to help you resolve them, and then continue with the configuration.

Enable Universal Password

Once all the pieces are in place, you are ready to enable universal password. To enable universal password, complete the following steps:

1. Launch iManager, open the NMAS Management link, and select Universal Password Configuration.

2. Specify the container for which you want to enable universal password, and click View.

3. Select the Enable radio button, and click Apply and OK.

Once enabled, the NetWare 6.5 Novell Client software will start using universal password automatically. When you reset a password, you will actually be resetting the universal password, which will transparently synchronize the traditional NetWare and Simple passwords for your users. They won't notice any difference in behavior. However, this transparent synchronization is fully operational only when running NetWare 6.5 with the latest Novell client software (version 4.9 or later for Windows 2000/XP clients and version 3.4 or later for Windows 95/98 clients). For more information on the specific capabilities of universal password when used in different combinations of NetWare, Novell Client, and various client services, see the NetWare 6.5 online documentation.

eDirectory Login Controls

In addition to the actual login process, eDirectory provides a variety of login controls designed to help secure the network. Those controls are found in the properties of each User object. The various types of restrictions offered by eDirectory include

► Password restrictions

► Login restrictions

► Time restrictions

► Address restrictions

► Intruder lockout

NOTE You will also see an Account Balance tab. This is a leftover from a server accounting feature that is no longer supported in NetWare 6.5.

You can manage the various login controls from iManager or ConsoleOne. Login controls can be set on individual User objects, or they can be defined at the container level, where they will be automatically applied to all users in that container. To get to the login restrictions pages available through eDirectory, complete the following steps:

1. Launch iManager and select the View Objects icon. Locate the object for which you want to set login controls.

2. Click the object and select Modify Object.

3. Select the Restrictions tab and you will see a subpage for each of the controls listed previously. Select the appropriate page.

4. Make your desired changes and click OK to save your changes.

Each of the login control pages is described in more detail in the following sections.

Password Restrictions

The Password Restrictions page allows you to set password characteristics for eDirectory users, as shown in Figure 6.2. By default, the only selected option is Allow User to Change Password. However, this will not provide any significant degree of security, so you will want to enable some of the other options.

▶ *Allow User to Change Password*: Checking this box permits the user to change the password associated with the User object.

▶ *Require a Password*: Checking this box forces the user to set an account password. It also enables all other password options. Associated with this option is a Minimum Password Length field, which can be used to require passwords of at least a given number of characters. The default is five, but the value can be set from 1 to 128 characters.

▶ *Force Periodic Password Changes*: This field allows you to require users to change their passwords regularly. Associated with this option is a Days Between Forced Changes field, which defines how often the password must be changed. The default is 40, but the value can be set between 1 and 365 days.

▶ *Date Password Expires*: With this option you can define specific password expiration. It also shows when the password will next expire. When the user resets a password, the system will automatically reset this date forward by the number of days specified in the days between forced changes field.

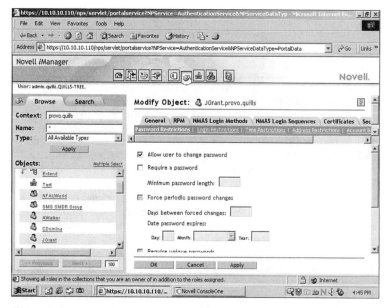

FIGURE 6.2
Password Restrictions page in iManager.

▶ *Require Unique Passwords*: Checking the Require Unique Passwords option allows eDirectory to track the last eight passwords used with this account and prevents the user from re-using these old passwords.

> **NOTE** eDirectory does not implement any pattern recognition algorithms that force users to change the password to a significantly different value. Users can change the value by a single character and eDirectory will not complain. Similarly, eDirectory does not have an option for requiring numeric or special characters as part of the password.

▶ *Limit Grace Logins*: This option limits the number of times a user is allowed to log in after his password has expired. Associated with it are two fields. The Grace Logins Allowed field allows the administrator to set how many grace logins are permitted. The default is six, but the value can be set between 1 and 200. The Remaining Grace Logins field tracks how many grace logins remain before the account is locked out. The administrator can also reset this value in order to give an expired account more time to reset the password, if necessary.

▶ *Set Password* (link): The Set Password link will open a Java utility to change the user's password. You must first supply the existing password, and then the new password.

Time Variables with ConsoleOne

Time values in ConsoleOne are interpreted as UTC time, or Greenwich Mean Time (GMT). This affects how you set any type of expiration parameter. For example, if you want a user's password to expire at a specific time, you need to take into account the time zone offset between your location and GMT. Mountain Standard Time (MST) is seven hours earlier than GMT, so if you want the password to expire at 1:00am in Utah you have to set the expiration time to 8:00am GMT (8:00 – 7:00 = 1:00).

It is possible to force ConsoleOne to use the local time rather than UTC by setting an environment variable on the workstation from which ConsoleOne is running. Consult the documentation for your particular workstation operating system to determine how this is done.

Because ConsoleOne is Java-based, and not a native Windows application, it does not recognize the Windows-based time zone information. In order to set system-level time zone information for Windows 95/98 or Windows NT/2000, add the TZ= environment variable to a login script or the AUTOEXEC.BAT file. For example, SET TZ=MST7MDT will instruct the system to use Mountain Standard Time instead of GMT when displaying time information. This information will be available to non-Windows applications such as ConsoleOne.

Login Restrictions

The Login Restrictions page allows you to control the capability of a user to log in to the network, as shown in Figure 6.3.

▶ *Account Disabled*: Checking this box disables the user account and prevents future login attempts. However, this will not affect a user who is currently logged in.

▶ *Account Has Expiration Date*: Checking this box allows you to set a date when the user account will be automatically disabled. This option might be used for contract employees or consultants who will be working for a predefined period of time.

▶ *Limit Concurrent Connections*: Check this box to define how many times the same account can be used to log in from different workstations simultaneously. If enabled, the default is 1, but any value between 1 and 32,000 can be selected.

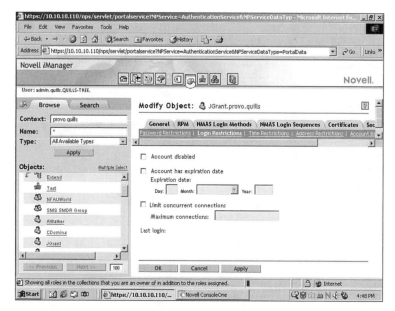

FIGURE 6.3
Login Restrictions page in iManager.

Time Restrictions

The Time Restrictions page enables you to limit the time(s) of day when a user can access the network, as shown in Figure 6.4. By default, there are no restrictions.

To set a time restriction, click the box for which you want the restriction to occur, and then click Update to reflect the change. To select a range of time, hold down the Shift key while moving the mouse over the time range. Each block is 30 minutes. When finished, make sure to select OK to save the new restrictions out to eDirectory. If a user is logged in when her lockout period is reached, she will be issued a five-minute warning, after which she will be automatically logged out.

NOTE One important caveat to time restrictions is that they are governed by the user's home time and not his current time. For example, if a user in New York, takes a trip to Los Angeles, and is going to dial in to his home network, the time in New York rather than the time in Los Angeles will determine the time restriction. A 6:00 p.m. EST time restriction would shut the user down at 3:00 p.m. PST. Although that might give your employee time to get in a round of golf, it might not be what you intended when configuring the time restriction in the first place.

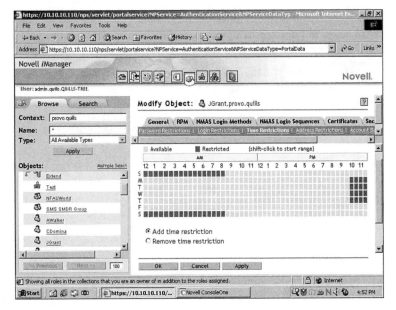

FIGURE 6.4
Time Restrictions page in iManager.

Address Restrictions

The Address Restrictions page can be used to tie a user account to a specific workstation, as shown in Figure 6.5, thereby forcing users to log in from that hardware location only.

In today's world of dynamic addressing and roaming users, this option is not as useful as it once might have been, but in very security-conscious environments, it can still be necessary. However, TCP/IP functionality is severely limited by the fact that the utility assumes a Class B subnet mask (255.255.0.0) for all IP addressing—not very practical in today's overloaded IP world.

Intruder Lockout

The Intruder Lockout page is useful only after a user account has been disabled. Intruder lockout refers to the disabling of a user account after a certain number of unsuccessful login attempts have been made. To re-enable a locked-out account, the administrator unchecks the Account Locked box on this page. The other three entries simply provide information about the status of the locked account.

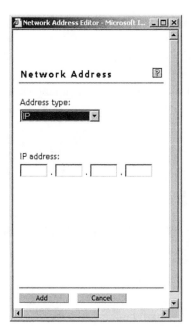

FIGURE 6.5
Address Restrictions page in iManager.

The actual intruder detection system is configured at the container level rather than at the user level. In order to configure your intruder detection environment, complete the following steps:

1. Launch iManager and select the View Objects icon. Locate the container for which you want to set intruder detection.

2. Click the object and select Modify Object.

3. Select the Intruder Detection link, as shown in Figure 6.6.

4. Make your desired changes and click OK.

   ▶ *Detect Intruders*: Check this box to enable the intruder detection system for this container. Associated with this check box are fields that allow you to set the number of incorrect login attempts before intruder lockout is activated—the default is 7—and the interval within which the unsuccessful attempts must occur—the default is 30 minutes.

   ▶ *Lock Account After Detection*: Check this box to enable the account lockout feature. Associated with this check box are fields that allow you to specify the time period for which the account will remain locked—the default is 15 minutes. At the end of this period, the account will be reactivated automatically.

Once configured, intruder lockout makes it much more difficult for would-be hackers to perform dictionary or other brute force attacks against one of your network accounts.

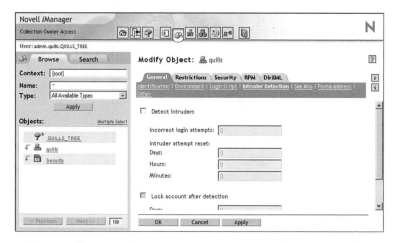

FIGURE 6.6
Enabling intruder detection features in iManager.

Authorization

Now that users have authenticated to the network, you must provide them with access to all the resources they need. This also entails preventing them from accessing resources that they do not need. It wouldn't do to have sensitive documents describing future products open to and accessible to just anyone. The reality of the corporate world is that some resources must be maintained as "need to know."

Although determining exactly who needs access to what is a decision beyond most network administrators, Novell eDirectory provides powerful tools for implementing those decisions. This section discusses eDirectory access control concepts and how they work together to provide proper access to objects in the eDirectory tree.

Access Control Lists

Access control lists (ACLs)are stored in each eDirectory object to identify those other objects that have been granted some sort of control over it. Each object in an eDirectory tree maintains two types of access rights. The first set of rights is entry rights. Entry rights define how an object can be manipulated by other directory entities, as described in Table 6.1.

TABLE 6.1 Valid Entry Rights in eDirectory

ENTRY RIGHT	DESCRIPTION
Browse	Allows a trustee to discover and view the object in the eDirectory tree.
Create	This right applies only to container objects. It allows the trustee to create new objects within the container.
Delete	Allows a trustee to delete the object.
Rename	Allows a trustee to rename the object.
Supervisor	Allows a trustee full access to the object and its attributes.

The second set of rights is property rights. Property rights define how the attributes associated with an object can be manipulated. eDirectory property rights are described in Table 6.2.

TABLE 6.2 Valid Property Rights in eDirectory

PROPERTY RIGHT	DESCRIPTION
Compare	Allows a trustee to compare, or see if an attribute contains a given value.
Read	Allows a trustee to read an attribute value. This right confers the Compare right.
Write	Allows a trustee to add, delete, or modify an attribute value. This right confers the add or delete Self right to the attribute.
Self	Allows a trustee to add or delete its name as an attribute value (if applicable).
Supervisor	Assigns a trustee all attribute rights.

When entry and/or property rights are conferred to an eDirectory entity, it becomes a trustee of the conferring object. The list of trustees, and the specific object and property rights they have been granted, are maintained in an access control list associated with each eDirectory object. Figure 6.7 shows a representative ACL as seen from iManager.

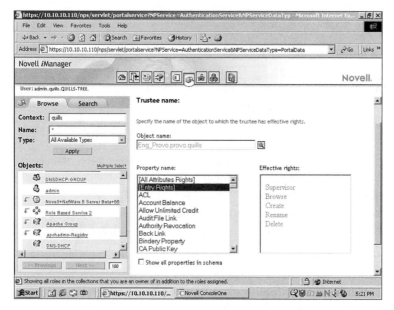

FIGURE 6.7
eDirectory access control list in iManager.

As shown in Figure 6.7, the ACL maintains three pieces of information about a trustee assignment: object name, property name, and effective rights.

▶ *Object Name*: This field identifies the object that is being granted rights. It can also contain one of the special entry references outlined in Table 6.3.

▶ *Property Name*: This field specifies the type of right that is being granted. It also specifies how that right is to be applied. Rights can be assigned to a specific property, to all properties, or to the object itself.

▶ *Effective Rights*: This field lists the rights that have been granted for a given property. In the eDirectory schema, most object classes specify a default access template that is used to create an ACL attribute for a new object. This default template provides basic access control for the new entry, allowing it to function in the directory. Different object classes have different default ACL templates to reflect their different needs. For example, the default ACL template for the User object grants the Write right to its own login script attribute. This allows users to change their personal login scripts as necessary.

TABLE 6.3   Special Trustee References in eDirectory

REFERENCE	DESCRIPTION
Inherited rights filter	eDirectory uses this reference to mask or filter privileges rather than granting rights.
[Public]	eDirectory uses this reference to grant rights to all objects in the eDirectory tree, including both authenticated and non-authenticated objects.
[Root]	eDirectory uses this reference to grant rights to all authenticated entries.
Creator	eDirectory uses this reference to grant all rights to the client that created the object.
Self	eDirectory uses this reference to allow objects to add or delete themselves as values of attributes and to grant the object rights to its own attributes.

Inheritance

Inheritance is one of the most powerful—and sometimes frustrating—concepts in eDirectory security planning. It is similar to the security equivalence concepts (discussed previously) in that it deals with the determination of effective rights at any given point in the eDirectory tree. On the one hand, inheritance promises to save untold amounts of work by automating the assignment of rights in the eDirectory tree. On the other hand, because of the way that inheritance works, things sometimes don't happen exactly as you might have planned.

Novell has been using inheritance for a long time to apply rights to the NetWare file system. If a user was granted rights at a specific directory, those rights implicitly applied to everything from that point down in the directory structure—until explicitly removed. The same principle applies to eDirectory: If a user is granted rights at a given container object, those rights are implicitly applied to each object in the tree from that point downward—until explicitly removed.

eDirectory implements inheritance through a dynamic model. This means that rights are calculated in real-time whenever an eDirectory object attempts to perform any directory operation. To do this, eDirectory starts at [Root] and walks the tree down to the object, building a set of effective rights for that object along the way. If the effective rights for that object permit the requested operation, it is allowed to continue. If not, the operation is denied.

At first, it might seem very inefficient to traverse the eDirectory tree from [Root] each time effective rights need to be calculated—and it would be—except that eDirectory resolves this inefficiency through the use of external references.

External references exist to protect database integrity by storing information about partitions that do have local replicas. In other words, the Master replica of a child partition will maintain an external reference to [Root]. In order to determine the effective rights for a user, eDirectory need only consult the locally stored external references instead of potentially crossing the entire network to find the information it needs. This reduces network traffic and increases the speed of eDirectory tremendously. For more information on external references, see Chapter 5, "Novell eDirectory Management."

Inherited Rights Filters

Inherited Rights Filters (IRFs) are used to restrict inheritance in a directory tree. IRF use looks pretty straightforward on the surface, but it can cause all kinds of interesting situations to arise. More calls have been logged to Novell's Technical Support groups because administrators got carried away with controlling every single aspect of eDirectory security instead of just trusting the environment to handle things properly.

WARNING Don't implement IRFs unless you are absolutely sure you understand the consequences of doing so.

That said, it is sometimes desirable to limit the flow of rights through the eDirectory tree—either to segment administration or to isolate portions of the tree. If this becomes necessary, IRFs are the way to go. Just remember that less is usually more in this case. If you find yourself creating a large number of IRFs, it might be a sign of some fundamental eDirectory design issues. See Chapter 5 for more information on eDirectory tree design.

The first thing to recognize about IRFs is that they can filter supervisory rights in eDirectory, unlike supervisory rights in the NetWare file system. This makes it possible to limit the control of Admin users higher up in the tree, but it also threatens to destroy your capability to administer the directory tree properly.

To configure an IRF, complete the following steps:

1. Launch iManager and select the View Objects icon. Locate the container or object for which you want to set an IRF.

2. Click the object and select Modify Inherited Rights Filter.

3. Click Add Property to create an IRF.

4. Select the property for which you want to define an IRF and click OK. You can create an IRF for entry rights, for all properties, or for specific properties.

5. Uncheck those rights that you want to be blocked by the IRF and select OK to save your changes. The IRF properties page is shown in Figure 6.8.

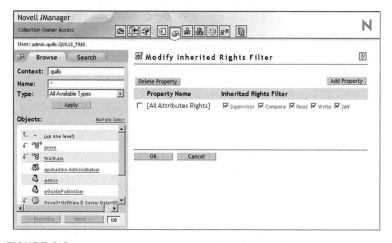

FIGURE 6.8
Modifying IRF properties in iManager.

WARNING It is very important that you remember the dynamic nature of rights calculation in eDirectory. For example, if you are going to create a container administrator and filter administrative rights to that container from above, create the new Admin object first. If you set the IRF first, you will find yourself locked out—unable to define a user with administrative control for the container. An IRF is a two-edged sword.

Explicit Rights

Explicit rights are specifically assigned to an object at some point in the eDirectory tree. When one object is given specific rights to another, it is called a *trustee*. To assign explicit rights, complete the following steps:

1. Launch iManager and select the View Objects icon. Locate the container or object for which you want to add a trustee.

2. Click the object and select Modify Trustees.

3. Click Add Trustee. Browse to the eDirectory object to which you want to assign trustee rights and click OK. You can select multiple objects if desired.

4. Click the Assigned Rights link next to each object, specify the appropriate rights for this trustee, and then click Done (see Figure 6.9).

   ▶ *Property and Rights*: Specify the rights you want to grant for this trustee. If you want to assign specific property rights only, click Add Property to select specific properties from a list. You can assign entry rights, all property (attribute) rights, specific property rights, or any combination of the three.

   ▶ *Inheritable*: If you are assigning a trustee to a Container object, you can check the Inheritable box if you want those rights to flow down to other objects within the container.

Assigning explicit rights is a very straightforward process, but as with IRFs, there are some caveats. For example, unlike security equivalence, explicit assignments are not cumulative. An explicit assignment preempts the implicit rights that a user might have had through inheritance. Making explicit rights assignments can easily eliminate rights that existed previously. Make sure you understand what is being provided through inheritance and security equivalence, and how your explicit assignment will affect those existing rights, before making manual changes to trustee rights.

Security Equivalence

Security equivalence in eDirectory is used to assign one object identical eDirectory rights to those already assigned to another object. eDirectory offers explicit and implicit security equivalence. Under the rules of inheritance described previously, security equivalence will continue to flow down from the point it is granted. In other words, if JHarris in Provo.Quills is granted equivalence to the Admin object, those rights will be granted at [Root] just like they are for Admin. Equivalence provides a method to grant users in one area of the eDirectory tree rights to objects in another.

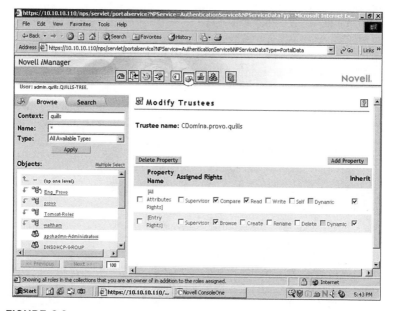

FIGURE 6.9
Assigning explicit trustee rights in iManager.

TIP Using security equivalence is not an efficient way to manage access. If you find yourself using lots of security equivalences, it is a strong indication of a poor eDirectory tree design. See Chapter 5 for more information on eDirectory design.

Implicit security equivalence occurs automatically when an object is inserted into the eDirectory tree. Every eDirectory object has security equivalence with the following objects:

▶ The [Root] object

▶ The [Public] trustee

▶ Each container between it and [Root]

Security equivalence to [Root] and [Public] provides basic access to eDirectory so that the new object can perform basic network tasks, such as navigating the directory, locating servers, and initiating an authentication request. All specific rights are derived from the inheritance from the container object(s) within which the object exists.

Explicit security equivalence is identical to implicit security equivalence, except the network administrator has to assign the equivalence manually. Use explicit security equivalence whenever one user needs identical explicit rights as another but cannot get those rights through normal inheritance or implicit security equivalence. To assign explicit security equivalence, complete the following steps:

1. Launch iManager and select the View Objects icon. Locate the container or object to which you want to grant security equivalence.

2. Click the object and select Modify Object.

3. Select the Security tab and click Security Equal To.

4. Specify the object to which this object will be security-equivalent and click OK.

5. Click OK to save the security equivalence.

Explicit security equivalence is most often used with Group objects, which were discussed earlier in this chapter. Each member of an eDirectory group is assigned as security equal to the Group object. In this way each user receives the rights associated with that group. Contrary to rights assignment, security equivalence is cumulative. This means that an object's implicit and explicit security equivalence will be added together in order to determine its effective rights.

The Danger of Explicit Security Equivalence

Not all uses of explicit security equivalence are appropriate. For example, some administrators have used security equivalence to make their User object equivalent to the Admin object. This gives them all rights associated with the Admin object. The danger in this is that when you derive your rights from another object, those rights are never specifically recorded in your object. For example, if JHarris.Provo.Quills is security equal to Admin.Quills, whenever JHarris attempts to perform some directory operation, eDirectory will look at the effective rights of Admin. If Admin has sufficient rights to perform the operation, JHarris, as a security equal, is granted permission as well.

Can you see the danger? Sometime down the road, JHarris is happily administering eDirectory. Why keep the Admin object around when it is never used? Except that the instant the object is deleted, JHarris loses all his administrative rights because they are derived from the Admin object and not explicitly assigned.

Even worse, unless some other object has been explicitly granted supervisory rights to the eDirectory tree, deleting the Admin object might delete the ability to administer eDirectory.

Explicit security equivalence can be a powerful tool, but you can end up laying a trap for yourself, or others who might come after you. In most cases, the explicit security equivalence should be restricted to use with Group objects. For applying specific rights to a single object, it is often best to assign those rights explicitly, rather than relying on another object to supply them.

Effective Rights

The whole point of all the preceding rights controls is to ensure that a given user, or other eDirectory object, has the appropriate rights on the network to do what's needed. Effective rights are the cumulative result of all the different rights tools working together. In the end, there are eight ways that one object can get rights to another:

▶ Object 1 is a trustee of Object 2. Therefore, Object 1 has explicit rights to Object 2.

▶ A parent container of Object 1 is a trustee of Object 2. Therefore, Object 1 has rights to Object 2 due to implicit security equivalence.

▶ Object 1 has explicit security equivalence to Object 3, which is a trustee of Object 2. Therefore, Object 1 has trustee rights to Object 2, which are equivalent to Object 3.

▶ [Public] is a trustee of Object 2. Therefore, Object 1 has rights to Object 2 through implicit security equivalence to [Public].

▶ [Public] is a trustee of a parent container of Object 2, and those rights flow down the tree due to inheritance. Therefore, Object 1 has rights to Object 2 through the combination of implicit security equivalence and inheritance.

▶ Object 1 is a trustee of one of Object 2's parent containers, and those rights flow down the tree to include Object 2 due to inheritance.

▶ A parent container of Object 1 is a trustee of a parent container of Object 2. Therefore, Object 1 has rights to Object 2 through a combination of explicit rights, implicit security equivalence, and inheritance.

▶ Object 1 is security equivalent to Object 3, which is a trustee of a parent container of Object 2. Therefore, Object 1 has rights to Object 2 through the combination of explicit security equivalence and inheritance.

NOTE Inherited rights filters cannot affect the effective rights in the first four cases because no inheritance is being used. However, IRFs can modify or eliminate the effective rights provided in last four cases because they depend on inheritance.

With eight ways to derive effective rights between two objects, it's easy to see how rights issues can get complicated very quickly. In most cases, the best solution is to let inheritance do the work of assigning rights wherever possible. The default combination of implicit security equivalence and dynamic inheritance is suitable for 90% of the directory installations out there.

Assign rights through containers and let them flow downward. As your directory tree evolves over time, situations can arise that cannot be satisfied by inheritance alone. If this happens, use groups, explicit assignments, and IRFs sparingly to address these exceptions.

When using IRFs, be careful that a single object doesn't become a point of failure. Consider what might happen if a User object is corrupted, or if that user becomes malicious. Always have a second or third option for accessing a branch of the tree that is restricted. Just as the military establishes a chain of command so that the mission can continue if one person is lost, eDirectory administrators have to make sure that proper access can continue—or at least be repaired—if the default method of access is lost.

TIP One way of doing this is to create a secondary User object with full administrative rights, and then add a Browse IRF to that object. This effectively hides the secondary Admin from view, but provides emergency administrative access should it be necessary.

Role-Based Administration

One exciting instance of authorization is the capability to assign specific administrative roles to users in the eDirectory tree. Although this was possible in a limited fashion with the use of organizational roles, iManager offers you a previously impossible level of control and ease-of-use. You can now define most any network activity as a *role*, and assign the eDirectory rights necessary to perform that activity to a user or group of users. For more information on configuring role-based administration with iManager, see Chapter 3.

Data Security

The whole point of eDirectory-based security concepts such as authentication and authorization is to provide a secure environment within which data can be used and protected. The mantra of the 21st century is "information is power," and you want to be sure you aren't sharing your competitive advantage with your competitors.

NetWare 6.5 leverages eDirectory to extend the idea of authorization to the server file system. The NetWare file system is manageable through the Server, Volume, Folder, and File objects in eDirectory. In this way, you can manage file access through the same tools used to manage the rest of your network.

You can implement two types of security tools in the file system, either together or separately, to protect your files:

▶ *Trustee rights*: These are equivalent to entry rights for eDirectory objects. Trustee rights define the possible actions that can be taken with Volume, Folder, and File objects, and who or what can perform those actions.

▶ *Attributes*: Unlike trustee rights, which define acceptable behavior for different users and groups, attributes define the characteristics of individual Volume, Folder, or File objects. Because attributes trump trustee rights, they control the activities of all users, regardless of which trustee rights are assigned.

File System Trustee Rights

File system trustee rights allow users and groups to work with files and directories in specific ways. Each right determines whether a user can do things such as see, read, change, rename, or delete the file or directory. File system rights obey inheritance rules just like directory rights. When rights are assigned to a file, they define a user's allowable actions for that file only. When rights are assigned to a directory, they affect a user's allowable actions on not only the directory itself but also everything stored within that directory.

Although file system rights are similar in nature to the eDirectory rights for objects and properties (described earlier in this chapter), they are not the same thing. File system rights are separate from eDirectory rights. They affect only how users work with files and directories. eDirectory rights affect how users work with other eDirectory objects.

There are eight file system trustee rights. You can assign any combination of those file system rights to a user or group, depending on how you want that user or group to work.

Table 6.4 describes the available file system rights and how they affect directory and file access.

TABLE 6.4 File System Rights

FILE SYSTEM RIGHT	ABBREVIATION	DESCRIPTION
Read	R	Directory: Allows the trustee to open and read files in the directory. File: Allows the trustee to open and read the file.
Write	W	Directory: Allows the trustee to open and write to (change) files in the directory. File: Allows the trustee to open and write to the file.
Create	C	Directory: Allows the trustee to create subdirectories and files in the directory. File: Allows the trustee to salvage the file if it was deleted.
Erase	E	Directory: Allows the trustee to delete the directory and its files and subdirectories. File: Allows the trustee to delete the file.
Modify	M	Directory: Allows the trustee to change the name, directory attributes, and file attributes of the directory and its files and subdirectories. File: Allows the trustee to change the file's name or file attributes.

FILE SYSTEM RIGHT	ABBREVIATION	DESCRIPTION
File Scan	F	Directory: Allows the trustee to see the names of the files and subdirectories within the directory. File: Allows the trustee to see the name of the file.
Access Control	A	Directory: Allows the trustee to change the directory's IRF and trustee assignments. File: Allows the trustee to change the file's IRF and trustee assignments.
Supervisor	S	Directory: Grants the trustee all rights to the directory, its files, and its subdirectories. It cannot be blocked by an IRF. File: Grants the trustee all rights to the file. It cannot be blocked by an IRF. Note that an explicit Supervisor right can be added or removed only at the entry point to the file system (where you go from directory object to file system object).

Inheriting File System Rights

Just like eDirectory rights, file system rights can be inherited. This means that if you have file system rights to a parent directory, you can also inherit those rights and exercise them in any file and subdirectory within that directory. Inheritance keeps you from having to grant users file system rights at every level of the file system.

You can block inheritance by removing the right from the IRF of a file or subdirectory. As with directory objects, every directory and file has an inherited rights filter, specifying which file system rights can be inherited from a parent directory. By default, file and directory IRFs allow all rights to be inherited.

Inheritance can also be blocked by granting a new set of trustee rights to a subdirectory or file within the parent directory. As with the eDirectory rights, inherited and explicit file system rights are not cumulative. Explicit assignments replace the inherited rights from a parent directory.

File System Security Equivalence

Security equivalence for file system rights works the same way as security equivalence for eDirectory rights (explained earlier in this chapter). You can assign one user to have the same eDirectory rights and file system rights as another user by using the Security Equal To Me tab in an object's properties page.

NOTE Remember: You are still subject to the shortcomings of security equivalence as described previously.

File System Effective Rights

Just as with eDirectory rights, determining which file system rights a user can actually exercise in a file or directory can be confusing at first. A user's *effective file system rights* are the file system rights that the user can ultimately execute in a given directory or file. The user's effective rights to a directory or file are determined in one of two ways:

▶ A users' inherited rights from a parent directory, minus any rights blocked by the subdirectory's (or file's) IRF

▶ The sum of all rights granted to the user for that directory or file through direct trustee assignment and security equivalences to other users

Working with File System Trustee Rights

iManager can't yet take you into the NetWare file system. You can assign rights at the volume level, but not at the directory or file level. Use ConsoleOne to work with file system rights. To see or change a user's trustee assignments, complete the following steps:

1. Launch ConsoleOne and browse to the point in the file system, volume, folder, or file with which you want to work.

2. Right-click the folder/file and select Properties. Select the Trustees tab.

3. Click Effective Rights. Browse to the User object for which you want to view file system rights and click OK.

4. The user's effective rights will be listed in black type, as shown in Figure 6.10.

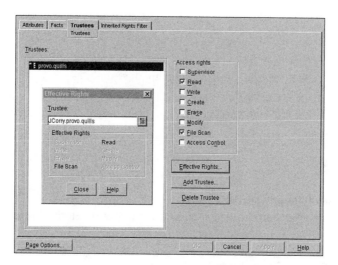

FIGURE 6.10
Working with file system trustee rights in ConsoleOne.

You can make a user a trustee of a File System object by doing the following:

1. From the Trustees page, click Add Trustee. Browse to the desired User object and click OK.

2. Check those explicit file system rights that you want to grant the user and click OK.

If the user is already a trustee, simply highlight the appropriate User object in the Trustees window and perform step 2.

Changes to explicit security equivalence are done using the same process described previously in the "Authorization" section of this chapter.

File and Directory Attributes

Another important NetWare security tool for securing files and directories is attributes. *Attributes* are properties of files and directories that control what can happen to those files or directories. Attributes, which are also called *flags*, are different from trustee rights in several ways:

▶ Attributes are assigned directly to files and directories, whereas rights are assigned to users.

▶ Attributes override rights. In other words, if a directory has the Delete Inhibit attribute, you can't delete the directory even if you've been granted the erase right.

▶ Likewise, attributes don't grant rights. Just because a file has the read-write attribute doesn't mean you can write to it if you don't have the Write right.

▶ Attributes affect all users, including the Admin user.

▶ Attributes affect some aspects of the file that rights do not, such as determining whether the files in a directory can be purged immediately upon deletion.

Knowing these distinctions between file attributes and trustee rights will help you better understand the behavior of the NetWare file system.

File and Directory Attribute Types

There are eight attributes that apply to either files or directories. There are an additional six that apply only to files. These attributes are listed in Table 6.5.

TABLE 6.5   File and Directory Attributes

ATTRIBUTE	FILE	DIRECTORY	DESCRIPTION
Archive needed	X		Indicates that the file has been changed since the last time it was backed up.
Execute- only	X		Prevents an executable file from being copied, modified, or deleted. Use with caution! Once assigned, it cannot be removed, so assign it only if you have a backup copy of the file. You may prefer to assign the Read-only attribute instead of the Execute-only attribute.
Read-only	X		Allows the file to be opened and read, but not modified. All NetWare files in SYS:SYSTEM, SYS:PUBLIC, and SYS:LOGIN are read-only. Assigning the Read-only attribute automatically assigns delete inhibit and rename inhibit.

ATTRIBUTE	FILE	DIRECTORY	DESCRIPTION
Sharable	X		Allows the file to be used by more than one user simultaneously. Useful for utilities, commands, applications, and some database files. All NetWare files in SYS:SYSTEM, SYS:PUBLIC, and SYS:LOGIN are shareable. Most data and work files should not be shareable, so that users' changes do not conflict.
Hidden	X	X	Hides the file or directory so it isn't listed by the DOS DIR command or in the Windows File Manager and can't be copied or deleted.
System	X	X	Indicates a system directory that might contain system files (such as DOS files). Prevents users from seeing, copying, or deleting the directory. (However, does not assign the System attribute to the files in the directory.)
Transactional	X		When used on database files, allows NetWare's Transaction Tracking System (TTS) to protect the files from being corrupted if the transaction is interrupted.
Purge immediate	X	X	Purges the file or directory immediately upon deletion. Purged files can't be salvaged.
Delete inhibit	X	X	Prevents users from deleting the file or directory.
Rename inhibit	X	X	Prevents users from renaming the file or directory.

TABLE 6.5   Continued

ATTRIBUTE	FILE	DIRECTORY	DESCRIPTION
Don't migrate	X	X	Prevents a file or directory from being migrated to another storage device.
Immediate compress	X	X	Compresses the file or directory immediately.
Don't compress	X	X	Prevents the file or directory from being compressed.
Don't suballocate	X		Prevents a file from being suballocated. Use on files, such as some database files, that need to be enlarged or appended to frequently. (See Chapter 8 for information on block suballocation.)

Assigning File and Directory Attributes

To assign attributes to a file or directory, complete the following steps:

1. Launch ConsoleOne and browse to the folder or file with which you want to work.

2. Right-click the object and select Properties.

3. Select the Attributes tab, which is shown in Figure 6.11. Check the desired attributes and select OK to accept your changes.

There are three File Status boxes on the Attributes page. These are informational and indicate the following:

▶ *File Compressed*: Indicates whether the selected file or folder is stored in a compressed format on the NetWare volume.

▶ *Can't Compress*: Indicates that selected file compression would not achieve any significant space savings on this file.

▶ *File Migrated*: Indicates that the selected file has been moved to a secondary storage system, such as tape.

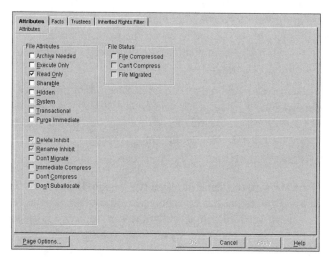

FIGURE 6.11
Working with the file and folder attributes in ConsoleOne.

Login Scripts

One other point of interaction between directory and file system is the login script. The eDirectory login script is a batch file that outlines basic operations that should be performed every time the user logs in to the network. Login script operations can include environment variables, drive mappings, program execution, and message display. Details of login script operation and configuration are available in Appendix B.

NCP Packet Signature

NCP Packet Signature is a feature designed to prevent a would-be hacker from spoofing a network connection. Spoofing involves hijacking a connection by forging network packets that appear to be from a legitimate user connection. This feature requires workstations and servers to automatically "sign" each NCP packet with a signature and to change the signature for every packet.

Packet Signature is an optional security feature and can slow down network performance on busy networks. Because spoofing requires access to a physical network connection, you might prefer not to use packet signatures if your network is in a relatively trusted environment, or if the threat of intruders stealing sensitive information is low.

There are four levels of NCP Packet Signature, which must be set on both workstations and servers. If the levels on the workstation and server don't form an allowable combination, the two computers will not be able to communicate with each other.

To set the signature level on a server, launch NoRM and select Set Parameters in the left navigation frame. Select NCP in the right frame. Look for NCP Packet Signature Option. You can also set the packet signature level from the server console prompt by typing:

```
SET NCP PACKET SIGNATURE OPTION=number
```

Replace *number* with the signature level (0 through 3) you want the server to use. After the server has been booted, you can execute the SET command to increase the signature level. If you want to decrease the level, however, you have to reboot the server. Table 6.6 shows the NCP Packet Signature levels.

TABLE 6.6   Server Levels for NCP Packet Signature

LEVEL	DESCRIPTION
0	Does not sign packets
1	Signs packets only if so requested by other entity
2	Prefers to sign packets, but will still communicate with an entity that cannot sign
3	Both entities must sign packets

To set the signature level on a Windows workstation, complete the following steps:

1. Right-click the red N in the system tray and select Novell Client Properties.

2. Select the Advanced Settings tab and browse to Signature Level.

3. Select the appropriate level, 0–3, and click OK to save your changes.

Figure 6.12 shows how the signature levels on servers and workstations combine to either allow unsigned packets, force signed packets, or deny login.

Workstation Level

		0	1	2	3
	0	Unsigned	Unsigned	Unsigned	Login Denied
Server Level	1	Unsigned	Unsigned	Signed	Signed
	2	Unsigned	Signed	Signed	Signed
	3	Login Denied	Signed	Signed	Signed

FIGURE 6.12
Packet signature interactions between server and client.

Novell Cryptographic Services

Starting with NetWare 5, Novell has provided a comprehensive security infrastructure. It provides the foundation for delivering advanced security solutions with NetWare and eDirectory. The Novell International Cryptographic Infrastructure (NICI) provides all cryptography-related services to eDirectory and its related services. Novell Certificate Server provides a public key infrastructure that integrates with today's standards-based security systems.

NICI and Certificate Server work largely behind the scenes to provide critical services to your network. Hopefully, you won't have to do much with them directly, but it is good to know a little about them in order to better understand how your network operates.

NICI

NICI is a modular security framework that is responsible for all cryptographic services in the NetWare and eDirectory environments. The advantage of using NICI as a security foundation is that it eliminates the need to build cryptographic functionality into each application. Because of varied export laws across countries, applications would have to be written in several versions if they were to be used worldwide.

NICI consolidates all cryptographic functionality into eDirectory. Applications leverage the existing cryptographic infrastructure and do not have to worry about multiple versions. It also means that all security management can take place from eDirectory management tools. The modular nature of NICI allows for the support of varied cryptographic export laws through the policy manager in NICI. NICI prevents the insertion and use of cryptographic modules that would violate export laws. Because of this, NICI has received export approval from the United States. All applications that leverage NICI for their cryptographic functions will only need to pass a cursory export review, rather than having to endure the whole process.

Certificate Server

Certificate Server is a set of services that implements a Public Key Infrastructure (PKI) to create key public key-pairs, generate certificates, import externally generated certificates, and revoke expired or invalid certificates.

PKI is also referred to as *asymmetric encryption*. Asymmetric encryption algorithms were developed in the 1970s as a way to avoid having to transmit cryptographic keys to those who needed to be able to decrypt secure messages. Asymmetric encryption utilizes a mathematically related key-pair instead of a single key in order to provide the encryption and decryption capabilities. When a message is encrypted using an asymmetric key, it can only be decrypted using the other half of the key-pair.

In a PKI, each person is assigned a key-pair and one of those keys is published as the public key (see Figure 6.13). The other is carefully guarded as the private key. If someone wants to send you a secure message, he encrypts it using your public key and sends it out. The sender knows the only person who can decrypt that message is the person with the other half of the key-pair—you!

Switching to the receiving end of that secure message (see Figure 6.14), you decrypt the message using your private key and find out that it is a note from the sender—except that you can't be sure he was actually the person that authored it. What if someone is attempting to impersonate the sender by sending you a forged message? Well, PKI also solves this problem by providing the capability to electronically "sign" a message.

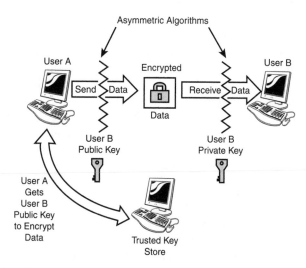

FIGURE 6.13
Asymmetric encryption in action.

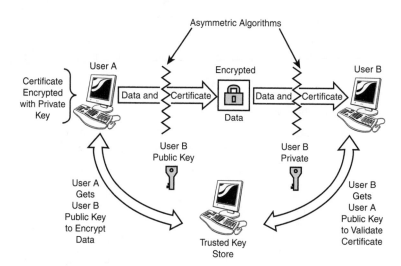

FIGURE 6.14
Digital certificates in action.

The next hurdle for PKI is creating repositories for all the public keys that are in use. Public keys are stored, together with vital statistics about the owner, in a standard certificate format known as X.509. These certificates can then be stored in large databases known as Certificate Authorities (CA). Certificate Server provides organizations the capability to use eDirectory as a CA. Cryptographic keys and certificates can be created and/or managed by eDirectory. Certificate Server can also interact with external entities such as VeriSign or Entrust through the use of standard communication protocols and certificate formats. Certificate Server supports the dominant standards in the security space. You can make eDirectory the hub for all your security needs from secure authentication and resource access, to secure communications with external parties and non-repudiation of business-critical communications.

Creating Server Certificates

When NetWare 6.5 is installed, all the necessary security objects are created automatically, including an organizational certificate authority and the necessary key-pairs to support cryptographic activities. During the installation, two server certificates are created: one for DNS and one for IP. These certificates are used to create secure SSL connections with client workstations. You can also create other server certificates, as needed, to support additional secure services on your NetWare 6.5 servers. To create a server certificate, complete the following steps:

1. Make sure you are logged in to the eDirectory tree as an administrator with supervisory rights to the container in which the server resides.

2. Launch iManager and open the Novell Certificate Server link in the left navigation frame.

3. Select Create Server Certificate. After the Server Certificate Wizard opens, specify the requested information and click Next.

   ▶ *Server*: Specify the server that will own the certificate that is being created.

   ▶ *Certificate Nickname*: Specify the name of your server certificate. This name will be combined with the server name to create a unique name for the Server Certificate object.

   ▶ *Creation Method*: Select the method for creating the certificate. Standard uses typical certificate parameters, whereas Custom lets you define each option manually. Import lets you specify a PKCS#12 file from which to get the necessary data.

Follow the prompts from there to complete the installation. If you select Custom, be prepared to supply the following information:

- ▶ CA that will sign the certificate (default: your organizational CA)
- ▶ Key size (default: 2048 bits)
- ▶ Key type (default: SSL)
- ▶ Algorithm for creating the certificate (default: SHA-1)
- ▶ How long the certificate will remain valid (default: 2 years)
- ▶ Certificate root (default: your organizational certificate)

Creating User Certificates

In order to make use of a PKI, users must have key-pairs and certificates of their own. Complete the following steps to create a user certificate:

1. Make sure you are logged in to the eDirectory tree as a user with supervisory rights to the User objects as well as rights to read objects in the security container.

2. Launch iManager and open the Novell Certificate Server Management link in the left navigation frame.

3. Select Create User Certificate. After the User Certificate Wizard opens, specify the user object(s) for which you want to create a digital certificate and click Next.

4. Specify the requested information and click Next.

   - ▶ *Server*: Specify the server that will own the certificate that is being created.

   - ▶ *Certificate nickname*: Specify the name of the user certificate. This name will be combined with the User object name to create a unique Certificate object name.

   - ▶ *Creation method*: Select the method for creating the certificate. Standard uses typical certificate parameters, whereas Custom lets you define each option manually.

Follow the prompts from there to create the user certificate(s). If you selected Custom, be prepared to provide the same type of information as previously specified for the server certificate.

Audit

With the release of Novell Advanced Audit Services (NAAS) in NetWare 6, Novell has been making a move toward providing an effective, eDirectory-based audit solution for NetWare environments. However, the release of NetWare 6.5 indicates that the answer isn't here yet. So, to give you the audit tools you need without any further delay, Novell has included a special NetWare 6.5 version of LT Auditor+ from Blue Lance, Inc. (www.bluelance.com). Blue Lance has long been one of Novell's corporate partners, and is a leader in network audit software.

This version of LT Auditor+ was developed exclusively for Novell, but is not as robust as the Enterprise Edition of LT Auditor+. However, it will get you down the auditing road enough that you can better decide how you want to move forward.

LT Auditor+ for NetWare is a server-centric version of the software that offers reporting of audit events on a per-server basis, but lacks the capability to consolidate audit information from across the network. Each NetWare 6.5 server with the LT Auditor+ agent installed reports auditable events to a management console where they can be logged and tracked.

For more information on NAAS and LT Auditor+ for NetWare, see the NetWare 6.5 online documentation.

CHAPTER 7

NetWare Printing Services

Instant Access

Installing and Configuring iPrint

▶ Install iPrint as part of the server installation, or install it after the fact through iManager.

▶ Configure the Broker, Print Manager, and Printer objects through iManager.

▶ After the Broker and Print Manager are created, load BROKER.NLM and NDPSM.NLM on your NetWare 6.5 server to enable NetWare print services.

▶ Use the Manage Printers page in iManager to configure printer objects.

▶ Use the RPM Configuration page in iManager to configure automatic printer support for workstations.

Working with iPrint

▶ IPPSRVR.NLM will be loaded automatically on the NetWare server that hosts the Print Manager for that printer.

▶ The iPrint client is required to access and manage iPrint printers. Install the client by going to the iPrint home page on your NetWare 6.5 server at `http://<server_IP_address or DNS_name>:631/ipp`.

Defining Print Options

▶ To tell the printer how to print a job (the paper form to use, format, and so on), open iManager >> Manage Printer. Specify the printer and select the Configurations page to change printer configuration.

Printing Jobs

▶ To print files from within an application, simply follow the application's normal printing procedures (making sure the application is configured to print to a network printer).

▶ To cancel or move a print job, open iManager >> Manage Printer. Specify the printer and select the Printer Control >> Jobs page.

Introduction to NetWare Printing

Along with file sharing, printer sharing was one of the original value propositions of NetWare back in the early 1980s. NetWare 6.5 continues to deliver a powerful printing solution that allows users to print to any network printer to which they have been given rights—even if that printer is on the other side of the world! NetWare 6.5 uses iPrint as its default print environment. iPrint leverages the powerful foundation of Novell Distributed Print Services (NDPS), but puts a Web face to printing and removes the dependence on the Novell client for print services. With iPrint, mobile employees, business partners, and even customers can access your printers through existing Internet connections. iPrint uses the Internet Printing Protocol (IPP), an industry standard, to make it possible to seamlessly print over the Internet, thus making location-based printing a reality.

The benefits of IPP include the following:

▶ Enjoys broad vendor support

▶ Works over local networks as well as the Internet

▶ Provides encrypted print services via SSL or TLS

▶ Provides accessibility to print services from any platform (Windows, Macintosh, Linux, Unix, and so on)

However, because iPrint is implemented on the foundation of NDPS, you get all the advantages of robust network printing services coupled with the interoperability and ease-of-use of an Internet standard. So, through the combination of IPP and NDPS, you get the following capabilities:

▶ Global access to printers managed through eDirectory

▶ Web-based printer location tool and driver installation

▶ Capability to print from anywhere to anywhere

▶ Web-based user controls and printer status

▶ Printers don't have to be IPP-aware to function with iPrint

Practically, this means that once your iPrint environment is configured, you can enjoy powerful printing options suitable for the Web-based business world, such as:

▶ *Printing across the Internet*: Remote employees can actually print directly to a printer located at the office because iPrint resources are available as standard Web URLs. Simply enter the appropriate URL for a company's print services, locate the printer to which you want to print, and iPrint takes care of the rest—including the installation of the iPrint client software, if necessary.

▶ *Printing away from "home"*: Setting up printing when visiting a different company location used to be an ordeal. No more. Now, simply access the company's print services URL, browse to the office at which you are currently located, and use the office map to locate the printer closest to you. Selecting the printer will install the necessary driver software automatically.

▶ *Printing instead of faxing:* Because you can now print across the Internet, you can effectively print instead of FAXing. All you need is an iPrint printer to which you can connect. With the Web-based iPrint tools it is possible to monitor the print job remotely and then email the intended recipient when the print job has finished.

iPrint provides the robust printing environment you expect from NetWare while at the same time integrating with modern printing standards that extend NetWare printing capabilities to the Internet.

iPrint Components

Because iPrint leverages NDPS, you might recognize several of the components that have been around since NetWare 5. In order to properly manage and route network print jobs from multiple users to multiple printers, NDPS uses the following software components:

▶ *Printer Agent*: A printer agent is simply software that manages a printer. Every printer must have a printer agent in the iPrint world. A printer's printer agent does the following:

   ▶ Manages the printer's print jobs

   ▶ Responds to client queries about print jobs or printer capabilities

   ▶ Communicates with the printer and is notified when something goes wrong, or when some other monitored event occurs so it can be communicated to those interested in such things

▶ *Gateways*: The gateway handles communication between the Print Manager and the printer. Novell provides a default gateway that will work in most situations (NDPSGW.NLM), but some printer vendors have their own custom gateway software that provides proprietary printer-specific information. For information on using a vendor-specific gateway, consult the printer documentation.

▶ *Print Manager*: The Print Manager controls all printer agents installed on a given server. Server-based printer agents are required for printers that are not NDPS-aware. NDPS-aware printers include their own printer agents, so one is not needed on the server.

▶ *Broker*: The NDPS broker provides centralized management of printing services for all the printers on the network. Because every server doesn't need to be a broker, the network is analyzed to determine whether a broker needs to be installed. A new broker will not be installed if an existing broker is within three network "hops" of the server currently being installed. However, there might be situations where you want to create an additional broker anyway; for example, to provide fault tolerance and reliability to the printing environment. The broker provides three services:

   ▶ *Resource management service*: This service allows resources such as printer drivers, fonts, print job banners, and so on to be installed in a central location and then downloaded to clients, printers, or any other entity on the network that needs them.

   ▶ *Event notification service*: This service receives notifications from the printer agents and distributes them to users and network administrators via predetermined methods.

Notification methods might include NetWare pop-up messages, entries in log files, email messages, or any other custom delivery method that can be created.

▶ *Service registry service*: Printers advertise their availability and attributes, such as make, model, and address, through this service.

TIP **If you are managing printers at multiple sites, you should plan to have a broker at each geographical location to reduce printing-related traffic over your WAN links.**

In addition to the previous NDPS components, iPrint adds the following components:

▶ *IPPSRVR.NLM*: This module provides the IPP compatibility for the iPrint environment, and generates a URL for the printer whereby it can be accessed through iPrint's Web-based tools. It will be loaded on any server that hosts a Print Manager for printers configured to use the IPP protocol.

▶ *iPrint Web pages*: These pages are used to install the iPrint client software and printers, and to view and manage print jobs. The look and feel of these pages is customizable with any HTML editor you might want to use.

▶ *Print provider and Web browser plug-ins*: These are the only client-side pieces necessary to leverage the iPrint environment. As previously mentioned, the Novell client is not required.

With this introduction to iPrint components you are now ready to start working with the printing capabilities of NetWare 6.5.

Installing iPrint

If you didn't select iPrint during the server installation, you can install it after the fact from iManager. To install iPrint from iManager, complete the following steps:

1. Launch iManager and open the Install and Upgrade link, and then select Install NetWare 6.5 Products.

2. Click Remote Product Install in the right frame.

3. Browse to the location of the NetWare 6.5 Operating System CD-ROM and click OK.

4. Browse to and select the server to which you want to install iPrint and click Next. Authenticate as an Admin user to the server you selected.

5. At the Components screen, select only iPrint, and click Next.

6. At the Summary screen, select Copy Files to install iPrint. You will need to insert, or specify the location of, the NetWare 6.5 Products CD-ROM.

7. When the iPrint installation is complete, click Close.

With iPrint installed on your NetWare 6.5 server, you are now ready to start configuring your iPrint environment.

Configuring iPrint

There are a few general tasks involved in setting up an iPrint environment. All of them can be performed through iManager.

▶ Create a broker.

▶ Create a Print Manager.

▶ *(Optional)* Set up DNS: Although not technically required, it will be a lot easier for your users to access Web-based iPrint tools if DNS is configured on your network. Otherwise, they will have to specify IP addresses to get to iPrint services. If the IP address changes for any reason, users will have to re-install their printers. For more information about configuring DNS, see Chapter 5, "Novell eDirectory Management."

▶ Create printer objects.

▶ Install iPrint support on workstations.

The following sections take a look at each of these tasks and describe how you can accomplish each of them.

Configuring the Broker

To create a new broker for your iPrint environment, complete the following steps:

1. Launch iManager and open the iPrint link.

2. Select Create Broker. At the Create Broker page, provide the necessary information and click OK (see Figure 7.1).

▶ *Broker name*: Specify a name for the Broker object.

▶ *Container name*: Specify a location for the Broker object in the eDirectory tree.

▶ *Enable services*: Select the services that you want to load on this broker. Broker services have been described previously. If you enable the Resource Management Service (RMS), you need to specify the volume on which the RMS database is stored. The volume name must include server name and directory context. For example:

```
PRV-SERV1_PRV_DATA.PROVO.QUILLS
```

3. Click OK to complete the process.

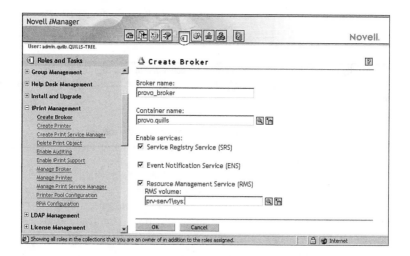

FIGURE 7.1
Creating an iPrint broker in iManager.

4. Load BROKER.NLM on the appropriate server using the following syntax. Table 7.1 lists the switches you can use when loading BROKER.NLM.

```
broker <broker name> /[startup parameter]
```

TABLE 7.1   BROKER.NLM Load Switches

STARTUP PARAMETER	DESCRIPTION
Noui	Loads the broker without displaying the user interface.
Noipx	The NDPS manager will not support the IPX protocol.
Noip	The NDPS manager will not support the IP protocol.
allowdup	The NLM will not check for two brokers using the same Broker object.
noadvert	Broker will not be advertised on the network with SLP or SAP.
ipaddress	If the server has multiple IP addresses, lets you specify which IP address the broker should use.

TIP Modify the AUTOEXEC.NCF file and add the command to load BROKER.NLM, with all the appropriate information, if you want print services to load automatically whenever the server starts.

Once installed, the NDPS broker provides the foundation for your NetWare printing environment, including centralized management of printing services for all the printers on the network.

Adding Printer Drivers or Other Resources to the Broker

NetWare 6.5 ships with many printer drivers for common printers. However, as printer manufacturers release new printers and updated drivers, you might need to add a driver that is not included with the default set that shipped with NetWare 6.5.

You can also add new banner pages to the broker using the same procedure. To see the list of existing printer drivers and banners, and to add a new driver or banner to the broker, complete the following steps:

1. Launch iManager and open the iPrint link.

2. Click Manage Broker. Specify or browse to your NDPS Broker object and click OK.

3. Select the Resource Management Service tab to add a resource to your broker, as shown in Figure 7.2.

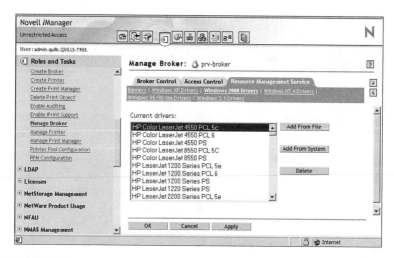

FIGURE 7.2
Adding a new printer resource to the iPrint broker with iManager.

4. Select the subpage for the type of resource you want to add. A list appears, showing all resources of that type that are currently loaded.

5. Click Add from File or Add from System and specify the driver you want to add. Click OK and follow the prompts to add the driver or banner to your broker. Add from File means you have a separate driver available. Add from System means you want to extract the appropriate resource driver from a system .CAB file.

The new driver or banner will appear in the list of available resources in the Resource Management database.

Disabling a Broker Service

By default, all three of the broker's services are enabled when the broker is installed. If you want to disable (or re-enable) a service, you can do so from iManager by completing the following steps:

1. Launch iManager and open the iPrint link.

2. Click Manage Broker. Specify or browse to your NDPS Broker object and click OK.

3. Select the Broker Control tab and uncheck the service that you want to disable.

4. Click Apply to disable the specified service for the selected Broker.

WARNING You should disable a broker service only if you're sure you do not need that service on your network, or if another broker is available that is no more than three hops away.

The specified broker services will be unloaded from the NetWare 6.5 server.

Creating a Print Manager

Once you have created and loaded your NDPS broker, you are ready to create a Print Manager on your server. To do this, create a Print Manager object in the eDirectory tree and then load NDPSM.NLM on the server by completing the following steps:

1. Launch iManager and open the iPrint link.

2. Select Create Print Manager. At the Create Manager page, provide the necessary information and click OK (see Figure 7.3).

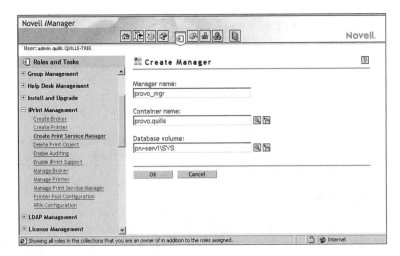

FIGURE 7.3
Creating a Print Manager in iManager.

- ▶ *Manager name*: Specify a name for the Print Manager object.

- ▶ *Container name*: Specify a location for the Print Manager object in the eDirectory tree.

▶ *Database volume*: Specify the location of the RMS database that you specified when creating the NDPS broker.

3. Click OK to return to the iManager home page.

4. From the console of the appropriate server, load NDPSM.NLM using the following syntax (see Table 7.2 for the switches to use when loading NDPSM.NLM):

```
load ndpsm <Manager name> /[startup parameter]
```

TABLE 7.2   NDPSM.NLM Load Switches

PARAMETER	DESCRIPTION
nodatabase	Loads the NDPS manager without opening the database. The Database Options menu is displayed, which lets you examine, back up, restore, resynchronize, and uninstall the NDPS manager database. See earlier sections in this chapter for more information about the NDPS manager database.
noipx	The NDPS manager will not support the IPX protocol.
noip	The NDPS manager will not support the IP protocol.
dbvolume=full_DNS_volume name	Downloads the database from eDirectory and reconnects pointers to the local server where the command is executed. This is useful for moving the NDPS manager to a new volume.
dbvolume=nocheck	The NDPS manager will not validate that the database volume is local. This is used with clustering.
setens=broker_name	Sets the event notification service to the specified broker for all printers associated this NDPS manager.
nosrs	Disables communication with Server Registry.
noens	Disables communication with Event Notification Service.

TABLE 7.2   Continued

PARAMETER	DESCRIPTION
Qloadbalance	The NDPS manager evenly distributes the waiting print jobs among printers that are ready. This is used when pooling printers.
ipaddress	Specifies which IP address on the server iPrint will use.
dnsname=NDPSM_DNS_name	This sets a DNS name to an NDPS Manager object. You will need to include the DNS information in your DNS lookup tables. If you included the DNS name before deploying printing with this manager, you can easily move the NDPS manager to another server without disrupting printing.

TIP   You should modify AUTOEXEC.NCF to load NDPSM.NLM automatically whenever the server restarts.

The Print Manager will control all printer agents that you install on your NetWare 6.5 server. Server-based printer agents are required for printers that are not NDPS-aware.

Setting Up DNS for the Print Manager

Each server that is running the Print Manager loads IPPSRVR.NLM when iPrint is enabled for a printer associated with that manager. To provide additional stability to the printing environment, you should assign a DNS name for each Print Manager that will host IPP printers. That way, if the Print Manager is moved to a different server, the iPrint URLs for associated IPP printers will still work.

To enable DNS for each Print Manager, first load NDPSM.NLM with the /dnsname command-line switch using the following syntax:

```
NDPSM <NDPS_Manager> /dnsname=<DNS Name>
```

Once the Print Manager is loaded with a DNS name, add a new resource record (A Rec) to your DNS name server that links the new DNS name to the IP address of the NetWare 6.5 server hosting the Print Manager. For more information on configuring DNS, see Chapter 5.

Creating Network Printers

To create an iPrint printer, you must first create a Printer object in the eDirectory tree, and you must have already created a Print Manager object. To create a Printer object using iManager, complete the following steps:

1. Launch iManager and open the iPrint link.

2. Select Create Printer. At the Create Printer page, specify the required information and click Next.

   ▶ *Printer name*: Specify a name for the Printer object.

   ▶ *Container name*: Specify a context where the Printer object will be located.

   ▶ *Manager name*: Specify the name of the Print Manager that will manage this printer.

   ▶ *Gateway type*: This specifies the printer gateway that will be used with this printer. Only the Novell LPR gateway is available through iManager. Third-party gateways from specific printer manufacturers must be installed from the server console. For more information on third-party gateways, see the NetWare 6.5 online documentation and the documentation that came with your printer.

3. Specify the IP address or DNS name of your printer and click Next.

4. Select the appropriate printer driver(s) from the driver lists and click Next. You can select a driver for each type of Windows workstation platform: Windows XP/2000, Windows 95/98/Me, and Windows 3.1. These are the drivers that will be automatically downloaded to the client workstations when they install the printer.

5. Click OK to return to the iManager home page.

Once the printer is created, make sure spooling is configured properly by completing the following steps:

1. From iManager, select iPrint Configuration and click Manage Printer.

2. Specify the printer you just created and click OK.

3. At the Manage Printer page, select the Configuration tab and choose the Spooling page.

4. From the Spooling page you can set the location of the spooling area (it defaults to the same location as the Print Manager), restrict the amount of space available for spooling, and determine the print-scheduling algorithm (default is First In, First Out).

IPP support is now enabled automatically when a new printer object is created. However, you can disable/re-enable IPP support from the Client Support tab in the Manage Printers page.

If you need to service legacy print queues, select the Client Support tab from the Manage Printer page and click the QMS Support subpage. From there you can specify the print queues that you want this printer to service. iPrint offers PSERVER emulation through NDPS, so you don't need to load PSERVER.NLM on the server.

Once your printers have been installed, managing them is relatively easy. Everything you need is located in iManager. The Printer Management links, shown in the left side of the navigation frame in Figure 7.3, are a one-stop shop for managing user access, printer configuration, and print service support.

Printer Pooling

iPrint lets you create a pool of printers to share print duties. Users install one of the printers associated with a pool. When a print job is sent, if the installed printer is busy, the Print Manager can automatically redirect that print job to an idle printer in the pool. Pool printers need to use the same print driver and be of a similar make and model to be sure that print jobs will print correctly. All printers in a pool must be assigned to the same Print Manager.

To create a printer pool, complete the following steps:

1. From iManager, select iPrint and then click Printer Pool Configuration.

2. Specify the Print Manager for which you are creating a printer pool. Select Create Pool from the drop-down list, and click OK.

3. Specify a name for the printer pool, and select the printers that should be included in the pool. Click Next.

4. Click OK to return to the iManager home page.

Once created, the printer pool will transparently share jobs among all printers in the pool when necessary.

Automatically Installing Printer Support

After creating printers, iPrint allows you to designate specific printer drivers to be automatically downloaded and installed on workstations so that the users don't have to worry about installing their own printer support. The printers you specify will appear automatically on the user's installed printers list. This feature is known as Remote Printer Management (RPM). You can also use Remote Printer Management to designate a default printer and remove printers from workstations.

NOTE You aren't required to designate printers to download and install automatically. Users can also install printer support manually. However, depending on your network, it might save time to designate one or more automatic downloads.

With Remote Printer Management, you configure printer drivers and other information you want to be installed. When a user logs in, the workstation software checks the user's container object for any new printer information. If new printer information (such as a new driver to be downloaded) exists, the workstation is automatically updated.

You can access Remote Printer Management from iManager by completing the following steps:

1. From iManager, select iPrint and click RPM Configuration.

2. Specify the object for which you want to configure Remote Printer Management and click OK. Valid object selections include Organization, Organizational Unit, Group, or User. Your choice will determine how broadly the RPM rules are applied.

3. At the RPM Configuration page, as shown in Figure 7.4, specify your desired configuration and click OK. You can enable/disable RPM, specify printers to install automatically, select a default printer, and even specify printers that should be removed if currently installed.

Once configured, Remote Printer Management will automatically apply the printer configuration you have specified to any workstation logged into by a user within the scope at which the RPM configuration has been applied.

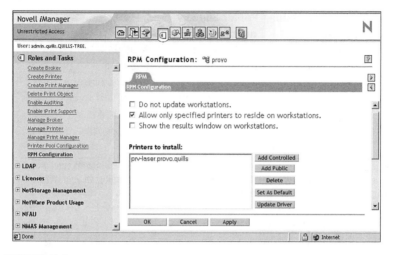

FIGURE 7.4
RPM configuration in iManager.

Manually Installing Printer Support

If a required printer driver isn't automatically downloaded, users can still install the printer support on their workstations manually. This involves using the standard Windows printer installation tools to locate, specify, and install the appropriate print drivers.

This method requires knowledge about the printer they are trying to install and access to appropriate print drivers, which are often available from Windows printer libraries.

Accessing iPrint Printers

In order for users to use iPrint, they need two components:

▶ The Novell iPrint client

▶ A printer to which they can print

When a user selects a printer to be installed by iPrint, iPrint determines whether the Novell iPrint client is installed. If it is not installed, iPrint will walk the user through the client installation. Following this, the printer driver is downloaded and the printer is installed in the user's Printers folder.

iPrint client files and printers can be quickly and easily installed from a Web page.

TIP The iPrint client and appropriate printer drivers can also be distributed using ZENworks for Desktops. If you have this additional Novell product, consult the Novell online documentation for more information on automating client delivery and installation with ZENworks for Desktops.

The iPrint client has the following requirements for installation:

▶ Windows 95/98/Me or Windows XP/2000/NT

▶ Web browser with JavaScript enabled, such as Microsoft Internet Explorer 5.0 or later

From such a workstation, users browse to the iPrint URL, which, by default, is the following: `http://<server_IP_address or DNS_name>/ipp`. Figure 7.5 shows a sample iPrint printers home page.

FIGURE 7.5
A sample iPrint printers home page.

The iPrint printers home page displays a listing of available printers and a link to install the iPrint client. Users simply select Install iPrint Client and follow the prompts to complete the client installation. If they try to install a printer before installing the iPrint client, they will be prompted to install the client first.

NOTE The iPrint client requires the workstation to reboot to complete the installation. The iPrint client can be removed through the standard Remove Programs option in the Windows Control Panel. There is also an Uninstall option under the Novell iPrint program group in the Start menu.

After the client is installed, users return to the same iPrint URL to install the necessary printer support. If you have associated a printer driver with each of your iPrint printers, it is automatically installed on the users' workstations. If a printer driver already exists on the workstations, it will be overwritten.

When the printer driver installs, a Printer icon is added to the users' Printers folder. From that point on, users access the printer through all the normal avenues.

Default Printer Driver Options

You can control how printer driver options are set when the printer driver is installed on a workstation. Printer driver defaults are kept in the INST.HTM file, which is stored in **SYS:APACHE2\HTDOCS\IPPDOCS** on your iPrint server. Complete the following steps to change the printer driver default settings:

1. Open **SYS:\APACHE2\HTDOCS\IPPDOCS\INST.HTM** using any text editor.

2. Search for the section heading **PARAM NAME=driver-options**, as shown in Figure 7.6.

3. Replace the value after the colon (:) with the desired parameter for each option you want to change. Supported parameter values are listed in Table 7.3.

4. Save and close INST.HTM.

FIGURE 7.6
Printer driver options portion of INST.HTM.

TABLE 7.3 Supported Printer Parameters for iPrint Printers

PARAMETER	SUPPORTED VALUES
Orientation	landscape, portrait
Paper size	letter, lettersmall, tabloid, ledger, legal, statement, executive, A3, A4, A4small, A5, B4, B5, folio, quatro, 10x14, 11x17, note, env_10, env_12, env_14, csheet, dsheet, esheet, env_dl, env_c5, env_c4, env_c3, env_c65, env_b5, env_b6, env_italy, env_monarch, env_personal, fanfold_us, fanfold_std_german, fanfold_lgl_german, iso_b4, japanese_postcard, 9x11, 10x11, 15x11, env_invite, letter_extra, legal_extra, tabloid_extra, A4_extra, letter_extra_transverse, a_plus, b_plus, letter_plus, A4_plus, A5_transverse, B5_transverse, A3_extra, A5_extra, B5_extra, A2, A3_transverse, A3_extra_transverse
Copies	Enter the number of copies you want printed
Color	yes=color; no or false=monochrome
Duplex	simplex, horizontal, vertical
Collate	yes or true=collate; no=do not collate

With your preferred settings defined in the INST.HTM file, workstations will receive your preferred configuration automatically.

iPrint Client Updates

Periodically, users will need to update their iPrint client. Each time a user starts his or her workstation, the iPrint client checks with the default printer to determine whether a newer version of the iPrint client exists. If necessary, a newer version of the client can be installed. You can control how this update takes place with the IPRINT.INI file.

IPRINT.INI is stored in `SYS:\APACHE2\HTDOCS\IPPDOCS` on each server where iPrint is installed. It lets you specify whether the user should be prompted before a new client is installed, or if the update should be a "hands-free" process.

Descriptive text for each entry in IPRINT.INI is included in the file. You can view and edit the file using a text editor.

WARNING The IPRINT.INI file should be synchronized across all servers on which iPrint is running.

Location-Based Printing

Location-based printing is one of the key values of iPrint. It lets users easily locate and install printers using one of two methods:

► *Printer list views*: With list views, you configure printer lists so that they make the most sense for your users, such as by building, by office location, or by eDirectory context.

► *Printer maps*: Using the iPrint Map Designer, you can create maps of printer locations by using drag-and-drop technology. Once created, the maps are posted on a Web server for users to access. By looking at the maps, they locate a printer close to their location and simply click the Printer icon. The printer driver and iPrint client, if necessary, are then installed on the users' workstations.

Each of these methods is discussed in the following sections.

Creating Printer Lists

iPrint provides a default list of printers organized by the Print Manager. In order to create a custom list, you can modify the HTML of the iPrint page and create links to individual printers' IPP URLs. When you create an iPrint printer, a URL is listed in the accepted IPP URL list. This is the URL you will specify when creating a customized printer list.

Using the iPrint Map Designer tool, you can quickly create a map showing printer locations. The tool lets you import floor plans that can be
used to drag and drop printers to actual locations. These maps are then
published on a Web server so that users can install printers that are closest to their location.

Creating Printer Maps

Creating printer maps requires that you use Microsoft Internet Explorer
5.5 or later and have the iPrint client installed on the workstation from
which you will be creating the maps.

The iPrint Map Designer lets you create maps showing the physical locations of printers in a building by using background images of the building's floor plan. Once the map is created, use the iPrint Map Designer to
modify or update your maps as necessary.

To create a printer map for your iPrint users, complete the following
steps:

1. Get graphic images of your building floor plan(s). iPrint supports
   images in JPEG, GIF, and BMP formats. Copy all of the floor plan
   images to your iPrint servers and store them in
   `SYS:APACHE2\HTDOCS\IPPDOCS\IMAGES\MAPS`.

2. To access the iPrint Map tool, do one of the following:

   ▶ Map a drive to `SYS:APACHE2\HTDOCS\IPPDOCS\` and open
     MAPTOOL.HTM with Microsoft Internet Explorer.

   ▶ With Microsoft Internet Explorer, open the `http://`
     `<server_address>:631/login/ippdocs/maptool.htm` iPrint
     URL, with `<server_address>` as the IP address or DNS name
     of the server where Print Manager is running.

3. Select Background from the navigation frame on the left. Select a
   floor plan image from those you have copied to `SYS:APACHE2\`
   `HTDOCS\IPPDOCS\IMAGES\MAPS`. Alternatively, you can retrieve and
   modify an existing map file by selecting Open and specifying
   (browsing to) the directory where the map is located.

4. To add a printer to the map, provide the following information:

   ▶ *Printer icon*: Select the type of printer icon you want to use.

   ▶ *Printer list*: Click the Browse icon and enter the DNS name of
     the appropriate Print Manager. Click OK. You can also enter
     the IP address or DNS name of the NetWare 6.5 server where

Print Manager is running. From the printer list, select the printer agent you want associated with this printer icon. If the printer is not listed, make sure you have IPP enabled for that printer.

NOTE To add printers from different Print Managers to the same map, first add the printers from the first Print Manager, and then click the Browse icon and select a different manager.

- ▶ *Printer URL*: This field will be populated automatically by the URL created for the printer when IPP is enabled for the printer. You should not need to change the URL.

- ▶ *Mouse over text*: This field is populated automatically by the printer agent's name. You can override this information and enter any descriptive text you want to display when a user moves the mouse over the Printer icon.

- ▶ *(Optional) Printer caption field*: Enter the information to display, using Enter to parse the information onto multiple lines.

5. Click Save, and save the map to SYS:APACHE2\HTDOCS\IPPDOCS\.

WARNING If you click Refresh or exit Internet Explorer without saving the map, all changes since the last time the map was saved will be lost.

Repeat step 4 for each printer you want to place on your map. You can edit a printer's information at any time by clicking the appropriate printer icon and changing the printer information fields as required. If you need to add or modify printers from a previously used Print Manager, click a printer icon from that manager and the printer list will be populated with printers from that manager.

Hosting the Maps on a Web Server

After creating your maps, you need to post them on a Web server. Copy the contents of the \IPPDOCS directory and its subdirectories to the Web server in order for your maps and iPrint to work properly. You can link to your maps from your company's internal Web page or send the URL out to your users.

Printer Availability on Workstations

You might want printers to remove themselves automatically from a workstation. For example, you have a printer in your lobby for customers to use. When the customer leaves, you want the printer to be removed from the customer's laptop. Setting the persistence of the printer allows you to automatically remove the printer when the customer reboots his or her laptop.

Complete the following to set the persistence of a printer:

1. Using a text editor, open `SYS:APACHE2\HTDOCS\IPPDOCS\INST.HTM`.

2. Edit the file by searching for `persistence=`.

3. Replace the printer setting value—located after the comma (,)—with `volatile-reboot`.

4. Save the file.

Doing this will instruct an installed printer driver to automatically remove itself when the workstation is rebooted.

Setting Up a Secure Printing Environment

iPrint is designed to take full advantage of eDirectory security and ease of management. Setting up a secure printing environment can be done on three levels:

▶ *Print access control*: Create a secure printing management infra-structure by assigning users to User, Operator, or Manager roles. This restricts the list of those who can control printers, Print Managers, and brokers.

▶ *Printer security levels*: Printer security levels control how access to printers is managed. By default, the client application will control print security, but this responsibility can be moved to the Print Manager to provide greater security.

▶ *Securing iPrint with SSL*: This option not only encrypts print com-munications over the wire, but also requires users to authenticate before installing and printing to a printer.

Each of these levels is discussed in the following sections.

Print Access Control

Printer security is ensured through the assignment of the Manager, Operator, and User Access Control roles, and by the strategic placement of printers and printer configurations. For more information on eDirectory access control in general, see Chapter 6, "Users and Network Security."

The access controls for iPrint allow you to specify the access each User, Group, or Container object will have to your printing resources. It is important to remember that all iPrint print roles function independently. For example, assigning someone as a printer manager does not automatically grant said person the rights of a printer user.

In most cases, the default assignments will prevent any problems that this role independence might cause. For example, a printer manager is automatically assigned as a printer operator and user for that printer. Similarly, a printer operator is automatically assigned as a user of that printer as well. You cannot remove the user role from an operator, and you cannot remove the operator and user roles from a manager.

The creator of an iPrint object is automatically assigned to all supported roles for the type of object being created.

You can assign multiple Printer objects to a given printer agent, but simultaneously make different access control assignments to each Printer object. This means that users in different containers can be assigned different trustee rights to the same printer.

Printer Roles

As previously alluded to, there are three roles associated with iPrint printing services: Manager, Operator, and User. Table 7.4 describes the rights granted to each role.

TABLE 7.4   NDPS Print Roles and Their Associated Rights

ROLE	ASSOCIATED RIGHTS
Manager	NDPS tasks performed exclusively by the printer manager are those that require the creation, modification, or deletion of NDPS Printer objects, as well as other eDirectory administrative functions. Printer managers are automatically designated as printer operators and users as well, so they can perform all tasks assigned to the operator role. Typical manager functions include the following:

TABLE 7.4 Continued

ROLE	ASSOCIATED RIGHTS
	▶ Modifying and deleting Printer objects ▶ Adding or deleting operators and users for a printer ▶ Adding other managers ▶ Configuring interested-party notification ▶ Creating, modifying, or deleting printer configurations
Operator	Print operators cannot create, modify, or delete eDirectory objects or perform other eDirectory administrative functions. Their management tasks include the following: ▶ Performing all of the functions available through the Printer Control page ▶ Pausing, restarting, or reinitializing printers ▶ Reordering, moving, copying, and deleting jobs ▶ Setting printer defaults, including locked properties ▶ Configuring print job spooling
User	Print users only have rights to submit and manage print jobs that they own. Users cannot copy, move, reorder, or remove jobs they do not own. To simplify administration, the container within which a printer resides is automatically assigned as a user for that printer. That way, all users in that container inherit printer user rights. You can delete the Container object as a printer user in order to block access to the printer for users in that container.

To define the role assignment for a printer, complete the following steps:

1. From iManager, select iPrint and click Manage Printer.

2. Specify the printer for which you want to configure access controls and click OK.

3. At the Manage Printer page, select the Access Control tab, as shown in Figure 7.7.

4. Make your desired changes by adding or deleting members from the User, Operator, and Manager roles for this printer. eDirectory objects that can be assigned in these roles include User, Group, or Container objects. Click OK to save your changes.

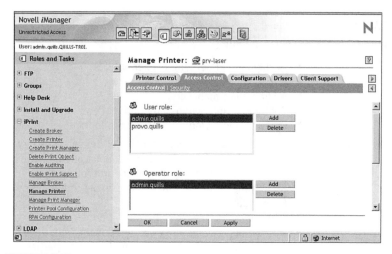

FIGURE 7.7
Access Control tab for defining printer management roles in ConsoleOne.

Following these changes, printer access will be granted according to the access controls you have defined.

Print Manager Access Controls

Print Manager security is provided exclusively through the printer manager role in iManager. The printer manager role was discussed previously in the "Printer Roles" section. Refer to Table 7.4 for more information on iPrint administrative roles in iManager. For more information on role-based administration with iManager, see Chapter 3, "Novell Management Tools." Common administrative tasks related to the print manager include the following:

- ▶ Creating printer agents and NDPS Manager objects
- ▶ Adding or deleting operators and users for a printer
- ▶ Adding other managers
- ▶ Configuring interested-party notification
- ▶ Creating, modifying, or deleting printer configurations

You should plan on assigning users who need to perform these types of tasks as occupants of the printer manager role.

NDPS Broker Access Controls

There are two roles associated with the NDPS Broker object. The printer manager role was discussed previously in the "Printer Roles" section. Refer to Table 7.4 for more information on iPrint administrative roles in iManager:

▶ *Manager*: NDPS tasks performed exclusively by the broker manager require the creation, modification, or deletion of Broker objects, as well as those that involve other eDirectory administrative functions. Typical manager functions include the following:

  ▶ Creating, modifying, and deleting Broker objects

  ▶ Adding other managers

  ▶ Enabling or disabling brokered services

  ▶ Adding resources to the Resource Management Service

  ▶ Assigning or changing a broker password

▶ *Public access user*: A public access user is a role assigned to all individuals on the network who are users of printers receiving services and resources provided by the broker. This role is assigned by default and does not require specific administrative action by the broker manager.

You can also assign a password to the broker interface for increased security. After the broker loads on your NetWare server, navigate to the Broker screen and press F4.

Printer Security Levels

Printer security levels affect how rights to a printer are determined and enforced. There are three security levels:

▶ *Low*: Security is enforced by the client applications only.

▶ *Medium (default)*: Security is enforced by the NDPS manager if print data integrity is involved. If print data integrity is not involved, security is enforced by the client applications.

▶ *High*: Security is enforced by the NDPS manager for all operations.

As noted, the default security level is Medium. For sensitive print data, you can set the security level to High, but there is a trade-off between print performance and print security. To set a printer's security level, complete the following steps:

1. From iManager, select iPrint Management and click Manage Printer.

2. Specify the printer for which you want to change security levels and click OK.

3. At the Manage Printer page, select the Access Control tab and click the Security subpage.

4. In the Security Level field, set the level of security for this printer and click OK to save your changes.

The printer will now adhere to the security characteristics defined by the security level you have applied to that printer.

WARNING As you can see, making security level changes will affect all print jobs going to this printer, so make sure you consider the consequences carefully.

Securing iPrint with SSL

Secure printing takes advantage of SSL, which requires users to authenticate using their eDirectory usernames and passwords. Users must authenticate once per eDirectory tree per session. The print data is encrypted, and all print communications use port 443. Without secure printing, the printer is available to anyone on the local network and print communications are not encrypted. Secure printing works in conjunction with the security level set for the printer.

Table 7.5 shows how access is determined, depending on the level of printer security and if secure printing is enabled or disabled. Printer security levels were discussed in a previous section.

TABLE 7.5 Effects of Printer Security and Secure Printing Options

PRINTER SECURITY LEVEL	SECURE PRINTING DISABLED (NO SSL)	SECURE PRINTING ENABLED (WITH SSL)
Low	Full access	eDirectory authentication.
Medium	Check of users' effective rights	eDirectory authentication and check of users' effective rights.
High	Users must use SSL and authenticate to eDirectory	Users will receive an error if they do not use SSL. eDirectory authentication, check users' effective rights, and connection verification are all required.

To enable SSL support for a given printer, or for all printers associated with a given print manager, complete the following steps:

1. From iManager, select iPrint and click Enable iPrint Support.

2. Specify the print service manager for which you want to enable IPP printing.

3. At the Enable iPrint Support page, check the box next to Enabled and click OK. This will enable IPP on all printers assigned to this print service manager. You can also select printers individually by checking the box from the Enabled column next to each printer you want iPrint enabled.

4. *(Optional)* Use the same check box procedure in the Secure column to enable secure printing as needed for printers associated with this print manager. More information on securing your printing services was provided earlier in this chapter.

5. Click OK to return to the iManager home page.

As you probably noted, this same routine can also be used to disable/ enable iPrint support for a printer should that be necessary.

Providing Transparent Access

In This Part

Up to this point, the book has focused on the specific components and tasks necessary to get NetWare 6.5 ready to support the business needs of the 21st century. Part III looks at the specific features and offerings in NetWare 6.5 that make it the preeminent network operating system for conducting eBusiness.

Think for a minute about what you need to do business in today's world. You have far-flung employees, mobile users moving from site to site, partners and suppliers that need to provide and receive critical information, and the open access Internet—across which you need to send mission-critical and often confidential information. To manage all this, you need to develop a new paradigm—a new way of looking at things—and NetWare 6.5 does just that.

Chapter 8 introduces you to the powerful features of Novell Storage Service (NSS), which provides unparalleled flexibility and security for your critical business data. In addition to NSS, NetWare 6.5 offers some exciting new options like NetWare distributed file system and storage area network capabilities through iSCSI. After all, the data is what the network is all about, right?

Chapter 9 introduces the NetWare 6.5 Apache Web server and Tomcat Servlet engine. NetWare 6.5 now uses the Apache Web server for NetWare for both its internal management tools and any external Web services you might want to create. This chapter also presents an overview of the Web services options that are included with NetWare 6.5 to make it one of the most powerful Web services platforms available today—all right out of the box!

Chapter 10 introduces the file access options in NetWare 6.5 in support of Novell's One Net vision. These tools make it possible to seamlessly and securely provide users with access to the information they need, regardless of location, time, or anything else. After all, your job as a network administrator revolves around making sure that users can access what they need when they need it—nothing more than that.

NetWare 6.5 can make your job a whole lot easier.

CHAPTER 8

File Storage and Management

Instant Access

Managing Logical Volumes

▶ To create, delete, or enlarge a logical volume, use the volume management options in iManager, or the console-based NSSMU.

▶ To mount/dismount, or activate/deactivate a logical volume, use the volume management options in iManager, or the console-based NSSMU.

▶ To move or split a logical volume, use the volume management options in iManager.

▶ To mount a server's DOS partition as a logical volume, load DOS-FAT.NSS at the server console.

Managing Disk Space

▶ To manage file compression, use NoRM to set file compression SET parameters.

▶ To limit users' disk space, use volume management options in iManager.

Managing Files

▶ To salvage or purge deleted files, use the NetWare Utilities option in the Novell client or ConsoleOne.

▶ To display information about files and directories, use ConsoleOne.

Using Distributed File System

▶ To create and manage DFS junctions, use ConsoleOne.

Using iSCSI

▶ Configure iSCSI partitions with NoRM or the console-based NSSMU.

▶ Configure an iSCSI initiator with the iSCSI Services options in NoRM.

Backing Up and Restoring Files

▶ To back up and restore network files, use SBCON from the server console (or a remote RConsoleJ session). For a more comprehensive backup/restore solution, use a third-party backup product that is SMS-compliant.

▶ Use file and pool snapshots to make it much easier to back up network data.

Understanding the NetWare File System

File storage and management is the core of any network server, and NetWare has long offered the capability to manage files in many ways. Answering questions about file security, file criticality, available disk space, and the potential for offline or near-line storage can go a long way in helping you to determine how best to configure and manage your file system environment.

The first step toward planning and managing an effective file system is to understand the Novell Storage Services (NSS). First released in limited fashion with NetWare 5, NSS provides tremendous flexibility to the NetWare file structure. But beyond NSS, there are also issues of archiving data, and newer network-based storage options.

This chapter looks at the various file storage options available in NetWare 6.5 and discusses the advantages and potential pitfalls of each. You will note that this chapter doesn't include a discussion of traditional NetWare volumes. This topic has been discussed for 20 years, and there isn't a lot left to say. Furthermore, traditional volumes are lacking when compared to the NSS option. However, for further information on traditional NetWare volumes, there is a library of information available, and Appendix E can point you in the right direction.

Novell Storage Services

Novell Storage Services (NSS) is a powerful storage and file system that provides an efficient way to use all the space on your storage devices. The first concept with which you should become familiar in the NetWare file system is the *volume*. A NetWare volume is the highest level in the file system hierarchy, and is the structure within which directories and files are maintained. Each NetWare server will have at least one volume, SYS, which contains all the NetWare system files and utilities. You can then create additional volumes on the server as necessary to serve your file-management needs.

The volume is the last link in the NSS chain. Figure 8.1 gives a high-level view of the NSS architecture.

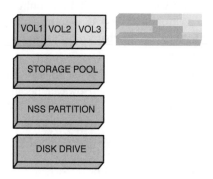

FIGURE 8.1
A high-level view of the NSS architecture.

▶ *NSS partitions*: A *partition* is a logical organization of space on a hard disk, and represents the lowest level of organization for disk storage. Partitions prepare space on storage devices to be used in an organized and structured way by defining the ways in which the file system will interact with the storage devices.

▶ *NSS storage pools*: NSS storage pools are created in partitioned space. A *storage pool* is a specified amount of space you obtain from all your storage devices. Within the storage pool, you will create the NSS volumes you need on the server. Only one storage pool can exist on a partition, but you can create an unlimited number of NSS volumes in each storage pool, thereby removing partition constraints to the number of volumes that can be created.

▶ *NSS volumes*: The volumes you create from NSS storage pools are called *logical volumes*. As noted in Figure 8.1, they are logical volumes because the space used to create a given volume can come from a variety of storage devices. It is not contiguous space. A logical volume can be set to a specific size, or allowed to grow dynamically according to the amount of physical space assigned to the pool. This lets you add and store any size or any number of files you need without having to create other partitions. You can add any number of volumes to a storage pool as long as you have available physical space in the pool.

Beyond these three NSS building blocks, you should be aware of several concepts related to the configuration and management of NSS volumes:

▶ *NSS management*: You will use NoRM for configuring and managing your NSS environment. It gives you the ability to control and change your server's storage characteristics from any place with an Internet connection.

▶ *Overbook your storage pool*: Individual logical volumes cannot exceed the size of a storage pool. However, because you can create multiple logical volumes in a single storage pool, NetWare 6.5 permits the total space allocated to logical volumes to exceed the actual pool size. This feature, called *overbooking*, can be an efficient way to manage your file system because it lets your volumes grow organically over time instead of being locked into a rigid structure that can leave space unused.

▶ *Deactivate/activate logical volumes and storage pools*: You might need to temporarily prevent user access to storage pools or volumes to perform maintenance. Instead of bringing down the server, you can deactivate individual storage pools. When you deactivate a storage pool, users will not have access to any of the volumes in that pool.

▶ *Fast error correction and data recovery*: Because NSS is a journaled file system, it can quickly recover data after a file system crash. Instead of scanning the file system for corruption, NSS replays the latest set of changes to make sure they were written correctly. The file system either recovers the changed information or returns it to its original condition prior to the transaction.

▶ *Immediately save data to disk*: The Flush Files Immediately feature saves your file data to disk immediately after you close the file instead of caching it in memory and waiting for the next disk write cycle. This prevents your data from being at risk between disk write cycles, at the cost of slower file system performance overall.

▶ *Retain previously saved files (Snapshot)*: The File Snapshot feature keeps an original copy of all open files so they can be archived by your backup utility. By capturing the most recent closed copy of the file, Snapshot guarantees that you still have a solid copy of the file with which to work. NetWare 6.5 also offers pool snapshots, so you can preserve a view of an entire storage pool at any point in time. This option can be a valuable addition to your data protection and archive capabilities.

▶ *Transaction Tracking System (TTS)*: Transaction Tracking System protects database applications by backing out transactions that are incomplete due to a system failure. To enable TTS for an NSS volume, type the following command at the server console. You can also place the NSS transaction command in your AUTOEXEC.NCF so that TTS starts automatically.

```
nss /transaction=<volume name>
```

▶ *Review the modified file list*: NSS maintains a list of files that have been modified since the previous backup. To save time, your backup utility has to review only this list rather than scanning the entire file system for modified files.

▶ *Enable file compression*: NSS supports file compression. This lets you decide whether to compress the files in your volumes for more efficient use of storage device space. Once it's enabled, however, you cannot disable file compression without re-creating the volumes.

▶ *Data shredding*: The data shredding feature overwrites purged disk blocks with random patterns of hexadecimal characters. This is a security option that helps prevent the use of a disk editor to attempt to recover purged files. You can require up to seven random shred patterns be written over deleted data.

- *User space restrictions*: From iManager, you can now limit the amount of space available to an individual user on a logical volume.

- *Directory space restrictions*: From iManager, you can now limit the space that can be assigned to a given directory or subdirectory.

- *CD-ROMs as read-only logical volumes*: NSS offers full CD-ROM support for ISO9660 and HFS formats. Simply insert the CD-ROM into the server-mounted CD-ROM drive and it will be automatically mounted as a new NSS volume.

- *No memory required for mounting volumes*: NSS does not require large amounts of memory to mount volumes because it does not scan the entire file system during the mounting process. After the mounting is complete, NSS does not load files into memory until you access them. Therefore, no additional memory is required when you add files and mount volumes.

- *Hot fix*: Over time, sections of your server hard disks might start to break down and lose their ability to reliably store data. NSS supports hot fix to prevent data from being written to unreliable blocks. Hot fix redirects the original block of data to the hot fix redirection area, where the data can be stored correctly. To redirect a block of data, the operating system records the address of the defective block. Then the server no longer attempts to store data in that block. By default, two percent of a disk's space is set aside as the hot fix redirection area. You can increase or decrease this amount. If hot fix is enabled, it is always active unless the disk fails or the redirection area is full. You can view hot fix activity in NoRM by selecting the Disk/LAN Adapters link. Click on the disk adapter to which the drive is attached and click the appropriate drive link. The Redirection Blocks column will show you how many blocks have been redirected to the hot fix area.

WARNING If you notice the number of redirected blocks increasing, it's a sign that your drive is ready to fail. You should immediately back up your data and replace the drive to prevent an unplanned outage.

TIP You can disable the hot fix redirection area when you create disk partitions, which will save partition space. This can be useful if you are using a RAID system that provides its own fault tolerance. If you do not enable hot fix when the partition is created, you can add it later only by deleting the volumes from the partition, adding hot fix, and restoring the volumes from a backup.

▶ *Repair storage pools instead of individual volumes*: Use the repair utilities VERIFY and REBUILD to repair NSS systems. VERIFY and REBUILD function on the pool level rather than the individual volume level. Unlike VREPAIR for traditional NetWare volumes, these utilities should be used only as a last resort to recover the file system after data corruption.

> ▶ VERIFY checks the file system integrity for an NSS pool by searching for inconsistent data blocks or other errors. This utility indicates whether there are problems with the file system.

> ▶ REBUILD verifies and uses the existing leaves of an object tree to rebuild all the other trees in the system. You need to deactivate pools (and all the volumes in the pools) before you run REBUILD so that users cannot access the volumes you are rebuilding. When you deactivate a storage pool, all the volumes in the pool automatically deactivate.

▶ *RAID support*: NSS provides software support for RAID 0 (data striping), RAID 1 (data mirroring), and RAID 5 (data striping with parity) to give you a robust set of options for protecting your server data. You can create and manage software RAID through iManager or through the console-based NSS Management utility (NSSMU).

Understanding these NSS concepts will make it easier for you to plan and manage your NetWare file system.

Planning the File System

Now that you know a little about NSS, you can start planning your NetWare 6.5 file system. Consider the following tips for creating a robust, accessible, and easy-to-manage file system:

▶ If possible, place SYS in its own storage pool and segregate it from the rest of the non-NetWare applications and data that will be on your NetWare 6.5 server. This will help ensure that the system always has the space it needs for internal operations and promote a stable storage environment for NetWare 6.5 services and utilities.

▶ To simplify data backup, separate applications and data into distinct volumes. Application volumes will be relatively stable over time, so they can be backed up less frequently than a data volume in which files are changing constantly. For more information about backing up files, see the "Backing Up and Restoring Files" section later in this chapter.

▶ If different applications will be available to different groups of users, try to organize the applications' directory structures so that you can assign comprehensive rights in a parent directory. This can help prevent you from having to create multiple individual rights assignments at lower-level subdirectories. For more information about file system rights, see Chapter 6, "Users and Network Security."

▶ If you want to use file compression to compress less frequently used files, try to group those types of files into directories separate from other files that are used more often. That way you can turn on compression for the less-used directories and leave it turned off for the frequently used directories. For more information about file compression, see the "File Compression" section later in this chapter.

▶ Decide whether you want users' daily work files to reside in personal directories, in project-specific directories, or in some other type of directory structure. Encourage your users to store their files on the network so that the network backup process can back up those files regularly, and so the files can be protected by NetWare security.

▶ Decide whether you want users to have their own individual home directories.

TIP You can have home directories created automatically when you create a new user, as explained in Chapter 6.

These tips can help you effectively plan your file system. In addition, you should take into consideration the directories that NetWare creates automatically during installation, as well as plan for directories that will contain applications. These issues are described in the following sections.

NetWare System Directories

When you install a NetWare server for the first time, there are several directories created by the system with which you should be familiar. These directories contain most of the tools, utilities, and configuration files that you need to configure, monitor, and manage your NetWare 6.5 server. All NetWare system-related directories are created in volume SYS:, a few of which include the following:

▶ SYSTEM holds nearly all the NLMs and utilities that you will use to configure, manage, and monitor a NetWare 6.5 server. You will become familiar with SYS:SYSTEM as you look for files, compare file versions, and perform other troubleshooting operations.

▶ PUBLIC holds all the NetWare tools, utilities, and user-related files for a NetWare 6.5 network. Any user created in a NetWare environment will have default access to SYS:PUBLIC so that he can access the tools he needs to set up his client access. Over time, you can add other utilities to this directory if you want all users to have access to them.

▶ ETC is similar to the /ETC file in a Unix environment. It mostly holds configuration files related to network communications such as protocol configuration, routing tables, DNS and DHCP configuration, audit files, and backup configuration files. It also holds several of the default NetWare log files, such as CONSOLE.LOG.

▶ LOGIN holds those files to which users need access even though they are not yet logged in to the NetWare environment. This includes language-specific files, the graphic elements used with NoRM's Java-based interface, and the basic utilities necessary to help accomplish a NetWare login.

▶ APACHE2 and ADMINSRV hold the system files related to the Apache Web server. This includes the Apache admin server, which supports all NetWare 6.5 Web-based administrative tools such as Web Manager, NoRM, and iManager, and the Apache Web server used for creating an actual Web site and providing Web services hosted on NetWare 6.5. For more information on Apache Web server, see Chapter 9, "NetWare 6.5 Web Services."

▶ TOMCAT holds the system files related to the Tomcat Servlet engine. For more information on Tomcat, see Chapter 9.

WARNING Because the SYS volume contains many directories containing files required for running and managing your NetWare network, do not rename or delete any of them without making absolutely sure they're unnecessary in your particular network's situation. This is another good reason not to mix your business applications and data with the system files on SYS.

There are many other directories related to specific services that you can load on a NetWare 6.5 server, and you can create additional directories and subdirectories in volume **SYS**, if desired.

Nonsystem Directories

For files not directly related to NetWare, or your network environment, it makes more sense to create a separate file structure. That way there will be fewer chances for problems to be introduced into your core NetWare system through extraneous installation, configuration, or management activities.

You need to consider application and file placement when planning your NetWare file system. By doing so, you can create a file structure in which it is much easier to assign proper trustee rights so that users have access to what they need, but without granting them access to things they don't. For example, general-use applications can be organized in an **APPS** volume, each in its own subdirectory. That way, rights to these applications can be easily assigned high in the directory structure where they will flow down, through inheritance, to all subdirectories. For more information about file system rights, see Chapter 6.

If an application requires that it be installed at the root of a file system, NetWare gives you the flexibility of installing the application where it makes sense and then creating a root drive mapping to fool the application into thinking it is operating from a root location in the file system. Creating a root drive mapping requires the redirector capabilities of either the Novell client or the NetDrive client. See Chapter 2, "Novell Clients," for more information on the Novell client. See Chapter 10, "NetWare File Access," for more information on NetDrive.

You can create a map root from the client, but if it is needed for a large number of users, a much better way is to include the **map** command in the appropriate login script. That way the **map** operation will be performed automatically when each user logs in and you don't have to worry about making changes to every workstation. For example, you can add the following command to a container login script to map a root drive for all users within the container:

```
MAP ROOT S16:=VOL1:APPS\ABC
```

For more information about login scripts, see Appendix B.

If you decide to host an application from the NetWare server, you should flag the application's executable files as Shareable, Read-Only (S, Ro). This allows the application to be used by multiple users simultaneously, but prevents users from inadvertently deleting or modifying it. This is an additional layer of protection beyond that provided by restricting access to the files at the directory level. For more information on file system rights, see Chapter 6.

Working with NSS Volumes

The first NSS volume, SYS:, was created automatically when you installed NetWare 6.5. However, you can also create additional storage structures as needed, both during the installation process and after the server installation is complete. Given that, it is probably a good idea to understand the technology and storage concepts a little before you start doing a lot of storage management. You can configure and manage NSS after installation with iManager or the console-based NSS Management utility (NSSMU).

With NSS, you use partitions, storage pools, and logical volumes. You create logical volumes in storage pools that are composed of free space from the various storage devices in your server.

NSS uses free space from multiple storage devices. NSS allows you to mount up to 255 volumes simultaneously and store up to eight trillion files in a single volume—up to 8TB (terabytes) in size.

The main components of the NSS file system were introduced at the beginning of this chapter. The following sections explain how to create and work with NSS resources.

NetWare Partitions

With NSS, you probably won't have to manage NetWare partitions directly because they are automatically created to support the storage pools you define. However, if you want a partition-level view or you want to create non-NSS partitions, you can do so from NoRM by following these steps:

1. Launch NoRM and select Partition Disks from the left navigation frame.

2. At the Partition Disks page, you can create a new partition by clicking the Create link next to any of the listed available free space (see Figure 8.2).

3. At the File System Creation Operations page, specify the type of volume you want to create, and click the creation operation you want to perform. You can choose from NSS, traditional NetWare, and iSCSI partition types. Based on your choice, you will see different options for proceeding with the partition creation process.

It's easier to work with NSS partitions through iManager because all the tools for pool and volume management are there as well. iSCSI is discussed later in this chapter. For more information on traditional NetWare volumes, see the NetWare 6.5 online documentation.

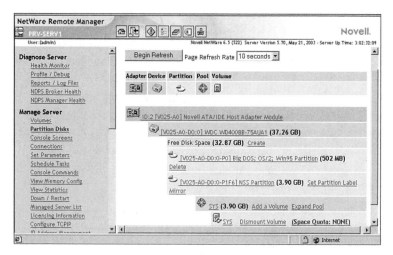

FIGURE 8.2
Using partition disks to manage partitions from NoRM.

Storage Pools

A *storage pool* is a specific amount of space you obtain from one or more storage devices in your server. NetWare 6.5 has integrated the partition-creation process into the process for creating storage pools. NSS storage pools provide the flexibility of NSS. They can be created to span one or multiple partitions on the hardware side, and can be divided into one or multiple logical volumes on the user side.

After a pool is created, you can add storage devices to your server and then expand the pool to include the space available on the new storage device. To create a new storage pool, complete the following steps:

1. Launch iManager, open the Storage link, and select Pools in the left navigation frame.

2. At the Pool Management page, specify the server with which you want to work. This will bring up the storage pool information for that server, as shown in Figure 8.3.

3. Click New to create a new storage pool.

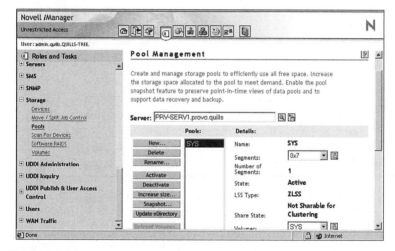

FIGURE 8.3
Managing storage pools from iManager.

4. Specify the name of the storage pool and click Next. Make sure to follow the naming conventions as outlined.

5. At the Select Device and Space page, choose the storage device(s) from which the new storage pool will get its space, and specify the amount of space for each device, and then click Finish. Check Activate on Creation if you want the pool to be available as soon as it is created.

Once created, you will be returned to the Pool Management page, from which you can perform various configuration tasks on storage pools and view the characteristics of pools that have been created. Configuration options include the following:

▶ *New*: Lets you create new storage pools, as described previously.

▶ *Delete*: Lets you delete an existing storage pool. You cannot delete the SYS pool in this way because that would remove the NetWare operating system.

▶ *Rename*: Lets you rename an existing storage pool.

▶ *Activate*: Makes a pool, and all volumes associated with that pool, available for use.

▶ *Deactivate*: Removes a pool, and all volumes associated with that pool, from service. Users cannot access data on an inactive pool. This might be done so you can perform maintenance on the pool or its associated volumes.

▶ *Increase Size*: Lets you add space to a storage pool.

▶ *Snapshot*: Creates a point-in-time view of an active storage pool. This is very helpful for backing up pool data because your backup application can back up the snapshot so you do not have to worry about open file issues and other snags that can make backing up network data so difficult. A pool snapshot will be visible from the Pools view in iManager as a separate storage pool. Information about backing up network data with Novell's Storage Management Services (SMS) is provided later in this chapter.

▶ *Update eDirectory*: If you have modified or renamed a storage pool, use this option to update the eDirectory pool object with the new information and characteristics.

▶ *(Conditional) Deleted Volumes*: If you have deleted volumes from a storage pool, you can use this option to salvage or purge those deleted volumes.

▶ *(Conditional) Offline*: If you select a pool snapshot, this option is available to take the selected snapshot offline.

These options give you granular control over the management and performance of the storage pools on your NetWare server.

Logical Volumes

Once a storage pool has been created, you are ready for NSS logical volumes. NSS volumes can be set to a specific size or set to grow dynamically within the storage pool according to the amount of storage space that is needed over time. When set to grow dynamically, NSS volumes can automatically take advantage of new storage devices once their space is added to their associated storage pool.

After you've created the volume, you must mount it before network users can access it. To create and mount a new NSS volume, complete the following steps:

1. Launch iManager, open the Storage link, and select Volumes in the left navigation frame.

2. At the Volume Management page, specify the server with which you want to work. This will bring up the volume information for that server, as shown in Figure 8.4.

3. Click New to create a new volume.

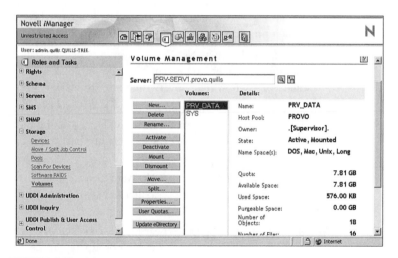

FIGURE 8.4
Managing server volumes from iManager.

4. Specify the name of the volume and click Next. Make sure to follow the naming conventions as outlined.

5. At the Select a Pool and Volume Quota page, provide the required information and click Next.

- *Storage pool*: Check the box next to the storage pool from which the volume will be created. You can also click the New Pool button to create a new storage pool for this volume. Doing this will drop you into step 4 of the storage pool creation process, discussed previously.

- *Allow Volume Quota to Grow to Pool Size*: If you don't want to specify a volume quota, check this box to let the volume grow dynamically to fit the available pool space.

6. At the Attribute Information page, make your desired selections and click Finish.

- *Backup*: This option marks the volume data for backup, similar to setting the Archive bit on a file or directory.

- *Compression*: Turns data compression on for this volume. Compression will use volume space much more efficiently at the cost of read performance. If volume data is not used constantly, compression can be a good idea.

- *Data shredding*: Instructs NetWare to overwrite deleted data with random characters to prevent recovery with disk reader software. Specify how many overwrite passes to make (1–7).

- *Directory quotas*: Sets a limit on the amount of space that any directory can occupy. This might be useful for restricting the size of application, log, or user directories you don't want to grow beyond a certain point.

- *Flush files immediately*: Instructs NetWare to write data to disk immediately upon file close, rather than waiting for the next write cycle.

- *Migration*: Enables support for near-line storage, such as optical subsystems. Migration creates a look-up key in the volume's File Allocation Table (FAT) that describes how to retrieve the data from the near-line storage system.

- *Modified file list*: Displays a list of files modified since the last backup cycle. This is useful for archive utilities, so they don't have to scan the entire volume for changed files.

- *Salvage files*: Instructs NetWare to keep deleted files until the space is needed for new data, so they can be recovered if necessary.

▶ *Snapshot—file level*: Instructs NetWare to keep a copy of the last closed version of each open file in this volume. That way, archive utilities can save the copy to provide some protection in the event of data loss.

▶ *User space quotas*: Allows you to set usage limits for individual eDirectory users. When a quota is reached, users will be unable to save any more files until they have made space for them by removing other files.

▶ *User-level transaction model*: Enables NetWare's Transaction Tracking System (TTS) for the volume. This helps protect databases from corruption that might occur if a failure happens during a database transaction. With TTS turned on, an incomplete transaction is completely backed out and restored to its original state prior to the transaction. TTS protects data by making a copy of the original data before it is overwritten by new data. Then, if a failure of some component occurs in the middle of the transaction, TTS restores the data to its original condition and discards the incomplete transaction.

NOTE TTS is enabled on volume SYS: by default because it is used to protect the eDirectory database from corruption.

▶ *On creation*: Allows you to specify whether to activate and/or mount the new volume upon creation. Activating a volume is what makes it available for use. Mounting a volume is a trivial exercise that sets a pointer in the Volume Mapping Table so that NetWare knows how to access it. If left unchecked, you can activate and mount a volume from the Volume Management page in iManager.

Once the volume has been created, you will be returned to the Volume Management page, from which you can perform various configuration tasks on existing volumes and view the characteristics of volumes that have been created. Configuration options include the following:

▶ *New*: Lets you create new volumes, as described previously.

▶ *Delete*: Lets you delete an existing volume. You cannot delete volume SYS: in this way because that would remove the NetWare operating system. All data on a deleted volume is removed, but salvage and purge options for deleted volumes are available at the storage pool level.

▶ *Rename*: Lets you rename an existing volume.

▶ *Activate*: Makes a volume available for mounting and use by the server.

▶ *Deactivate*: Makes a volume temporarily unavailable for use by the server. A volume cannot be mounted while it is deactivated.

▶ *Mount*: Makes a volume available for use by network users, who can then access the volumes through any of the access methods supported by NetWare 6.5.

▶ *Dismount*: Makes a volume temporarily unavailable for use by network users.

▶ *Move*: Made possible by the NetWare Distributed File System (DFS), the Move option allows you to move an existing volume from its current storage pool to another pool, either on the same server or a different server in the same eDirectory tree. After a move operation, all data is moved automatically, but users can continue to access the data as if it were still in its original location. DFS performs a transparent redirection of requests to the new volume location. DFS is discussed in more detail later in this chapter.

▶ *Split*: Also leveraging DFS, the Split option allows you to select any portion of an existing volume, at the directory level, and install it into a new volume, either on the same server or on another server in the same eDirectory tree. After a split operation, all data is moved automatically, but users can continue to access the data as if it were still in its original location. DFS performs a transparent redirection of requests to the new volume location. DFS is discussed in more detail later in this chapter.

▶ *Properties*: This option lets you make changes to volume attributes, as defined when the volume was created. Volume attributes were discussed previously, during the volume creation process.

▶ *User quotas*: If you have enabled the User Space Restrictions attribute on a volume, use this option to set those space restrictions. This is often useful for limiting the amount of space available to users' home directories. For more information on user home directories, see Chapter 6.

▶ *Update eDirectory*: If you have modified or renamed a volume, use this option to update the eDirectory volume object with the new information and characteristics.

These volume configuration options give you granular control over the management and performance of the volumes on your NetWare servers.

Mounting a DOS Partition as an NSS Volume

If desired, you can mount a server's DOS partition as an NSS volume so that you can access its files like any other network volume. To do this, you need to load DOSFAT.NSS on the NetWare 6.5 server. Type the following command at the server console:

DOSFAT.NSS

This command loads the necessary NLMs to support the DOS partition as a logical volume. It also mounts the DOS partition as a volume with the name DOSFAT_*x*, where *x* is the drive letter of the DOS partition—usually C.

Repairing NSS Pools with REBUILD

When a problem occurs in the NSS environment, repairs are made at the storage pool level rather than at the volume level. This is a change for those of you familiar with VREPAIR.NLM from older versions of NetWare. NSS provides two tools to perform these repair operations:

▶ VERIFY: This utility checks the file system integrity for an NSS pool by searching for inconsistent data blocks or other errors. This utility indicates if there are problems with the file system.

▶ REBUILD: This utility actually makes repairs to the NSS storage pool should they prove necessary. You need to deactivate pools (and all the volumes in the pools) before you run REBUILD so that users do not attempt to access the volumes you are rebuilding. When you deactivate a storage pool, all the volumes in the pool automatically deactivate. REBUILD also copies errors and transactions into an error file called *volume_name*.RLF at the root of the DOS drive on your server. Every time you rebuild a particular NSS volume, the previous error file is overwritten. If you want to keep old error files, move them to another location. You can check the error file whenever an NSS volume does not come up in active mode after a rebuild.

> **NOTE** REBUILD should be a last resort and is seldom necessary. The NSS file system is *journaled*, meaning that it keeps a log of disk activities while they are executing. When a disk crash or other problem occurs, NSS automatically rolls the file system state back to a known good state and then re-executes the operations in the journal to bring the system back up to date.

To run VERIFY, which is a read-only assessment of the storage pool, type the following command at the server console:

```
nss /poolverify
```

NSS provides a list of pools from which you can select. The VERIFY operation will return a summary screen of storage pool information, as shown in Figure 8.5.

FIGURE 8.5
Summary report from the console-based VERIFY.

Should it become necessary, you can run REBUILD by typing the following command at the server console:

```
nss /poolrebuild
```

NSS provides a list of pools from which you can select. REBUILD verifies and accounts for all data blocks in the storage pool. If there are any errors, the errors appear on the screen; otherwise, it reverts to the active state. You must re-activate the pool and remount volume(s) before users can access them again.

NOTE There are many other NSS options available from the command line in addition to REBUILD and VERIFY, but much of this functionality is more easily accessible from your Web-based management tools. For more information on NSS command-line functions, see the NetWare 6.5 online documentation.

Saving Disk Space

NetWare 6.5 offers a few simple features to help you to conserve disk space if it becomes an issue:

▶ File compression, which compresses less frequently used files, has been shown to conserve up to 63% of your hard disk space. However, your specific experience will vary depending on the types of files being stored on the server.

▶ Restricting users' disk space enables you to decide how much room user data can consume on a given volume.

▶ Purging files lets you free up disk space by removing files that have been deleted but are still retained in a salvageable state. (You can also salvage deleted files, instead of purging them, but of course that doesn't free up any disk space.)

Although none of these is a replacement for adding disk space to your server, they can help you keep things running smoothly while you prepare to upgrade your hardware.

File Compression

File compression typically can save up to 63% of the server's hard disk space by compressing unused files. Compressed files are automatically decompressed when a user accesses them, so the user doesn't necessarily know that the files were compressed.

Volumes are automatically enabled to support compression should you enable that attribute when the volume is created. You can also enable support for compression after the fact by modifying a volume's properties with iManager.

Once compression is enabled on a volume, it cannot be disabled, except at the server level, using the following SET parameter:

```
SET Enable File Compression = ON¦OFF
```

This parameter can be set using NoRM and selecting Set Parameters. It is found in the Common File System section. Changing this SET parameter to OFF will suspend compression activities only. There is no way to remove compression capabilities from a volume, except to delete and re-create the volume.

Managing Compression

By default, once the volume is enabled and compression is turned on, files and directories are compressed automatically after they've been untouched for 14 days.

You can change several aspects of file compression, however, such as how long the files wait before being compressed, the time of day the compression activity occurs, and which files never get compressed. To control file compression, you can use two file and directory attributes and several SET parameters.

To specify compression for specific files or directories, you can assign them the following file and directory attributes with NoRM. To do this, select the Volumes link in the left navigation frame, and browse to the directory or file for which you want to set the compression attributes:

- ▶ *Don't Compress*: Instructs NetWare to never compress the file or directory, even if compression is turned on for a parent directory.

- ▶ *Immediate Compress*: Instructs NetWare to compresses the file or directory immediately, without waiting the standard inactivity period.

The SET parameters that affect file compression let you control compression characteristics for all enabled volumes on the server. You can set options such as when compression happens, how many files can be compressed at the same time, how many times a file must be accessed before it is decompressed, and so on. The easiest way to view and change these parameters is with NoRM, but you can also use MONITOR.NLM or the appropriate SET console command at the server console.

NOTE Remember that if you change a SET parameter, the change affects all files and directories in all volumes on the server that have been enabled for compression.

To change the SET parameters, complete the following steps:

1. Launch NoRM and click the Set Parameters link in the Navigation frame.

2. In the Set Parameter Categories window, click Common File System.

3. Modify any of the following compression-related SET parameters by clicking the value currently associated with that parameter.

   ▶ *Compression Daily Check Stop Hour=HOUR:* Specifies the hour when the file compressor stops searching volumes for files that need to be compressed. If this value is the same as the Compression Daily Check Starting Hour value, the search starts at the specified starting hour and goes until all compressible files have been found. The default is 6 (6:00 a.m.). Values range from 0 (midnight) to 23 (11:00 p.m.).

   ▶ *Compression Daily Check Starting Hour=HOUR:* Specifies the hour when the file compressor begins searching volumes for files that need to be compressed. The default is 0 (midnight). Values range from 0 to 23 (11:00 p.m.).

   ▶ *Minimum Compression Percentage Gain=NUMBER:* Specifies the minimum percentage that a file must be able to be compressed in order to remain compressed. The default is 20. Values range from 0 to 50.

   ▶ *Enable File Compression=ON|OFF:* When set to On, file compression is allowed to occur on volumes that are enabled for compression. If set to Off, file compression won't occur, even though the volume is still enabled for compression. The default is On.

   ▶ *Maximum Concurrent Compressions=NUMBER:* Specifies how many volumes can compress files at the same time. Increasing this value can slow down server performance during compression times. The default is 2. Values range from 1 to 8.

   ▶ *Convert Compressed to Uncompressed Option=NUMBER:* Specifies how a compressed file is stored after it has been accessed. The default is 1. Values range from 0 = always leave the file compressed; 1 = leave the file compressed after the first access within the time frame defined by the Days Untouched Before Compression parameter, and then leave the file uncompressed after the second access; 2 = change the file to uncompressed after the first access.

▶ *Decompress Percent Disk Space Free to Allow Commit=NUM-BER*: Specifies the percentage of free disk space that is required on a volume before committing an uncompressed file to disk. This helps you avoid running out of disk space by uncompressing files. The default is 10. Values range from 0 to 75.

▶ *Decompress Free Space Warning Interval=TIME*: Specifies the interval between warnings when the volume doesn't have enough disk space for uncompressed files. The default is 31 min 18.5 sec. Values range from 0 sec (which turns off warnings) to 29 days 15 hours, 50 min 3.8 sec.

▶ *Deleted Files Compression Option=NUMBER*: Specifies how the server handles deleted files. The default is 1. Values range from 0 = don't compress deleted files; 1 = compress deleted files during the next day's search; 2 = compress deleted files immediately.

▶ *Days Untouched Before Compression=DAYS*: Specifies how many days a file or directory must remain untouched before being compressed. The default is 14. Values range from 0 to 100000.

These SET parameters give you robust control over the compression process. However, you should always remember that enabling compression can lead to slower file system performance due to the processor-intensive nature of file compression/decompression.

Restricting Users' Disk Space

You can restrict how much disk space a user can fill up on a particular volume. This can help prevent individual users from using an excessive amount of disk space. NSS volumes let you enable/disable this support through the User Space Restrictions attribute.

To set space restrictions, use the Volume Management page in iManager. Click the User Quotas option to open a page from which you can select users and assign them a maximum amount of disk space they can use on a given volume (see Figure 8.6). You can also see how existing restrictions have been set and how much space each user has available in their quota.

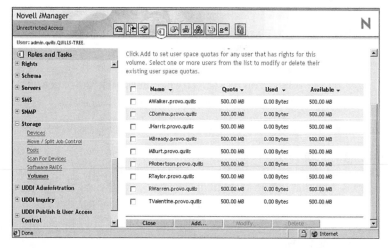

FIGURE 8.6
Using NoRM to set and view user volume quotas.

Purging and Salvaging Files

When files are deleted from a NetWare server, they are not actually removed from the server's hard disk. Instead, they are retained in a salvageable state. Deleted files are usually stored in the same directory from which they were originally deleted. If, however, the directory itself was also deleted, the deleted files are stored in a special directory called DELETED.SAV at the volume's root.

Exceptions to the Salvageable State

Deleted files are maintained in this salvageable state unless one of the following occurs:

▶ The file is salvaged, restoring it to its original form.

▶ The server runs out of free space on the disk and begins to overwrite files that have been deleted for a specified period of time. The oldest deleted files are overwritten first. A configurable **SET** parameter defines the amount of time a file must remain deleted before it can be overwritten.

▶ The administrator or user purges the file. (When purged, a file is completely removed from the disk and cannot be recovered.) You can purge files with ConsoleOne.

▶ The Immediate Purge attribute can be set at the file, directory, or volume level to prevent files from being salvaged. You can set this attribute with ConsoleOne.

▶ The administrator uses SET Immediate Purge of Deleted Files = ON. All volumes on that server will immediately purge deleted files. (The default for this parameter is Off.)

Once any one of these events occurs, the file is no longer salvageable.

Purging and Salvaging Files

You, or any user, can use the Novell client utilities to either purge or salvage a deleted file or directory. To do so, right-click the red N in the system tray, select NetWare Utilities, and choose either Salvage or Purge.

You can also use ConsoleOne to salvage and purge files by completing the following steps:

1. Launch ConsoleOne and browse to the directory containing the files or directories you want to salvage or purge.

2. From the View menu, select Deleted File View.

3. In the View window (right side), select a file or directory.

4. Click either the Salvage or Purge button on the ConsoleOne toolbar, as shown in Figure 8.7.

5. If you salvage files from an existing directory, the files are restored to that directory. If you salvage files from a deleted directory, the files are restored into the DELETED.SAV directory at the root of the volume.

This provides both users and administrators with a tool for recovering deleted files.

NOTE If you have data shredding enabled, it will occur when a file is purged, not when it is deleted. If you have very sensitive materials on which you want to use data shredding, it might be a good idea to enable the Immediate Purge attribute for the file or directory where such data is stored.

Salvage   Purge

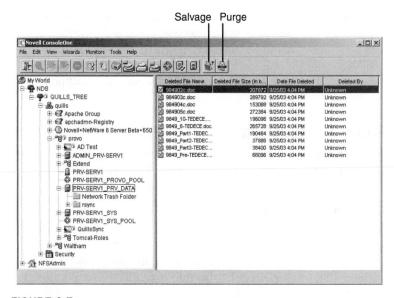

FIGURE 8.7
Using ConsoleOne to salvage or purge deleted files.

NetWare Distributed File System

Distributed File System (DFS) for NetWare 6.5 effectively allows you to directory-enable your NetWare volumes. It lets you create virtual directory structures of data that in reality exist on multiple servers in the eDirectory tree. A DFS junction can be applied at any point in your file system. All it does is point to the actual location of the volume referred to by the junction. In effect, it is a file system alias.

It is DFS and the DFS junction that makes it possible to move and split NetWare volumes, as mentioned previously. When a junction is created, a unique ID for the junction is stored in the Volume Location Database (VLDB). When a user requests access to data through a junction, the Novell client uses to junction's unique ID to search the VLDB for the path to the physical location of the data. It then retrieves and displays the data from its physical location transparently.

Junctions eliminate the need for a user to understand where data is stored on the network. By creating junctions, it is possible to make all a user's data appear as if it is located on a single server, when in fact it is distributed across several servers. This can greatly simplify the interface to network-stored data and reduce the complexity of drive mappings that must be managed by your IT staff.

Using DFS Junctions

NetWare 6.5 does not include a Web-based interface for performing DFS management, so you have to use ConsoleOne if you are going to use DFS. There are a few tasks associated with using DFS, described next.

Create a DFS Management Context

You must create at least one DFS management context in your eDirectory tree. The DFS management context will hold the VLDB. You can create more than one if you want to better support a dispersed network infra-structure. That way, VLDBs can be controlled locally. To create a manage-ment context, complete the following steps:

1. Launch ConsoleOne and browse to the container object—organization (O) or organizational unit (OU)—that you want to use as the DFS management context.

2. Right-click the container and select New >> DFS Management Context.

3. At the Select the Servers screen, select a server or servers to host the VLDB and click Next. Use the right and left arrows to select and deselect servers.

4. At the Specify Database Location screen, specify where you want to store the VLDB on the server, and click Finish. The default location is SYS:\ETC. Make sure you check Load NLMs automatically when the server restarts if you want VLDB.NLM to load automatically when the server boots.

Once created, you can view VLDB information and perform a few basic VLDB tasks by right-clicking the Server object that is running VLDB and selecting Properties. Double-click the Supported Services tab and select NSS VLDB.

Create a DFS Junction

Once the DFS management context is created, and the service is started on the server you selected, you can create DFS junctions. To create a DFS junction, complete the following steps:

NOTE Only NetWare 6 or newer servers can host DFS junctions, but junctions can point to both NSS and Traditional NetWare 5.1 volumes.

1. Launch ConsoleOne and browse to the subdirectory where you want to create a DFS junction. You can also create a new subdirectory for this purpose. You can also select a Volume object to create a junction at the root of a volume.

2. Right-click the subdirectory and select New >> Shortcut >> Junction.

3. At the Target Information screen, browse to the volume to which you want the junction to point, and click Next.

4. Specify the name of the Junction object, and click Finish. Once the junction is created, you might need to refresh ConsoleOne before you will see the new object.

Once created, a DFS junction appears as any other directory or folder in your file system. You can leverage DFS junctions using the latest Novell client, the Microsoft Windows CIFS protocol, or using the XTier protocol for Web services. If you attempt to use a DFS junction from some other method, you will see a small file but will not be able to read or open it.

Moving and Splitting Volumes

Moving and splitting volumes provides unsurpassed flexibility in managing the location of data on your NetWare servers. Moving a volume involves transferring all the data associated with a given NetWare volume to another location, which can be on the same server or a different server in the same directory tree. When a volume is moved, a junction is left behind to point to the new location of the data.

Splitting a volume allows you to move some portion of an NSS volume to a different location, which can be on the same server or a different server in the same directory tree. When a volume is split, a junction is left behind to point to the new location of the data.

A few caveats exist with moving and splitting volumes. They include the following:

▶ You can move or split volumes only to a destination NSS volume. The source volume for a split must be NSS, but for a move it can be either NSS or traditional.

▶ When you specify the context for a source volume, use the full context with both leading and trailing dots.

▶ DFS supports the capability to resume an operation if a server crash or some other type of event interrupts it. When the server restarts, the DFS operation will continue where it left off.

▶ If at all possible, DFS operations should only be performed during off hours when files in the affected volume are closed. DFS cannot transfer open files, although it can keep track of them and allow you to deal with them manually. For more information, see the NetWare 6.5 online documentation.

Volume moves and splits are performed from iManager. To move a volume, complete the following steps:

1. Launch iManager, open the Storage link, and select Volumes in the left navigation frame.

2. Specify the server that holds the volume you want to Move.

3. Select the volume you want to move and click Move.

4. Specify the name of the server to which you want to move the volume and click Next. If you want to schedule the move operation to take place at some later time, you can specify that as well.

5. Specify the name of the moved volume on the new server and click Next. The volume name must be unique on the destination server and follow all standard volume naming conventions.

6. Specify the storage pool into which the new volume will be created and click Next. You can also create a new storage pool, if desired.

7. Select the appropriate volume attributes for the new volume and click Finish.

At this point, all volume data, attributes, and access controls are moved to the new server. To split a volume, complete the following steps:

1. Launch iManager, open the Storage link, and select Volumes in the left navigation frame.

2. Specify the server that holds the volume you want to split.

3. Select the volume you want to move and click Split.

4. At the Split Volume page, specify the name of the server to which you want to move the split portion of the volume, and then specify the directory at which the split should occur. Click Next. If you want to schedule the move operation to take place at some later time, you can specify that as well.

5. Specify the name of the split volume and click Next. The volume name must be unique on the destination server and follow all standard volume naming conventions.

6. Specify the storage pool into which the split volume will be created and click Next. You can also create a new storage pool, if desired.

7. Select the appropriate volume attributes for the new volume and click Finish.

At this point, the split portion of the volume will be moved to the location specified. A DFS junction is left at the point of the split so that the data from the split volume will still be accessible as if it were still in its original location.

Network Attached Storage with iSCSI

iSCSI is a new service offered with NetWare 6.5. *SCSI*, or *Small Computer System Interface*, is a standard for connecting storage devices to a computer. The SCSI standard requires a specialized 50-pin connector and ribbon cable between the SCSI controller and the hard drive. Given this limitation, SCSI devices typically have to be connected directly, and in close proximity to, the computer for which they are providing disk storage.

iSCSI is an exciting new standard that makes it possible to transmit SCSI communications over a network by encapsulating them in standard TCP/IP data packets. This lets you create a low-cost Storage Area Network (SAN) using regular high-speed network hardware, and avoid the considerable costs previously associated with fiber-based SAN architectures. A SAN allows you to consolidate network storage resources for multiple NetWare 6.5 servers.

iSCSI can be configured in a variety of ways, including a nondedicated system in which the iSCSI disk array is accessed through the normal network backbone; a dedicated system in which the iSCSI disk array is accessed through a separate network dedicated to serving the needs of the iSCSI environment; and a storage router option in which the dedicated iSCSI network uses specialized iSCSI router hardware to achieve even greater performance. You can evaluate your needs and choose the iSCSI solution that makes the most sense to you.

iSCSI Basics

There are two main components to the NetWare 6.5 iSCSI environment. The software necessary to use a NetWare 6.5 server is installed with the NetWare 6.5 operating system. You don't have to do any special installation routine in order to use iSCSI.

Initiator software is installed on each server that will use the shared iSCSI storage. The initiator software allows a NetWare 6.5 server or cluster to communicate with an iSCSI storage server or other iSCSI target over a normal TCP/IP network. At this time, the initiator software is only supported on NetWare 6.5.

Target software is installed on a NetWare server that will act as a disk controller for the shared iSCSI storage. A shared disk subsystem is attached directly to the NetWare 6.5 server running the target software. The target software allows external initiators to access the shared disk system.

Alternatively, a dedicated iSCSI router can be used for the target, in which case the NetWare 6.5 target software is unnecessary. The iSCSI router must comply with iSCSI Internet Draft Specification 20. A shared disk subsystem is attached directly to the iSCSI router according to the manufacturer's instructions.

Configuring the iSCSI Environment

Once you have determined the best iSCSI architecture for your needs, you are ready to configure the iSCSI environment. If you have chosen to use an iSCSI router as an iSCSI target, refer to the iSCSI storage router documentation for configuration details.

Configuring an iSCSI Target

There are three main steps to configuring NetWare 6.5 as an iSCSI target:

1. Create an iSCSI partition
2. Load iSCSI target software
3. Create storage pools and logical volumes on the target disk subsystem

You can use either NoRM or the console-based NSS Management utility (NSSMU) to create the iSCSI partition on your target subsystem. To create an iSCSI partition with NoRM, complete the following steps:

1. Launch iManager and open the Servers link in the left navigation frame. Click Launch NetWare Remote Manager.

2. Specify the server that will function as the iSCSI target and click OK. This will ensure that you are running NoRM for the correct server.

3. In NoRM, select Partition Disks in the left navigation frame.

4. In the right frame, locate the disk subsystem that will be used for iSCSI and click the Create link next to the free space associated with the device.

5. In Partition Type, select Novell iSCSI and click Create a New Partition.

6. Specify the size of the iSCSI partition and click CREATE.

   With the iSCSI partition created, load the iSCSI target software on the server by entering the following command at the server console:

   `ton`

   You can unload the iSCSI target software by typing the following at the server console:

   `toff`

7. With the iSCSI target software loaded, use iManager to create NSS partitions, storage pools, and logical volumes on the iSCSI partition. The iSCSI partition will appear as a separate disk device to iSCSI initiators, so you still need to create an NSS partition on the iSCSI partition. The process for creating NSS partitions, pools, and volumes was discussed previously in this chapter.

Configuring iSCSI Initiators

To configure a NetWare 6.5 server as an iSCSI initiator, you must first load the initiator software on the server by entering the following at the server console:

ion

To configure the initiator software, use NoRM to complete the following steps:

1. Launch iManager and open the Servers link in the left navigation frame. Click Launch NetWare Remote Manager.

2. Specify the server that will function as the iSCSI target and click OK. This will ensure that you are running NoRM for the correct server.

3. Select the iSCSI Services link in the left navigation frame.

4. In the right frame, click Add Target.

5. Specify the IP address of the iSCSI target that is connected to the shared storage system and click Next. If the iSCSI disk subsystem is connected to a NetWare 6.5 server, the IP address is that of the NetWare server. If you are using an iSCSI router, the IP address is that of the iSCSI router.

6. Select the target(s) with which you want this initiator to establish an iSCSI session and click Next. Each target listed corresponds to an iSCSI partition you have created, so you can potentially have multiple targets associated with a single IP address.

7. At the server console of the initiator, use the List Devices command to have the server locate the new iSCSI storage device. The iSCSI subsystem will be listed along with other storage devices directly connected to the server.

With the target and initiator configured, you can access the iSCSI disk subsystem as if it were a directly attached resource on each NetWare 6.5 server configured as an initiator for that iSCSI device. Mapping drives, trustee rights, and directory and file attributes will all work identically to a directly connected storage device.

Backing Up and Restoring Files

Although current storage technologies, such as RAID, hot-swappable hard drives, and network-attached storage are making servers ever more secure in their capability to maintain data, there are still many ways in which data can be lost or corrupted. For those situations, it is necessary to have a backup of your network data so that lost files can be recovered.

NetWare 6.5 provides a data backup-and-restore infrastructure known as Storage Management Services (SMS). SMS makes it possible to copy your network data, including files, directories, the eDirectory database, and even data from other servers and clients, to an offline storage system such as tape or optical disk. With a well-developed backup strategy, you can be confident that you will always have a current copy of your network data, so you can restore files should the unthinkable occur.

There are several network backup solutions on the market today. The third-party backup solutions for NetWare build upon the SMS foundation to deliver their solutions. NetWare 6.5 includes a fairly basic server-based backup interface called **SBCON**. This utility will get the job done, but it lacks many of the conveniences, such as flexible scheduling options, that third-party products have.

Backing up network files involves more than just making a copy of the files. It's important to use a backup product, such as **SBCON**, that backs up not just the files but also the NetWare information associated with those files, such as trustee rights, inherited rights filters, and file and directory attributes.

A solid backup strategy is critical to the well being of your network. The following section describes backup strategies that can be employed to protect your valuable data.

Planning a Backup Strategy

Planning is critical to developing an effective backup strategy. A well-planned backup strategy will avoid those headaches associated with finding and restoring files should that be necessary. It will reduce the time it takes to perform data backups and help keep your network humming along. When planning your backup strategy, consider the following:

- How frequently should you make backups?
- What type of medium are you going to use to back up your data?

▶ How should you rotate your backup media?

▶ Where will your backup copies be stored?

▶ How and when will you test the restore procedure?

TIP Although it is possible to backup eDirectory database files, restoring them is a prescription for major grief. Rather than trying to restore eDirectory objects from tape, use partition replication to restore objects to a server. For more information on eDirectory design and replication, see Chapter 5.

Planning a Backup Schedule

An important part of determining how often you need to back up your data revolves around how rapidly significant changes to your data occur, and how important those changes are. A lot of this depends on your line of business. If your data changes rapidly, and those changes must be protected, you should plan on daily backups of that information. If your data changes more slowly, or if re-creating the lost data isn't a big deal, perhaps a weekly backup schedule will do the trick.

Backup products let you determine not only when to back up your network, but also what types of information you back up each time. There isn't much point in backing up all your network data every night if only a few of the files are changing each day.

If you don't need a full backup every time, you can perform what is known as an *incremental* backup. In an incremental backup, changed files are detected, and only they are backed up. One particularly efficient way of backing up your network involves both incremental and full backup routines.

One day a week, you perform a full backup of the network. Then, on each subsequent day during that week, perform an incremental backup of only those files that have changed. Using this strategy, you can restore your entire system, if necessary, by first restoring the weekly backup, and then applying each daily backup to get your files back to their state the day prior to the system failure. This achieves full data protection while minimizing the time it takes to perform the daily backup routines.

Finally, a *differential* backup is a twist on the incremental backup. Differential backups are the same as incremental backups except that the archive bit is not reset as part of the backup process. This means that each differential backup will include all changed data since the last full backup, eliminating the need to restore multiple backup sessions in order to recover all file changes since the last full backup.

> **TIP** Backup products that are NSS-aware can speed up incremental backups significantly by leveraging the NSS Modified File List (MFL). The MFL maintains a list of changed files so that the backup software doesn't have to review every file manually to see which have changed since the last backup.

Another tip for minimizing backup time is to organize your directory (folder) structure so that often-changed files are separate from seldom-changed files. For example, there's no point in wasting your time by frequently backing up files such as applications and utilities, which seldom change. If you put applications in one directory and work files in another, you can skip the application directory completely during incremental backups, making the process go faster.

Finally, be sure to document your backup schedule and keep a backup log. A written record of all backups and your backup strategy can help someone else restore the files if you aren't there.

Choosing Your Backup Medium

Before purchasing a backup device, you must decide what kind of backup medium you want to use. Many manufacturers' backup products can back up data onto a variety of storage media, but it's a good idea to know what you want before you buy something that limits your choices. The medium you choose will probably depend on the following factors:

▶ How much you're willing to spend.

▶ How large your network is.

▶ How long you need to retain your backed-up data. (Some media deteriorate after a few years; other media have a 100-year guarantee.)

Tape is still the most common backup medium in use today, especially in small- to medium-sized businesses. Tapes are relatively easy to use, can be used in any size network, and are fairly inexpensive.

> **NOTE** One of the downsides of tape is that backup manufacturers may use different, proprietary tape formats that aren't compatible with each other. Two tape standards have been established (one from Novell and another from Microsoft), so some efforts have been made to standardize on one or the other, but there are still differences between manufacturers. Be sure any backup product you buy is compatible with any other system with which you need to share tapes.

You should study the pros and cons of the various tape formats to find the best balance between cost and performance before making a decision. For example, SBCON supports the following tape formats:

- ▶ 0.25" TapQuarter-Inch Cartridge
- ▶ 4mm (use only Digital Data Storage–certified tapes)
- ▶ 8mm

If you are interested in very long-term storage, tapes suffer because they will break down over time. Optical storage such as CD-writeable disks and DVDs provide a storage medium that is much more resistant to the ravages of time. However, these solutions are typically significantly more expensive than tape solutions, and SBCON does not currently support an optical backup method. You will need to use a third-party solution in this case.

If you are unsure about the best storage medium for you, talk to your resellers about your specific needs, and let them help you choose the best fit for your storage needs.

Planning the Media Rotation

When you are using re-writeable media, such as tapes, plan to have multiple sets of backup media that can be rotated. This way you keep multiple datasets available at all times. If your current backup is corrupted for any reason, you can still fall back to an older copy. Many network administrators use three or more sets of backup media and cycle through them, one each week. That way, three or more backup datasets are available at any given time. The number of tapes or disks you need depends on the rotation schedule you select.

Some backup products offer preset rotation schedules for you. They will automatically prompt you for the right set of media and keep track of the schedule.

Deciding Where to Store the Backups

Another important aspect of your backup strategy is to plan where to store your backups. If you have backups of noncritical data, you might be comfortable keeping them on-site. However, when storing backups on-site, you should at least store them in a room separate from the server's room. If a fire breaks out in the server room, your backup tapes won't do you much good if they're lying melted beside the server.

For mission-critical data, you might need to keep backups in an off-site location. That way, if a physical disaster occurs (such as a fire, flood, or earthquake), they'll be safe. If the data is critical enough to store off-site, but you also want to have immediate access to it, consider making two copies and storing one off-site and the other on-site.

Testing the Restore Process

A backup is useful only if the data in it can be restored successfully. Too many people discover, too late, a problem with their backups when they're in the middle of an important data restore process. One way to avoid this is to practice restoring files in a lab environment. This will not only familiarize your staff with the process, but will also test the quality and integrity of your backup data. By practicing, you can identify problems you didn't realize you had. Don't wait until it's too late.

The correct frequency for testing your restore process is dependent upon the frequency of your backups and the criticality of your data. For very sensitive systems, monthly tests might be necessary, but for most environments, a quarterly test of your restore process will probably be sufficient.

Preparing to Use SBCON

SBCON is a console-based utility included in NetWare 6.5 that can be used to back up all the different types of files that can be stored on your server: DOS, Macintosh, Windows NT/2000/XP, Windows 95/98, and Unix.

There are five major steps involved in configuring the NetWare 6.5 backup system for use:

1. Install the Storage Management Services (SMS) on a NetWare 6.5 server. SMS is the collection of files and utilities that comprise the NetWare backup solution. It also provides a foundation and common interface for third-party vendors that allow their backup applications to communicate with NetWare.

2. Install a backup device and load the device's drivers on a server. This server will be the host server (the backup server).

3. Load the necessary backup NLMs on the host server.

4. Load the appropriate Target Service Agents (TSAs) on any servers or workstations whose files you want to back up. These servers and workstations are called *targets*.

5. Launch the Storage Management Engine (SME) on either the host server or a workstation. The SME is the interface from which you will run backup and restore operations. **SBCON** is the NetWare 6.5 SME.

You will perform the first three steps in this process whether you choose to use **SBCON** or some other utility as your preferred SME. Several third-party vendors offer backup/restore utilities that function as SMEs. They have designed their systems to integrate with the NetWare SMS so that they don't have to re-create the low-level interface with the operating system.

Installing Storage Management Services

You can install SMS during the installation of NetWare 6.5, by choosing it as an optional Novell service. You also can install SMS after the fact through iManager or the graphical server console. To install SMS through iManager, complete the following steps:

1. Insert the NetWare 6.5 Operating System CD-ROM into your workstation.

2. Launch iManager and open the Install and Upgrade link in the left navigation frame.

3. Select Install NetWare 6.5 Products, and then click Remote Product Install in the right frame.

4. At the Target Server screen, select the server to which you want to install SMS and click Next. Authenticate as an Admin user for your eDirectory tree and click OK.

5. At the components screen, click Clear All and select only Storage Management Services. Click Next.

6. At the Summary screen, click Copy Files. You will be prompted to insert the NetWare 6.5 product's CD-ROM. After the SMS files are copied, click Close to complete the installation.

With SMS installed, you are now ready to configure the backup/restore environment on your NetWare 6.5 server.

Setting Up the Host Server and Targets

Before you can run **SBCON**, you must first prepare the host server and any targets you want to back up, by completing the following steps:

1. Attach the backup device (tape or disk drive) to the host server, following the manufacturer's instructions.

2. Load the necessary backup device drivers on the host server, again following manufacturer's instructions.

3. Confirm that the device is loaded, and recognized by NetWare, by launching NoRM and opening Partition Disks. You should see the backup device listed as a device. If you don't see your backup device listed, use the following console command to register the device with NetWare:

   `SCAN FOR NEW DEVICES`

TIP Place the commands that load the backup device drivers in the server's STARTUP.NCF file if you want them to load automatically when the server is rebooted.

4. SMS includes SMSSTART.NCF to load the basic SMS modules on a NetWare 6.5 server. It is stored in `SYS:SYSTEM`. You can put the `SMSSTART` command in your AUTOEXEC.NCF if you want to load SMS modules automatically when the server boots.

   ▶ *SMDR.NLM*: This is the SMS Data Requester. It automatically creates an SMS SMDR Group object in the server's context. The SMS SMDR Group object will contain each server and workstation to be backed up by this host server.

   ▶ *TSAFS.NLM*: This is the TSA for NetWare 6.5 servers. This module lets you back up data stored on this server.

Additional SMS modules might also be needed, depending on your specific needs. They must be loaded manually from the server console or the AUTOEXEC.NCF. These optional SMS modules include the following:

   ▶ *SMSDI.NLM*: This is the SMS Device Interface module, which will let the `SBCON` program communicate with the backup device:

   ▶ *QMAN.NLM*: This is the SMS Queue Manager, which will create a job queue for the backup utility to use. The backup queue object is named *<servername> Backup Queue* (where *<servername>* is the name of the server on which QMAN.NLM is running).

   ▶ *TSANDS.NLM*: This TSA lets you back up the eDirectory database. It's usually best to load this on a server that contains a replica of the eDirectory tree's largest partition.

NOTE Because NSS supports mounting the DOS partition as a logical volume, you can use the `nss /DOSFAT` command to make the DOS partition accessible to your SMS backup operations.

---

5. *(Optional)* If you are going to back up any other target servers from this host server, you need to load the appropriate TSA(s) on the target server. The TSA modules that might be appropriate for a target server, which is not also functioning as a host, include the following:

   ▶ **TSA600**: Load on NetWare 6 target servers.

   ▶ **TSA500**: Load on NetWare 5 target servers.

   ▶ **TSA410**: Load on NetWare 4 target servers.

   ▶ **TSADOSP**: Load on a target server if you want to back up its DOS partition. This NLM is necessary only on older versions of NetWare.

When these steps are completed, the host server is prepared, and the target server is ready to be backed up.

Backing Up Files with SBCON

After you've loaded the necessary NLMs on the host server and loaded a TSA on the target server or workstation, you are ready to back up the target's files. NetWare 6.5 provides SBCON.NLM as a console-based utility for backing up network data.

SBCON enables you to select the type of backup you want to perform. There are three choices (all of which can be customized for your particular needs):

▶ *Full backup.* This option backs up all network files. It removes the Archive file attribute—assigned to a file whenever the file is changed—from all files and directories. When the file is backed up, most backup products can remove the attribute so that the next time the file is changed, the attribute is once again assigned.

▶ *Differential backup.* This option backs up only files that were modified since the last full backup. It does not remove the Archive attribute from these files.

▶ *Incremental backup*. This option backs up only files that were modified since the last full or incremental backup. It removes the Archive attribute from these files.

SMS is cluster-enabled, meaning that it can run on a server cluster. It is also capable of backing up cluster-enabled pools by using the same procedure outlined next for regular SMS targets. For more information on Novell Cluster Services (NCS), see Chapter 11, "Multiprocessor Support and Clustering."

To use **SBCON** to back up files, complete the following steps:

1. Load **SBCON** from the server console. You can also perform these tasks remotely using RConsoleJ. For more information on RConsoleJ, see Chapter 3.

2. From the main menu, choose Job Administration, and then choose Backup.

3. At the Backup Options screen, configure the backup session (see Figure 8.8). When finished, press Esc to save your options.

FIGURE 8.8
The Backup Options screen in SBCON is used to create a new backup job.

▶ *Target service*: Select the target server to back up. Enter a suitable username and password for the target. Specify the user's full name, with context and a leading dot.

▶ *What to back up*: Press Enter to open the List Resources box. Press Ins and browse the list of volumes, directories, and files until you locate what you want to back up. Press Enter to select the item and Esc to move it to the List Resources box.

When you have selected all the resources you want to back up, press Esc to return to the Backup Options menu.

▶ *Description*: Enter a descriptive name for this backup session. This description will be used during a restore process, so be as specific as possible. Include dates and specific paths included in the backup session if possible.

▶ *Device/media name*: Choose the backup device and medium you will use. If only one device is available, the backup program will choose it for you. Specifying wildcard characters (*.*) will select the default device.

4. Open the Advanced Options menu to select specific session characteristics for the backup. Press Esc to save your choices.

▶ *Backup type*: Specify Full, Differential, or Incremental backup.

▶ *Subsets of what to back up*: Specify Include and Exclude options to customize what you want to back up. Use Exclude options when you want to back up most of the file system while omitting only a small part. Everything that you don't specifically exclude is backed up. Use Include options when you want to back up only a small portion of the file system. Everything you don't specifically include is excluded.

▶ *Scan options*: Specify what types of data to exclude from the backup process. Options include subdirectories, trustee rights, hidden files, and the like.

▶ *Execution time*: Specify the time you want the backup to occur. If you don't modify this, it will start immediately.

▶ *Scheduling*: Specify a schedule for the job you are creating, if you want it to run on a regular basis without having to reconfigure it each time.

5. Next to Append Session, select Yes if your backup device allows you to put multiple sessions on a medium, and if one or more sessions are already on the medium you're using. Select No to overwrite any existing sessions.

6. When asked if you want to submit a job, select Yes to submit it to the SMS queue.

Once the job is submitted, **SBCON** runs the backup session as configured, at the time specified.

Restoring Files with SBCON

To restore files from a backup, you need to prepare the host server and
targets the same way you did for the backup procedure.

After you've loaded the necessary NLMs on the host server and loaded a
TSA on the target server or workstation, use SBCON to restore files. To use
SBCON to restore files to an SMS target server, complete the following
steps:

1. Load SBCON from the server console.

2. From the main menu, choose Job Administration, and then choose
   Restore.

3. At the Restore Options screen, configure the restore session (see
   Figure 8.9). When finished, press Esc to save your options.

FIGURE 8.9
The Restore Options screen in SBCON is used to restore a backup to an
SMS target.

▶ *Target service*: Select the target server. Enter a suitable username and password for the target. Specify the user's full
  name, with context and a leading dot.

▶ *Description*: Specify the name for this restore session. This
  name can be used to identify the restore session in the SBCON
  job queue.

▶ *Device/media name*: Choose the backup device and medium
  from which you will restore the data. If only one device is
  available, the backup program will choose it for you.
  Specifying wildcard characters (*.*) will select the default
  device.

▶ *Session to Restore*: Specify the name of the session that you want to restore. Press Enter to see a list of all available sessions on the device/media you have chosen. You will see the description names you specified when each backup session was created.

4. Advanced Options is the last option on the Restore Options screen. Use it to configure the specific session characteristics for the restore operation. Press Esc to save your choices.

▶ *Rename data sets*: If you want to restore the data to a different location, specify the specific path here.

▶ *Subsets of what to restore*: Specify Include and Exclude options to customize what you want to restore. Use Exclude options when you want to restore most of the file system while omitting only a small part. Everything that you don't specifically exclude is restored. Use Include options when you want to restore only a small portion of the file system. Everything you don't specifically include will not be restored.

▶ *Open mode options*: Specify what types of data to exclude from the restore process. Options include data streams, trustee rights, space restrictions, and the like.

▶ *Overwrite parent*: Specify whether you want to overwrite existing data that might exist for parent objects, which include servers, volumes, and directories.

▶ *Overwrite child*: Choose whether to overwrite files without regard for last backup time or date of existing file.

▶ *Execution time*: Specify the time you want the restore operation to occur. If you don't modify this, it will start immediately.

▶ *Scheduling*: Specify a schedule for the job you are creating if you want it to run on a regular basis without having to reconfigure it each time.

5. When asked if you want to submit a job, select Yes to submit the restore operation to the SMS queue.

As with the backup process, upon submission, **SBCON** runs the restore session as configured, at the time specified.

CHAPTER 9

Open Source Web Services

Instant Access

Installing Apache Web Server and Tomcat Servlet Engine

▶ Install Apache Web server and Tomcat Servlet engine using iManager or the graphical server console.

Managing Apache Web Server

▶ To manage Apache Web Server, use Apache Manager, which is accessible through Web Manager.

▶ Use the options in Server Preferences to configure the behavior of the Web server.

▶ Use the options in Content Management to manage Web server content and applications.

▶ Use the options in Server Logs to configure and view Apache Access and Error logs.

Working with NetWare Web Search Server

▶ Creates a Web search engine for use by internal users (indexes relevant Internet Web sites) or by external users (indexes your Web server information so that it can be effectively searched).

▶ Configured and managed through the Web search management pages, which are accessible from Web Manager after Web Search Server is installed.

Introduction to NetWare 6.5 Web Services

There are four main components of the NetWare 6.5 Web services model:

▶ *Apache Web Server for NetWare*: The Apache Web server is an open source (read: *free*) Web server that is responsible for serving more than 60% of all Web content on the Internet. In NetWare 6.5, Apache provides support for all NetWare 6.5 Web-based management tools, and support for regular Web server functionality for providing Web services and applications.

▶ *Tomcat Servlet Engine for NetWare*: Tomcat was developed by the same folks who gave us Apache and is used to serve up Web applications. As with Apache, Tomcat is used internally for NetWare Web-based management tools, and can be used externally to provide Web-based services.

▶ *NetWare Web Search Server*: Web Search Server offers a powerful, full-text search engine that you can use to add search capabilities to your Internet or intranet Web sites.

▶ *Additional Web Services*: NetWare 6.5 includes several other pieces to the Web services puzzle, including MySQL database, OpenSSH, and scripting support through Perl and PHP. These services are introduced briefly in this chapter.

This chapter looks at Apache Web server for NetWare and Tomcat Servlet Engine for NetWare because they form the foundation for delivering Web services on the NetWare 6.5 platform. Several of the powerful NetWare 6.5 services rely on Apache and Tomcat, including

▶ iManager

▶ iFolder

▶ iPrint

▶ NetWare Web Search Server

▶ Virtual Office

The chapter also takes a look at NetWare Web Search Server, which allows you to create powerful search services for your internal and external Web sites, thereby making them much more usable to your employees, partners, and customers.

Finally, this chapter briefly introduces several of the other Web services that are available to provide more specific tools and development functionality to your network environment.

Apache Web Server for NetWare

Apache Web Server for NetWare replaces the NetWare Enterprise Web server, and is the only HTTP stack provided for NetWare 6.5. The Apache Web server is an open source Web server used by more than two-thirds of the Internet's Web servers. As such, it runs on all major server platforms and can scale to support thousands of simultaneous connections.

Apache Web server is a complex and full-featured Web server, so there is a lot more to it than can be covered here. However, because Apache is an open source application, most anything you want to know about it is available on the Web. You should take some time to look through the open source Apache documentation in order to become familiar with architecture and capabilities, particularly if you are going to implement a more complex Web environment. The Apache Web server documentation is available online at http://httpd.apache.org/docs-2.0.

Apache Web server is used in two separate ways on NetWare 6.5. First, one instance of Apache is installed automatically as a dedicated Web server to support the administration tools for NetWare 6.5 and its related products and services. You can find all files related to this instance of Apache in the SYS:ADMINSRV directory. The admin server supports Web Manager, iManager, iFolder, and iPrint, and other NetWare 6.5 services that need a Web interface.

A second instance of Apache can optionally be installed on NetWare 6.5 that will function as a dedicated Web server for hosting your organization's Web services, such as a corporate intranet, external Web site, or any other Web service. You can find all files related to this instance of Apache in the SYS:APACHE2 directory.

When you use iManager, accessible from any Web browser (including the new Web browser now available from the NetWare GUI), it is the Admin instance of the Apache Web server that is serving up the data between the Web browser and NetWare 6.5.

Installing Apache Web Server

If you are interested in using Apache only as the foundation for your NetWare 6.5 tools and services, you don't have to do anything to get Apache up and running. The admin server instance of Apache is installed automatically during the NetWare 6.5 installation.

However, if you want to create a dedicated Web server on NetWare 6.5, you need to specify the installation of the second instance of Apache. If you didn't select Apache as one of the NetWare 6.5 components to install during the initial server installation, you can install it after the fact through iManager. To install Apache Web server through iManager, complete the following steps:

1. Insert the NetWare 6.5 Operating System CD-ROM into your workstation.

2. Launch iManager and open the Install and Upgrade link in the left navigation frame.

3. Select Install NetWare 6.5 Products, and then click Remote Product Install in the right frame.

4. At the Target Server screen, select the server to which you want to install Apache Web server and click Next. Authenticate as an Admin user for your eDirectory tree and click OK.

5. At the components screen, click Clear All and select only Apache2 Web Server and Tomcat 4 Servlet Container. Click Next.

6. At the Summary screen, click Copy Files. You will be prompted to insert the NetWare 6.5 product's CD-ROM. After the Apache and Tomcat files are copied, click Close to complete the installation.

Once Apache Web server is installed, the following commands are inserted into the server's AUTOEXEC.NCF to load Apache and Tomcat automatically whenever the server starts:

```
AP2WEBUP
SYS:\TOMCAT\4\BIN\TOMCAT4.NCF
```

The full path for TOMCAT4.NCF is optional because a **SEARCH ADD** path for this directory is also provided. However, by default, the TOMCAT4.NCF load statement includes the path.

To unload Apache Web server and Tomcat, use the following console commands:

```
AP2WEBDN
TC4STOP
```

The admin server instance of Apache and Tomcat are also loaded automatically from the AUTOEXEC.NCF with the following commands:

```
ADMSRVUP
TCADMUP
```

To unload the admin server and Tomcat, use the following commands:

```
ADMSRVDN
TCADMDN
```

Apache Web Server Configuration

Apache Web servers are managed through a configuration file: HTTPD.CONF. NetWare 6.5 stores HTTPD.CONF in `SYS:APACHE2\CONF\`. Typically, this means that you manually edit the configuration file to configure Apache. However, NetWare 6.5 offers Apache Manager, which puts a browser-based face on the HTTPD.CONF file. Apache Manager not only reduces the potential for errors, but also lets you manage your Web server environment from any Web browser.

> **NOTE** The admin server instance of Apache Web server also uses a configuration file `SYS:ADMINSRV\CONF\ADMINSERV.CONF`. However, you will likely not have to modify this file as part of your network administration duties.

Apache Manager operates in two modes: File and Directory. If you are running a single Web server, you can use the File mode to modify the HTTPD.CONF and store it directly on the Web server. To launch Apache Manager in File mode, complete the following steps:

1. On the server running Apache Web server, open NetWare Web Manager by typing the following. For more information on Web Manager, see Chapter 3, "Novell Management Tools."

   ```
   https://www.quills.com:2200
   ```

   or

   ```
   https://137.65.192.100:2200
   ```

2. Log in as an Admin user in the eDirectory tree.

3. Open the Open Source link in the left navigation frame and select Apache 2.0.

4. In the yellow box, click Administer Single Apache Server. This will open Apache Manager, as shown in Figure 9.1.

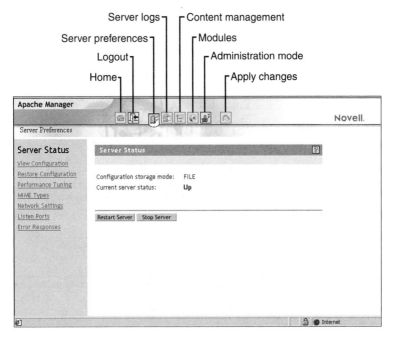

FIGURE 9.1
Apache Manager running in File mode.

From this page, you can perform all the necessary configuration and management activities associated with Apache Web server. When changes are made, they will be written to the HTTPD.CONF file on the Apache Web server. However, if you are running multiple Apache Web servers in your environment, consider using Apache Manager in Directory mode. Directory mode lets you share configurations between several Apache Web servers by storing the configuration file in eDirectory.

In Directory mode, a configuration daemon imports the contents of the HTTPD.CONF file from each Web server into eDirectory.

To launch and configure Apache Manager in Directory mode, you should first load the configuration daemon on each Apache Web server in your environment:

1. From the console of each Apache Web server you want to manage, load **AP2WEBMAN** to load the configuration daemon on the server.

2. Enter a password for the configuration file on this server.

3. Press Y and then Enter to create a directory object for this server's configuration file.

Once this has been done on all Apache Web servers, all configuration files will be stored in eDirectory. Once this is done, you are ready to run Apache Manager in Directory mode:

1. Launch Apache Manager in File mode as described previously.

2. Click the Administration Mode button in the header (see Figure 9.1).

3. Select the storage mode for the Apache configuration and click Save.

   ▶ *File*: This is the default option, and suitable for managing Apache on a single server. Apache configuration will be kept in the HTTPD.CONF file on the server.

   ▶ *eDirectory*: This option will switch Apache configuration to the configuration stored in eDirectory. The eDirectory configuration is first created when you load **AP2WEBMAN** on the server and create an eDirectory object for Apache management.

   ▶ *eDirectory Import Wizard*: If you want to update the Apache configuration in eDirectory as part of your switch to eDirectory Storage mode, select eDirectory Import Wizard and follow the prompts to import the current Apache configuration into eDirectory.

4. When the Storage mode is changed, Apache Manager will automatically refresh. When it does, it will re-open in Multiple Server mode using the configuration stored in eDirectory.

With the complete Apache Web server configuration file in eDirectory, the configuration can now be applied to a single server, to a group of servers, or to all servers in your Web environment. Apache Manager lets you define groups of servers and apply a consistent configuration to all servers in the group. When a change is made to the configuration file, the configuration daemon will make sure that the change is replicated to each server in the group so that everything stays consistent.

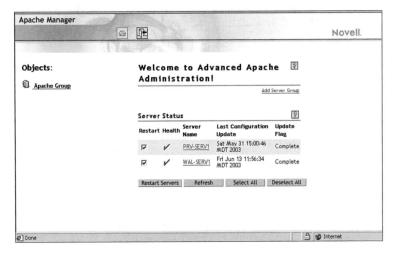

FIGURE 9.2
Apache Manager running in Directory mode.

However, the aspects of the configuration are identical whether you are using File or Directory mode for doing the management of your Apache Web servers. So, for simplicity's sake, the actual Apache Web server configuration issues are discussed from the perspective of File mode. For more information on using Apache Manager in Directory mode, see the NetWare 6.5 online documentation.

Storing Web Content

The most important aspect of running a Web server is making sure that the various Web pages are available to your Web users. Although the art of creating Web pages is beyond the scope of this book, you need to know the basics about storing files on Apache Web servers so that pages will be available as needed. There are three main Web server directory features with which you should become familiar to do this: Document Root, Additional Document Directories, and User Home Directories.

Document Root

The home page associated with your Web server's IP address and/or DNS name is stored in the document root with the name INDEX.HTM (or .HTML). From the home page, you can create links to other pages, graphics, and applications as needed. Secondary resources can have any filename.

The document root, also called the *primary document directory*, is where a Web server will start looking for requested Web pages and resources. By default, Apache Web server document root is set to the following location:

`SYS:APACHE2\HTDOCS`

Because it's not necessarily a good idea to use the **SYS:** volume for storing your Web pages, you can change the document root to another volume and directory by completing the following steps:

> **NOTE** For the best Web server performance, you should keep the document root as high in the directory structure as possible to reduce document search times.

1. From Apache Manager (see Figure 9.1), click the Content Management button in the header.

2. Specify the new document root in the Document Root field and click Save. Use the following syntax to specify the document root: *<volume>*:*<directory>**<subdirectory>*. For example:

   `PRV_DATA:\APACHE2\DOCS`

> **NOTE** The path specified for the document root must already exist. There is no option to create a new path on the fly as part of this process.

3. Click Save, and then select Save and Apply to reset the document root on the Web server.

Apache will be restarted so that the change will take effect.

Additional Document Directories

You can also create additional document directories for those who want to publish their own content, but to whom you don't want to grant access to the document root. This also lets you easily distribute the responsibility of Web content to those responsible for it.

> **NOTE** Additional directories don't even have to be located on the Web server. You can specify another server's volume and directory so long as that server is accessible from the Web server via TCP/IP.

To set an additional document root, complete the following steps:

1. From Apache Manager, click the Content Management button in the header.

2. Select Additional Document Directories from the left navigation frame.

3. Specify the required information and click Save. Click Save and Apply to restart Apache so that the changes will take effect.

   ▶ *URL prefix*: Specify the URL prefix or keyword you want to use to represent the path. This is appended to your root domain name.

   ▶ *File Path*: Specify the complete (absolute) path of the directory to which you want to map the URL prefix. Use the `volume:\directory\subdirectory` syntax.

You will see a list of all additional document directories that are currently defined for this Apache Web server. In addition to creating new document directories, you can configure those that have already been defined.

User Home Directories

This feature lets you to set up document directories for each user in your eDirectory tree. This lets users access their own files from a Web browser. Effectively, users can have their own personal Web sites. To create a document directory for a user, complete the following steps:

1. If you haven't already done so, use iManager to create a home directory for every user who will provide Web access to files.

2. In the user's home directory, create a `PUBLIC_HTML` directory. Copy an INDEX.HTM file to it. This can be any simple HTML template that the Web server can use to display the user's content. Users will typically modify the default file as they build their personal Web page.

3. Specify how Apache will authenticate to eDirectory in order to query for user home directories. Apache can use the default Public User object in eDirectory, or you can create a generic User object specifically for use by Apache. If you decide to create a generic User object, use iManager to create the user before continuing.

4. From Apache Manager, click the Content Management button in the header.

5. Select User Home Directories from the left navigation frame.

6. Specify the required information and click Save.

   ▶ *Status*: Check On to enable support for user home directories.

   ▶ *User URL Prefix*: Specify the character to be used to indicate that the following text refers to a user home directory. The default character, and the one most commonly used in this situation is the tilde (~), but you can specify any character or number.

   ▶ *Subdirectory*: Specify the name of the directory you created for each user as the primary document directory. By default, this is `public_html`.

   ▶ *User Search Contexts*: Specify the search context where your user objects are stored. Apache uses LDAP to locate the specified context, so use LDAP syntax, with commas (,) as delimiters instead of periods (.). For example:

   `o=quills,ou=provo`

   ▶ *Configuration Option*: Specify the method you have chosen to log Apache in to eDirectory. Assign Public Rights uses the Public object, whereas Username and Password lets you specify a generic User object for use by Apache.

WARNING The username and password information is stored, in plain text, in the HTTPD.CONF file. Make sure you have properly protected this file so that it cannot be accessed except by authorized administrative users. Generic User objects should only have rights to browse user directories, and no other areas of the NetWare 6.5 file system. For more information on setting file rights, see Chapter 6.

7. Click Save, and then Save and Apply to reset the User Home Directory settings on the Web server.

Apache will be restarted so that the change will take effect. Once enabled, users can view the content of their user home directory by typing the domain name, followed by a slash (/), followed by ~usersname. For example:

`http://www.quills.com/~jharris`

Hosting Multiple Web Sites

Apache supports *virtual servers* to host multiple Web sites on a single physical server. This lets a single NetWare 6.5 server potentially host all your Web server needs. This is useful if you need to let different divisions or departments host their own Web resources, or if you are an ISP and need to host multiple Web sites for your clients without having a separate physical server for each one of them.

You can host two types of virtual servers on your NetWare server:

▶ *Hardware virtual servers*: This option lets you define multiple IP addresses and assign each to a different document root. Hardware virtual servers require fewer system resources than multiple instances of the Web server, but all hardware virtual servers must share the same configuration. If you want to set up different servers for different purposes, this might not be the best solution.

NOTE To create a secondary IP address for use by a hardware virtual server, use the following console command:

add secondary IPaddress <*IP address*>

To have the server bind the additional IP address(es) each time it starts, add the command to the **AUTOEXEC.NCF**. It should be placed after the LOAD and BIND statements (or after the **INITSYS.NCF** statement, if INETCFG is being used).

▶ *Software virtual servers*: This option lets you map a single IP address to multiple server names by assigning each server a distinct port number. Each software virtual server can have its own home page, which allows you to host multiple Web sites from one IP address. However, to do this, your Web clients (the Web browsers) must support the HTTP host header in order to distinguish between one software virtual server and the next.

NOTE To support software virtual servers, configure Apache to listen on the additional ports by using the Listen Ports link in Apache Manager. From this page, you can define all the ports to which the Apache Web server should listen for incoming requests.

For more information on both of these virtual server options, see the Novell online documentation.

To set up a virtual server, complete the following steps:

1. From Apache Manager, click the Content Management button in the header.

2. Select Virtual Hosts from the left navigation frame.

3. Specify the required information and click Save.

   ▶ *IP address:port*: Specify the IP address of your Apache Web server, followed by a colon (:) and the port number you want to use. If you don't specify a port, Apache will assume port **80**. If you want to have Apache listen on both a secure and an unsecure port, enter both IP address and port combinations separated by a space.

   ▶ *Server name*: Specify the hostname (DNS) of your Apache Web server.

   ▶ *Host TYPE*: Specify the name-based option to set up a software virtual server. Specify IP-based to set up a hardware virtual server.

4. Click Save and Apply to create the virtual server.

Apache will be restarted so that the new virtual server can be loaded as configured.

NOTE For more information on both hardware and software virtual servers, you should review the Apache documentation on the subject at `http://httpd.apache.org/docs-2.0/vhosts/`.

Apache Modules

The Apache Web server has been developed with a component architecture that permits functionality to be added through the addition of a functionality-specific module. A *module* is a specially developed extension for Apache Web server that provides new or expanded functionality.

Requests directed to an Apache Web server pass through a series of stages as they are handled. Some of the Apache stages include authentication, authorization, and access control. Modules can be inserted at these, or any other, stage to provide increased functionality.

There are several modules available for use with Apache Web server on NetWare 6.5:

▶ `mod_ldap_auth` enables LDAP authentication support to Apache Web server.

▶ `mod_edir` builds upon `mod_ldap_auth` to provide eDirectory authorization capabilities to Apache Web server.

▶ `mod_cache` enables an HTTP content cache that can be used to cache either local content or content available through a proxy.

▶ `mod_perl` enables support for the Perl scripting language on Apache Web server.

▶ `mod_php` enables support for the PHP scripting language on Apache Web server.

▶ `mod_nsn` enables support for the Novell Script for NetWare (NSN) scripting language on Apache Web server.

▶ `mod_dav` provides WebDAV (Web-based Distributed Authoring and Versioning) functionality for the Apache Web server.

Selecting the Modules button in the header of Apache Manager can enable the caching module and the three scripting modules. For more information on using Apache modules, see the NetWare 6.5 online documentation and visit the Apache Web server documentation site at `http://httpd.apache.org/docs-2.0/mod/`.

Adding Content to Your Web Site

After Apache Web server has been installed and enabled, you can immediately access a sample Web page and some subpages that are included for demonstration. The default Web pages look just like Web Manager, but lack the links to the management utilities that are available through the secure interface. This content is stored in the default document root at `SYS:APACHE2\HTDOCS`.

To view the sample Web site, open a client Web browser on a workstation in your network and enter your NetWare server's IP address or DNS name. For example:

`http://<server_IP_address>`

or

`http://<domain_name>`

Once your Web server is running, you can start posting content for your Web server audience to access—whether that's your department, your company, or the whole world. Do this by placing files in the Web server's primary or additional document directories.

For example, suppose you created a new HTML file called MKTG_DOCS.HTM that includes links to the marketing collateral for your organization. You would probably copy that file to the additional document directory assigned to the marketing organization; for example, `PRV_DATA:\WEB_PAGES\MARKETING`.

Once the file is stored in the additional document directory, users can access the file by entering the Web server's DNS name together with the additional document directory identifier and the filename. For example:

`HTTP://WWW.QUILLS.COM/MARKETING/MKTG_DOCS.HTM`

The same general process governs the creation of any Web content, whether that content is an Internet site, a corporate intranet, a departmental page, or even a personal Web page. What differentiates one Web site from another is how it is available (internally versus externally) and what type of server it is running on. External sites and larger corporate sites are usually run on dedicated Web servers or hardware virtual servers, whereas smaller departmental sites work well on software virtual servers where users can easily create personalized pages, if necessary.

Publishing Content to a Web Site

When you are configuring an internal Web site, you will often have areas of a Web site that are available for contributors to publish their content. This makes it possible for users to communicate within a department, share information with other departments, and communicate items of general interest.

NOTE Virtual Office is a powerful new feature for NetWare 6.5 that makes it much easier to create temporary or ad hoc portals for information sharing purposes. For more information on Virtual Office, see Chapter 10.

Web content contributors have several options for publishing content to your Web server. For example:

- ▶ Mapping a network drive and creating or copying the content to the desired directory
- ▶ Using Internet Explorer 5.0 or higher
- ▶ Using Novell NetDrive to map a drive

Additionally, users who are familiar with Web publishing tools can choose any of those with which they are familiar.

Publishing Content Using a Mapped Drive

If your contributors are using the Novell Client, this is one way of providing access to Web content areas. Use iManager to assign the appropriate rights to Web content contributors and provide users with the correct network path so they can map a drive to the content directory. You can also set up the drive mapping in a login script. For more information on login scripts with the Novell Client, see Appendix B.

Publishing Content Using Internet Explorer

Web-distributed authoring and versioning (WebDAV) is an industry-standard protocol that enhances HTTP, turning the Web into a document database that enables collaborative creation, editing, and searching from remote locations.

WebDAV support is provided on NetWare 6.5 through NetStorage. With NetStorage enabled, you can publish content directly to a specified document directory from Internet Explorer. For more information on NetStorage, see Chapter 10.

Publishing Content with NetDrive

Novell NetDrive lets you map a drive to any server without using the traditional Novell Client. This means that with NetDrive, you can access your files on any server and modify them through standard Windows utilities such as Windows Explorer. The NetDrive client can be installed from the Novell client's CD-ROM. For more information on NetDrive, see Chapter 10.

Securing Web Content

Once you have content organized and published, you should immediately start looking for ways to prevent unauthorized access and malicious tampering with your Web resources. There are three main areas that affect the security of Apache Web server: authentication, authorization, and encryption.

Authentication

As mentioned previously, Apache Web server integrates with any LDAP directory to provide authentication services through the `mod_ldap_auth` module. This makes it possible to integrate Apache with most any directory service that is available, including Novell eDirectory. Apache will refer to the LDAP directory to determine access controls, authentication credentials, and so on. The `mod_ldap_auth` module, discussed previously, provides this support.

Authorization

Apache must be able to access both eDirectory and remote server file systems in order to determine access rights to Web resources that a user might request when he or she visits an Apache-hosted Web site. The `mod_edir` module provides Apache with the capability to access both eDirectory and remote file systems in order to determine user rights. Two authorization modes are supported: Anonymous and Authenticated.

Anonymous Mode

Instead of using a username and password to authenticate to eDirectory or the remote file system, Anonymous mode lets Apache leverage [`Public`] rights to access eDirectory and remote files systems. However, in order to use Anonymous mode, you must do two things. First, you must grant [`Public`] access to the Home Directory attribute associated with every User object in the eDirectory tree. This is necessary in order to provide users with access to their home directories through the Web server.

Second, in order to access a remote server's file system, the NetWare 6.5 server running Apache must be able to log in to the remote server. To make this possible, make sure the Apache server hosts a local eDirectory replica and grant the Apache Web server's eDirectory object Read and File Scan rights to all remote file systems it will need to access.

Authenticated Mode

Instead of relying on [`Public`] access rights, Authenticated mode leverages a username and password that you create specifically for the Apache Web server. This username and password are stored in the Apache Web server's HTTPD.CONF file. This information must match an eDirectory user object that is created for the Apache Web server to use. This User object is then assigned rights to access the Home Directory attribute of all User objects in eDirectory, and Read and File Scan rights to all remote file systems that it will need to access.

Because storing an eDirectory username and password in HTTPD.CONF poses a significant security lapse, you should restrict access to the HTTPD.CONF file to only those with administrative rights to your Web server environment. You can also create a separate .CONF file that only holds the Apache directives necessary to specify the user ID and password to the Apache User object. Then you can reference this .CONF file from HTTPD.CONF whenever it is necessary.

Encryption

Encryption is the third aspect of a sound Web server security policy. Apache Web server can take advantage of the robust cryptographic foundations provided by NetWare 6.5, including the cryptographic keys and certificates provided by Novell Certificate Server. Certificate Server lets you create and securely store server certificates that can be used to encrypt Web server communications with SSL. Once enabled, SSL requires that you use the HTTPS:// prefix rather than the standard HTTP:// prefix when specifying URLs. For more information on Certificate Server, see Chapter 6.

SSL communications require a separate HTTP port than that used for unencrypted communications. Port numbers enable IP packets to be routed to the correct process on a computer. A total of 65,535 port numbers are available. Some port numbers are permanently assigned to a specific process; for example, email data under SMTP goes to port number 25. Other processes, such as Telnet sessions, receive a temporary port number during initialization. The Telnet port is reserved for use by the Telnet process only while the session is active. When the Telnet session terminates, the port is released for potential use by another process.

By default, unencrypted HTTP uses port **80** and encrypted HTTP (SSL) uses port **443**. To configure a secure port on which Apache can listen for secure communications, complete the following steps:

1. From Apache Manager, click the Server Preferences button in the header, and select Listen Ports in the left navigation frame.

2. At the Add Listen Port page, provide the necessary information and click Save (see Figure 9.3).

   ▶ *Listen Port*: Specify the IP address and port combination that you want to configure for Apache listening. If you don't specify an IP address, the port configuration is applied to all IP addresses bound to the Apache Web server. If you don't specify a port number, the default port **80** is used.

WARNING Don't configure port 80 for encrypted communications. Port 80 should be used for unencrypted HTTP communications.

▶ *Encryption*: Select On to use SSL encryption with this port.

▶ *Server certificates*: From the drop-down list, select the certificate you want to use for Web server encryption.

3. Click Save, and then Save and Apply to save the new settings and restart the Web server. This will enable listening on the new port.

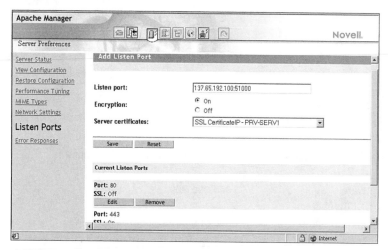

FIGURE 9.3
Configuring listening ports in Apache Manager.

In the Add Listen Port page, you will see a list of all currently configured listening ports for Apache. From this page, you can also edit or delete existing listen ports, as needed. You should be careful as you create new listening ports that you aren't creating any conflicts with existing IP services.

Some ports in the NetWare 6.5 environment can be reassigned, whereas others are permanent. Table 9.1 shows the default port assignments for NetWare 6.5 Web services as a starting point for planning the installation and configuration of your Web services.

TABLE 9.1   Default Port Assignments

SERVICE	PORT NUMBER(S)	CONFIGURABLE?
Apache	80 and 443	Yes
Domain Name Service (DNS)	53	No

TABLE 9.1   Continued

SERVICE	PORT NUMBER(S)	CONFIGURABLE?
File Transfer Protocol (FTP)	20 and 21	No
iFolder	Uses LDAP and Apache ports	Indirectly by changing LDAP and/or Apache ports
iMonitor	80	Yes
iPrint	631 and SSL port	Indirectly by changing the SSL port
Lightweight Directory Access Protocol (LDAP)	389 and 636	Yes
NetWare Core Protocol (NCP)	524	No
NetWare File System	20, 111, and 2049	Only 2049 is configurable
NetWare Graphical User Interface	9000 and 9001	Yes
NetWare Remote Manager (NRM)	8008 and 8009	Yes
NetWare Web Access	Uses Apache port	Indirectly by changing the Apache port
Network Time Protocol (NTP)	123	No
RConsoleJ	2034, 2036, and 2037	Yes
Compatibility Mode Driver (CMD)	2302	No
Service Location Protocol (SLP)	427	No
Simple Network Management Protocol (SNMP)	161	No
Telnet	23	No
Tomcat	8080	Yes
Web Manager	2200	Yes

Apache Web Server Management

There are several pages of configuration options for the Apache Web server. They are organized into groups that correspond to the various buttons in the Header frame. In each group, the Navigation frame on the left provides links to specific configuration pages for Apache Web server. The following sections describe those features, not previously discussed, which are available in each group.

Server Preferences

This group of settings allows you to configure specific server-level settings that govern the behavior of the Web server itself. Server Preferences is the default group when the Apache Web server management interface is opened.

Server Status

This page shows you the current status of the Web server (Up or Down) and allows you to stop and restart the Web server remotely. It also tells you the configuration file management option that is currently in use (File or Directory).

View Configuration

This page gives you easy access to the server configuration parameters stored in HTTPD.CONF. It displays an abbreviated look at Apache's configuration parameters, showing some of the more important Web server settings (see Figure 9.4). Clicking any of the links displays a page that allows you to modify the information in these files. Make any necessary changes, click Save, and then choose Save and Apply to restart the server with the new settings.

Restore Configuration

If you have made changes to your server that have caused unwanted results, the Restore Configuration page can help you get back on track (see Figure 9.5). On this page, you will see a list of versions, dates, and change log notes indicating what was changed in Apache's configuration file each time. These are backups of every configuration that your server has had.

Apache saves a backup copy of HTTPD.CONF each time you make a change. These previous versions are stored in SYS:\APACHE2\CONF\ BACKUP. By clicking the Restore button for a particular date and time, you can restore your server to the exact configuration it had at that time.

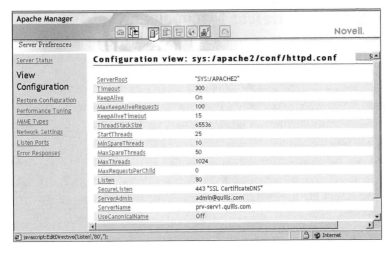

FIGURE 9.4
The View Configuration page in Apache Manager.

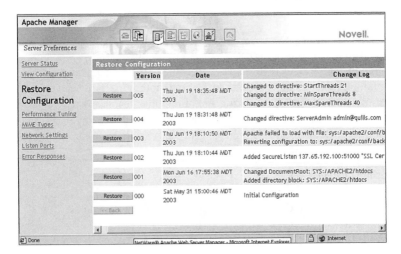

FIGURE 9.5
Restoring previous versions of HTTPD.CONF with Apache Manager.

Performance Tuning

The Performance Tuning page enables you to make some basic performance adjustments to Apache Web server. However, the changes available
through the Performance Tuning page are only the tip of the iceberg

when compared to the options available by editing HTTPD.CONF directly. However, this can also lead quickly to problems if you are not very
familiar with Apache server directives. Before going down that path,
review the relevant material on the Apache documentation Web site at
`http://httpd.apache.org/docs-2.0`.

NOTE You will have much greater control over HTTPD.CONF if you are using Apache
Manager in Directory mode as opposed to File mode. Directory mode was discussed earlier in this chapter.

MIME Types

Also known as context labels, MIME (Multipurpose Internet Mail
Extension) types specify the file types that Apache Web server
recognizes and supports. The MIME Types configuration file is
`SYS:APACHE2\CONF\MIME.TYPES`. If you want to put MP3 files on your
server, for example, you must add the MP3 extension to your MIME
types. If this extension is not added, the server transfers the file to the
user as text, instead of as a sound file. The Global MIME Types page
makes it easy to add new types. From this page, you can also delete or
modify existing types.

To add a new MIME type to your Web server, provide the following
information:

- ▶ *Content Type*: Specify the type of content for which you are creating a new MIME type. When a Web server sends a document to a
  client, it includes metadata that identifies the document's type so
  the client can handle the document correctly. Some common content types include

  - ▶ `text/plain`
  - ▶ `text/html`
  - ▶ `image/jpeg`
  - ▶ `image/gif`
  - ▶ `application/x-tar`
  - ▶ `application/postscript`
  - ▶ `application/x-gzip`
  - ▶ `audio/basic`
  - ▶ `lang` (used to specify a specific language)
  - ▶ `enc` (used to specify that the file is compressed)

NOTE The official list of context types is maintained by the Internet Assigned Numbers Authority (IANA), and can be found at www.iana.org.

▶ *Suffix*: In the File Suffix field, enter the file extension associated with the context label you have specified.

Once you have entered the information, click New and your new MIME type will be added.

Network Settings

This page lets you specify three settings for your Apache Web server:

▶ *Server Admin*: Specify the email address of the Web administrator who should be notified if problems are encountered on a Web site. This email address will be included with HTTP error messages sent to Web clients.

▶ *Server-Side Includes*: Enables server-side includes (SSI) on Apache Web server. SSI is code that is executed on the Web server rather than the Web client. The results are then passed to the client. SSI is disabled by default because the parsing of SSI code can be processor-intensive and result in slower Web server performance.

▶ *SSI File Extensions*: Specify the extension that will be used to denote Web content that uses SSIs. Typically this is .SHTML, but you can specify a different extension if you want.

Listen Ports

This page lets you configure the various ports that Apache Web server uses to listen for incoming requests. This information was discussed previously.

Error Responses

Typical HTTP error messages are pretty generic and do not give much information. Use the Error Responses page to customize error messages and potentially redirect the client to a location where more help is available. When a server cannot complete a request, it can send one of the following four error messages to the client:

▶ *Unauthorized (HTTP 401)*: Occurs when a user tries unsuccessfully to access a file in a secure area of the Web server.

▶ *Forbidden (HTTP 403)*: Occurs when the server does not have file system rights sufficient to read the requested data.

- ▶ *Not found (HTTP 404)*: Occurs when a user tries to access data that does not exist.

- ▶ *Server (HTTP 500)*: Occurs when the server is improperly configured or when a fatal error occurs (such as the system running out of memory).

There are many situations in which you might want to use custom messages. For example, if users are denied access, instead of receiving a message that simply says "Unauthorized," they could receive a custom error message that explains the reason they were denied access and points them to the help desk to have an account created.

To change the error response for your server, complete the following steps:

1. Select the error response you want to change.

2. In the appropriate dialog box, enter the path\filename or URL that you want to replace the default message. All errors except HTTP 401 also permit you to simply enter the text of the message directly into the dialog box.

3. Repeat this process for each error message you want to change.

4. When finished, click Save and then Save and Apply to restart the Web server with the new settings.

If you want to return to the default error messages, simply delete the custom information in the dialog box and click Save.

Server Logs

Apache Web server provides two types of server logs for tracking what is happening in your Web server environment. To view the error logs, click the Server Logs button in the header of Apache Manager.

Access Log

Select View Access Log in the left navigation frame to see Apache's access log. The access log records information about Web clients that access your Web server, and records client information such as IP addresses and date and time of access. By default, the access log is
SYS:\APACHE2\LOGS\ACCESS_LOG.

Select Log Preferences in the left navigation frame to configure access log settings. From this page, you can enable/disable access logging, change the log filename and location, manage log file rotation scheme to prevent files from getting too big, and specify what information is logged.

Error Log

Select View Error Log in the left navigation frame to see Apache's error log. The error log records diagnostic information related to errors that occurred while processing requests. The error log is very important because it often contains details of what went wrong and how to fix it. By default, the error log is SYS:\APACHE2\LOGS\ERROR_LOG.

From View Error Log, you can also set the number of entries to display on a page, as well as filter entries for specific content, such as a specific error code.

Select Error Preferences in the left navigation frame to configure error log settings. From this page, you can change the log filename and location, manage the log file rotation scheme to prevent files from getting too big, and set the log level, or level of detail, you want included in the error log.

Content Management

Apache Web server offers many options for configuring and storing your Web content. To access these options, click the Content Management button in the header of Apache Manager.

Primary Document Directory

This page lets you set the primary storage location for Web server content, and was discussed previously.

Additional Document Directories

This page lets you set secondary document locations for Web server content, and was discussed previously.

User Home Directories

This page lets you configure locations where individual users can manage and access their own Web content. This information was discussed previously.

Document Preferences

Use this page to set the default Web page that Apache Web server will look for if no specific file is specified in a client's request. By default, this is INDEX.HTML, but you can set this to any filename you want.

URL Forwarding

Forwarding URLs is a common task on the Internet because Web sites move to new locations for various reasons. URL forwarding enables you to specify a forwarding address for any URL on your server. That way, if you move your Web site, a user can still type the old URL, but her browser automatically connects to the new location. To forward a URL, simply provide the pathname of the content that has moved, and then specify the new location for that content. Then, when a Web client requests the content, Apache returns the new URL to the client, which then requests it from the new location.

CGI Extensions

Common Gateway Interface (CGI) provides a very common method for adding dynamic content to a Web site. The CGI Extensions page lets you specify how Apache Web server handles CGI scripts. To configure a CGI interpreter, simply provide the required information and click Add.

- ▶ *CGI Path*: Specify a complete (absolute) path to the CGI interpreter. NetWare 6.5 includes `SYS:\PERL\PERLCGI\PERLCGI.NLM` for this purpose.

- ▶ *Extension*: Specify the file extension that will be associated with CGI scripts. Typically, (CGI) this is .CGI.

Virtual Hosts

This page lets you configure software and hardware virtual hosts. Virtual hosts were discussed previously in this chapter.

Tomcat Servlet Engine for NetWare

Tomcat was first introduced to NetWare as part of NetWare 6. As with Apache, Tomcat is an open source application. Its specific function is servlet container. A *servlet* is a server-side program that generates dynamic Web pages based upon user input. Tomcat provides a runtime environment within which servlets can execute and be managed. Apache Web server depends upon Tomcat to process servlets and JavaServer Pages (JSP).

As with Apache, two instances of Tomcat can be loaded on a NetWare 6.5 server. The first is an admin instance that is used in conjunction with the Apache admin server to support the various management tools and other services available with NetWare 6.5. The admin instance of Tomcat is loaded automatically when NetWare 6.5 is installed.

The second instance is a public copy that is used in support of Web applications that are served from the NetWare 6.5 server. You will use this version to build your own Web environment.

> **NOTE** Tomcat provides basic servlet and JSP support for NetWare 6.5. For a more robust Web application development environment, Novell offers Novell exteNd Application Server. For more information on Novell exteNd offerings, see the NetWare 6.5 online documentation, and visit http://www.novell.com/solutions/extend/.

Installing and Configuring Tomcat

Because Tomcat is useless without a Web server with which to interoperate, Tomcat is installed automatically with Apache Web server. For information on installing Apache and Tomcat, see the Apache installation section earlier in this chapter.

By default, Tomcat files are installed into a directory structure starting at SYS:\TOMCAT. Both the admin and public versions of Tomcat will share this directory.

Similar to Apache Web server, Tomcat offers two utilities to help you configure and use the Tomcat servlet container:

- ▶ *Tomcat Admin*: Provides Web-based configuration of the Tomcat environment. Tomcat Admin is not a Novell utility. It was created by the Apache Foundation so that Tomcat could be managed from any Web browser. Tomcat Admin is accessible from Web Manager by selecting the Open Source link, selecting Tomcat in the left column, and then clicking Tomcat Admin in the yellow box on the right.

- ▶ *Tomcat Manager*: Provides Web-based deployment and management of servlets and Web applications. Tomcat Manager is accessible from Web Manager by selecting the Open Source link, selecting Tomcat in the left column, and then clicking Tomcat Manager Application in the yellow box on the right.

> **TIP** For more information on Tomcat, see the NetWare 6.5 online documentation, and visit the comprehensive Tomcat documentation site at http://jakarta.apache.org.

NetWare Web Search Server

Although Web Search Server isn't a required Web service for NetWare 6.5, it is all about making your Web resources available to employees and customers as quickly and accurately as possible. Supporting everything from simple internal search solutions to complex search services that you can offer to organizations for a fee, Web Search Server is one of the fastest and most accurate search engines currently available.

Web Search Server offers a powerful, full-text search engine that you can use to add search capabilities to your Internet or intranet Web sites. Compatible with the Apache Web server, you can create custom search forms and search result pages either from scratch or by using the included templates.

This section introduces you to Web Search Server and its basic installation and configuration. However, for comprehensive information, see the NetWare 6.5 online documentation.

Web Search Server Capabilities

With NetWare Web Search Server, you can

- ▶ Support searching multiple language indexes from a single interface
- ▶ Host search services for multiple organizations
- ▶ Organize collections of related files from diverse sources as a single document
- ▶ Create custom search and print results and error and response messages and apply them to individual language searches or across all supported languages
- ▶ Gather customer metrics by reviewing searches to identify what your customers look for the most
- ▶ Improve employee productivity by helping them find information more quickly

Installing Web Search Server

NetWare Web Search Server can be installed as an optional component during the NetWare 6.5 installation, or it can be installed after the fact through iManager or the graphical server console.

To install Web Search Server using iManager, complete the following steps:

1. Insert the NetWare 6.5 Operating System CD-ROM into your workstation.

2. Launch iManager and open the Install and Upgrade link in the left navigation frame.

3. Select Install NetWare 6.5 Products, and then click Remote Product Install in the right frame.

4. At the Target Server screen, select the server to which you want to install Web Search Server and click Next. Authenticate as an Admin user for your eDirectory tree and click OK.

5. At the components screen, click Clear All and select only NetWare Web Search Server. Click Next.

6. At the Summary screen, click Copy Files. You will be prompted to insert the NetWare 6.5 Products CD-ROM. After the Web Search Server files are copied, click Close to complete the installation.

Once the installation is complete, restart the NetWare 6.5 server where Web Search Server is installed.

Web Search Basics

Before you get started creating and managing search sites, you should understand the basics of Web searches. Web searches are driven by the idea of a *search site*. By definition, a search site is a collection of one or more indexes and their related configuration files. A typical search site consists of the following:

▶ *Indexes*: Indexes are at the heart of a search site. An index is an optimized binary file that contains keywords found in documents hosted on a Web or file server. Indexes are used by Web Search to return search results to users.

NOTE When you install NetWare Web Search Server, some of your server's content is automatically indexed and appears on the default search form as the "NetWare Web Search" and "Doc Root" indexes.

▶ *Log files*: A log file keeps record of search statistics and performance of the search site.

▶ *Search and print templates*: These are templates that become populated with the results of a search and then are displayed to the user. Depending on which templates are used, the level of detail displayed in search and print results varies.

▶ *Scheduled events*: Index management, such as updating or regenerating, can be automated to occur at specific intervals using the Scheduling feature.

▶ *Themes*: A theme instantly adds a common look and feel to your search page, search and print results pages, and response and error message pages.

Testing Web Search

Once you start Web Search Server, you can open the search page using your Web browser and perform a search against the content that has been automatically indexed. To test NetWare Web Search Server using the default search page, do the following:

1. Point your browser to the default search page at `http://<server DNS name of IP address>/novellsearch`. Remember that the URL is case sensitive. For example:

   `http://prv-serv1.quills.com/novellsearch`

2. In the Search field, type **NetWare** and click Search.

The results of this search will be collected from the newly created index in Web Search Server.

Working with Web Search Server

Once installed, you can manage Web Search Server through Web Search Manager. That way, Web Search Manager is available from NetWare 6.5 Web Manager. To open Web Search Manager, launch Web Manager and select Web Search 3.0 in the left navigation frame. Then click the Web Search Administration link in the right frame. The Web Search Manager interface is shown in Figure 9.6.

The default Web Search Manager page is also what you get when you click List in the left navigation frame. There are four primary tasks associated with configuring and managing Web Search Server:

▶ Creating a search site

▶ Creating and managing indexes

▶ Generating indexes

▶ Scheduling index events

Each of these is described in the following sections.

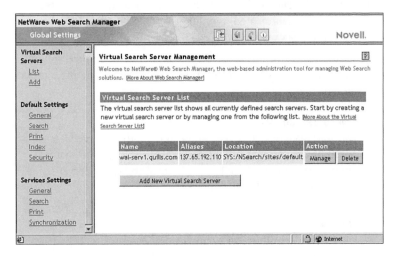

FIGURE 9.6
Web Search Manager interface.

Creating a Search Site

Using Web Search Manager, you can create and configure search sites, also called *virtual search servers*, and then begin adding indexes to them. To create a new search site, click the Add button in the header frame, or select Add under the Virtual Search Server heading in the left navigation frame. The Add Site page is shown in Figure 9.7. Provide the following information:

▶ *Name*: Specify a name for the new search site. This is typically the DNS or domain name of your server. When Web Search Server receives a query, it must determine which of the available search sites it should use to handle the request. There are two ways to do this:

  ▶ Matching the domain name in the search query with a search site name in Web Search

  ▶ Using the SITE=*searchsitename* query parameter to find matching search site names

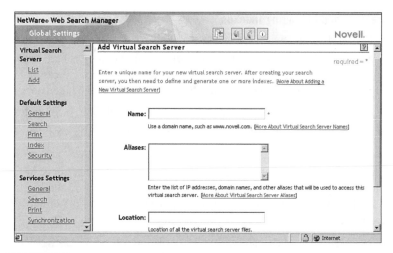

FIGURE 9.7
Adding a new search site in Web Search Manager.

▶ *Aliases*: Specify a secondary name for the search site. This is typically the IP address of your server. An alias name typically follows
one of two conventions:

  ▶ An IP address could be used either in the domain name portion of a URL or be included in a search query using the
  &site query parameter. Using an IP address in place of a
  domain name to select a search site works only in a hardware
  virtual server configuration where each search site has its
  own unique IP address. For more information on virtual Web
  servers, see the discussion on Apache Web server earlier in
  this chapter.

  ▶ Any other numeric or textual value that can be passed as the
  value of the **&site** query parameter.

▶ *Location*: Specify the path to where you want the index and configuration files to be stored. If this field is left blank, Web Search will
store the search site files in **SYS:NSEARCH\SITES\<NAME>**, where
<NAME> is the name you have assigned to this search site. The location can be set to any volume on the server where Web Search is
installed, but not on other servers.

Creating and Managing Indexes

Web Search Server supports two types of indexes:

▶ *Crawled*: Follows hypertext links until it reaches a dead end. Web Search Server can crawl one or more Web sites, specific areas of a Web site, or specific URLs, all the way down to specific filenames.

▶ *File system*: Indexes content on a file server. Web Search can index one or more paths on multiple volumes, including Storage Area Network (SAN) systems.

There are two forms you can use to create each type of index: the standard form and the advanced form. The standard form is discussed here. For information about the advanced form, see the NetWare 6.5 online documentation.

Web Search Server can search across multiple indexes within a single search site, but cannot search across multiple search sites.

TIP   Searching a single index is generally faster than searching across multiple indexes.

To create a new crawled index, complete the following steps:

1. Launch Web Search Manager and select List in the left navigation frame. Click the Manage button next to the site for which you want to create an index.

2. In the Define a New Index box, select New Crawled Index and click Define Index.

3. In the Define Crawled Index screen, provide the required information and click Apply Settings.

    ▶ *Index name*: Specify a name for the new index. The name can be a word, phrase, or a numeric value. If you are going to have a large number of indexes, you should use a naming scheme so that you can effectively manage your indexes. Keep in mind that the index name will be visible to users, so you might want to choose a name that will mean something to them.

    ▶ *URL of Web site*: Specify the URL of the Web site you want to index. You can enter a URL by itself or include a path down to a specific file level. The standard index form includes two

URL fields. Click Add more URLs to specify more than two
URLs to be indexed.

To create a new file system index, complete the following steps:

1. Launch Web Search Manager and select List in the left navigation
    frame. Click the Manage button next to the site for which you want
    to create an index.

2. In the Define a New Index box, select New File System Index and
    click Define Index.

3. In the Define File System Index screen, provide the required infor-
    mation and click Apply Settings.

    ▶ *Index name*: Specify a name for the new index. The name can
      be a word, phrase, or a numeric value. If you are going to
      have a large number of indexes, you should use a naming
      scheme so that you can effectively manage your indexes.
      Keep in mind that the index name will be visible to users, so
      you might want to choose a name that will mean something
      to them.

    ▶ *Server path to be indexed*: Specify the absolute path to the
      folder containing the information that you want indexed; for
      example, `SYS:\MARKETING\COLLATERAL`.

    ▶ *Corresponding URL prefix*: Specify the URL that should be
      used by the search results page to access the individual files.
      This corresponds to a document directory (Document Root)
      that has been defined on the Web server. For more informa-
      tion on document directories, see the discussion on Apache
      Web Server earlier in this chapter.

You can specify multiple paths for a single index by clicking Add More
Paths.

Generating Indexes

Once you define an index, you must generate it before it can be used for
searching. This is the actual process of examining Web site content or
Web server files to gather keywords, titles, and descriptions and to place
them in the index file.

To generate a newly defined index, complete the following steps:

1. Launch Web Search Manager and select List in the left navigation frame. Click Manage next to the search site for which you want to generate an index.

2. Click Generate next to the specific index that you want to generate.

At the Active Jobs screen, you will see the status of the current indexing jobs. If there is no current index job, the status page will read *No indexing jobs are currently running or defined*. To cancel the current indexing jobs, click the Cancel link in the Status column.

Scheduling Index Events

Web Search Server can automatically update your indexes on specific dates and times by scheduling events. To configure an automatic generation event, complete the following steps:

1. Launch Web Search Manager and select List in the left navigation frame. Click Manage next to the search site for which you want to schedule an indexing operation.

2. Select Scheduling in the left navigation frame and click Add Event.

3. At the Schedule a New Event screen, provide the required information and click Apply Settings.

   ► *Dates, days of week, and time*: Specify the month, days, days of the week, or time (in hours and minutes) when you want Web Search Server to run the event. You can use the Ctrl and Shift keys to select multiple dates and times.

   ► *Operation*: Select the type of operation you want performed on your indexes. Update will add any new content from the Web site or file system to the index file. Optimize will remove unnecessary content and make the index file smaller and faster. Regenerate replaces the existing index with a new one.

   ► *Perform operations on*: Determine whether you want the chosen operation performed on all indexes (collections) in the search site, or only on specified indexes. If you have large indexes, it might be best to create multiple events to update indexes at different times.

Once the schedule is configured, the index will be automatically updated at the frequency specified in the schedule.

Managing Web Search Server

Services settings give the Web Search Server administrator global control over the search services provided by NetWare Web Search Server, including the capability to completely disable searching. These pages also control overall performance of the Web Search Server.

Services settings are organized under the Services Settings heading in the left Navigation frame. There are four categories of services settings available for Web Search Server.

General

General service settings define error log and site list settings for all search sites. The General services Settings page is shown in Figure 9.8.

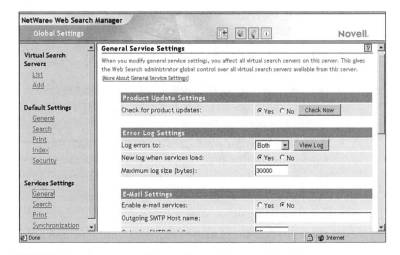

FIGURE 9.8
General Service Settings page in Web Search Manager.

▶ *Product Update Settings*: This option lets you automatically receive notifications of updates to Web Search Server software as they become available.

▶ *Error Log Settings*: The following settings let you configure the error log on Web Search Server.

　▶ *Log Errors To*: Select where you want log results displayed. You can choose to log errors to a file, to the console, or both.

Click the View Log button to see the error log directly from Web Search Manager.

▸ *New Log When Services Load*: When set to Yes, this option starts a new log file each time you restart the Web Search Server.

▸ *Maximum Log Size (Bytes)*: Limit the size of the log file to the size you specify (in bytes).

▸ *Email Settings*: These settings allow you to set up email notifications for errors that occur on Web Search Server.

  ▸ *Enable Email Services*: Enables/disables email notifications for Web Search Server. Note that this is a global setting that affects all search sites configured in Web Search Server.

  ▸ *Outgoing SMTP Hostname*: Specify the DNS name of the outgoing SMTP mail server.

  ▸ *Outgoing SMTP Port #*: Specify the port to which the SMTP mail server is listening. Default: port **25**.

  ▸ *Outgoing SMTP User ID (conditional)*: If the SMTP server requires authentication, specify a valid user ID for use by Web Search Server here.

  ▸ *Outgoing SMTP Password (conditional)*: If the SMTP server requires authentication, provide the password associated with the user ID provided for use by Web Search Server.

▸ *Server Management Settings*: The following settings define some general characteristics of the Web Search Server:

  ▸ *Maximum Number of Active Index Jobs*: Limits the number of indexing jobs that can run at the same time. Default is 5.

  ▸ *Default Location of Virtual Search Servers*: Specifies the path to where you want all search site files to be stored, including index and configuration files. Changing this setting won't move existing sites to a new location, but all new search sites will be placed here.

  ▸ *Detect Manual Search Server Changes*: When set to Yes, this option directs Web Search Server to reload configuration files that are modified manually, instead of using Web Search Manager.

▶ *Seconds Between Checking for Changes*: Specifies how often Web Search Server will look for manually modified configuration files, in seconds.

▶ *Detect Template Changes*: When set to Yes, this option directs Web Search Server to automatically check for modifications to search, print, or error templates used by Web Search Server.

▶ *Seconds Between Checking for Template Changes*: Specifies how often Web Search Server should reload search, print, results, and error templates, in seconds. Any changes to templates will be recognized within the time period specified here.

When you are done making changes, click Apply Settings.

Search

Search service settings let you turn search capabilities on or off and manage debugging and statistics settings. The Search service settings are shown in Figure 9.9.

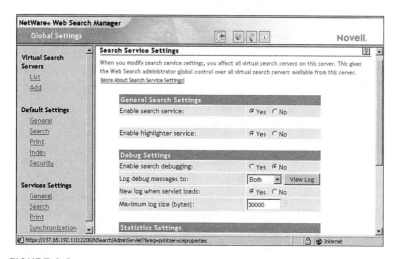

FIGURE 9.9
Search Service Settings page in Web Search Manager.

▶ *General Search Settings*: These settings let you enable/disable the primary search features of Web Search Server:

► *Enable Search Service*: Enables search services for all search sites on the Web Search Server.

► *Enable Highlighter Service*: This option configures Web Search Server to highlight instances of the search term or phrase within the searched documents.

► *Debug Settings*: These settings let you keep a log of all searches and query results going to all search sites. Typically, this option is used only when troubleshooting a problem with a search because the log file can grow very quickly.

  ► *Enable Search Debugging*: Enables/disables debugging of searches.

  ► *Log Debug Messages To*: Specifies whether debug messages should be logged to a file, to the server console, or both. Server console messages are viewable from the view them from the Tomcat servlet container console screen.

  ► *New Log When Servlet Loads*: Specifying Yes will restart the debug file whenever Web Search Server is restarted.

  ► *Maximum Log Size (Bytes)*: Specifies the size of the debug file, in bytes.

► *Statistics Settings*: Search statistics can provide you with information that can help you optimize Web Search Server over time to improve search performance.

  ► *Enable Search Statistics Logging*: When set to Yes, this setting generates an updated log file containing statistics about searches performed against all search sites on your Web Search Server.

  ► *Seconds Between Statistics Updates*: Specifies the time, in seconds, between updates of the statistics log file.

  ► *Log Statistics To*: Specifies whether statistics log messages should be logged to a file, to the server console, or both. Server console messages are viewable from the Tomcat servlet container console screen.

  ► *Maximum Log Size (Bytes)*: Specifies the size of the statistics log file, in bytes.

  ► *New Log When Servlet Loads*: Specifying Yes will restart the statistics log file whenever Web Search Server is restarted.

> ► *Log Error If Search Time Exceeds (Seconds)*: Specifies the
> timeout, in seconds, before Web Search Server should record
> the current search as exceeding the specified time limit on
> the statistics display.

When you are done making changes, click Apply Settings.

Print

This page manages Print services and has the same type of options and
parameters described in the Search section. Click Apply Settings to save
any changes you make to this page.

Synchronization

Web Search Synchronization lets you manage multiple Web Search
Servers from a single administration interface. Changes made to one server are automatically replicated to the other servers in the cluster. You can
also synchronize Web Search files across multiple Web Search Servers,
including generated indexes, configuration settings, and search results
templates. For more information on using Web Search Synchronization,
see the NetWare 6.5 online documentation.

Managing Search Sites

The default site settings define characteristics for search sites that are created on Web Search Server. Changes to the parameters defined on these
pages will be automatically applied to any new search sites that are created, unless overridden through the use of the Advanced Index definition
form.

In this way, you can manage your search sites by exception, rather than
by having to define every setting for every site manually when it is created. There are five categories of default site settings, which are detailed in
the following sections.

General

General settings let you manage query, response, and error log settings
for all newly created search sites. The general default site settings are
shown in Figure 9.10.

> ► *Default Query Encoding*: Specifies an encoding that represents the
> character set encoding that most of your user queries will use.
> Default is UTF-8.

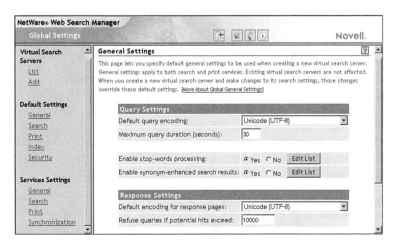

FIGURE 9.10
Default general settings in Web Search Manager.

▶ *Maximum Query Duration (Seconds)*: Specifies the maximum duration of any query, in seconds. Any query that reaches this limit will terminate whether or not the query has actually finished. Default is 30 seconds. This option helps you protect server resources from malicious rogue searches, which are intended to slow site performance by consuming server resources.

▶ *Enable Stop-Words Processing*: This option instructs Web Search Server to ignore insignificant search words (stop-words), such as articles, conjunctions, or prepositions. A list of common stop words is configured by default, but you can modify the list by clicking Edit List.

▶ *Enable Synonym-Enhanced Search Results*: This option lets search users expand their search results to include synonyms of the original search terms. This is kind of like doing a Thesaurus search that can help uncover related information using similar, but not exact, words to those being searched for. You can modify the synonym list by clicking Edit List.

▶ *Default Encoding for Response Pages*: Specifies the encoding Web Search Server will use when responding to user queries with Search and Print Results templates, and Error and Response Messages templates. Default is Unicode (UTF-8).

▶ *Refuse Queries If Potential Hits Exceed*: Specifies the maximum effective size of a search for Web Search Server. Use this field to cancel the processing of search results that might take a long time to complete because a large number of hits are being returned. Users should modify their queries in this case.

▶ *Maximum Log Size (Bytes)*: Specifies the maximum size, in bytes, to which Web Search Server will allow the log file to grow. This protects your server hard drive resources, particularly on a busy search server.

When you are done making changes, click Apply Settings.

Search

Search default site settings let you turn search capabilities on or off and manage debugging and statistics settings. The Default search settings are shown in Figure 9.11.

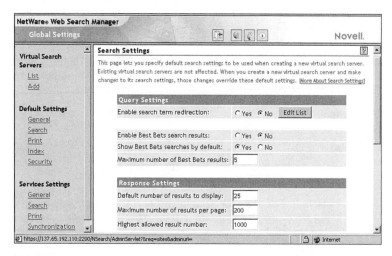

FIGURE 9.11
Default search settings in Web Search Manager.

▶ *Query Settings:* These options let you configure some additional features to improve search performance and usability:

▶ *Enable Search Term Redirection*: Lets you set up common search terms to go to a specific URL. For example, the term *programming* might take a user straight to your Developer Web site.

▶ *Enable Best Bets Search Results*: Enables/disables Best Bets. *Best Bets* are common search destinations that can be displayed in addition to a user's specific results. They are generated from a special index just for that purpose.

▶ *Show Best Bets Searches by Default*: Enables/disables showing Best Bets by default.

▶ *Maximum Number of Best Bets Results*: Specifies the number of Best Bets results to display.

▶ *Response Settings*: These options configure the default format for replying to a search request.

▶ *Default Number of Results to Display*: Specifies the number of search results that will be displayed on each search results page.

▶ *Maximum Number of Results Per Page*: Sets a limit on the number of results allowed on any results page.

▶ *Highest Allowed Result Number*: Specifies the maximum number of results that will be returned for any query.

▶ *Enable Search Terms Highlighter*: Specifies whether the search term highlighter is a default option for search sites configured on this Web Search Server.

▶ *Template Settings*: Sets basic information about the template used by Web Search Server.

▶ *Templates Directory*: Specifies the location of the Web Search Server templates files. The default path is SYS:\Nsearch\Templates.

▶ *Default Encoding for Templates*: Specifies the character set in which your templates are written. This is a default value that will be used with templates that do not specify a specific encoding.

▶ *Default Search Page Template*: Specifies the name of the search page template file you want to use.

▶ *Default Search Results Template*: Specifies the name of the search results template file you want to use.

▶ *Default Highlighter Template*: Specifies the name of the highlighter template file you want to use.

▶ *Template to Use If No Results Returned*: Specifies the name of the template file to be used if no results are found.

▶ *Template to Use If Error Occurs*: Specifies the name of the template file to be used if there are errors while processing a query.

When you are done making changes, click Apply Settings.

Print

The default print settings let you manage print results templates and parameters that affect result printing. The Print Settings page is shown in Figure 9.12.

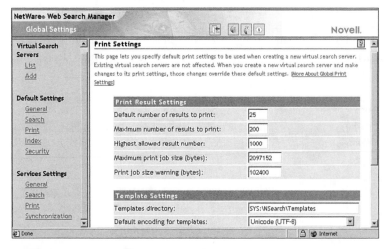

FIGURE 9.12
Default Print Settings in Web Search Manager.

▶ *Print Result Settings*: These options let you configure some basic print settings for the Web Search Server environment:

  ▶ *Default Number of Results to Print*: Specifies the number of print results that you want displayed on each print results page.

  ▶ *Maximum Number of Results to Print*: Sets a limit on the number of results allowed on any results page.

  ▶ *Highest Allowed Result Number*: Specifies the maximum number of results that will be returned for any query.

▶ *Maximum Print Job Size (Bytes)*: Specifies the largest allowable print job size, in bytes. Any request for a print job larger than this value will receive an error message.

▶ *Print Job Size Warning (Bytes)*: When a print job exceeds the specified size, in bytes, Web Search Server will send a warning message to the user via the ResponseMessageTemplate.html file. It then prompts the user to confirm the print job before continuing.

▶ *Template Settings*: These settings provide the same type of information described previously in the section on Search settings.

When you are done making changes, click Apply Settings.

Index

The index default site settings make the process of creating indexes easier by letting you configure common default settings. The Index default site settings are shown in Figure 9.13.

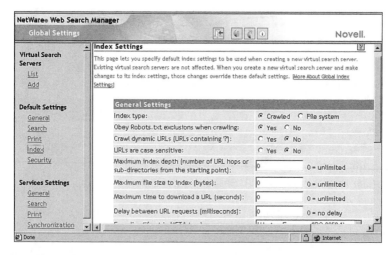

FIGURE 9.13
Default index settings in Web Search Manager.

▶ *General Settings*: These options define the basic default features for indexes used by Web Search Server.

    ▶ *Index Type*: Specifies the default index as either Crawled or File System.

► *Obey Robots.txt Exclusions When Crawling*: Enable this
option to have Web Search Server obey instructions in a
Robots file. The Robots.txt file lets a Web site administrator
specify URLs that should not be indexed by a search engine.

► *Crawl Dynamic URLs (URLs Containing '?')*: Enable this
option if you want Web Search Server to crawl and index
dynamically generated Web pages as well as standard static
Web pages. Indexes are sometimes less effective with dynamic pages because the content can change at any time.

► *URLs Are Case Sensitive*: Check this box if you want Web
Search Server to distinguish between URLs that are different
only in character case. Leaving this unchecked can help
indexing duplicate information that comes from URLs that
use different cases but point to the same information.

► *Maximum Index Depth (Number of URL Hops or Sub-
Directories from the Starting Point)*: Specifies the maximum
number of hypertext links from the starting URL that Web
Search Server will follow before it stops indexing.

► *Maximum File Size to Index (Bytes)*: Specifies the largest file,
in bytes, that Web Search Server will index.

► *Maximum Time to Download a URL (Seconds)*: Specifies the
maximum time, in seconds, that Web Search Server will
attempt to download a URL before it bypasses indexing of
that URL.

► *Delay Between URL Requests (Milliseconds)*: Specifies the
amount of time Web Search Server should pause between
requests for URLs that it is trying to index.

► *Encoding (If Not in META Tags)*: Specifies the encoding to be
used when indexing files that do not contain an encoding
specification. Usually, HTML files will specify their encoding
with a Content-Type META tag.

► *Synchronization Settings*: Enable this option if you want this index
to be copied to other Web Search Servers in the synchronization
cluster.

► *Rights-Based Search Results*: These options let you restrict the ability to search sites with sensitive information. If users have rights to
the restricted directory, they can perform a search against that data.
If not, their request is denied.

▸ *Authorization Checking*: To enable rights-based searches, select By Index and specify the file to be used in verifying user access. Make sure you assign the appropriate user rights to that file. For more information on NetWare file rights, see Chapter 6.

▸ *Unauthorized Hits Filtered By*: Specify how unauthorized search requests are handled. Selecting Engine performs the index search, but will prevent users from seeing any of the restricted results without first logging in. Selecting Template will force users to log in before the index search will be performed.

When you are done making changes, click Apply Settings.

Security

Default security settings manage access to indexed content by requiring users to authenticate to a server before seeing rights-protected search results. The security default site settings are shown in Figure 9.14.

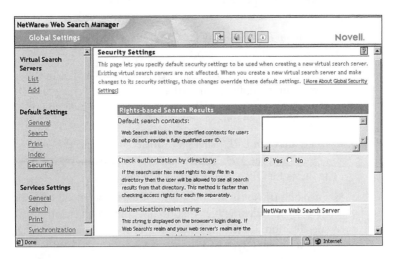

FIGURE 9.14
Default security settings in Web Search Manager.

▸ *Rights-Based Search Results*: These options let you configure search results based on the rights granted to the user who is performing the search:

▸ *Default Search Contexts*: Specify default context(s) for Web Search Server to search for user information. This way, users have to provide only their common name and not their fully qualified User ID.

▸ *Check Authorization by Directory*: Enabling this option lets Web Search Server speed up the authorization process by allowing a user who has rights to any file in a directory access to all files in that directory. This way, each file doesn't have to be authorized separately.

▸ *Authentication Realm String*: Defines the responsible authentication system accepted by Web Search Server. By default, Web Search Server will perform authentication itself, but you can set the Apache server authentication realm string in this field, so users who authenticate to NetWare Enterprise Web server won't have to authenticate again when using Web Search Server to search and access protected information.

▸ *Connection Settings*: These options provide additional security to Web searches:

  ▸ *Require HTTPS*: Select Yes if you want to protect usernames and passwords via SSL as they are sent across the network or Internet.

  ▸ *Auto-Logout Time (Minutes)*: Specifies the amount of time, in minutes, that users can be idle before they are logged out of Web Search Server.

When you are done making changes, click Apply Settings.

Additional NetWare 6.5 Web Services

NetWare 6.5 includes several other pieces to the Web services puzzle, including MySQL database, OpenSSH, and scripting support through Perl and PHP. Although an in-depth discussion of these utilities is beyond the scope of this book, a brief introduction to these services and their capabilities is in order.

MySQL

MySQL is an open source SQL (Structured Query Language) database. It is easy to install and use, but offers exceptional power, security and scalability. In fact, because of its small size and speed, it is an ideal platform for delivering database capabilities to your Web sites—and because it's an open source application, and free with NetWare 6.5, the potential return on investment (ROI) doesn't get much better.

MySQL runs on a wide variety of operating systems other than NetWare, making it ideal for today's heterogeneous network environments. You don't have to learn different database systems just because you have different platforms. MySQL platforms include, in addition to NetWare, Microsoft Windows NT/2000, Linux, Sun Solaris, IBM AIX, FreeBSD, OS/2, and others.

MySQL can be installed during the NetWare 6.5 installation, or anytime thereafter through iManager or the GUI server console.

OpenSSH

OpenSSH is an open source encryption service that has been integrated with NetWare 6.5. It leverages the Novell International Cryptographic Infrastructure (NICI) to provide a secure shell suitable for both administrators and users who need to access their NetWare servers in a way that provides secure access and data transmission.

For example, network admins can use OpenSSH to copy files to and from any server in their networks. Users can securely access and copy files to and from their home directories, or any other directory to which they have rights. OpenSSH makes all of this possible without using a Web browser or any NetWare-specific client.

To do this, OpenSSH provides secure versions of several common file transfer protocols that use unencrypted transmission channels and clear text passwords that pose a significant security risk. OpenSSH offers SFTP to replace FTP, SSH to replace Telnet and Rlogin, and SCP to replace RCP. There are several SSH-compatible client utilities that you can choose from, including PuTTy, RedHat Linux OpenSSH clients, Absolute Telnet, and MindTerm, to name a few.

OpenSSH can be installed during the NetWare 6.5 installation, or anytime thereafter through iManager or the GUI server console. Novell recommends that you install Apache Web Server on your NetWare 6.5 server prior to installing OpenSSH.

Perl and PHP Scripting Support

Common Gateway Interface (CGI) scripting is the most common way for a Web server to interact with users. It provides the capability to create dynamic content and increase the sophistication and functionality of your Web pages.

In addition to the Web application, scripting is also a valuable tool for automating network administrative functions and parsing and generating reports based on network activities. Because of this, Novell offers multiple scripting languages with NetWare 6.5, with the goal of not making you learn yet another coding method in order to get your job done.

The most commonly recognized of Novell's scripting languages, outside of the NetWare world, are Perl (Practical Extraction and Report Language) and PHP (Hypertext Preprocessor).

Perl is an open source language that was originally created specifically to process text. Because of this, it is particularly good at text parsing and report generation. It is also very good at Web page generation and task automation.

PHP is a server-side HTML-embedded scripting language. It can be used to create dynamic Web pages, collect form data, and receive cookie information. It can also be used for talking to other services through protocols such as IMAP, SNMP, and HTTP. PHP supports a wide range of Web servers and databases, but is most commonly used with Apache Web server and MySQL. This makes it a natural choice for the NetWare 6.5 Web services environment.

Both Perl and PHP support for NetWare 6.5 is provided in the Novell Developer Kit (NDK) that is included with NetWare 6.5. For more information on the NDK, see the NetWare 6.5 online documentation, and visit `http://developer.novell.com/ndk`.

CHAPTER 10

NetWare File Access

Instant Access

Using NetStorage

▶ NetStorage provides a WebDAV server interface for all NetWare 6.5 files and directories.

▶ Use any WebDAV-compliant application, such as Web browsers, Windows Explorer (My Network Places), or Office 2000 to access NetWare 6.5 files and folders.

▶ NetStorage can provide clientless access to iFolder files.

▶ NetStorage provides the WebDAV support for the NetDrive client.

Working with NetDrive

▶ NetDrive client is available on the NetWare 6.5 client's CD-ROM.

▶ Supports access of NetWare 6.5 files and folders using standard protocols: FTP, WebDAV, or iFolder.

Synchronizing Files with Novell iFolder

▶ Synchronize files between remote clients and a centralized iFolder server, so that user data is available anytime, from anywhere.

▶ Configure and manage iFolder server through the iFolder management console, available through Web Manager after iFolder is installed.

▶ Use iFolder client to provide synchronization between the iFolder server and regularly used machines.

▶ If you are using a machine for one-time access, use NetStorage to access the iFolder server without having to synchronize all files.

▶ Use NetDrive to access the iFolder server without synchronizing the entire directory. Useful when the desktop application is not WebDAV-aware.

▶ iFolder access requires that the iFolder server be installed and configured prior to use.

Using Virtual Office

▶ Use preconfigured services to make NetWare 6.5 files, as well as common services such as NetStorage, iPrint, and email, available through a single portal Web site.

▶ Configure Virtual Office through the Virtual Office Management link in iManager.

▶ *Virtual teams* are a specialized instance of Virtual Office that you can use to create ad-hoc portals to support a community, group, or team focused on a specific project or topic of discussion.

Introduction to NetWare File Access

One of the major tenets of Novell's one Net philosophy is that users should have access to their files and data at anytime, from anywhere. To help you reach this goal, NetWare 6.5 includes a host of methods for accessing network data.

In keeping with Novell's open standards approach to network services, these access methods are designed to use Internet standards, Web browsers, and thin clients, thereby minimizing the need to add large amounts of workstation software in order to access network resources. Those access methods that do require a client of some sort make installation and configuration as easy as possible, so users can get on with their business.

This chapter takes a look at the new and nontraditional forms of file access available in NetWare 6.5. These include

▶ NetStorage

▶ Novell NetDrive

▶ Novell iFolder

▶ Virtual Office

▶ NetWare FTP server

NetStorage

NetStorage provides a transparent WebDAV interface to NetWare files. This is probably one of the most exciting NetWare 6.5 features that you've never heard of. Effectively, NetStorage lets you access files on a NetWare 6.5 server without a NetWare client. NetStorage is integrated with iFolder, NetDrive, and Virtual Office to make accessing your network files as easy and seamless as possible—all without using the traditional Novell Client.

NetStorage leverages a middle-tier architecture, also called *X-tier*, to provide its services. This same architecture is used to support some of the functionality for Novell's ZENWorks line of management solutions.

Installing NetStorage

NetStorage can be installed during the installation of the NetWare 6.5 server, or after the fact through iManager or the graphical server console. Typically, you will need to install NetStorage only on one NetWare 6.5 server in your eDirectory tree, or on one server at each geographical site, although very heavy usage might require more than one per site.

To install NetStorage through iManager, complete the following steps:

1. Insert the NetWare 6.5 Operating System CD-ROM into your workstation.

2. Launch iManager and open the Install and Upgrade link in the left navigation frame

3. Select Install NetWare 6.5 Products, and then click Remote Product Install in the right frame.

4. At the Target Server screen, select the server to which you want to install NetStorage and click Next. Authenticate as an Admin user for your eDirectory tree and click OK.

5. At the components screen, click Clear All and select only Novell NetStorage. Click Next.

6. At the Summary screen, click Copy Files. You will be prompted to insert the NetWare 6.5 Products CD-ROM.

7. At the NetStorage Install screen, specify the required information, and click Next. You can change these settings after the installation through iManager by opening the NetStorage link and selecting Authentication Domains.

   ▶ *Primary eDirectory Server*: Specify the DNS name or IP address of a server in your eDirectory tree that hosts a master or a read/write replica of eDirectory. This does not have to be the server where NetStorage is being installed. NetStorage will use this server to authenticate users when they attempt to log in to NetStorage.

TIP If you want NetStorage to search a specific eDirectory context for user information, you can add that context to the end of the DNS name or IP address, separated by a colon (:). If no context is specified, NetStorage searches the entire eDirectory partition stored on the specified eDirectory server for user information.

   ▶ *(Optional) Alternate eDirectory Server*: Specify up to two other eDirectory servers to use for user authentication. These can be different servers entirely, or the same server but a different associated context.

   ▶ *(Optional) iFolder Server*: Specify the DNS name or IP address of your iFolder server, as well as the port number used by the iFolder service. This will make iFolder contents available via NetStorage (WebDAV). More information on iFolder is available later in this chapter.

WARNING If you install NetStorage after the NetWare 6.5 installation, you must restart your NetWare 6.5 server after completing the NetStorage installation.

At the Installation Complete screen, click Close to complete the installation of NetStorage.

Configuring NetStorage

Use iManager to configure and manage your NetStorage environment by opening the NetStorage link in the left navigation frame. There really isn't much in the way of required configuration, but it's nice to understand the control you do have over NetStorage.

▶ *Authentication Domains*: This page lets you add/remove/modify authentication domains to NetStorage. These are eDirectory servers that NetStorage will search for user authentication information.

▶ *Browse Files*: This page lets you actually view the available NetStorage files. You will be required to authenticate as a valid user, and the user must exist in one of the authentication domains defined for this NetStorage server.

▶ *Current Sessions*: Shows a list of current NetStorage sessions.

▶ *General*: This page lets you configure some basic NetStorage parameters. In most cases you won't have to change any of these, but they are available if necessary.

▶ *iFolder Storage Provider*: This page lets you review and change basic iFolder parameters that relate to its operation with NetStorage. In most cases you won't have to change any of these, but they are available if necessary.

▶ *NetWare Storage Provider*: This page lets you review and change basic parameters related to the use of NetWare mapped drives with NetStorage. In most cases you won't have to change any of these, but they are available if necessary.

▶ *Resource Usage*: This page shows server resources being used in support of the NetStorage middle-tier server environment. It is useful for keeping track of how server resources are being used for troubleshooting server issues.

▶ *Statistics*: Displays a report with information about server up time, login failures, number of NetStorage sessions, and so on.

▶ *Storage Locations*: Use the Storage Locations pages to create/delete/modify storage location objects in your eDirectory tree. Storage location objects are pointers to NetWare directories that can be given more useful names than those typically seen when looking at NetStorage resources. This is particularly useful for common directories shared by multiple users.

▸ *WebDAV Provider*: This page lists the location of the NetStorage WebDAV provider (XDAV.NLM) and the location of NetStorage template files used for building the NetStorage Web interfaces.

For more detailed information on any of these parameters, see the NetWare 6.5 online documentation.

Using NetStorage

In order to avoid timestamp issues and confusion over the most current version of a file, Novell recommends that the date and time on the NetStorage server and the WebDAV client be reasonably close, within a few hours of each other.

You can access NetStorage from any WebDAV client. Two of the most obvious of which are Web browsers and Microsoft Windows Web folders. However, there are WebDAV clients for Macintosh and Unix/Linux systems as well. The following process is equally applicable to those environments.

1. From your WebDAV client, enter the magic NetStorage URL, which is the DNS name or IP address of your NetStorage server with /oneNet/NetStorage appended to the end. Remember to include the http:// prefix and remember that URLs are case sensitive. For example:

   `http://wal-serv1.quills.com/oneNet/NetStorage`

NOTE To use Web folders in Windows 2000, open My Network Places (the Windows WebDAV client) and double-click Add Network Place. This opens a wizard for creating a new folder in My Network Places.

2. At the authentication screen, specify your eDirectory username and password. This User object must be accessible from the eDirectory server(s) you specified during the NetStorage installation.

Once authenticated, your WebDAV client displays the network files and folders that are currently accessible. To do this, NetStorage reads the user's NetWare login script to determine drive mappings, reads eDirectory User object properties to determine the path to the user's home directory, and then displays a list of files and folders based on mapped drives and home directories. Figure 10.1 shows NetStorage views from both a Web browser and Windows Web folders.

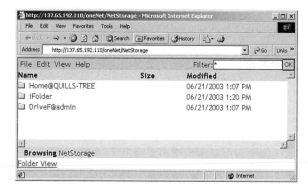

FIGURE 10.1
Accessing NetWare folders through NetStorage.

TIP If you specified eDirectory servers from different eDirectory trees during the NetStorage installation, NetStorage will read the user login script from only the primary eDirectory server when calculating mapped drives to display. However, NetStorage will read User object properties from all trees and display multiple home directories—as long as the User object has the same name in each tree. This is useful if a user normally logs in to more than one eDirectory tree.

If you have an iFolder account, you will see an iFolder folder in addition to your mapped drives and home directory, as shown in Figure 10.1. The first time you open the iFolder folder, all you will see is a file called PASSPHRASE.HTM. To access the contents of your iFolder directory, open PASSPHRASE.HTM, as shown in Figure 10.2, and specify the passphrase of your iFolder account.

This lets NetStorage decrypt your iFolder files so that it can interpret them properly. The passphrase for NetStorage is stored as an encrypted attribute on your User object, so it is not at risk of discovery.

Once connected to your NetWare files through WebDAV, you have full access to them. You can browse, open, and close folders; copy files to your local drive; and open files with WebDAV-compliant applications such as Web browsers, Microsoft Office 2000, and so on.

In addition, if you use Microsoft Windows Web folders, you can use all the normal Windows mechanisms for copying, cutting, pasting, and renaming files. To perform similar actions from a browser interface, click the Down arrow next to the file or folder with which you want to work.

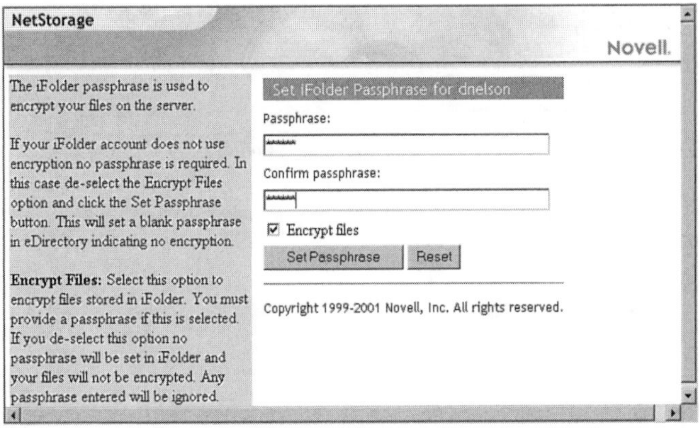

FIGURE 10.2
Specifying your passphrase to access iFolder from NetStorage.

If you need to use a file with a non-WebDAV application, you will need to copy the file to your local drive so that the application can use normal operating system mechanisms for working with the file. This is the only real drawback to NetStorage: It does not provide low-level integration with the operating system, such as creating a drive letter that lets applications access the files as if they were local.

Novell helps you resolve this issue for Windows workstations with NetDrive, which is described in the next section. The trade-off is having full access to network files as if they were local versus having a clientless solution for accessing your network files.

Novell NetDrive

Novell NetDrive lets you to map a network drive to any NetWare 6.5 server without using Novell client software. This means that with NetDrive, you can access and modify your files from any workstation using just an Internet connection. Once a network drive is mapped, the drive letter that you assigned during the mapping appears in Windows Explorer and functions just like those that are mapped through Novell client. Basically, the capability to map drives has been extracted from the Novell client where it can be used independent of all the other Novell client features. For more information on the Novell client, see Chapter 2.

NetDrive Prerequisites

NetDrive runs on any Windows workstation, including Windows 95/98/Me and Windows XP/2000/NT. You need only 2MB of available space on your hard drive to install and run the NetDrive client.

WARNING If you are installing the NetDrive client on a Windows 95 workstation, make sure you have installed the Winsock 2 update from Microsoft. It is available on the Microsoft Web site.

NetDrive supports three protocols for accessing network files:

▶ *WebDAV*: NetDrive integrates with NetStorage to provide a comprehensive file-access solution with very little client overhead. NetStorage must be installed and configured prior to using NetDrive with WebDAV.

▶ *FTP*: NetDrive can access network files using the standard File Transfer Protocol (FTP). An FTP server must be installed and configured on your network before using NetDrive with FTP. You can use the NetWare FTP server, described earlier in this chapter, to provide this type of access.

▶ *iFolder*: NetDrive can access files from your directory on the iFolder server. iFolder must be installed, and your iFolder account configured, prior to using NetDrive with iFolder.

The choice of protocol depends largely on your network environment. One is not preferable to another. Use the protocol that best fits your network strategy.

Installing NetDrive

The NetDrive client is available on the Novell client's CD-ROM. To install the NetDrive client, complete the following steps:

1. Insert the Novell client's CD-ROM. The CD-ROM will auto-play and present you with the Novell Client Installation menu. If the CD-ROM does not auto-play, run WINSETUP.EXE from the root of the CD-ROM.

2. At the Client Installation screen, select Novell NetDrive Client 4.1.

3. Select the language for the installation and click OK.

4. At the Welcome screen, click Next. At the License Agreement screen, click Yes.

5. At the Destination Location screen, specify the location where the NetDrive client should be installed and click Next.

After your workstation reboots, you are ready to use NetDrive to access your files over the network.

Using NetDrive

With the NetDrive client installed, you can access files on your NetWare 6.5 servers using standard Internet protocols. However, not every protocol is supported on every version of Windows.

▶ *iFolder*: Windows NT and 2000

▶ *FTP*: Windows 95, 98, Me, NT, and 2000

▶ *WebDAV (HTTP)*: Windows 95, 98, Me, NT, and 2000

▶ *Secure WebDAV (SSL)*: Windows NT and 2000

The NetDrive installation inserts an icon in the Windows system tray (lower-right corner of the Explorer window). To configure NetDrive and begin using it to access your network files, complete the following steps:

1. Click the NetDrive icon in the system tray.

2. From the main NetDrive window, as shown in Figure 10.3, you can create new sites, map network drives, and configure and manage the Web sites to which you have mapped drives.

Each of these functions is discussed in the following sections.

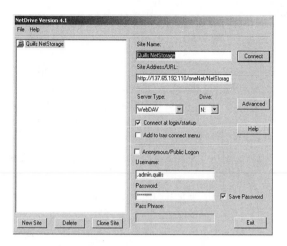

FIGURE 10.3
The NetDrive 4.1 configuration window.

Adding a Site to NetDrive

This makes a NetWare 6.5 site available to NetDrive so that drive mapping can take place. To add a site to NetDrive, complete the following steps:

1. In the main NetDrive window, click New Site.

2. At the Add New Site screen, enter the requested information, and click Finish.

   ▶ *Name for your new site*: Enter a descriptive name for the new NetDrive site.

   ▶ *Address/URL*: For an FTP connection, specify the DNS name or IP address of your FTP server (`ftp://ftp.quills.com/files`). For a WebDAV connection, specify the DNS name or IP address of the server where NetStorage is installed, along with the NetStorage access path (`http://ormserv2.quills.com/oneNet/NetStorage`). For iFolder, specify the DNS name or IP address of your iFolder service (`http://ifolder.quills.com`). If you omit the FTP or HTTP prefix, NetDrive defaults to FTP. If you want to use a nonstandard HTTP port, make sure you append it to the end of the URL.

NOTE If you want to connect with WebDAV and SSL encryption, remember to specify the HTTPS prefix as part of the URL.

Once you have created a site, the name of the new site and the URL of the NetWare 6.5 server are listed in the main NetDrive window. The rest of the page defaults to common connection options for the file protocol you have chosen (refer to Figure 10.3). However, you can change any of this information after the fact:

▶ *Server Type*: Specify the protocol that you will use to access this site.

▶ *Drive*: Specify the drive letter that you want to use for the mapped drive.

▶ *Connect at Login/Startup*: Check this box to have NetDrive map its drive automatically when your workstation starts.

▶ *Add Tray Connect Menu*: If you right-click the NetDrive icon in the system tray, you will see a Connect To option. Check this box to add the site to those listed in the Connect To menu.

▶ *Anonymous/Public Logon*: Check this box to bypass user authentication for an FTP connection. Both WebDAV and iFolder access require specific user authentication. Leave this box unchecked if you want to require authentication in order to access the site. If you do this, you will have to enter a valid username and password.

▶ *(Conditional) Passphrase*: If you are connecting to an iFolder server, enter a passphrase. This is used to encrypt your files as they are transferred over the Internet. iFolder is discussed later in this chapter.

▶ *Save Password*: Check this box if you want NetDrive to remember your authentication password.

Click the Advanced button to set optional download, caching, and file-locking parameters for the NetDrive site. You won't normally have to do anything in the Advanced area.

When you are finished configuring site properties, click Connect to actually map the drive. When NetDrive maps the drive, Windows opens a new window corresponding to the drive letter that you have just mapped.

Once NetDrive has successfully mapped a drive to the site, the Monitor window appears. It provides you with connection status, file transfer statistics, and a connection log. With the newly mapped drive, you can copy, cut, and paste files as you would in any other Windows drive.

> **TIP** If you have problems viewing the mapped directory or connecting to a server using FTP, specify the server IP address instead of the URL. You might also need to enable passive mode if the problem does not go away. Click Advanced and select PASV–Passive Mode. Then try connecting to the Web server again.

For more information on the advanced options available with NetDrive, see the NetWare 6.5 online documentation.

Novell iFolder

Novell iFolder gives you automatic, secure, and transparent synchronization of files between your hard drive and the iFolder server, which results in easy access to personal files anywhere, anytime.

Being able to access your files from any computer, in any location, eliminates mistakes and the updating that is frequently necessary when your local files are not accessible over the network.

There are three components to Novell iFolder:

> ▶ *iFolder server software*: Once you have installed the iFolder server software on your server, users can install the iFolder client in order to access their iFolder files. Administrators use the iFolder Management console and the iFolder Web site to manage iFolder user accounts.

> **NOTE** The iFolder Management console lets you perform administrative tasks for all iFolder user accounts. From the iFolder Web site, iFolder users download the iFolder client. It is also where you can access the Java applet and view your iFolder files from a browser. The iFolder Web site can, and should, be customized to fit the look, and feel of your organization.

> ▶ *iFolder client software*: Novell iFolder client is compatible with Windows 95/98/Me and Windows XP/2000/NT workstations. The iFolder client must be installed on every workstation that you will use to access your iFolder files. When the iFolder client is installed, it does three things:

▶ It creates a shortcut to your iFolder directory on your desktop. The iFolder directory, which by default is located in `My Documents\iFolder\userid\Home`, is where you will keep the files you want to synchronize with the iFolder server. When a file is placed in the iFolder directory, it is synchronized out to the iFolder server, from which it can be accessed by all workstations that are logged in to your iFolder account.

▶ An iFolder icon is placed in the workstation system tray. Right-clicking the system tray icon gives users access to their user-configurable preferences and the iFolder status screen, which displays a history of the transactions that have occurred between the iFolder server and the client.

▶ A user account is created on the iFolder server. iFolder user accounts are created automatically when a user downloads and installs the iFolder client. When you log in, iFolder asks you for a username and a password. Next, iFolder prompts you for a passphrase. This passphrase is used to encrypt files that are uploaded to the server.

NOTE Uninstalling the iFolder client does not delete the associated user account on the iFolder server. This can be done only from the iFolder Management console.

▶ *iFolder Java applet*: Use the iFolder Java applet to access iFolder files from a workstation on which the iFolder client is not installed.

iFolder Prerequisites

Remember the following prerequisites when you are installing iFolder:

▶ iFolder requires Internet Explorer 5.0 or 5.5 to be installed on every workstation where you are installing the iFolder client.

▶ You need 10MB of free space on the `SYS:` volume where you plan to install iFolder.

▶ Novell iFolder is compatible with Windows XP/2000/NT, and 95/98/Me workstations. The iFolder client requires about 2MB of free space on your workstation.

NOTE If you are installing the iFolder client on a Windows 95 workstation, make sure you have installed the Winsock 2 update from Microsoft. It is available on Microsoft's Web site.

Installing iFolder

Novell iFolder can be installed as part of the NetWare 6.5 server installation, or it can be installed after the fact through either iManager or the graphical server console. To install iFolder with iManager, complete the following steps:

1. Insert the NetWare 6.5 Operating System CD-ROM into your workstation.

2. Launch iManager and open the Install and Upgrade link in the left navigation frame.

3. Select Install NetWare 6.5 Products, and then click Remote Product Install in the right frame.

4. At the Target Server screen, select the server to which you want to install iFolder and click Next. Authenticate as an Admin user for your eDirectory tree and click OK.

5. At the Components screen, click Clear All and select only Novell iFolder Storage Services. Click Next.

6. At the Summary screen, click Copy Files. You will be prompted to insert the NetWare 6.5 product's CD-ROM.

7. At the iFolder Server Options screen, as shown in Figure 10.4, provide the required information and click Next.

   ▶ *LDAP Hostname or IP*: Enter the hostname or IP address of the eDirectory server that will authenticate your iFolder users. This server must have a replica of your eDirectory root partition.

   ▶ *LDAP Port*: Enter the LDAP port you want to use. Use the default LDAP port (**389**) for unencrypted communications or port **636** for SSL-encrypted communications. If you use port **389**, make sure that your LDAP environment allows clear text passwords. Similarly, if you use port **636**, make sure that your LDAP server is configured to support SSL.

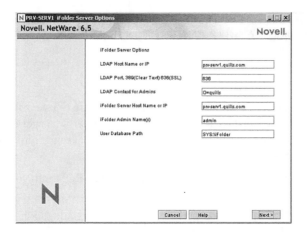

FIGURE 10.4
iFolder server configuration options during installation.

> **TIP** Unencrypted LDAP communications (port 389) is a good choice if iFolder and LDAP are running on the same server, and no LDAP communications have to cross the network. For more information on LDAP configuration, see Chapter 5, "Novell eDirectory Management."

- ▶ *LDAP Context for Admins*: Specify the context for all Admin users who need rights to modify iFolder user account information.

- ▶ *iFolder server Hostname or* IP: Specify the domain name or IP address of the server on which iFolder services will be running.

- ▶ *iFolder Admin name(s)*: Specify the User objects that will act as iFolder administrators. Separate multiple names with semi-colons, but no spaces.

- ▶ *User Database Path*: Enter the path to the directory where you want the iFolder user data to be stored on the iFolder server.

At the Installation Complete screen, click Close to complete the installation of iFolder.

Configuring iFolder

The first time the iFolder client is installed, a user account is automatically created on your iFolder server. In addition to the default iFolder Web site, another Web site is available for performing server management.

Once iFolder is installed, you can access the iFolder Management console through the following URL: `https://<ifolder server DNS or IP address>/iFolderServer/Admin`. For example:

`https://prv-serv1.quills.com/iFolderServer/Admin`

The initial view of iFolder Management console shows you the types of tasks you can perform, but you won't be able to actually do anything until you actually log in via LDAP. Use an administrative user account you specified during the iFolder installation. Once authenticated, you will get a new authenticated view of iFolder Management console that lets you actually perform the various iFolder administrative tasks (see Figure 10.5). There are four types of iFolder management activities:

- ▶ Global settings
- ▶ User management
- ▶ System monitoring
- ▶ Reporting

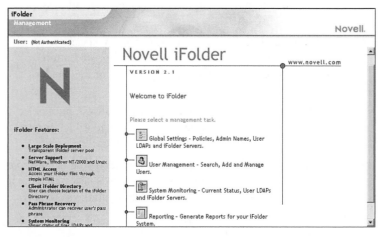

FIGURE 10.5
iFolder Management console.

Global Settings

When you click the Global Settings button, you will see five links in the left navigation frame (see Figure 10.6):

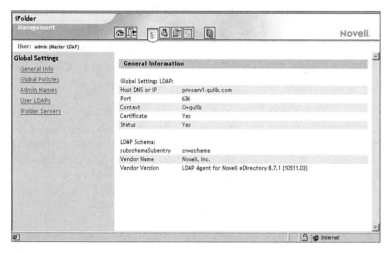

FIGURE 10.6
Configuring iFolder global settings with the iFolder Management console.

- ▶ *General Info:* The General Info link provides basic information about the iFolder server, including DNS name or IP address, port being used, and so on.

- ▶ *Global Policies*: With the Global Policies page, you can set both server and client policies by clicking the appropriate button. These settings define the default configuration for the iFolder environment.

- ▶ *Admin Names*: This page lets you modify the list of Admin objects defined for iFolder. These objects must be located in the Admin context defined during the installation of iFolder.

- ▶ *User LDAPs*: The User LDAPs page lets you define the LDAP server that iFolder will use to authenticate users. This is necessary only if your LDAP server and iFolder are not running on the same server.

- ▶ *iFolder Servers*: This page lets you add new iFolder servers to the iFolder environment as they are installed.

Use the global settings links to configure the primary characteristics of your iFolder environment.

User Management

Before your users can start using iFolder, you have to enable their User objects from the User Management button in the iFolder Server Management console. You can select users individually or in groups. To enable user objects to work with iFolder, complete the following steps:

1. Launch iFolder Server Management and click the User Management button.

2. Click Advanced Search in the left navigation frame.

3. Specify how you want iFolder to search for users and then click Search. You can search by a name, a portion of a name, the context, or even the entire server. Once you perform the search, all user objects located within your defined criteria will be listed (see Figure 10.7).

4. Click Enable All Found Users as iFolder Users to allow the User objects that have been found to use iFolder. Alternatively, you can check the boxes next to only those user objects for which you want to provide iFolder access and click Enable Checked Users as iFolder Users.

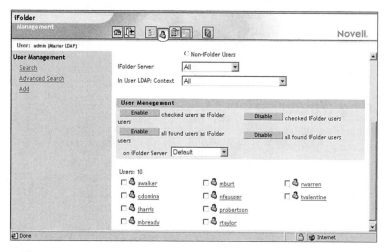

FIGURE 10.7

Configuring iFolder users with the iFolder Management console.

NOTE As new User objects are configured on your network, you will have to add those users in order for them to have access to iFolder. iFolder access is not granted by default.

System Monitoring

The System Monitoring button provides a real-time view of the status of your iFolder environment. From this page, you can see a list of all iFolder and LDAP servers in your environment, along with important characteristics of each.

Reporting

The Reporting button allows you to take the information you can see from System Monitoring and capture it in report format. You can create reports in four categories:

▶ *General Information*: This report gives you information about the status of your entire iFolder environment.

▶ *iFolder Servers*: This report provides configuration information for each iFolder server in your environment.

▶ *User LDAPs*: This report provides configuration information for each LDAP server being used by your iFolder environment for user authentication.

▶ *User Accounts*: This report provides information about each user object that is using your iFolder environment and how it is making use of iFolder resources.

You can configure the iFolder reporting environment to fit the needs of your network environment.

Using iFolder

Once iFolder is installed and configured on the server and user access has been defined, your users can begin to take advantage of iFolder's file synchronization capabilities. The first thing iFolder users need to do is install the iFolder client. The iFolder client is available from Web Manager. To install the iFolder client, complete the following steps:

1. From Web Manager, click the iFolder link in the left navigation frame.

2. In the box entitled iFolder Links, select Download iFolder Client.

3. At the File Download screen, choose to either save the client file to disk or run it directly from the server, and then click OK. If you are accessing the server from a remote location, it will probably be faster to download the file prior to installing the iFolder client. If you do this, specify a location for the file. Once the download is complete, execute the file you downloaded.

4. If you get a Security Warning screen from Windows, click Yes.

5. At the Welcome screen, click Next.

6. At the License Agreement Language screen, select the language in which to view the license agreement and click Next. This will open a browser window with the iFolder license agreement. To continue the installation, close the browser window.

7. At the License Agreement screen, click Yes to accept the agreement.

8. At the Destination Location screen, specify the location where you want the iFolder client files to be installed and click Next.

9. At the Installation Complete screen, select Yes, I Want to Restart My Computer Now and click Finish.

10. After your workstation reboots, you will see a Setup Complete message, with instructions on using iFolder. Click Continue to finish the installation.

11. The Login screen will be displayed, as shown in Figure 10.8. Specify the required information and click Login. You will provide a username (typically your NetWare username) and password. Typically, the iFolder server information will be provided for you.

FIGURE 10.8
The iFolder Login screen.

12. At the iFolder Location screen, specify the location on your local drive to which your iFolder files will be synchronized and click OK.

13. If you use encryption, provide a passphrase and click OK. The passphrase is used as the cryptographic key to encrypt your files on the iFolder server.

Once you log in, you will see new iFolder icons on your desktop and in the Windows system tray (lower-right corner of the desktop). The desktop icon is a shortcut to your iFolder files. The system tray icon gives you access to iFolder user account information and configuration parameters. To do this, right-click the iFolder icon that appears on the system tray of your workstation. The following major menu options are available:

▶ *Logout/login*: If currently logged in, the Logout option is displayed, which will log you off of the iFolder server and stop all iFolder synchronization. If currently logged out, the Login option is displayed, which allows you to log in to the iFolder and initiate synchronization activities.

▶ *Sync Now*: Forces synchronization between the workstation and the iFolder server to begin immediately.

▶ *Account Information*: This option lets you view account settings and synchronization activity, as well as allows you tob set account synchronization preferences. The Account Information screen is shown in Figure 10.9. From the Account Information screen, you can do the following:

   ▶ *Account Information tab*: Displays basic account information, including username, iFolder directory location, iFolder servername, account space statistics, and to-be-synchronized statistics.

   ▶ *View Activity tab*: Lets you view, save, and clear your iFolder account activity log. The log is automatically cleared each time you log in to iFolder.

   ▶ *Preferences tab*: Lets you enable/disable automatic synchronization and define how often files will be synchronized to/from the iFolder server. You can also choose to have the iFolder client remember your iFolder password and passphrase so that you don't have to type them each time you log in.

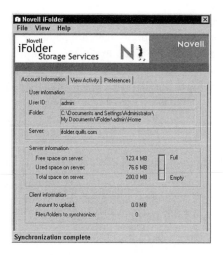

FIGURE 10.9
The iFolder Account Information screen.

▶ *Open iFolder*: Opens the iFolder directory associated with your iFolder client account. This is equivalent to double-clicking the iFolder icon that is created, by default, on the Windows desktop.

▶ *View Conflict Bin*: The conflict bin exists to save files that were deleted or changed during an iFolder synchronization. You can manually review the files in the conflict bin to make sure that the correct version of the file has been synchronized.

▶ *About iFolder*: Provides version information for the iFolder client.

▶ *iFolder Web Site*: Selecting this option opens the iFolder Web site associated with your iFolder server. From this page, you can download the iFolder client, view iFolder product information and instructions, and access your iFolder account via a Web browser.

▶ *Help*: Opens the iFolder client help file.

▶ *Exit*: This option closes the iFolder client interface, and effectively logs you out of the iFolder server. The icon will disappear from the system tray, so in order to restart the iFolder client, you have to click Start >> Programs >> Novell iFolder >> iFolder Client.

As you can see, nearly every feature needed by a user is available through the iFolder icon in the Windows system tray.

Accessing iFolder Through a Browser

iFolder has a browser-based option that eliminates the need for the iFolder client in order to access files in your account on the iFolder server. With iFolder Web access, you can download only the files that you need, as opposed to synchronizing the entire directory. With the iFolder Web access, all you need is Internet access to get to your iFolder account.

To access your iFolder account through a Web browser, complete the following steps:

1. From Web Manager, click the iFolder link in the left navigation frame.

2. In the box entitled iFolder Links, select Open iFolder WebAccess. If a security warning appears, click Yes.

3. Enter your iFolder username, password, and passphrase, and click Connect.

Once logged in, you will see your iFolder files, listed in a directory structure in the browser window, as shown in Figure 10.10. Expand folders by double-clicking them.

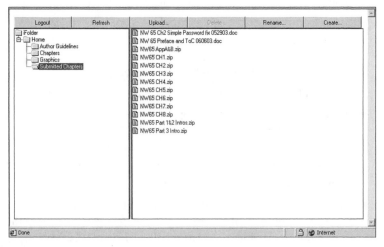

FIGURE 10.10
Web interface to iFolder.

From the browser interface, you can download, upload, delete, create, and rename files. However, after downloading a file, changes will not be synchronized automatically. Make sure you upload files after making changes, so they can be synchronized to all other workstations where you have installed the iFolder client.

Accessing iFolder from NetStorage or NetDrive

Accessing an iFolder server from either NetStorage or NetDrive was described earlier in this chapter in the sections for each of those products. However, the important thing to remember is that you are accessing files on the server only. You don't get the effects of synchronization between client and server as you do with the iFolder client.

The advantage of this scenario is that you can access files from any workstation without fear of accidentally leaving data on a foreign machine. This might lead some to consider using iFolder without installing the iFolder client. This is a possible solution, but remember that files are not replicated to multiple locations. If the server experienced a problem, or you forget your passphrase, files on the iFolder server could be lost or unrecoverable.

TIP The best solution is one that uses each technology where it makes sense, without relying too heavily on only one type of file-access solution.

Novell Virtual Office

Novell Virtual Office allows network administrators to quickly and easily provide browser-based access to network resources. Effectively, Virtual Office lets you to create personalized user portals through which users can access their data and applications from a single Web site. Not only that, but Virtual Office also provides the capability to create *virtual teams*, or ad-hoc shared portals that can support a project or any other group that needs access to shared resources.

Virtual Office provides services that allow you to access network resources through the Virtual Office interface. *Services* are little Java-based servlets or applications that provide access to specific types of network resources. NetWare 6.5 includes several default Virtual Office services for accessing network resources and performing common network tasks:

▶ *NetStorage*: Provides access to the Novell NetStorage service. NetStorage provides Internet-based access to file storage on a NetWare 6.5 server, including access to iFolder. Both NetStorage and iFolder were discussed earlier in this chapter.

▶ *iPrint*: Provides access to Internet printing via iPrint. For more information on iPrint, see Chapter 7, "NetWare Printing Services."

▶ *Email and calendaring*: Provides support for popular email applications and protocols, including Novell GroupWise, Microsoft Exchange, Lotus Notes, Novell Internet Messaging System (NIMS), POP3, and IMAP.

▶ *eGuide*: Provides a simplified screen to access phone numbers and other user information stored in eDirectory. For more information on eGuide, see the NetWare 6.5 online documentation.

▶ *Password*: Links to a page where users can change their password in eDirectory.

▶ *ZENWorks*: Provides integration with Novell ZENWorks for Desktops functionality, such as application delivery, through the Virtual Office interface.

Perhaps most important to you as a network administrator, Virtual Office doesn't require any complicated Web development or programming. It's pretty much ready to go right out of the box.

Installing Virtual Office

Virtual Office can be installed as an optional component during the NetWare 6.5 installation or it can be installed later through iManager or the graphical server console.

NOTE For most networks, you will need to install Virtual Office on only one server in each eDirectory tree.

The only requirement for WebAccess, beyond the minimum requirements for a NetWare 6.5 server, is a browser (Netscape v4.7 or later, or Internet Explorer v5.5 or later). To install Virtual Office using iManager, complete the following steps:

1. Insert the NetWare 6.5 Operating System CD-ROM into your workstation.

2. Launch iManager and open the Install and Upgrade link in the left navigation frame.

3. Select Install NetWare 6.5 Products, and then click Remote Product Install in the right frame.

4. At the Target Server screen, select the server to which you want to install Virtual Office and click Next. Authenticate as an Admin user for your eDirectory tree and click OK.

5. At the components screen, click Clear All and select only Novell Virtual Office. Click Next.

6. At the Summary screen, click Copy Files. You will be prompted to insert the NetWare 6.5 product's CD-ROM. When the Installation Complete screen appears, click Close.

Once loaded, you can access a default Virtual Office Web page by pointing your browser to the following page: http://*<server DNS name or IP address>*/vo. For example:

http://wal-serv1.quills.com/vo

This page will include links to all the gadgets you can use from the Virtual Office portal.

Preparing Virtual Office for Use

There are two aspects to configuring your Virtual Office environment: configuring Virtual Office itself, and configuring Virtual Office services. Most of these tasks are handled through iManager.

Configuring Virtual Office

To perform the initial configuration of Virtual Office, complete the following steps:

1. Launch iManager and open the Virtual Office Management link.

2. Select Environment Administration (see Figure 10.11).

3. Use each of the tabs provided to configure your general Virtual Office environment:

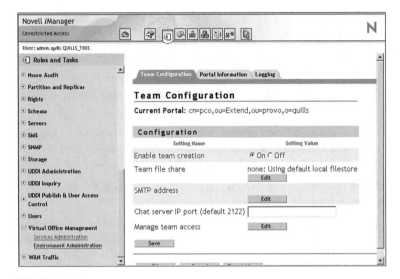

FIGURE 10.11
Configuring the Virtual Office environment in iManager.

▶ *Team Configuration*: Virtual teams let you create virtual ad-hoc groups that can share resources and information through a centralized portal dedicated for that purpose. More information on virtual teams is provided later in this chapter. To configure your virtual team environment, provide the requested information and click Save.

   ▶ *Enable Team Creation*: Lets you enable virtual team creation. This is enabled by default. When disabled, no virtual team functionality is available.

   ▶ *Team File Share*: Click Edit to specify the location where virtual team members will be allowed to store shared files. File sharing requires the Native File Access Protocols (NFAP) capabilities of NetWare 6.5 because the location to which virtual team files will be stored must be configured as a CIFS share point. For more information on NFAP and configuring a CIFS share point, see Chapter 2.

   ▶ *SMTP Address*: Click Edit to specify the IP address or DNS name of your SMTP mail server. This is required if you want Virtual Office to be able to send email notifications to virtual team members.

▶ *Chat Server IP Port*: Specifies the TCP port that will be used for chat communications for virtual teams.

▶ *Manage Team Access*: Click Edit to specify those users who have rights to configure virtual teams.

▶ *Portal Information*: This page lets you define how your Virtual Office portal can be used. There are three options on this page:

▶ *Portal Containers*: Sets those contexts from which users can log in and access Virtual Office. Effectively, this restricts the list of potential Virtual Office users to those within the contexts you specify.

▶ *Portal Locations*: If you are running Virtual Office on multiple servers, make sure that all portal addresses are listed here. Remember, you can specify the same storage location for multiple Virtual Office portals.

▶ *Teams*: Lists all virtual teams that have been created on the selected Virtual Office portal.

▶ *Logging*: This page lets you configure the information that will appear in Virtual Office log reports. Virtual Office logs can help you track service usage and diagnose problems. Typically, you won't use logging because of the overhead that it requires, but it is useful for gathering environment and troubleshooting information.

▶ *Logging*: Check this box to enable logging.

▶ *Logging Level*: Sets the level of logging that will be performed. There are three levels of information you can obtain from the logging report. It's counter-intuitive, but selecting Low will log all available information, Medium limits logging output, and High restricts log output even more.

▶ *Logging Modules*: Lets you specify the specific Virtual Office modules that you want to include in the logging. Leave the field blank to log all modules.

▶ *Logging to Standard Error*: Check this box to log to the defined Standard Error device. By default, this is the Tomcat logger screen.

▶ *Logging to Standard Out*: Check this box to log to the defined Standard Out device. By default, this is the Tomcat logger screen.

▶ *Logging to File*: Check this box to send the log to a file. By default, the log file is SYS:\TOMCAT\4\WEBAPPS\NPS\ WEB-INF\DEBUG.XML.

Once you have completed the initial configuration of Virtual Office, you can move on to the configuration of the services available through the Virtual Office portal.

Configuring Virtual Office Services

There are several default Virtual Office services that ship with NetWare 6.5, but in order to use each you must perform some basic configuration, primarily centered around enabling the service and specifying the location of the service on the network.

NOTE If you are interested in doing more advanced customization, or in developing your own Virtual Office services, you can use the Novell exteNd development tools for doing this.

Some Virtual Office services are configured through iManager, and others are configured directly from the Virtual Office home page. To configure Virtual Office services from iManager, complete the following steps:

1. Launch iManager and open the Virtual Office Management link.

2. Select Services Administration (see Figure 10.12).

3. Use the eight tabs provided to configure the Virtual Office services. If you uncheck the Enable box on any of these tabs, that service will be removed from your Virtual Office Web page.

   ▶ *Company Info*: Use this option to specify the information that will appear in the News field in the Virtual Office Web page. Enter regular text or HTML in the text box to specify the information that should appear in the News field.

   ▶ *NetStorage*: You must have NetStorage installed and configured before enabling this service. More information on NetStorage is provided earlier in this chapter. Specify the location of the NetStorage service to be used by Virtual Office. You can run NetStorage from the same server that is running Virtual Office, from a different server, or specify a custom location for the NetStorage service. Unless you are using the default local location for NetStorage, you will have to provide the complete IP or DNS path to the NetStorage service.

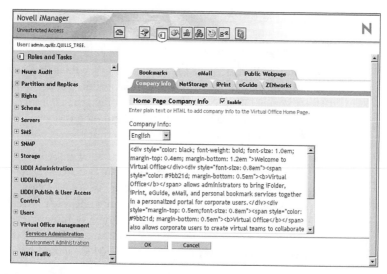

FIGURE 10.12
Configuring Virtual Office services in iManager.

▶ *iPrint gadget*: You must have NDPS and Novell iPrint
installed and configured before enabling this service. For
more information on iPrint, see Chapter 7. Specify the location of the iPrint service to be used by Virtual Office. You can
run iPrint from the same server that is running Virtual Office,
from a different server, or specify a custom location for the
iPrint service. Unless you are using the default local location
for iPrint, you will have to provide the complete IP or DNS
path to the iPrint service.

▶ *eGuide gadget*: You must have eGuide installed and configured before enabling this service. For more information on
eGuide, see the NetWare 6.5 online documentation. Specify
the location of the eGuide service to be used by Virtual
Office. You can run eGuide from the same server that is running Virtual Office, from a different server, or specify a custom location for the eGuide service. Unless you are using the
default local location for eGuide, you will have to provide the
complete IP or DNS path to the eGuide service.

▶ *ZENWorks*: You must have ZENWorks for Desktops installed
and configured before enabling this service. When enabled,

certain ZENWorks services can be accessed through Virtual
Office, such as application distribution. For more information, see the NetWare 6.5 online documentation.

▶ *Bookmarks*: Virtual Office lets you specify Web links that you
want to appear on the Virtual Office Navigation bar and/or a
User's Virtual Office Web page. You can only enable/disable
this service from iManager. Actual configuration is done
directly from the Virtual Office Web page.

▶ *Email*: You must have an email service installed and configured before enabling this service. There are two steps to making a user's email available through Virtual Office, as follows.
First, you specify the type of email system with which Virtual
Office will integrate, and then you click the Edit button next
to the server link to specify the type and location (IP or DNS
name) of the mail server to which Virtual Office should
attach.

▶ *Public Web Page*: Virtual Office allows individual users to
configure personal Web pages that will be accessible through
Virtual Office. You can only enable/disable this service from
iManager. Actual configuration is done directly from the
Virtual Office Web page.

Virtual Office also permits customization of services directly through the
Virtual Office Web page. Users can launch the Virtual Office Web page,
which is available at `http://<server DNS name or IP address>/vo`
by default.

▶ *Bookmarks*: Click View and Manage My Bookmarks in the Virtual
Office, and then click the Personalize link (see Figure 10.13). From
this page, you can add, edit, or delete the Web links that will
appear on your Virtual Office Web page and/or Menu bar.

▶ *Change Password*: This link lets you reset your user password
through Virtual Office.

▶ *View and Edit My Webpage*: This link lets you specify the personal
information that will be presented when a link to your User object
is clicked in Virtual Office.

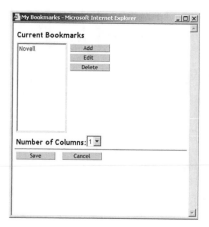

FIGURE 10.13
Adding bookmarks to your Virtual Office portal.

Virtual Teams

A *virtual team* is an ad-hoc shared portal that can support a project or any other group that needs access to shared resources. To create a virtual team, complete the following steps:

1. Launch the Virtual Office Web page, which is available at
   `http://<server DNS name or IP address>/vo` by default.

2. Select Create Virtual Teams in the left navigation bar.

3. Specify a name for the new virtual team and click Create. You can also enter a description for the team you are creating.

Within a virtual team, team members can exchange information, share files, and maintain a calendar of events. Virtual Office lets you create and manage your own virtual teams and/or become a member of teams created by others.

Configuring Virtual Team Services

There are certain services that are available only within the context of a virtual team. These special services are designed to enhance communication and productivity between the members of a virtual team. Selecting the Team link in the left navigation frame (see Figure 10.14) will open a Web page from which the team-specific services are available:

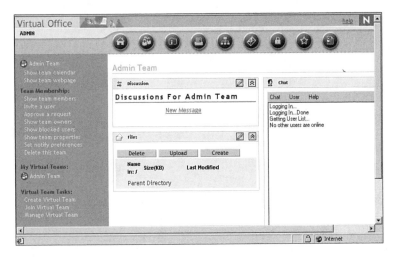

FIGURE 10.14
Default virtual team portal in Virtual Office.

▶ *Discussion*: Team members can use the Discussion service as a Web log of sorts to capture online discussions, and exchange ideas and messages. The discussion threads are accessible by all members of the team.

▶ *Files*: Team members can use the Files service as a Web-based file-sharing tool. Files can be created, uploaded, deleted, and browsed through this service. The Files service uses the Team File Share location specified during the configuration of Virtual Office, discussed previously.

▶ *Chat*: Lets members of a virtual team communicate through instant messaging. With the Chat service, you can do instant messaging with the members of your virtual team, but the instant message capabilities have been enhanced so that you can save conversations, invite multiple users to join a single chat session, and indicate when you are not available to chat.

▶ *Links*: The Links service lets you create a list of team-related links that can be shared among team members to facilitate research or collaboration.

In addition to the team-specific services available through the Virtual Team link, there are two other resources available to virtual team members:

► *Calendar*: From the left navigation frame, select Show Team Calendar. From this page, you can schedule team-related events and appointments and share this information with team members.

► *Team Web Site*: From the left navigation frame, select Show Team Webpage. The team Web page provides basic information about the virtual team, including its purpose, team members, and lists of published Web links and files that the team wants to make readily available.

Managing Virtual Teams

As the owner of a virtual team, there are several management tasks available to you for configuring and managing your virtual team. Once you have created a virtual team, open the team Web page to perform one or more of the following tasks:

► *View Team Membership*: From the Team Membership column, select Show Team Members, and then click Membership.

► *Invite Someone to Join a Team*: From the Team Membership column, select Invite a User, and then click Add. Once invited, a user can choose to accept or reject the invitation.

► *Accept or Reject a Membership Request*: From the Team Membership column, select Approve a Request, and then click Approve or Deny.

► *Add Team Owners*: From the Team Membership column, select Show Team Owners, and then click Add. Once added, new team owners have the same rights you do, including the capability to remove you as an owner! For this reason, make sure team ownership is handed out carefully.

► *Block Users from a Team*: From the Team Membership column, select Show Blocked Users, and then click Add. This option lets you manage team membership by exception, rather than having to specify each user who should be a member.

► *Edit Team Properties*: From the Team Membership column, select Show Team Properties. From this page, you can update the name, description, or services associated with a virtual team.

► *Set Notify Preferences*: From the Team Membership column, select Set Notify Preferences and select each event for which you want team members automatically notified via email.

▶ *Delete a Virtual Team*: From the Team Membership column, select Delete this Team, and then click Delete twice more. Once a virtual team has served its purpose, you can delete it very easily.

As you can see from this list, virtual team owners have several tools at their disposal to manage the operation of the team portal, control access to the team portal, and make sure that usage of the team portal is only for designated purposes.

Joining a Virtual Team

You must be a member of a virtual team to have access to information and services associated within that virtual team. To request membership in a virtual team, complete the following steps:

1. Launch the Virtual Office Web page, which is available at `http://<server DNS name or IP address>/vo` by default.

2. Select Join Virtual Team in the left navigation bar.

3. Select the team you want to join from the list of available teams, and click Join.

4. Request membership from the owner of the team and click OK. After the owner approves your request, you become a member of the team and will have access to the virtual team resources.

Any user can request membership to virtual teams, but membership is granted only when approved by the virtual team owner.

NetWare FTP Server

NetWare FTP server is based on the standard ARPANET file transfer protocol that runs over TCP/IP and conforms to RFC 959. You can perform file transfers from any FTP client by using the FTP server to log in to the Novell eDirectory tree.

FTP server is a fully functional FTP with many features, such as those in following list. This section provides basic installation and configuration information so you can use FTP file access with NetDrive.

▶ *iManager-based management*: Use iManager to start and stop FTP server, and configure server, security, user, and log settings. For more information on iManager, see Chapter 3.

▶ *Run multiple copies of FTP server*: Multiple instances of NetWare
FTP server software can be loaded on the same NetWare server,
providing different FTP services to different sets of users.

▶ *FTP access restrictions*: FTP access can be restricted at various levels through comprehensive access rights controls.

▶ *Intruder detection*: Intruder hosts or users who try to log in using
an invalid password can be detected and restricted.

▶ *Remote server access*: FTP users can navigate and access files from
other NetWare servers in the same eDirectory tree, and even from
remote IBM servers. Remote servers don't have to be running an
FTP server.

▶ *Anonymous user access*: Anonymous user accounts can be set up to
provide users with basic access to public files.

▶ *Special quote site commands*: These are special, NetWare-specific
commands used to change or view some NetWare-specific
parameters.

▶ *Firewall support*: If the FTP client is behind a firewall, FTP server
supports passive mode data transfer and the configuration of a
range of passive data ports.

▶ *Active sessions display*: View details of all active FTP instances in
real-time. This includes such information as a list of all instances,
details of each instance, all sessions in an instance, and details of
individual sessions within an instance.

▶ *Name space support*: FTP server supports both DOS and long name
spaces. The FTP user can dynamically change the default name
space by using one of the quote site commands.

▶ *SNMP error reporting*: Simple Network Management Protocol
(SNMP) traps are issued when an FTP login request comes from an
intruder host or from a node address restricted through Novell
eDirectory. SNMP traps can be captured and viewed by any SNMP-
compliant management console.

▶ *FTP logs*: The FTP service maintains a log of several activities,
including FTP sessions, unsuccessful login attempts, active sessions
details, and system error and FTP server-related messages.

▶ *Cluster services support*: NetWare FTP server can be configured
with Novell Cluster Services (NCS) for high availability.

For detailed information on all FTP server features, see the NetWare 6.5 online documentation.

Installing FTP Server

The FTP server can be installed as an optional component during the NetWare 6.5 installation or it can be installed later through iManager or the graphical server console. To install the FTP server using iManager, complete the following steps:

1. Insert the NetWare 6.5 Operating System CD-ROM into your workstation.

2. Launch iManager and open the Install and Upgrade link in the left navigation frame.

3. Select Install NetWare 6.5 Products, and then click Remote Product Install in the right frame.

4. At the Target Server screen, select the server to which you want to install FTP server and click Next. Authenticate as an Admin user for your eDirectory tree and click OK.

5. At the Components screen, click Clear All and select only NetWare FTP Server. Click Next.

6. At the Summary screen click Copy Files. You will be prompted to insert the NetWare 6.5 product's CD-ROM.

After the FTP server files are copied, click Close to complete the installation.

Configuring FTP Server

Before you start the NetWare FTP server software, you should configure it by setting the configuration parameters in the configuration file. The default configuration file is SYS:/ETC/FTPSERV.CFG. The parameters in this configuration file are commented with their default values.

When the NetWare FTP server is started, the IP address of the host (HOST_IP_ADDR) and the port number of the NetWare FTP server (FTP_PORT), as defined in the configuration file, are used to bind to and listen for FTP client connection requests. If these parameters are not defined in the configuration file, the FTP server binds to all configured network interfaces in the server and uses the standard FTP ports.

Multiple instances of the NetWare FTP server can run on a single machine with different IP addresses or port numbers. The various parameters in the configuration file along with the default values are described in the tables presented later in this chapter.

You can use iManager as an access point for administering the NetWare FTP server. To do so, launch iManager and select File Protocols > FTP in the left navigation frame. The FTP server utility is shown in Figure 10.15.

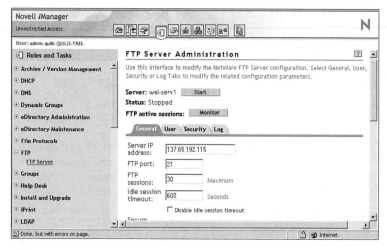

FIGURE 10.15
FTP Server Administration page in iManager.

The FTP server configuration file can be edited manually with any text editor. However, it is much easier to configure and manage FTP server from iManager. iManager also gives you the freedom to manage the FTP server from any network connection and Web browser.

From the FTP Server Administration page, you can start and stop the FTP server as necessary. This loads or unloads NWFTPD.NLM on the NetWare 6.5 server running FTP services. You can also use the Monitor button to view a list of active FTP sessions, with statistics on each.

The server reads the default configuration file SYS:/ETC/FTPSERV.CFG and configures itself accordingly. If there is any change in the FTP configuration file, you should stop and restart the FTP server.

There are four pages of configuration options available to configure and manage FTP server from iManager. Each provides access to specific types of configuration parameters and information, as described in the following sections.

General Settings

Click the General tab to access general FTP server settings. When finished, click Save to record your settings or click Reset to revert to the previous settings. Table 10.1 lists the available server settings, with a brief description and the equivalent setting in the configuration file.

TABLE 10.1 Server Settings Parameters in iManager

PARAMETER	CONFIG FILE	DEFAULT VALUE	DESCRIPTION
Server IP address	HOST_IP_ADDR	N/A	Sets the IP address that will be used for the FTP server. If left blank, FTP server will bind to every IP address on the NetWare server.
FTP Port	FTP_PORT	21	Specifies the port that FTP server will use to listen for FTP requests.
FTP sessions (maximum)	MAX_FTP_ SESSIONS	30	Maximum number of FTP sessions that can be active at any point of time. Minimum value is 1.
Idle session timeout (seconds)	IDLE_SESSION_ TIMEOUT	600	Duration in seconds that any session can remain idle. Check the Disable Idle Timeout box if you don't want FTP sessions to time out. This sets the FTPSERV value to –1.

TABLE 10.1 Continued

PARAMETER	CONFIG FILE	DEFAULT VALUE	DESCRIPTION
Secure connections only	SECURE_ CONNECTIONS_ ONLY	Disabled	Forces all FTP sessions to use a secure (SSL) connection. Nonsecure sessions are rejected.
Default Namespace	DEFAULT_NS	Long	The default namespace. The valid values are DOS and LONG.
Data buffer size (KB)	DATA_BUFF_ SIZE	64	Sets the size of the FTP transfer buffer. Valid sizes range from 4KB to 1020KB.
Keep-alive time (minutes)	KEEPALIVE_ TIME	10	Sets the interval at which the FTP server will check active connections to see whether they have been broken from the other side. Values can be 5 minutes to 120 minutes.
Welcome banner file	WELCOME_ BANNER	SYS:/ETC/ WELCOME.TXT	When the FTP client establishes a connection, the content of this file is displayed.
Directory message file	MESSAGE_ FILE	MESSAGE.TXT	When the user changes the directory, the contents of this file are displayed. For this, the file with that name should exist in the directory.

TABLE 10.1 Continued

PARAMETER	CONFIG FILE	DEFAULT VALUE	DESCRIPTION
Minimum port	PASSIVE_ PORT_MIN	1	Minimum port number used for establishing passive data connection. The port value range is 1 to 65534. The minimum value should always be less than or equal to the maximum value.
Maximum port	PASSIVE_ PORT_MAX	65534	Maximum port number used for establishing passive data connection. The port value range = 1 to 65534. The maximum value should always be greater than or equal to the minimum value.
File permissions	PSEUDO_FILE_ PERMISSIONS	644	If enabled, this will display file rights in the standard Unix format rather than in the NetWare trustee rights format.
Directory permissions	PSEUDO_DIR_ PERMISSIONS	755	If enabled, this will display directory rights in the standard Unix format rather than in the NetWare trustee rights format.

User Settings

Click the User tab to access parameters that control file access and user authentication for FTP server. When finished, click Save to record your settings or click Reset to revert to the previous settings. Table 10.2 lists the available user settings, with a brief description and the equivalent setting in the configuration file.

TABLE 10.2   User Settings in Web Manager

PARAMETER	CONFIG FILE	DEFAULT VALUE	DESCRIPTION
Use FTP for Web publishing	N/A	No	Sets home directory to `SYS:/APACHE2/HTDOCS/FTPWEBS`. Lets content publishers copy files to a Web server via FTP.
Default home server	`DEFAULT_USER_HOME-SERVER`	`Server where FTP is running`	Specifies the name of the server that the default home directory is on.
Default home directory	`DEFAULT_USER_HOME`	`SYS:\PUBLIC`	The default home directory for FTP users.
Always use Default Home Directory instead of user's home directory from eDirectory	`IGNORE_REMOTE_HOME`	No	Specifies whether to ignore the home directory and go to the default directory.
Use FTP Default Home Directory if user's eDirectory home directory is not on the FTP server	`IGNORE_HOME_DIR`	No	Specifies whether to ignore the home directory, if it is on a remote server, and go to the default directory.

TABLE 10.2 Continued

PARAMETER	CONFIG FILE	DEFAULT VALUE	DESCRIPTION
Default FTP context	`DEFAULT_FTP_CONTEXT`	N/A	Sets the container in which FTP server will look for users. This must be a fully distinguished container name in eDirectory (with leading dot).
Search List	`SEARCH_LIST`	N/A	A list of fully distinguished names of containers in which FTP users will be looked for, separated by commas. The length of this string including the commas should not exceed 2048 bytes. You can specify a maximum of 25 containers.
FTP user restrictions file	`RESTRICT_FILE`	`SYS:/ETC/FTPREST.TXT`	FTP server can define access restrictions to various levels of users, hosts, and so on. These restrictions are defined in a file, which can be specified here.

TABLE 10.2   Continued

PARAMETER	CONFIG FILE	DEFAULT VALUE	DESCRIPTION
Anonymous users	ANONYMOUS_ ACCESS	No	Specifies whether anonymous user access is allowed.
Anonymous user directory	ANONYMOUS_ HOME	SYS:/PUBLIC	The Anonymous user's home directory.
Require email for password	ANONYMOUS_ PASSWORD_ REQUIRED	Yes	Specifies whether to ask for an email ID as the password for Anonymous user to log in.

Security Settings

Click the Security tab to access intruder detection parameters for FTP server. When finished, click Save to record your settings or click Reset to revert to the previous settings. Table 10.3 lists the available security settings, with a brief description and the equivalent setting in the configuration file.

TABLE 10.3   Security Settings in Web Manager

PARAMETER	CONFIG FILE	DEFAULT VALUE	DESCRIPTION
Intruder list	N/A - Clear	N/A	Clears the [button] intruder list that is maintained by FTP server.
Host intruder detection	See next parameter	Yes	Turns intruder detection on/off for other FTP hosts that access the FTP server.

TABLE 10.3 Continued

PARAMETER	CONFIG FILE	DEFAULT VALUE	DESCRIPTION
Login attempts for host intruder detection	INTRUDER_ HOST_ATTEMPTS	20	The number of unsuccessful login attempts for intruder host detection. When set to 0, intruder host login detection is disabled.
Login disable time after detection	HOST_RESET_ TIME	5	Time interval in minutes during which the intruder host is not allowed to log in.
User intruder detection	See next parameter	Yes	Turns intruder detection for FTP clients that access FTP server.
Login attempts for user intruder detection	INTRUDER_USER_ ATTEMPTS	5	The number of unsuccessful login attempts for intruder host detection. When set to 0, intruder host login detection is disabled.
Login disable time after detection	USER_RESET_ TIME	10	Time interval in minutes during which the intruder user is not allowed to log in.

Log Settings

Click the Log tab to access log file parameters for FTP server. All FTP logs are created automatically. You control only the types of messages that are logged and how large the log files will grow. When finished, click

Save to record your settings. You can also view current log files by selecting the log you want to see and clicking the View button.

Table 10.4 lists the available log settings, with a brief description and the equivalent setting in the configuration file.

TABLE 10.4   Log Settings in Web Manager

PARAMETER	CONFIG FILE	DEFAULT VALUE	DESCRIPTION
Log directory	`FTP_LOG_DIR`	`SYS:\ETC`	Specifies the directory in which FTP log files will be stored.
Maximum log size (KB)	`MAX_LOG_SIZE`	`1024`	Maximum size to which an FTP log file will grow. Range from 1KB to 4194303KB.
Messages of type	`LOG_LEVEL`	Errors, Warnings, and Information	Indicates the types of messages that are logged.
Daemon log file	`FTPD_LOG`	`ftpd`	Specifies the name of the FTP daemon log file.
Audit log file	`AUDIT_LOG`	`ftpaudit`	Specifies the name of the FTP audit log file.
Intruder log file	`INTRUDER_LOG`	`ftpintr`	Specifies the name of the FTP intruderlog file.
Statistics log file	`STAT_LOG`	`ftpstat`	Specifies the name of the FTP statistics log file.

To view any of the log files mentioned in Table 10.4, select it from the Log File drop-down menu and click the View button.

This information will give you an FTP server suitable for use with NetDrive, which was discussed earlier in this chapter. For more information on using an FTP server in more general situations, see the NetWare 6.5 online documentation.

Delivering Business Continuity

In This Part

Today it seems like it's all about the network. The Internet has created an environment in which the network really is the computing platform of the 21st century. With this emphasis on the network, you better keep yours up all the time. Many organizations that rely on their networks for customer interaction now measure network outages in thousands, or even millions, of dollars per hour. Obviously, these types of mission-critical environments require network components that are always available.

NetWare 6.5 offers powerful, high-availability solutions to help you keep your network ready for high profile attention. Chapter 11 discusses the multiprocessing and clustering technologies available in NetWare 6.5. These technologies let you do a lot more with the hardware and server space you have, remove bottlenecks to efficient server operation and generally makes life much easier for users of busy networks. Furthermore, Novell Cluster Services (NCS), when used in conjunction with Network Attached Storage (NAS) or Storage Area

Network (SAN) technologies, can create a network-computing infrastructure that is virtually indestructible from the client perspective. Services and data are always available; servers are always up. Business processes, therefore, run more efficiently—ensuring the network infrastructure is helping, rather than hindering, an organization's business imperatives.

Finally, Chapter 12 discusses two additional Novell technologies that will take you even further into Novell's One Net vision: Nterprise Branch Office and DirXML Starter Pack. Nterprise Branch Office is an appliance especially designed to deliver all the network features necessary while being remotely managed from your central office. DirXML is Novell's award-winning directory solution that lets you configure eDirectory as a central meta-directory through which data shared among disparate systems can be synchronized. Two powerful network solutions offered for the first time ever as part of the NetWare product bundle!

CHAPTER 11

Multiprocessor and Clustering Support

Instant Access

Introducing Multiprocessor-Enabled Services

▶ The integrated Multiprocessing Kernel (MPK) is responsible for providing all multiprocessing capabilities in the NetWare 6.5 environment.

▶ All core NetWare 6.5 services are multiprocessor-enabled, including the TCP/IP protocol stack, Novell eDirectory, and the NetWare Core Protocol (NCP) engine.

▶ NetWare 6.5 accommodates both multiprocessor-aware and non-multiprocessor applications. Non-multiprocessor applications are simply funneled to processor 0, where they execute as if they were on a uniprocessor system.

Understanding Multiprocessor Concepts

▶ Threads are the basis for multiprocessing. A *thread* is a single flow of execution within a server, responsible for completing one very specific task.

▶ NetWare 6.5 uses a scheduler process and multiple local thread queues to distribute threads to processors for execution.

▶ NetWare 6.5 uses a load-balancing algorithm to make sure that no processor is overloaded.

Multiprocessor Hardware Support

▶ Platform Support Modules (PSM) provide a "driver" for multiple processors that abstracts the NetWare 6.5 operating system away from complexity of the multiprocessor hardware itself.

▶ NetWare 6.5 provides a PSM compatible with the Intel Multiprocessor Specification (MPS), which will support any hardware designed using this specification.

Installing NetWare Cluster Services

▶ You can install NetWare Cluster Services (NCS) from iManager. NetWare 6.5 ships with a license for a two-node cluster. Clusters of a larger size require additional licenses, which are purchased separately.

▶ If you are upgrading an existing cluster environment to NetWare 6.5, make sure you perform the pre-upgrade routine in iManager prior to upgrading the cluster.

Configuring Clusters

▶ Configure your cluster environment from the Cluster Config page in NoRM.

▶ Cluster-enable a volume (storage pool) by selecting New Cluster Volume from the Cluster Config page in NoRM.

▶ Cluster-enable an application or service by selecting New Cluster Resource from the Cluster Config page in NoRM.

▶ Configure parameters for individual cluster resources in NoRM by selecting the resource from the Cluster Config page.

Monitoring Clusters

▶ Monitor you cluster environment from the Cluster Management page in NoRM.

▶ View the status of the cluster and the various cluster resources from the Cluster Management page in NoRM.

NetWare Multiprocessing

NetWare 6.5 provides robust multiprocessor support that was first released with NetWare 6. However, multiprocessor support of some type has been available in the NetWare operating system since the time of NetWare 4. This chapter presents an overview of the NetWare 6.5 multiprocessor environment and how some common multiprocessor issues have been resolved.

Novell first introduced multiprocessor functionality, in a limited fashion, with NetWare 4. Although NetWare 4 provided multiprocessor capabilities, all its own core operating system processes were not multiprocessor-enabled. External multiprocessor applications could leverage secondary processors, but all operating system processes, such as disk access, network I/O, and so on, had to be funneled through the primary processor, also known as *processor 0*.

With the release of NetWare 5, multiprocessor functionality was rewritten and integrated with the NetWare operating system kernel to create the MPK. This effort made all but a few of the native NetWare 5 processes multiprocessor compatible. Unfortunately, two of the most important processes, namely LAN drivers and disk drivers, remained tied to processor 0.

Finally, with the release of NetWare 6, all core operating system processes are multiprocessor compliant. This means that the entire path between network wire and server storage is now multi-processor aware and can take advantage of multiple processors in the server hardware.

Multiprocessing Improvements

The core of the NetWare operating system is the integrated multiprocessing kernel. The MPK provides symmetric multiprocessing to the NetWare environment. As such, the MPK manages threads, schedules processor resources, handles interrupts and exceptions, and manages access to memory and the I/O subsystems.

As previously mentioned, all NetWare 6.5 software subsystems are now multiprocessor-enabled. NetWare 6.5 can itself take full advantage of the power of a multiprocessing system. Table 11.1 lists many of the NetWare 6.5 services that are multiprocessor-enabled.

TABLE 11.1   Multiprocessor-Enabled Services in NetWare 6.5

SERVICE TYPE	SERVICE COMPONENTS
Protocol stacks	NetWare Core Protocols (NCP) Service Location Protocols (SLP) IP stack HTTP Ethernet connectivity Token ring connectivity Web Distributed Authoring and Versioning (WebDAV) Lightweight Directory Access Protocol (LDAP)
Storage services	Novell Storage Services (NSS) Distributed File Service (DFS) Protocol services Request dispatcher Transport service Fiber channel disk support
Security services	Novell International Cryptographic Infrastructure (NICI) Authentication ConsoleOne authentication snap-ins
Miscellaneous services	Novell eDirectory Novell Java Virtual Machine (JVM) Web engines Additional Web features

In addition to improved performance and greater scalability, NetWare 6.5 multiprocessing offers these benefits:

▶ Complete backward compatibility with applications written for the older SMP.NLM (written for NetWare 4.11), as well as any legacy CLIB application that does not support multiprocessing (they are just funneled to processor 0).

▶ An integrated Multiprocessing Kernel (MPK) that supports both uniprocessing and multiprocessing platforms.

▶ Kernel-level support for preemption. NetWare 6.5 supports applications written for a preemptive multitasking environment natively.

▶ A single Platform Support Module (PSM) provides full integration between the multiprocessing hardware and the NetWare MPK.

Running Programs on a Multiprocessor System

When you install NetWare 6.5 on multiprocessor hardware, the MPK determines how many processors are in the system. Next, the kernel scheduler determines the processor on which to run the waiting threads. This decision is based on information about the threads themselves and on the availability of processors.

Three types of programs can run on NetWare 6.5:

▶ *Multiprocessor safe*: Multiprocessor Safe programs are typically NLMs that are not multiprocessing-enabled, but are safe to run in a multiprocessing environment. These programs run on processor 0, which is home to all multiprocessing safe programs. NetWare 6.5 is very accommodating to programs that were written prior to the introduction of the NetWare MPK. These non-multiprocessing-aware applications are automatically scheduled to run on processor 0 upon execution.

▶ *Multiprocessor compliant*: Multiprocessor compliant programs are specifically written to run in a multiprocessing environment. When one of these programs loads, the NetWare 6 scheduler automatically assigns the different threads to available processors. The Intel MPS specification allows programs to indicate whether their specific threads want to run on a specific processor. In this case, the NetWare scheduler will assign that thread to run on the requested processor. Although this functionality is available in NetWare 6.5 for those multiprocessing utilities and other programs that require the ability to run on a specific processor, Novell discourages developers from writing programs this way.

NOTE When a multiprocessing-compliant program is loaded, the NetWare scheduler checks for an available processor on which to run the thread (provided its threads don't request a specific processor). If the first available processor is processor 3, the thread is scheduled to run there. The next thread would go to processor 4, and so on. This assumes that the processors make themselves available in consecutive order. If the system has only one processor, all the applications' threads will be queued up to run on processor 0, which is always the first processor regardless of whether it is an MP or non-MP environment.

▶ *NetWare OS*: Lastly, the NetWare OS is completely MP compliant, allowing its multitude of threads to run on available processors as needed.

All processes that run on your NetWare 6.5 server will fit into one of these categories.

Multiprocessing Concepts

In order to understand multiprocessing in general, and the NetWare multiprocessing architecture in particular, you should be familiar with the multiprocessing concepts described in the following sections.

NOTE Many people assume that a multiprocessor server with two processors will be twice as powerful as the same server with a single processor. Although this may be the theoretical goal of multiprocessor hardware engineers, you won't see this linear increase in performance in our imperfect world. Generally, as the number of processors in a server increases, the processing power of the system also increases, although to a lesser degree. Practically, this means that a two-processor system gives you about 1.8 times the processing power as the same system with a single processor. A four-processor system delivers roughly 3.5 times as much processing power, and a six-processor system offers about 5.2 times the processing power.

NetWare 6.5 supports up to 32 processors in a single server, which works out to a whole lot of processing horsepower!

Threads

A thread is not some bit of code that the processor is executing. Rather, a thread represents an independent stream of control within the processing environment. Since NetWare was first released, it has been using threads to allow operating system processes to function efficiently. Here's how they work:

► Processes and threads are not equivalent, but they are similar. The main difference between the two is that a process can typically be swapped out of memory to make room for another process (preemptive), whereas a thread is normally allowed to run to completion once it starts (non-preemptive).

► NetWare 6.5 keeps track of all the threads that run in the server environment with a scheduler and thread queues. The scheduler is multiprocessor-enabled itself, and an integral part of the NetWare 6.5 MPK. As a result, each processor maintains its own scheduler for managing its thread execution.

► Each processor also maintains three thread queues for organizing thread execution. The three queues are the Run queue, the Work To Do queue, and the Miscellaneous queue.

▶ The threads in the Run queue have priority over threads in the other two queues. Run queue threads are non-blocking, meaning that they do not relinquish control of the processor until they are done. The Run queue is typically reserved for critical systems such as protocol stacks and many of the other NetWare kernel processes.

▶ When a Run queue thread completes, the processor checks for additional threads in the Run queue. If no threads are currently in the Run queue, the processor looks in the Work To Do queue. Unlike the Run queue, Work To Do threads can relinquish control of the processor if they rely on less-important functions that can be blocked by the scheduler. The Work To Do queue is usually used by noncritical NetWare services and NLMs.

▶ Finally, the Miscellaneous queue is checked after the Work To Do queue. The Miscellaneous queue holds most application threads that are running in the NetWare environment.

NOTE NetWare Loadable Modules (NLMs) often establish multiple threads, each representing a distinct path of execution. Make sure you don't equate a thread with NLM execution.

In a multiprocessing environment, there are two methods for managing the execution of individual threads:

▶ *Global Run queues*: This approach to distributing threads has the advantage of automatic load balancing. Waiting threads are automatically doled out to the processor that becomes available first. Unfortunately, the Global queue itself becomes the bottleneck as the number of processors and the number of executing threads increases in a system.

▶ *Local Run queues*: This approach does not have the bottleneck problem associated with the Global queue because a Run queue is created for each processor in the system. It also makes it possible to preferentially schedule threads on the processor on which they last ran, which can increase the efficiency of the system as a whole. The downside to Local queues, however, is it becomes necessary to manually spread the load on the processors as evenly as possible. Without a load-balancing mechanism, threads might pile up at one processor while another processor remains idle.

NetWare uses Local queues in NetWare 6.5 because of the scalability advantages over a Global queue solution.A sophisticated load-balancing algorithm was built on top of the Local queue solution to help prevent processor imbalances from occurring.

Load Balancing

When Novell engineers began considering the details of their load-balancing algorithm, they identified two primary requirements:

▶ *Stability*: Load balancing would do little good for the system if it reacted to small changes in thread balance by wasting large amounts of time moving threads back and forth between processors.

▶ *Quick distribution*: When the scheduler identifies a situation that requires load balancing, the algorithm better be able to make the necessary changes very quickly so as not to affect the overall performance of the system.

NetWare 6.5 addresses the issue of stability by using a threshold. The threshold determines how far out of balance the thread distribution must get before the system takes action to fix the situation. The next issue became where to set the threshold.

A low threshold would keep processors in closer balance at the risk of causing excessive thread movement due to frequent load balancing. A high threshold would greatly reduce the risk of excessive thread movement at the risk of having some processors with a significantly higher load than others, reducing the overall performance of the system. To resolve this problem, NetWare 6.5 defines its threshold as a range within which a processor load is deemed acceptable.

To determine where in the load spectrum the threshold should be placed, the scheduler calculates the system-wide load and from that the average processor load, on a regular basis. The average processor load becomes the midpoint of the threshold range, as shown in Figure 11.1.

The upper and lower bounds of the threshold become high/low trigger points for the load balancing system. A processor is overloaded when its load exceeds the high trigger. A processor is underloaded when it is below the low trigger.

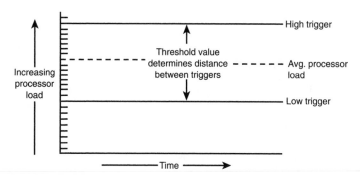

FIGURE 11.1
How processor load balancing works in NetWare 6.5.

When this happens, the scheduler moves threads from the overloaded processor to the underloaded processor to bring the system back into balance. You can actually configure the load-balancing threshold in NoRM by completing the following steps:

1. From NoRM, select the Set Parameters page and click Multiprocessor.

2. Click the value currently listed for the System Threshold parameter.

3. Specify a new value and click OK.

The updated threshold parameters will take effect immediately.

WARNING Novell strongly recommends using the default value, unless you have carefully considered your reasons for changing it and tested the new setting in a lab environment before committing it to your production server(s). For more information on multiprocessor SET parameters, see Appendix C.

Preemptive Thread Execution

As mentioned previously, when discussing the NetWare MPK queues, NetWare 6.5 does allow certain noncritical threads to be preempted, or blocked, in order to make operation of the system as a whole more efficient.

Earlier versions of NetWare multiprocessor support did not support process preemption. Rather, they implemented a round-robin (first-in, first-out) scheduling policy where threads were scheduled to run in the order they entered the Run queue. This makes for a simple and very fast operating environment, but at the expense of overall flexibility.

To support a preemptive environment, applications must be explicitly written to identify those critical sections that cannot be blocked. These sections are identified to the scheduler so the thread cannot be preempted while in a critical section.

NetWare will preempt an application thread only under the following conditions:

▶ The code where the thread is running must be preemptable. This is indicated by a flag set in the module's NLM file format. When the code is loaded into memory, the memory pages are flagged as preemptable.

▶ The thread cannot be in a critical section of the code.

▶ The thread has run long enough to qualify for preemption. The scheduler checks the elapsed time with every tick.

Support for preemption provides

▶ An execution environment that allows simplified application development. Developers can rely on the Scheduler to handle preemption.

▶ A way to forcibly manage modules that are monopolizing the processor.

NOTE The NetWare kernel itself cannot be preempted.

Multiprocessing Memory Issues

In a uniprocessing environment, there is no problem with memory management because a single processor controls all interaction with system memory. Unfortunately, in a multiprocessing environment, things get a lot more complicated, with multiple processors competing for the use of system memory and the I/O channel. Because of this, NetWare must have control logic to manage processor interaction with other subsystems to prevent memory corruption (process crashes) and, basically, to keep the whole thing from melting down.

For example, it is possible for a single application to have multiple threads running on multiple processors simultaneously. In this situation, it is possible that multiple threads need to update the same memory location at the same time. This is known as a *race condition*. Without the proper thread management, you could easily end up with bad data being written to memory.

To avoid this type of dangerous condition, NetWare 6.5 requires that threads emanating from the same connection run on the same processor. By doing this, NetWare ensures that application threads are queued up and run sequentially to eliminate the possibility of memory corruption.

Beyond this, NetWare 6.5 also has to manage requests for server subsystems between all the application threads that might be executing at any given time. To do this, NetWare 6.5 uses what are known as *synchronization primitives*, which are processes that manage access to shared resources, so everything stays in sync. Synchronization primitives include the following:

▶ *Mutually exclusive lock (mutex)*: This mechanism ensures that only one thread can access a shared resource at a time, such as system memory or the I/O channel.

▶ *Semaphores*: These are somewhat similar to mutexes, but semaphores use counters to control access to RAM memory or other protected resources.

▶ *Read-write locks*: Similar to mutexes, read-write locks work with mutexes to ensure that only one thread at a time has access to a protected resource.

▶ *Condition variables*: These are based on an external station. In so doing, they can be used to synchronize threads. Because they are external to the thread synchronization code, they can be used to ensure that only one thread accesses a protected resource at a time.

NetWare 6.5 also uses two other synchronization primitives that are restricted to the kernel address space (ring 0): spin locks and barriers. These primitives are not accessible to applications that run in a protected address space.

Platform Support Modules

Besides NetWare, all that is necessary to enable multiprocessing on a multiprocessor computer is the Platform Support Module (PSM) for your specific hardware platform and NetWare. No other modules are required.

The PSM is a kind of device driver for the processors in your multiprocessing server. It provides an abstraction layer between the multiprocessor hardware and the NetWare 6.5 operating system that shields NetWare from the details and intricacies of the vendor-specific multiprocessing implementation. It also enables secondary processors to be brought online and taken offline without having to shut down the server.

During installation, NetWare detects multiple processors by reading the multiprocessor configuration table in the server's BIOS. From that information, it determines which of the available NetWare PSM drivers matches the particular multiprocessing hardware platform.

Once installation is complete, you can choose not to load the PSM, which results in NetWare running only on processor 0. By default, the NetWare 6.5 installation routine will add the PSM load line to the STARTUP.NCF so that it will load whenever the server is started.

Novell provides MPS14.PSM, which supports any hardware platform that complies with the Intel Multiprocessor Specification (MPS) v1.1 and v1.4. Compaq also provides a PSM for its specific multiprocessing system requirements.

Intel MPS v1.4 defines an environment in which all the processors in the system work and function together similarly. All the processors in the system share a common I/O subsystem and use the same memory pool. MPS-compatible operating systems, such as NetWare 6.5, can run on systems that comply with this specification without any special modifications.

Because NetWare 6.5 complies with Intel's specification, it will automatically take advantage of all the processors in your MPS-compliant hardware. At this time, most major computer manufacturers already offer multiprocessing systems compatible with the Intel specification.

TIP More information on the Intel MPS v1.4 specification is available from Intel at http://developer.intel.com/design/intarch/MANUALS/242016.htm.

NetWare Cluster Services

In order to remain competitive, your organization needs to provide customers and employees uninterrupted access to data, applications, Web sites, and other services 24 hours a day, seven days a week, 365 days a year.

This makes high availability of your organization's services more than a technical issue. It's a business issue that requires a reliable solution.

Novell Clustering Services (NCS) is a multi-node clustering system for NetWare 6.5 that is integrated with Novell eDirectory. NCS ensures high availability and manageability of critical network resources including data (server volumes), applications, and NetWare 6.5 services. NCS supports failover, failback, and migration (load balancing) of individually managed cluster resources.

NOTE A license for a two-node NCS cluster is included with NetWare 6.5. Licenses for additional cluster nodes must be purchased separately from Novell.

Clustering Benefits

NCS allows you to configure up to 32 NetWare servers into a high-availability cluster, where resources can be dynamically switched or moved to any server in the cluster. Resources can be configured to automatically switch or move to another node in the event of a server failure. They can also be moved manually, if necessary, to troubleshoot hardware or balance server workload.

One of the best things about NCS is that it lets you create a high-availability environment from off-the-shelf components. You don't have to spend millions when you create a cluster, and you can add servers to the cluster as your needs change and grow over time.

Equally important is the capability to greatly reduce unplanned service outages that result from server failures of some sort. You can even reduce the frequency of planned outages for software and hardware maintenance and upgrades because individual nodes can be removed from the cluster without affecting service availability to network users.

NCS provides the following advantages over a nonclustered environment:

- ▶ Increased availability
- ▶ Improved performance
- ▶ Low cost of operation
- ▶ Scalability
- ▶ Disaster recovery
- ▶ Data protection
- ▶ Shared resources

Because of these advantages, clustering systems are becoming mandatory for environments in which system availability is a must.

Clustering Fundamentals

Suppose you have configured a two-node cluster, with a Web server installed on each of the nodes. Each of the servers in the cluster hosts two Web sites. All the content for all four Web sites is stored on a shared disk subsystem connected to each of the servers in the cluster. Figure 11.2 shows how such an environment might look.

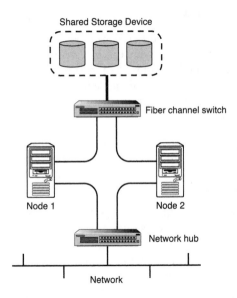

FIGURE 11.2
The basic cluster architecture.

During normal operation, each clustered node is in constant communication with the other nodes in the cluster through periodic polling. In this way, a node can quickly detect whether something happens to another node in the cluster.

If node 2 fails due to some hardware or software problems, users currently attached to the Web server will lose their connections. The IP address associated with node 2, and all its services, are migrated to node 1. Users would likely have to reload their Web pages, which would be available from the new node within a few seconds.

Once the problem in node 2 is located and repaired, it is restarted and automatically re-inserts itself back into the cluster. Node 1 detects the return of node 2 and seamlessly passes back all the addresses and services originally assigned to node 2. The cluster returns to its normal configuration without any administrator intervention.

Clustering Terminology

We all know that clustering provides a high-availability platform for your network infrastructure. High availability is becoming increasingly important for two purposes: file access and network services. The following sections discuss NCS configuration for both of these situations. However, before you start working with an NCS cluster, you should be familiar with the terms described in the following sections.

Master Node

The first server that comes up in an NCS cluster is assigned the cluster IP address and becomes the *master node*. (Other nodes in the cluster are often referred to as *slave* nodes.) The master node updates information transmitted between the cluster and eDirectory, and monitors the health of the cluster nodes. If the master node fails, NCS migrates the cluster IP address to another server in the cluster, and that server becomes the master node.

Cluster-Enabled Volume

A *cluster-enabled* volume is an NSS volume configured to provide location-transparent access to NetWare file services. The volume is associated with an eDirectory virtual server object that provides a unique secondary IP address for locating the volume on the cluster's shared storage device. The volume provides read-write file access to users.

> **NOTE** NetWare 6.5 clusters failover storage pools. This means you can migrate more than one volume at a time to another node if they are part of the same storage pool. For more information on NetWare Storage Services (NSS), see Chapter 8, "File Storage and Management."

Cluster Resource

A *cluster resource* is an object in eDirectory that represents an application or other type of service (such as DHCP or the master IP address) that you can migrate or failover from one node to another in an NCS cluster. The cluster resource object includes scripts for unloading the service from one node and loading it on another node. In most cases, make sure the service is installed on all nodes in the cluster that will host the service.

Heartbeats and the Split-Brain Detector

NCS uses heartbeats on the LAN and a Split-Brain Detector (SBD) on the shared storage device to keep all services highly available on the cluster when a node fails. NCS determines when a node fails over the LAN and casts off the failed node through the following process:

▶ Every second (by default), each node in an NCS cluster sends out a heartbeat message over the network.

▶ The master node monitors the heartbeats of all other nodes in the cluster to determine whether they are still functioning.

▶ If a heartbeat is not received from a node during a predefined time-out (8 seconds by default), that node is removed (cast off) from the cluster, and migration of services begins.

NOTE If the master node fails to send a heartbeat within the predefined timeout, it is cast off, and another node takes over as the master node.

NCS also uses the SBD to determine when a node fails through the following process:

▶ Each node writes an epoch number to a special SBD partition on the shared storage device. An epoch occurs each time a node leaves or joins the cluster. The epoch number is written at half the predefined timeout value (4 seconds by default).

▶ Each node reads all epoch numbers for all other nodes in the SBD partition.

▶ When the master node sees an epoch number for a specific node that is lower than the others, it knows that the node has failed, and the node is cast off.

Fan-Out Failover

When a node fails in an NCS cluster, the cluster-enabled volumes and resources assigned to that node are migrated to other nodes in the cluster. Although this migration happens automatically, you must design and configure where each volume and resource migrates during failover.

TIP You will probably want to distribute, or *fan out*, the volumes and resources to several nodes based on factors such as server load and the availability of installed applications. NCS relies on you to define where clustered resources will be assigned should a failure occur.

Installing NetWare Cluster Services

The following list specifies the minimum hardware requirements for installing NCS:

▶ A minimum of two NetWare 6.5 servers.

▶ At least 512MB of memory on all servers in the cluster. This provides sufficient memory to support failover of multiple applications to the same server node.

▶ At least one local disk device on which the **SYS:** volume will be installed for each node.

▶ A shared disk system, either Storage Area Network (SAN) or iSCSI, is required for each cluster in order for all cluster data to be available to each node. This is how high availability ofdata is achieved.

NOTE NCS will create a special cluster partition using one cylinder of one drive of the shared disk system. This will require roughly 15MB of free disk space on the shared disk system for creating the cluster partition.

▶ Make sure the disk system is installed and configured properly. You can verify that all servers in the cluster recognize the drives in the shared disk system by using the **LIST DEVICES** console command. For more information on this command, see Appendix C.

▶ Make sure that the disks in the shared disk system are configured in some type of fault tolerant configuration, such as mirroring or RAID 5. If this is not done, a single disk error can potentially cause a volume failure across the entire cluster.

Preparing an Existing Cluster

If you have an existing NCS cluster, using NetWare 5.1 Cluster Services, you need to prepare the existing cluster for the upgrade procedure. The preparation process performs the following tasks:

▶ Saves all trustee assignments so that they will not be lost during the upgrade.

▶ Identifies shared partitions so that NetWare 6.5 safety features can be installed.

▶ Deactivates the cluster in preparation for the upgrade.

This process also assumes that you are already running Novell eDirectory.

1. Launch iManager and select Install and Upgrade in the left navigation frame. Make sure you have the NetWare 6.5 Operating System CD-ROM loaded and accessible.

2. Select Prepare Cluster for Upgrade, and click Prepare a Cluster in the right frame.

3. At the Welcome screen, select Next.

4. At the NCS Cluster Selection screen, specify the required information and click Next.

   ▶ *Cluster object name*: Specify the name of the existing Cluster object in your eDirectory tree.

   ▶ *Directory services tree*: Specify the name of your eDirectory tree.

   ▶ *Directory services context*: Specify the context of the Cluster object.

5. At the Down Servers screen, choose whether you want the clustered servers you are working with to go down after the pre-upgrade procedure. Click Next.

Bringing down all cluster servers before an upgrade ensures NSS volumes on shared storage devices are deactivated prior to the NCS upgrade.

TIP   If you choose to not to take down all clustered servers after the pre-upgrade, you must do it manually before upgrading cluster servers to NetWare 6.5.

Installing a Cluster

NetWare 6.5 includes an NCS installation program that you use to do the following:

▶ Create a cluster

▶ Add nodes to an existing cluster

▶ Upgrade NCS software in an existing cluster

To install Novell Cluster Services, complete the following steps:

1. Launch iManager and select Install and Upgrade in the left naviga-tion frame. Make sure you have the NetWare 6.5 Operating System CD-ROM loaded and accessible.

2. Select Install or Upgrade a Cluster, and click Install or Upgrade a Cluster in the right frame.

3. At the Welcome screen, click Next.

4. At the NCS Action screen, select the installation option you want to use and click Next.

   ▶ *Create new cluster*: Choose this option to create a new cluster in your network.

   ▶ *Add New Nodes to Existing Cluster*: Check this option to add another node to an existing cluster.

   ▶ *Upgrade Software in Existing Cluster*: Choose this option to upgrade an existing cluster to NetWare 6.5 NCS. Make sure that you have performed the pre-upgrade, if necessary.

NOTE Checking Skip File Copy prevents NCS files from being copied during the instal-lation. Because NCS files are copied to a NetWare 6.5 server during its original installa-tion, you normally don't have to copy the files again. However, if you want to refresh the NCS files on a server, you can uncheck this box.

5. At the NCS Cluster Selection screen, specify the required informa-tion and click Next.

   ▶ *If this is a new cluster*: Specify a name for the Cluster object, the name of your eDirectory tree, and the context for the Cluster object.

   ▶ *If you are adding nodes*: Specify the name of the Cluster object to which you want to add nodes, your eDirectory tree, and the context of the Cluster object.

   ▶ *If you are upgrading software*: Specify the name of the Cluster object to be upgraded, your eDirectory tree, and the context of the Cluster object. Skip to step 9.

6. At the NCS Cluster Node Modification screen, click the Browse button to open a secondary window from which you can select all the server objects you want to add to the cluster. You must select at

least two servers. Click OK to exit the secondary window and Next to continue with the installation.

NOTE You can remove a node from the cluster by selecting it from the NetWare Servers in Cluster list and clicking Remove. NCS automatically detects the IP address of a server that is added to a cluster. If a specified server has more than one IP address, you will be prompted to select the IP address you want Novell Cluster Services to use.

7. At the Cluster IP Address Selection screen, specify a unique IP address for the Cluster object and click Next. The cluster IP address is separate from the server IP address. ConsoleOne and NoRM use it for cluster management functions. The cluster IP address will be bound to the master node and will remain with the master node, even as it moves from server to server during failover events.

8. *(Conditional)* If you are creating a new cluster, specify the requested information and click Next.

   ▶ Specify whether the cluster will be using a shared storage device such as a SAN or shared SCSI system. If you do have shared media, select the shared device from the drop-down list.

   ▶ Choose whether you want to mirror the cluster partition. If you do want to mirror the cluster partition, select a location for the mirror partition from the drop-down list.

WARNING As previously mentioned, you must have roughly 15MB of free (unpartitioned) space on one of the shared disk drives to create the cluster partition. If no free space is available, Novell Cluster Services can't use the shared disk drives.

9. At the Start Clustering screen, choose whether you want the servers you are upgrading or adding to your cluster to start NCS software after the installation, and then click Next. If you choose not to start NCS, you will need to manually start it after the installation. You can do this by typing **LDNCS** from the server console of each cluster server.

10. *(Conditional)* If you are creating a cluster with more than two nodes, browse to and select the Cluster Server License files and click Add. NCS licenses are available separately from Novell. If you

do not install NCS licenses during installation, you can add them later from iManager. However, NCS will not function until proper licenses are installed.

11. At the Summary screen, click Finish to install NCS. At the Installation Complete message, click Close.

Once NCS is installed and running, you will have access to a new Clustering section in the left navigation frame of NoRM.

Configuring NetWare Cluster Services

There are some general configuration options for your NCS environment of which you should be aware. All of these configuration options are available from the Cluster Config page, shown in Figure 11.3.

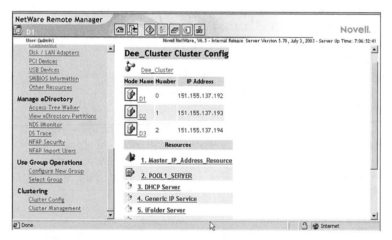

FIGURE 11.3
Cluster Config page in NoRM.

These configuration parameters configure the entire cluster environment. To view these options, select the Cluster object link from the Cluster Config page. This will open the Cluster Configuration fields, shown in Figure 11.4. The various configuration settings available from this page are described next.

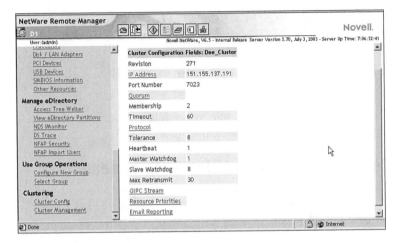

FIGURE 11.4
Cluster configuration fields in NoRM.

IP Address

You can view and change the IP address and port assigned to the Cluster object when you installed NCS. The Cluster IP address normally does not need to be changed, but can be if needed.

The default cluster port number is **7023**, and is automatically assigned when the cluster is created. The cluster port number should not be changed unless there is a TCP port conflict with another resource using the same port. If there is a conflict, you can change the port number to any other value that doesn't cause a conflict.

Quorum

The Quorum configuration is used to define two trigger values that are used during the startup of the cluster.

▶ *Membership*: The quorum membership is the number of nodes that must be running in the cluster before resources will start to load. When you first bring up servers in your cluster, NCS reads the number specified in the Membership field and waits until that number of servers is up and running in the cluster before it starts loading resources. Set the membership value to a number greater than 1 so that all resources don't automatically load on the first server that is brought up in the cluster.

▶ *Timeout*: Timeout specifies the amount of time to wait for the number of servers defined in the Membership field to be up and running. If the timeout period elapses before the quorum membership reaches its specified number, resources will automatically start loading on the servers that are currently up and running in the cluster.

Protocol

You can use the Protocol link to view or edit the transmit frequency and tolerance settings for all nodes in the cluster, including the master node.

▶ *Tolerance*: Specifies the amount of time the master node gives all other nodes in the cluster to signal that they are alive. For example, setting this value to 4 means that if the master node does not receive an "I'm alive" signal from a node in the cluster within 4 seconds, that node will be removed from the cluster.

▶ *Heartbeat*: Specifies the amount of time between transmits for all nodes in the cluster except the master. For example, if you set this value to 1, nonmaster nodes in the cluster will send a signal that they are alive to the master node every second.

▶ *Master Watchdog*: Specifies the amount of time between transmits for the master node in the cluster. For example, if you set this value to 1, the master node in the cluster will transmit an "I'm alive" signal to all the other nodes in the cluster every second.

▶ *Slave Watchdog*: Specifies the amount of time the master node has to signal that it is alive. For example, setting this value to 5 means that if the nonmaster nodes in the cluster do not receive an "I'm alive" signal from the master within 5 seconds, the master node will be removed from the cluster and one of the other nodes will become the master node.

▶ *Max Retransmits*: This option is not currently used with Novell Cluster Services but will be used for future versions.

The master node is generally the first node brought online in the cluster, but if that node fails, any of the other nodes in the cluster can become the master.

GIPC Stream

The GIPC Stream page lets you view, but not change, the script used to configure the cluster protocol parameters for your cluster. The script is created based on the settings you make in the protocol settings, described previously.

Resource Priority

The Resource Priority page allows you to control the order in which multiple resources start on a given node when the cluster is brought up, or during a failover or failback. For example, if a node fails and two resources failover to another node, the resource priority will determine which resource loads first. This is useful for ensuring that the most critical resources load first and are available to users before less critical resources.

Priority settings can range between 0 (lowest priority) and 65535 (highest priority). Note that the Master IP Address Resource is always the highest priority. To set/change the priority for a resource, enter the new priority value in the dialog box next to that resource. Click Apply when finished.

Email Reporting

NCS can automatically send out email messages for certain cluster events such as cluster and resource state changes or nodes joining or leaving the cluster.

- ► *Admin Email Addresses for SMTP*: Specify the email address that should receive notifications in the field provided. Repeat this process for each address you want on the notification list. You can provide up to eight email addresses.

- ► *XML Format*: Check this box if you want administrators to receive notifications in XML format. XML messages can be interpreted and formatted in a way that lets you customize the message information for your specific needs.

- ► *Notification*: The settings in this section allow you to configure the types of messages that will be sent.

- ► *None*: Check this box to effectively disable email notifications.

- ► *Critical*: Check this box if you want administrators to receive notification of only critical events like a node failure or a resource going comatose.

▶ *Verbose*: Check this box if you want administrators to receive notification of all cluster state changes, including critical events, resource state changes, and nodes joining and leaving the cluster.

Cluster Node Properties

The IP address of an individual cluster node can be configured by selecting the desired node from the Cluster Config page. This is the only setting available for individual nodes.

IP Address specifies the IP address for the selected node. Make sure you click Apply to save any changes.

Click Delete to remove this node from the cluster. Once this is done, you must unload and reload NCS on each server in the cluster in order for the node deletion to take effect. To do this, run UNLDNCS.NCF from the console of each server in the cluster. Reload NCS by running LDNCS.NCF from the console of each server in the cluster.

Always Available File Access

To make network data constantly available through your newly created cluster, you need to create and configure shared cluster volumes. To create a cluster-enabled volume, complete the following steps:

1. Launch NoRM and select Partition Disks in the left navigation frame.

2. Select the Server object of one of the nodes in the cluster, and click Device Disk Management on the ConsoleOne toolbar.

3. Locate the device that corresponds to your shared storage. Click Create next to the free space on that device where you want to create the shared partition.

4. Click Create New Pool and Volume.

5. Provide the required pool information and click Create. For more information on each of the pool configuration parameters, see Chapter 8. You can either select Cluster Enable Pool now or cluster-enable the pool later. You **must** cluster-enable a pool in order for it to failover during a failure.

6. (*Optional*) If you choose to cluster-enable the storage pool now, you have to provide the following information:

- *(Optional) Virtual Server Name*: Change the name of the default Virtual Server object. When you cluster-enable a pool, the Virtual Server object is named by combining the Cluster object name and the Pool object name. For example: `QuillsCluster_SharePool_Server`.

- *Advertising Protocols*: Specify how you want the shared storage pool to advertise its existence to clients. NCP is used by the Novell client, CIFS is used by Microsoft Windows, and AFP is used by Macintosh clients.

- *(Conditional) CIFS Server Name*: If you select CIFS as an advertisement protocol, specify a server name that CIFS clients will see for this storage when browsing the network.

- *Auto Pool Activate*: Select this option to have the pool activate automatically upon creation.

The whole point in creating a cluster is to provide constant access to network resources. Because one of the principal resources on a network is data, cluster-enabling a storage pool will likely be one of the things you do first.

Cluster-Enabling a Volume After Creation

If you chose not to cluster-enable a shared volume when it was initially created, you can do so after the fact from NoRM. Make sure you deactivate the pool and dismount the volume(s) before cluster-enabling them. To cluster-enable an existing volume, complete the following steps:

1. Launch NoRM and select Cluster Config in the left navigation frame. Click New Cluster Volume in the right frame.

2. In the dialog box, specify the path in which the volume that you want to cluster-enable resides.

3. In the drop-down list, select the volume you want to cluster-enable and click Select.

4. Specify the IP address to assign to the cluster-enabled volume and click Save. This IP address is actually assigned to the storage pool associated with the volume you have selected. Any volume in the same pool that is cluster-enabled will share the same IP address. Checking the Auto-Online check box will cause the resource to automatically start once it is created.

You can delete cluster-enabled volumes and pools in the same way that you delete standard NSS volumes and pools. When a cluster-enabled resource is deleted, NCS will automatically modify its load scripts to remove that resource.

Modifying Node Assignment for a Storage Pool

When you cluster-enable a storage pool, all nodes in the cluster are automatically assigned to the pool. The order of assignment is the order in which the nodes appear in the list. To assign or un-assign nodes, or to change the failover order, complete the following steps:

1. Launch NoRM and select Cluster Config from the left navigation frame.

2. In the right frame, select the Virtual Server object associated with your cluster-enabled storage pool from the Resources list.

3. Click the Nodes link. Configure the nodes for the cluster-enabled volume as needed and click Apply. The first server in the Nodes list will be the preferred node for the cluster-enabled storage pool. Failover will occur sequentially down the list.

Configuring Storage Pool Policies

Once a storage pool has been cluster-enabled, you can configure the start, failover, and failback parameters. To do this, complete the following steps:

1. Launch NoRM and select Cluster Config from the left navigation frame.

2. In the right frame, select the Virtual Server object associated with your cluster-enabled storage pool from the Resources list.

3. Click the Policies link. Configure the Virtual Server policies as you want them and click Apply.

   ▶ *Ignore Quorum*: Check this box if you don't want the cluster-wide timeout period and node number limit enforced. This makes sure the resource is launched immediately as soon as any server in the Assigned Nodes list is brought online. You can modify the quorum values from the Cluster Configuration Fields page in NoRM.

   ▶ *Start*: When set to Auto, the resource will start automatically whenever the cluster is brought online. When set to Manual,

you must start the device after the cluster comes online. The
default is Auto.

▶ *Failover*: When set to Auto, the resource will automatically
move to the next server in the Assigned Nodes list if the node
it is currently running on fails. When set to Manual, you will
intervene after a failure and re-assign the resource to a functioning node. The default is Auto.

▶ *Failback*: When this is set to Auto, the cluster resource will
migrate back to its preferred node when it comes back
online. The preferred node is the first node listed in its
Assigned Nodes table. When set to Manual, the cluster
resource will not failback until you allow it to happen. When
set to Disable, the cluster resource will not failback to its
most preferred node when the most preferred node rejoins
the cluster. The default is Disable.

▶ *Master only*: Select this option if you want the resource to
run only on the master node in the cluster. If the master node
fails, the resource will failover to the node that becomes the
new master node in the cluster.

These settings allow you to configure the behavior of your clustered storage pools to cluster-specific events.

Always Available Network Services

When you are ready to start loading applications and services in a clustered environment, there are some extra steps you have to take beyond
the standard installation and configuration provided by the application or
service. As with a cluster volume, you will most likely need to cluster-
enable the application or service. You might also have to make some
changes to the Cluster object and the cluster nodes so that they can
properly support the new application or service.

Cluster Resource Applications

When creating a resource for an NCS cluster, you need to be familiar
with the following types of applications:

▶ *Cluster-aware*: Cluster-aware applications are specifically designed
to take advantage of a clustered environment. These applications
and services recognize when they are running on a cluster. They

will automatically tweak their internal settings to be more tolerant of communication lapses that occur in a clustered system.

▶ *Cluster-naive*: Although you can cluster-enable any application, if it is not designed to recognize that it is running on a cluster, the application is referred to as *cluster-naive*. For a cluster-naive application or service, NCS does all the work to ensure that the resource is reloaded on another node if the assigned cluster node fails.

There are many NetWare 6.5 services, and some third-party applications as well, that are designed to take advantage of Novell Clustering Services when it is detected:

▶ Apache Web server and Tomcat Servlet Engine

▶ AppleTalk Filing Protocol (AFP)

▶ BorderManager (proxy and VPN)

▶ DHCP server

▶ GroupWise (MTA, POA, GWIA, WebAccess)

▶ iFolder

▶ iManager

▶ iPrint

▶ NetWare FTP server

▶ Common Internet File System (CIFS)

▶ NFS 3.0

▶ NDPS

▶ Novell clients (Windows 98 and Windows XP/2000)

▶ Pervasive Btrieve

▶ Symantec Norton AntiVirus

▶ NetStorage

▶ ZENWorks for Servers

▶ ZENWorks for Desktops

As you can see from this list, you can leverage the advantages of clustering with many types of applications, thereby making your entire network more resilient to failures.

Cluster-Enabling an Application

You cluster-enable a service or application by creating a Cluster Resource object for it in eDirectory.

To create a cluster resource for an application, complete the following steps:

1. Launch NoRM and select Cluster Config from the left navigation frame.

2. In the right frame, click New Cluster Resource.

3. At the New Cluster Resource screen, supply the necessary information and click Apply.

   ▶ *Resource Name*: Specify a name for the new cluster resource.

   ▶ *(Optional) Template*: If a resource template already exists for the resource you are creating, select it from the drop-down list.

   ▶ *Create Resource Template*: Similar to templates for other eDirectory objects, cluster resource templates simplify the process of creating similar or identical cluster resources. If you want to create multiple instances of the same resource on different servers, you can create a template that will automatically assign all the necessary properties when the resource object is created, rather than having to set each one up manually.

NOTE NCS includes resource templates for DHCP, iFolder, MySQL database server, and generic IP services. The generic IP service template can be used when configuring certain server applications to run on your cluster. You can edit and customize any of the templates for your specific needs.

   ▶ *Define Additional Properties*: If a resource template does not exist, check this box so that you can set the Cluster Resource object properties after it is created. This opens the Resource Information screen to configure resource properties, just as if you were configuring an existing cluster resource.

The cluster resource includes a unique IP address, which lets it be migrated from node to node within the cluster, as necessary. Cluster resources are created for both cluster-aware and cluster-naive applications.

Assign Nodes to the Cluster-Enabled Resource

When you create a cluster-enabled resource, all nodes in the cluster are automatically assigned to the resource. The order of assignment is determined by the order the nodes appear in the Assigned Nodes list. To assign or un-assign nodes, or to change the failover order for the resource, complete the following steps:

1. Launch NoRM and select Cluster Config from the left navigation frame.

2. In the right frame, select the Virtual Server object associated with the cluster resource from the Resources list.

3. Click the Nodes link. Configure the nodes for the cluster-enabled volume as needed and click Apply.

The first server in the Nodes list will be the preferred node for the cluster-enabled storage pool. Failover will occur sequentially down the list.

Configure Clustered Resource Policies

Once a storage pool has been cluster-enabled, you can configure the start, failover, and failback parameters. To do this, complete the following steps:

1. Launch NoRM and select Cluster Config from the left navigation frame.

2. In the right frame, select the Virtual Server object associated with your cluster resource from the Resources list.

3. Click the Policies link. Configure the Virtual Server policies as you want them and click Apply.

   ▶ *Ignore Quorum*: Check this box if you don't want the cluster-wide timeout period and node number limit enforced. This makes sure the resource is launched immediately as soon as any server in the Assigned Nodes list is brought online. You can modify the quorum values from the Cluster Configuration Fields page in NoRM.

   ▶ *Start*: When set to Auto, the resource will start automatically whenever the cluster is brought online. When set to Manual, you must start the device after the cluster comes online. The default is Auto.

▶ *Failover*: When set to Auto, the resource will automatically move to the next server in the Assigned Nodes list if the node it is currently running on fails. When set to Manual, you will intervene after a failure and re-assign the resource to a functioning node. The default is Auto.

▶ *Failback*: When this is set to Auto, the cluster resource will migrate back to its preferred node when it comes back online. The preferred node is the first node listed in its Assigned Nodes table. When set to Manual, the cluster resource will not failback until you allow it to happen. When set to Disable, the cluster resource will not failback to its most preferred node when the most preferred node rejoins the cluster. The default is Disable.

▶ *Master only*: Select this option if you want the resource to run only on the master node in the cluster. If the master node fails, the resource will failover to the node that becomes the new master node in the cluster.

These settings give you granular control over the behavior of your clustered storage pools.

Migrating a Cluster Resource

A node doesn't have to fail in order to migrate a resource from one node to another. To migrate a cluster resource, complete the following steps:

1. Launch NoRM and select Cluster Management from the left navigation frame.

2. In the right frame, select the cluster resource that you want to migrate.

3. Select a server from the list of cluster nodes and click Migrate to move the resource to the selected server. If you click Offline instead of Migrate, the resource will be unloaded, and will not load again until it is manually reloaded into the cluster. If you need to modify the resource configuration, Offline lets you take the resource out of the cluster in order to do so. Cluster resources can't be modified while loaded or running in the cluster.

You might want to do this in order to perform some type of maintenance on one of the nodes or just to balance out the node workload, if one is getting too busy.

Configuring Load and Unload Scripts

Load scripts are required for each resource or volume in your cluster. The load script specifies the commands to start the resource or mount the volume on a node. Unload scripts are used to ensure that when a resource is removed from a node, all modules and resources are properly cleaned up in the process.

TIP Load and unload scripts are created automatically for disk pools when they are cluster-enabled. Because of this, you shouldn't have to mess with scripts for cluster-enabled volumes and pools.

To view or edit a script, complete the following steps:

1. Launch ConsoleOne and browse to the appropriate Cluster Resource object.

2. Right-click the Cluster Resource object and select Properties.

3. Double-click the Scripts tab. Select either Cluster Resource Load Script or Cluster Resource Unload Script.

4. Edit or add the necessary commands to the script to load or unload the resource on a node. Some commands might require command-line input. You can add << to a command to indicate command-line input. For example: **LOAD SLPDA <<Y**. This means that when the module **SLPDA** is loaded, it will receive a **Y** response to its command-line prompt, presumably to a question that needs a yes answer. You can string multiple inputs together by specifying them on subsequent lines, as follows (a string up to 32 characters in length):

```
LOAD SLPDA <<Y
<<Y
<<N
```

5. Specify a timeout value. The timeout value determines how much time the script is given to complete. If the script does not complete within the specified time, the resource becomes comatose. The default is 600 seconds (10 minutes).

You use the same commands in a load script that you would use to create any other NetWare configuration file that runs from the server console (such as AUTOEXEC.NCF). Applications and services will often include pre-built NCF files for loading and unloading application modules. You can use these as a template for creating load and unload scripts. Consult the application or service documentation for information on necessary load and unload commands.

Understanding Resource States

When running or testing an NCS cluster, you can view valuable information about the current state of your cluster, and its various resources, from the Cluster Management view in NoRM (see Figure 11.5).

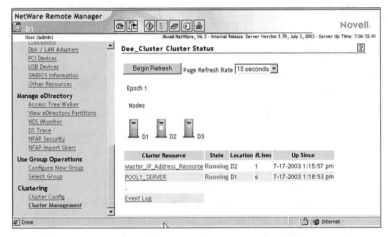

FIGURE 11.5
View of cluster status in NoRM.

Some of the specific cluster information you can gather from the Cluster Management view includes the following:

▶ An icon represents each node in your cluster. The yellow disk indicates the node that is functioning as the master server in the cluster. The master server can change over time due to failover or migration events that take place.

▶ Epoch indicates the number of times the cluster state has changed. The epoch number will increment each time a node joins or leaves the cluster.

▶ The Event Log link provides a detailed history of your cluster. Every time the cluster state changes, a new event is added to the event log.

▶ Next to each loaded cluster resource is an associated resource state.

Table 11.2 describes different resource states you might see in the Cluster Management view of NoRM and provides some possible actions for each state.

TABLE 11.2   Cluster Resource States

RESOURCE STATE	DESCRIPTION	ACTION
Alert	One of the resource policies has been set to Manual. The resource is waiting for admin instructions.	Click the Alert Status indicator and you will be prompted to start, failover, or failback the resource.
Comatose	The resource is not running and requires administrator intervention.	Select the Comatose Status indicator and take the resource offline. After resource problems are resolved, the resource can be put back online.
Unloading	The resource is un-loading from the server on which it was running.	None.
Running	The resource is in a normal running state.	Select the Running Status indicator, and you can choose to migrate the resource to a different node or take the resource offline.
Loading	The resource is loading on a server.	None.
Unassigned	None of the nodes in the Assigned Node list is currently online.	Select the Unassigned Status indicator and you can take the resource offline. This will prevent the resource from running on any of its preferred nodes should one or more of them rejoin the cluster.
NDS_Sync	The properties of the resource have changed and the changes are still being synchronized in eDirectory.	None.

TABLE 11.2   Continued

RESOURCE STATE	DESCRIPTION	ACTION
Offline	The resource is shut down or is in a dormant or inactive state.	Select the Offline Status indicator and, if desired, click the Online button to load the resource. NCS will choose the best node possible, given the current state of the cluster and the resource's Assigned Nodes list.
Quorum wait	The resource is waiting for a quorum to be established so that it can begin loading.	None.

CHAPTER 12

Advanced Network Services

Instant Access

Installing Nterprise Branch Office

▶ Create an Nterprise Branch Office appliance by using the Nterprise Branch Office CD-ROM to re-image your computer's hardware and load the necessary software.

▶ Synchronize your branch office data back to a central office server by installing and configuring `rsync`.

Managing Nterprise Branch Office

▶ Use Nterprise Branch Office Web Administrator to configure and manage a branch office appliance

▶ A command-line management option is available for use with Telnet connections.

Installing DirXML Starter Pack

▶ Install the DirXML engine from the DirXML Starter Pack CD-ROM at the NetWare 6.5 graphical console.

▶ Install DirXML drivers and management plug-ins (for iManager) from the DirXML starter pack CD-ROM at the Application server or workstation destination.

Configuring DirXML Starter Pack

▶ Use the DirXML management plug-ins to configure and manage your DirXML environment from iManager.

Nterprise Branch Office

Nterprise Branch Office, originally released as a standalone product, is now included as part of NetWare 6.5. Nterprise Branch Office lets you simplify the management and integration of remote locations by creating a multifunction appliance that efficiently links your branch offices to your HQ, using the Internet as your link. This way, existing security and management policies can be transparently extended to your branch offices without requiring a bunch of additional infrastructure to make it happen.

Nterprise Branch Office software combines with your hardware to create a branch office server appliance that is designed to provide those network services that are best provided locally (such as authentication, file access, and printing), while letting the central office manage more strategic services (such as security, directory management, and file replication). The basic architecture of an Nterprise Branch Office solution is shown in Figure 12.1.

Users access file and print services from Nterprise Branch Office using the same tools that can be used with a standard NetWare 6.5 file server. They can authenticate through multiple protocols, including HTTP, CIFS, NCP (Novell Client), FTP, AFP, and NFS and access their files in the method with which they are familiar.

Installing Nterprise Branch Office

There are just two tasks related to installing Nterprise Branch Office:

▶ Creating the branch office appliance
▶ Installing the central office software

Depending on how you plan to use the Nterprise Branch Office appliance, there may be some other supporting tasks that you need to perform. The Nterprise Branch Office appliance can be installed either standalone, or as an integral part of your central office infrastructure, as shown in Figure 12.1. The process of creating the appliance is similar, but central office integration requires a few additional tasks in order to prepare the central office to communicate with and support the branch office appliance.

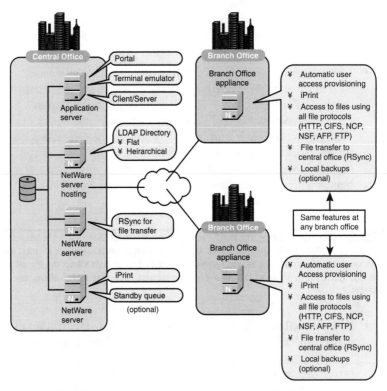

FIGURE 12.1
How Nterprise Branch Office works.

Extending Authentication to the Branch Office

In order to leverage the same user authentication provided by the
eDirectory environment at your central office, the User Access Provisioner
on the branch office appliance will automatically create accounts for
users the first time they log into the appliance. These branch office
accounts will have the same username and passwords that are used at the
central office so that users don't have to manage multiple accounts. In
order to support the proper creation of these new branch office accounts,
do the following:

> ▶ *Configure an LDAP server*: The branch office appliance will authen-
> ticate users using the LDAP protocol to communicate with your
> central office eDirectory tree. Therefore, your central office must
> have at least one LDAP server with which the branch office

appliance can communicate. For more information on creating an LDAP server on NetWare 6.5, see Chapter 5, "Novell eDirectory Management."

▶ *Universal passwords*: Several potential authentication protocols, such as CIFS and HTTP, require the use of the simple password capabilities of NetWare 6.5. Simple password is introduced in Chapter 2, "Novell Clients." To effectively manage the needs of these protocols, enable universal passwords on the central office servers. This will allow you to synchronize and manage passwords regardless of the method that users might use to authenticate at the branch office. For more information on Universal Passwords, see Chapter 6, "Users and Network Security."

NOTE If your branch office users will use the Novell client for their first login attempt to the branch office appliance, make sure that NMAS is disabled at the client in order for the user account provisioning to work properly. You can disable NMAS from the Novell client property pages at the workstation. For more information on the Novell client, see Chapter 2.

▶ *Install an SSL certificate*: In order to communicate authentication information with your central office server, the branch office appliance requires an appropriate SSL certificate. Your NetWare 6.5 server will create an SSL certificate automatically during its installation. Use ConsoleOne or iManager to export this certificate to a binary .DER file. Subsequently, you will install this certificate as part of the branch office appliance initialization. To export an SSL certificate with iManager, complete the following steps:

1. Launch iManager and click the View Objects button in the header frame.

2. In the left navigation frame, browse to the container in which your LDAP server is located. The SSL certificate for the LDAP server will be in the same context. The SSL certificate object will have a name of the form (where *<servername>* is the name of your LDAP server):

   `SSL CertificateIP-<servername>`

3. Click the SSL Certificate object and select Modify Object.

4. Select the Certificates tab in the right frame and click Export.

5. Select No to export the private key with the certificate, and click Next.

6. Select File in binary DER format and click Next.

7. Click Save the exported certificate to a file. Save the certificate file to your local drive or to a floppy disk. When the file has been created, click Close to exit the Certificate Export Wizard.

With these preparatory tasks out of the way, your branch office appliance will be ready to perform authentication based on user credentials initially created at your central office. Existing usernames, passwords, and rights can all be leveraged to jumpstart your branch office environment.

Replicating Branch Office Data to the Central Office

One critical requirement of a branch office server is that branch office data be protected just as carefully data at the central office. Prior to Nterprise Branch Office, this required a separate data backup/restore solution for remote servers. However, Nterprise Branch Office solves this problem by making it possible to synchronize branch office data to a central office server where it can be backed up and archived at the same time as the rest of the central office data. The result is that you no longer require someone at the branch office to manage the storing and changing of backup tapes or other media in order for the backup routine to run smoothly.

Nterprise Branch Office leverages a technology known as rsync to accomplish the transparent synchronization of data from the branch office appliance to a designated central office server. rsync is an open source technology that performs incremental data replication from one file system to another. The incremental nature of rsync means that, once the initial replication is complete, subsequent updates can occur very quickly, because only changes are replicated instead of entire files or directories.

To use rsync, the chosen central office server must be configured as an rsync server. To configure an existing server as an rsync server, complete the following steps. You can also configure a new server as an rsync server by installing the rsync server option during the NetWare 6.5 installation. For more information on NetWare 6.5 installation, see Chapter 1.

1. Insert the NetWare 6.5 Operating System CD-ROM into your workstation.

2. Launch iManager and open the Install and Upgrade link in the left navigation frame.

3. Select Install NetWare 6.5 Products, and then click Remote Product Install in the right frame.

4. At the Target Server screen, select the server to which you want to install Nterprise Branch Office and click Next. Authenticate as an Admin user for your eDirectory tree and click OK.

5. At the Components screen, click Clear All and select only Nterprise Branch Office—rsync Server. Click Next.

6. At the Summary screen, click Copy Files. You will be prompted to insert the NetWare 6.5 Products CD-ROM.

7. At the Rsync License Agreement screen, click I Accept.

8. At the Installation Complete screen, click Close to complete the installation of **rsync** server.

Once installed, make sure that **rsync** is loaded, and that the configuration pages are available from NoRM by loading the following **rsync** modules at the server console:

```
SYS:RSYNC\RSYNCST.NLM
RSYNCNRM.NLM
```

For best results, insert these commands into your central office server's AUTOEXEC.NCF so that they load automatically each time the server starts.

With **rsync** loaded, you can now finish the configuration from NoRM. To do so, complete the following steps:

1. Launch NoRM and select RSync Configuration in the left navigation frame. The **rsync** options are grouped under the Manage Applications heading.

2. Select Global Configuration in the right frame (see Figure 12.2). The Global settings will be applied to all branch office appliances linked to this **rsync** server. Provide the required information and click Apply to save your settings:

   ▶ *RSync IP Address*: Provide the IP address of the **rsync** server that you are installing at the central office.

   ▶ *Port*: Provide the port number that will be used by **rsync** activities. By default, **rsync** will use port **873**.

▶ *Enable SSL*: Check this box to use an SSL connection when replicating data via **rsync**. This option is enabled by default.

▶ *Enable Progress Logging*: Check this box to create a detailed log of data transfer activities. This log can get very large and require significant server resources. Because of this, it is typically only used while troubleshooting an **rsync**-related issue.

▶ *Log File*: Specify the location of the log file that will be used for progress logging. The log is stored as a text file and can be viewed with any text editor.

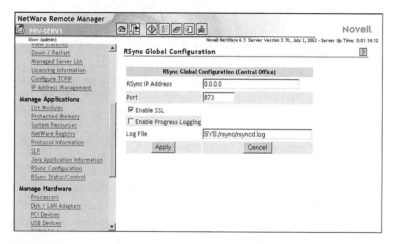

FIGURE 12.2
RSync global configuration settings in NoRM.

3. Select Branch Office Configuration in the right frame and click Add Branch Office. At the Branch Office Name and Volume screen, provide the required information and click Apply to save your settings:

▶ *Branch Office Name*: Type the branch office appliance name that you want to replicate to this **rsync** server. The appliance name is case-sensitive, so make sure you enter the *same value* as that entered when initializing the actual branch office appliance. For more information on initializing the branch office appliance, see "Creating the Branch Office Appliance," later in this chapter.

▶ *Volume for File Transfer*: Specify the volume on the central office server where you want replicated files to be stored. rsync does not use encryption, so this volume must be large enough to hold all data from the branch office appliance.

WARNING The volume used for rsync replication should be restricted so that only administrator's have access. Otherwise, potentially sensitive data from the branch office could be exposed to unauthorized users in the central office.

4. At the RSync Branch Office Configuration screen (see Figure 12.3), provide the required information and click Apply to save your settings:

▶ *Branch Office Name*: This is the name of the branch office appliance (provided previously).

▶ *File Transfer Path*: Specify the path to which rsync will replicate the branch office appliance data. By default, rsync appends the following path to the volume you chose previously:

   \rsync\<Branch Office name>

▶ *(Optional) Comment*: Provide any type of descriptive comment about the branch office appliance.

▶ *Transfer Logging*: Check this box to create a detailed log of data transfer activities. This log can get very large and require significant server resources. As such, it is typically only used while troubleshooting some rsync-related issue.

▶ *Branch Office IP Address*: Specify the IP address of the branch office appliance. This must be a public IP address through which the appliance will be accessible. If your branch office uses Network Address Translation (NAT), specify the public IP address and not the private server address.

▶ *Timeout*: Specify the amount of time, in seconds, that the rsync server will wait while attempting to contact a branch office appliance. If your Internet connection is slow, this value should be set fairly high. The default setting of 3600 seconds is the maximum timeout value.

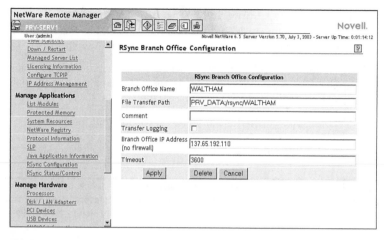

FIGURE 12.3
Branch office appliance configuration settings in NoRM.

5. Export the SSL IP certificate from your **rsync** server. This certificate will be needed during the branch office appliance configuration, and before the first data replication can occur. The process for exporting a server certificate was described previously.

At this point, your central office is configured to support branch office appliances. The following sections look at the installation and configuration of the branch office appliances themselves.

Creating the Branch Office Appliance

The Nterprise branch office appliance is created by installing a preconfigured image onto existing computer hardware so that it will function as a branch office appliance. NetWare 6.5 includes the Nterprise Branch Office CD-ROM, which is a bootable CD that launches the imaging process automatically. Because, under the covers, the branch office appliance is a limited functionality NetWare server, Novell recommends the following minimum hardware requirements:

▶ Server class PC with a Pentium II or AMD K7 processor (up to 32 processors).

▶ Minimum 512MB RAM (1GB recommended).

▶ Minimum 9GB local storage. The operating system will occupy 4GB of this space, with the rest available for user data. You should assume 1–2GB per user for data storage.

▶ Bootable CD-ROM drive and floppy drive. Make sure the BIOS settings for the appliance hardware list the CD-ROM as the first boot device, and then the hard drive, and then the floppy disk.

▶ Up to four Novell PCI Ethernet network boards. The branch office appliance can recognize up to four network adapters and provide automatic failover should one board fail.

▶ SVGA display adapter and monitor, keyboard, and mouse.

To create a new branch office appliance, complete the following steps:

WARNING The branch office appliance is a dedicated server device, and any existing operating systems or data will be deleted as part of the imaging process. Make sure that you back up any existing data that you might want to keep prior to starting the installation routine.

---

1. Insert the Nterprise Branch Office CD-ROM into the system that will become your new branch office appliance and reboot the system.

2. At the prompt, type **Y** to re-image the machine as an Nterprise Branch Office server.

   At this point, the branch office appliance image will create new disk partitions to support Nterprise Branch Office, and overwrite all data on the destination hard drive with the appropriate appliance files. This process might take some time. Once the imaging process is complete, the appliance will automatically reboot and move on to an automated configuration routine. Following this you will continue with the installation process.

3. When they are displayed, review both the Nterprise Branch Office and the rsync license agreements. You can also elect to press **C** to bypass the actual reading part and get on with the installation.

4. Press **Y** to accept the Novell License Agreement. Press **Y** to accept the rsync license agreement.

5. Enter the IP address of the branch office appliance.

6. Enter the subnet mask of the branch office appliance.

7. Enter the IP address of the default gateway.

   At this point, the appliance is installed and you are ready to move onto the Web-based appliance configuration. You can access the configuration utility from your Web browser by entering the following URL:

```
https://<server IP address>:2222
```

8. Authenticate as user Supervisor with no password to enter the appliance configuration utility, as shown in Figure 12.4. You will be able to set the password as part of the configuration process.

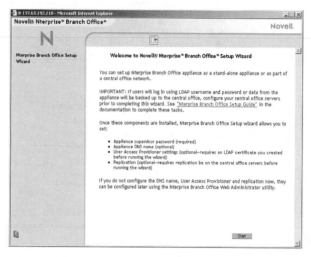

FIGURE 12.4
The initial Web-based branch office appliance configuration screen.

9. Click Start to begin the appliance configuration wizard.

10. At the Set General Settings screen (see Figure 12.5), provide the required information and click Next.

   ▶ *Supervisor Password*: Specify a password that will be used to access the appliance configuration wizard.

   ▶ *Appliance Name*: Specify a unique name of the branch office appliance. If you are going to use **rsync** with this server, make certain that the name specified matches the one provided in the **rsync** server configuration, described previously. Names are *case sensitive!*

   ▶ *(Optional) DNS Name, Domain, and DNS Server Address*: Provide the requested DNS information if users will use DNS to access printers within the branch office firewall. The

Nterprise branch office appliance provides iPrint functionality for network printing.

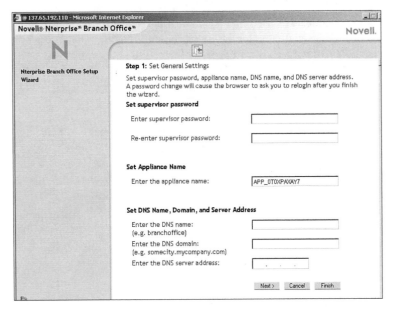

FIGURE 12.5
Configuring general settings on the branch office appliance.

11. *(Optional)* At the Setup User Access Provisioner screen, provide the required information and click Next (see Figure 12.6). The User Access Provisioner is necessary if you want to allow the branch office appliance to recognize LDAP users from an existing eDirectory tree at the central office.

   ▶ *Central office LDAP Server Information*: Provide the IP address, SSL port (default **636**), and SSL certificate for the LDAP server at the central office.

   ▶ *(Conditional) LDAP Context for User Access Provisioner*: If all the LDAP users who will authenticate to the branch office appliance are in a single container, provide the appropriate context here. Be sure to use the LDAP syntax (comma delimiters) instead of the familiar eDirectory syntax (period delimiters).

► *(Conditional) LDAP ID for Use by User Access Provisioner*: If
you want the branch office appliance to search multiple containers during LDAP user authentication, provide a valid user
ID and password that the appliance will use to connect to the
LDAP tree and query for users. This LDAP user must have
sufficient rights to read and scan all common names in the
central office LDAP-enabled tree.

NOTE The LDAP user ID and password will not be stored in the branch office appliance configuration file, for security reasons. If an appliance is ever restored from the
central office, this information will have to be provided manually before the User Access
Provisioner will work again.

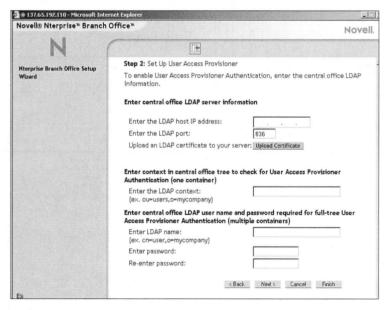

FIGURE 12.6
Configuring user access provisioner settings on the branch office
appliance.

12. *(Optional)* At the Setup Replication screen, provide the required
information and click Finish. Configure these settings is you are
using **rsync** to replicate branch office appliance data to a central
office server.

▶ *Central Office rsync Server Information*: Provide the IP
address, SSL port (default **873**), and SSL certificate for the
`rsync` server at the central office.

Once the configuration is complete, the branch office appliance will save
all the specified settings and reboot one more time to start up with the
specified settings. You will be prompted to authenticate to the appliance
again. Remember to use the user ID Supervisor, and the password that
you specified during the appliance configuration. Once you've been
authenticated, you will see the Nterprise Branch Office Web
Administrator, as shown in Figure 12.7.

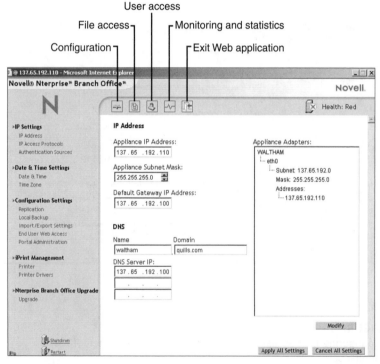

FIGURE 12.7
Nterprise Branch Office Web Administrator interface.

Configuring Nterprise Branch Office

Nterprise Branch Office is relatively easy to configure from a Web inter-face. As you navigate and configure the appliance, changes are tracked and stored in a local buffer. With the exception of printing and date/time settings, changes are not actually applied until you click the Apply All Settings button at the bottom of the content frame (right side). Because some settings require the appliance to restart, accumulating changes can make the configuration process a lot more efficient. Similarly, clicking Cancel All Settings will ignore accumulated changes.

At the bottom of the navigation frame, you will see links that will let you shut down or restart the appliance. As you can see, these options make it possible for the appliance to function in a "headless" environment such as a rack-mounted server room. Broad control over the appliance is pro-vided through the Branch Office Web Administrator. The following sec-tions look at the various pages and options available through the Web Administrator.

Configuration

This is the default view when Web Administrator is launched. Configuration page options are available as links in the left navigation frame:

▶ *IP Address*: This page, the default page shown in Figure 12.7, lets you configure the basic IP environment for your appliance, includ-ing IP addresses, subnet masks, gateway servers, DNS information, and Ethernet adapter settings.

▶ *IP Access Protocols*: This page lets you select and configure the pro-tocols that can be used for file access and administrative access on the branch office appliance. You can also add IP addresses to your appliance and configure protocols per IP address. Supported file access protocols include AFP, NFS, HTTP, FTP, HTTPS, NCP, and CIFS. Administrative protocols include HTTPS, FTP, and Telnet.

▶ *Authentication Sources*: Selects and configures the authentication protocols that will be supported by the branch office appliance. Options include LDAP, NIS, and NT DOMAIN.

▶ *Date & Time*: Configures the time synchronization environment for the branch office appliance. The appliance can locate NetWare or NTP time sources automatically, or you can specify a particular server. For more information on time synchronization, see Chapter 4.

▶ *Time Zone*: Configures the time zone and daylight saving time options for the branch office appliance. These settings will be used in the appliances time calculations to determine whether it is in proper time synchronization.

▶ *Replication*: Configures data replication from the branch office appliance to a central office `rsync` server. For more information on data replication, see "Replicating Branch Office Data to the Central Office," earlier in this chapter.

▶ *Local Backup*: If you choose not to replicate data to the central office, you should configure a local backup/restore device and attach it to the branch office appliance so that data will be properly protected.

▶ *Import/Export Settings*: Creates (exports) or imports a settings file that contains a branch office appliance configuration. These settings files can be used to store a specific configuration. They can also be used, after some modification, to configure another appliance with similar settings to those configured on the source appliance.

▶ *End User Web Access*: Provides some basic portal configuration for the branch office appliance. You can customize the company logo that will appear on the branch office portal Web page, and define a set of shared Web links that will be accessible by all branch office users.

▶ *Portal Administration*: This link will take you to more advanced portal configuration options from which you can customize most any aspect of the branch office appliance portal. As you will see, Branch Office leverages Novell Portal Services to provide its portal environment.

▶ *Printers*: Lets you add, delete, modify, and manage branch office printers. Nterprise Branch Office leverages iPrint to deliver its print services. For more information on iPrint, see Chapter 7.

▶ *Printer Drivers*: Lets you manage printer drivers available from the iPrint system.

▶ *Upgrade*: Allows you to apply Novell appliance upgrade files to your branch office appliance.

As you can see, most of the configuration necessary to get your branch office appliance up and running is available from this page.

File Access

This page, shown in Figure 12.8, provides the branch office appliance administrator with access to the appliance's file system. As you can see from the left navigation frame, the same file management options are available for the branch office appliance as are used with a regular NetWare 6.5 server.

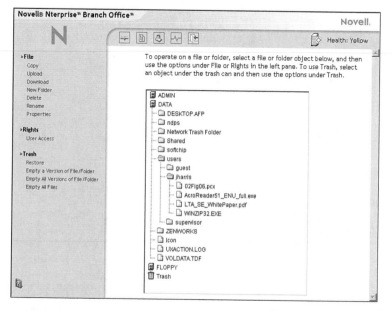

FIGURE 12.8

Nterprise Branch Office file access options from Branch Office Web Administrator.

From these pages you can manipulate folders and files, configure folder and file properties, configure user access rights, and recover deleted files. For more information on file access and security, see Chapter 6.

User Access

This page, shown in Figure 12.9, lets the branch office appliance administrator manage users and groups within the appliance environment, including creation, deletion, and modification of users and groups.

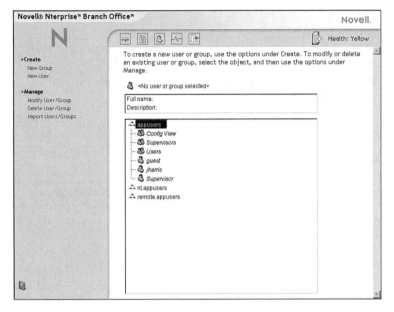

FIGURE 12.9
Nterprise Branch Office user access options from Branch Office Web Administrator.

From here, you can also reset user passwords if necessary. Users and groups on the branch office appliance function in exactly the same way as they do in a regular Novell network. For more information on users and groups, see Chapter 6.

Monitoring and Statistics

This page, shown in Figure 12.10, lets the branch office appliance administrator monitor appliance activity and performance, gather statistics on disk usage, and perform basic troubleshooting tasks should the need arise.

Monitoring and statistics options are organized into five categories in the left navigation frame:

▶ *Status*: The default page (see Figure 12.10) gives you a quick view of the status of the primary systems in the appliance so that you can be aware of any potential problems. Selecting any of the health indicators will show the characteristics included in the indicator.

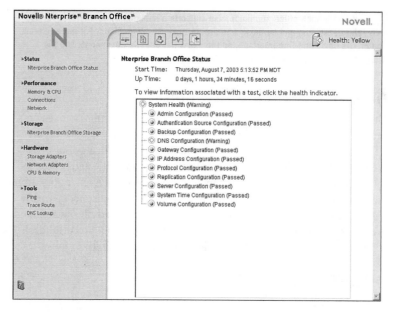

FIGURE 12.10
Nterprise Branch Office monitoring and statistics options from Branch Office Web Administrator.

▶ *Performance*: Provides graphical views of CPU, memory, connection, and network performance over time. Click the appropriate link to view the performance of that appliance subsystem.

▶ *Storage*: Provides graphical views of the various storage resources available to the branch office appliance, including data volumes and floppy drives.

▶ *Hardware*: Provides basic configuration information concerning storage adapters, network adapters, CPU, and memory.

▶ *Tools*: Provides three basic tools for testing your network environment, and provides information for troubleshooting problems in the branch office. The Ping utility lets you see if IP communications are occurring normally. Trace Route records the path of an IP packet from source to destination computer and displays the time necessary to make the trip. DNS Lookup lets you test the DNS environment to see whether addresses can be properly converted into IP addresses and vice versa.

NOTE The branch office appliance also supports a command-line interface for use with Telnet sessions, and by those who are particularly masochistic. For more information on the command-line interface, and to see a list of valid commands, see the Nterprise Branch Office online documentation.

Nterprise Branch Office Portal

One of the easiest ways for users to access their data and resources on the branch office appliance is through the branch office portal (see Figure 12.11). Based on Novell Portal Services, the branch office portal is completely customizable, and provides Web-based, authenticated access to folders and files stored on the branch office appliance. As mentioned previously, you can customize the branch office portal to display company logos and deliver other common content such as shared files and shared Web links. You can make the branch office portal into a powerful desktop that provides users with everything they need to do their jobs.

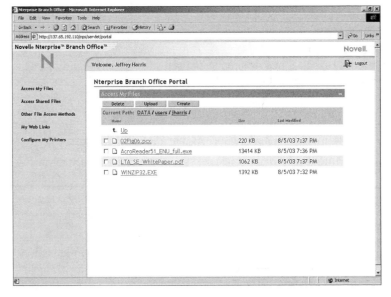

FIGURE 12.11
Nterprise Branch Office portal interface.

To access the branch office portal, users simply point their Web browsers to the IP address of DNS name of the branch office appliance. You can configure the portal to accept either secure (HTTPS) or insecure (HTTP) connections. For example:

```
https://137.65.192.110
```

or

```
http://www.waltham.quills.com
```

For more information, see "Configuring Nterprise Branch Office," earlier in this chapter.

DirXML Starter Pack

Originally released in the fall of 1991, DirXML has become an award-winning and groundbreaking tool for integrating the diverse systems in today's modern networks. NetWare 6.5 includes, for the first time, a fully functional version of DirXML suitable for linking some of today's most common directory systems into a cohesive whole.

Derived from DirXML 1.1a, the DirXML Starter Pack lets you bi-directionally synchronize data and passwords between Novell eDirectory, Microsoft Active Directory, and Microsoft Windows NT domains. In addition to the "big three," Starter Pack includes several other system drivers that are provided with 90-day evaluation licenses so they can be tried out in a lab environment, including GroupWise, Exchange 5.5 and Exchange 2000, Lotus Notes, LDAP, Delimited Text, JDBC, PeopleSoft, SAP HR, NIS, IBM Websphere MQ, and SIF.

How DirXML Works

DirXML Starter Pack allows you to link your disparate network data sources together using Novell eDirectory as the central repository for sharing data, as shown in Figure 12.12.

The DirXML architecture is comprised of several components that work together to achieve effective data and password synchronization:

- ▶ *DirXML Engine*: Running on NetWare 6.5, the DirXML engine functions as the communications hub that provides data and password synchronization between your central eDirectory tree and any participating external systems. The DirXML engine uses Extensible Markup Language (XML) to create object models of any data event. It then applies a set of rules to determine if, and how, the data modifications are sent to participating systems. The centralized DirXML engine makes sure that data events are processed consistently throughout your network environment.

SUBSCRIBER / PUBLISHER

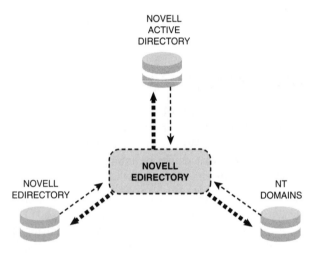

FIGURE 12.12
Logical DirXML architecture—Hub and Spoke.

▶ *DirXML Drivers*: Customized to each system that will participate in DirXML synchronization, the DirXML drivers act as communications "spokes," or channels between your central eDirectory tree and any participating external systems. DirXML drivers are configured to subscribe to data changes made in the central eDirectory tree, and publish data changes that occur locally to the central eDirectory tree. This publish/subscribe model gives you complete control over the nature and direction of data synchronization.

NOTE To simplify configuration, DirXML Starter Pack provides configuration files that you can import into a driver during installation to automatically set up driver rules, filters, and transformation documents that dictate what data from this system should be exchanged with other systems, and how this data should be exchanged.

▶ *Filters*: Filters specify which objects and attributes can be shared between the central eDirectory tree and a given target system. Each DirXML driver supports two sets of filters. The Subscriber filter determines the objects and attributes that are shared from eDirectory to the target system. The Publisher filter determines the objects and attributes that are shared from the target system to eDirectory. A list of default attribute mappings for Active Directory and NT Domain drivers is provided in Table 12.1.

▶ *Rules*: Rules are used to specify requirements for the management of object creation, matching, and placement that take place as part of a data synchronization event. For example, a Creation rule might specify that any User object created through a synchronization event must first have certain attributes defined, such as Surname and Email address.

▶ *Style Sheets*: Style Sheets use Extensible Stylesheet Language Transformations (XSLT) documents to transform XML events and data as needed to suit the needs of the various DirXML-integrated systems. For example, XSLT can be used to transform data received from one system into a format consumable by another system to which the data must be synchronized.

▶ *Password Synchronization Filters and Agents*: PasswordSync filters capture changes to passwords and pass these changes to PasswordSync agents over secure channels. PasswordSync integrates with DirXML drivers to determine how password changes should be applied across systems. For example, changing the password for `JHARRIS` in an NT domain could mean the new password should be sent to `JLHARRIS.PROVO.QUILLS.COM` in the eDirectory environment.

▶ *Remote Loader Service*: The Remote Loader Service is a communications mechanism whereby the DirXML engine and central eDirectory tree can effectively communicate with a DirXML driver that is actually loaded and running on a separate server. For example, the DirXML engine leverages the Remote Loader Service to communicate with the DirXML driver for Active Directory, which is loaded on a Windows 2000 Active Directory server.

TABLE 12.1 DirXML Starter Pack Configuration Files Set Bi-Directional Synchronization Between the Following Object Attributes

EDIRECTORY OBJECT ATTRIBUTES	ACTIVE DIRECTORY	NT DOMAINS
User	User	User
CN	userprincipalName	Name
Description	description	Comment
DirXML-ADAliasName	sAMAccountName	NT4AccountName
Facsimile Telephone Number	facsimileTelephone Number	FullName
Full Name	displayName	
Given Name	givenName	
Group Membership	memberOf	Logon Disabled
Login Disabled		nadLoginName
nadLoginName		
Owner	userAccountControl	PasswordChange
Password Allow Change	nadLoginName	PasswordRequired
Password Required	managedBy	
Physical Delivery Office Name	I	
Postal Code	postalCode	
Post Office Box	postOfficeBox	
S	st	
SA	streetAddress	
See Also	seeAlso	
Surname	sn	
Telephone Number	telephoneNumber	
Title	title	
Unique ID	mailNickname	
Group	Group	
CN	cn	
Member	member	
Organizational Unit	Organizational Unit	
OU	ou	

Installing the DirXML Engine

DirXML Starter Pack components are installed on those servers that will participate in the data synchronization process. iManager components must also be installed on your iManager server if it is different from the server running the DirXML engine. To install the DirXML engine on your NetWare 6.5 server, complete the following steps:

1. At the NetWare 6.5 server where you want to install DirXML, insert the DirXML Starter Pack CD-ROM.

2. From the GUI server console, click the Novell button and select Install.

3. At the Installed Products screen, click Add.

4. At the Source Path screen, browse to the DirXML Starter Pack CD-ROM, select `\NW\PRODUCT.NI`, and then click OK twice.

5. At the DirXML Starter Pack Product Installation page, click Next.

6. At the License Agreement screen, select the appropriate language to view the license agreement. Once you have reviewed the agreement, click I Accept.

7. On the Components page, select the DirXML components you want to install and click Next. As mentioned previously, DirXML drivers and management components can be installed on separate servers from the DirXML engine if desired.

8. On the Schema Extension page, provide the user ID and password of a user with administrative rights to the root of your eDirectory tree, and then click Next.

9. At the Components screen, select the DirXML drivers you want to install and click Next. Typically, you will only be installing the eDirectory DirXML driver for now. All other drivers are product-specific and require those products to be present.

NOTE DirXML drivers that cannot be installed on a NetWare server cannot be selected. All drivers marked Evaluation are subject to a 90-day evaluation license, and should be used only in a lab environment.

10. (*Conditional*) If you have chosen to install one or more pre-configured DirXML drivers, select those drivers at the Components screen, and click Next.

11. Review the information on the Installation Summary screen, and click Finish. At this point, eDirectory will be shut down so that the schema extensions can be applied, and the file copy will occur.

12. At the Installation Complete screen, click Close.

13. *(Conditional)* If you have chosen to install the iManager plug-ins for DirXML, restart your Web services by typing the following commands at the NetWare 6.5 server console:

```
TC4STOP
TOMCAT4
```

With Tomcat restarted, when you load iManager, you will see two new DirXML options in the left navigation frame: DirXML Management and DirXML Planning. These will be used for configuring the actual data synchronization process, described later in this chapter.

Installing Remote Loaders and Drivers

With the DirXML engine installed, you can install DirXML drivers on those are ready to start configuring your DirXML environment. The first step in doing this is to make sure that the Remote Loader is installed on any systems that will use it. For both Active Directory and NT domain synchronization, the DirXML driver and Remote Loader must be installed on an appropriate Domain Controller. The Domain Controller should have the following characteristics:

- ▶ *Active Directory*: Domain Controller running Windows 2000 Server with Support Pack 1 and Internet Explorer 5.5 or later

- ▶ *NT Domain*: Primary Domain Controller (PDC) running Windows NT 4 with Service Pack 6a or later

To install Remote Loader and DirXML driver on a Windows 2000 server running Active Directory, complete the following steps. For more information on performing the same type of installation on an NT 4 server, see the NetWare 6.5 online documentation.

1. At the Windows 2000 server that will host the driver, insert the DirXML Starter Pack CD-ROM. After a few moments, the DirXML Starter Pack Installation screen will appear. Click Next.

2. At the License Agreement screen, select the appropriate language to view the license agreement. Once you have reviewed the agreement, click I Accept.

3. On the Components screen, select DirXML Remote Loader and Drivers, and click Next.

4. At the Location screen, specify the path to which the Remote Loader will be installed, and click Next. It is usually best to just accept the default path.

5. At the Select Drivers for Remote Loader Install screen, select DirXML Remote Loader Service and DirXML Driver for Active Directory, and then click Next.

6. Review the information on the Installation Summary screen, and click Finish. You will see a warning about LDAP conflicts. Click OK to close the message box.

7. At the Create Shortcut screen, click Yes. This will create a shortcut on your Windows desktop to the Remote Loader Configuration wizard.

8. At the Installation Complete screen, click Close.

9. Launch the DirXML Remote Loader Configuration Wizard. At the Welcome page, click Next.

10. At the Command Port screen, click Next. This is the port that will be used by this instance of the remote loader to listen for DirXML activity. Novell recommends keeping the default port.

11. At the Configuration File screen, click Next. This is the name and location of the log file that will be used to record Remote Loader configuration options.

12. At the DirXML Driver screen, select Native and make sure that ADDRIVER.DLL is listed in the drop-down list. Click Next.

13. At the Connection to DirXML screen, provide the required information and click Next.

   ▶ *Port*: Specify the port that Remote Loader will use to listen for the DirXML engine. Novell recommends keeping the default port.

   ▶ *Address*: Specify the IP address that Remote Loader will use to communicate with the DirXML engine.

   ▶ *Use SSL*: Check the Use SSL box if you want secure communications between the DirXML engine and Remote Loader. You will have to provide the self-signed certificate from the DirXML server in order to use SSL. For more information on using SSL, see the NetWare 6.5 online documentation.

14. At the Tracing screen, specify the level of tracking data that you want recorded, the location of the trace file, and click Next. You will likely want to set up tracing while installing and configuring your driver. However, once configured, you will probably want to set the trace level to 0 to prevent the log file from growing to fill your entire hard drive over time.

   ▶ *Level 0*: No information display or tracking

   ▶ *Level 1*: General informational messages about processing

   ▶ *Level 2*: Displays messages from level 1 plus the XML documents that are passed between the engine and driver

   ▶ *Level 3*: Displays messages from level 2 plus documents sent and received between the Remote Loader and the DirXML engine

   ▶ *Level 4*: Displays messages from level 3 plus information about the connection between the Remote Loader and the DirXML engine

15. At the Install as a Service screen, check Mark Install the Remote Loader Instance as a Service, and click Next. Doing this lets Remote Loader continue to run even after you have logged out of the Windows system.

16. At the Passwords screen, specify the password you want to set for access to Remote Loader and the Driver object, and click Next.

17. At the Summary screen, review your configuration settings, and click Finish. When prompted, click Yes to start the Remote Loader service. This will launch the Remote Loader trace screen, as shown in Figure 12.13.

With Remote Loader configured, DirXML will now be able to synchronize data between your central eDirectory tree and your secondary Active Directory environment. Data is mapped from one directory structure to the other as discussed previously (see Table 12.1). The Remote Loader trace screen will show you the communication activities between the two directory environments.

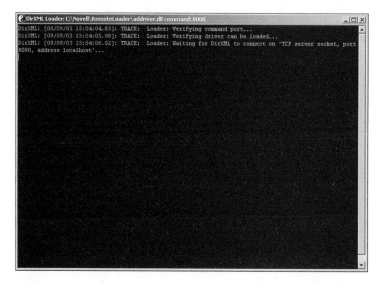

FIGURE 12.13
Remote Loader trace screen.

Installing DirXML on a Secondary eDirectory Tree

Each eDirectory tree that you want to synchronize with DirXML must
have a DirXML driver installed and configured on a replica server of the
secondary eDirectory tree. The first DirXML driver for eDirectory was
installed as part of the DirXML engine installation, described previously.
The DirXML driver installation for eDirectory will vary based on the version of NetWare that the host server is running. DirXML supports the following NetWare versions:

▶ NetWare 5.1 SP6 or later

▶ NetWare 6.0 SP3 or later

▶ NetWare 6.5

For more information on installing the DirXML driver in a secondary
eDirectory tree, see the NetWare 6.5 online documentation.

Configuring a DirXML Driver

Now that all the DirXML components are in place, you can do the actual
DirXML driver configuration. This is done through the iManager plug-ins

for DirXML that were installed previously. You can also use ConsoleOne to do the DirXML configuration if desired.

In order to simplify the configuration process, you can import the pre-configured driver settings that you have copied to your systems as part of the DirXML installation process, described previously. To import a pre-configured DirXML driver, complete the following steps:

1. Launch iManager from the server where the DirXML plug-ins have been installed.

2. Open the DirXML Management link in the left navigation frame and click Import Drivers.

3. Select the radio button next to In a New Driver Set, and click Next.

4. Provide the required information and click Next.

   ▶ *Name*: Provide a name for the driver set.

   ▶ *Context*: Specify the context in which you want the driver set object to be created.

   ▶ *Server*: Specify the server object on which DirXML is installed.

   ▶ *Create a new partition on this driver set*: Selecting this option will create a new directory partition in which DirXML data will be stored, where it can be isolated from the rest of the day-to-day eDirectory activity. Novell recommends that you configure DirXML in this way.

5. Select the specific driver configuration file you want to import and click Next. You can select multiple drivers, if desired.

6. Provide the required information to configure the driver and click Next. If you have selected multiple drivers, you will have fill out the appropriate configuration information for each driver. For more information on the specific information requested by each driver type, see the NetWare 6.5 online documentation.

7. Provide the required information to configure administrative rights for the DirXML driver and click Next.

   ▶ Click Define Security Equivalence, add Admin, and click OK. This grants the DirXML driver security equivalence to Admin in eDirectory so that sufficient rights are granted the driver to perform its synchronization operations.

   ▸ Click Exclude Administrative Roles, add Admin, and click
     Next. You should add any objects with administrative roles to
     this list in order to avoid problems with similar objects that
     may exist in other directories. Typically, administrative roles
     are specific to a given directory tree and don't need to be syn-
     chronized.

  8. At the Summary screen, click Finish. You can also click Finish with
     Overview if you want to view a synopsis of the driver's settings.

With the DirXML driver configured, you will see a new driver set in the
DirXML Overview screen. From here you can enable the driver, and then
perform synchronization tests to make sure the driver is functioning
properly. You can use the driver's trace screen to monitor activities as well
as the Trace options in iMonitor. For advanced settings and detailed
information on DirXML driver configuration, see the NetWare 6.5 online
documentation.

DirXML Password Synchronization

In addition to the synchronization of data between disparate systems
such as eDirectory, Active Directory, and NT domains, DirXML Starter
Pack also enables you to synchronize passwords between these systems.
DirXML Password Synchronization for Windows, known as
PasswordSync, allows passwords to be transparently and securely synchronized between eDirectory and the Active Directory/NT domains for
which you have DirXML drivers configured.

PasswordSync uses filters and agents to capture changes to passwords
and securely pass those changes to included systems. DirXML is capable
of understanding object mappings across systems so that each user object
is associated with the proper object in every other system. Because of
this, synchronizing passwords across the systems becomes much easier.

The specifics of how PasswordSync is installed depends on the systems
involved. For example, because Microsoft clients forward password
change requests to their respective Domain Controllers for processing,
PasswordSync Filters are installed on all Domain Controllers in Active
Directory and NT environments. On the other hand, because Novell
clients never send passwords across the network, PasswordSync filters for
eDirectory are installed on the client workstation and are part of the
Novell clients that ship with NetWare 6.5.

Unfortunately, because password synchronization with DirXML relies on PasswordSync filters and agents communicating the changes throughout the environment, if a password is synchronized through an unsupported mechanism, the synchronization will not occur. One example of this is an LDAP client such as Novell eGuide. Using an LDAP client to change your eDirectory password will not be synchronized to your Active Directory and/or NT Domain environments because the PasswordSync filters are never involved in the process. Similarly, if a password is changed from a non-Windows environment, the change will not be synchronized.

Bottom line here: Use Password Sync if you can be confident that password changes will only occur in one of the Windows methods supported by PasswordSync. For example:

- ▶ Workstation running the Novell client

- ▶ Workstation not running the Novell client

- ▶ Windows server or workstation running Microsoft Management Console

- ▶ Windows workstation or server running ConsoleOne

- ▶ Workstation or server running Novell iManager

For more information on configuring and using PasswordSync, see the NetWare 6.5 online documentation.

PART V

Appendices

APPENDIX A

Novell Client Properties

The Novell clients for Windows 9x and Windows 2000/XP contain a large number of configuration parameters to optimize the operation of the client for specific workstation and network configuration. These configuration options are available through the Novell client property pages. To access the Novell client property pages, right-click the red Novell N in the system tray and select Novell Client Properties.

This appendix provides a comprehensive listing of Novell client configuration options for the Novell Client v3.4 for Windows 9x, and Novell Client v4.9 for Windows 2000/XP. This information might vary for older, or newer, versions of the Novell client software. However, much of the information is accurate across multiple versions of the client.

The material has been organized under headings that correspond to the various property pages (tabs) that are available. For each option on a given tab, the following information is specified, where applicable: Default Value, Value Range, and Description.

NOTE The client options for Windows 9x and Windows 2000/XP vary significantly due to differences in operating system architecture. Items that do not apply to both versions of the Novell client are so identified.

Client Tab

First Network Drive

- ▶ *Default Value*: F
- ▶ *Range*: A–Z (only allow non-local drives)
- ▶ *Description*: This parameter sets the first network drive to the drive letter of your choice when you connect to a NetWare server. The first network drive applies to any user logging in to the network using the workstation where it is set.

Preferred Server

- ▶ *Default Value*: N/A
- ▶ *Range*: N/A
- ▶ *Description*: Legacy setting used to specify the server that eDirectory should authenticate the user to when the Novell client is started. The corresponding Default Location Profile value takes precedence over this setting.

Preferred Tree

- ▶ *Default Value*: N/A
- ▶ *Range*: N/A
- ▶ *Description*: Legacy setting used to specify the Directory tree that eDirectory should authenticate the user to when the Novell client is started. The corresponding Default Location Profile value takes precedence over this setting.

Client Version

- ▶ *Default Value*: 3.40.0.0 (Windows 9x) or 4.90 (Windows 2000/XP)
- ▶ *Range*: 0–9999
- ▶ *Description*: Shows the version information for the Novell client (derived from both external and internal versioning).

Support Pack

- ▶ *Default Value*: 0
- ▶ *Range*: 0–9999

▶ *Description*: Displays both the support pack version information as well as providing a button-activated list of the patched files.

Name Context

▶ *Default Value*: N/A

▶ *Range*: N/A

▶ *Description*: Legacy setting used to specify the eDirectory context that should be used when eDirectory attempts to authenticate a user during the initial Novell client startup. The corresponding Default Location Profile value takes precedence over this setting.

Tree/Name Context Pairs

▶ *Default Value*: N/A

▶ *Range*: N/A

▶ *Client Version*: 2000/XP v4.3 and higher

▶ *Description*: List of the most recently used context for the eDirectory tree(s) into which the Novell client has logged in. There is a single entry for each tree. Each tree/context pair will have a string value with the name of the tree and its associated Name context.

Location Profiles Tab

List of Location Profiles

▶ *Default Value*: N/A

▶ *Range*: N/A

▶ *Description*: Location profiles allow a network administrator to save the information from a user's specific login into one profile. When the user selects this profile when logging in, the profile automatically sets up login information such as the user's name, server, context, login script, and other applicable information so that the user does not have to type this information. For information on setting Location Profiles, see the Novell online documentation.

Advanced Login Tab

Initial Novell Login

- ▶ *Default Value*: 1 (Checked)
- ▶ *Range*: 0 = Unchecked, 1 = Checked
- ▶ *Description*: Enables/disables the Novell client login screen during workstation startup. If disabled, users will have to launch the login manually after authenticating to the workstation.

NMAS Authentication

The NMAS client, which is installed as part of the default installation of the Novell client, must be installed for NMAS authentication to appear.

- ▶ *Default Value*: 1 (Checked)
- ▶ *Range*: 0 = Unchecked, 1 = Checked
- ▶ *Description*: Enables/disables the use of NMAS authentication during the login. If NMAS is not being used on the network, NMAS can cause login delays.

OEM Extended ASCII Password

- ▶ *Default Value*: 0 (Unchecked)
- ▶ *Range*: 0 = Unchecked, 1 = Checked
- ▶ *Description*: Enables/disables the use of OEM extended ASCII characters in a password. OEM extended ASCII characters are already supported through the Unicode code pages in the Novell client, so this option should be needed only rarely with older software that requires the OEM ASCII codes.

Default Policy Support

- ▶ *Default Value*: 0 (Unchecked)
- ▶ *Range*: 0 = Unchecked, 1 = Checked
- ▶ *Description*: If enabled, the Novell client will attempt to read `SYS:PUBLIC\CONFIG.POL` on the authentication server after a user has successfully authenticated.

Policy Path and Filename

▶ *Default Value*: \System32

▶ *Range*: N/A

▶ *Description*: If the Default Policy Support is disabled, you can spec-ify the path to the Configuration Policy file. The specified path must be provided in UNC format and include the server name, volume/share, directory, and filename. For example, \\serv1\sys\ policies\policy.cfg.

Location List

▶ *Default Value*: 0 (Unchecked)

▶ *Range*: 0 = Unchecked, 1 = Checked

▶ *Description*: Specifies whether the Location list in the Login dialog box is enabled. The list shows Location Profiles that have been con-figured on this workstation and allows the user to select one for login. (Location Profiles store many login settings such as Preferred Server, Tree, and Context.) After the initial installation, there is only one Location Profile enabled—called the Default Location Profile. However additional Location Profiles can be configured manually or by using ZENWorks.

Advanced Button

▶ *Default Value*: 1 (Checked)

▶ *Range*: 0 = Unchecked, 1 = Checked

▶ *Description*: Specifies whether the Advanced button on the Login dialog box is enabled. This button leads to various tabs that help you to specify advanced login parameters.

Variables Button

▶ *Default Value*: 1 (Checked)

▶ *Range*: 0 = Unchecked, 1 = Checked

▶ *Description*: Specifies whether the Variables button in the Login dialog box is enabled. The button allows you to define the %2, %3, %4, and %5 login script variables used when the user logs in.

Clear Connections

▶ *Default Value*: 0 (Unchecked)

▶ *Range*: 0 = Unchecked, 1 = Checked

▶ *Description*: Specifies whether the Clear Connections check box appears in the Login dialog box. The check box allows you to clear all previous connections when you create a new connection to the network (clears printer captures, drive mappings, and network drive search path entries from the Environment Search PATH).

Workstation Only (Windows 2000/XP Only)

▶ *Default Value*: 1 (Checked)

▶ *Range*: 0 = Unchecked, 1 = Checked

▶ *Description*: Check this box if you want the Workstation Only check box to be available when users log in. This determines whether the option is available; it does not set the value of the Workstation Only setting. It only allows the user to see the check box and change it.

Suppress Single Sign-On for this Login (Windows 2000/XP only)

▶ *Default Value*: 1 (Checked)

▶ *Range*: 0 = Unchecked, 1 = Checked

▶ *Description*: Check this box if you want the Suppress Single Sign-On for This Login check box to be available when users log in. Even if selected, this check box will be available only if single sign-on has been enabled on the Single Sign-On tab.

Tree (Windows 2000/XP Only)

▶ *Default Value*: 1 (Checked)

▶ *Range*: 0 = Unchecked, 1 = Checked

▶ *Description*: Enables/disables the Tree dialog box that allows users to specify an eDirectory tree other than the default.

Tree Button (Windows 2000/XP Only)

▶ *Default Value*: 1 (Checked)

▶ *Range*: 0 = Unchecked, 1 = Checked

▶ *Description*: Enables/disables the Tree button that allows users to select a tree from the list of available trees on the network.

Context (Windows 2000/XP Only)

▶ *Default Value*: 1 (Checked)

▶ *Range*: 0 = Unchecked, 1 = Checked

▶ *Description*: Enables/disables the Context dialog box that allows users to specify an eDirectory tree other than the default.

Context Button (Windows 2000/XP Only)

▶ *Default Value*: 1 (Checked)

▶ *Range*: 0 = Unchecked, 1 = Checked

▶ *Description*: Enables/disables the Context button that allows users to browse to a specific context with the selected tree.

Force Logoff Button (Windows 2000/XP Only)

▶ *Default Value*: 0 (Unchecked)

▶ *Range*: 0 = Unchecked, 1 = Checked

▶ *Description*: Check this box if you want the Force Logoff button to be available from the Login page. Force Logoff lets you terminate an open Novell client session even if the workstation is locked. Any unsaved work may be lost if this is done.

Welcome Screen Bitmap Filename (Windows 2000/XP Only)

▶ *Default Value*: NWELCOME.BMP

▶ *Range*: N/A (Any valid string is allowed)

▶ *Description*: Specifies the bitmap that appears on the welcome screen when you start Windows 2000/XP. You can specify any bitmap located in the \WINNT directory.

Welcome Screen Caption (Windows 2000/XP Only)

▶ *Default Value*: Begin Login

▶ *Range*: N/A (Any valid string is allowed)

▶ *Description*: Specifies the text that appears in the header on the welcome screen that appears when you start Windows 2000/XP.

Service Location Tab

Scope List

- ▶ *Default Value*: N/A

- ▶ *Range*: N/A

- ▶ *Description*: This is a list of scope names to be reported to SLP applications on this workstation. Multiple scope names are allowed. The list order reflects the preference order. Scopes can also be configured via DHCP or discovered dynamically from Directory Agents (unless the Active Discovery option has been disabled), although dynamically discovered scopes are not displayed here (can only be viewed with the **SLPINFO** command).

Static (Check Box in Scope List Window)

- ▶ *Default Value*: 0 (Unchecked)

- ▶ *Range*: 0 = Unchecked, 1 = Checked

- ▶ *Description*: Check the Static check box if you don't want the list to be supplemented by scopes that are discovered dynamically from Directory Agents; otherwise, the client will use all scopes that the discovered Directory Agents service.

Directory Agent List

- ▶ *Default Value*: N/A

- ▶ *Range*: N/A

- ▶ *Description*: This is a list of SLP Directory Agent addresses. Multiple Directory Agent addresses are allowed and the SLP User Agent/Client will contact each of these DAs when performing a service query, so it is not recommended to assign more than two or three DAs. Each address is a fully qualified domain name (DNS), or a dotted decimal IP address. Directory Agents can also be configured via DHCP, or discovered dynamically.

Static (Check Box in Directory Agent List Window)

- ▶ *Default Value*: 0 (Unchecked)

- ▶ *Range*: 0 = Unchecked, 1 = Checked

- ▶ *Description*: If you check the Static check box for the Directory

Agent list, SLP requests will be sent to the Directory Agents whose addresses or DNS names have been configured in the list. Otherwise, SLP will send requests to all discovered (statically or dynamically) Directory Agents (DA) in the network.

Active Discovery (Check Box in Directory Agent List Window)— Windows 9x Only

▶ *Default Value*: 1 (Checked)

▶ *Range*: 0 = Unchecked, 1 = Checked

▶ *Description*: Controls whether SLP is allowed to use multicast to look up services. If it is set to ON, the SLP namespace provider can send multicast requests to Server Agents (SA) in the event the service could not be found using a Directory Agent (DA). Setting this to ON also allows the SLP User Agent (UA) to attempt to locate a DA using multicast. If this is set to OFF, the SLP namespace provider must send unicast service requests to DAs and is *not* allowed to send multicast requests to SAs. This setting has been moved to the Advanced Setting tab in the 2000/XP client, and is listed as SLP Active Discovery.

Registration Filter Scope List (Windows 2000/XP Only)

▶ *Default Value*: N/A

▶ *Range*: Any valid scope string name

▶ *Description*: This parameter is available when you select the Filters button on the Service Location tab of the client properties. It stores a list of SLP scopes to which this workstation can register SLP services. If there are any entries in this parameter, the SLP Server Agent (SA) will only register services to the scopes listed here, even if there are other scopes listed in the Common Scope List. The typical workstation will not be registering SLP services, typically only servers do this, but the Novell client does support SLP service registration from the workstation. An example of workstation registered SLP services includes the **SAPSRV.NOVELL** service, which is used for IPX compatibility and lists all IPX SAPs that are normally advertised over IPX.

Filtered Service Type List (Windows 2000/XP Only)

▶ *Default Value*: OFF

▶ *Range*: ON, OFF

▶ *Description*: Similar in functionality to the `SERVICE REGISTER` command used in `SLP.CFG` on NetWare servers. It is available only if you highlight a scope name that was added to the Registration Filter Scope List. Its purpose is to filter or restrict the registration of specified SLP service types to the specified scopes. For example, you can force the registration of all `SAPSRV.NOVELL` to the `IPXCMD` scope. This definition would affect only the `SAPSRV.NOVELL` SLP service; all other service types would be registered either to the Common Scope List or to the General Registration Scope List, which is displayed as Registration Filter Scope List under the Filters button in the Service Location tab of the client properties.

NOTE If there are entries in both Filtered Service Type List and Registration Filter Scope List, SLP service registration will be handled differently than if there were just entries in the Registration Filter Scope List. If there are only entries in the Registration Filter Scope List, all SLP services advertised on the workstation will be registered *only* to the scopes listed there and not to any of the scopes listed on the Common Scope List. If there are entries on both the Registration Filter Scope List and the Filtered Service Type List, all SLP service types defined in the Filtered Service Type List will be registered to the scopes in the Registration Filter Scope List. Likewise, all other SLP service types not defined will be registered to the Common Scope List.

Use Strict Registration Filtering (Windows 2000/XP Only)

▶ *Default Value*: 0 (Unchecked)

▶ *Range*: 0 = Unchecked, 1 = Checked

▶ *Description*: See the preceding note for background understanding. The Use Strict Registration Filtering setting prevents all SLP services not explicitly listed in the Filtered Service Type List from being registered with the Common Scope List. It behaves the same as if there were entries in both the Filtered Service Type List and Registration Filter Scope List, except that any SLP service types not defined in the Filtered Service Type List are not registered with any entry in the SLP Common Scope List. It is possible to add an entry in the Registration Filter Scope List and not assign any service types to it. In this scenario, any service types that were not assigned to a specific entry or entries in the Registration Filter Scope List would go into the entry that has no specific service types assigned to it. If you don't make a specific assignment, it assumes *all* service types. Once you make an assignment, it becomes exclusive.

Advanced Settings Tab

Alert Beep (Windows 9x Only)

- ▶ *Default Value*: ON
- ▶ *Range*: ON, OFF
- ▶ *Description*: Specifies whether an audible beep should be sounded when a pop-up message is displayed.

Auto Reconnect

- ▶ *Default Value*: 3
- ▶ *Range*: 0–5 (0–1 for 2000/XP)
- ▶ *Description*: Specifies the level of the Client Auto Reconnect feature to use. The levels of Auto Reconnect are as follows:
    - ▶ 0 = Disable/no Auto Reconnect
    - ▶ 1 = Devices (connections, drive mappings, printer captures) only
    - ▶ 2 = Devices and files opened for read-only
    - ▶ 3 = Devices and all opened files and file locks
    - ▶ 4 = Devices, all opened files/file locks, and guaranteed file write data recovery
    - ▶ 5 = Devices, all opened files/file locks, guaranteed file write data recovery, and capability to write network files to local disk and then resync files to the network later

NOTE Current Novell clients and NetWare 6.5 only support Auto Reconnect levels 0–3. Levels 4 and 5 are for potential future implementation. The Windows 2000/XP client only allows you to enable/disable Reconnect level 3. If you select 1, level 3 is enabled. If you select 0, Auto Reconnect is disabled.

Auto Reconnect Timeout (Windows 9x Only)

▶ *Default Value*: 120

▶ *Range*: 120–65535

▶ *Description*: How long (in minutes) the Auto Reconnect feature will continue to attempt to reconnect to lost resources before timing out.

Broadcast Mode (Windows 9x Only)

▶ *Default Value*: 0

▶ *Range*: 0, 1, 2 (0=All, 1=Server Only, 2=None)

▶ *Description*: Broadcast Mode controls what type of incoming pop-up messages a workstation can receive. When set to All, the workstation receives all messages from users and servers. Server Only accepts messages only from servers and None rejects all incoming pop-up messages from users and servers.

Bad Server Name Cache Enabled (Windows 2000/XP Only)

▶ *Default Value*: ON

▶ *Range*: ON, OFF

▶ *Description*: Enables/disables the caching of server names that the Novell client has been unable to resolve.

Bad Server Name Cache Timeout (Windows 2000/XP Only)

▶ *Default Value*: 300 (seconds)

▶ *Range*: 0–4294967295 seconds

▶ *Description*: Sets the time period for which server names will be kept in the Bad Server Name cache before being removed.

Burst Mode (Windows 2000/XP Only)

▶ *Default Value*: 1

▶ *Range*: 0, 1 (0 = OFF, 1 = ON)

▶ *Description*: The Burst Mode parameter controls the use of the packet burst protocol for file read/write. Generally, packet burst reduces overall network traffic and improves performance. Novell strongly recommends enabling packet burst to improve file read/write performance from NetWare servers.

Cache NetWare Password (Windows 9x Only)

▶ *Default Value*: ON

▶ *Range*: ON, OFF

▶ *Description*: Specifies whether the NetWare credentials (name and password) from the initial login are stored in memory (cache) and used to authenticate to additional NetWare resources. If this is disabled, when users use Network Neighborhood to browse to NetWare servers or trees, they will be required to re-enter their names and passwords before access is granted.

Cache Writes (Windows 9x Only)

▶ *Default Value*: ON

▶ *Range*: ON, OFF

▶ *Description*: Improves performance for writing files to the network by allowing the client to save changes to workstation memory before saving them to the network. If this is disabled, the Novell client must submit the file write changes to the server before being allowed to continue (will create a longer delay in the time applications pause during a file write). This is not the same as the True Commit parameter, which goes a step further and requires that the server acknowledge that the file changes have actually been committed to the volume on the server (not just submitted) before being allowed to continue.

Checksum (Windows 9x Only)

▶ *Default Value*: 1

▶ *Range*: 0–3

▶ *Description*: Provides a higher level of data integrity by validating NCP packets.

Close Behind Ticks (Windows 9x Only)

▶ *Default Value*: 400

▶ *Range*: 0–65535

▶ *Description*: The time (in ticks) the client waits after a file is closed before flushing the file from cache and writing it to disk. Increasing this value will improve file performance where files are opened, changed, closed, and then reopened frequently (such as with a database). There are about 18 ticks per second.

Cluster Connection Validation Interval (Windows 2000/XP Only)

▶ *Default Value*: 20 seconds

▶ *Range*: 0–300 seconds

▶ *Description*: Specifies how often TCP keep-alive packets will be sent to the cluster server to confirm that the cluster connection is still valid. A value of 0 will disable TCP keep-alive packets.

Delay Writes (Windows 9x Only)

▶ *Default Value*: ON

▶ *Range*: ON, OFF

▶ *Description*: Delay Writes keeps the files in cache for the amount of time specified by Close Behind Ticks after the application closes the file. This is used for applications that repeatedly close and reopen files, such as overlay files.

Disable Account Creation—Local (Windows 9x Only)

▶ *Default Value*: OFF

▶ *Range*: ON, OFF

▶ *Description*: Disables the creation of Disconnected Authentication accounts for users who do not currently have an account on the workstation, and who attempt to log in locally while the workstation is disconnected from the network.

Disable Account Creation—Network (Windows 9x Only)

▶ *Default Value*: OFF

▶ *Range*: ON, OFF

▶ *Description*: Disables the creation of Disconnected Authentication accounts for users who do not currently have an account on the workstation, and attempt to authenticate to the network. This is valid only during the initial login.

Disable Windows Password Cache (Windows 9x Only)

▶ *Default Value*: OFF

▶ *Range*: ON, OFF

▶ *Description:* Disables the Windows user profile password file. This prevents others from potentially obtaining a user's eDirectory password, but other applications will not be able to use the Windows password cache.

DOS Long Name Support (Windows 2000/XP Only)

▶ *Default Value*: ON

▶ *Range*: ON, OFF

▶ *Description*: This parameter allows long filenames to appear in the DOS window.

DOS Name

▶ *Default Value*: WIN98 (Windows 9x client), WINNT (Windows 2000/XP)

▶ *Range*: N/A

▶ *Description*: DOS Name is the operating system used by the %OS parameter.

Enable Disconnected Authentication (Windows 9x Only)

▶ *Default Value*: OFF

▶ *Range*: ON, OFF

▶ *Description:* Forces user to authenticate even if the workstation is not connected to the network, so that unauthorized users cannot log in to the workstation and access another user's profile.

End Of Job (Windows 9x Only)

▶ *Default Value*: OFF

▶ *Range*: ON, OFF

▶ *Description*: Causes an End of Job (EOJ) command to be sent to the file server when a process has completed (such as a print job, file read/write, and so on) that releases all resources allocated on the file server to the current task. This setting was implemented to help accommodate applications that did not properly release resources on the network.

Environment Pad (Windows 9x Only)

▶ *Default Value*: 17

▶ *Range*: 17–512 bytes

▶ *Description*: Environment Pad specifies the number of bytes added to a DOS program's environment space before executing the program. If there are several environment variables (created using SET statements), this value might need to be increased to accommodate them; otherwise, some of the variables might not be available to the DOS program.

File Cache Level (Windows 9x Only)

▶ *Default Value*: 3

▶ *Range*: 0–3

▶ *Description*: Specifies the type of file caching used at the client. The larger the value, the more aggressive the client will be in caching files for better performance. Some applications might be intolerant of aggressive file caching and might require this setting to be disabled (0).

File Caching (Windows 2000/XP Only)

▶ *Default Value*: ON

▶ *Range*: ON, OFF

▶ *Description*: This controls whether the client will cache files locally. This parameter is equivalent to the Opportunistic Locking setting in the Windows 9x client.

File Commit (Windows 2000/XP Only)

▶ *Default Value*: OFF

▶ *Range*: ON, OFF

▶ *Description*: This controls whether buffers flushed by an application are committed immediately to disk on the server. Setting this value to ON will ensure data integrity at the expense of significantly reduced file write performance. This is because when this is set to ON, the client must immediately commit the file changes to disk on the server and must wait until the server acknowledges that the changes have been written instead of just requiring an acknowledgment from the server that the write request has been received (shows as disk request and then as dirty cache buffer if it sits long enough). This parameter is similar to the True Commit parameter offered in the Windows 9x client.

File Write Through (Windows 9x Only)

▶ *Default Value*: OFF

▶ *Range*: ON, OFF

▶ *Description*: Controls whether all files are opened in write-through mode.

Force First Network Drive (Windows 9x Only)

▶ *Default Value*: OFF

▶ *Range*: ON, OFF

▶ *Description*: Specifies the network drive letter the SYS:LOGIN directory is mapped to after logging out. ON maps SYS:LOGIN to the First Network Drive. OFF maps SYS:LOGIN to the current drive letter in use.

Give Up on Requests to SAs

▶ *Default Value*: 15

▶ *Range*: 1–60000 seconds

▶ *Description*: This parameter specifies the maximum amount of time SLP will take to send requests to Server Agents (SAs).

Handle Net Errors (Windows 9x Only)

▶ *Default Value*: OFF

▶ *Range*: ON, OFF

▶ *Description*: Determines whether the client handles network critical errors or returns an INT 24 to the application making the network request (thereby allowing the application to handle the network critical error).

Hold Files (Windows 9x Only)

▶ *Default Value*: OFF

▶ *Range*: ON, OFF

▶ *Description*: Specifies whether files opened by a program using FCB_IO are held open until the program exits or are closed before the program exits. ON will hold them open until the program exits. OFF means that they can be closed by the program before it exits.

IP Address Costing

▶ *Default Value*: 2

▶ *Range*: 0–2

▶ *Description*: This parameter controls the method used to estimate the cost of sending address referrals from SLP, DNS, and eDirectory via a given network route.

  ▶ 0 = Disable IP address costing

  ▶ 1 = Calculate the address cost via sorting by subnet mask

  ▶ 2 = Calculate the address cost via an ICMP ECHO packet

Large Internet Packet Start Size

▶ *Default Value*: 65535

▶ *Range*: 512–65535

▶ *Description*: Large Internet Packet (LIP) Start Size determines the starting value for negotiating the LIP size. Setting this value can shorten the initial negotiation time for packet size over slow links.

Large Internet Packets

▶ *Default Value*: YES (ON)

▶ *Range*: YES, NO (GUI shows this as ON, OFF; Registry uses YES, NO)

▶ *Description*: When Large Internet Packets is ON, it uses the maximum packet size negotiated between the NetWare server and the workstation, even across routers, bridges, and switches. If the maximum packet size supported by the network is smaller than the negotiated packet size, the size supported by the network is used.

Limit SAP Broadcast Queries (Windows 2000/XP Only)

▶ *Default Value*: ON

▶ *Range*: ON, OFF

▶ *Description*: Use this setting to limit SAP so that it locates servers only on connections where the bindery is present. Disable this parameter if you want SAP to find servers if the bindery query fails.

Link Support Layer Max Buffer Size

▶ *Default Value*: 4736

▶ *Range*: 638–24682 bytes

▶ *Description*: Specifies the maximum supported packet size in bytes. Use this setting to optimize performance for media (primarily token ring) that can use packets that are larger than the default size. If your network uses bus-mastering, increasing the settings increases system memory usage. Otherwise, system memory usage is usually unaffected by this setting.

Lock Delay (Windows 9x Only)

▶ *Default Value*: 1

▶ *Range*: 1–65535 ticks

▶ *Description*: Determines the delay (in ticks) to retry the open or lock of a file after a **SHARE** failure. Increase this value if you receive **SHARE** errors. There are approximately 18 ticks per second.

Lock Retries (Windows 9x Only)

▶ *Default Value*: 5

▶ *Range*: 1–65535 retries

▶ *Description*: Determines the number of retries to open or lock a file after receiving a **SHARE** failure. Increase this value if you receive **SHARE** errors.

Log File (Windows 9x Only)

▶ *Default Value*: NULL

▶ *Range*: N/A

▶ *Description*: Specifies the location and filename used to store Novell client diagnostic information (for example, `C:\NOVELL\ CLIENT32\NIOS.LOG`). In addition to setting this value, you must also put the `NWEnableLogging=True` line in the `[386Enh]` section of the SYSTEM.INI file before the Novell client will begin writing information to the log file.

Log File Size (Windows 9x Only)

► *Default Value*: 65535

► *Range*: 0–1048576 bytes

► *Description*: Determines the maximum size of the log file used for Novell client diagnostic information before it begins to wrap around to the beginning of the file.

Login Attempt Retry Count (Windows 9x Only)

► *Default Value*: 3

► *Range*: 0–200

► *Description:* Specifies the number of failed login attempts allowed before the user is prompted to shut down and restart the workstation. To use this parameter, you must have Disconnected Authentication enabled, and the NICI client must be installed on the workstation.

Long Machine Type

► *Default Value*: IBM_PC

► *Range*: N/A

► *Description*: Tells the Novell client for Windows 9x what type of machine is being used each time the %MACHINE variable is accessed. Use this setting to set the machine's search path to the correct version of DOS.

Max Cache Size (Windows 9x only)

► *Default Value*: 0 (dynamically sized by Novell client)

► *Range*: 0–49152 KB

► *Description*: Determines the largest size the NetWare cache is allowed to use. Setting to 0 allows the client to dynamically allocate available memory for caching. Setting a larger value improves network file access performance, but decreases the memory available for running applications or caching files on local drives.

Max Cur Dir Length (Windows 9x Only)

► *Default Value*: 64

► *Range*: 64–255 characters

▶ *Description*: Sets the maximum length of the DOS prompt. Some applications do not function correctly if this is set higher than 64.

Max Read Burst Size (Windows 2000/XP Only)

▶ *Default Value*: 36000

▶ *Range*: 1–65536 bytes

▶ *Client Version*: 2000/XP v4.3 and higher

▶ *Description*: Specifies the maximum read burst window size that the client can request from the server. This value controls the maximum size only for a packet burst read window; the actual value in use will depend on network conditions (the client reduces the size used when packets are lost or data in the packet is incomplete). Max read burst size values smaller than the maximum packet size supported by the medium effectively disable packet burst for file reads. The client will try to request a read burst of the maximum size only if network conditions allow it.

Max Write Burst Size (Windows 2000/XP Only)

▶ *Default Value*: 15000

▶ *Range*: 1–65536 bytes

▶ *Description*: Specifies the maximum write burst size that the client can request from the server. This value controls the maximum size only for a packet burst write window; the actual value in use will depend on network conditions (the client reduces the size used when packets are lost or data in the packet is incomplete). Max write burst size values smaller than the maximum packet size supported by the medium effectively disable packet burst for file writes. The client will try to request a write burst of the maximum size only if network conditions allow it. Increasing this value beyond its default might be detrimental to server performance.

Message Timeout (Windows 9x Only)

▶ *Default Value*: 0 (user must clear the message manually)

▶ *Range*: 0–10000 ticks

▶ *Description*: Defines the time (in ticks) before pop-up messages are cleared from the screen without user intervention. Setting this to 0 will leave messages on the screen until the user manually clears the message. There are approximately 18 ticks per second.

Minimum Time to Net

▶ *Default Value*: 0

▶ *Range*: 0–65535 milliseconds

▶ *Description*: Used for bridged WAN/satellite with time-to-net values set too low for workstations to make a connection under either of the following conditions:

> ▶ The server on the other side of the link is not running packet burst.

> ▶ The transfer rate for the link is 2400 baud or less. For 2400 baud, set this parameter to 10000 milliseconds.

Name Cache Level (Windows 9x Only)

▶ *Default Value*: 1

▶ *Range*: 0, 1, 2 (0 = disabled, 1 = enabled, 2 = enabled with persistence)

▶ *Description*: Specifies the level of name caching to be used by the client. Name caching refers to the mapping of a service name to an address (IP or IPX). For example, mapping the server named PRV-SERV1 to the IP address of 151.155.204.32. Setting this to 2 allows the client to store service names and their address(es) in a file that will be read the next time the machine is booted, which can result in significantly reduced login times and network traffic.

Name Resolution Timeout (Windows 2000/XP Only)

▶ *Default Value*: 10

▶ *Range*: 1–180 seconds

▶ *Description*: The time in seconds the client will wait for the config-ured namespace providers to resolve the specific name to an address.

NCP Max Timeout (Windows 9x Only)

▶ *Default Value*: 30

▶ *Range*: 0–65535 seconds

▶ *Description*: The amount of time the client is allowed to retry a net-work connection before an error message is displayed.

Net Status Busy Timeout (Windows 9x Only)

▶ *Default Value*: 180

▶ *Range*: 1–600 seconds

▶ *Description*: Specifies the number in seconds to wait for a non-busy response from a server before the client displays an error message.

Net Status Timeout (Windows 9x Only)

▶ *Default Value*: 30

▶ *Range*: 1–600 seconds

▶ *Description*: Specifies the number of seconds to wait for a response from the network to an application's request before the client displays an error message. The difference between this setting and the Net Status Busy Timeout is that this setting is used when there has been *no* response from the server. The Net Status Busy Timeout is used when there has been a Server Busy/Choke/Request Being Processed reply from the server for a request, but the actual requested information has not yet been provided.

NetWare Protocol (Windows 9x Only)

▶ *Default Value*: NDS BIND

▶ *Range*: NDS BIND, BIND NDS, NDS, BIND

▶ *Description*: Legacy setting that controlled in what order the *namespace providers* (formerly NetWare name services) are accessed. This is now controlled on the Name Resolution Order on the Protocol Preferences tab.

Network Printers (Windows 9x Only)

▶ *Default Value*: 3

▶ *Range*: 0–9 printers

▶ *Description*: Sets the number of logical LPT ports the Novell client can capture/redirect. This parameter allows you to capture and redirect LPT1 through LPT9.

Opportunistic Locking (Windows 9x Only)

▶ *Default Value*: OFF

▶ *Range*: ON, OFF

▶ *Description*: If enabled, allows the client to detect opportunities to exclusively cache network files locally. Setting this to ON can dramatically improve file access performance. This parameter has been renamed *File Caching* on 2000/XP clients v4.7 and higher.

Packet Burst (Windows 9x Only)

▶ *Default Value*: 1

▶ *Range*: 0, 1 (0 = OFF, 1 = ON)

▶ *Description*: The packet burst parameter controls the use of the packet burst protocol for file read/write. Generally, packet burst reduces overall network traffic and improves performance. Novell strongly recommends enabling packet burst to improve file read/write performance from NetWare servers.

Packet Burst Read Window Size (Windows 9x Only)

▶ *Default Value*: 24

▶ *Range*: 3–255 packets

▶ *Description*: Specifies the maximum number of packets used in a read burst window size that the client can use. This value controls only the maximum number of packets for a packet burst read window; the actual value in use will depend on network conditions (the client reduces the value used when packets are lost or data in the packet is incomplete). Increasing this value beyond its default might be detrimental to server performance because the client will continue to attempt to increase this value if it has previously backed off because of network problems.

Packet Burst Write Window Size (Windows 9x Only)

▶ *Default Value*: 10

▶ *Range*: 3–255 packets

▶ *Description*: Specifies the maximum number of packets used in a write burst window that the client can use. This value controls the maximum number of packets only for a packet burst write window; the actual value in use will depend on network conditions (the client reduces the value used when packets are lost or data in the packet is incomplete). Increasing this value beyond its default might be detrimental to server performance because the client will continue to attempt to increase this value if it has previously backed off because of network problems.

Polled Broadcast Message Buffers (Windows 9x Only)

▶ *Default Value*: 0

▶ *Range*: 0–100

▶ *Description*: Sets the maximum number of broadcast messages to be saved on the client when Broadcast Message Mode (value in the broadcast packet, not the same as Broadcast Mode) is set to Polled. If more uncleared messages are received than this value allows, subsequent messages will be discarded.

Print Header (Windows 9x Only)

▶ *Default Value*: 64

▶ *Range*: 0–1024 bytes

▶ *Description*: Sets the size of the buffer (in bytes) that holds the information used to initialize the printer for each print job. Increase this value if you are using a complex print job, or when printing to a PostScript printer.

Print Tail (Windows 9x Only)

▶ *Default Value*: 16

▶ *Range*: 0–1024 bytes

▶ *Description*: Sets the size of the buffer (in bytes) that holds the information used to reset the printer after a print job.

Quit Idle Connects (Windows 2000/XP Only)

▶ *Default Value*: 5

▶ *Range*: 1–60000 minutes

▶ *Description*: Time (in minutes) for DAs and SAs to close idle TCP connections.

Read Only Compatibility (Windows 9x Only)

▶ *Default Value*: OFF

▶ *Range*: ON, OFF

▶ *Description*: Determines whether a file marked read-only can be opened with a Read/Write access call. Some applications require this parameter to be ON to function properly.

Receive Broadcast Messages (Windows 2000/XP Only)

▶ *Default Value*: 0

▶ *Range*: 0, 1, 2 (0 = All, 1 = Server Only, 2 = None)

▶ *Description*: Tells the client which broadcast messages, if any, to receive. You can choose one of the following settings: All (receive all broadcast messages), Server Only (receives broadcast messages sent by the server only), or None (do not receive any broadcast messages).

Remove Drive From Environment (Windows 9x Only)

▶ *Default Value*: ON

▶ *Range*: ON, OFF

▶ *Description*: Controls whether network drive letters—all drive letters between the First Network Drive and **Z:**—are removed from the **PATH** variable during login or when a drive mapping is removed/deleted. If the AUTOEXEC.BAT file defines a **PATH** statement that includes a network drive letter that points to a non-NetWare server during the persistent drive reconnecting, it will be removed during login to Netware unless this parameter is set to OFF.

Replica Timeout

▶ *Default Value*: 0

▶ *Range*: 0–1000 (minutes)

▶ *Description*: Amount of time for which the client will attempt to log in to the eDirectory replica previously used as the Primary eDirectory server. By doing this, you can force the client to first attempt to use the same replica for all of its eDirectory operations. When set to 0, the client will use the first replica to respond to a given request.

Resolve Name Using Primary Connection (Windows 9x Only)

▶ *Default Value*: ON

▶ *Range*: ON, OFF

▶ *Description*: Controls whether Resolve Name requests will be done only over the primary connection/primary eDirectory server. If set to OFF, Resolve Name requests can be done over all connections.

Search Dirs First (Windows 9x Only)

▶ *Default Value*: OFF

▶ *Range*: ON, OFF

▶ *Description*: When the Novell client attempts to locate a file/directory request from an application, it does not yet know if it is a file or directory. It first attempts to find the requested path/file as a file and if that fails, it attempts to locate it as a directory. Setting this parameter to ON will change the client to search for a file/directory request as a directory first and a file second. Unless you open more directories than files, leave this setting at its default.

Search Mode (Windows 9x Only)

▶ *Default Value*: 1

▶ *Range*: 1–7

▶ *Description*: Alters the method for finding a file if it is not in the current directory or path. Search Mode has five settings that range from 1, 2, 3, 5, and 7. The default is 1.

  ▶ Mode 1 looks in the search drives only when the application specifies no path and the file is not in the default directory.

  ▶ Mode 2 prevents the Novell client from looking in any search drives for auxiliary files (do not search mode).

  ▶ Mode 3 is similar to mode 1, but it focuses only on read-only search requests.

  ▶ Mode 5 searches on all open paths, even if the application also specifies a path.

  ▶ Mode 7 is similar to mode 5, but it focuses on read-only requests.

Server Cache Timeout (Windows 2000/XP Only)

▶ *Default Value*: 21

▶ *Range*: 0–60

▸ *Description*: Number of days before a server entry, which relates the server name to an IP/IPX address, is cleared out of the file cache. This parameter controls how long an unused entry is stored before it is removed.

Set Station Time

▸ *Default Value*: ON

▸ *Range*: ON, OFF

▸ *Description*: Synchronizes the client workstation date and time with the NetWare server that the client workstation initially attaches to. Setting the value of this parameter to OFF disables synching time from the server to the workstation and allows the workstation time to differ significantly from the network servers.

Short Machine Type

▸ *Default Value*: IBM

▸ *Range*: N/A (Any valid string)

▸ *Description*: Specifies which overlay files to use with the specific machine type of your client workstation. This setting is similar to Long Machine Type, except that it is used specifically with overlay files. The value for this setting can be up to four characters long. Use this setting when the %MACHINE variable is accessed.

Shrink Path to Dot (Windows 9x Only)

▸ *Default Value*: ON

▸ *Range*: ON, OFF

▸ *Description*: Allows network search drives in the DOS PATH variable to either be truncated to a dot or be left with the full directory path.

Signature Level

▸ *Default Value*: 1

▸ *Range*: 0–3 (0 = Disabled, 1 = Enabled, but not preferred, 2 = Preferred, 3 = Required)

▸ *Description*: Determines the level of enhanced security support. Enhanced security includes the use of a message digest algorithm and per-connection/per-request session state. Options 2 and 3 will increase security at the cost of performance.

SLP Active Discovery (Windows 2000/XP Only)

- ▶ *Default Value*: ON
- ▶ *Range*: ON/OFF
- ▶ *Description*: Controls whether SLP is allowed to use multicast to look up services. If it is set to ON, the SLP namespace provider can send multicast requests to Server Agents (SA) in the event the service could not be found using a Directory Agent (DA). Setting this to ON also allows the SLP User Agent (UA) to attempt to locate a DA using multicast. If this is set to OFF, the SLP namespace provider must send unicast service requests to DAs and is not allowed to send multicast requests to SAs.

SLP Cache Replies

- ▶ *Default Value*: 1
- ▶ *Range*: 1–60 minutes
- ▶ *Description*: When SLP receives a service request from a User Agent (UA), the SLP reply is saved for the amount of time specified by the SLP Cache Replies parameter. If SLP receives a duplicate of the request, the cached reply is sent so that the same reply does not have to be generated again.

SLP Default Registration Lifetime

- ▶ *Default Value*: 10800
- ▶ *Range*: 60–60000 seconds
- ▶ *Description*: The Novell clients include the capability to advertise SLP services from workstations (not just servers). In the event an application requests the client to register an SLP service with a DA, this setting controls the time (in seconds) for the default registration lifetime (time before the DA expires/invalidates the service).

SLP Maximum Transmission Unit

- ▶ *Default Value*: 1400
- ▶ *Range*: 576–4096 bytes

▶ *Description*: This parameter specifies the maximum transmission unit (MTU) for the link layer used. Erroneously setting this parameter either too large or too small will adversely affect performance of SLP. This parameter only affects SLP traffic using the UDP protocol; the TCP protocol negotiates its own MTU during connection creation.

SLP Multicast Radius

▶ *Default Value*: 32

▶ *Range*: 1–32

▶ *Client Version*: 9x v3.0 or higher, 2000/XP v4.5 or higher

▶ *Description*: This parameter is a number specifying the maximum number of subnets (number of routers plus 1) that SLP's multicast packets can traverse. This is accomplished by setting the Time to Live (TTL) of the multicast packet equal to this parameter. A value of 1 confines multicasting to the local segment only (all routers will discard the multicast request).

Synch NDS Password (Windows 9x Only)

▶ *Default Value*: ON

▶ *Range*: ON/OFF

▶ *Description:* Updates the Disconnected Workstation Authentication password with the eDirectory password. Synch NDS Password does not alter the Windows User Profile password. To use this parameter, you must have Disconnected Authentication enabled, and the NICI client must be installed on the workstation.

True Commit (Windows 9x Only)

▶ *Default Value*: OFF (NO)

▶ *Range*: ON/OFF (YES/NO)

▶ *Description*: This controls whether buffers flushed by an application are committed immediately to disk on the server. Setting this value to ON will ensure data integrity at the expense of significantly reduced file write performance. This is because when this is set ON, the client must immediately commit the file changes to disk on the server and must wait until the server acknowledges that the changes have been written instead of just requiring an acknowledgment from the server that the write request has been received (shows as disk request and then as dirty cache buffer if it sits long enough). This parameter is similar to the File Commit functionality used in the Windows 2000/XP client.

UNC Path Filter (Windows 2000/XP Only)

▶ *Default Value*: ON

▶ *Range*: ON, OFF

▶ *Description*: Enables/disables the UNC path filter. Filters requests for UNC path resolution sent to the Client for Microsoft Networks (Microsoft Redirector). When enabled, UNC path queries sent to the Microsoft Redirector will first be filtered by the Novell client to see whether the Novell client knows the server name. If the server name is known, the Microsoft Redirector will not attempt a name resolve. If the server name is not known, the usual name resolution process will occur. This can dramatically increase the speed of network file operations and resource mappings.

Use DHCP for SLP

▶ *Default Value*: ON

▶ *Range*: ON, OFF

▶ *Description*: This parameter controls whether the Dynamic Host Configuration Protocol (DHCP) can be used for obtaining SLP Scope and Directory Agent configuration. This is accomplished by the client sending a DHCP Inform Req for the DHCP Option 78 (SLP DA) and 79 (SLP Scope).

Use Extended File Handles (Windows 9x Only)

▶ *Default Value*: ON (YES)

▶ *Range*: ON/OFF (YES/NO)

▶ *Description*: If set to ON, allows the Novell client to open multiple files up to the server parameter MAXIMUM FILE LOCKS PER CONNECTION.

Use Video BIOS (Windows 9x Only)

▶ *Default Value*: OFF

▶ *Range*: ON, OFF

▶ *Description*: Specifies whether the client uses BIOS or Direct Video Memory calls when a pop-up message is displayed. The BIOS method is slower than the Direct Video Memory calls.

Wait Before Giving Up on DA

▶ *Default Value*: 5

▶ *Range*: 1–60000 seconds

▶ *Description*: This parameter specifies the amount of time that SLP will wait before giving up on a request to a Directory Agent.

Wait Before Registering on Passive DA

▶ *Default Value*: 2

▶ *Range*: 1–60000 seconds

▶ *Description*: Specifies the range of time for the random delay interval before a Server Agent reregisters its service with the Directory Agent.

Workstation Manager Login Events (Windows 2000/XP Only)

▶ *Default Value*: OFF

▶ *Range*: ON, OFF

▶ *Description*: Enables/disables Novell client login event notifications to be sent to Workstation Manager. These events allow the ZENWorks Policy Scheduler to launch policies scheduled for these event types. If you disable the Initial Novell Login or if users log in to eDirectory from the red N menu, you should enable this setting so that login events will be forwarded to Workstation Manager.

Advanced Menu Settings Tab

Cancel Desktop Login (Windows 9x Only)

▶ *Default Value*: OFF

▶ *Range*: ON/OFF (YES/NO)

▶ *Description*: Allows/disallows the canceling of the desktop login.

Change Password

- ▶ *Default Value*: ON
- ▶ *Range*: ON, OFF
- ▶ *Description*: Enables/disables the Change Password button in the Novell Password Administration dialog box (available when right-clicking the Novell red N in the system tray [Systray] and selecting User Administration for [your_eDirectory_Tree]). If disabled, the Change Password button is still displayed in the Novell Password Administration dialog box, but it is grayed out (disabled) and cannot be selected.

Display Bindery Services Page

- ▶ *Default Value*: ON
- ▶ *Range*: ON, OFF
- ▶ *Description*: Enables/disables the Bindery Services configuration page.

Display Container Page

- ▶ *Default Value*: ON
- ▶ *Range*: ON, OFF
- ▶ *Description*: Displays the Bindery Container page. The Container page is accessed by selecting Properties from the context menu of the selected container icon in Network Neighborhood.

Display DFS Junction Information Page

- ▶ *Default Value*: ON
- ▶ *Range*: ON, OFF
- ▶ *Description*: Enables/disables the DFS Junction Information tab. When enabled, this tab is available from the DFS Junction Properties page associated with a DFS Junction object.

Display Directory Map Object Page

- ▶ *Default Value*: ON
- ▶ *Range*: ON, OFF
- ▶ *Description*: Enables/disables the NetWare Directory Map Object Information page for the Directory Map object. This property page

shows the full eDirectory object Path (context) and eDirectory tree as well as the server, volume, and directory path the Directory Map Object references. Disabling this property page does not disable other property pages (such as NetWare Info or NetWare Rights), nor does it restrict a user's ability to use this Directory Map Object (eDirectory rights/ACL).

Display Directory Services Page

▶ *Default Value*: ON

▶ *Range*: ON, OFF

▶ *Description*: Enables/disables the properties page for the Novell Directory Services selection. The Novell Directory Services selection is available under Network Neighborhood, Entire Network, and NetWare Services. Disabling this setting does not prevent a user from opening the Novell Directory Services selection and browsing within the eDirectory tree, only from viewing the properties.

Display NetWare Information Page

▶ *Default Value*: ON

▶ *Range*: ON, OFF

▶ *Description*: Enables/disables the NetWare Info page for a volume, directory, or file object when browsing within Network Neighborhood. This property page shows the namespaces loaded, the assigned owner, space restrictions, space available, create/last modified dates, and NetWare directory/file attributes. Disabling this property page does not disable other property pages (such as NetWare Rights), nor does it restrict a user's ability to use the volume, directory, or file (managed using eDirectory rights/ACL).

Display NetWare Rights Page

▶ *Default Value*: ON

▶ *Range*: ON, OFF

▶ *Description*: Enables/disables the NetWare Rights page for a volume, directory, or file object when browsing within Network Neighborhood. This property page shows the direct trustee assignments, inherited rights filters, and effective rights (for the logged-in user). Disabling this property page does not disable other property pages (such as NetWare Info), nor does it restrict a user's ability to use the volume, directory, or file (managed using eDirectory rights/ACL).

Display Server Page

- ▶ *Default Value*: ON
- ▶ *Range*: ON, OFF
- ▶ *Description*: Enables/disables the properties page for a NetWare Server object when browsing within Network Neighborhood. This page is normally viewed when browsing inside of Network Neighborhood, either browsing inside eDirectory containers or under NetWare servers. The NetWare Server Information property page shows the server name, company, version, revision date, network address(es) (both IPX/IP), connections in use, max licensed connections, eDirectory tree, and full eDirectory Server object name/context. Disabling this property does not restrict a user's ability to use the server.

Display Tree Page

- ▶ *Default Value*: ON
- ▶ *Range*: ON, OFF
- ▶ *Description*: Enables/disables the properties page for a NetWare Tree object when browsing within Network Neighborhood. This page is normally viewed when browsing inside of Network Neighborhood, either browsing inside eDirectory containers or under NetWare servers. The NetWare Tree Information property page shows the company and tree name. Disabling this property page does not restrict a user's ability to use the tree.

Display Volume Information Page

- ▶ *Default Value*: ON
- ▶ *Range*: ON, OFF
- ▶ *Description*: Enables/disables the NetWare Volume Information page for a Volume object when browsing within Network Neighborhood. This property page shows the volume name, storing server, namespaces, volume number, block size, installed features (suballoc, compression), user restrictions, and free/used disk for the

user. Disabling this property page does not disable other property pages (such as NetWare Volume Statistics, NetWare Info, or NetWare Rights), nor does it restrict a user's ability to use the volume (managed using eDirectory rights/ACL).

Display Volume Statistics Page

▶ *Default Value*: ON

▶ *Range*: ON, OFF

▶ *Description*: Enables/disables the NetWare Volume Statistics page for a Volume object when browsing within Network Neighborhood. This property page shows the volume name, disk total space, free space, compressed space, purgeable space, used space, total directory entries, available directory entries, and used directory entries. Disabling this property page does not disable other property pages (such as NetWare Volume Information, NetWare Info, or NetWare Rights), nor does it restrict a user's ability to use the volume (managed using eDirectory rights/ACL).

Enable Authenticate to Server

▶ *Default Value*: ON

▶ *Range*: ON, OFF

▶ *Description*: Enables/disables the selection for Authenticate when right-clicking a NetWare server in Network Neighborhood. If disabled, the selection for Authenticate is still displayed when right-clicking a NetWare server, but it is grayed out.

Enable Authenticate to Tree

▶ *Default Value*: ON

▶ *Range*: ON, OFF

▶ *Description*: Enables/disables the selection for Authenticate when right-clicking an eDirectory tree in Network Neighborhood. If disabled, the selection for Authenticate is still displayed when right-clicking an eDirectory tree, but it is grayed out.

Enable Browse To Dialog

▶ *Default Value*: ON

▶ *Range*: ON/OFF (YES/NO)

▶ *Client Version*: 9x v3.2 or higher, 2000/XP v4.7 or higher

▶ *Description*: Enables/disables the selection for Browse To when right-clicking the Novell red N in the system tray. If disabled, the selection for Browse To is still displayed when right-clicking the Novell red N, but it is grayed out.

Enable Capture Dialog

▶ *Default Value*: ON

▶ *Range*: ON, OFF

▶ *Description*: Enables/disables the selection for Novell Capture Printer Port when right-clicking the Novell red N in the system tray (Systray). If disabled, the selection for Novell Capture Printer Port is still displayed when right-clicking the Novell red N, but it is grayed out.

Enable Change Context Dialog

▶ *Default Value*: ON

▶ *Range*: ON, OFF

▶ *Description*: Enables/disables the selection for Change Context when right-clicking an eDirectory tree in Network Neighborhood. If disabled, the selection for Change Context is still displayed when right-clicking an eDirectory tree, but it is grayed out.

Enable Disconnect Dialog

▶ *Default Value*: ON

▶ *Range*: ON, OFF

▶ *Description*: Enables/disables the selection for Disconnect Network Drive when right-clicking the Novell red N in the system tray. If disabled, the selection for Disconnect Network Drive is still displayed when right-clicking the Novell red N, but it is grayed out.

Enable End Capture Dialog

▶ *Default Value*: ON

▶ *Range*: ON, OFF

▶ *Description*: Enables/disables the selection for Novell End Capture when right-clicking the Novell red N in the system tray. If disabled, the selection for Novell End Capture is still displayed when right-clicking the Novell red N, but it is grayed out.

Enable Group Membership Dialog

- ▶ *Default Value*: ON
- ▶ *Range*: ON, OFF
- ▶ *Description*: Enables/disables the selection for Group Memberships when right-clicking the Novell red N in the system tray and selecting User Administration for [your_eDirectory_Tree]. If disabled, the selection for Group Memberships is still displayed when right-clicking the Novell red N, but it is grayed out.

Enable Inherited Rights Dialog

- ▶ *Default Value*: ON
- ▶ *Range*: ON, OFF
- ▶ *Description*: Enables/disables the selection for Inherited Rights and Filters when right-clicking the Novell red N in the system tray and selecting NetWare Utilities. If disabled, the selection for Inherited Rights and Filters is still displayed when right-clicking the Novell red N, but it is grayed out.

Enable Login Administration

- ▶ *Default Value*: ON
- ▶ *Range*: ON, OFF
- ▶ *Description*: Enables/disables the selection for Login Account Information when right-clicking the Novell red N in the system tray and selecting User Administration for [your_eDirectory_Tree]. If disabled, the selection for Login Account Information is still displayed when right-clicking the Novell red N, but it is grayed out.

Enable Login Dialog

- ▶ *Default Value*: ON
- ▶ *Range*: ON, OFF
- ▶ *Description*: Enables/disables the selection for NetWare Login when right-clicking the Novell red N in the system tray. If disabled, the

selection for NetWare Login is still displayed when right-clicking the Novell red N, but it is grayed out.

Enable Login to Server

- ▶ *Default Value*: ON
- ▶ *Range*: ON, OFF
- ▶ *Description*: Enables/disables the selection for Login to Server when right-clicking a NetWare server in Network Neighborhood. If disabled, the selection for Login to Server is still displayed when right-clicking a NetWare server, but it is grayed out.

Enable Logout of Server

- ▶ *Default Value*: ON
- ▶ *Range*: ON, OFF
- ▶ *Description*: Enables/disables the selection for Logout when right-clicking a NetWare server in Network Neighborhood. If disabled, the selection for Logout is still displayed when right-clicking a NetWare server, but it is grayed out.

Enable Logout of Tree

- ▶ *Default Value*: ON
- ▶ *Range*: ON, OFF
- ▶ *Description*: Enables/disables the selection for Logout when right-clicking an eDirectory tree in Network Neighborhood. If disabled, the selection for Logout is still displayed when right-clicking an eDirectory tree, but it is grayed out.

Enable Map Dialog

- ▶ *Default Value*: ON
- ▶ *Range*: ON, OFF
- ▶ *Description*: Enables/disables the selection for Novell Map Network Drive when right-clicking the Novell red N in the system tray. If disabled, the selection for Novell Map Network Drive is still displayed when right-clicking the Novell red N, but it is grayed out.

Enable Modify Container Script

- ▶ *Default Value*: ON
- ▶ *Range*: ON, OFF
- ▶ *Description*: Enables/disables the selection for Edit NDS Container Login script when right-clicking an eDirectory Container object in Network Neighborhood. If disabled, the selection for Edit NDS Container Login Script is still displayed when right-clicking an eDirectory Container object, but it is grayed out.

Enable NDS Login To Tree

- ▶ *Default Value*: ON
- ▶ *Range*: ON, OFF
- ▶ *Description*: Enables/disables the selection for Login to NDS tree when right-clicking an eDirectory Tree object in Network Neighborhood. If disabled, the selection for Login to NDS tree is still displayed when right-clicking an eDirectory tree, but it is grayed out.

Enable NDS Mailing Information

- ▶ *Default Value*: ON
- ▶ *Range*: ON, OFF
- ▶ *Description*: Enables/disables the selection for Mailing Information when right-clicking the Novell red N in the system tray and selecting User Administration for [your_eDirectory_Tree]. If disabled, the selection for Mailing Information is still displayed when right-clicking the Novell red N, but it is grayed out.

Enable NDS Personal Information

- ▶ *Default Value*: ON
- ▶ *Range*: ON, OFF
- ▶ *Description*: Enables/disables the selection for Personal Information when right-clicking the Novell red N in the system tray and selecting User Administration for [your_eDirectory_Tree]. If disabled, the selection for Personal Information is still displayed when right-clicking the Novell red N, but it is grayed out.

Enable NDS Work Information

- ▶ *Default Value*: ON
- ▶ *Range*: ON, OFF
- ▶ *Description*: Enables/disables the selection for Work Information when right-clicking the Novell red N in the system tray and selecting User Administration for [your_eDirectory_Tree]. If disabled, the selection for Work Information is still displayed when right-clicking the Novell red N, but it is grayed out.

Enable NetWare Connections Dialog

- ▶ *Default Value*: ON
- ▶ *Range*: ON,OFF
- ▶ *Description*: Enables/disables the selection for NetWare Connections when right-clicking the Novell red N in the system tray. If disabled, the selection for NetWare Connections is still displayed when right-clicking the Novell red N, but it is grayed out.

Enable NetWare Copy Dialog

- ▶ *Default Value*: ON
- ▶ *Range*: ON/OFF (YES/NO)
- ▶ *Client Version*: 9x v3.2 or higher, 2000/XP v4.7 or higher
- ▶ *Description*: Enables/disables the selection for NetWare Copy when right-clicking the Novell red N in the system tray and selecting NetWare Utilities. If disabled, the selection for NetWare Copy is still displayed when right-clicking the Novell red N, but it is grayed out.

Enable NetWare Utilities

- ▶ *Default Value*: ON
- ▶ *Range*: ON, OFF
- ▶ *Description*: Enables/disables the selection for NetWare Utilities when right-clicking the Novell red N in the system tray. If disabled, the selection for NetWare Utilities is still displayed when right-clicking the Novell red N, but it is grayed out.

Enable Novell Client Help

- ▶ *Default Value*: ON

- ▶ *Range*: ON, OFF

- ▶ *Description*: Enables/disables the selection for Novell Client Help when right-clicking the Novell red N in the system tray. If disabled, the selection for Novell Client Help is still displayed when right-clicking the Novell red N, but it is grayed out.

Enable Novell Client Properties

- ▶ *Default Value*: ON

- ▶ *Range*: ON, OFF

- ▶ *Description*: Enables/disables the selection for Novell Client Properties when right-clicking the Novell red N in the system tray. If disabled, the selection for Novell Client Properties is still displayed when right-clicking the Novell red N, but it is grayed out.

Enable Object Properties Dialog

- ▶ *Default Value*: ON

- ▶ *Range*: ON, OFF

- ▶ *Description*: Enables/disables the selection for Object Properties when right-clicking the Novell red N in the system tray and selecting NetWare Utilities. If disabled, the selection for Object Properties is still displayed when right-clicking the Novell red N, but it is grayed out.

Enable Password Administration

- ▶ *Default Value*: ON

- ▶ *Range*: ON, OFF

- ▶ *Description*: Enables/disables the selection for Novell Password Administration when right-clicking the Novell red N in the system tray and selecting User Administration for `[your_eDirectory_Tree]`. If disabled, the selection for Novell Password Administration is still displayed when right-clicking the Novell red N, but it is grayed out.

Enable Purge Dialog

- ▶ *Default Value*: ON
- ▶ *Range*: ON, OFF
- ▶ *Description*: Enables/disables the selection for Purge when right-clicking the Novell red N in the system tray and selecting NetWare Utilities. If disabled, the selection for Purge is still displayed when right-clicking the Novell red N, but it is grayed out.

Enable Salvage Dialog

- ▶ *Default Value*: ON
- ▶ *Range*: ON, OFF
- ▶ *Description*: Enables/disables the selection for Salvage when right-clicking the Novell red N in the system tray and selecting NetWare Utilities. If disabled, the selection for Salvage is still displayed when right-clicking the Novell red N, but it is grayed out.

Enable Send Message

- ▶ *Default Value*: ON
- ▶ *Range*: ON, OFF
- ▶ *Description*: Enables/disables the selection for Send Message when right-clicking the Novell red N in the system tray and selecting Send Message. If disabled, the Send Message option is still displayed when right-clicking the Novell red N, but it is grayed out.

Enable Send Message To Server Dialog

- ▶ *Default Value*: ON
- ▶ *Range*: ON, OFF
- ▶ *Description*: Enables/disables the selection for To Server Console when right-clicking a NetWare Server object in Network Neighborhood and selecting Send Message or when using the Send Message selection by right-clicking the red N in the system tray and selecting NetWare Utilities and Send Message. If disabled, the selection for To Server Console is still displayed in the Send Message menu, but it is grayed out.

Enable Send Message To User Dialog

▶ *Default Value*: ON

▶ *Range*: ON, OFF

▶ *Description*: Enables/disables the selection for To Users when right-clicking a NetWare Server object in Network Neighborhood and selecting Send Message or when using the Send Message selection by right-clicking the red N in the system tray and selecting NetWare Utilities and Send Message. If disabled, the selection for To Users is still displayed in the Send Message menu, but it is grayed out.

Enable Set Current Tree

▶ *Default Value*: ON

▶ *Range*: ON, OFF

▶ *Description*: Enables/disables the selection for Set Current Tree when right-clicking an eDirectory tree in Network Neighborhood. If disabled, the selection for Set Current Tree is still displayed when right-clicking an eDirectory tree, but it is grayed out.

Enable Set Default Context

▶ *Default Value*: ON

▶ *Range*: ON, OFF

▶ *Description*: Enables/disables the selection for Set Default Context when right-clicking an eDirectory Container object in Network Neighborhood. If disabled, the selection for Set Default Context is still displayed when right-clicking an eDirectory Container object, but it is grayed out.

Enable Show Parent Context

▶ *Default Value*: ON

▶ *Range*: ON, OFF

▶ *Description*: Enables/disables the selection for Show Parent Context when right-clicking an eDirectory Container object in Network Neighborhood. If disabled, the selection for Show Parent Context is still displayed when right-clicking an eDirectory Container object, but it is grayed out.

Enable Systray Config Dialog

- ▶ *Default Value*: ON
- ▶ *Range*: ON, OFF
- ▶ *Description*: Enables/disables the selection for Configure System Tray Icon when right-clicking the Novell red N in the system tray. If disabled, the selection for Configure System Tray Icon is still displayed when right-clicking the Novell red N, but it is grayed out.

Enable Trustee Rights Dialog

- ▶ *Default Value*: ON
- ▶ *Range*: ON, OFF
- ▶ *Description*: Enables/disables the selection for Trustee Rights when right-clicking the Novell red N in the system tray and selecting NetWare Utilities. If disabled, the selection for Trustee Rights is still displayed when right-clicking the Novell red N, but it is grayed out.

Enable Update Novell Client

- ▶ *Default Value*: ON
- ▶ *Range*: ON, OFF
- ▶ *Description*: Enables/disables the Update Novell Client menu option that is available by right-clicking the Novell red N in the system tray.

Enable Who Am I Dialog

- ▶ *Default Value*: ON
- ▶ *Range*: ON, OFF
- ▶ *Description*: Enables/disables the selection for WhoAmI when right-clicking an eDirectory tree or NetWare server in Network Neighborhood. If disabled, the selection for WhoAmI is still displayed when right-clicking an eDirectory tree or NetWare server, but it is grayed out.

Filter User List

- ▶ *Default Value*: OFF
- ▶ *Range*: ON, OFF

▶ *Description*: Has the same functionality as the selection for Show Only User Objects in List when right-clicking the Novell red N in the system tray and selecting NetWare Utilities, Send Message, and then To Users. If this is enabled, only user objects will be shown in the Send Message dialog box.

Force Bindery Connections

▶ *Default Value*: OFF

▶ *Range*: ON, OFF

▶ *Description*: Forces the Novell Login dialog box to utilize Bindery login credentials to authenticate, rather than using eDirectory authentication.

Force Login Dialog (Windows 9x Only)

▶ *Default Value*: OFF

▶ *Range*: ON, OFF

▶ *Description*: Forces the Login dialog box on initial login. Setting this parameter to ON forces the login at initial login rather than attempting a background authentication. This is only utilized when the Primary Network Logon is *not* set to Novell's provider.

Show Bindery Servers

▶ *Default Value*: ON

▶ *Range*: ON, OFF

▶ *Description*: Enables/disables the option for NetWare servers in the Network Neighborhood Entire Network/NetWare Services (still leaves the option for Novell Directory Services). When the option for NetWare servers is selected, it will attempt to locate all NetWare servers on the network using the enabled namespace providers. When IPX is enabled on the server, this allows the client to issue a bindery scan request for type **0004** (NW File Server SAP). If this occurs frequently enough, it can increase server utilization and reduce server performance/responsiveness.

Show Current Connections

▶ *Default Value*: ON

▶ *Range*: ON, OFF

▶ *Description*: Enables/disables the display of the currently connected NetWare servers and eDirectory trees when opening Network Neighborhood.

Show Edit Login Script Item

▶ *Default Value*: ON

▶ *Range*: ON, OFF

▶ *Description*: Enables/disables the selection for Edit Login Script when right-clicking the Novell red N in the system tray and selecting User Administration for `[your_eDirectory_Tree]`. If disabled, the selection for Edit Login Script is still displayed when right-clicking the Novell red N, but it is grayed out.

Show NDS Description

▶ *Default Value*: OFF

▶ *Range*: ON, OFF

▶ *Description*: Shows the Description eDirectory attribute of all leaf objects under the Comment column when browsing contexts inside the eDirectory tree using Network Neighborhood. The Comments column is visible only when the Network Neighborhood view is set to Details (under the View drop-down menu). Even when set to Details, this will not display the Description attribute of Container objects (Country, Organization, and Organizational Unit)—only the Description attribute of Leaf objects.

Show NDS Objects

▶ *Default Value*: ON

▶ *Range*: ON, OFF

▶ *Description*: Enables/disables the display of all eDirectory type objects in Network Neighborhood. This includes eDirectory trees, containers, any eDirectory Leaf objects, and the removal of the Novell Directory Services option under NetWare Services. When this setting is disabled, all views displayed are using bindery namespace providers.

Show Novell System Tray Icon

- ▶ *Default Value*: ON
- ▶ *Range*: ON, OFF
- ▶ *Description*: Enables/disables the display of the red N in the system tray. Disabling this will not affect the user's ability to perform the same tasks using other methods (such as mapping a drive in Network Neighborhood); it only disables this interface.

Show Scheduler System Tray Icon

- ▶ *Default Value*: ON
- ▶ *Range*: ON, OFF
- ▶ *Description*: Disables/enables the display of the ZEN for Desktops icon, previously known as the Workstation Manager Scheduler.

Show User Administration Menu

- ▶ *Default Value*: ON
- ▶ *Range*: ON, OFF
- ▶ *Description*: Enables/disables the selection for User Administration for [your_eDirectory_Tree] when right-clicking the Novell red N in the system tray. If disabled, the selection for User Administration for [your_eDirectory_Tree] is still displayed when right-clicking the Novell red N, but it is grayed out.

Use NDS Dot Format for Browsing

- ▶ *Default Value*: ON
- ▶ *Range*: ON, OFF
- ▶ *Description*: When enabled, eDirectory contexts will be built using the familiar dot notation. If disabled, backslashes (\) will be used.

Default Capture Tab

Number of Copies

- ▶ *Default Value*: 1
- ▶ *Range*: 1–255
- ▶ *Description*: Specifies the number of copies to print.

Form Feed

- ▶ *Default Value*: 0 (Unchecked)
- ▶ *Range*: 0, 1 (0 = Unchecked, 1 = Checked)
- ▶ *Description*: If you want the printer to add a blank piece of paper at the end of the print job, enable this check box.

Enable Tabs

- ▶ *Default Value*: 0 (Unchecked)
- ▶ *Range*: 0, 1 (0 = Unchecked, 1 = Checked)
- ▶ *Description*: If you want to print the specified number of spaces in place of tab characters, enable this check box. If you don't want spaces to be printed in place of tabs, disable this check box. Byte-stream print jobs do not require tabs to be enabled. Some graphics print data contain tab characters, so this option might cause some graphics jobs to print incorrectly.

Number of Spaces

- ▶ *Default Value*: 8
- ▶ *Range*: 1–18 spaces
- ▶ *Description*: Specifies the number of spaces that are printed in place of tab characters. You must check the Enable Tabs check box for this setting to take effect.

Enable Banner

- ▶ *Default Value*: 0 (Unchecked)
- ▶ *Range*: 0, 1 (0 = Unchecked, 1 = Checked)
- ▶ *Description*: If you want a banner page for each print job, enable this check box.

1st Banner Name

- ▶ *Default Value*: NULL
- ▶ *Range*: Any valid string
- ▶ *Description*: Specifies the text printed on the upper half of the banner page. This text can be up to 12 characters long.

2nd Banner Name

▶ *Default Value*: NULL

▶ *Range*: Any valid string

▶ *Client Version*: 9x v2.5 or higher, 2000/XP v4.3 or higher

▶ *Description*: Specifies the text printed on the lower half of the banner page. This text can be up to 12 characters long.

Hold

▶ *Default Value*: 0 (Unchecked)

▶ *Range*: 0, 1 (0 = Unchecked, 1 = Checked)

▶ *Client Version*: 9x v2.5 or higher, 2000/XP v4.3 or higher

▶ *Description*: To put a user hold on print jobs, enable this check box.

Keep

▶ *Default Value*: 0 (Unchecked)

▶ *Range*: 0, 1 (0 = Unchecked, 1 = Checked)

▶ *Description*: If you want to keep jobs in the print queue after they have completed printing, enable this check box.

Notify

▶ *Default Value*: 1 (Checked)

▶ *Range*: 0, 1 (0 = Unchecked, 1 = Checked)

▶ *Description*: If you want to receive a pop-up message when the print job is printed, enable this check box.

Seconds Before Timeout (Windows 9x Only)

▶ *Default Value*: 0

▶ *Range*: 0–1000 seconds

▶ *Description*: Specifies the number of seconds the operating system waits after the last data is received before closing the print job.

Protocol Preferences Tab

Name Resolution Order (Windows 9x Only)

- ▶ *Default Value*: NWHOST, SLP, DNS, DHCP, NDS, BIND, SAP

- ▶ *Range*: Any combination of the previous entries in any order.

- ▶ *Description*: The list specifies the order in which namespace providers are used to attempt to resolve service names. All configured name service providers (NSP) are queried asynchronously in order to resolve a service name to an address. They are first queried with a cache flag that allows NSPs who maintain a cache to attempt to resolve the name. If no NSP resolves the name, they are queried again without the cache flag, allowing NSPs to attempt to resolve the name on the network. The client either waits the time specified by the Name Resolution Timeout value or until all the queried NSPs respond with a `NOT_FOUND` or `NO_MORE` status.

Preferred Network Protocol (Windows 2000/XP Only)

- ▶ *Default Value*: IP

- ▶ *Range*: IP, IPX

- ▶ *Description*: The client will wait up to one quarter of the Name Resolution Timeout value to resolve the specified name to an address of the preferred network type.

Protocol Component Settings (Windows 2000/XP Only)

- ▶ *Default Value*: CLSID for this namespace provider service.

- ▶ *Range*: N/A

- ▶ *Description*: This list specifies the order in which name service providers (NSPs) are queried to resolve a network name.

LDAP Contextless Login (Windows 2000/XP Only)

Enable LDAP Treeless Login

- ▶ *Default Value*: OFF
- ▶ *Range*: ON, OFF
- ▶ *Description*: Check this box to enable a treeless login, which lets users log in without specifying an eDirectory tree.

Enable LDAP Contextless Login

- ▶ *Default Value*: OFF
- ▶ *Range*: ON, OFF
- ▶ *Description*: Check this box to enable a contextless login, which lets users log in without specifying an object context. This option requires LDAP services for eDirectory on the server hosting a replica of the tree to which you want to authenticate.

Enable LDAP Context Search Scope

- ▶ *Default Value*: OFF
- ▶ *Range*: ON, OFF
- ▶ *Description*: This option allows you to restrict the scope of the LDAP search to a specific context, set of contexts, or sub-trees.

Trees

- ▶ *Default Value*: N/A
- ▶ *Range*: N/A
- ▶ *Description*: Specifies the directory tree, or trees, that will participate in the LDAP contextless login.

Servers

- ▶ *Default Value*: N/A
- ▶ *Range*: N/A
- ▶ *Description*: Specifies the server, or servers, associated with the eDirectory tree that will be searched during the authentication process.

Settings Button

▶ *Default Value*: N/A

▶ *Range*: N/A

▶ *Description*: Provides an additional page of options for configuring the LDAP login process, including attributes that will be displayed during login and those attributes that can be used to search for the requested LDAP object in order to perform the login.

Single Sign-On Tab (Windows 2000/XP Only)

Enable Single Sign-On

▶ *Default Value*: OFF

▶ *Range*: ON, OFF

▶ *Description*: The Single Sign-On tab is available as a convenience for NMAS users authenticating via a biometric login method.

DHCP Settings Tab (Windows 2000/XP Only)

Use Server

▶ *Default Value*: OFF

▶ *Range*: ON, OFF

▶ *Description*: Enabling this parameter overrides the DHCP Option Tag 85 (Preferred Server) with the value of the selected Location Profile Login Service. It discards any Preferred Server value passed in from DHCP. It is possible to enable this parameter without specifying Login Service. In this case, the Novell client will behave as if neither Login Service Server nor DHCP Option Tag 85 parameter were set.

Use Server from Login Service

▶ *Default Value*: Undefined

▶ *Range*: Undefined or Default

▶ *Description*: Determines what Location Profile Login Service is accessed for the Server value.

Use Tree

▶ *Default Value*: OFF

▶ *Range*: ON, OFF

▶ *Description*: Enabling this parameter overrides the DHCP Option Tag 86 (Preferred Tree) with the value of the selected Location Profile Login Service. It discards any Preferred Tree value passed in from DHCP. It is possible to enable this parameter without specifying Login Service. In this case, the Novell client will behave as if neither Login Service Tree nor DHCP Option Tag 86 parameter were set.

Use Tree from Login Service

▶ *Default Value*: Undefined

▶ *Range*: Undefined or Default

▶ *Description*: Determines which Location Profile Login Service is accessed for the Tree value.

Use Context

▶ *Default Value*: OFF

▶ *Range*: ON, OFF

▶ *Description*: Enabling this parameter overrides the DHCP Option Tag 87 (Name Context) with the value of the selected Location Profile Login Service. It discards any Name Context value passed in from DHCP. It is possible to enable this parameter without specifying Login Service. In this case, the Novell client will behave as if neither Login Service Context nor DHCP Option Tag 87 parameter were set.

Use Context from Login Service

▶ *Default Value*: Undefined

▶ *Range*: Undefined or Default

▶ *Description*: Determines which Location Profile Login Service is accessed for the Context value.

DSCAT Contextless Login Tab

Enable

▶ *Default Value*: OFF

▶ *Range*: ON, OFF

▶ *Description*: Check this box to enable contextless login. Contextless login makes it possible to log in to the network without specifying an eDirectory context. Contextless login requires the catalog and dredger services to be configured on a NetWare server and will not work without this preparation.

Wildcard Searching Allowed

▶ *Default Value*: OFF

▶ *Range*: ON, OFF

▶ *Description*: Available only if the contextless login is enabled. If enabled, a user can use wildcards in the username, rather than having to enter the entire username. For example, a user with the username JHARRIS could enter JHAR* as the search string.

Search Timeout (Sec)

▶ *Default Value*: 2 (seconds)

▶ *Range*: 0–999 seconds

▶ *Description*: Specifies that maximum amount of time that you want the Novell Login to search eDirectory for the specified user. If your searches are timing out before the user is located, increase this setting to allow more time. However, setting this value too high will create extended delays when searching for an invalid or unavailable user.

Tree/Catalog Key Pair

▶ *Default Value*: N/A

▶ *Range*: N/A

▶ *Description*: During a login session, usable catalogs are automatically found. You can specify tree and catalog pairs to force contextless logins to use a specific catalog for each tree in the list. For each tree/catalog pair, there will be a string value with the name of the tree and the value of the catalog.

Update Agent

Enable Automatic Update Agent

▶ *Default Value*: OFF

▶ *Range*: ON, OFF

▶ *Description*: Enables/disables the Novell Automatic Update Agent on this workstation. If enabled, the Agent loads during the login process.

Update Agent Launch Interval (Days)

▶ *Default Value*: 7 (days)

▶ *Range*: 0–999 days

▶ *Description*: If the Update Agent is enabled, specify the interval at which the agent will check for an updated client. Setting a value of 0 effectively disables the Update Agent.

Update Location

▶ *Default Value*: OFF

▶ *Range*: ON, OFF

▶ *Description*: Enabling Update Location lets you specify a specific path to the new client files. If more than one of the three Update Sources is enabled, Update Location is the first in order of precedence. Specify the location of the new client files in the associated dialog box. This can be a UNC path, a mapped drive, or a URL.

Previous Install Location

- ▶ *Default Value*: OFF
- ▶ *Range*: ON, OFF
- ▶ *Description*: Enabling Previous Install Location instructs the Update Agent to look for updated client files at the same location from which the Novell client was previously installed. If more than one of the three Update Sources is enabled, Previous Install Location is the second in order of precedence. This path is not editable.

Unattend File

- ▶ *Default Value*: N/A
- ▶ *Range*: N/A
- ▶ *Description*: Specifies the name of the Unattend file that should be used with the client update. The Unattend file must reside in the same location specified by the Update Location or the Previous Install Location. Unattend files will not be used with the Novell Client Update Web Site.

Suppress Update Prompt

- ▶ *Default Value*: OFF
- ▶ *Range*: ON, OFF
- ▶ *Description*: Enabling this option prevents the Update Agent from querying the user before the client update routine starts. It will begin automatically without user intervention.

Support Pack Update

- ▶ *Default Value*: OFF
- ▶ *Range*: ON, OFF
- ▶ *Description*: Enabling this option lets the Update Agent go directly to a support pack subdirectory and review/update only the support pack files rather than having to review every client file. To do this, the support pack directory, named \SP, must be in the location specified by the Update Location or Previous Install Location.

Administrator Rights

- ▶ *Default Value*: ON

- ▶ *Range*: ON, OFF

- ▶ *Description*: If the user who logs in to the workstation does not have administrative rights to the workstation, check this box to grant administrative rights to the Update Agent during a client upgrade. Administrative rights are required during the client upgrade routine.

NetWare Login Scripts

When a user successfully logs in to the network, Novell Login executes one or more login scripts that automatically set up the workstation environment. Login scripts are similar to batch files and are executed by the Novell Login utility. You can use login scripts to map drives and search drives to directories, display messages, set environment variables, and execute programs or menus. Login scripts are properties of specific eDirectory objects.

Working with Login Scripts

There are four types of login scripts:

- *Container*: Sets the general environment for all users in that container. Novell Login executes container login scripts first. Container login scripts can be associated with Organization or Organizational Unit objects. A user login will use only the container login script for the container in which their object resides.

- *Profile*: Sets environments for several users at the same time. Novell Login executes a profile login script after the container login script. Profile login scripts are associated with profile objects. A user can be assigned only one profile login script but can choose other profile login scripts.

- *User*: Sets environments (such as printing options or an email username) specific to a single user. Novell Login executes the user login script after any container and profile login scripts have executed.

User login scripts are associated with User objects. A user can have only one user login script.

▶ *Default*: Contains only essential commands, such as drive mappings to NetWare utilities, and cannot be edited. It runs if a user (including user admin) doesn't have a user login script, even if a container or profile login script exists. You can prevent the default login script from running by placing the `NO_DEFAULT` command in a container or profile login script.

NOTE Before you create or modify login scripts, you must have the Write property right to the object that will contain the login script. The Organization, Organizational Unit, Profile, or User object that you plan to assign the login script to must exist.

Creating or Modifying a Login Script

To create or modify a login script with ConsoleOne, follow these steps:

1. Launch iManager and click View Objects in the header frame.

2. Browse to the object whose login script you want to create or modify.

3. Click the object and select Modify Object. Select the Login Script tab to open the login script editor.

4. Enter the login script commands and information into the Login Script text box, or specify a profile script to associate with this object. Click OK to save your changes when finished.

Maintaining many user login scripts can be time-consuming. Therefore, you should try to include as much customization information as possible in the container and profile login scripts, which are fewer in number and easier to maintain. For example:

▶ If all users need access to the NetWare utilities in the same volume, put the search drive mapping to that volume in a single container login script rather than in every user login script.

▶ Create profile login scripts if multiple objects have identical login script needs.

▶ In user login scripts, include only those individual items that can't be included in profile or container login scripts.

▶ If you don't want to create any user login scripts and you don't want the default login script to execute for any users, you can disable the default login script by including the `NO_DEFAULT` command in the container or profile login script.

WARNING Because up to three login scripts can execute whenever a user logs in, conflicts can occur and consecutive login scripts can overwrite drive mappings. It is important to note that the last login script to execute (usually the user login script) overrides any conflicting commands in a previous login script.

Login Script Conventions

When creating login scripts, you must follow certain conventions. These conventions are as follows:

▶ *Minimum login script*: There is no minimum. You may choose whether to utilize login scripts, and all types of login scripts are optional. Login scripts can vary in length from one line to many lines and can be quite complex. There are no required commands.

▶ *Case*: You can use uppercase or lowercase when writing login scripts. There is one exception to this rule. Identifier variables enclosed in quotation marks and preceded by a percent sign (%) must be uppercase.

▶ *Characters per line*: You can have a maximum of 512 characters per line, including any variables after they are replaced by their values. However, it's probably better to limit line length for readability.

▶ *Punctuation and symbols*: You must type all symbols (#, %, ", _) and punctuation exactly as shown in examples and syntax.

▶ *Commands per line*: You should use one command per line. Start each command on a new line. It is important to note that lines that wrap automatically are considered one command.

▶ *Sequence of commands*: You should enter commands in the order you want them to execute. If you use # (or @) to execute an external program, the command must follow any necessary `MAP` commands. If sequence is not important, group similar commands, such as `MAP` and `WRITE`, together to make the login script easier to read.

▶ *Blank lines*: Blank lines don't affect login script execution. You can use them to visually separate groups of commands.

▶ *Remarks (REMARK, REM, asterisks, and semicolons)*: As with all scripts, lines beginning with `REMARK`, `REM`, an asterisk, or a semicolon are comments, and are not displayed when the login script executes. You can use remarks to record the purpose of each command or group of commands or to temporarily keep certain lines from executing.

▶ *Identifier variables*: Identifier variables allow you to replace the variable with specific information, such as a user's last name or the workstation's operating system. This makes the login script more flexible. When the login script executes, it substitutes real values for the identifier variables. By using the variable, you can make the same login script command applicable to multiple users. More information on identifier variables appears later in this appendix.

▶ *eDirectory attributes*: Any eDirectory attribute value can be read from a login script. This includes extended names. The login utility does not store the Novell names but it takes the attribute name and tries to read it. The syntax for accessing eDirectory attributes is identical to common script variables with the following exceptions:

▶ If the name contains a space, you can replace it with an underscore (_).

▶ The eDirectory attribute must be at the end of the string.

▶ If multiple variables are required, such as in required a WRITE statement, they must be in separate strings.

▶ You must use the actual eDirectory attribute value names. You cannot use localized names or nicknames.

▶ You must have Read rights to read the value of objects other than values associated with your own.

Following these conventions will help you develop well-written login scripts and help you avoid potential difficulties.

Commands for Network Connection and Resource Access

The commands for network connection and resource access are as follows:

▶ ATTACH

▶ CONTEXT

▶ DRIVE

▶ MAP

▶ TREE

Each of these commands is covered in detail in the following sections.

ATTACH

ATTACH establishes a connection between a workstation and a NetWare server. If the server is not in the current tree, a bindery connection is made. This is mostly for NetWare 3 servers. NetWare 4 and higher servers no longer need to attach separately to multiple servers and do not need to use the ATTACH command. If users want to connect to multiple trees, use the TREE command. If users are trying to create persistent drive mappings, use the MAP command.

CONTEXT

CONTEXT sets a user's current context in the eDirectory tree.

```
CONTEXT <desired eDirectory context>
```

To change the current eDirectory context, replace *context* with the context you want the user to see after login. For example, to set the current context to the organizational unit Orem, under the organization Quills, add the following line to the login script:

```
CONTEXT .Orem.Quills
```

You can also type a single period instead of a container name to indicate that you want to move up one level. For example, if you are in the context SysTest.Testing.Provo.Quills and you want to move up one level to Testing.Provo.Quills, you type

```
CONTEXT .
```

You can use multiple periods to move up multiple levels in the tree.

DRIVE

DRIVE changes the default drive while the login script is executing. If this command is not included in the login script, the default drive will be set to the first network drive, which is often assigned to the user's home directory. If you don't want the default drive to be the first network drive, map a drive in the login script to the directory you want to be the default; then use the DRIVE command to change the default drive.

Instead of specifying a drive letter such as F: or G:, you can use an asterisk followed by a number *n* to represent the *n*th network drive (for example, ***3**). This allows drive letters to reorder themselves automatically if previous drive mappings are deleted or added.

```
DRIVE [drive letter ¦*n]
```

Replace **drive letter** with a local or network drive letter, or replace *n* with a drive number. The use of either is dependent on their already being assigned within the login script.

MAP

MAP assigns drive letters to network directories. Placing **MAP** statements in the login script eliminates the need to map drives every time a user logs in. If you do not want the result of each mapping to be displayed as it is executed, add the **MAP DISPLAY OFF** command at the beginning of the login script. When all drive map assignments have been completed, add the line **MAP DISPLAY ON** for a cleaner display for users as they log in.

Instead of specifying drive letters such as F: or G:, you can use an asterisk followed by a number *n* to represent the *n*th network drive. For example, if the first network drive is F:, using **MAP *3:=** would assign H: (1 2 3 = F G H). Or, if the first network drive is D:, using **MAP *4:=** would assign G: (1 2 3 4 = D E F G).

This allows drive letters to reorder themselves automatically when local drives are removed or added or when the first network drive is changed. This also allows users to log in from workstations with a different number of local drives than their regular workstation. Use the following syntax:

```
MAP [[options]¦[parameter][drive:=path]
```

Replace **drive** with any valid network drive letter, local drive letter, or search drive number.

Replace **path** with a drive letter, a full directory path, or a Directory Map object. When mapping a drive to a directory on an eDirectory server, begin the path with the volume object's name or **<server name>\<volume name>**. More than one command can be on the map line if a semicolon (;) separates the commands:

```
MAP *1:=SYS:PUBLIC;*2:=SYS:PUBLIC\DOS
```

Replace *options* with **DISPLAY ON¦OFF** or **ERRORS ON¦OFF**. **DISPLAY ON¦OFF** determines whether drive mappings are displayed on the screen when the users log in. The default setting is **ON**. **ERRORS ON¦OFF** determines whether **MAP** error messages are displayed when the users log in. **MAP ERROR OFF** must be placed before **MAP** commands in the login script. The default setting is **ON**.

Replace *parameter* with one of the following:

▶ **INS**: Inserts a drive mapping between existing search mappings.

▶ **DEL**: Deletes a drive mapping, making that drive letter available for other mapping assignments.

▶ **ROOT** or **R**: Maps a fake root. Some applications require their executable files to be located in a root directory. Because you might not want users to have rights at the root directory, you can map a fake root to a subdirectory instead. The Windows NT native environment forces a map root on all drives. To prevent a forced map root in a Windows NT environment, set the **MAP ROOT OFF = 1** environment variable. All drives are then mapped as specified, and only explicit map root drives are rooted.

▶ **C** (**CHANGE**): Changes a search drive mapping to a regular mapping, or a regular mapping to a search drive mapping.

▶ **P** (**PHYSICAL**): Maps a drive to the physical volume of a server, rather than to the volume object's name. A Volume object's name might conflict with a physical volume name. (For example, object **ACCT** is an Accounting volume, but there is also an **ACCT** that is a physical volume.) Therefore, if you prefer to map a drive to the physical volume name, use **MAP P**.

▶ **N** (**NEXT**): When used without specifying a drive number or letter, maps the next available drive.

TREE

Use the **TREE** command to attach to another eDirectory tree within the network and to access its resources. The **TREE** command changes the focus of the login script so that all eDirectory object references in subsequent script commands (for drive mappings, print captures, and so on) apply to the eDirectory tree specified in the **TREE** command. You can include multiple **TREE** commands within a login script, either to attach to additional trees or to switch the login script's focus back to a tree that the user is already attached to. Use the following syntax:

```
TREE tree_name[/complete_name]
```

Replace **tree_name** with the name of the eDirectory tree that you want the user to attach to.

Replace **complete_name** with the user's Distinguished Name (DN) for the eDirectory tree that the user is attaching to. The DN establishes the user's context in the tree. If you do not include the complete name, the user will be prompted for a DN during login script execution.

The TREE command will always prompt the users for their eDirectory password.

Login Script Commands for Login Script Execution

The following script commands are available for login script execution:

- ▸ BREAK
- ▸ FIRE or FIRE PHASERS
- ▸ IF...THEN
- ▸ INCLUDE
- ▸ NO_DEFAULT
- ▸ PAUSE
- ▸ PROFILE

Each of these commands is covered in detail in the following sections.

BREAK

BREAK ON allows the users to terminate login script execution. The default is BREAK OFF. If BREAK ON is included in a login script, the users can press Ctrl+C or Ctrl+Break to abort the normal execution of the login script.

FIRE or FIRE PHASERS

FIRE or FIRE PHASERS emits a phaser sound by playing the phasers.wav sound file. Use FIRE or FIRE PHASERS with the IF...THEN command to make the sound execute a different number of times depending on the circumstances of the login.

FIRE *n* soundfile

Replace *n* with the number of times you want this sound to occur.

Replace *soundfile* with the name of the sound file you want to play when this command is executed. You can use any .WAV or platform-compatible sound file. For example

FIRE 3 RIFLE.WAV

To use a variable as the number of times to fire, use % before the variable identifier. This allows you to vary the fire number based on some other conditional event.

FIRE %variable

For more information about using variables, see the section called "Identifier Variables" later in this appendix.

IF...THEN

IF...THEN performs an action only under certain conditions. For example:

IF MEMBER OF "SALES" THEN

In this statement, some action is performed if the user who logged in belongs to the Group object named SALES. You might also use IF...THEN to specify a specify time or date. For example:

IF DAY_OF_WEEK="MONDAY"

In this statement, the equal sign (=) indicates the relationship between the variable (DAY_OF_WEEK) and its value (MONDAY). Note that the value (MONDAY) is placed inside quotation marks. The values of conditional statements must be enclosed in quotation marks. Furthermore, when using IF...THEN statements, you can use AND or OR to include two or more conditionals in an IF...THEN statement.

Finally, values of conditional statements are compared with the assumption that the values are characters, not numeric values. The value of 21, therefore, is considered greater than the value of 100 when comparing these two characters. To ensure that the system properly calculates numeric values instead of character values, use the **VALUE** modifier in the **IF...THEN** statement.

The **ELSE** statement is optional. When used, the **IF**, **ELSE**, and **END** commands must be on separate lines. **THEN** does not need to be on a separate line. If you include a **WRITE** command as part of the **IF...THEN** command, the **WRITE** command must be on a separate line.

IF...THEN statements can be nested (up to 10 levels). If your **IF...THEN** statement consists of only one line, you do not need to include **END** even if that line wraps. If your **IF...THEN** statement must be on more than one line (for example, if you used **ELSE** or **WRITE**, which must be on separate lines), you must include **END**.

Six Boolean operators can be used between the elements of an **IF...THEN** statement. They are

- ▶ **=** Equals
- ▶ **< >** Does not equal
- ▶ **>** Is greater than
- ▶ **>=** Is greater than or equal to
- ▶ **<** Is less than
- ▶ **<=** Is less than or equal to

When using **IF...THEN** statements, use the following syntax:

```
IF conditional [AND¦OR [conditional]] THEN
commands
[ELSE
command]
[END]
```

Replace *conditional* with identifier variables. Replace *commands* with any login script commands that you want to be executed if the specified condition is true. For example, if you place the following command in a login script, the message "**Status report is due today**" appears when the user logs in on Friday and "**Have a nice day!**" appears on other days:

```
IF DAY_OF_WEEK="FRIDAY" THEN
    WRITE "Status report is due today."
ELSE
    WRITE "Have a nice day!"
END
```

You can also nest **IF...THEN** statements. Notice that if there are multiple **IF** statements, each must have its own **END** statement:

```
IF DAY_OF_WEEK="FRIDAY" THEN
    WRITE "Status report is due today."
    IF MEMBER OF OPERATIONS THEN
        WRITE "Your report is due immediately!"
    END
END
```

Conditionals can be joined with commas, the word **AND**, or the word **OR** to form compound conditionals. The first line of the following **IF...THEN** statement is a compound conditional that means "If it is the evening of the first day of the month":

```
IF GREETING_TIME="EVENING" AND DAY="01" THEN
    WRITE "The system will be backed up tonight."
END
```

An **IF...THEN** statement can include several commands that must be executed if the conditional is true.

The following example shows two commands that are executed on Tuesdays: a **WRITE** command that displays a message about a staff meeting, and an **INCLUDE** command that tells the login script to process any commands or messages contained in the file **SYS:PUBLIC\UPDATE.TXT**.

```
IF DAY_OF_WEEK="TUESDAY" THEN
    WRITE "Staff meeting today at 10 a.m."
    INCLUDE SYS:PUBLIC\UPDATE.TXT
END
```

INCLUDE

INCLUDE executes independent files or another object's login script as a part of the login script currently being processed. These can be text files that contain valid login script commands (any of the commands explained in this section) or login scripts that belong to a different object you have rights to. Text files that contain login script commands and other objects' login scripts can be used as subscripts. Subscripts do not have to have any particular filenames or extensions.

The INCLUDE command executes the login script commands contained in the subscript. It does not display the text of the subscripts. If the subscript is a text file, users must have at least File Scan and Read rights to the directory containing the subscript. If you are using another object's login script as a subscript, users must have the Browse right to the object whose script you are including and the Read right to the object's Login Script property.

INCLUDE [*path*]*filename*

or

INCLUDE *object_name*

Replace *path* with either a drive letter or a full directory path beginning with the NetWare volume name. To use a text file as a subscript, replace *filename* with the complete name (including the extension) of the text file. See the example in the IF...THEN section.

Alternatively, you can replace *object_name* with the name of the object whose login script you want to use.

NO_DEFAULT

NO_DEFAULT in a container or profile login script indicates that do not want to create any user login scripts, and you do not want the default login script to run. To use NO_DEFAULT, add this command to either the container or the profile login script. If you have created a user login script for someone, that login script executes whether or not the NO_DEFAULT command is in the container or profile login script.

PAUSE

PAUSE creates a pause in the execution of the login script. You can add PAUSE to the login script following a message so that the user has time to read the message before it scrolls off the screen. If you include PAUSE, the message "Strike any key when ready..." appears on the workstation screen. NetWare login then waits for a key to be pressed before it executes the rest of the login script.

PROFILE

Using **PROFILE** in a container script overrides a user's assigned or command line-specified profile script. This is useful when defining a group profile. Use the following syntax:

PROFILE *profile_object_name*

Replace *profile object name* with the name of the profile that you want to override the default profile script that is assigned to a given user.

Commands for Workstation Environment

The following commands are for the workstation environment:

▶ SET

▶ SET_TIME

Each of these commands is covered in detail in the following sections.

SET

SET assigns an environment variable to a specified value. When you use **SET** in a login script, you must enter quotation marks (" ") around the values. **SET** commands do not have to be defined in a login script. For example, you can **SET** environment variables in a workstation's AUTOEXEC.BAT file. Where you use **SET** commands depends upon your individual needs.

> **NOTE** If a variable is set to a path that ends in \ ", these two characters are interpreted as an embedded quote preceded by an escape character. To avoid this problem, use two backslashes before the ending double quotes (\ \ ").

After you use the **SET** command to assign a value to an environment variable, you can use that variable in other login script commands. To include an environment variable as an identifier variable in a command, enclose the name of the variable in angle brackets (for example, <engineer>). Use the following syntax:

SET *name*="*value*"

Replace *name* with an environment parameter that identifies the environment you want to change. Replace *value* with identifier variable substitutions. Values must be enclosed in quotation marks.

To temporarily assign an environment setting for the duration of the login script only, use the optional keyword TEMP at the start of the SET line.

```
TEMP SET name="value"
```

SET_TIME

SET_TIME sets the workstation time equal to the time on the NetWare server to which the workstation first connects. If you include SET_TIME OFF in the login script, the workstation time does not update to the server's time.

Commands for Text File Usage

The following commands are for text file usage:

- ▶ #
- ▶ @
- ▶ DISPLAY
- ▶ EXIT
- ▶ FDISPLAY
- ▶ TERM
- ▶ WRITE

Each of these commands is covered in detail in the following sections.

The # Symbol

The # symbol executes a program that is external to the login script and waits until it is finished running before continuing with other login script commands.

```
# [path] filename [parameter]
```

Replace *path* with a drive letter. Replace *filename* with the executable file. It isn't necessary to include the extension, but doing so can speed up the execution of the external program. Replace *parameter* with any parameters required by the executable file.

TIP Use the @ command, described in the following section, instead of the # command if an external program will remain open for any length of time. Otherwise, the login script will remain "open" until the external program closes (login scripts cannot be edited when they are held open).

The @ Command

The @ command executes a program that is external to the login script and then continues with the script (similar to the Startup group in Windows).

@ [*path*] *filename* [*parameter*]

Replace *path* with a drive letter. Replace *filename* with an executable. Do not include the extension. Replace *parameter* with any parameters required by the executable file. For example, if you want to start the GroupWise program from within the login script, use the following command:

@SYS:\APPS\GROUPWISE\GRPWISE

DISPLAY

DISPLAY shows the contents of a text file when the user logs in. All characters in the file, including any printer and word processing codes, appear.

DISPLAY [*path*] *filename*

Replace *path* with either a drive letter or a full directory path beginning with the volume name. Replace *filename* with the complete name (including the extension) of the file you want to display. For example, you can put messages in a file SYS:PUBLIC\MESSGES\NEWS.TXT. To have the messages shown to users when they log in on Monday, add the following lines to the container login script:

```
IF DAY_OF_WEEK="Monday" THEN
  DISPLAY SYS:PUBLIC\MESSAGES\NEWS.TXT
END
```

EXIT

Use EXIT to terminate execution of the login script.

WARNING You cannot use EXIT in a login script to stop the login script and execute a program. EXIT only terminates the execution of the login script. If you want to execute a program after exiting the login script, use # or @ followed on the next line by EXIT.

FDISPLAY

FDISPLAY shows the text of a word processing file when the user logs in. When you use FDISPLAY to display a word processing file, the text is filtered and formatted so that only the text is displayed.

```
FDISPLAY [path] filename
```

Replace *path* with either a drive letter or a full directory path beginning with the volume name. Replace *filename* with the complete name (including the extension) of the file you want to display. For example, you can put messages in a file SYS:PUBLIC\MESSGES\NEWS.DOC. To have the messages shown to users when they log in on Monday, add the following lines to the container login script:

```
IF DAY_OF_WEEK="Monday" THEN
   FDISPLAY SYS:PUBLIC\MESSAGES\NEWS.DOC
END
```

TERM

TERM is normally used only for Application Launcher scripts, a component of Novell ZEN for Desktops (ZfD). Use the TERM command in a login script to stop the login script and return an error code. You can also use TERM in an IF...THEN statement, so that the login script stops and an error code is returned only if a condition is true (that is, if a certain condition exists). If the condition doesn't occur the login script skips the TERM command and continues executing.

WARNING Because TERM stops the login script, be sure to put this command either at the end of the login script or at a point within the script where you intend execution to stop. Do not nest the TERM command in the login script. If you add TERM to a container login script, it prevents other profile or user login scripts from running. If you put TERM in a profile login script, it prevents the user login script from running.

WRITE

WRITE displays messages on the workstation screen when a user logs in to the network. Text you want to display must be enclosed in quotation marks (" ").

There are several ways to display variables in the text message. The way you enter the variable in the WRITE command determines the display format, as follows:

▶ To simply display the variable value onscreen, type the identifier variable with no accompanying punctuation.

▶ To combine regular text with an identifier variable, precede the variable with a percent sign (%), type it in uppercase letters, and enclose the identifier variable inside quotation marks. Both text and the variable can be enclosed in the same quotation marks.

▶ To join several text strings and identifier variables into a single display without enclosing the variables in quotation marks, use a semicolon between the text and the variables.

▶ If you have several WRITE commands, each one appears on a separate line on the user's workstation. However, if you put a semicolon at the end of all but the last WRITE commands, the commands all appear as one continuous sentence or paragraph (although they might wrap onto additional lines on the workstation's screen).

Text strings can include the following special characters:

▶ \r Causes a carriage return

▶ \n Starts a new line of text

▶ \" Displays a quotation mark on the screen

▶ \7 Makes a beep sound

In addition to the semicolon, you can use other operators to join text and identifier variables into one command. These operators are listed in order of precedence:

▶ * / % Multiply, divide, modulo

▶ + - Add, subtract

▶ >> << Shift left or right (1000 >> 3 becomes 1)

For example:

```
WRITE "[text][%identifier] [;][identifier]"
```

Replace *text* with the words you want to display on the screen. Replace *identifier* with a variable you want to display. For example, to display the message "Hello," along with the user's last name, add the following line to the login script:

```
WRITE "Hello, ;%LAST_NAME"
```

To make a beep sound occur while the phrase "Good morning" appears on the screen, add the following line to the login script:

```
WRITE "Good %GREETING_TIME \7"
```

Other Login Script Commands

The following are other login script commands, which are described in the following sections:

▶ LASTLOGINTIME

▶ REMARK

LASTLOGINTIME

LASTLOGINTIME displays the last time the user logged in.

REMARK

REMARK, REM, an asterisk (*), or a semicolon (;) allows you to include explanatory text in the login script or to keep a line from being executed during testing. Any text that follows these symbols is ignored. If a remark is several lines long, begin each line with the remark keyword (REMARK, REM, an asterisk, or a semicolon).

WARNING This command and its associated text must be the only entry on a line. Placing remarks on the same line as other login script commands can cause errors.

Identifier Variables

Identifier variables are used most often with commands such as
IF...THEN, MAP, and WRITE. They allow you to create one login script for
multiple users by replacing the variable with other text or information.
You need to make sure you type the variable exactly as shown. Identifier
variables can be placed within literal text strings in a WRITE statement.
Literal text must be enclosed in quotation marks and the identifier must
be preceded by a percent sign (%). For example, using the %LAST_NAME
variable, substitutes the user's actual last name for the LAST_NAME variable. In a login script, WRITE "HELLO, "%LAST_NAME displays a Hello,
JONES message on Mary Jones' workstation screen when she logs in.
Tables B.1 through B.6 contain the identifier variables that can be used in
NetWare 6 login scripts.

TABLE B.1   Date Variables

IDENTIFIER VARIABLE	FUNCTION
DAY	Day in number format (01 through 31)
DAY_OF_WEEK	Day of the week (Monday, Tuesday, and so on)
MONTH	Month number (01 through 12)
MONTH_NAME	Month name (January, February, and so on)
NDAY_OF_WEEK	Weekday in number format (1 through 7; 1=Sunday)
SHORT_YEAR	Last two digits of the year (99, 00, 01)
YEAR	All four digits of the year (1999, 2000, 2001)

TABLE B.2   Time Variables

IDENTIFIER VARIABLE	FUNCTION
AM_PM	Day or night (a.m. or p.m.)
GREETING_TIME	Time of day (morning, afternoon, evening)
HOUR	Hour (12-hour scale; 1 through 12)
HOUR24	Hour (24-hour scale; 00 through 23)
MINUTE	Minute (00 through 59)
SECOND	Second (00 through 59)

TABLE B.3   User Variables

IDENTIFIER VARIABLE	FUNCTION
CN	User's full login name as it exists in eDirectory.
FULL_NAME	User's unique username. It is the value of the FULL_NAME property for eDirectory.
LAST_NAME	User's surname in eDirectory.
LOGIN_CONTEXT	User's context.
LOGIN_NAME	User's unique login name (long names are truncated to eight characters).
MEMBER OF "group"	Group object to which the user is assigned.
NOT MEMBER OF "group"	Group object to which the user is not assigned.
PASSWORD_EXPIRES	Number of days before password expires.
REQUESTER_CONTEXT	Context when login started.
USER_ID	Number assigned to each user.

TABLE B.4   Network Variables

IDENTIFIER VARIABLE	FUNCTION
FILE_SERVER	NetWare server name
NETWORK_ADDRESS	The internal number assigned by the network specifying where a device can be located in the network cabling system

TABLE B.5   Workstation Variables

IDENTIFIER VARIABLE	FUNCTION
MACHINE	Type of computer (IBM_PC, and so on)
OS	Type of operating system on the workstation
OS_VERSION	Operating system version on the workstation
P_STATION	Workstation's node number (12-digit hexadecimal)
PLATFORM	Workstation's operating system platform
SMACHINE	Short machine name (IBM, and so on)
STATION	Workstation's connection number
WINVER	Version of the workstation's Windows operating system

TABLE B.6 Miscellaneous Variables

IDENTIFIER VARIABLE	FUNCTION
ACCESS_SERVER	Shows whether the access server is functional (TRUE = functional; FALSE = nonfunctional).
ERROR_LEVEL	An error number (0 = no errors).
%n	Replaced by parameters used during login. When a user logs in, additional parameters can be entered that the login utility passes to the login script. The login utility then substitutes these parameters for any %n variables in the login script. These variables are replaced in order by the parameters the user entered when logging in.
	Users can change only four variables (%2 to %5) in the login screen. The %0 variable is replaced by the name of the NetWare server entered in the login dialog box, and %1 is replaced by the user's fully distinguished login name. The remaining variables change, depending on what the user types when executing the login utility. The %n variables must precede all command-line options.
property name	You can use property values of eDirectory objects as variables. Use the property values just as you do any other identifier variable. If the property value includes a space, enclose the name in quotation marks.
	To use a property name with a space within a WRITE statement, you must place it at the end of the quoted string.

NetWare Console and SET Commands

NetWare 6 console commands and **SET** parameters are two of the primary tools at your disposal for tuning, optimizing, and customizing your NetWare 6.5 servers. It is invaluable as a network administrator to understand the configurable parameters of your NetWare 6.5 server, and the tools you can use to make modifications and changes should it be necessary. This appendix describes the primary console commands and **SET** parameters available in NetWare 6.5.

NetWare Console Commands

Console commands, such as **MOUNT**, are executed by typing a command at the server console. You can also execute console utilities from remote sessions, through NoRM or ConsoleOne.

In general, you use console commands to change some aspect of the server or view information about it. Console utilities are built into the core NetWare 6.5 operating system modules, such as SERVER.EXE, DS.NLM, NSS.NLM, and so on. As such, no additional files are loaded in order to execute them. For convenience, and in addition to the console commands, a few executable and NCF files have also been listed, for lack of a better category in which to put them.

Use the **HELP** command to see a list of all console utilities, or type **HELP** *<utility* name> to see a brief synopsis a console utility. For example:

```
HELP mount
```

This section does not list every single console command due to the sheer number of them. NetWare 6.5 currently has upward of 200 console commands. Rather, we have tried to include the most relevant, and also the lesser known, console commands related to administration of a NetWare 6.5 server. Some commands that are left over from prior versions, or that relate more to development than administration, have been excluded.

ABORT REMIRROR

Stops disk partitions from remirroring. Use the following command format, replacing *number* with the number of the logical disk partition you want to stop from remirroring:

```
ABORT REMIRROR number
```

ACTIVATEMODULE

Allows you to manually load a driver that is normally pre-loaded from the STARTUP.NCF file. It is useful for testing new configurations or load options on pre-loaded drivers.

```
ACTIVATEMODULE <module name>
```

ADD PROGRAM

Adds a specified program to the stage *n* load template. Make sure that your NLM is compatible with the type of NLM required at the specific stage, or it will not load. Use the following syntax, replacing *program name* with the name of the NLM to load and *n* with the stage at which the NLM should be loaded:

```
ADD PROGRAM <program name> TO STAGE <n>
```

For more information on NetWare 6.5 load stages, see the **LOADSTAGE** command.

ALERT

Controls how the server handles alerts if you are using SNMP network management tools. You can turn on and off specified types of alerts, control where they are displayed or recorded, and so on. Use the following command format, substituting the alert number for *nmID* (optional) and one of the options listed in Table C.1 for *option*. Then choose ON or OFF for the specified alert and option you have chosen. You can specify only one option at a time, unless you use the **ALL** option, which sets the Log, Console, Everyone, and Bell options simultaneously. To specify more than one option, repeat the **ALERT** command multiple times, using a different option in each command.

```
ALERT <nmID> <option> ON|OFF
```

TABLE C.1 ALERT Commands

OPTION	DESCRIPTION
Event	When set to ON, generates an event when the alert occurs. When set to OFF, an event is not generated.
Log	When set to ON, records the alert message in a log file.
Everyone	When set to ON, sends the alert to all network users who are logged in.
Console	When set to ON, displays the alert message on the server's console.
Bell	When set to ON, sounds a warning noise when the alert occurs.
ID	When set to ON, displays ID information (used only in older alert messages).
Locus	When set to ON, displays locus information (used only in older alert messages).
Alert	When set to ON, generates the alert.
Nmid	When set to ON, causes the alert nmID to appear in the alert message.
All	When set to ON, turns on the Log, Console, Everyone, and Bell commands at the same time.

ALIAS

Creates a shortcut to a particular console utility or command. Use the following syntax, replacing *alias* with the new command you want to be able to type, and replacing *command* with the original utility name or command you want to execute when you type the alias:

```
ALIAS <alias> <command>
```

APPLET or APPLETVIEWER

Used to execute a Java-based applet. Type the following command, substituting the applet's filename for *html_file*:

```
APPLET <html_file>
```

To execute a Java application, see the JAVA console utility.

BIND

Assigns a protocol, such as IP or IPX, to a LAN driver or network board. Any configuration parameters you specify when you load the LAN driver must also be added to the **BIND** command so that the protocol is bound to the correct board. You can place **BIND** commands in AUTOEXEC.NCF so that they are permanent.

Use the following syntax, replacing *protocol* with the name of the protocol, *driver* with the name of the LAN driver or network board, and *parameters* with any necessary driver or protocol parameters:

BIND *protocol driver parameters*

Table C.2 describes the most common **BIND** parameters for the different protocols.

TABLE C.2 Common BIND Parameters

DRIVER PARAMETER	DESCRIPTION
DMA=*number*	Indicates the DMA channel the board should use.
FRAME=*type*	Indicates the frame type (Ethernet or token ring) this board should use. The available frames types are Ethernet_II (default for IP) Ethernet_802.2 (default for IPX) Ethernet_802.3 Ethernet_SNAP Token Ring Token-Ring_SNAP
INT=*number*	Indicates the interrupt (in hex) the board should use.
MEM=*number*	Indicates the memory address the board should use.
NODE=*number*	Indicates the board's node address.
PORT=*number*	Indicates the I/O port the board should use.
SLOT=*number*	Indicates the slot in which the board is installed.

BINDERY

Adds or deletes a bindery context in the list of bindery contexts this server uses. To add a bindery context to a server, use the following command format, substituting a valid context for *context*:

`BINDERY ADD CONTEXT = <context>`

To delete a bindery context from a server, type

`BINDERY DELETE CONTEXT = <context>`

BROADCAST

Sends a short message from the server console to users on the network. To send a message to a user, use the following command format, replacing *message* with the message you want displayed (no more than 55 characters long) and *user* with either the name of the user or the workstation's connection number:

`BROADCAST "message" <user>`

To send the message to multiple users, separate each username or connection number with a comma or space. To send the message to all users, don't specify a username. (You can also use the **SEND** console utility to accomplish the same thing.)

C1START.NCF

Starts the graphical server desktop and loads ConsoleOne at the same time. Java-based applications, such as ConsoleOne, can execute only from the graphical server desktop.

CDBE

There are four hidden commands associated with the Configuration Database Engine (CDBE.NLM). CDBE manages the loading of NLMs during the NetWare 6.5 startup sequence. Information includes version number, location, and database file information. Little explanation of the commands is available, but they are **CDBE EDIT**, **CDBE ERRLVL**, **CDBE INFO**, and **CDBE VALIDATE**.

CLEAR STATION

Closes a workstation's open files and removes the workstation's connection from the server. This is necessary only if the workstation has crashed and left files open and the user can't log out normally.

Use the following syntax, replacing *number* with the workstation's connection number (as seen in MONITOR.NLM) or the word **ALL** to clear all connections:

`CLEAR STATION number`

CLS

Clears the server's console screen.

CM BUSY

Displays a list of all connections that are currently using server processing cycles.

CM CONN

Displays current information about the specified connection number, including node address and status. Use the following syntax:

```
CM CONN <connection number>
```

You can find connection numbers with NoRM, in the Connections page, or with MONITOR.NLM; select Connections.

CM KILL

Kills the specified connection number. Use the following syntax:

```
CM KILL <connection number>
```

You can find connection numbers with NoRM, in the Connections page, or with MONITOR.NLM; select Connections.

CM STATS

Displays current Connection Manager statistics.

CONFIG

Displays configuration information about the server. This utility displays the following information:

- ▶ The server's name
- ▶ The server's internal network number
- ▶ The LAN drivers that are loaded on the server
- ▶ The server's hardware settings
- ▶ The protocols the server is currently supporting
- ▶ The node address of each network board installed in the server
- ▶ The server's tree name
- ▶ The server's bindery context

CPUCHECK

Displays information about the server's processor, such as the CPU speed, model, and cache. If the server has more than one processor, typing CPUCHECK will display information about all the server's processors. To see information about only one of the processors, use the following command format, substituting the processor number for *number*:

CPUCHECK <number>

CSET

Lets you to display and set server (SET) parameters by category. Use the following syntax, substituting the parameter category for *category*:

CSET <category>

For example, to see each server parameter in the Memory category, and to be given the opportunity to change each one as it is displayed, type

CSET MEMORY

This is much easier done from NoRM or even MONITOR.NLM. For a complete list of SET parameter categories, see the NetWare SET parameters section later in this appendix.

CWD

Current Working Directory. This command displays the current default DOS path. Usually this is C:\NWSERVER.

DELAY

This command is typically used in NCF files to delay execution of a command in order to let another complete. You can delay up to 300 seconds. Use the following syntax:

DELAY <number of seconds>

DISABLE LOGIN

Prevents users from logging in to the server (such as when you want to perform maintenance on the server). Users who are already logged in won't be affected, but additional users cannot log in. To allow users to log in again, use ENABLE LOGIN.

DISABLE TTS

Disables TTS (NetWare's Transaction Tracking System) on traditional NetWare volumes. If you want to use TTS with NSS logical volumes, you need to use **DISABLE TTS** to shut TTS down on any traditional volumes you might have. Refer to Chapter 8, "File and Storage Management," for more information.

DISMOUNT

Dismounts a volume (usually in preparation for repairing or deleting a volume). Use the following command format, replacing *volume* with the name of the volume you want to dismount:

```
DISMOUNT <volume>
```

DISPLAY

There are several commands associated with displaying certain server statistics, configuration, or service information in NetWare 6.5. A few of the more interesting ones include

▶ **DISPLAY DEVICE STATS**: Displays basic statistics on individual storage devices attached to the server. Information is organized by device ID.

▶ **DISPLAY ENVIRONMENT**: Displays the current values of all server parameters.

▶ **DISPLAY INTERRUPTS**: Displays information about the interrupt handler and interrupt statistics on the server. To see more detailed information, use the following syntax, substituting one of the options listed in Table C.3 for *option*:

```
DISPLAY INTERRUPTS <option>
```

TABLE C.3   DISPLAY INTERRUPTS Options

OPTION	DESCRIPTION
n	Displays information for the specific interrupt number (replace n with the interrupt number). To display information for more than one interrupt, separate each interrupt number with a space.
ALL	Displays information about all interrupts.
ALLOC	Displays information for allocated interrupts.
PROC	Displays interrupt information by processor.
REAL	Displays the interrupts that occurred while the operating system was in real mode, and that were sent to protected mode for servicing.

▶ DISPLAY MODIFIED ENVIRONMENT: Displays the server parameters that have been changed from their default values. This utility displays both the current value and the original default value. You can also view this information from NoRM in the **SET** parameters page.

▶ DISPLAY NETWORKS: Displays a list of all the networks (shown by their network numbers) that this server recognizes. It also displays how many hops (different network segments separated by a router) away these networks are, and the time in ticks (1/18 of a second) it takes for a packet to reach these networks.

▶ DISPLAY SERVERS: Displays a list of all the servers that this server recognizes and records in its router table. It also displays how many hops (different network segments separated by a router) away those servers are. Use the following syntax:

DISPLAY SERVERS *<server>*

To see information about a single server, or subset of servers that start with the same letters, replace *<server>* with a server's name, or use the wildcard character to display multiple servers that begin with the same letters, such as **B***.

DOWN

Shuts down the server cleanly. This command closes any open files, writes any data left in the cache buffers to the disk, and so on, so that server files will not be damaged when you shut down the server.

After you've brought down the server with the **DOWN** command, you can safely turn off the computer.

ECHO OFF

Disables the displaying of the commands that are executed from NCF files. Similar in operation to the **Echo** command in DOS.

ECHO ON

Enables the displaying of the commands that are executed from NCF files. This is the default. Similar in operation to the **Echo** command in DOS.

ENABLE LOGIN

Allows users to log in using this server. This is necessary only if you have used **DISABLE LOGIN** to prevent logging in.

ENABLE TTS

Restarts TTS (Transaction Tracking System) on traditional NetWare volumes after it has been disabled. Remember, you can enable transaction tracking for either traditional or logical volumes, not both simultaneously. Refer to Chapter 8 for information on enabling TTS on logical volumes.

ENVSET

Displays and modifies global environment variables for the server. To display all environment variables, type

```
ENVSET
```

To set or modify an environment variable, type the following command, substituting the variable you want for *variable*, and substituting a string or value for *value*:

```
ENVSET <variable> = <value>
```

If you leave *value* blank after the equal sign, the variable is removed from the environment.

EXTCHECK

Performs a Java Extensions Directory Check. Use the following syntax:

```
EXTCHECK -verbose <jar file>
```

FILE SERVER NAME

Sets the server's name. Use the following command format, substituting the new server name for *name*:

```
FILE SERVER NAME <name>
```

> **WARNING** Changing the name of your NetWare 6.5 server will break all your license associations in eDirectory. You will have to use iManage to reassign the appropriate licenses. For more information on licensing, refer to Chapter 1, "NetWare 6.5 Server Installation."

HELP

Provides help for console commands. To see a list of available console utilities, type HELP. To display help for a specific console utility, use the following syntax, replacing *utility* with the name of the console utility whose help file you want to read:

```
HELP <utility>
```

HTTPBIND

Binds the specified IP address to HTTPSTK.NLM for use by HTTP services. Use the following syntax, substituting the IP address you want to bind
for *ip address*:

```
HTTPBIND <ip address> [/KEYFILE: <key filename>]
```

The optional **KEYFILE** parameter lets you specify the server certificate
object that will be used with this IP address for SSL communications. For
example:

```
HTTPBIND 137.65.192.4 /KEYFILE: "SSL Certificate IP"
```

HTTPCLOSEPORT

Closes the TCP port on all IP addresses bound to the protocol stack
HTTPSTK.NLM. Use the following syntax, substituting the port number
you want to close for *IP Port*.

```
HTTPCLOSEPORT <IP Port>
```

HTTPOPENPORT

Opens a TCP port on all IP addresses bound to the protocol stack HTTP-
STK.NLM. Use the following syntax, substituting the port you want to
open for *IP Port*:

```
HTTPOPENPORT <IP Port> [/SSL]
```

The optional **/SSL** parameter enables SSL on the port you are opening.

HTTPUNBIND

Unbinds the specified IP address from HTTPSTK.NLM. Use the following
syntax, substituting the address you want to unbind for *ip address*:

```
HTTPUNBIND <ip address>
```

IDCACHE CONN

Displays legacy fileserver ID cache information for the specified connection number. Use the following syntax:

```
IDCACHE CONN <connection number>
```

You can find connection numbers with NoRM (Connections page) or
with MONITOR.NLM (select Connections).

PART V Appendices

IDCACHE STATS

Displays legacy fileserver ID cache statistical information.

```
IDCACHE STATS <connection number>
```

You can find connection numbers with NoRM, in the Connections page, or with MONITOR.NLM; select Connections.

IPX INTERNAL NET

Sets the server's internal IPX network address. NetWare 6.5 refers to this parameter as the *network number*.

JAR

This utility lets you create Java Archive files (.JAR). See the Novell documentation for more information.

JAVA

Use this command to execute a Java-based application. The version of the command you type depends on how you want the application to run. If the application doesn't require user input, or if it runs in a graphical user interface, type the following command, substituting the application's name for *class*:

```
JAVA class
```

If you want to use options with this command, use the following command format, substituting one of the options in Table C.4 for *options*. Remember to precede each option with a minus sign (–).

TABLE C.4   JAVA Options

OPTION	DESCRIPTION
–HELP	Displays help for the JAVA command.
–NWHELP	Displays help for NetWare-specific options for the JAVA command.
–CLASSPATH *dir;dir;...*	Specifies the directories in which to search for classes.
–D*property=value*	Redefines a property's value.
–DEBUG	Enables remote Java debugging.
–ENV*variable*	Sets an environment variable for the Java application.

OPTION	DESCRIPTION
-EXIT	Exits all currently running Java applications and unloads Java from the server.
-KILL*id*	Kills a running Java application. (To see the *id* of a particular Java application, use the -SHOW option.)
-MS*number*	Sets the initial Java heap size.
-MX*number*	Sets the maximum Java heap size.
-NOASYNCGC	Prevents asynchronous garbage collection.
-NOCLASSGC	Prevents class garbage collection.
-NOVERIFY	Prevents verification of any class.
-NS	Brings up a separate console screen for the application. Use if the application is text-based and requires user input.
-OSS*number*	Sets the Java stack size for a process.
-PROF	Sends profiling data to ./java.prof.
-SHOW	Displays all currently running Java applications.
-SS*number*	Sets the C stack size of a process.
-VERBOSE	Turns on verbose mode (which displays informational messages).
-VERBOSEGC	Displays a message whenever garbage collection occurs.
-VERIFY	Verifies all classes when they are read in.
-VERIFYREMOTE	Verifies classes that are read in over the network (this is the default setting).
-VERSION	Displays the build version number of Java.
-Vm*size*	Specifies a specific amount of virtual memory for the Java application to use. Substitute the amount of memory (in megabytes) for *size*. The default size is 32MB.

KF8 OFF

Disables pausing between commands executed from NCF files.

KF8 ON

Enables pausing between commands executed from NCF files.

LANGUAGE

Changes the language that displays when NLMs are loaded. This will not change the language of the operating system or of NLMs that are already loaded. It only affects the NLMs that are loaded after this utility is executed. To display the current language being used by NLMs, type

LANGUAGE

To display a list of all available languages, type

LANGUAGE LIST

To change the language to be used by subsequently loaded NLMs, use the following command format, replacing *name* with either the name or number of the language:

LANGUAGE <*name*>

LIST DEVICES

Displays a list of all the storage devices you have installed on the server, such as CD-ROM drives, disk drives, tape drives, and external storage systems.

LIST FAILOVER DEVICES

Displays a list of all the failover devices found, and the paths associated with each device. Use the following syntax:

LIST FAILOVER DEVICES <*device id*>

<*device id*> is optional. If included, only the paths associated with the specified device will be displayed.

LIST PARTITIONS

Displays all partitions associated with storage devices attached to this server. User the following syntax:

LIST PARTITIONS <*deviceid*>

<*device id*> is optional. If included, only the partitions associated with the specified device are displayed.

LIST STORAGE ADAPTERS

Lists all the server's storage adapters and HAMs (host adapter modules), and their associated storage devices.

LIST STORAGE DEVICE BINDINGS

Lists all the HAMs (host adapter modules) that are bound to a storage device, such as a disk drive. Use the following command format, substituting the storage device's number for *number*:

```
LIST STORAGE DEVICE BINDINGS <number>
```

To see the device number for a storage device, use the **LIST DEVICES** console utility.

LOAD

Used to load NLMs on the server. However, in NetWare 5, using the **LOAD** command is optional; you can load NLMs simply by typing their name. If you want to use **LOAD**, use the following syntax, replacing *module* with the name of the NLM you're loading (you don't need to include the .NLM extension in the module name):

```
LOAD <module>
```

To unload an NLM, use the **UNLOAD** console utility.

LOADSTAGE

Executes a specific NetWare 6.5 load stage. What happens during a given load stage is governed by the load order template. The template consists of 32 stages. Stages 0–5 are defined as kernel stages, and stages 6–31 are user stages. Stages consist of template entries for each NLM to be loaded, the NLM load order, and a path to the NLM. Subsequent load stages generally have dependencies on all stages that execute previously.

▶ *STAGE K (Kernel Startup stage)*: This is the first stage to execute and is not configurable. It loads the NetWare Configuration DataBase Engine (CDBE.NLM). After the kernel initializes, it loads NWKCFG.NLM, which starts loading NLMs by stage. NWKCFG.NLM uses the CDBE engine to determine when to load each NLM.

▶ *STAGE 0*: This stage executes prior to the STARTUP.NCF. It generally loads extended kernel services, which have no dependencies except storage services. The only functions required by Stage 0 NLMs are provided by the OS kernel (memory, threads, and so on).

▶ *STAGE 1*: This stage executes after the STARTUP.NCF and before SYS volume mounts. NLMs that load during this stage, such as FILESYS.NLM, require only kernel services and storage services.

▶ *STAGE* 2: This stage executes after SYS volume mounts but before AUTOEXEC.NCF runs. Examples include NCP.NLM and UNI-CODE.NLM.

▶ *STAGE* 3: This stage executes before the AUTOEXEC.NCF and before the Name Service Loader. Examples include DSLOADER.NLM and SLP.NLM.

▶ *STAGE* 4: This stage executes after the Name Service Loader but before the AUTOEXEC.NCF. Examples include DS.NLM and TIME-SYNC.NLM.

▶ *STAGE* 5: This stage executes after the AUTOEXEC.NCF has run. Examples include HWDETECT.NLM and LOADIMG.NLM.

Use the following syntax, substituting the name of the stage or the word ALL for *name*:

LOADSTAGE *<name>*

For more information on adding NLMs to a specific stage, see **ADD PROGRAM**.

LOGGERPATH

Specifies the directory where LOGGER.TXT is stored. By default, LOGGER.TXT is stored in **C:/NWSERVER**. If the path you specify does not exist, it will be created. You can specify any directory on **SYS:** or the DOS partition. Use the following syntax:

LOGGERPATH = *<path to location for logger.txt>*

LOGGERSAVE

Saves the logger screen buffer to the file LOGGER.TXT. By default, LOGGER.TXT is stored in **C:\NWSERVER**. However, this location can be changed with the **LOGGERPATH** command.

MAGAZINE

If the server prompts you to insert a new media magazine during some task, use this utility to indicate to the server that you've inserted or removed a media magazine. Use the following command format, replacing *option* with one of the options listed in Table C.5:

MAGAZINE *<option>*

TABLE C.5   MAGAZINE Options

OPTION	DESCRIPTION
Inserted	Tells the server you've inserted the media magazine.
Not Inserted	Tells the server that you have not inserted the media magazine.
Removed	Tells the server that you have removed the media magazine.
Not Removed	Tells the server that you have not removed the media magazine.

MAILTO

Mails a message to the specified user on the network. Use the following syntax:

`MAILTO <mail to> <mail subject> <message> ¦ @filename`

- ▶ *mail to*: Specify the name of the network user.

- ▶ *mail subject*: Specify the contents of the email subject line.

- ▶ *message*: Specify the message to be sent.

- ▶ *@filename*: (*Optional*) You can append a file attachment by specifying the full path and name of the file to attach.

MEDIA

If the server prompts you to insert a specified storage medium during some task, use this utility to indicate to the server that you've inserted or removed the medium. Use the following command format, replacing *option* with one of the options listed in Table C.6:

`MEDIA <option>`

TABLE C.6   MEDIA Options

OPTION	DESCRIPTION
Inserted	Tells the server you've inserted the medium.
Not Inserted	Tells the server that you have not inserted the medium.
Removed	Tells the server that you have removed the medium.
Not Removed	Tells the server that you have not removed the medium.

MEMORY

Displays the total amount of memory (RAM) currently installed in the server.

MEMORY MAP

Displays how memory is allocated between the DOS environment and the server environment.

MIRROR STATUS

Lists all the disk partitions on the server and display their mirror status. The following five states are possible:

▶ *Being remirrored*: This means the disk partition is being synchronized with another partition and will soon be mirrored.

▶ *Fully synchronized*: This means the disk partitions are mirrored and working correctly, so that both partitions contain identical data.

▶ *Not mirrored*: This means the disk partition isn't mirrored with any other partition.

▶ *Orphaned state*: This means the disk partition used to be mirrored with another, but isn't now. The integrity of this partition's data might not be ensured.

▶ *Out of synchronization*: This means the two disk partitions that are mirrored do not have identical data and, therefore, need to be remirrored.

MM

There are several commands associated with configuring the Media Manager in NetWare 6.5. For more information on using these commands, see the NetWare 6.5 online documentation. Use the following syntax:

```
MM <option> <option-specific parameters>
```

MODULES

Displays a list of all the NLMs currently loaded on the server. If you want to see information about a single NLM, use the following command format, replacing *module_name* with an NLM's name:

```
MODULES <module name>
```

You can use the wildcard character to display multiple NLMs that begin with the same letter or letters. For example, to see all the loaded NLMs that start with the letters **DS**, type

```
MODULES DS*
```

MOUNT

Mounts a volume on a server so that network users can access it. Use the following command format, replacing *volume_name* with the volume's name (or with **ALL** to mount all volumes):

```
MOUNT <volume name>
```

NAME

Displays the server's name.

NATIVE2ASCII

Converts a native-language file to ASCII format. Use the following command format, substituting the file's name for *filename*:

```
NATIVE2ASCII <filename>
```

NCP ADDRESSES

Displays a list of all known NCP network service addresses.

NCP DUMP

Records all NCP standard deviation statistics in a specified file. Use the following command format, substituting the file's name for *filename*:

```
NCP DUMP <filename>
```

NCP STATS

Displays all NCP statistics for incoming NCP requests. To reset the counter for these statistics, type the following command:

```
NCP STATS RESET
```

NCP TRACE

Decodes incoming NCP packets and displays them on an active server screen. You can also send the data to a file. Use the following command format to display the information on the screen:

```
NCP TRACE ON¦OFF
```

To send the information to a file, type the following, substituting the
name of the file for *filename*:

```
NCP TRACE ON <filename>
```

NSS

Views and sets parameters for the NetWare Storage System environment
on NetWare 6.5. For more information on NSS, see Chapter 8. Although
there are numerous parameters for NSS, the two to be most interested in
are

▶ *nss /poolrebuild*: The REBUILD utility goes through the storage
  pool that you specify, checking and repairing any errors it finds.
  REBUILD will keep an error log of any errors it finds. The error log
  file is located in the SYS volume, and is named with the volume's
  name, followed by the extension .RLF. For example, if your NSS
  volume is named NSSVOL, the error log will be named
  NSSVOL.RLF.

▶ *nss /poolverify*: Verify the integrity of an NSS storage pool. Use it
  when you suspect a volume is corrupted, or want to verify that a
  volume is intact after REBUILD.

NWTRAP

There are several commands associated with configuring the Simple
Network Management Protocol (SNMP) environment in NetWare 6.5.
For more information on using these commands, see the NetWare 6.5
online documentation. Use the following syntax:

```
NWTRAP <option> <option-specific parameters>
```

OFF

Clears the server's console screen, similar to CLS.

PAUSE

Similar to its DOS counterpart, this command is used in NCF files to halt
execution until a key is pressed.

POLICYTOOL

This is the Java Security Policy Tool. It is a graphical tool that allows you
to add, edit, or remove a policy from your keystore file. For more information, see the Novell documentation.

PROTECT

Used to specify that all NLMs loaded from within an NCF file should be loaded in a protected address space. For more information about protected address spaces, refer to Chapter 4, "NetWare 6.5 Server Management." Use the following syntax, substituting the name of the NCF file for *filename*:

```
PROTECT <filename>
```

PROTECTION

Used to list information about the protected address spaces currently being used on the server.

PROTOCOL

Registers a new protocol or frame type for the server to support. You don't need to use this utility to register IPX, IP, or AppleTalk because they are registered automatically during installation or configuration, but you might need to use this if you use a different protocol. See the protocol's manufacturer for more details.

To list all the protocols that are currently registered on the server, type

```
PROTOCOL
```

To register a new protocol, use the following command format, replacing *protocol* with the name of the protocol, *frame* with the frame type, and *id* with the protocol ID (PID, also called Ethernet Type, E-Type, or SAP) number assigned to the protocol:

```
PROTOCOL REGISTER <protocol> <frame> <id>
```

PSM

Loads a PSM (platform support module). PSMs are used for multi-processor support in NetWare 6.5. To see all the PSM commands available, type **PSM?**.

PURGESET

Removes unowned **SET** commands from the server. This is useful if the server is serving a specific purpose and you don't want extraneous **SET** commands causing confusion. Use the following syntax:

```
PURGESET [SET parameter] [ALL]
```

The [ALL] parameter can be used instead of specifying a specific SET parameter. It will locate all unowned SET parameters automatically.

PVER

Displays the NetWare product information for the version of NetWare that you are running on this server. For example, the shipping version of NetWare 6.5 displays the following:

```
Product Version Information:
    Product ID : 30
    Product Major Version Number :6
    Product Minor Version Number :50
    Product Revision Number :00
    Product Description: Novell NetWare 6.5
```

RECORD

The RECORD family of console commands allows you to record a series of commands for execution in an .NCF file. Table C.7 shows the various RECORD commands.

TABLE C.7 RECORD Commands in NetWare 6.5

COMMAND	DESCRIPTION
RECORD	Displays all command recording sessions currently in progress.
RECORD KILL <session name>	Terminates the specified recording session. See session names with the RECORD command.
RECORD SAVE <session name>	Saves the contents of a command recording session to an .NCF file.
RECORD START <session name>	Starts a command recording session with the name specified.
RECORD STOP <session name> {NCF}	Stops a command recording session. Use the NCF tag to save session to an .NCF file.
RECORD TYPE <session name>	Displays the contents of a command recording session.

REGISTER MEMORY

Use this utility on older ISA (AT bus) servers to register memory above 16MB so that NetWare can address it. On a PCI computer, NetWare automatically recognizes up to 64MB.

Use the following command format, replacing *start* with the hexadecimal address of where the memory above the limit begins. For ISA servers this will be 16MB, or 1000000 Hex. For PCI systems this will be 64MB, or 4000000 Hex. Table C.8 shows some common *length* numbers for different memory amounts.

`REGISTER MEMORY <start> <length>`

TABLE C.8   Hexadecimal Length Values for Memory

TOTAL MEMORY IN SERVER (MB)	*LENGTH* VALUE FOR ISA	*LENGTH* VALUE FOR PCI
128	7000000	4000000
256	F000000	C000000
512	1F000000	1B000000
1024	3F000000	3B000000
2048	7F000000	7B000000
4096	FE000000	FB000000

REMIRROR PARTITION

Restarts the remirroring process if something halted the server's remirroring of its disk partitions. Use the following command format, replacing *number* with the number of the disk partition you want to remirror:

`REMIRROR PARTITION <number>`

REMOVE NETWORK ADAPTER

Unloads one instance of a LAN driver, when the LAN driver has been loaded multiple times for use with more than one network board. This command unloads the driver from one board, but leaves the driver bound to the other boards. Use the following command, substituting the filename of the LAN driver for *driver* and, if necessary, the instance number of the board for *board_name* if there are multiple boards of the same type.

`REMOVE NETWORK ADAPTER <board number>`

You can find the board number for each network adapter in your server by using NoRM or MONITOR.NLM.

▶ *NoRM*: Open the Disk/LAN Adapters page and click the network adapter you want to remove.

▶ *MONITOR.NLM*: Select LAN/WAN drivers and select the driver you want to remove.

REMOVE NETWORK INTERFACE

Unloads a single frame type from a LAN driver, if that LAN driver has been loaded with multiple frame types. (Each time a driver is loaded with a frame type, it is called a *logical board*. Therefore, you can have several logical boards loaded, even though there is only one physical adapter in the server.)

This command unloads one frame type from the LAN driver, but leaves the LAN driver loaded with the other specified frame types. Use the following command, substituting the logical board number for **board**:

```
REMOVE NETWORK INTERFACE board
```

You can find the board number for each network adapter in your server by using NoRM or MONITOR.NLM.

▶ *NoRM*: Open the Disk/LAN Adapters page and click the network adapter you want to remove.

▶ *MONITOR.NLM*: Select LAN/WAN drivers and select the driver you want to remove.

REMOVE PROGRAM

Removes a specified program from the stage *n* loading template. See **ADD PROGRAM** and **LOADSTAGE** for more information about load stages. Use the following syntax:

```
REMOVE PROGRAM <program name> FROM STAGE n
```

REMOVE STORAGE ADAPTER

Unloads a single instance of a storage driver. If that storage driver has been loaded for use with more than one storage device, only the instance you specify will be unloaded. The other devices will still remain intact, with the storage driver active. If this storage driver is bound to only one storage device, the entire driver is unloaded.

Use the following syntax, substituting the adapter number for *n*:

REMOVE STORAGE ADAPTER A<*n*>

You can find the *An* number of each instance of the storage driver with **LIST STORAGE ADAPTERS**. The *An* number is enclosed in square brackets at the beginning of the adapter's name.

REMOVEMODULE

Allows you to manually unload a driver that is normally pre-loaded from STARTUP.NCF, or was loaded using the **ACTIVATEMODULE** command. It is useful for testing new configurations or load options on pre-loaded drivers.

REMOVEMODULE <module *name*>

REPLACE

Unloads and then reloads the specified NLM module, using the following syntax:

REPLACE <*NLM Name*>

REPLAY

Replays a recorded command session, using the following syntax:

REPLAY <*session name*>

For more information on recording commands, see **RECORD**.

RESET ENVIRONMENT

Restores all server (**SET**) parameters to their original default values.

RESET NETWORK ADAPTER

Used to stop whatever task a network board was doing, and reset it to a clean state. You might want to do this if you suspect something is wrong with the board. Use the following syntax, substituting the filename of the board's LAN driver for *driver* and, if necessary, the instance number for *board* if there are multiple boards of the same type.

RESET NETWORK ADAPTER <*driver*> <*board*>

You can find the board number for each network adapter in your server by using NoRM or MONITOR.NLM.

▶ *NoRM*: Open the Disk/LAN Adapters page and click the network adapter you want to remove.

▶ *MONITOR.NLM*: Select LAN/WAN drivers and select the driver you want to remove.

RESET NETWORK INTERFACE

Restarts a logical board that was previously shut down using the SHUTDOWN NETWORK INTERFACE utility. You can restart the logical board without having to reload and bind the LAN driver. Use the following syntax, substituting the logical board number for *board*:

RESET NETWORK INTERFACE <board>

You can find the board number for each network adapter in your server by using NoRM or MONITOR.NLM.

▶ *NoRM*: Open the Disk/LAN Adapters page and click the network adapter you want to remove.

▶ *MONITOR.NLM*: Select LAN/WAN drivers and select the driver you want to remove.

RESET ROUTER

Clears the router table and forces a new table to be built on the server, updating any changes to servers or routers that have gone down or come back up. The table is automatically rebuilt every two minutes, so you need to use this utility only if you don't want to wait for the next automatic rebuild.

RESET SERVER

Brings down the server and does a warm reboot of the computer. You can use RESTART SERVER to bring down and restart the server without booting the machine. This option is also available from NoRM.

RESTART SERVER

Restart the server after you have brought it down. Supports three startup options: -na starts the server without running AUTOEXEC.NCF; -ns starts the server without running STARTUP.NCF; and -d starts the server and loads the debugger.

SCAN ALL

Searches for and displays all Logical Unit Numbers (LUNs) on SCSI adapters in the server. A LUN is used to designate an individual device attached to a SCSI bus. To display all LUNs on all SCSI adapters in the server, type

```
SCAN ALL
```

To display all LUNs on a particular SCSI adapter, type the following command, substituting the number of the adapter for *n*:

```
SCAN ALL An
```

You can find the *An* number of each instance of the storage driver with **LIST STORAGE ADAPTERS**. The *An* number is enclosed in square brackets at the beginning of the adapter's name.

SCAN FOR NEW DEVICES

Instructs the server to look for and recognize any new storage devices (disk drives, CD-ROM drives, and so on) that have been added since the server was booted.

SEARCH

Sets the paths that the server should search through when looking for NCF files, NLMs, or Java applications. The default search path is **SYS:SYSTEM**. If SYS isn't mounted, the default search path becomes the DOS boot directory on the server. To display the server's current search paths, type **SEARCH**.

To add a search path, use the following command format, replacing *path* with the directory path you want the server to search. This command is regularly used in the AUTOEXEC.NCF to define a permanent search path.

```
SEARCH ADD path
```

To delete a search path, use the following command format, replacing *number* with the number of the search drive you want to remove (drive numbers are displayed when you type **SEARCH**):

```
SEARCH DEL number
```

SECURE CONSOLE

Prevents anyone from loading NLMs from anywhere but **SYS:SYSTEM**. (This prevents unauthorized users from loading NLMs from an area where they may have more rights than in **SYS:SYSTEM**, such as from a disk in the server's disk drive.) This utility also prevents anyone from accessing the operating system's debugger from the server's keyboard, and allows only the administrator to change the server's date and time. To disable this feature, reboot the server.

SEND

Sends a short message from the server console to users on the network. To send a message to a user, use the following command format, replacing *message* with the message you want displayed (no more than 55 characters long) and *user* with either the name of the user or with the workstation's connection number:

```
SEND "message" <user>
```

To send the message to multiple users, separate each username or connection number with a comma or space. To send the message to all users, don't specify a username. (You can also use the **BROADCAST** console utility to accomplish the same thing.)

SERIALVER

This utility is the Java Serial Version Command. See the Novell documentation for more information.

SERVER.EXE

Loads the NetWare server from DOS. When the server computer first boots up, it is running DOS. From DOS, you change to the NWSERVER directory, and then type **SERVER** to load the network operating system.

Usually, the **SERVER** command is added to the AUTOEXEC.BAT file so that the server loads automatically when the computer is booted.

You can also specify how to execute the server's startup files by using the load options listed in Table C.9.

TABLE C.9   SERVER.EXE Load Options

OPTION	DESCRIPTION
–NA	Prevents the AUOTEXEC.NCF file from executing.
–NL	Prevents the Novell logo screen from displaying while the server is starting up.
–NS	Prevents both the AUOTEXEC.NCF file and the STARTUP.NCF file from executing.
–S filename.ncf	Specifies a different .NCF file to execute instead of STARTUP.NCF.

SET

Changes performance parameters for the server. This can be accomplished more easily from NoRM or MONITOR.NLM.

See the **SET** parameters section later in this appendix for more information.

SET TIME

Changes the server's date and time. If you are using time synchronization on your network, you should use this command with caution or time sync problems can result. Use the following syntax:

```
SET TIME <month/day/year> <hour:minute:second>
```

SET TIMEZONE

Changes the server's time zone information. Replace the variables in the following command syntax with the correct information:

```
SET TIMEZONE <zone> <hours> <daylight>
```

▶ Replace *zone* with the three-letter abbreviation for your time zone (such as EST, CST, MST, or PST).

▶ Replace *hours* with the number of hours you are east or west of Greenwich Mean Time (GMT). Precede *hours* with a – (minus) sign if your time zone is east of GMT.

▶ Replace *daylight* with the three-letter abbreviation for your area's daylight saving time (only if you are currently on daylight saving time).

For example, to set the time zone to eastern daylight saving time, type:

```
SET TIMEZONE EST5EDT
```

SHUTDOWN NETWORK INTERFACE

Shuts down a logical board, while leaving its resources intact on the server. This allows the logical board to be restarted, with the **RESET NETWORK INTERFACE** utility, without having to reload and bind the LAN driver. Use the following syntax, substituting the logical board number for *board*:

```
SHUTDOWN NETWORK INTERFACE <board>
```

You can find the board number for each network adapter in your server by using NoRM or MONITOR.NLM.

- ▶ *NoRM*: Open the Disk/LAN Adapters page and click the network adapter you want to remove.

- ▶ *MONITOR.NLM*: Select LAN/WAN drivers and select the driver you want to remove.

SLP

There are several commands associated with configuring the Service Location Protocol (SLP) environment in NetWare 6.5. For more information on using these commands, see the NetWare 6.5 online documentation. Use the following syntax:

```
SLP <option> <option-specific parameters>
```

SPEED

Displays the server processor speed.

START PROCESSORS

Starts all secondary processors in a multiprocessor server. Use the following command format, substituting the number of each processor you want to start for *number*. To specify more than one processor, separate each number with a space. To start all processors, leave *number* blank.

```
START PROCESSORS <number>
```

STARTX.NCF

Starts the graphical server desktop. Java-based applications, such as ConsoleOne, can execute from the graphical server desktop.

STOP PROCESSORS

Stops all secondary processors in a multiprocessor server. Use the following syntax, substituting the number of each processor you want to stop for *number*. To specify more than one processor, separate each number with a space. To stop all secondary processors, leave *number* blank.

```
STOP PROCESSORS <number>
```

SWAP

View, create, and delete virtual memory swap files. For example, to see information about a server's swap files, type the following:

```
SWAP
```

To create a new swap file, type the following, substituting the name of the volume for *volume*:

```
SWAP ADD <volume>
```

By default, this command will create a swap file with a minimum size of 2MB, a maximum size of 5MB, and will leave a minimum of 5MB of free space on the volume. To change any of these parameters (all of which are optional), type the following command instead (substituting the number of megabytes for *size*). You can use any (or all) of these optional parameters.

```
SWAP ADD <volume> MIN=<size1> MAX=<size2> MIN FREE=<size3>
```

To delete a swap file from a volume, type

```
SWAP DEL volume
```

You can do all this much easier with NoRM. Open the View Memory Config page and click Swap File Size.

TIME

Displays the server's date, time, Daylight Saving Time status, and time synchronization information. (To change the date or time, use the SET TIME console utility. To change the server's time zone information, use the SET TIMEZONE console utility.)

UNBIND

Unbinds a protocol, such as IPX or AppleTalk, from a network board. Use the following command format, replacing *protocol* with the name of the protocol, *driver* with the name of the LAN driver or network board from which you want the protocol unbound, and *parameters* with the same parameters you originally specified when you loaded the driver (so that the UNBIND command knows exactly which LAN driver or network board you intend):

```
UNBIND <protocol> FROM <driver parameters>
```

See the BIND section in this appendix for more information about driver parameters.

UNLOAD

Unloads an NLM that's been previously loaded. Use the following syntax, replacing *module* with the name of the NLM you want to unload (you can omit the .NLM extension of the NLM's filename):

UNLOAD *<NLM name>*

VERSION

Displays the version of NetWare running on the server.

VMINFO ON

Enables the NetWare virtual memory information screen in NetWare 6.5.

VMINFO OFF

Disables the virtual memory information screen in NetWare 6.5.

VOLUME

Displays a list of all the volumes currently mounted on the server. The display also indicates which namespaces each volume supports.

NetWare SET Parameters

When you first install NetWare 6.5, the operating system is tuned by default so that its performance is optimized for most systems. Over time, the server optimizes itself according to the network usage it encounters. Occasionally, however, you might find that you want to make manual changes to your system in some aspect of the server's operation. This is particularly true if you are reconfiguring a server specifically to run a different set of service than what is currently configured.

For this reason, there are numerous server parameters you can set to change the way the server handles things such as memory or file locks. These server parameters, also called **SET** parameters, can be set in several ways:

- ▶ *NoRM*: Open the SET parameters page to access all NetWare 6.5 **SET** parameters, by category.

- ▶ *MONITOR.NLM*: Provides menu-driven access to **SET** parameters from the server console. Select Server Parameters from the main menu.

- ▶ *SET console command*: You can change any **SET** parameter individually by using the following general syntax:

SET *<parameter name>* = *<value>*

In most cases, you might not need to change any server parameters. However, if you need to change them, each server parameter is explained in this appendix. There are 14 **SET** parameter categories in NetWare 6.5. Within each category there are hidden and unhidden parameters. Hidden parameters are viewable through NoRM by selecting the View Hidden **SET** Parameters setting on the Set Parameters page. However, information is limited for these parameters and they should be adjusted only if you are absolutely sure of the consequences. The following sections list some, but not all, of the hidden parameters. Use NoRM for a complete listing of potential settings.

Common File System

This category sets basic file system parameters common to both NSS and traditional volumes, including compression characteristics. Table C.10 describes the Common File System parameters.

TABLE C.10   Common File System SET Parameters

PARAMETER	VALUES	DESCRIPTION
Maximum transactions	100 to 10000 (Default: 10000)	Specifies how many transactions can occur simultaneously across all connections.
Maximum concurrent directory cache writes	5 to 500 requests (Default: 75)	Sets the maximum number of write requests that can be stored before the disk head begins a sweep across the disk.
Minimum file delete wait time	0 sec–7 days (Default: 1 min. 6 sec)	Specifies how long a deleted file must be stored before it can be purged.
Immediate purge of deleted files	ON|OFF (Default: OFF)	Specifies whether files are purged immediately when they are deleted or stored in a salvageable state. If turned ON, this parameter purges delet-ed files immediately, and they cannot be salvaged.

TABLE C.10 Continued

PARAMETER	VALUES	DESCRIPTION
Compression daily check stop hour	0–23 (Default: 6)	Specifies the hour, using a 24-hour clock, when the file compressor stops searching volumes for files that need to be compressed. If this value is the same as the Compression daily check starting hour value, the search starts at the specified starting hour and goes until all compressible files have been found.
Compression daily check starting hour	0–23 (Default: 0)	Specifies the hour, using a 24-hour clock, when the file compressor begins searching volumes for files that need to be compressed.
Minimum compression percentage gain	0–50 (Minimum 20)	Specifies the minimum percentage that a file must be able to be compressed in order to remain compressed.
Enable file compression	ON|OFF (Default: ON)	When set to ON, file compression is allowed to occur on volumes that were previously enabled for compression (during installation). Just because a volume is enabled for compression doesn't mean compression will actually occur. This parameter must be turned ON for compression to occur. For more information about file compression, see Chapter 8.

PARAMETER	VALUES	DESCRIPTION
Maximum concurrent compressions	1–8 (Default: 2)	Specifies how many volumes can compress files at the same time. Increasing this value might slow down server performance during compression times.
Convert compressed to uncompressed option	0–2 (Default: 1)	Specifies how a compressed file is stored after it has been accessed. 0 = always leave the file compressed; 1 = leave the file compressed after the first access within the time frame defined by the Days untouched before compression parameter and then leave the file uncompressed after the second access; 2 = change the file to uncompressed after the first access.
Decompress percent disk space free to allow commit	0–75 (Default: 10)	Specifies the percentage of free disk space that is required on a volume before committing an uncompressed file to disk. This helps you avoid running out of disk space by uncompressing files.
Decompress free space warning interval	0 sec–29 days 15 hours, 50 min 3.8 sec. (Default: 31 min 18.5 sec)	Specifies the interval between warnings when the volume doesn't have enough disk space for uncompressed files.

TABLE C.10   Continued

PARAMETER	VALUES	DESCRIPTION
Deleted files compression option	0–2 (Default: 1)	Specifies how the server handles deleted files. 0 = don't compress deleted files; 1 = compress deleted files during the next day's search; 2 = compress deleted files immediately.
Days untouched before compression	-0–100000 (Default: 14)	Specifies how many days a file or directory must remain untouched before being compressed.

Communications

Communication parameters configure the way the operating system handles communication buffers. Table C.11 describes the communication parameters that are available.

TABLE C.11   Communication SET Parameters

PARAMETER	VALUES	DESCRIPTION
IPX CMD Mode Routing	ON|OFF (Default: OFF)	When set to ON, turns on IPX Compatibility Mode routing.
SPX Maximum Window Size	0–16 (Default: 0)	Sets the maximum SPXS window size.
Load Balance Local LAN	ON|OFF (Default: OFF)	Turns load balancing on or off.
Maximum Pending TCP Connection Requests	ON|OFF (Default: OFF)	Determines whether IPX Compatibility Mode routing is enabled.
BSD Socket default Buffer Size in Bytes	4096 to 1073741824 bytes (Default: 32768)	This parameter is used to set the BSD socket default send and receive buffer size. The constraint is given in bytes.

PARAMETER	VALUES	DESCRIPTION
Discard Oversize PING Packets	ON|OFF (Default: ON)	Determines whether to discard ping packets larger than Largest Ping Packet Size.
Largest Ping Packet Size	The range is 0 to 65535	This option sets the largest ping packet size that can be received by the server.
TCP Defend Land Attacks	ON|OFF (Default: ON)	Sets whether TCP defends against land attacks.
IP Wan Client Validation	ON|OFF (Default: OFF)	Sets whether IP WAN clients are validated when they dial in to the network remotely via NetWare Connect.
TOS for IP Packets	0 to 127 (Default: 0)	This SET option is used to set the Type of Service (TOS) in the IP header for all outgoing packets for all available interfaces.
Arp Entry Update Time	240 to 14400 (Default: 300)	This parameter is used to change the update time of Address Resolution Protocol (Arp) entries in seconds. It is recommended that the Arp entry update time be greater than or equal to the Arp entry expiry time.
Arp entry expiry time	240 to 14400 (Default: 300)	This option is used to change the expiry time of Arp entries in seconds. It is recommended that the Apr entry expiry time be less than or equal to the Arp entry update time.

TABLE C.11   Continued

PARAMETER	VALUES	DESCRIPTION
ICMP Redirect Timeout	0–525600 (Default: 3)	Allows ICMP learned routes to expire. 146 = 1 sec.
Largest UDP Packet Size	0–36992 (Default: 16384)	Set maximum allowable UDP packet for this server.
Discard Oversized UDP Packets	ON|OFF (Default: ON)	Discards UDP packets larger than Largest UDP Packet Size.
TCP UDP Diagnostic Services	ON|OFF (Default: OFF)	Allows you to start or stop diagnostic servers over TCP and UDP.
TCP Path MTU Black Hole Detection and Recovery	ON|OFF (Default OFF)	This option is used to enable or disable Path Maximum Transmission Unit (MTU) Black Hole Detection and Recovery feature. This feature aids in resolving the problems of datagrams being sent out, but no replies come back.
TCP Max Port Limit	4999–54999 (Default: 54999)	Defines the upper limit for ephemeral, or user-configurable, TCP ports.
TCP Sack Option	ON|OFF (Default: ON)	This SET option is used to enable or disable Selective Acknowledgment (Sack) support. This set option will not change the behavior of existing connections.
TCP Large Window Option	ON|OFF (Default: ON)	Use this parameter to enable or disable Large Window support. This set option will not change the behavior of existing connections.

PARAMETER	VALUES	DESCRIPTION
Maximum RIP SAP Events	1 to 100000 (Default: 100)	Limits the SAP and RIP traffic on network.
IPX Router Broadcast Delay	0, 1, 2 (Default: 0; Adjust based on size of RIP/SAP tables)	Sets how long the IPX router waits between SAP/RIP broadcast packets.
IPX NETBios replication option	0–3 (Default: 2) 0 = no replication of broadcasts; 1 = replicate broadcasts; 2 = replicate broadcasts, but suppress duplicate broadcasts; 3 = same as 2, but do not replicate to WAN links	Sets how the IPX router handles replicated NetBIOS broadcasts.
Use old watchdog packet type	ON|OFF (Default: OFF)	Sets server to use type 0 instead of type 4 watchdog packets. Use this option if you use older router hardware that filters out type 4 IPX packets.
Reply to get nearest server	ON|OFF (Default: ON)	When set to ON, this server will respond to workstations that request a connection to their nearest server.
Number of watchdog packets	5–100 (Default: 10)	Sets the number of watchdog packets the server sends to an unresponsive workstation before clearing the workstation's connection.
Delay between watchdog packets	9.9 sec to 10 min 26.2 sec (Default: 59.3)	Sets the time the server waits before sending each watchdog packet.

TABLE C.11   Continued

PARAMETER	VALUES	DESCRIPTION
Delay before first watchdog packet	15.7 sec to 14 days (Default: 4 min 56.6 sec)	Sets the time the server waits before sending the first watchdog packet to an unresponsive workstation.
Console display watchdog logouts	ON|OFF (Default: OFF)	When set to ON, a console message is displayed when the watchdog clears a workstation's connection.
Maximum packet receive buffers	50 to 4294967295 (Default: 500)	Sets the maximum number of packet receive buffers the server can allocate.
Minimum packet receive buffers	10 to 4294967295 (Default: 128)	Sets the minimum number of packet receive buffers that the server can allocate. This number is allocated automatically when the server is booted.
Maximum physical receive packet size	618 to 24682 bytes (Default: 4224)	Sets the largest size of packets that can be received by an MLIB. Default size is acceptable for Ethernet and token ring boards. If some boards on the network can transmit more than 512 bytes of data per packet, use the largest packet size.
New packet receive buffer wait time	0.1 to 20 sec (Default: 0.1)	Sets the time the operating system waits after allocating the minimum number of buffers before granting the next packet receive buffer.

PARAMETER	VALUES	DESCRIPTION
Maximum interrupt events	1 to 1000000 (Default: 10)	Sets the maximum number of interrupt time events (such as IPX routing) that occurs before a thread switch is guaranteed to have occurred.

Directory Services

Directory Caching parameters enable you to configure how directory cache buffers are used to optimize access to frequently used directories. A *directory cache buffer* is a portion of server memory that holds a directory entry that is accessed frequently. A directory entry held in memory is accessed faster than a directory entry stored on the hard disk. Table C.12 describes the Directory Caching parameters that are available.

TABLE C.12 Directory Services SET Parameters

PARAMETER	VALUES	DESCRIPTION
NDS trace to screen	ON|OFF (Default: OFF)	When set to ON, the NDS trace screen, which displays information about NDS events, is turned on.
NDS trace to file	ON|OFF (Default: OFF)	When set to ON, the NDS trace information is sent to a file in the SYS: SYSTEM directory, named DSTRACE.DBG by default.
NDS trace filename	Path and filename (Default: SYS: SYSTEM\DSTRACE.DBG)	Specifies a different pathname or filename for the NDS trace file.
Bindery context	Name of Bindery Context(s) (Default: None)	Specifies which containers and their objects will be used as the server's "bindery" when the server provides bindery services. You can include up to 16 containers as part of this server's bindery context. Separate each context with a semicolon.

TABLE C.12 Continued

PARAMETER	VALUES	DESCRIPTION
NDS external reference life span	1–384 hours (Default: 192)	Sets the number of hours that unused external references (local IDs assigned to users when they access other servers) can exist before they are removed.
NDS inactivity synchronization interval	2–1440 minutes (Default: 60)	Sets how many minutes can elapse between exhaustive synchronization checks. Set high (up to 240 minutes) if replicas have to synchronize across WAN connections to reduce network traffic.
NDS synchronization restrictions	ON|OFF (Default: OFF)	When set to OFF, the server synchronizes with all versions of NDS that are available on the network. When this parameter is ON, the server synchronizes only with the versions of NDS specified (such as "On, 489, 492, 599").
NDS servers status	UP|DOWN (Default: None)	Sets the status of all Server objects in the local NDS database as either up or down, so you can force the network to recognize that a particular server is up when the network thinks it is down.

PARAMETER	VALUES	DESCRIPTION
NDS janitor interval	1–10080 minutes (Default: 60)	Specifies how often, in minutes, the janitor process runs. The janitor process cleans up unused records, reclaims disk space, and purges deleted objects.
NDS Distributed reference link interval	1–10080 minutes (Default: 780)	Specifies how often, in minutes, the NDS distributed reference link consistency check is performed.
NDS Bindery QoS Mask	0–4294967295 (Default: 8)	Selects which eDirectory objects should be subject to the bindery quality of service delay.
NDS Bindery QoS Delay	0–60000 msec (Default: 150)	Specifies the delay between successfully finding a requested bindery object and returning it to the requesting process.
NDS backlink interval	1–10080 minutes (Default: 780)	Specifies how often, in minutes, backlink consistency is checked. Backlinks indicate that an object in a replica has an ID on a server where the replica does not exist.
NDS trace file length to zero	ON|OFF (Default: OFF)	When set to ON, the server deletes the contents of the NDS trace file (but does not delete the trace file itself). To delete the file contents, also set the NDS Trace to File parameter to ON, so that the file will be open for the deletion process.

TABLE C.12 Continued

PARAMETER	VALUES	DESCRIPTION
NDS bootstrap address	IP address (Default: None)	Specifies the address of a remote server with which this server can perform tree connectivity operations. Set only if this server does not hold a replica.

Disk

Disk parameters allow you to control several aspects of your disk drive operation and configuration, including disk mirroring for fault tolerance. Table C.13 describes the SET parameters available in the Disk category.

TABLE C.13 Disk SET Parameters

PARAMETER	VALUES	DESCRIPTION
Auto Scan of CDM Modules	ON|OFF (Default: ON)	When set to ON, the server automatically scans and loads defined generic Custom Device Modules (CDMs). If turned off, the desired CDMs must be loaded manually, or added to the STARTUP.NCF file.
Sequential elevator depth	0–294967295 (Default: 8)	Sets the number of sequential requests that the Media Manager will send to the same device. If another device in the mirror group is idle when the first device contains this number of requests, Media Manager will begin sending requests to the idle device.

PARAMETER	VALUES	DESCRIPTION
Enable IO handicap attribute	ON|OFF (Default: OFF)	When set to ON, it allows drivers and applications to set and use an attrib- ute to inhibit (or handi- cap) read requests from one or more devices. When turned off, NetWare can treat the device like any other device. Do not turn this parameter on unless instructed to by the manufacturer.
Mirrored devices are out of sync message frequency	5–9999 minutes (Default: 28)	Specifies how often devices are checked for out-of-sync status.
Remirror block size	1–8 (Default: 1)	Specifies the remirror block size in multiples of 4K. 1 = 4K, 2 = 8K, 3 = 12K, and so on.
Ignore Partition Ownership	ON|OFF (Default: OFF)	When set to ON, partitions owned by other servers in a cluster can be activated on this server.
Concurrent remirror requests	2–32 (Default: 32)	Sets the number of simultaneous remirror requests that can occur per logical disk partition.
Ignore disk geometry	ON|OFF (Default: OFF)	When set to ON, allows the creation of nonstan- dard and unsupported partitions on the server's hard disk.
Enable Hardware Write Back	ON|OFF (Default: OFF)	Enables storage drivers to use the hardware write- back feature if they sup- port it. This allows I/O write requests to be cached and processed before the data is actually written to the disk, which can increase performance.

TABLE C.13 Continued

PARAMETER	VALUES	DESCRIPTION
Enable disk read after write verify	ON|OFF (Default: OFF)	Specifies whether data written to disk is compared with the data in memory to verify its accuracy. If set to ON, this parameter tells the driver to perform the highest level of read-after-write verification that it can. If set to OFF, this parameter turns off any form of read-after-write verification that the driver performs. If the disk controller has a built-in function for read-after-write verification, leave this parameter OFF.

Error Handling

Error-handling parameters let you manage log files and error recovery options in NetWare 6.5. Table C.14 describes the error-handling parameters available in NetWare 6.5.

TABLE C.14 Error-Handling SET Parameters

PARAMETERS	VALUES	DESCRIPTION
Server log file state	0–2 (Default: 1)	Specifies what action to take when the server log, SYS$LOG.ERR, reaches its maximum size. 0 = take no action; 1 = delete the log file; 2 = rename the log file.
Server log file overflow size	65536–4294967295 bytes (Default: 4194304)	Specifies the maximum size of SYS$LOG.ERR.

PARAMETER	VALUES	DESCRIPTION
Boot error log file state	0–3 (Default: 3)	Specifies what action to take when the boot log, BOOT$LOG.ERR, reaches its maximum size. 0 = take no action; 1 = delete the log file; 2 = rename the log file; 3 = start a new log file each time the server reboots.
Boot error log file overflow size	65536 to 4294967295 bytes (Default: 4194304)	Specifies the maximum size of BOOT$LOG.ERR.
Boot error log	ON|OFF (Default: ON)	When turned on, specifies that all console error messages are saved in the BOOT$LOG.ERR file. When turned off, only error messages that occur during the boot procedure are saved in this file.
Hung unload wait delay	0 sec–1 min 58.3 sec (Default: 30 sec)	Specifies how long the system will wait for a hung NLM to unload before asking the user whether to shut down the NLM's address space. Used only for NLMs loaded in protected memory spaces.
Auto Restart Down Timeout	0–600 sec (Default: 180)	Specifies the time that a server will wait before automatically restarting after an ABEND. This prevents the server from hanging if a problem occurs while it is trying to go down.

TABLE C.14   Continued

PARAMETER	VALUES	DESCRIPTION
Auto restart after ABEND delay time	2–60 minutes (Default: 2)	Sets the time that the server will wait before automatically shutting down and restarting after an ABEND occurs.
Auto restart after ABEND	0–3 (Default: 1)	Determines whether the server automatically attempts to recover if an ABEND occurs. 0 = the server does not restart itself; 1 = the server determines the ABEND cause, and then either keeps the computer running or shuts it down and restarts; 2 = the server attempts to recover, and then shuts down and restarts the server in the configured amount of time; 3 = the server immediately shuts down and restarts.

Licensing Services

Licensing Services parameters provides a few Novell Licensing Services (NLS) configuration parameters. Table C.15 describes the licensing services parameters available in NetWare 6.5.

TABLE C.15   Licensing Services SET Parameters

PARAMETER	VALUES	DESCRIPTION
NLS search type	0–1 (Default: 0)	Specifies where to stop the upward tree search for license objects. 0 = stop search at tree root, 1 = stop search at partition root. Setting this parameter to 1 will limit

PARAMETER	VALUES	DESCRIPTION
		the scope of a license search to the current partition.
`Store NetWare 5 Conn SCL MLA usage in NDS`	ON|OFF (Default: OFF)	Setting this to ON moves MLA-type server connection licenses (SCL) for NetWare 5 servers into eDirectory where they can be more easily managed.
`NLSTRACE`	0–2 (Default: 0)	Specifies if/how NLS trace files should be managed. 0 = no trace, 1 = trace to screen, 2 = trace to screen and file (`SYS:SYSTEM\NLSTRACE.DBG`).

Memory

Memory parameters enable you to configure how the server's memory is managed. There are also a bunch of hidden **SET** parameters in this category, which are viewable through NoRM but not Monitor. Table C.16 describes the memory parameters available in NetWare 6.5.

TABLE C.16   Memory SET Parameters

PARAMETER	VALUES	DESCRIPTION
`VM garbage collector period`	10 sec–23 h 59 m 29 s (Default: 5 min)	Specifies how often the Virtual Memory (VM) garbage collector will run. The VM garbage collector analyzes virtual memory, identifying memory contents that are no longer in use, cleaning them up.
`VM garbage collector looks`	1–1048576 memory pages (Default: 10000)	Each time the VM garbage collector runs, this variable determines how many memory pages are examined.

TABLE C.16   Continued

PARAMETER	VALUES	DESCRIPTION
Interactive screen timeout	0 sec–2730+ days (Default: 1 hour)	Specifies the amount of time that the current interactive screen will wait for some type of user input.
Average page in alert threshold	1 to 4294967295 memory pages (Default: 2000)	Specifies the average number of incoming virtual memory pages that will trigger an alert to the system console.
Restart server on address space cleanup failure	ON|OFF (Default: OFF)	When set to OFF, the server will isolate address spaces that cannot be cleaned up completely. When set to ON the server will react according to the Auto Restart settings in the Error, Handling SET Parameters. See the Error Handling section for more information.
Memory protection ABEND after restart count	ON|OFF (Default: OFF)	If set to ON, the server will ABEND if an address space restarts more than the number of times specified in Memory protection restart count, within the time interval specified by Memory protection no restart interval.
Memory protection restart count	1–1000 (Default: 1)	Specifies the number of restarts allowed during Memory Protection No Restart Interval. An address space will restart if a protection fault occurs. This param-eter limits the number of

PARAMETER	VALUES	DESCRIPTION
		the number of errors that can occur during the defined interval.
Memory protection no restart interval	0–60 minutes (Default: 1)	Specifies the interval over which the number of address space restarts are tracked. If the number of restarts exceeds `Memory protection restart count` during the interval, the address space will not be restarted. Setting the parameter to 0 turns the interval off, allowing the address space to restart regardless of faults.
Memory protection fault cleanup	ON|OFF (Default: ON)	When set to ON, specifies that an address space is removed and its NLMs unloaded if an NLM in the space attempts to violate memory protection. When set to OFF, the address space isn't cleaned up, and the problem is left to be handled by the normal ABEND recovery process.
Garbage collection interval	1 min–1 hour (Default: 5 min)	Sets the maximum time between garbage collections.
Alloc memory check flag	ON|OFF (Default: OFF)	When set to ON, the server is set to do corruption checking in the alloc memory nodes.
Reserved buffers below 16 meg	8–2000 (Default: 300)	Reserves the specified number of cache buffers in lower memory for device drivers that do not support memory access above 16MB.

Miscellaneous

The Miscellaneous category includes all those "other" parameters that don't fit in a specific category. Table C.17 describes the Miscellaneous SET parameters available in NetWare 6.5.

TABLE C.17 Miscellaneous SET Parameters

PARAMETER	VALUES	DESCRIPTION
Display incomplete IPX packet alerts	ON|OFF (Default: ON)	When set to ON, alert messages are displayed when IPX receives incomplete packets.
Enable SECURE.NCF	ON|OFF (Default: OFF)	When set to ON, causes the SECURE.NCF file to be executed when the server boots. This file is used to set configuration parameters necessary for a C2 security-compliant system. See the NetWare security documentation for more information.
Allow audit passwords	ON|OFF (Default: OFF)	When set to ON, allows audit password requests to be used.
Command line prompt default choice	ON|OFF (Default: ON)	Sets the default input for the conditional execution ("?") console command. ON = Yes, OFF = No.
Command line prompt time out	0 to 4294967295 sec (Default: 10)	Sets the number of seconds the conditional execution ("?") will wait before using the default answer.
Sound bell for alerts	ON|OFF (Default: ON)	When set to ON, a sound emits whenever an alert message appears on the server's console screen.

PARAMETER	VALUES	DESCRIPTION
Replace console prompt with server name	ONIOFF (Default: ON)	When set to ON, the server's name is displayed as the console prompt on the server command line.
Alert message nodes	10–256 (Default: 20)	Determines how many alert message nodes are pre-allocated. This sets aside memory to receive alert messages.
Classic work to do Pre Check Flag	ONIOFF (Default: OFF)	If an event is scheduled using the classic NetWare WorkToDo method, setting this to ON causes the process scheduler to see if the event is already on the scheduler list.
Worker thread execute in a row count	1–20 (Default: 10)	Determines how many times in a row the scheduler dispatches new work before allowing other threads to execute.
Halt system on invalid parameters	ONIOFF (Default: OFF)	When set to ON, the system stops whenever invalid parameters or conditions are detected. When this parameter is set to OFF, the system displays an alert message but continues running if an invalid parameter is detected.
Display relinquish control alerts	ONIOFF (Default: OFF)	When set to ON, messages are displayed when an NLM uses the server's processor for more than 0.4 seconds without giving up control to other processes. This command is useful if you are writing your own NLMs and want to see if your NLM is using the CPU correctly.

TABLE C.17 Continued

PARAMETER	VALUES	DESCRIPTION
Display old API names	ON|OFF (Default: OFF)	When set to ON, messages are displayed when API calls from older versions of NetWare are used by an NLM. If you receive these messages, you might want to contact the NLM manufacturer for an upgrade that uses current the current API set, which will provide better performance.
CPU hog timeout amount	O sec–1 hour (Default: 1 min)	Sets the amount of time the system waits before terminating a process that has not relinquished control of the CPU. If set to 0, this option is disabled.
Developer option	ON|OFF (Default: OFF)	When set to ON, options that are associated with a developer environment are enabled.
Display spurious interrupt alerts threshold	1–1000000 per sec (Default: 200)	Specifies how many spurious interrupts per second must occur before a spurious interrupt alert is sent to the console.
Display lost interrupt alerts threshold	1–1000000 per sec (Default: 10)	Specifies how many lost interrupts per second must occur before a lost interrupt alert is sent to the console.

PARAMETER	VALUES	DESCRIPTION
Display spurious interrupt alerts	ON|OFF (Default: OFF)	When set to ON, error messages are displayed when the server hardware creates an interrupt that has been reserved for another device. If you receive this error, remove all add-on boards and run SERVER.EXE (the NetWare operating system). If the message doesn't appear after you remove everything, add the boards one at a time until you locate the board that is generating the message. Then contact the board's vendor or manufacturer for assistance.
Display lost interrupt alerts	ON|OFF (Default: OFF)	When set to ON, error messages are displayed when a driver or board makes an interrupt call but drops the request before it's filled. To identify the problem driver, unload all drivers, and then reload them one at a time. When you locate the driver that is generating the message, contact the driver's manufacturer.
Pseudo preemption count	1–4294967295 (Default: 40)	Sets how many times threads can make file read or write system calls before they are forced to relinquish control.

TABLE C.17 Continued

PARAMETER	VALUES	DESCRIPTION
Global pseudo preemption	ON|OFF (Default: ON)	When set to ON, all threads are forced to use pseudo preemption.
Minimum service processes	10–500 (Default: 25)	Sets the minimum number of service processes the server can allocate without waiting for the amount of time specified in the New service process wait time parameter.
Maximum service processes	5–1000 (Default: 500)	Sets the maximum number of service processes the server can create. Increase this parameter if the number of service processes (as shown in NoRM) is at the maximum
New service process wait time	.3 sec–20 sec (Default: 2.2 sec)	Determines how long the server waits to allocate another service process after receiving an NCP request. If a service process is freed up during this time, a new one will not be allocated.
Allow unencrypted passwords	ON|OFF (Default: OFF)	When set to ON, the server will accept unencrypted passwords. This is only required for ancient versions of NetWare, which you shouldn't be using anymore anyway.

Multiprocessor

Multiprocessor parameters enable you to configure settings for servers with multiple processors. Table C.18 describes the Multiprocessor SET parameters in NetWare 6.5.

TABLE C.18 Multiprocessor SET Parameters

PARAMETER	VALUES	DESCRIPTION
System threshold	0–102400 (Default: 1536)	Specifies the threshold for calculating thread shedding for load balancing. *Thread shedding* is the process of transferring process threads to another processor when a processor starts to get overloaded.
Auto clear interrupt statistics	ON|OFF (Default: ON)	When set to ON, the detailed statistics for an offline processor or removed interrupt handles are removed from memory. When set to OFF, the statistics are retained in memory. Must be set in START-UP.NCF. Changes will take effect when server is rebooted.
Auto start processors	ON|OFF (Default: ON)	When set to ON, secondary processors are automatically started when the PSM (Platform Support Module) is loaded. When set to OFF, you must use the console command **START PROCESSORS** to start secondary processors.

NCP

NCP (NetWare Core Protocol) parameters enable you to configure NCP packets, control boundary checking, and change NCP Packet Signature security levels on the server. Table C.19 describes the NCP **SET** parameters in NetWare 6.5.

TABLE C.19   NCP SET Parameters

PARAMETER	VALUES	DESCRIPTION
NCP exclude IP addresses	max 191 char (Default: None)	Specifies IP addresses over which NCP is disabled. All other IP addresses on this server will accept NCP traffic. NONE indicates that no bound IP addresses on this server will disable NCP. ALL indicates that NCP is disabled on all bound IP addresses. Addresses listed here have priority over the SET NCP Include IP Addresses command.
NCP include IP addresses	max 191 char (Default: All)	Specifies IP addresses over which NCP is enabled. NONE indicates that NCP is disabled on all bound IP addresses. ALL indicates that NCP is enabled on all bound IP addresses.
NCP over UDP	ON|OFF (Default: ON)	This parameter enables NCP packets over the UDP transport.
NCP TCP keep alive interval	0 sec–16 hours (Default: 9 min 53 sec)	Specifies how long before "TCP keep-alive" closes idle NCP connections. A value of 0 indicates that idle connections are never closed.
Minimum NCP TCP receive window to advertise	256–16384 (Default: 4096)	Sets the minimum receive window to advertise on NCP connections.
NCP TCP receive window	1400–65535 (Default: 23360)	Sets the advertised receive window on NCP connections.

PARAMETER	VALUES	DESCRIPTION
Enable UDP checksums on NCP packets	0–2 (Default: 1)	Specifies how check-summing of NCP UDP packets is handled. 0 = no checksums; 1 = checksums performed if enabled at the client; 2 = checksums required.
Enable IPX checksums	0–2 (Default: 1)	Sets the IPX checksum level. 0 = no checksums; 1 = checksums performed if enabled on the client; 2 = checksums required.
Enable task zero checking	ON|OFF (Default: OFF)	This is a read-only parameter and is provided for informational purposes only.
NCP packet signature option	0–3 (Default: 1)	Sets the server's NCP packet signature security level. 0 = don't do packet signatures; 1 = do packet signatures only if the client requires them; 2 = do packet signatures if the client can, but don't require them if the client doesn't support them; 3 = require packet signatures. After startup, you can only increase the level.
Client file caching enabled	ON|OFF (Default: ON)	When set to ON, allows clients to cache open files locally, thereby increasing file access performance.
NCP protocol preferences	IPX, TCP, UDP (Default: None)	Specifies the preferred protocol order of the loaded transports. List each transport separated by a space.

TABLE C.19   Continued

PARAMETER	VALUES	DESCRIPTION
NCP file commit	ON|OFF (Default: OFF)	When set to ON, an application is allowed to issue a File Commit NCP and flush the file immediately from cache to disk.
Display NCP bad component warnings	ON|OFF (Default: OFF)	When set to ON, NCP bad component alert messages are displayed.
Reject NCP packets with bad components	ON|OFF (Default: OFF)	When set to ON, the server rejects NCP packets that fail component checking.
Display NCP bad length warnings	ON|OFF (Default: OFF)	When set to ON, NCP bad-length alert messages are displayed.
Reject NCP packets with bad lengths	ON|OFF (Default: OFF)	When set to ON, the server rejects NCP packets that fail boundary checking.
Maximum outstanding NCP searches	10–1000 (Default: 51)	Determines the maximum number of NCP directory searches that can be performed at the same time.
Allow change to client rights	ON|OFF (Default: ON)	When set to ON, a job server is allowed to assume a client's rights for NCP Packet Signature. If you are concerned that a job or print server may forge packets, turn off this parameter.
Allow LIP	ON|OFF (Default: ON)	When set to ON, support for Large Internet Packets is enabled.

Novell Storage Services

A new category, added for NetWare 6.5, is Novell Storage Services (NSS).
This category introduces 23 new parameters to allow customization of
NSS. Table C.20 describes the NSS parameters available in NetWare 6.5.

TABLE C.20 NSS SET Parameters

PARAMETER	VALUES	DESCRIPTION
NSS auto locks CD-ROM disc in device	ON|OFF (Default: OFF)	Disables the ability to eject a CD-ROM that is mounted as an NSS logical volume.
NSS auto update CD9660 volume objects to NDS	ON|OFF (Default: OFF)	Automatically mounts a 9660 format CD-ROM when it is inserted into the server's CD-ROM reader.
Emulate classic NetWare directory quotas	ON|OFF (Default: OFF	Setting this parameter ON instructs the server to emulate pre–NetWare 6.5 disk quotas.
NSS work to do count	5–100 entries (Default: 40)	This parameter determines the number of WorkToDo entries that can be concurrently executing.
NSS maximum cache balance buffers per session	16–1048576 buffers (Default: 1024)	This parameter limits the number of cache buffers used during a cache balance operation.
NSS cache balance timer	1–3600 sec (Default: 30)	This parameter sets the cache balance timer.
NSS cache balance percent	1–99 percent (Default: 60)	This parameter sets what percentage of free memory NSS will use for its buffer cache.
NSS cache balance enable	ON|OFF (Default: ON)	This parameter sets the dynamic balancing of free memory for the NSS buffer cache.

TABLE C.20   Continued

PARAMETER	VALUES	DESCRIPTION
NSS buffer flush timer	1–3600 sec (Default: 1)	Specifies the delay before flushing modified cache buffers to disk.
NSS minimum OS cache buffers	256–1048576 entries (Default: 256)	Specifies the minimum number of NetWare buffer cache entries.
NSS minimum cache buffers	256–1048576 (Default: 256)	Specifies the minimum number of NSS buffer cache entries.
NSS file flush timer	1–3600 sec (Default: 10)	Specifies the delay before flushing modified open files to disk.
NSS closed file cache size	0–1000000 (Default: 50000)	Specifies the number of closed files that can be cached in memory.
NSS open file hash shift	8–25 (Default: 16)	Specifies the size of the Open File hash table in powers of 2. For example, a setting of 10 indicates 210, or 1024 bytes.
NSS auth cache size	16–50000 entries (Default: 1024)	Specifies the number of authorization cache entries.
NSS ASCII name cache enable	ON|OFF (Default: ON)	This parameter enables or disables ASCII name caching.
NSS name cache enable	ON|OFF (Default: ON)	This parameter enables or disables name caching.
NSS name cache size	3–65521 entries (Default: 2111)	This parameter sets the number of name cache entries.
NSS low volume space alerts	ON|OFF (Default: ON)	This parameter enables or disables sending messages warning of low storage space to all users.

PARAMETER	VALUES	DESCRIPTION
NSS low volume space warning reset threshold	0–1000000 MB (Default: 15)	This parameter sets the threshold, above which a low storage space warning is reset.
NSS low volume space warning threshold	0–1000000 (Default: 10)	This parameter sets the threshold below which a low storage space warning will be issued.

Service Location Protocol

Service Location Protocol (SLP) parameters enable you to configure SLP values. Table C.21 describes the SLP parameters in NetWare 6.5.

TABLE C.21   Service Location Protocol SET Parameters

PARAMETER	VALUES	DESCRIPTION
SLP exclude IP addresses	Max 191 char (Default: NONE)	Specifies IP addresses over which SLP is disabled. All other IP addresses on this server will accept SLP traffic. NONE indicates that SLP is enabled on all addresses. ALL indicates that SLP is disabled on all bound IP addresses. This setting overrides SLP include IP addresses.
SLP include IP addresses	Max 191 char (Default: ALL)	This parameter allows you to specify IP addresses over which SLP is enabled. All other IP addresses on this server will ignore SLP traffic. If you specify NONE, it indicates that SLP is disabled on all IP addresses. Specifying ALL enables SLP over all bound IP addresses on this server.

TABLE C.21   Continued

PARAMETER	VALUES	DESCRIPTION
SLP agent IP address	Max 31 char (Default: FIRST)	This SET parameter specifies the IP address of the SLP Directory Agent (DA) on this server. You specify FIRST to use the first bound non-excluded IP address. FOLLOW may be specified to use the IP address of the received DA service request.
SLP API handicap	1–100000 (Default: 50)	The maximum number of UA requests before SLP starts slowing them down.
SLP nwserver NLM names	ON|OFF (Default: OFF)	This parameter enables or disables the nwserver.novell service, which includes NLM names as an SLP attribute.
SLP maximum WTD	1–64 (Default: 10)	Sets the maximum number of controlled WorkToDos supported on this server.
SLP reset	ON|OFF (Default: OFF)	Forces the service agent to send new service registers. Forces the directory agent to send DA Advertise. After execution, flag is reset to OFF.
SLP scope list	Max 185 char (Default: NA)	Holds a comma-delimited list of Service Agent scopes.
SLP close idle TCP connections time	0–86400 sec (Default: 300)	Specifies how many seconds the system must wait before closing idle TCP connections.

PARAMETER	VALUES	DESCRIPTION
SLP DA heart beat time	0–65535 sec (Default: 10800)	Specifies how many seconds the system must wait before sending the next DA heartbeat packet.
SLP DA event timeout	0–120 sec (Default: 15)	Specifies how many seconds the system must wait before timing out a DA packet request.
SLP event timeout	0–120 sec (Default: 3)	Specifies how many seconds the system must wait before timing out a multicast packet request.
SLP SA default lifetime	0–65535 sec (Default: 3600)	Specifies the default lifetime for service registers.
SLP retry count	0–128 (Default: 3)	Specifies the maximum number of retry attempts.
SLP debug	0–65535 (Default: 0)	When set to 0, turns off debug mode. When set to a number, turns on debug mode. Bit 0x01 = COMM; 0x02 = TRAN; 0x04 = API; 0x08 = ERR; 0x20 = SA.
SLP rediscover inactive directory agents	0–86400 (Default: 60)	Specifies how many seconds the system must wait before issuing service requests to rediscover inactive DAs.
SLP multicast radius	0–32 (Default: 32)	Specifies the multicast radius.
SLP DA discovery options	0–8 (Default: 7)	Sets the DA discovery option bit flag. Bit 0x01 = use multicast DA advertisements; 0x02 = use DHCP discovery; 0x04 = use static file SYS:ETC\SLP.CFG; 0x08 = scopes required.

TABLE C.21 Continued

PARAMETER	VALUES	DESCRIPTION
SLP MTU size	0–24682 bytes (Default: 1450)	Specifies the maximum transfer unit size.
SLP broadcast	ON|OFF (Default: OFF)	When set to ON, tells SLP to use broadcast packets instead of multicast packets. When set to OFF, tells SLP to use multicast packets.
SLP TCP	ON|OFF (Default: OFF)	When set to ON, tells SLP to use TCP packets instead of UDP packets when possible. When set to OFF, tells SLP to use UDP packets.

Time

Initially, you set up time services on the server during installation. Time services are controlled by TIMESYNC.NLM, which is loaded automatically when the server is started up. To modify time synchronization after installation, use the Time SET parameters, which are described in Table C.22.

All parameters that start with the word TIMESYNC are elements of the TIMESYNC.CFG file. NetWare 6.5 now updates the TIMESYNC.CFG file automatically when you make changes to these settings. You can use EDIT.NLM to modify the TIMESYNC.CFG file directly.

TABLE C.22 Time SET Parameters

PARAMETER	VALUES	DESCRIPTION
TIMESYNC configuration file	path\filename (Default: SYS: SYSTEM\ TIMESYNC.CFG)	Specifies the directory and filename of the time synchronization configuration file.
TIMESYNC configured sources	ON|OFF (Default: OFF)	When set to ON, the server ignores SAP (Service Advertising Protocol) time sources and instead accepts time sources configured with the

PARAMETER	VALUES	DESCRIPTION
		TIMESYNC Time Source parameter. When this parameter is turned OFF, it causes the server to listen to any advertising time source.
Start of daylight savings time	Max 79 char (First Sunday in April @0200)	Indicates the day that daylight saving time begins locally. To specify the beginning of daylight saving time so it recurs every year, enclose the date and time in parentheses, and use the following format: (April Sunday First 2:00:00 a.m.). If you do not enclose the date in parentheses, the change will occur only in the current year. "April Sunday First" indicates that the change occurs on the first Sunday in April.
End of daylight savings time	Max 79 char (Default: Last Sunday in October @0200)	Indicates the day that daylight saving time ends locally. To specify the end of daylight saving time so it recurs every year, enclose the date and time in parentheses, and use the following format: (October Sunday Last 2:00:00 a.m.). If you do not enclose the date in parentheses, the change will occur only in the current year. "October Sunday Last" indicates that the change occurs on the last Sunday in October.

TABLE C.22   Continued

PARAMETER	VALUES	DESCRIPTION
Daylight savings time offset	+or- hour:minute: second (Default: +1:00:00)	Specifies the offset applied to time calculations when daylight saving time is in effect, causing UTC time to be recalculated from local time.
Daylight savings time status	ON|OFF (Default: NA)	When set to ON, this parameter indicates that daylight saving time is currently in effect. Changing this parameter does not change the local time on the server.
New time with daylight savings time status	ON|OFF (Default: ON)	When set to ON, the local time on the server is adjusted by adding or subtracting the time indicated in the Daylight saving time offset parameter.
TIMESYNC directory tree mode	ON|OFF (Default: ON)	When set to ON, time synchronization ignores SAP (Service Advertising Protocol) packets that don't originate from within the server's Directory tree. When this parameter is set to OFF, the server accepts SAP packets from any time source on the network, regardless of the tree from which it originates. If SAP is turned on, this parameter should also be set to ON.
TIMESYNC polling count	1–1000 packets (Default: 3)	Specifies the number of time packets to exchange while polling. Increasing this number might increase unnecessary traffic on the network.

PARAMETER	VALUES	DESCRIPTION
TIMESYNC polling interval	10 to 2678400 sec (Default: 600)	Determines the polling interval, in seconds. All servers in the tree must use the same polling interval. Maximum works out to 31 days.
TIMESYNC RESET	ON|OFF (Default: OFF)	When set to ON, all servers are removed from the time source list, and time synchronization is reset. This parameter automatically resets itself to OFF after execution.
TIMESYNC restart flag	ON|OFF (Default: OFF)	When set to ON, the TIMESYNC service automatically restarts. This parameter automatically resets itself to OFF after execution.
TIMESYNC service advertising	ON|OFF (Default: ON)	When set to ON, SAP (Service Advertising Protocol) is turned on, meaning Single Reference, Reference, and Primary time sources advertise using SAP. Set this parameter OFF if you are using a configured list of time sources.
TIMESYNC synchronization radius	0 to 2147483647 msec (Default: 2000)	Determines the maximum time that a server is allowed to drift from network time while still being synchronized. Do not set this parameter for under two seconds (2000 milliseconds) unless you have an application that uses synchronized time stamps that will not tolerate a two-second deviation between time sources.

TABLE C.22   Continued

PARAMETER	VALUES	DESCRIPTION
TIMESYNC time adjustment	+or- hour:minute: second [at month/ day/year hour: minute:second]	Determines when a time adjustment will take place. This parameter does not apply to Secondary time servers. Use sparingly to correct network-wide time errors. Overuse can corrupt time synchronization. The default date and time is six polling intervals or one hour (whichever is longer) from the current time.
TIMESYNC time sources	Max 150 char (Default: ;)	Specifies a server, or servers, as accepted time sources. If used at the console, and no server name is entered, the parameter displays the list of configured servers. To specify multiple servers, separate each one by a semicolon (;). The list of servers must contain at least one semicolon, even if only one server is listed. A semicolon alone clears the list of servers.
TIMESYNC type	Single, Reference, Primary, Secondary	Specifies the type of time sync role this server will play in the network. Default is Single for the first server in the tree, and Secondary for all subsequent servers. See Chapter 6 for more information on time synchronization.

PARAMETER	VALUES	DESCRIPTION
Time zone	Max 80 char (Default: NA)	Specifies the abbreviation for the server time zone, its offset from UTC (Universal Coordinated Time, which used to be called Greenwich Mean Time), and the daylight savings abbreviation, if applicable. For example: *zone* is MST7MDT for mountain standard time in the U.S.A. Mountain standard time is offset seven hours from UTC, and the abbreviation used when daylight saving time is in effect is MDT.
Default time server type	Max 50 char (Default: Secondary)	Specifies the type of time server for this server.

Traditional File System

A new category with NetWare 6.5, Traditional File System, includes all kinds of parameters relating to traditional NetWare volumes. If you are familiar with **SET** parameters from NetWare past, this category combines parameters from several different areas. So, if you can't find it, it might very well be right here. Table C.23 describes the traditional file system parameters in NetWare 6.5.

TABLE C.23   Traditional File System SET Parameters

PARAMETER	VALUES	DESCRIPTION
Purge files on dismount	ON|OFF (Default: OFF)	Automatically purges all deleted files on a volume when it is dismounted.
Volume log file state	0–2 (Default: 1)	Specifies what action to take when VOL$LOG.ERR reaches its maximum size. 0 = take no action; 1 = delete the log file; 2 = rename the log file.

TABLE C.23   Continued

PARAMETER	VALUES	DESCRIPTION
Volume TTS log file state	0–2 (Default: 1)	Specifies what action to take when TTS$LOG.ERR reaches its maximum size. 0 = take no action; 1 = delete the log file; 2 = rename the log file.
Volume log file overflow size	65536 to 4294967295 bytes (Default: 4194304)	Specifies the maximum size of VOL$LOG.ERR.
Volume TTS log file overflow size	65536 to 4294967295 bytes (Default: 4194304)	Specifies the maximum size of TTS$LOG.ERR.
Auto TTS backout flag	ON|OFF (Default: ON)	When set to ON, incomplete transactions can be backed out automatically when a downed server is rebooted.
TTS abort dump flag	ON|OFF (Default: OFF)	When set to ON, the TTS$LOG.ERR file is created to record backout data in the event of a failure.
TTS unwritten cache wait time	11 sec–10 min 59 sec (Default: 59 min 19 sec)	Sets the time that a block of transactional data can be held in memory.
TTS backout file truncation wait time	1 min 6 sec– 26 hours 21 min 51 sec (Default: 59 min 19 sec)	Sets the minimum amount of time that allocated blocks remain available for the TTS backout file.
Dirty directory cache delay time	0–10 sec (Default: 0.5 sec)	Specifies how long a directory table write request is kept in memory before it is written to disk.

PARAMETER	VALUES	DESCRIPTION
Directory cache allocation wait time	0.5 sec–2 min (Default: 2.2 sec)	Specifies how long the server waits after allocating one directory cache buffer before allocating another one.
Directory cache buffer nonreferenced delay	1 sec–1 hour (Default: 5.5 sec)	Sets how long a directory entry is held in cache before it is overwritten.
Directory cache allocation wait time	0.5–2 min (Default: 2.2 sec)	Specifies how long the server waits after allocating one directory cache buffer before allocating another one.
Directory cache buffer nonreferenced delay	1 sec–1 hour (Default: 5.5 sec)	Sets how long a directory entry is held in cache before it is overwritten.
Maximum directory cache buffers	20–200000 (Default: 500)	Sets the maximum number of directory cache buffers that the server can allocate. Prevents the server from allocating so many directory cache buffers that other server processes run out.
Minimum directory cache buffers	10–100000 (Default: 150)	Sets the minimum number of directory cache buffers to be allocated by the server before the server uses the Directory cache allocation wait time to determine if another directory cache buffer should be allocated. Allocating buffers too quickly will cause the server to eat up memory resources during peak loads. Waiting too long can cause a delay in file

TABLE C.23   Continued

PARAMETER	VALUES	DESCRIPTION
		searches. This wait time creates a leveling factor between peak and low access times.
Maximum number of internal directory handles	40–1000 (Default: 100)	Sets the maximum number of directory handles that are available to internal NLMs that use connection 0. A directory handle is allocated each time an NLM accesses a file or directory. Allocating directory handles decreases the time required to gain access rights.
Maximum number of directory handles	20–1000 (Default: 20)	Sets the maximum number of directory handles that each connection can obtain.
Maximum record locks per connection	10–100000 (Default: 500)	Sets the number of record locks a workstation can use simultaneously.
Maximum file locks per connection	10–1000 (Default: 250)	Sets the number of opened and locked files a workstation can use simultaneously.
Maximum record locks	100–400000 (Default: 20000)	Sets the number of record locks the server can support simultaneously.
Maximum file locks	100–100000 (Default: 10000)	Sets how many opened and locked files the server can support simultaneously.

PARAMETER	VALUES	DESCRIPTION
Read ahead enabled	ON|OFF (Default: ON)	When set to ON, background reads can be done during sequential file access so that blocks are placed into the cache before they are requested.
Read ahead LRU sitting time threshold	0 sec–1 hour (Default: 10 sec)	Sets the time the server will wait before doing a read ahead. (LRU means *Least Recently Used*.)
Minimum file cache buffers	20–2000 (Default: 20)	Sets the minimum number of cache buffers that must be reserved for file caching.
Maximum concurrent disk cache writes	10–4000 (Default: 750)	Sets the maximum number of write requests that can be stored before the disk head begins a sweep across the disk.
Dirty disk cache delay time	0.1 sec–10 sec (Default: 3.3 sec)	Sets how long the server will keep a write request in memory before writing it to the disk.
Minimum file cache report threshold	0–2000 (Default: 20)	Sets how close to the minimum number of allowed buffers the system can drop before a warning message is sent.
Auto Mount mirrored volume containing inactive device	ON|OFF (Default: OFF)	Automatically mounts a volume detected to have a mirrored partition with an inactive device associated with it.
Automatically repair bad volumes	ON|OFF (Default: ON)	When set to ON, automatically runs VREPAIR.NLM when a volume fails to mount.

TABLE C.23 Continued

PARAMETER	VALUES	DESCRIPTION
File delete wait time	0 sec–7 days (Default: 5 min 29.6 sec)	Sets the maximum amount of time a deleted file must be stored in a salvageable state. After this time has elapsed, the file can be purged if the space is needed.
Allow deletion of active directories	ON|OFF (Default: ON)	When set to ON, a directory can be deleted even if a user has a drive mapped to it.
Maximum percent of volume space allowed for extended attributes	5–50 percent (Default: 10)	Limits the percentage of disk space that can be used to store extended attributes.
Maximum extended attributes per file or path	4–512 attributes (Default: 16)	Specifies the maximum number of extended attributes that can be assigned to a file or a subdirectory (path) on any of the server's volumes.
Fast volume mounts	ON|OFF (Default: ON)	When set to ON, allows the server to mount volumes more quickly by not checking certain less-important fields. This parameter should be on only if the volume was dismounted normally the last time.
Maximum percent of volume used by directory	5–85 percent (Default: 13)	Limits the percentage of disk space that can be used as directory space.
Maximum subdirectory tree depth	10–100 subdirectories (Default: 25)	Sets the maximum level of subdirectories the server can support.

PARAMETER	VALUES	DESCRIPTION
Volume low warn all users	ON|OFF (Default: ON)	When set to ON, all users are notified when the free space on a volume reaches a minimum level.
Volume low warning reset threshold	0–100000 blocks (Default: 256)	Specifies the number of disk blocks above the Volume low warning threshold value that must be freed up to reset the low volume warning. This parameter controls how often you receive the low volume warning if your free space is fluctuating around the threshold.
Volume low warning threshold	0–1000000 blocks (Default: 256)	Sets the minimum amount of free space (in blocks) that a volume can have before it issues a warning that it is low on space.
Turbo FAT re-use wait time	0.3 sec–1 hour 5 min 54.6 sec (Default: 5 min 29.6 sec)	Sets how long a turbo FAT (File Allocation Table) buffer stays in memory after an indexed file is closed.
Allow unowned files to be extended	ON|OFF (Default: ON)	When set to ON, files can be changed even if their owner has been deleted.

eDirectory Reference Materials

As you probably know by now, eDirectory is an extremely complex environment. Fortunately, it is largely self-sufficient. Most of the day-to-day tasks of maintaining and protecting directory data are handled automatically and transparently. Not only does eDirectory have many built-in integrity features, but it also employs several background processes that keep the directory environment stable and healthy.

eDirectory Background Processes

This section provides a look at the main background processes that do all the heavy lifting associated with eDirectory operations. They are

- ▶ Database initialization
- ▶ Flat cleaner
- ▶ Janitor
- ▶ Replica sync
- ▶ Replica purger
- ▶ Limber
- ▶ Backlinker
- ▶ Schema sync
- ▶ Time sync

When you use the various eDirectory monitoring and repair tools, of which some were discussed in Chapter 5, "Novell eDirectory Management," and more are discussed later in this appendix, these background processes and their effects are what you monitor and repair. For this reason, it's a good idea to know a little bit about what you are looking at.

Database Initialization

The Database Initialization (DB Init) background process is automatically initiated whenever the file system is mounted on the eDirectory server. It also executes any time the eDirectory database is opened or when eDirectory is reloaded. DB Init is responsible for

- ▶ Verifying the usability of the eDirectory database files on this server
- ▶ Scheduling the running of other eDirectory background processes
- ▶ Initializing the various global variables and data structures used by eDirectory
- ▶ Opening the eDirectory database files for use by the version of eDirectory running on this server

DSTrace provides the capability to monitor the DB Init process directly.

Flat Cleaner

The Flat Cleaner background process is used to eliminate eDirectory variables and attributes that are no longer needed by the database. Flat Cleaner is responsible for

- ▶ Eliminating unused bindery and external reference (X-ref) objects and/or attributes.
- ▶ Making sure that each of the objects in a partition replica maintained on this server has a valid public key attribute.
- ▶ Eliminating X-ref obituaries that have been set as purgeable.
- ▶ Making sure that the Server objects in partition replicas hosted on this server have maintained accurate Status and Version attributes. The Server object maintains an attribute that specifies server status—up, down, initializing, and so on. It also keeps a record of the version of eDirectory running on that server.

Flat Cleaner can be indirectly monitored through the use of Check External References in `DSRepair`. `DSTrace` also provides the capability to monitor the Janitor process directly.

Janitor

As its name implies, the Janitor process is responsible for routine cleanup of eDirectory environment. Janitor is responsible for

▶ Monitoring the value of the NCP status attribute maintained in the eDirectory Server object for this server.

▶ Keeping track of the `[Root]`-most partition replica on the server and the overall replica depth of the server. The `[Root]`-most partition is the partition root object highest in the tree (closest to `[Root]`). *Replica depth* describes how many levels down from [Root] the highest partition replica hosted by that server is.

▶ Executing the Flat Cleaner process at regular intervals.

▶ Optimizing the eDirectory database at regular intervals.

▶ Reporting synthetic time use by a partition replica on the server. Synthetic time occurs when a server clock set to a future time is reset to the correct time. Any eDirectory changes made while the clock was set at the future time will bear incorrect timestamps. This problem will self-correct as long as the gap between current and synthetic time is not too large.

▶ Making sure the inherited rights for each partition root object on this server are properly maintained.

Like Flat Cleaner, Janitor can be monitored indirectly by examining the Replica Ring repair options, Time Synchronization status, and Replica Synchronization status operations with `DSRepair`. `DSTrace` also provides the ability to monitor the Janitor process directly.

Replica Sync

The Replica Synchronization background process is responsible for two primary tasks:

▶ Distributing modifications to eDirectory objects contained within partition replicas maintained by the eDirectory server

▶ Receiving and processing partition operations involving partition replicas hosted by the eDirectory server

DSRepair can report the status of the replica synchronization process from a number of different perspectives:

▶ Report synchronization status

▶ Report synchronization status of all servers

▶ Report synchronization status on the selected server

DSTrace also provides the ability to monitor the Replica Synchronization process directly.

Replica Purger

Replica Sync schedules the execution of the Replica Purger background process. It is responsible for

▶ Purging any unused objects and/or attributes that exist in eDirectory partition replicas hosted on this server

▶ Processing obituaries for objects maintained within partition replicas hosted on this server

DSTrace also provides the ability to monitor the Replica Purger process directly, commonly referred to as *Skulker*.

Limber

After questioning several sources, it is still unclear why this process is named Limber, so that will remain a mystery for now. However, naming issues aside, Limber is responsible for

▶ Making sure that the eDirectory referral information for this server is properly maintained in each partition hosted on this server.

▶ Making sure that the server hosting the Master replica of the partition in which the Server object for this server resides has the correct Relative Distinguished Name (RDN) for this server. The RDN identifies a target eDirectory object's context in relation to the context of the source eDirectory object. For example, the Admin object in O = Quills would receive the following RDN for CN = jharris.OU = Education.OU = Provo.O = Quills: jharris.Education.Provo. The O = Quills is assumed from the location of the Admin object itself.

▶ Making sure the server object in eDirectory correctly reflects the operating system version and network address in use on this server.

► Making sure the name of the eDirectory tree in which this server resides is correctly reported.

► Monitoring the external reference/DRL links between this server and the partition replica that holds this server's eDirectory Server object. This is done to make sure that the eDirectory server can be properly accessed via its eDirectory object.

► Making sure this server's identification information is correct.

Limber can be monitored indirectly through Check External Reference, Report Synchronization Status, and Replica Ring repair options in DSRepair. DSTrace also provides the ability to monitor Limber directly.

Backlinker

The Backlinker background process helps maintain referential integrity within the eDirectory environment. Backlinker is responsible for

► Making sure that all external references (X-refs) maintained by this server are still required.

► Making sure that each X-ref is properly backlinked to a server that hosts a partition replica that holds the eDirectory object specified in the X-ref.

► Eliminating X-refs that are no longer necessary. As part of doing this, the server hosting the partition replica that holds the referenced eDirectory object is notified of the elimination of the X-ref.

Backlinker can be monitored indirectly through Check External References in DSRepair. DSTrace also provides the ability to monitor Backlinker directly.

Schema Sync

The Schema Sync background process is responsible for synchronizing the schema updates received by this server with other eDirectory servers. DSTrace also provides the ability to monitor Schema Synchronization directly.

Time Sync

Although time sync is not an eDirectory process, it is necessary in order to perform some partition operations such as moves and merges. The underlying time sync mechanism is not important as long as the eDirectory servers are, in fact, synchronized. Time sync can be monitored directly through the Time Synchronization option in `DSRepair`.

DSTrace with iMonitor

Now that you have been introduced to the most common eDirectory processes, it's important that you know how to keep track of the health and general operation of those processes. To do this you can use iMonitor. iMonitor is presented in Chapter 3, "Novell Management Tools," as one of the principal management tools for NetWare 6.5. However, this section focuses on the iMonitor options for monitoring eDirectory processes and activities. Refer to Chapter 3 for information on iMonitor installation, general interface, and additional capabilities. For detailed feature information, see the NetWare 6.5 online documentation.

iMonitor is a Web-based replacement for several of the console-based management utilities used with previous versions of NetWare, including `DSBrowse`, `DSTrace`, and `DSDiag`. Because the eDirectory processes discussed previously run on each eDirectory server, iMonitor provides a server-level view of eDirectory health as opposed to a tree-level view. You can view the health of processes running only on the server from which you are running iMonitor. To view another server, launch iMonitor from that server.

Prior to using `DSTrace` from iMonitor, you must configure the utility and specify the activity that you want to monitor. This is accomplished from the Trace Configuration page, shown in Figure D.1.

When you go into Trace Configuration, you will see four new links in the left navigation frame:

▶ *Trace Configuration*: This is the default view you will see when entering the Trace Configuration page. From this page, you can define the server-based eDirectory events and processes that you want to trace. The following configuration options are available from this page:

   ▶ *Trace On/Off*: Enables/disables DSTrace monitoring. When DSTrace is enabled, you will see a Trace button (big lightning bolt) in iMonitor's header frame that you can use to view the active trace (see Figure D.2).

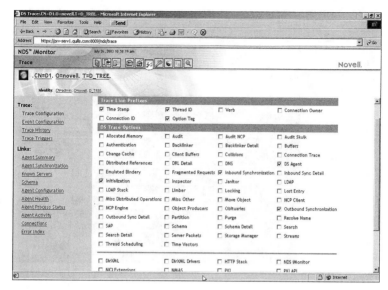

FIGURE D.1
Trace Configuration page in iMonitor.

NOTE DSTrace can increase CPU utilization significantly and reduce performance, so you should trace only when you are actively looking for something, and not as a standard practice.

▶ *Update*: Applies new configuration options to an existing trace.

▶ *Trace Line Prefixes*: These options let you specify what type of descriptive information to include with each trace line. These prefixes allow you to identify event sequence, group related messages together, and determine how long ago a problem occurred. This can be critical when analyzing DSTrace data, particularly historical trace data.

▶ *DSTrace Options*: Specifies the eDirectory activities that you want to trace for this particular eDirectory server. In order to control the amount of data that you will have to sift through in DSTrace, it's best to restrict tracing to only those specific events that are of interest instead of tracing everything. Table D.1 provides a brief description of many of the common trace options.

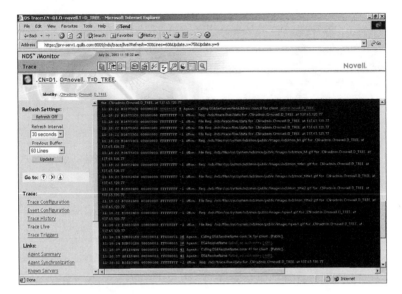

FIGURE D.2
Active DSTrace view in iMonitor.

▶ *Event Configuration*: This link provides a view similar to Trace Configuration, but it lets you select eDirectory events that you want to trace. eDirectory events include such things as adding/deleting objects, modifying attributes, and changing a password. The same configuration options described for Trace Configuration are available for Event Configuration, except that instead of listing DSTrace options, DS Events are listed.

▶ *Trace History*: From this page you can view a list of previous traces. A timestamp indicating the period of time during which the trace was gathered identifies each trace.

▶ *Trace Triggers*: This page lists some common DS Agent activities and identifies the DSTrace options that must be selected in order to trace that type of DS Agent activity. Selecting trigger options and clicking Submit will add those DSTrace options to the list of active DSTrace options, if they are not already active.

TABLE D.1 Common DSTrace Options

OPTION NAME	DESCRIPTION
Allocated Memory	Trace messages related to allocation of memory for eDirectory processes.
Audit	Trace messages related to the eDirectory audit process.
Audit NCP	Trace Audit NCP (NetWare Core Protocol) events.
Audit Skulk	Trace audit messages related to the replica sync process.
Authentication	Trace messages related to eDirectory authentication events.
Backlinker	Trace messages related to the Backlink process.
Buffers	Trace messages related to allocation of inbound and outbound packet buffers related to eDirectory requests.
Change Cache	Trace messages related to the changing of the eDirectory memory cache.
Client Buffers	Events related to memory buffers maintained for client connections.
Collisions	Trace messages related to the receipt of duplicate update packets. These duplicate packets usually occur on very busy networks.
Distributed References	Trace messages related to Distributed Reference Link operations.
DNS	Trace messages related to Domain Name Service requests.
DS Agent	Trace messages related to general eDirectory agent activities on this server.
Emulated Bindery	Trace messages related to Bindery Emulation.
Fragmented Requests	Trace messages related to the packet fragmenter that breaks up eDirectory messages for transmission in multiple packets.
Inbound Synchronization	Trace messages related to incoming eDirectory synchronization requests.
Initialization	Trace messages related to the opening of the local eDirectory database.

TABLE D.1   Continued

OPTION NAME	DESCRIPTION
Inspector	Messages related to the Inspector process. Inspector is part of the Janitor that verifies the structural integrity of the eDirectory database.
Janitor	Trace Janitor messages. The Janitor cleans up eDirectory by removing objects that are no longer needed.
LDAP	Trace messages related to LDAP communications.
LDAP Stack	Trace messages related to the memory stack associated with LDAP operations.
Limber	Trace Limber messages. The Limber monitors connectivity between all replicas.
Locking	Trace messages related to manipulation of the local eDirectory database locks.
Lost Entry	Trace messages related to obituaries, eDirectory attributes, and stream files.
Move Object	Trace messages related to eDirectory object move operations.
NCP Engine	Trace messages related to the NCP engine.
Outbound Synchronization	Trace messages related to background replica synchronization.
Partition	Trace partition operations and messages.
Purge	Trace replica purger messages.
Resolve Name	Trace messages related to eDirectory name resolution when traversing the eDirectory tree.
SAP	Trace messages related to the SAP protocol.
Schema	Trace schema modification and synchronization messages.
Server Packets	Trace messages related to server packets.
Streams	Trace messages related to stream attributes in eDirectory.
Thread Scheduling	Trace messages related to the management of processor threads used with eDirectory.
Time Vectors	Trace messages related to transitive vectors, which describe how caught up the replica is in the synchronization process.
Wanman	Trace messages related to WAN Traffic Manager.

Repairing eDirectory with DSRepair

Every database needs a tool for repairing inconsistencies when they occur. DSRepair has been serving in this capacity as long as eDirectory has existed. Even though Novell is shifting its focus toward Web-based tools, DSRepair is still essential for working on your eDirectory on a day-to-day basis. DSRepair offers three main groups of features:

▶ Unattended full repair

▶ eDirectory monitor operations

▶ eDirectory repair operations

To load DSRepair on your NetWare 6.5 server, load DSREPAIR.NLM at the server console. Throughout this section, when describing steps for performing a DSRepair operation, it is assumed that you have already loaded the utility. Figure D.3 shows the main menu of DSRepair.

FIGURE D.3
DSRepair main menu.

All DSRepair operations and results can be logged to file for review. The default log file is SYS:SYSTEM\DSREPAIR.LOG. DSRepair on NetWare has a menu for configuring the log file. To access this menu, select the Advanced Options Menu, and then select Log File and Login Configuration.

This following three sections describe the features available in each of the three main categories of DSRepair operations: Unattended Full Repair, eDirectory Monitor Operations, and eDirectory Repair Operations.

Unattended Full Repair

The Unattended Full Repair (UFR) is probably the most-used feature in DSRepair—although the huge database sizes now being supported by eDirectory might change that. UFR checks for and repairs most noncritical eDirectory errors in the eDirectory database files of a given server. UFR is activated by selecting Unattended Full Repair from the main DSREPAIR menu.

The UFR performs eight primary operations each time it is run, none of which requires any intervention by the administrator. These operations are described in Table D.2. During some of these operations, the local database is locked. UFR builds a temporary set of local database files and runs the repair operations against those files. That way, if a serious problem develops, the original files are still intact. When complete, a UFR log file will be generated that outlines all the activities that have gone on, errors that were encountered, and other useful information in reviewing the state of your eDirectory environment.

TIP Rebuilding the operational indexes used by eDirectory is possible only when the local database is locked. Given this, it is good to schedule a locked database repair on a regular basis, even in large eDirectory environments.

TABLE D.2 Operations Performed by Unattended Full Repair

OPERATION	LOCKED?	DESCRIPTION
Database structure and index check	Yes	Reviews the structure and format of database records and indexes. This ensures that no structural corruption has been introduced into the eDirectory environment at the database level.
Rebuild the entire database	Yes	This operation is used to resolve errors found during structure and index checks. It restores proper data structures and re-creates the eDirectory database and index files.

TABLE D.2 Continued

OPERATION	LOCKED?	DESCRIPTION
Perform tree structure check	Yes	Examines the links between database records to make sure that each child record has a valid parent. This helps ensure database consistency. Invalid records are marked so that they can be restored from another partition replica during the eDirectory replica synchronization process.
Repair all local replicas	Yes	This operation resolves eDirectory database inconsistencies by checking each object and attribute against schema definitions. It also checks the format of all internal data structures.
		This operation can also resolve inconsistencies found during the tree structure check by removing invalid records from the database. As a result, all child records linked through the invalid record are marked as orphans. These orphan records are not lost, but this process could potentially generate a large number of errors while the database is being rebuilt. Do not be overly alarmed. This is normal and the orphan objects will be reorganized automatically over the course of replica synchronization.
Check local references	Yes	Local references are pointers to other objects maintained in the eDirectory database on this server. This operation will evaluate the internal database pointers to make sure that they are pointing to the correct eDirectory objects. If invalid references are found, an error is reported in DSREPAIR.LOG.

TABLE D.2 Continued

OPERATION	LOCKED?	DESCRIPTION
Repair network addresses	No	This operation checks server network addresses stored in eDirectory against the values maintained in local SAP or SLP tables to make sure that eDirectory still has accurate information. If a discrepancy is found, eDirectory is updated with the correct information.
Validate stream syntax files	Yes	Stream syntax files, such as login scripts, are stored in a special area of the eDirectory database. Validate stream syntax files checks to make sure that each stream syntax file is associated with a valid eDirectory object. If not, the stream syntax file is deleted.
Check volume objects and trustees	No	This operation first makes sure that each volume on the NetWare server is associated with a volume object in eDirectory. If not, it will search the context in which the server resides to see whether a Volume object exists. If no Volume object exists, one will be created.
		After validating the volume information, the list of trustee IDs is validated. Each object in eDirectory has a unique trustee ID. This ID is used to grant rights to other objects, including NetWare volumes, in the eDirectory tree. This task makes sure that each trustee ID in the volume list is a valid eDirectory object. If not, the trustee ID is removed from the volume list.

> **WARNING** When the local database is locked, no changes are permitted while the operations execute. Some of these operations, when performed on very large eDirectory databases, will take an extended period of time to complete. When working with a large eDirectory database, it is best to schedule these types of operations carefully so as not to disrupt network operations.

DSRepair Monitor Operations

DSRepair offers several partition, replica, and server operations that are available to monitor the health of the eDirectory environment. These operations can be performed individually or as groups to help keep eDirectory stable and healthy.

Some of the DSRepair operations described in this section are available only when DSRepair is loaded in advanced mode. This is done by typing the following at the server console:

```
DSREPAIR -a
```

The first category of operations can be loosely grouped into monitor operations that are designed to report eDirectory status and health. You will likely perform most of these tasks from iMonitor with NetWare 6.5, but they are still available from DSRepair. Table D.3 describes the monitor operations available with DSRepair.

TABLE D.3   DSRepair Monitor Operations on NetWare

OPERATION	HOW TO ACCESS	DESCRIPTION
Report sync status	Select Report Synchronization Stat	Reports the sync status for every partition that hosts a replica on this server.
Report sync status of all servers	Select Advanced Options Menu Select Replica And Partition Operations, and then select a partition Select Report Synchronization Status Of All Servers	Queries each server hosting a replica of the selected partition and reports the sync status of each replica.

TABLE D.3   Continued

OPERATION	HOW TO ACCESS	DESCRIPTION
Report sync status on selected server	Select Advanced Options Menu Select Replica and Partition Operations and then select a partition Select View Replica Ring and choose a server Select Report Synchronization Status on Selected Server	Reports the sync status of the replica hosted by this server for the selected partition.
Time sync	Load DSRepair at the NetWare console and select Time Synchronization	Reports status of time synchronization.
Perform database structure and index check	Select Advanced Options Menu, and then Repair Local DS Database	Reviews the structure and format of database records and indexes. This ensures that no structural corruption has been introduced into the eDirectory environment at the database level.
Perform tree structure check	Select Advanced Options menu, and then Repair Local DS Database	Examines the links between database records to make sure that each child record has a valid parent. This helps ensure database consistency. Invalid records are marked so that they can be restored from another partition replica during the eDirectory replica synchronization process.

TABLE D.3   Continued

OPERATION	HOW TO ACCESS	DESCRIPTION
Servers known to this database	Select Advanced Options menu, and then select Servers Known to This Database	Queries the local database and compiles a list of servers known to this partition.
View entire server name	Select Advanced Options menu, and then select Servers Known to This Database

Select a server, and then select View Entire Server's Name | Displays the distinguished eDirectory name for this server. |
| View replica ring | Select Advanced Options, and then select Replica and Partition Operations

Select a partition and then select View Replica Ring | Displays a list of all servers that host a replica of the selected partition. |
| View entire partition name | Select Advanced options menu, and then select Replica and Partition Operations; select a partition, and then select View Entire Partition Name | Displays the distinguished eDirectory name for this partition root object. |

DSRepair Repair Operations

Although monitoring the condition of the eDirectory database is important, it does little good if there are no tools for repairing inconsistencies
when they occur. DSRepair offers several eDirectory repair operations.
These repair operations can be organized into three categories:

▶ Database repair operations

▶ Partition and replica repair operations

▶ Other repair operations

Database Repair Operations

All database repair options are accessible from the same menu in
DSRepair, as shown in Figure D.4. Access these operations by selecting
Advanced Options Menu and then choosing Repair Local DS Database.

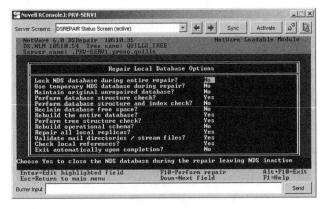

FIGURE D.4
Database repair options available from DSRepair.

Table D.4 describes the repair operations available from this menu.

TABLE D.4   DSRepair Database Operations on NetWare

OPERATION	DESCRIPTION
Rebuild entire database	This operation is used to resolve errors found during structure and index checks. It restores proper data structures and re-creates the eDirectory database and index files.
Repair all local replicas	This operation resolves eDirectory database inconsistencies by checking each object and attribute against schema definitions. It also checks the format of all internal data structures.
	Repairing all local replicas can also resolve inconsistencies found during the tree structure check by removing invalid records from the database. As a result, all child records linked through the invalid record are marked as orphans. These orphan records are not lost, but this process could potentially generate a large

TABLE D.4 Continued

OPERATION	DESCRIPTION
	number of errors while the database is being rebuilt. Do not be overly alarmed. This is normal and the orphan objects will be reorganized automatically over the course of replica synchronization.
Validate mail directories/syntax files	Both of these operations are only used with NetWare. By default, eDirectory creates mail directories in the SYS:Mail directory of NetWare servers in order to support legacy bindery users. Login scripts for bindery users are stored in their mail directory. Validate Mail Directories checks to make sure each mail directory is associated with a valid eDirectory User object. If not, the mail directory is deleted.
	Stream syntax files, such as login scripts, are stored in a special area of the eDirectory database. Validate Stream Syntax Files checks to make sure that each stream syntax file is associated with a valid eDirectory object. If not, the stream syntax file is deleted.
Check local references	Local references are pointers to other objects maintained in the eDirectory database on this file server. Check Local References evaluates the internal database pointers to make sure they are pointing to the correct eDirectory objects. If invalid references are found, an error is reported in DSREPAIR.LOG.
Reclaim database free space	This operation searches for unused database records and deletes them to free up disk space.
Rebuild operational schema	This operation rebuilds the base schema classes and attributes needed by eDirectory for basic functionality.

Partition and Replica Repair

In addition to these database repair options, DSRepair offers a menu of partition and replica operations designed to keep the distributed eDirectory environment functioning properly. This changes the focus from the local database to the partition—and all the replicas of that partition stored on servers across the network. To access these operations,

select Advanced Options, Replica and Partition Options, and then select
the partition with which you want to work, as shown in Figure D.5.

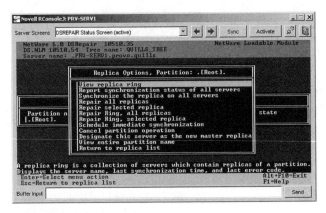

FIGURE D.5
DSRepair replica and partition options.

Table D.5 describes the various partition and replica operations available.

TABLE D.5   DSRepair Partition and Replica Operations

OPERATION	DESCRIPTION
Sync replica on all servers	Each server holding a replica of the selected partition is contacted and then a synchronization cycle is initiated.
Repair all replicas	This operation resolves eDirectory database inconsistencies by checking each object and attribute against schema definitions. It also checks the format of all internal data structures.
Repair selected replica	Performs a replica repair on the selected replica only.
Repair ring – selected replica	Performs a replica repair operation on each server that hosts a replica of the selected partition.
Repair ring – all replicas	Performs the replica ring repair operation for each replica ring in which this server participates.

TABLE D.5   Continued

OPERATION	DESCRIPTION
Schedule immediate sync	Initiates a replica synchronization cycle for each partition with a replica hosted on this server. This is useful for forcing the recognition of recent database changes.
Designate this server as new master replica	If the master replica of a given partition is lost due to hardware failure, this operation can be used to designate a new master in order for partition operations to function normally.

Three other replica operations are available by doing the following:

1. Select Advanced Options Menu, and then select Replica And Partition Operations.

2. Select a replica and then choose View Replica Ring.

3. Select a server from the list.

These three operations are described in Table D.6.

TABLE D.6   DSRepair Replica Ring Operations on NetWare

OPERATION	DESCRIPTION
Synchronize the replica on the selected server	Reports the synchronization status of the selected partition's replica that is hosted on this server.
Send all objects to every replica in the ring	The operation rebuilds every replica in the ring according to the objects found in this server's replica.
	Warning: Any changes made to other replicas that have not yet updated to this server will be lost.
Receive all objects for this replica	This operation rebuilds the local replica from object information received from the master replica.
	Warning: Any changes made to this replica that have not yet updated to the master replica will be lost.

Other Repairs

Finally, there are four miscellaneous repair operations that are accessible from other areas of the DSREPAIR utility. Table D.7 describes these operations.

TABLE D.7 Other DSRepair Operations

OPERATION	HOW TO ACCESS	DESCRIPTION
Repair all network addresses	Select Advanced Options Menu, and then Servers Known to This Database. Select a server from the list.	This operation checks server network addresses stored in all Root Partition objects in the tree against the values maintained in local SAP or SLP tables. If a discrepancy is found, eDirectory is updated with the correct information.
		If no corresponding SAP or SLP entry is found, DSRepair reports an error.
Repair selected server's network addresses	Select Advanced Options Menu, and then Servers Known to This Database. Select a server, and then select Repair Selected Server's Network Addresses.	Same as above, but only the Root Partition objects on the local server are checked.
Check volume objects and trustees	Select Advanced Options Menu, and then Check Volume Objects and Trustees.	Check Volume Objects and Trustees first makes sure that each volume on the NetWare server is associated with a Volume object in eDirectory. If not, it searches the context in which the server resides to see whether a Volume object exists. If no Volume object exists, one is created.
		After validating the volume information, the list of trustee IDs is validated. Each object in eDirectory has a unique trustee ID. This ID is used to grant

TABLE D.7 Continued

OPERATION	HOW TO ACCESS	DESCRIPTION
		rights to other objects, including NetWare volumes, in the eDirectory tree. This task makes sure that each trustee ID in the volume list is a valid eDirectory object. If not, the trustee ID is removed from the volume list.
Check external references	Select Advanced Options Menu, and then Check External References.	External references are to eDirectory objects not stored in partition replicas on this server. Check External References evaluates each reference to an external object to make sure that it is pointing to a valid eDirectory object.
		The external reference check also verifies the need for all obituaries maintained in the local database. An obituary is used to maintain database consistency while eDirectory is replicating changes such as object moves, deletes, or name changes. If a replica attempts to reference the changed object using old information because it has not received the replica sync yet, the obituary entry permits it to do so without generating an error. Once all replicas have synchronized with the new information, the Janitor process eliminates the obituary.

By using the operations described in this section, you will be able to manage most non-catastrophic problems in your eDirectory environment.

DSRepair Command-Line Switches

Novell recommends that some DSRepair operations be performed on a regular basis in order to keep the eDirectory tree healthy. To facilitate this, Novell has also made DSRepair functionality available through command-line switches. These switches make it possible to use batch schedulers to perform regular eDirectory tree maintenance automatically without any input from the administrator. Table D.8 describes the various command-line switches that are provided for automating basic DSRepair tasks.

TABLE D.8 Basic Command-Line DSRepair Switches

SWITCH	PARAMETER	DESCRIPTION
-L	Filename (with path)	Specify location for DSRepair log file. Appends to existing log file if it exists. Default is SYS:SYSTEM\DSREPAIR.LOG.
-U	None	Performs Unattended Full Repair and automatically unloads when complete.
-RC	None	Create an eDirectory dump file. This file is a snapshot of the local eDirectory database that can be used for troubleshooting. The dump file is stored as SYS:SYSTEM\DSR_DIB.
-RD	None	Repair Local Database. Executes using default database repair options, which includes Structure and Index Check, Rebuild Database, Tree Structure Check, Repair All Local Replicas, Validate Mail/Stream Files, and Check Local References.
-RN	None	Repair Network Addresses.
-RV	None	Perform Volume Object Repair.
-RVT	Volume Name	Perform Volume Object Repair and Trustee Check.

In addition to the numerous functions described in the previous sections, DSRepair also has some advanced features that are hidden from normal use. These advanced features are enabled through switches when loading the DSRepair utility. Table D.9 provides an overview of the advanced functionality available on each platform.

WARNING The features described in this section can—and will—cause irreversible damage to your eDirectory tree if used improperly. We recommend that these features be used only under the guidance of eDirectory professionals, such as the Novell Technical Services team, in order to resolve serious database issues. Always make a full backup of the eDirectory tree before using any of these features on a production tree. If you are going to use these features be sure you understand *all* the consequences before proceeding.

TABLE D.9 Advanced DSRepair Features

SWITCH	DESCRIPTION
-MR	Removes all "move inhibit" obituaries.
-N	Limits the number of days a User object can be connected to a given server to the number specified as a command-line argument. When this number is reached, the user connection is terminated. The default value is 60 days.
-RS	Removes the server identified by the Partition Root ID provided as a command-line argument from the replica ring for that partition. This might be necessary if a Read/Write replica becomes corrupt and needs to be eliminated.
-A	Load DSRepair with advanced options available. This uncovers additional menu options that are not normally visible. Select Advanced Options Menu, and then select Replica and Partition Operations and choose the partition with which you want to work. You will see the following additional menu items: ▶ Repair timestamps and declare a new epoch ▶ Destroy the selected replica on this server ▶ Delete unknown leaf objects This switch also allows the Designate This Server as the New Master Replica option to assign a Subordinate Reference as the new Master replica. Be careful!! If you select the View Replica Ring option and select a replica, you will see an additional option on that menu as well: —Remove this server from the replica ring
-XK2	Kill all eDirectory objects in this server's eDirectory database. This operation is used only to destroy a corrupt replica that cannot be removed in any other way.
-XK3	Kill all external references in this server's eDirectory database. This operation is used to destroy all external references in a nonfunctioning replica. If the references are the source of the problem, eDirectory can then re-create the references in order to get the replica functioning again.

These advanced options are seldom used because they are needed for only the most serious of cases. However, it is nice to know they exist when you get into a jam.

It is highly recommended that you work with these switches in a test environment and carefully study the ramifications of these radical operations. Sometimes the cure can be worse than the problem.

eDirectory Errors

There are a wide variety of error codes and conditions that can be reported in your Novell eDirectory environment. Specific information on each error is available in the Novell online documentation. You can also link to error code information from iMonitor by clicking an error from the Trace screen. eDirectory error codes are usually displayed in decimal numbers.

NOTE Because the eDirectory is designed as a loosely consistent database, temporary errors are normal. Don't be alarmed if temporary error conditions come and go as part of normal eDirectory operation. However, if errors persist for a significant period of time, you might need to take some action to resolve the problem.

eDirectory error codes can be categorized as shown in the following subsections.

eDirectory Agent Errors

These are the error codes with which you will typically work when tackling some eDirectory problem. They come in two ranges:

- ▶ –601 to –799
- ▶ –6001 or higher

The 6001 range is new to recent versions of eDirectory. These error codes identify errors originating in the eDirectory Agent running on your NetWare 6.5 server.

Operating System Errors

Certain eDirectory background processes or operations, such as network communications or time synchronization, require the use or functionality provided by the operating system on which eDirectory is running. These functions can return operating system–specific error codes to eDirectory. These error codes are passed on to the eDirectory process or operation that initiated a request.

Generally, negative numbers identify all eDirectory-generated operating system errors, whereas positive numbers identify all other operating system errors:

- ► *–1 to–256*: eDirectory-generated operating system errors
- ► *1 to 255*: Operating system–generated errors

This is an esoteric distinction for your information only. During troubleshooting, you should treat occurrences of operating system errors with the same number, whether negative or positive, as relating to the same event.

Client Errors

In some cases, an eDirectory server will function as a directory client in order to perform certain background processes or operations. This can result in client-specific error codes being returned to eDirectory background processes and operations. The eDirectory client that is built into DS.NLM generates these error codes. Client error codes fall in the range of –301 through –399.

Other eDirectory Errors

Some eDirectory background processes and operations require interaction with other NLMs running on the NetWare 6.5 server. Examples of this include TIMESYNC.NLM and UNICODE.NLM. If any of these external NLMs encounter an error, it can be passed on to DS.NLM. Errors in this category utilize codes ranging between –400 and –599.

Where to Go for More Information

NetWare 6.5 is a very large and complex product. It also includes a large number of services that many NetWare administrators might not have seen before. Fortunately, when a product becomes as popular and as widely used as NetWare, an entire support industry develops around it. If you are looking for more information about NetWare, you're in luck. You can go to a variety of places for help.

This appendix points you toward sources of information that will help you:

- ▶ Dig further into Novell's vision and strategy
- ▶ Find more information on NetWare 6.5 configuration and troubleshooting
- ▶ Get more information on the new products and services offered with NetWare 6.5

General Novell Product Information

The main Novell information number, 1-800-NETWARE, is your inroad to all types of pre-sales information about Novell or its products.

By calling this number, you can obtain information about Novell products, the locations of your nearest resellers, pricing information, and phone numbers for other Novell programs.

To access the online documentation for any current Novell product, visit Novell's online documentation site at

`http://www.novell.com/documentation/`

Novell on the Internet

There is a tremendous amount of information about Novell and NetWare products, both official and unofficial, on the Internet. Officially, you can obtain the latest information about Novell from Novell's Web site. Novell also helps support several user forums that deal specifically with NetWare or generally with networking and computers.

Novell's Web site is at

`www.novell.com`

Novell user forums can be found at

`support.novell.com/forums/`

These user forums are not managed directly by Novell employees, but offer users access to a wide variety of information and files dealing with NetWare and other Novell products, such as GroupWise. You can receive information such as technical advice from sysops (system operators) and other users, updated files and drivers, and the latest patches and workarounds for known problems in Novell products.

The Novell sites also provide a database of technical information from the Novell Technical Support division, as well as information about programs such as Novell Training classes and NetWare Users International (NUI). You can also find marketing and sales information about the various products that Novell produces.

Novell Cool Solutions

Novell Cool Solutions is another way of hooking up with Novell's broad community of users. It offers product reviews, tips, and tricks and the opportunity to share knowledge with Novell users all over the world.

Information is organized by solution set and by product, and there is a lot to see. To check out Novell's Cool Solutions, visit the Web site at

`http://www.novell.com/coolsolutions`

Novell AppNotes

Novell's Research Department produces a monthly publication called *Novell AppNotes*. Each issue of AppNotes contains research reports and articles on a wide range of topics. The articles delve into topics such as network design, implementation, administration, and integration. AppNotes are available online at

`http://developer.novell.com/research`

Novell Connection

Novell Connection magazine is a bi-monthly publication devoted to providing the latest and greatest strategy overviews, product reviews, and customer case studies. Novell Connection is written at a higher level than AppNotes, so it is ideal for helping you communicate IT messages to your business executives.

Best of all, Novell Connections is available online free! To check out the latest edition of Novell Connection, or check out past issues, visit the Web site at:

`http://www.novell.com/connectionmagazine/`

Novell Technical Support

If you encounter a problem with your network that you can't solve on your own, there are several places you can go for help:

▶ Try calling your reseller or consultant.

▶ Go online, and see if anyone in the online forums or Usenet forums knows about the problem or can offer a solution. The knowledge of the people in those forums is broad and deep. Don't hesitate to take advantage of it, and don't forget to return the favor if you know some tidbit that might help others.

▶ Call Novell technical support. You might want to reserve this as a last resort, simply because Novell technical support charges a fee for each incident (an incident can involve more than one phone call). The fee depends on the product for which you're requesting support.

When you call technical support, make sure you have all the necessary information ready, such as the versions of NetWare and any utility or application you're using, the type of hardware you're using, network or node addresses and hardware settings for any workstations or other machines being affected, and so on. You'll also need a major credit card.

Novell's technical support department also offers online information, technical bulletins, downloadable patches and drivers, and so on. They also offer the Novell Professional Resource Suite (NPRS). The NPRS is a collection of CDs, offered on a subscription basis, that includes the support knowledge base, product evaluation library, and other useful support tools to help you support your Novell environment and plan for the future.

To get in touch with Novell's technical support, or to find out more about Novell's technical support options, visit Novell's support Web site at

`http://support.novell.com`

To open a technical support incident call, call 1-800-858-4000.

Novell Ngage

Because of the complexity of many of the modern information solutions offered by Novell, it's not practical to assume that you are going to stay on top of every aspect of your modern network environment. To help you cope, and make the most of your investment in Novell solutions, Novell offers comprehensive, fee-based consulting services, marketed under the brand Novell Ngage, to help you with system planning and design, custom development, and comprehensive solution implementation.

For more information about Novell Ngage services, visit the Ngage Web site at

`http://www.novell.com/ngage/`

DeveloperNet: Novell's Developer Support

Developers who create applications designed to run on NetWare might qualify to join Novell's program for professional developers, called DeveloperNet. Subscription fees for joining DeveloperNet vary, depending on the subscription level and options you choose. If you are a developer, some of the benefits you can receive by joining DeveloperNet are

- ▶ Novell development CD-ROMs, which contain development tools you can use to create and test your applications in NetWare environments

- ▶ Special pre-releases and early access releases of upcoming Novell products

- ▶ Special technical support geared specifically toward developers

- ▶ Discounts on various events, products, and Novell Press books

For more information, visit Novell's developer Web site at

`http://developer.novell.com`

You can also apply for membership or order an SDK by calling 800-REDWORD.

Novell Training Classes and CNE Certification

If you are looking for a way to learn about NetWare in a classroom setting, Novell Training offers a variety of options with hands-on labs and knowledgeable instructors. As a pioneer of IT training and certification, Novell has a broad range of training opportunities available. For the most current information on Novell Training courses, certifications and materials, visit the Novell Training Web site at

`http://www.novell.com/training/`

NetWare classes are taught at more than 1,000 Novell Training Service Partners (NTSPs) throughout the world. They are also taught at more than 100 NATPs (Novell Academic Training Partner), which are universities and colleges that teach these courses.

Certification courses offer an excellent way to get some direct, hands-on training in just a few days. Classes are also available in Computer-Based Training (CBT) form, in case you'd rather work through the material at your own pace, on your own workstation, than attend a class.

These classes also help prepare you if you want to become certified as a CNE, signifying that you are a Novell professional.

The Novell CNE program provides a way to ensure that networking professionals meet the necessary criteria to adequately install and manage NetWare networks. To achieve CNE status, you take a series of exams on different aspects of NetWare. In many cases, you might want to take the classes Novell offers through its NTSPs to prepare for the exams, but the classes aren't required.

The classes and exams you take depend somewhat on the level of certification you want to achieve. Although certain core exams are required for all levels, you can also take additional electives to achieve the certification and specialization you want.

The following levels of certification are available:

▶ *CNA (Certified Novell Administrator)*: This certification is the most basic level. It prepares you to manage your own NetWare network. It does not delve into the more complex and technical aspects of NetWare. If you are relatively new to NetWare, the class offered for this certification is highly recommended.

▶ *CNE (Certified Novell Engineer)*: This certification level ensures that you can adequately install, manage, and support NetWare networks. While pursuing your CNE certification, you "declare a major," meaning that you choose to specialize in a particular Novell product family. For example, you can become a NetWare 6 CNE or a GroupWise CNE. There are several exams (and corresponding classes) involved in achieving this level of certification.

▶ *Master CNE*: This certification level allows you to go beyond CNE certification. To get a Master CNE, you declare a "graduate major." You will delve deeper into the integration- and solution-oriented aspects of running a network than does the CNE level.

▶ *CNI (Certified Novell Instructor)*: CNIs are authorized to teach NetWare classes through NTSPs. The tests and classes specific to this level ensure that the individual taking them will be able to adequately teach others how to install and manage NetWare.

▶ *Certified Directory Engineer*: A Novell elite training program for IT experts using directory-enabled solutions.

▶ *Specialist Certificates*: These one-course, one-test certificates provide you with the solution-focused training you need to implement Novell products and solutions.

CNEs and Master CNEs qualify for membership in the Network Professional Association (NPA), which is explained later in this appendix. For more information about Novell Training certifications, classes and programs, visit the Web site at

`http://www.novell.com/training/`

Numerous organizations also provide classes and seminars on NetWare products. Some of these unauthorized classes are quite good. Others are probably of lower quality, because Novell does not have any control over their course content or instructor qualifications. If you choose an unauthorized provider for your NetWare classes, try to talk to others who have taken a class from the provider before, so you'll have a better idea of how good the class is.

Advanced Technical Training

In addition to standard Novell Training courses, Novell also offers highly technical and specialized seminars known as Advanced Technical Training (ATT). ATT is the most advanced training offered by Novell, and covers a wide range of advanced topics including support issues, in-depth architectural reviews and advanced enterprise solutions. ATT is an excellent way to keep your skills, and those of your IT staff, in top form so that you are able to effectively support emerging technologies and complex network infrastructure solutions. For more information on ATT, visit the Web site at

`http://www.novell.com/training/pep/att/def.html`

Novell Users International

Novell Users International (NUI) is a nonprofit association for networking professionals. With more than 250 affiliated groups worldwide, NUI provides a forum for networking professionals to meet face to face, to learn from each other, to trade recommendations, or just to share war stories.

By joining the Novell user group in your area, you can build relationships and network with other Novell professionals in your area, attend regularly scheduled local user group meetings for training, and have access to regional NUI conferences, held in different major cities throughout the year. Best of all, there is usually little or no fee associated with joining an NUI user group.

For more information or to join an NUI user group, visit the NUI Web site at

`http://www.nuinet.com`

You can also call 800-228-4NUI.

Network Professional Association

If you've achieved, or are working toward, your CNE certification, you might want to join the Network Professional Association (NPA). The NPA is an organization for network computing professionals, including those who have certified as networking professionals in Novell, Microsoft, Cisco, and other manufacturers' products. Its goal is to keep its members current with the latest technology and information in the industry.

If you're a certified CNE, you can join the NPA as a full member. If you've started the certification process, but aren't finished yet, or if you are a CNA, you can join as an associate member (which gives you all the benefits of a full member except for the right to vote in the NPA's elections).

When you join the NPA, you can enjoy the following benefits:

▶ Local NPA chapters (more than 100 worldwide) that hold regularly scheduled meetings that include presentations and hands-on demonstrations of the latest technology

▶ A subscription to *Network Professional Journal*

▶ Access to NPA Labs that contain up-to-date technology and software for hands-on experience

▶ Job postings

▶ NPA's own professional certification programs

▶ Discounts or free admission to major trade shows and conferences, including NPA's own conferences

For more information on the NPA, visit the Web site at

`http://www.npanet.org`

INDEX

Symbols & Numbers

A

B

C

E

N

P

X-Y-Z